Everyman, I will go with thee,
and be thy guide

THE EVERYMAN
LIBRARY

The Everyman Library was founded by J. M. Dent
in 1906. He chose the name Everyman because he wanted
to make available the best books ever written in every
field to the greatest number of people at the cheapest possible
price. He began with Boswell's 'Life of Johnson';
his one-thousandth title was Aristotle's 'Metaphysics',
by which time sales exceeded forty million.

Today Everyman paperbacks remain true to
J. M. Dent's aims and high standards, with a wide range
of titles at affordable prices in editions which address
the needs of today's readers. Each new text is reset to give
a clear, elegant page and to incorporate the latest thinking
and scholarship. Each book carries the pilgrim logo,
the character in 'Everyman', a medieval morality play,
a proud link between Everyman
past and present.

William Langland

THE VISION OF PIERS PLOWMAN

A CRITICAL EDITION OF
THE B-TEXT BASED ON
TRINITY COLLEGE CAMBRIDGE MS B.15.17

Second Edition

Edited by
A. V. C. SCHMIDT
Balliol College, University of Oxford

EVERYMAN
J. M. DENT · LONDON
CHARLES E. TUTTLE
VERMONT

Introduction and other critical material © J. M. Dent 1995

First published in Everyman in 1978

This edition first published in Everyman in 1995

Reprinted 1997, 1998, 2000, 2001, 2002, 2003

J. M. Dent
Orion Publishing Group
Orion House
5 Upper St Martin's Lane
London WC2H 9EA
and
Tuttle Publishing,
Airport Industrial Park, 364 Innovation Drive,
North Clarendon, VT 05759-9436, USA.

Photoset by Deltatype Ltd, Birkenhead, Merseyside
Printed in Great Britain by
Clays Ltd, St Ives plc

British Library Cataloguing-in-Publication Data
is available upon request.

ISBN 0 460 87509 4

CONTENTS

For Judith

'Counseilleth me, Kynde', quod I, 'what craft be best to lerne?'
'Lerne to love,' quod Kynde, 'and leef alle othere.'

NOTE ON THE AUTHOR AND EDITOR

WILLIAM LANGLAND lived from *c.* 1330 to *c.* 1386. He was born near Malvern, in Worcestershire, and educated for a career in the Church, but appears to have married and never proceeded beyond minor orders. Little is known about his life apart from what can be learnt from the work on which he spent the years from 1360 or earlier to the time of his death, earning his living as a psalter-clerk in London, mainly, and possibly returning to the West Country in his last years. His great alliterative poem *Piers Plowman* exists in three versions, A, B and C (though recently a fourth version, called 'Z', has been claimed as his work, a version earlier than A). Of these only the B-text is extant in a completely revised form. It was this that was published in 1550 and has generally been regarded as the finest of the three as poetry.

Piers Plowman stands at the centre of medieval English literature along with Chaucer's *Canterbury Tales*, which in many ways it complements. It is unique in its impassioned concern for social justice, religious integrity and personal 'truth'; but its message inspires rather than compromises its poetic art, which is more varied and flexible than that of any other of the Alliterative Makers.

A. V. C. SCHMIDT taught at University College, Dublin and Exeter College, Oxford before becoming Andrew Bradley-James Maxwell Fellow in 1973 at Balliol College, Oxford, where he is Senior English Tutor. He was co-editor of *Medium Ævum* from 1981 to 1990 and his many articles and books on medieval literature include a study of Langland's poetic art, *The Clerkly Maker* (1987), a prose translation of the B-text (1992), and a parallel-text edition of *Piers Plowman: The A, B, C and Z Versions* (1995).

ACKNOWLEDGEMENTS

I wish to thank the Master and Fellows of Trinity College, Cambridge, for permission to publish their B-text of *Piers Plowman*, MS B.15.17. I am also grateful to the following for permission to print variant readings from *Piers Plowman* manuscripts belonging to them or in their care: the Bodleian Library, Oxford; the Syndics of Cambridge University Library; the Board of the British Library; the President and Fellows of Oriel College, Oxford and of Corpus Christi College, Oxford; the Principal and Fellows of Newnham College, Cambridge; and the Trustees of the Huntington Library, California.

In preparing this edition I have incurred many obligations, in particular to Professor John Burrow and Mr Edward Wilson, whose learning and care have greatly helped me; to Professor Derek Brewer, late Master of Emmanuel College, for help and hospitality in Cambridge; and to my mother-in-law, the late Mrs Yvonne Jackson, for typing the Index and Bibliography.

I am grateful to Oxford University and to Balliol College for sabbatical leave from teaching and administration; to the Librarian of Balliol College; and to students, undergraduates and graduates, who have studied the poem with me over the last twenty-five years, and whose enthusiasm and curiosity have been a constant stimulus and support.

Any editor of *Piers Plowman* must owe much to previous workers in the field. I apologize to all scholars whose studies I have drawn on without apparent acknowledgement; they are welcome to make as free with my work as I have with theirs. The debts I am most conscious of are to the editions of Skeat and of Bennett, with their inexhaustibly erudite and interesting notes, and to the great Athlone Press edition of Kane and Donaldson, which has brought about a revolution in our understanding of the text of *Piers Plowman*. To attempt to recover that text and elucidate its meaning is a rewarding, but also a daunting, task.

Without the work of the scholars I have named, I could not even have attempted an edition such as this.

My final acknowledgement is to my wife, who has shared the making of this book at every stage, helping in countless ways to enable me to get on with the task without distraction. It would be impossible to dedicate it to anyone else.

A. V. C. S.

PREFACE TO THE SECOND EDITION

Since its first publication in 1978, this book has been reprinted seven times. The 1987 reprint contained, as well as minor additions and corrections, a Glossary to supplement the marginal glosses. The latter have now been reduced in fullness to take account of this, making possible a less crowded page of text. However, the textual apparatus at the foot of the page has been somewhat expanded. Changes to the footnote translations have been few, nor have they been made to harmonize with the much freer version in my 1992 World's Classics translation, which serves a different but complementary purpose to that of the present volume.

The text itself has been completely revised, mainly as a result of working on a parallel-text edition of all four versions of *Piers Plowman*. Except that the spelling in the Everyman text replaces obsolete Middle English letters, the text is identical with that of the latter edition (Longman, 1995; hereafter *P-T*), and forms the basis of the Oxford translation. The changes to the 1978–87 text are so numerous that all printings before the current one are to be regarded as superseded. The consequences of this for the rest of the book are four. The content as well as the form of the critical apparatus is now new; the Textual Notes have been largely re-written; so, in particular, has the portion of the Introduction dealing with the text, which has been expanded, and will now serve by way of introduction to the fuller account that will appear in Volume II of *P-T*. Finally, the Literary and Historical Commentary has been greatly expanded. But the book is still intended to serve as a study edition for readers, many of whom will be coming to the poem for the first time. It would have been possible to alter the balance between explanatory and textual notes more drastically in this new edition; but discussion of major textual details remains of great importance, and questions about Langland's style, metre and language continue to be dependent on a text that can be seen to be soundly established. I am consoled for what may

appear shortcomings in the annotation by the fact that a fuller
commentary will appear in due course in Volume II of *P-T* and
also by the existence of further explanatory notes in the Oxford
translation. The latter, while necessarily overlapping with what
appears here, constitute an interpretative commentary which
complements rather than merely repeats it, and students should
find it worthwhile to acquire both books, in the reasonable
certainty of finding most of what they need at a modest price. For
this reason, too, I have left the other sections of the Introduction
substantially unaltered. Though my general understanding of the
meaning and style of *Piers Plowman* has inevitably developed
over the last fifteen years, the original Introduction still represents
my view of Langland as a poet. The Introduction to my Oxford
translation, which differs in form and approach, will also, I hope,
be found to complement not duplicate the interpretation
presented here.

For the rest, I have had to be content to correct as many errors
as I could find and bring the notes up to date wherever possible.
However, Langland scholarship has grown to the point where it
has not been possible to go into detailed problems of interpretation within the limits of this book. Readers will have, in time, the
fuller commentaries now being prepared, by myself and by other
Langland scholars; meanwhile they can explore for themselves
some of the excellent articles and books available, aided by the
helpful bibliographical guides published in the last few years.
Readers of the B-version will find much help in Derek Pearsall's
edition of the C-text, where learning and acute judgement are
everywhere evident, and I am happy to declare my indebtedness to
it in revising my notes for this edition. I would also acknowledge
the pioneering edition of the Z-version of *Piers Plowman*, by A.
G. Rigg and Charlotte Brewer (1983), which convinced me of the
need to examine the Z-text carefully in the light of the other
versions, and both to include Z in my parallel-text edition and cite
its readings in the apparatus here as part of the comparative
evidence for the establishing of the B-text itself. Although there
has been opposition, some of it vehement, to the authenticity of Z,
its arrival seems to me one of the most worthwhile additions to
our knowledge of *Piers Plowman* since the A-text appeared nearly
a hundred and thirty years ago.

The obligation to my wife expressed in the first edition has
grown considerably over the years. The mechanics of creating the

new textual apparatus required exceptional patience and skill; those who find this edition useful are greatly in her debt. I also wish to express my thanks to Dr Jennifer Fellows for her meticulous copy-editing of the whole book, and to my publishers for their patient and generous support of this revision.

A. V. C. S.

CHRONOLOGY OF *Piers Plowman*

1388	Merciless Parliament; Scots defeat English at Otterburn
1389	Richard's resumption of rule; d. John of Gaunt
1390	Gower's *Confessio Amantis*; Wycliffite Bible; ?*Pearl*
1392	Julian's *Revelations of Divine Love*
1399	Deposition and murder of Richard II; Henry IV king
1400	d. Chaucer

INTRODUCTION

i *The versions of* Piers Plowman

Piers Plowman exists in three versions known, ever since Walter Skeat named them over a century ago, as the A-, B- and C-texts, and a fourth, the Z-text, which is not universally accepted as authentic. Like Skeat and most students of the poem, I believe **A**, **B** and **C** to represent three successive states of a single work by one man. The A-version consists of a prologue and twelve passus, just over 2540 lines, and is unfinished. But in some MSS we find an 'A'-text supplemented or 'completed' by a text of another version. Thus Trinity College, Cambridge MS R.3.14 completes from C after A XI, while British Library MS Harley 3954 is a B-text up to about Passus V 125 and thereafter an A-text. **B** is a complete revision of **A** which adds eight passus, some 4880 lines. Three B-MSS, the closely related British Library MSS Additional 10574 and Cotton Caligula A xi, and the Bodleian MS Bodley 814, are B-texts from Passus III to the end, but have a C beginning (Prologue to II 128) followed by an A-text of II 86–208. The C- version is a further revision of **B**, only about seventy lines longer, but with much re-arrangement, new material, and minute verbal alteration. It has a prologue and twenty-two passus, though in many MSS, including the one Skeat printed, the Prologue is taken as Passus I and the total number of passus becomes twenty-three. The last two passus, corresponding to B XIX and XX, are almost unrevised. The Z-text is a version of 1515 lines preserved in one MS, Bodley 851. It consists of a Prologue and eight passus; it is followed by about 100 lines of A-text, and then the C-text from Passus X to the end. Although rejected by Skeat as merely a poor A-text, it has been accepted by some scholars, including the present editor, as an early, draft version of the poem, anterior to **A**.[1] Whether or not the C-version is the poet's final word, critics and readers generally seem to have agreed that of the longer versions the B-text is on the whole the most enjoyable, though C has distinctive merits which make it well worth reading.

It is, in fact, the B-text of *Piers Plowman* that was first printed, by Robert Crowley, in 1550, though Crowley knew other manuscripts and other versions of the poem. It was thus in the B-version that the poem became known to, and influenced, English poets such as Spenser, Marlowe and (possibly) Shakespeare. It was not until 1813 that a C-text was first printed, by Thomas Whitaker. In 1824 Richard Price discovered the version now called 'A' when editing Thomas Warton's *History of English Poetry*, and a manuscript of this was published by Skeat in 1867. In 1842 an early MS of the B-text, Trinity College, Cambridge MS B.15.17 (also the basis of the present edition), was published by Thomas Wright, with useful notes, and in 1869 Skeat printed B from Bodleian MS Laud Misc. 581, supplemented with readings from other MSS. In 1873 Skeat went on to print the C-text, regrettably from the same MS (Phillipps 8231) that Whitaker had used. In addition to his many valuable observations on the text, Skeat provided a massive body of notes containing lexical, historical and interpretative comment. This became the basis of modern study and appreciation of *Piers Plowman*, and much of it has not been entirely superseded.

It is in Skeat's editions for the Early English Text Society, in his two-volume Oxford 'parallel-text' edition, and in his school edition of the Prologue and Passus I–VII, that the poem has become familiar over the years to modern readers. But the progress of textual scholarship during this century has had the effect of rendering Skeat's texts obsolete. His A- and C-texts were, in any case, based on inferior manuscripts, which he printed with little correction from better ones. His B-text, by contrast, which was based on the best MSS, and which took careful account of many of the others, nonetheless contains the many errors that were present in the archetype of all the B-MSS. It was not until 1960, nearly a century after Skeat's A-text was made known, that there appeared the first volume of the Athlone Press edition of *Piers Plowman*, edited by George Kane. Much valuable work on the text had been done in the interim by, in particular, R. W. Chambers and J. G. Grattan, by Elsie Blackman, and by R. A. Knott and D. C. Fowler;[2] but Kane's book started afresh with a fundamental revaluation of the manuscript evidence and the problems of textual transmission. Its impact upon *Piers Plowman* studies, not to mention medieval literary scholarship as a whole, was dramatic, for Kane successfully showed the extent to which scribal corruption, unconscious or conscious, obstructed the recovery of the original by the traditional editorial method of recension. Kane further demonstrated the need for the editor of *Piers Plowman* to consider the use of reconstruction and conjecture where he recognized that the archetypal text itself had been corrupted by the same processes that had affected its descendants, the extant MSS and their putative group ancestors.

The methods pioneered by Kane in his edition were applied in a radical and extended fashion in the edition of the B-text by Kane and E. T. Donaldson published in 1975. Both works are intended for scholars and in their format and presentation are not without difficulties even for the specialist student, let alone the general reader. Nonetheless, their influence on all subsequent editions is bound to be deep and far-reaching. The basic arguments of Kane and Donaldson can only be accepted or refuted; they cannot be bypassed. There is now no way of 'going back to Skeat', and no point in reproducing his texts as the original work of the poet or, in matters of detail, anything approaching it. A summary of the processes of reasoning that lie behind my own editorial decisions will be found in section vii of the Introduction and in the Textual Commentary at the end of the book. I cannot claim to have solved all the major problems left unsolved by previous editors; but I hope I have not overlooked any. This edition is intended for the widest use, and it therefore attempts to supply both a modern text that takes account of advances in editorial method, and a concise commentary that will serve as a convenient basis for study of the poem and for both textual and literary criticism. The present revision (1995) is the result of a comprehensive re-examination of the B-version which has been carried out in the context of the Z-, A- and C-texts and in the light of developments in our understanding of Langland's language and metre over the past fifteen years.

ii *Authorship, audience and date*

Piers Plowman has a good claim to be the greatest English poem of the Middle Ages. It was certainly one of the most popular. Over sixty manuscripts survive, compared with over eighty of Chaucer's *Canterbury Tales* and sixteen of his *Troilus and*

Criseyde, and some forty of Gower's *Confessio Amantis*. Robert Crowley prefaced his 1550 printing of the poem with an enthusiastic introduction, and he met a receptive audience: the work was reprinted twice in the same year and then again by Owen Rogers in 1561. In these editions *Piers Plowman* became as accessible to the Elizabethan reader as the works of Chaucer. But even in its own day the poem appears to have made a powerful impact, as is attested by the well-known letter of the insurrectionary leader John Ball to the peasants of Essex. This is dated 1381 and so could allude to the B-text (see below), with its powerful dramatization of a conflict between the peasant hero Piers and a contemptuous priest in Passus VII:

> . . . stondeth togidre in Godes name, and biddeth Peres Ploughman go to his werk . . . And do wel and bettre, and fleth synne . . .[3]

The quarrel between Piers and the priest is removed from the C-text, and it is possible that one motive for revising the poem was the poet's wish to dissociate himself from the atrocities, including the murder of churchmen, which occurred during the Peasants' Revolt of 1381. It could indeed have been unsafe to be known as the author of a work the name of whose hero had been used as a slogan by dangerous revolutionary preachers, no matter what the actual intentions of the writer himself. This may be one reason why virtually nothing seems to be known about the poet except what can be deduced from the text itself. The many official documents which give a quality of historical solidity to Chaucer and Gower do not exist in the case of Langland.

The internal and external evidence for the authorship of *Piers Plowman* has been authoritatively studied and evaluated by George Kane. His conclusion is that the poem in all its versions is the work of William Langland, as Skeat and most subsequent scholars have believed. Such is the statement of one of the oldest and fullest ascriptions, that of the Trinity College, Dublin MS of the C-text, and since it is the strongest single piece of external evidence, I reproduce it here. It is written in a very early fifteenth-century hand on folio 89b of TCD MS 212 (D.4.1):

> Memorandum quod Stacy de Rokayle pater willielmi de Langlond qui stacius fuit generosus & morabatur in Schiptoun vnder whicwode tenens domini le Spenser in comitatu Oxoniensi qui predictus willielmus fecit librum qui vocatur Perys ploughman.[4]

(It is worth recording that Stacy de Rokayle was the father of William de Langlond; this Stacy was of gentle birth and lived in Shipton-under-Wychwood, a tenant of the Lord Spenser in the county of Oxfordshire. The aforesaid William made the book which is called *Piers Plowman*.)

The authority of this ascription has been convincingly defended by Kane. It is confirmed by the statement of the poem's narrator in Passus XV 152 of the B-text:

'I have lyved in londe,' quod I, 'my name is Longe Wille.'

Kane has shown (ch. 4) that it was the convention in French and English dream-vision poems of the period for the author to incorporate his 'signature' in the text, sometimes in an oblique fashion. B XV 152 both confirms the Christian name given in the Dublin ascription and also, if *Longe*, *londe* forms an (anagrammatic) signature, the surname. The word *Longe* also performs at least one other function, to note a personal feature of the poet known (presumably) to his immediate audience, his height. This 'fact' seems clearly confirmed by the so-called 'autobiographical' passage in the C-text: 'Y am . . . to long, lef me, lowe to stoupe' (V 23–4; all references to the other versions of the poem are to my parallel-text edition).

Apart from the bare fact of his name, there is no other early and reliable evidence of an external kind about Langland. Our knowledge of him must therefore be gathered from his own statements in the various versions of his poem or else deduced from such matters as his knowledge of the Bible, the law and religious and other writings in Latin and French. Here the assumptions we start with will inevitably tend to influence our conclusions. I assume, on the strength of Kane's arguments from literary history,[5] that the 'portrait' Langland gives of himself is likely to be *generally* true in its external particulars, though we cannot be certain if it is scrupulously autobiographical, and there is plainly considerable room for poetic distortion in the interests of ironic or didactic purposes. Thus, since the very conditions of medieval 'publication' presuppose that the *first* audience of a manuscript work would have had some personal knowledge of the author, such characteristics of Langland as his height, his being married and his having a daughter (like the plumpness and bookishness of 'Geffrey' in the poems of Chaucer) may be plausibly taken as 'authentic'. A number of other statements about himself also belong roughly to this category: that he was given a clerical education; that he sang psalms for a living; and that he lived in London but had lived in the country, specifically in the Malvern region. A passage from the C-text, extracted from the famous 'autobiographical' introduction to Passus V, will serve to give the flavour of the poet's self-revelations:

When Y yong, yong was, many yer hennes,   *years ago*
My fader and my frendes foende me to scole,   *provided; university*
Tyl Y wyste witterly what Holy Writ menede,
And what is beste for the body, as the Boek telleth,
And sykerost for the soule, by so Y wole contenue.   *surest; persevere*
And foend Y nere, in fayth, seth my frendes deyede,   *never; since*
Lyf that me lykede but in this longe clothes.
And yf Y be labour sholde lyven and lyflode deserven,

by; livelihood; win

The laboure that Y lerned beste, therwith lyven Y sholde:
In eadem vocacione qua vocati estis . . .
[Let every man abide in the same calling in which he
  was called (I Cor 7:20)]
And so Y leve yn London and opelond bothe.   *in the country*
The lomes that I labore with and lyflode deserve   *tools; win (by)*
Ys Paternoster and my prymer, *Placebo* and *Dirige*,

prayers (for the dead)

And my Sauter som tyme and my sevene psalmes.
This Y segge for here soules of suche as me helpeth,   *say*
And tho that fynden me my fode fouchen saf, Y trowe,

provide; guarantee

To be welcome when Y come, otherwile in a monthe,

make (me) welcome

Now with hym, now with here; on this wyse Y begge,
Withoute bagge or botel but my wombe one.   *stomach only*

(VI 35–52; spelling slightly modernized)

In this passage the poet, in defending himself against Reason's objections to his way of life, claims that, as an educated man, he is not obliged to perform manual labour to earn a living: a clerk like himself, he argues, moreover, should only receive the tonsure

yf he come were
Of frankeleynes and fre men and of folke ywedded. (C V 64)

This clearly seems to imply that the speaker could meet these criteria himself (for it is not challenged by Reason), and the word *frankeleyn* is a close vernacular equivalent of *generosus* in the

Dublin ascription. The phrase *folke ywedded* would seem, by the same token, to rule out the possibility of Langland's illegitimacy, something which may otherwise be suggested by his surname not being 'Rokayle', though it was not the case at this time that a man automatically took his father's surname rather than that of his place of birth.

We do not know when Langland was born, since the various references to the Dreamer's age, e.g. in B XI 47, are hard to interpret exactly. The only evidence for the date of his death is the statement of John But in a MS of the A-text (Oxford, Bodleian Library MS Rawlinson Poet. 137), which also contains a clear reference to other versions of the poem:

> Wille þurgh inwit [þo wiste] wel þe soþe –
> þat þis speche was spedelich, and sped him wel faste,   *profitable*
> And wrouȝthe þat here is wryten and oþer werkes boþe
> Of Peres þe Plowman and mechel puple also.
> And whan þis werk was wrouȝt, ere Wille myȝte aspie,
> Deþ delt him a dent and drof him to þe erþe   *blow*
> And is closed vnder clom – Crist haue his soule!   *'buried'*

This implies that the poet died suddenly, but that he had completed his work. If the John But who names himself in the line immediately following is the man identified by Edith Rickert[6] as having died in 1387, Langland's death would fall between then and the probable date of the C-text, about 1385. Since the poet describes himself as already old in the B-text (XX 186ff.), he would have been at least fifty in 1379, the likely date of completion of B. It seems safe to give the poet's approximate dates as 1330–86, but a certain margin of error must be allowed for.

The historical Langland is, if we ignore the internal evidence of the poem, little more than a name. By contrast with Chaucer, nothing is known of his descendants, if any survived him. But it is probable that he had patrons, though he does not speak directly of financial support from them. The number of extant copies of the poem in all its versions testifies to strong interest in his work, and while no manuscript (except perhaps that of Z) dates from his lifetime, the textual evidence indicates that one or more copies of the A- and B-texts were made by scribes and probably used by the poet. Kane and Donaldson have demonstrated that Langland used a scribal copy of the B-text when revising to C (pp. 98–127). The copying of so long a work would have been an expensive undertaking; while none of the surviving manuscripts are *de luxe* copies like the Ellesmere *Canterbury Tales* or the Corpus Christi, Cambridge *Troilus*, many are executed and rubricated by skilled professional scribes, and their careful if modest presentation is in keeping with what we know of the early owners of these and other (lost) manuscripts. As John Burrow has shown from a study of the wills of people who bequeathed *Piers Plowman* MSS,[7] these owners were, in the first instance, clerics, though some were educated laymen who were not courtiers, let alone magnates, but presumably people with an interest in Langland's religious themes. The original dialect of *Piers Plowman* was not such as to render it linguistically obscure to a *Southren man* (see Chaucer's *Parson's Prologue* (*CT* X.42), as a work like *Sir Gawain and the Green Knight* might have been. Its verse form, admittedly, might have been associated with the north and west of the country (see next section); but educated London readers would have experienced little difficulty with its language and style, and *Piers Plowman* has every appearance of being, like Gower's, 'A bok for Engelondes sake' (*Confessio Amantis* Prol. 24). When Robert Crowley printed it a hundred and fifty years later, he drew attention to the age of the poem's language, not the strangeness of its dialect: 'The Englishe is according to the time it was written in'; and he recommended the work not for its antiquarian appeal but for the direct relevance of its message to the religious concerns of contemporary readers: 'Loke not vpon this boke therfore, to talke of wonders paste or to come, but to amende thyne owne misse, which thou shalt fynd here most charitably rebuked' (printed in Skeat, Vol. II, pp. xxiii–xxiv).

The date of *Piers Plowman* has already been touched upon in connection with Langland's life. The Z-text cannot be earlier than 1362, since Z V 32 refers to a memorable south-western wind on a Saturday evening which is independently recorded by a chronicler as occurring on 15 January 1362 (a Saturday). J. A. W. Bennett has argued from other allusions for a date between 1367 and 1370 for the A-text, in which the same allusion occurs at V 14.[8] We do not know if Langland worked continuously on his poem, but a reference to the mayoralty of John Chichester as 'not long passed' (B XIII 268–70) serves to place the B-text securely after 1370. The Parliament of Rats and Mice in the Prologue very probably alludes to the Good Parliament of 1376, and in Passus XIX, as Bennett has shown convincingly, there are allusions to the warfare between the rival popes that broke out in April 1379 after the Great Schism of the previous year. This enables us to assign the writing of **B** to the years between 1377 and 1379. Kane argues for '1377, not 1378 or later' as the likely earliest date for the origin of the B MS tradition. His argument that Pr 110–11 (on the power of the cardinals to elect the Pope) alludes to ideas of John Wyclif 'abroad in the land' before being published in 1379–80, even if true, will suggest c. 1377 only for the beginning of *Piers Plowman*, since at least two years would have been needed for the composition of so long a work. This leaves 1379 unaffected as the likely date for its completion. An allusion to the warfare between the rival popes is more probably intended in XX 431ff. than one to papal campaigns in the 1360s or in 1377, as Kane contends.[9]

The C-text is harder to date from internal evidence. Its reference to the unpopularity of King Richard in III 207–9 made Skeat elect for a date about 1393; but it is clear that this passage, which speaks of 'custumes of coveytise the comune to destruye' and of 'Unsyttyng soffraunce', will fit well with conditions in 1384–5, when Richard and his court 'were giving rise to widespread anxiety'.[10] It is possible that Langland was no longer working on C by 1386; but this need not imply that 'all three forms ... were clearly current and being copied by the early 1380s', for the C-tradition could have been generated with great rapidity soon after the poet's death. It may be that the text of TCD MS 212 is 'at least five removes from any authorized exemplar' on grounds of date;[11] but the *text* of a MS can be some way from the original without a great period of time necessarily intervening, just as a MS (like Cambridge University Library Gg.4.31) may be two centuries from the original while being closer to it textually than another which is less than fifty years from it chronologically (Cambridge, Newnham College MS 070). 1386 as the date for the completion (or abandonment) of the C-text is also that to which two pieces of external evidence point. One is an allusion to a C-text passage in *The Testament of Love* by Thomas Usk, written perhaps a year before his execution in 1388. The other is the reference to Langland's death mentioned above, which, if its author is the John But who died in 1387, would indicate a date for C around 1385–6. By this time, Chaucer had completed *Troilus and Criseyde* and was about to begin work on the *General Prologue*. This is the first of his writings to show the possible influence of Langland, and it is not difficult to recognize in his portrait of the ideal ploughman a tasteful tribute to the work of his (?recently deceased) contemporary:

> A *trewe* swynkere and a good was he,
> Lyvynge in pees and *parfit charitee*. (*GP* 531-2)

The italicized words would have readily suggested to his audience the special qualities of Langland's hero and perhaps even helped to remove misgivings aroused by John Ball's use of Piers Plowman as a symbol of peasant militancy.

If the proposed dates for the four versions are correct, Langland will have spent the years of his maturity engaged in a single artistic enterprise. This was the construction of a poem which in depth and richness of organization challenges comparison with *Paradise Lost* and *The Divine Comedy*. We know of no 'earlier and other creation' by Langland; but with the Z-text, which bears all the marks of a work in progress, it is easier to account for our sense that A, an assured if undeveloped literary work, could not have been his first effort at writing a poem.[12]

iii *The literary tradition of* Piers Plowman

In all four texts Langland employed the dream-vision form which was the common property of medieval English poets, whether they wrote accentual-syllabic or alliterative verse and whether they lived in London or the north or west. Langland also used the verse form that he must have learnt in his youth in Worcestershire, the home of the early thirteenth-century Layamon, author of the *Brut*, and arguably of the whole Alliterative Movement. The works of the Alliterative Revival have received a comprehensive survey from Thorlac Turville-Petre, and Elizabeth Salter, S. S. Hussey and Derek Pearsall have all examined the question of Langland's debt to earlier alliterative poems.[13] It emerges that he probably owes little to the few he can be shown to have known, notably *Wynnere and Wastoure* (1352-3) and the semi-alliterative *The Simonie* (before 1350). On the other hand, several alliterative poets of the late fourteenth and early fifteenth century were clearly indebted to *Piers Plowman*. Five works, *The Crowned King, Pierce the Ploughmans Crede, Richard the Redeless, Mum and the Sothsegger* and *Death and Liffe*[14] may all be classed as written by followers, if not disciples, of Langland. It is not possible to examine here the points of contact between

Langland and such poets, but they are many and problematic. To take but one example, the line describing Elde in *The Parlement of the Thre Ages* (?late fourteenth century) –

He was ballede and blynde, and alle babirlippede (158)

is either derived from or else is the source of Langland's line describing the Sin of Envy:

He was bitelbrowed and baberlipped, with two blered eighen. (V 188)

The Langland line as quoted here has been reconstructed from the A- and C-texts, but in the B archetype (see section vii below) consists of two lines divided before *with*, the second line being completed with the phrase *as a blynde hagge*, which the present text rejects as scribal in character. In its archetypal form the line's closeness to that on Elde may point to indebtedness on the *Parlement*-poet's part rather than Langland's; what seems clear is that the lines are too close to have coincided simply through shared use of formula-like phrases.

In attempting to isolate the important *differences* between *Piers Plowman* and other alliterative poems, it is perhaps easier not to begin by stressing its obviously learned, Latinate qualities. These tend to be heavily concentrated in some passages and sections and totally lacking in others. Again, though Langland's Latin expressions, especially when embedded in the structure of a macaronic verse-line, give a characteristic and sometimes intense colouring to his poetry (as in Passus XVIII, discussed below), they are perhaps not the most fundamentally distinctive features of his style taken as a whole.[15] The features I select, though negative, *are* pervasive. One is the absence of the traditional ornamental diction which the Revival poets inherited from Old English poetry. The other, related to the first, is the lack of interest in description for its own sake, whether of clothing, scenery or architecture. (The second at least of these qualities *is* found even in his followers.) Langland did not lack visual imagination, as I shall argue in discussing his imagery in section vi; but his was not a pictorial poetry. In this he is closer to Shakespeare than to Spenser or the Chaucer of the *Knight's Tale* and the *General Prologue*. The second feature can be briefly illustrated by comparing the description, excellent in itself, of a beautiful natural scene that occurs in *Mum and the Sothsegger*, at lines

889ff., with the passage of *Piers Plowman* which clearly inspired it, Will's vision of nature in B XI 319ff.

The author of *Mum* shows a lively relish for particulars, as he describes

> The breris with thaire beries bent ouer the wayes
> As honysoucles hongyng vppon eche half,
> Chesteynes and chiries that children desiren
> Were loigged vndre leues ful lusty to seen. (898–901)

Langland can match the tactile immediacy of *bent* and *loigged*, as in his pungent evocation of greedy clerics:

> Thei ben *acombred* with coveitise, thei konne noght *out crepe*,
> So harde hath avarice *yhasped* hem togideres. (I 196–7)

But it is not clear in these lines whether we are to visualize a snail in its shell, a man locked in a chest, both, or neither. It is doubtful, in fact, whether we are meant to visualize at all. The images here are essentially half-realized, because they function as part of an imaginative metaphor, rich in suggestion, which subserves an intellectual and moral purpose. Similarly, in describing nature, Langland eschews the decorative possibilities afforded by the alliterative medium. His generalized vision of nature sweeps from 'the sonne and the see and the sond' to 'briddes and beestes' and 'Wilde wormes', through 'Man and his make', to terminate with characteristic emphasis in the social, moral and religious realities which were his ultimate concerns:

> Povertee and plentee, bothe pees and werre,
> Blisse and bale – bothe I seigh at ones.
> And how men token Mede and Mercy refused. (XI 331–3)

Langland's *emotional* world is, however, of immense circumference. One pole of this world is the all-too-human ridiculous of XX 195–8:

> For the lyme that she loved me fore, and leef was to feele –
> On nyghtes, namely, whan we naked weere –
> I ne myghte in no manere maken it at hir wille,
> So Elde and he[o] it hadden forbeten

with its rueful-ironic and mock-pathetic tones. The other is the religious sublime of XVIII 57–61, with its real pathos, tragic depth and stark grandeur:

'*Consummatum est*,' quod Crist, and comsede for to swoune,
Pitousliche and pale as a prison that deieth;
The lord of lif and of light tho leide hise eighen togideres.
The day for drede withdrough and derk bicam the sonne.
The wal waggede and cleef, and al the world quaved.

Langland's creative power displays itself as a complex holding-together of the multitudinous associations clustering around this climactic moment. The understatement of *swoune*, the recalling of the 'poor naked wretches' for whom Christ dies and with whom he is most closely identified in his desertion, are set against the hyperbole of a shrinking personified day and a vast cosmic upheaval in which man-made *wal* and God-made *world* are alliteratively bound so as to bring home the immensity and the closeness of the event, on which the salvation of each individual and all humankind depends. It is astonishing poetry, whether considered in its total effect or in such minutiae as the haunting phrase *leide hise eighen togideres*, which comes with poignant gentleness after the majestic extended half-line preceding. Such density of meaning cannot be paralleled even in *Sir Gawain* or *Pearl*; but it recalls the Old English *Dream of the Rood*, and it looks forward to Shakespeare's mature tragedies.

Langland was, it would seem, a poet of the capital, and not, in spite of his origins, a provincial writer. Yet he did not use the form of verse inherited from France by the leading writers of his day, the court poets Chaucer and Gower, and handled with fluent ease by anonymous redactors of romance such as the author of *Sir Orfeo* in the Auchinleck manuscript. But by using the alliterative long line, he achieved two things: he broadened and deepened the mainstream of English poetry by handling powerfully material of major significance left untouched by both Chaucer and Gower, and, by doing so, brought a form otherwise restricted to the provinces into the central tradition, where it remained stubbornly while the rest of alliterative poetry languished forgotten or unknown.

The artistic achievement of *Piers Plowman* is only now beginning to secure proper recognition. The more immediately appealing quality of the *Gawain–Pearl* poet, the most accomplished virtuoso amongst the alliterative masters, has tended to conceal from most readers the less obviously attractive but profounder virtues of Langland's work considered not as versified preaching but simply as poetry. Langland does not, admittedly,

have Chaucer's variety of form and mood; but he has a wider
emotional range, encompassing comedy, whether coarse or
sophisticated, and religious sublimity, both of which find expression characteristically in daring metaphor and wordplay.
Langland was in the alliterative tradition but not of it. While
rejecting many of the sensuous beauties of the form, he nevertheless opened up its hidden potential to express a wide range of
tones and inflexions in his exploration of the experience of
common humanity. His poem thus stands at the *centre* of
medieval English literature with the work of Chaucer. Gerard
Manley Hopkins, perhaps because he missed the qualities of
surface richness that he sought in his own poetry, dismissed *Piers
Plowman* as 'not worth reading'.[16] T. S. Eliot, however, who
alludes to Chaucer's *General Prologue* in the opening of *The
Waste Land*, acknowledged Langland in the opening lines of his
last poem, *Little Gidding*, which recall both Langland's Prologue
and his ecstatic lines on the Holy Ghost in Passus XVII:

> Midwinter spring is its own season
> Sempiternal though sodden towards sundown,
> Suspended in time, between pole and tropic.

In doing so, Eliot was showing a prophetic understanding of the
nature of poetic 'tradition'.

iv *The structure of* Piers Plowman

Few critics today would probably agree with C. S. Lewis's
provocative judgement that Langland is 'confused and monoto-
nous, and hardly makes his poetry into a poem'.[17] Some of the
best recent criticism, such as that of Burrow, Frank and
Simpson,[18] has brought out the poem's structural coherence, both
as a whole and at the level of individual visions. If 'confusions' still
exist, some are of the critics' making, and one even goes back to
Skeat. This is the practice of seeing *Piers Plowman* as formally
made up of a *Visio* (Prologue and Passus I–VII) and a *Vita* (Passus
VIII–XX). There is very little authority in the B-MSS for this
division, though the A- and C-MSS at the end of VII/IX have an
'Explicit Visio de Petro Plowman' and an 'Incipit Vita de Dowel,
Dobet & Dobest secundum Wyt & Reson' ('Incipit visio eiusdem
de Dowel' in C for the latter), and B-MS R's rubric to Passus VIII
resembles that of the C-version. Skeat, however, saw the *Vita* as

'altogether a new poem' though 'intended . . . to be the sequel and completion of the former portion' (Vol. II, p. li). If this was Langland's aim in **A** (which is doubtful), there is no sign that it was when he wrote **B**, while the evidence in **C** implies continuity rather than disjunction. The theme of Dowel, introduced by Holy Church as early as Passus I 128–33, is later affirmed in Truth's pardon to Piers at VII 110–14. Passus VIII, in which Will sets out 'for to seke Dowel', does not begin 'a new poem' but rather presupposes what has gone before and goes on to *develop* material latent in the first seven passus. Both the plan of the poem as a whole and the many verbal anticipations and echoes indicate that the B-text was intended to be read as a single, unified work of art. It does have great complexity, admittedly, a complexity Lewis mistook for confusion; but there are three structural principles which help the reader to grasp its no less fundamental unity.

The first of these principles is the protagonist's quest. Will is commonly called 'the Dreamer' and most of the work does indeed consist of his dream-visions; but some 230 lines are devoted to waking episodes. Some of these, like the long passage opening Passus XX and those placed between VII and VIII, help to impart a sense of Will's 'real' life advancing inexorably, with occasional spiritual setbacks, from youth to age, from 'intellectual' lust for knowledge to love and spiritual understanding.[19] There is, then, a real progression. Will first seeks 'wondres' (Pr 4); he proceeds to seek Dowel (VIII 2); after his visions of Patience and Charity he grows 'wery of the world' (XVIII 4). But whilst at his final awakening it is not he but Conscience who sets out as a pilgrim (XX 381), it has become clear by then that Will has proceeded from identification with the Folk of the Field (V 61) and later with their representative, the Active Man Haukyn, to real (if implied) identification with Conscience, the character who sets out to 'walken as wide as the world lasteth', just as Will in the Prologue 'wente wide in this world'. The opening quest 'wondres to here' has become a closing quest 'to seken Piers the Plowman' (XX 383).[20]

In addition to their purely narrative function in forwarding Will's 'pilgrimage', the waking episodes serve to introduce the themes of the succeeding, and reflect upon the significance of the preceding, dream-visions. The longest such episode, placed between Visions 2 and 3, indicates a major advance in understanding and a new vista opening out before Will. His dream experience has made him 'to studie/ Of that I seigh slepyng' (VII 144–5) and has left him 'pencif in herte' for Piers Plowman (a phrase strongly suggestive of love-melancholy). Only a passive recipient so far, he now becomes an active seeker. But in the continuation of the waking section that begins VIII, Will does not seek Piers; instead he asks all he meets who and where *Dowel* is. He goes on to have an (unsatisfactory) encounter with two Friars Minor who think they know, and then resumes the lonely wandering of the Prologue, before having his third dream. These waking episodes strengthen our sense of Will as a real man, no mere 'dreamer' in retreat from life, but a vexed individual striving to translate the truth of visions into the practice of daily living. The nameless narrator of the contemporary *Pearl* is rapt from his body to 'gon in Godes grace/ In aventure ther mervayles meven' (63–4), and after being wakened through his own rash impulse to 'hente' more than is his 'by right' (1195–6), he finds himself required to continue living without further visions, though not without the comfort of what he *has* seen. This character's unique experience serves to answer a particular 'wo' (56), just as a dream brings the narrator of Chaucer's *Book of the Duchess* relief for a particular 'sicknesse' (36) and that of *The Parliament of Fowls* light upon 'a certeyn thing' he has been attempting 'to lerne' (20). Langland's dreams seem to form part of a whole pattern of existence: Will's response to each helps to shape and precipitate the one that follows, just as each dream works to change the life on which it impinges.

The interplay between sleep and waking helps to impart dramatic urgency to the dreams themselves, which are the second main structural principle in the poem. They are eight in number, ten if we count the inner dreams of Visions 3 (3a) and 5 (5a), as numbers 4 and 6. Vision I occupies Passus I–IV; Vision 2 Passus V–VII; Vision 3 VIII–XII, enclosing the first inner dream (3a) at XI 4–404; Vision 4 occupies XIII–XIV. Vision 5 extends from XV to XVII and encloses the second inner dream (5a) at XVI 20–166. Visions 6, 7 and 8 each occupy one passus (XVIII, XIX, XX). Partition of the poem into 'vision' and *passus* ('step') appears within the text and seems to be reliably authentic. Some manuscripts additionally head the seven passus VIII–XIV 'Dowel', the four XV–XVIII 'Dobet', and the last two, XIX–XX, 'Dobest'. These titular divisions, which correspond respectively to Visions 3–4, 5–6 and 7–8, may well go back to authorial rubrics. They undoubtedly point up recognizable concentrations of interest in character and theme: 'Dowel' on Will and Haukyn, learning and patience; 'Dobet' on Piers and Christ, and charity; 'Dobest' on the Holy Ghost and the Church, and grace. But they will tend to mislead as much as help if they are taken to imply that there is an exclusive interest in Dowel, Dobet or Dobest in each passus group. The three ways are considered together, even if the *full* meaning of Dobest cannot be brought out until Christ's victory over death and his triumphant rule come to be finally expounded by Conscience to Will in terms of 'conquest'. Certainly, it would be incorrect to equate Charity, shown in XVII–XVIII as the highest virtue, potent where Faith and Hope fail, with Dobet *rather than* Dobest on the mere grounds that the Tree of Charity and the Samaritan, exemplar of Charity, happen to appear in the section headed 'Dobet'. Though less dubious than the term *Vita*, these headings too must be treated with some caution when analysing the structure of the poem in an attempt to elucidate its meaning.

That the last six visions have something like a new beginning is, however, signalized by the deliberate echoes in Passus VIII of the Prologue's *somer seson*, which advances during Will's search for Dowel. But Passus VIII clearly follows straight on from the concerns expressed in Passus VII, and if a major division is sought it cannot easily be found between what some critics still distinguish as *Visio* and *Vita*. Such a division, arguably, *does* exist between the first four and the last four visions (Pr–XIV, XV–XX). A key to this division would be the character Haukyn, whose appearance in XIII–XIV has long been seen as thematically linking the *Visio* and *Vita*. But even more than he *connects* separate sections (let alone separate poems), Haukyn serves to *conclude* a sequence of visions, the nature of which may be described as 'carnal' rather than 'ghostly'. For the tears Haukyn sheds at the end of XIV are properly 'religious' tears. They do not flow from fear of damnation, like Will's at V 61 or Robert the Robber's at V 463. They arise from an awareness, however rudimentary, of having betrayed God's love, which won the grace of salvation for men only at the heavy cost of Christ's death:

'Allas,' quod Haukyn the Actif Man tho, 'that after my cristendom I ne hadde be deed and dolven for Dowelis sake!' (XIV 320–1)

In the next passus (XV) Will, after hearing Anima's description of the Tree of Charity, 'swoons' at the name of Piers and experiences the most 'mystical' of his visions. This proves to be a deeply symbolic disclosure of the activation, to redeem mankind, of the same divine love that Haukyn had wept at betraying.

It is Piers who dominates the inner dream of XVI and saves Will from the error of men like the *Pearl*-dreamer who try to 'more hente/ Then moghte by ryght upon hem clyven' (1195). Piers states that the Tree is mysterious beyond man's grasp:

> 'the Trinite it meneth' –
> And egreliche he loked on me, and therfore I spared
> To asken hym any moore therof. (XVI 63–5)

And because Will has by now learnt patience, the virtue whose spiritual basis is humility, he does not 'ask any more'. Instead he *refrains* from re-enacting Adam's sin of concupiscence for the fruit of the tree of knowledge, the desire, stemming from pride, to 'be as gods, knowing good and evil' (Gen 3: 5). Will wants to taste not knowledge but charity, not to 'know' but to 'know how to love'. And his humility here saves him; though he must wake from the inner dream at 167, he will go on to receive a series of revelations which climax in the vision of Christ's victory over hell and death. And on seeing this victory, he can apply to himself the utterance of the privileged apostle Paul (I Cor 12: 4): 'I heard secret words which it is not granted to man to utter' (XVIII 396a). By *not* 'asking', Will has received.

This second inner dream, which leads to the disclosure of secret truths, is precipitated by Will's violent access of *pure joye* (XVI 18) at hearing Piers's name. The *first* inner dream also came after a powerful surge of emotion; but it contrasts sharply with the second, since the emotion there is not love but 'wo and wrathe' at Scripture's rebuke of him for lacking self-knowledge (XI 5). Thus, though 'ravysshed' into a vision of Middle Earth and of Nature, he is as yet spiritually unprepared to understand it; and though 'fet forth by ensaumples to knowe, / Thorugh ech a creature, Kynde my creatour to lovye' (XI 324–5), he cannot yet respond to the revelation of God in creation. He therefore fails at this stage to grasp Reason's profound affirmation, 'al that [God] wroughte was *well ydo*' (XI 396). This affirmation grounds Dowel, later shown as the charity of Christ, the 'new creation', in God's *initial* act of love, his creation of the world. Will thereupon awakens blushing with shame and says, much like the dreamer in *Pearl*:

Wo was me thanne
That I in metels ne myghte moore have yknowen. (XI 404–5)

The crucial change in Will that occurs before the *second* inner dream is his abandonment of his lust to know for humility before God's purposes. This he achieves through his experiences in Passus XIII with Patience, a crucial figure in the poem, whose name links him with the suffering God who has the right to take vengeance but refrains, shows mercy, and even dies for his enemies. As Reason says, preparing Will for his trying encounter with the gluttonous doctor of divinity: 'Who suffreth moore than God? ... no gome, as I leeve' (XI 379). To learn this truth properly is for Will to begin to be *symple of herte*, 'humble,' and humility, 'patience', as he discovers, is 'the pure tree' on which 'groweth the fruyt Charite' (XVI 8–9).

Much of *Piers Plowman*'s later visions is an elaboration of I Cor 8: 2–3: 'And if any man think that he knoweth any thing, he hath not yet known as he ought to know. But if any man love God, the same is known by him.' To be 'known by God' (= acknowledged, loved) is to 'know even as I am known' (I Cor 13: 12); and the way to that knowing is through charity, which 'is not puffed up', though '*knowledge* puffeth up' (8: 1), but 'is patient, is kind' (13: 4). When Will asks Kynde in XX 'what craft be best to lerne?' the answer he gets is 'Lerne to love' (207–8). The nature of this 'craft' Will learns in the four visions that come to him after learning patience. They could even be called 'love-dreams' (see XVI 20, which uses the phrase). In them, Will receives what St Paul calls 'spiritum sapientiae et revelationis, in agnitione eius ... illuminatos oculos cordis', 'a spirit of wisdom and of revelation, in the knowledge of [Jesus Christ] ... the eyes of [the] heart enlightened' (Eph 1: 17–18).

Will's development through his dreams and the waking vicissitudes that separate them gives the poem a distinct feeling of linear progression. This is true in spite of its also being a *dialogus*, as the colophon of the Trinity MS has it, tense with an almost dialectical alternation of attitudes. But *Piers Plowman* further shares with other fourteenth-century poems another structural principle, that of *circularity*. Fitt II of *Sir Gawain and the Green Knight*, for example, opens by contrasting nature's annual self-renewal with man's linear progress from cradle to grave. Its hero's own experience, however, is to meet at the end of his quest for the

Green Knight not the expected death, but an unexpected new birth into self-knowledge. Sir Gawain is able to discover two things: that perfection is not attained once for all in this life but can be lost, the loss entailing sin, shame and guilt; and also that failure can be redeemed, perfection re-won – and lost again.[21] In *Pearl*, the Dreamer tries to cross the river and break out of the inexorable quotidian cycle of repetition, a life grown empty without his beloved Pearl. But his impulse is not to God's *paye*, 'good pleasure', and he wakes abruptly back into that life. For all that, he is left, finally, with the consolation the vision brought. Further, in the daily recurrence of the liturgy of the Eucharist, which gives shape and meaning to historical time, he finds a figurative foreshadowing of the heavenly Jerusalem which also comforts him in his 'longeyng hevy' (1180), until the time of his release eventually arrives. Langland, too, uses a 'circular' structure; but because his poem consists of several visions and not just one, he has enough space to develop it into a new artistic principle, the principle of *recapitulation*.

Piers Plowman is a poem which traces the development not only of an individual but of a whole society, the historical community of Christians. It begins with things as they are: an individual who is a 'doted daffe' (I 140), forgetful of the truth necessary for salvation which Holy Church seems to repeat to him like a mnemonic formula for a child:

> When alle tresors arn tried, Treuthe is the beste. (I 85, 135, 207)

That the individual will can grow in appreciation of this profoundly simple and profoundly difficult affirmation is something that makes for progression and linearity; and the same is true also of the community. Thus in Passus V, Will and the folk repent; but Will behaves like a 'doted daffe' in succumbing to Fortune's false promises in XI. Likewise the folk of the field who, in V collectively and in XIV in the person of Haukyn, experience the 'sharp salve' of Shrift, fall in XX to the friar who 'gloseth there he shryveth' and 'clene foryeten to crye and to wepe.' Langland gives in the course of *Piers Plowman* many exemplars of heroic holiness – the hermit saints, the martyrs and, supremely, Christ. But he places in the foreground an image of common humanity, Will himself and, 'doubling' him, his surrogate Haukyn. The latter represents man immersed *in* the fleshly world *of* which he yet is not, cyclically washing his 'cote of cristendome' in confession yet unable to 'kepen it clene an houre' (XIV 12). Against Haukyn's cry, 'So hard it is . . . to lyve and to do synne./ Synne seweth us evere' (XIV 322–3), a cry just this side of despair, all that can be set is hope in God's grace. This, his faith assures the Dreamer, will not fail a man of good will, however heavy his burden of sin:

> The goode wil of a wight was nevere bought to the fulle:
> For ther nys no tresour therto to a trewe wille. (XIII 193–4)

It is a *trewe wille* that in the end will find the *tresor Truthe* and the *fruyt Charite*.

The faith on which human hope is to build is faith in the reality of the Incarnation, a mystery to be grasped in all its implications for man the sinner. This is the same 'kynde of Kryst' that 'comfort kenned' to the dreamer in *Pearl* when, like Haukyn's, his 'wreched wille in wo ay wraghte' (55–6). The chief of these implications is the dizzying notion that, if God became man, men can become like God. The reality of this implication is exemplified in the saints – whence the (otherwise surprising) preoccupation of medieval people with veneration of the saints. Langland also 'exemplifies' it in his rich and strange creation Piers Plowman. Piers begins as the servant of Truth (as the knightly hero Sir Gawain is the devotee and exemplar of the chivalric virtue of *trawthe*); yet even Piers can succumb to gluttony (VI 254–5) and, after receiving the pardon, resolves to abandon his 'bely joye' for 'preieres and penaunce' (VII 119–20). It is this Piers who in XIX 262–3 is to be made Grace's 'prowor and plowman . . . for to tilie truthe'. His 'spiritual' ploughing in XIX certainly recapitulates his 'earthly' ploughing in VI, but also grows out of it: for Grace builds upon nature. Thus, because Piers in his earthly rôle could 'travaille as Truthe wolde' and his 'teme dryve' (VI 139, 134) and, in spite of his aching belly in VI, could turn to God, he becomes the recipient in XIX of spiritual 'greynes – cardynales vertues', including Temperance, so that 'Sholde nevere mete ne meschief make hym to swelle' (285). And again, as Piers's earthly ploughing was menaced by 'wasters', so in XIX his effort under Grace 'to tilie truthe / And the lond of bileve, the lawe of Holy Chirche' (336–7) is menaced by the Deadly Sins under Pride:

> greven he thynketh
> Conscience and alle Cristene and Cardinale Vertues. (339–40)

Finally, as the sins of the Folk of the Field were repented with bitter tears, so Langland shows how in the early Church

> wellede water for wikkede werkes,
> Egreliche ernynge out of mennes eighen. (XIX 381–2)

But Langland was no nostalgic idealist. He understood that *Ecclesia semper reformanda est* ('the Church always needs to be reformed') for the simple reason that the human individuals who compose the Church remain always prone to sin. This constant awareness on the poet's part largely accounts for the sombre tone of *Piers Plowman*: the grotesque humanness of the Sins in Passus V, which modifies our sense of them as evil, is absent from the devilish crew who assault Unity in Passus XX. Yet Langland never entirely loses hope; and this is because his vision of Piers, the embodiment of man's hope of responding to grace and becoming like God, never finally deserts him.

I have been able to examine only one example of the principle of recapitulation in the poem; most of the others are noted in the Commentary as they occur. What I have been discussing here is the main design of *Piers Plowman*; but what is true of the whole can also be shown to be true of the parts, down to the smallest unit, as a detailed analysis of the Prologue would readily demonstrate. There is not space in this section for such an analysis; but in the next, which deals with the poem's themes, I shall inevitably be also considering, to some extent, the structure of the individual visions which present the themes. The lay-out of the entire work may very well be determined by a type of 'narrative' progression, the story of the growth of the dreamer's soul; but the plan of the dream-visions themselves will be found to be determined by more immediate thematic concerns – Meed, the Deadly Sins, Learning, Patience and Charity.

v *The poem's themes*

Vision 1 has three movements but really only one theme: the true purpose of, and value in life. The Prologue's *vision* sets individual and field of folk against the starl alternatives of heaven and damnation (tower and dungeon). Christians at all times risk becoming immersed in the world; but Langland seems to see obsession with wealth as the special problem of his day, when the Christian Church itself was becoming engrossed in temporal possessions. The rat fable does not disrupt the formal vision of society, since its concern is not merely topical politics but the perennial issue of power in this world and the perennial need for a central authority to maintain social order. Passus I is largely *explanation*: Holy Church answers Will's six urgent questions about the purpose of life and criticizes men for pursuing worldly 'treasure' (meed) instead of spiritual 'treasure' (truth). 'Truth' is a way of life as well as the object of man's search: 'tho that *werche wel* . . . And enden . . . in truthe . . . shul wende to hevene, / Ther Treuthe is in Trinitee' (130–3). Thus Holy Church introduces the notion of 'Dowel' in summarizing the demands of God's law. After 'things seen' (vision) and 'things said' (explanation), we have 'things done' (action). Passus II–IV take the form of a dramatic trial-at-law: Holy Church is the guardian of the true treasure; now we see being put to the test the claims of her antitype Lady Meed, personification of the false treasure men seek. The power and allure of money are symbolized by a woman in scarlet and gold radiating the pride of life and the lust of the flesh. Her trial ends with a (provisional) victory, as it seems, of Reason and Conscience over Meed in the high councils of national life.

Vision 2 considers the condition of the people as a whole. As Burrow has shown,[22] its action has four stages: the sermon, the confession, the pilgrimage and the pardon. A sustained personification-allegory like Vision 1, it also contains detailed realistic description of ordinary life in the confessions and the ploughing of the half-acre. Although it opens with 'Will's' repentance in response to Reason's sermon, its central figure is not the Dreamer, but the Ploughman. Piers enters at the very moment when the folk are trying to make satisfaction by following Reason's injunction, 'Seketh Seynt Truthe' (V 57). A model son of the Church, whose 'coveitise' (52) is not Meed but Truth, he demonstrates in action how to 'werche wel' so as to 'wende to hevene'. In return for such action he obtains Truth's 'pardon', which the Church's institutional representative, the priest, is unable to recognize as a 'true' pardon. Piers's tearing it, as Frank argues,[23] stands for his rejection of the idea of paper pardons as a substitute for doing well, not for a literal disagreement with the words contained in the pardon, words which in fact repeat Holy Church's teaching earlier. The scene graphically illustrates Langland's hatred of all that de-spiritualizes religion and substitutes outward form for inner substance, ceremony or procedure for integrity of heart; for it is this that is 'truth' operative in the individual.

The *waking interlude* after Vision 2 leads on to a *second prologue*. Will is to seek Truth in his own way, because each Christian must make a personal 'pilgrimage': a life of sincere obedience to God cannot be lived by proxy, and each individual must 'do well' for himself. Will, as a clerk, understandably chooses the intellectual way: he seeks, therefore, a formal *definition* of Dowel. This means, in practice, consulting the institutional representatives of knowledge and learning. *Vision 3* therefore has Will first thinking for himself ('meeting Thought'); then arriving at Knowledge or Understanding ('Wit'); next meeting Study and being sent on to Clergy and Scripture. But he is vexed by the discrepancy between what the educated know and the way they live, when he finds that 'clerkes of Holy Kirke that kepen Cristes *tresor*' (X 474) often have a less sure hold on 'truth' than the simple and the unschooled. Giving voice to his disillusionment with learning, he receives a sharp rebuke from Scripture for the wrong-headed spirit of his approach. As a result, he is plunged into an *inner dream*, in which the pagan emperor Trajan, who was saved from hell for '*lyvyng* in truthe' (XI 161), demonstrates the true nature of God's justice. Will now proceeds to question God's ways, asking why Nature should be free of the disorder and unreason that afflict man; Reason's rebuke to the rebuker wakes him abruptly back into the outer dream. Here the enigmatic figure Ymaginatif resolves Will's main doubts by showing knowledge of the 'truth' (in an intellectual sense) to be necessary, but not sufficient, for salvation: '*lyvyng* in truthe' is also essential. Ymaginatif thereby reconciles with the Church's doctrine of the necessity of baptism the salvation of the formally unbaptized Trajan, who exercised 'trewe truthe' (XII 287) as a 'tresor / To kepe with [his] comune' (XII 293–4).

After this protracted *dialogus*, *Vision 4* moves towards the mode of action. Passus XIII consists of two parts, linked by the imagery of food (material and spiritual); and it has two memorable characters, the gluttonous Doctor of Divinity and the Active Man. Each in turn is contrasted with Patience, who is strictly neither active nor contemplative in the traditional way, but who is *spiritually* 'active' because his 'food' is the word and sacrament of God. At Conscience's dinner it becomes clear that Dowel cannot be simply knowledge as such, but must be an active virtue (charity), the basis of which is found to be a passive one (patience). The Active Man Haukyn then appears to balance the learned but spiritually myopic friar: he is the type of the uneducated layman, whose Christian baptism does not by itself guarantee the 'well-doing' without which salvation cannot be attained. A second necessary sacrament, confession, therefore comes to the fore as the theme of XIV. Haukyn has to learn that the remedy for sin, of which the root is pride, is humility, which is the root of charity (this is what Patience means by 'poverty'). Haukyn, serving in part here as Will's surrogate, has advanced the Dreamer's 'quest' from one for Dowel (VIII 13) to one for Charity (XIV 97), which is to be found 'in poverte ther pacience is' (217). The nature of charity itself, the 'fruit' of the allegorical tree of patience, is the mysterious main theme to be dealt with in the next vision.

The foregoing outline of the thematic structure of the first four visions runs the risk, like all such summaries, of over-simplifying a complex and subtle organization. To counteract this danger, which is unavoidable if one attempts to clarify the themes for a reader unfamiliar with Langland and his world, I offer here a more extended analysis of the long *Vision 5*, before returning to a summary mode for the last three. This also provides an opportunity to look back over the earlier visions, which, as I argued in section iv, hang together in much the same way as do the last four, starting with Passus XV. The powerfully dramatic action of *Vision 6* flows from what is learnt of the nature of Charity in the discursive Fifth, where Piers returns as a crucial figure. But this fifth vision, which contains the 'mystical' inner dream (the second), opens with Will encountering a character, Anima, who distinctly recalls the personifications of intellectual faculties met with earlier in Vision 3. The difference, however – and it is an important one – is that Anima is more specifically the human soul as the theatre in which God's grace operates, rather than the rational mind as such. Having left behind in Vision 4 the exemplar of the outer life, Haukyn, we now enter an interior world. Nonetheless, in some ways Anima is really just a convenient mouthpiece for Langland's most sustained moral diatribe against the evils of his age. First, then, Anima attacks Will's own special vice, in which he repeats the original fault of Adam, 'Coveitise to konne and to knowe science', and which leads him away from holiness (doing well). Anima also attacks the institutional

Church, which, though it is the divinely ordained means of sacramental grace, can yet become a source of corruption, because its human agents, the clergy, set an evil example of teaching one thing and doing another and so, by their hypocrisy, infect the people. The image Anima uses is of a *tree* (XV 96–102). Will's own problem is not unrelated to this contemporary dilemma of a corrupt clergy: if 'charity' is something active, why can it not be experienced in operation in the real world?

Anima sets out to answer Will's questions, which keep raising themes first dealt with right at the beginning of the poem. Will has now resumed the rôle temporarily taken over by Haukyn in Vision 4, and his question at XV 176 echoes Haukyn's at XIV 101–2: is charity possible for the rich? It also recalls his own question to Holy Church in Passus I: what is the 'treasure' which saves the soul instead of destroying it? Her answer, 'Truth', Will had been unable to comprehend in more than a 'cognitive' sense, because of his undeveloped spiritual state at that point. As a consequence, the whole of Vision 3 had been spent exploring what could be learnt of Dowel, the way to Truth, by means of the exercise of the intellect. Yet Holy Church had also pointed out that Truth was essentially a matter of Love, the real content of the Old Law given to Moses and also the motive of Christ's Incarnation, culminating in his death, which established the New Law. To communicate this message, she had used the image of the plant of peace, the heavenly seed coming to eat the 'soil' of human nature and thereby grow into a potent, penetrating weapon of God's purpose. This purely verbal figure now evolves into the two great structural images of the Tree of Charity and of Christ as the jousting knight. In assuring Will that charity *is* possible to those who are not literally poor, Anima nonetheless emphasizes the need for detachment from the world. In doing so, he recapitulates Holy Church's earlier attack on the covetousness of the clergy; but he extends it further to argue that the contemporary clergy's obsession with material things has now destroyed their God-given power to evangelize. The modern clergy's inferiority to the saints of old is dramatically summed up in their inability to perform miracles, including the 'miracle' of suffering for Christ's sake. The 'red noble' (537) is 'reverenced' (a powerful word, suggesting idol-worship) before the bloodstained rood of Christ. The evil of clerical covetousness, Anima argues, stems from Constantine's original endowment of the Church, an action which had the unintended effect of allying the spiritual domain with the carnal, the City of God with the City of this World.

The extraordinary inner dream of Vision 5 is introduced, in Passus XVI, by Anima's reply to Will's question, What does charity mean? The mention of Piers's name which precipitates it is not the first in this vision: twice before, at XV 199 and 212, Anima has already spoken of the depth of Piers's vision and his understanding of the profound truth that charity can be 'known' 'Neither thorugh wordes ne werkes, but thorugh wil oone' (210). It is in this sense that the inner vision can be called a 'love-dream' (XVI 20): it is the revelation which can come only to a will purged by patience, not to an arrogant intellect that has taken much thought. The image of the tree of charity thus, inevitably, defies discursive explication; but this is not to say that it is incoherent or internally contradictory. The 'fruits' Will sees have to be actual human beings because the 'tree' grows in man's body, and it is from the actuality of human nature that God develops his great purpose, through the Incarnation of his Son. But human actuality is *historical*: it is thus, surely, a logical step for Langland to see and to wish us to see these fruits also in a historical perspective, extending from Adam to Christ. Piers's rôle in this action is perhaps the hardest to explain, if not actually to comprehend. One way of 'explicating' the scene would be to see XVI 86–8 as a vivid imaginative rendering of 'human nature taking into itself the divine', of the mystery of the Incarnation being viewed, so to speak, from man's side (since it is impossible to view it from God's). 'Piers' is perhaps more readily understood not as the human nature of Christ *per se* so much as that potential for becoming human which Christians believe was actualized in God's Word 'becoming flesh'. Langland sets out here to meditate dramatically on the dogma of the Incarnation, just as in XVII he will meditate on the dogma of the Trinity. As the very core of what is distinctive in Christianity, this 'mystery' cries out for interpretation, for re-presentation through imagery and action; and Langland's response is the inner vision open to 'wil oone'. Presumably its very nature is such that it *can* only be 'known' by 'wil oone': discursive analysis cannot get at the heart of what the dogma, any more than the vision, aims to teach about the 'revelation' or unveiling of God's love for man.

The strange image of the tree itself lasts for only a short while, as though, in Eliot's words, 'Human kind cannot bear very much reality': and Piers wards off Will's clumsy gesture at probing any further with the mind. The 'strange' accordingly dissolves, relapses into the familiar – the often-told story of Christ's passion and death; yet Langland somehow succeeds in his arduous task of revivifying this profound but by now hackneyed theme with an intensity of personal engagement which seems to be expressed above all in his audacious use of the figure of Piers Plowman. When the Dreamer wakes from the inner vision, the narrative has been abruptly stopped at the moment of Jesus' arrest on Holy Thursday. The Dreamer has by now advanced considerably under Piers's guidance; but he is not yet fully ready to meet the embodiment of charity, Jesus himself, 'face to face'. He first must be prepared, his rough ways made plain, by becoming more thoroughly acquainted with the prior workings of God's purpose in the Old Testament, for it was these that laid the basis for its fulfilment in the New. Hence Will must first encounter Abraham, exemplar of the faith on which charity is built. And Abraham's discourse leaves Will fully conscious of the sheer force of sin and like Haukyn at the end of Vision 4, weeping religious tears, 'gracious drops'. To grasp the strength of God's love he must first grasp the power of the stubborn opposition offered to that love by the human will and the diabolic will that uses it.

With an increasing sense of drama, Vision 5 proceeds towards the climactic disclosures of Passus XVIII. The quest of Hope and Faith for Jesus fuses with that of Will for Piers, whom he had lost at XVI 168; but first the object of both quests is *indirectly* encountered, in the person of the Good Samaritan. It is he who leads Will to see that there is no real contradiction between 'faith' and 'love' of God and neighbour (obedience to law through keeping the Commandments) as forms of Dowel. Both are to be seen as complementary and both are perfected by the active charity which is selfless, sacrificial love of all mankind, including one's enemies. This it is alone that *heals* wounded humanity. The power of sin, which had made Will weep, Langland vividly brings out by his image of 'unkindness', supremely manifested in the sin of murder. This act is a quenching of the very light and warmth of God's initiative to man (which theologians call grace), a piercing of the 'palm' of the Trinity, an attack on God's own 'kind' or nature, which is love, and of which the truest image is the created human being, our fellow-man. The Samaritan describes the very acts which have resulted in the wounding of the traveller whom he rescues. Against the energy of evil, that of the Devil and of a myriad human acts of will, only an immense act of divine power, what Langland calls a *maistrie*, will suffice; and it is this that the Crucifixion of Jesus, seen in terms of another great structural image, the chivalric metaphor of the 'joust' with Death, here constitutes.

Although the last three visions are relatively short and ostensibly self-contained, each occupying only one passus, they form together a single grand action, which began in XV with Anima and does not conclude till the last line of the poem. There is in these passus none of the variety and contrast which characterized the first four visions. Rather, a single concentrated purpose pervades and directs *Vision 6* – to give the audience experiential knowledge, *kynde knowyng*, of the nature of charity, God's love, in action. The narrative that unfolds is a story which occurred in time, and is 'recapitulated' annually in the liturgy, with a smaller, weekly cycle culminating in the 'Easter' of each Sunday throughout the Church's year. But it is a story with an end – and with it time is to end. Until then, there is only the 'cycle', as inexorable as the cycle of the seasons, of man sinning, repenting, being forgiven, falling again, sustained only by God's promise of ultimate release from sin. This promise is concretely embodied in the Eucharist, which is received with especial devotion at Easter. Vision 6 is very closely linked with the two visions that follow, and it displays the tightest thematic organization of any section of the poem. Earlier organizing devices had been the trial, the ploughing, the argument, the structural images of food and clothing, and the allegorical symbol of charity as a tree. This triple set of visions is built around a battle, or rather two battles. These are a 'joust', which is a victory for the hero (although he is seemingly overcome) and a siege, which is a real, if temporary, defeat for the hero's faithful followers, Conscience and the 'fools' who defend the house of Unity.

Throughout the increasingly urgent narrative action, links are also sustained with the themes of XVI and XVII, principally through the character Faith. For a mighty *argument* as well as an action is being worked out, as the debate of the Four Daughters of God and Christ's own 'debate' with Lucifer both demonstrate. God's purpose is to be vindicated completely because his 'act', to be a true *maistrie*, must be not a mere show of superior force, but rather an assertion of divine wisdom and truth over the falsity of the Devil. Thus Christ's 'binding' of Lucifer with chains is intended to be seen as both intellectually and dramatically satisfying. But the victory of Christ does not signify the victory of the Church in history: that is something that can only come at the end of time. The founding of the Church is, of course, God's initiative; but, from there on, man is to be an active partner in the work of salvation. And man's weaknesses inevitably form a part of the total *aventure* along with the strength which is divine in origin. In XIX, therefore, the action of Passus V is recapitulated *in reverse*. Piers is given the power of pardon by Grace *before* he begins to sow his field with his spiritual 'seeds'; but in so far as Piers represents the continuing human witness to Christ, with all its imperfections, his work will remain under a continual threat from the powers opposed to God: 'Now is Piers to the plow, and Pride it aspide' (XIX 338). With the passing of the Apostolic Age, the defence of Christianity is put into the hands of Conscience, the character who sums up all those who live out sincerely the faith that they outwardly profess. If these are few, as they seem to be in this age, then the Church will be weak. For, since grace requires man's free will to co-operate with it, there can be no triumph of the Church over the world like that of Christ once for all over the power of the Devil which assailed *him*. The holiness of the Church is seen to depend, therefore, on man as well as on God.

In *Vision 7* the focus has been on the Christian community in history. The final, eighth vision opens with Will being brought firmly back into the picture, and after this he is never completely lost sight of. We see the Dreamer afflicted by age and having to make his choice between the world and the spirit. But the chief protagonist in this vision nonetheless remains Conscience, whose rôle here corresponds closely to that of Piers in Passus VI. And as Piers earlier had called on Hunger for help against the 'wasters', Conscience now calls on Kynde to *desist* from punishing sinners with the plague. The Dreamer finds himself thereupon caught up in a world intoxicated with the 'pride of life' in its most basic sense – the sheer animal relief at having survived the Black Death which seems to have led to confidence in man's self-sufficiency, and also to a new recklessness in the pursuit of worldly enjoyment, and a new and total neglect of the spirit. In the fierce onslaught of Sin upon those who are seeking, within Unity, to lead a life according to God's will, the sacrament of penance, which had been shown to be vital to the individual Haukyn, is also asserted to be indispensable for the spiritual health of the community. The hypocrisy of the flattering friar, however, manages to corrupt this sacrament, which depends essentially on the sincerity of the penitent's inner contrition and on the maintaining of a 'truthful' relationship with God. Now the threat has come from 'within': for the friars are part of the Church. Even Conscience, it appears, can be deceived (though he cannot be destroyed). He cannot, in any fundamental sense, 'leave' Unity, but he must for the time turn aside from the clergy whose standing has been seen as gravely compromised by their venal attitude to spiritual things. Conscience's only resort in this final crisis is to the image of human charity in which the creative power of Kynde and the saving power of Grace are seen to unite. It is this that must inspire and sustain the Christian in the darkest moments of history as, in his old age, it must support the Dreamer, when physical power fails him and the 'death of kind' inexorably approaches. This 'image', *Piers*, now contains within itself the multiple significances which the developing understanding of Will and the power of Langland's poetry have given it. And it is Piers Plowman's name that is ringing in the Dreamer's ears as he awakes abruptly from his long series of visions. The waking is final; there is no epilogue.

vi *Langland's poetic art*

I have already touched briefly on the occasional sublimity of Langland's poetry in the B-text (section iii), a quality which has been appreciated by critics from Warton and Skeat to Lewis. His characteristic combination of the grand and the homely has been discussed with sensitivity by Nevill Coghill.[24] Looking in more detail now at the poetic art displayed in *Piers Plowman*, I wish to concentrate on four features which serve to distinguish Langland from both his fellow alliterative writers and his other great contemporaries Chaucer and Gower. Three of these features seem to ally him more closely not with these but with Shakespeare. They are his expressive verse rhythms, his frequent wordplay, and his use of expanded metaphor and thematic and structural imagery. The other feature, his peculiar use of Latin words and phrases as part of his English verse, suggests affinities with earlier traditions, notably those of medieval lyric poetry. I shall examine this first.

As the reader of Langland quickly notices, Latin quotations usually not forming part of the English verse play a major rôle in forwarding the argument of many passages in *Piers Plowman*.[25] But sometimes Langland fully integrates the quoted phrases into the structure of the alliterative line. In doing so, he does not necessarily expect his audience to *identify* the quotation: often he gives the source, and the effect is not quite that of an Augustan poet 'quoting' from a classical author to delight his educated readers; rather, he seems to be appealing to *several* levels of literacy in his audience. To take one example: when Anima is warning Will not to enquire too closely into God's secrets, he quotes from Proverbs a caution against eating too much honey and translates it for 'Englisshe men' (XV 55–9), reflecting in this the practice common in contemporary sermons of translating Latin Biblical passages for the *lewed* congregation. But when, just a few lines later, Anima quotes from St Bernard, he not only gives his authority, he also works the quoted text into the syntactical and metrical structure of the English sentence and offers no translation:

> '*Beatus est*,' seith Seint Bernard, '*qui scripturas legit
> Et verba vertit in opera* fulliche to his power.' (XV 60–1)

Other examples in Passus XV occur at 212, 215, 267–9 and 286, and their effect is to impart weight and authority to the speaker's statements. The clerkly tongue was above all the sacred speech of prayer and worship, and something of the lustre of liturgical Latin rubs off on words and phrases not actually from the liturgy.

Langland may have learnt this use of Latin to enrich English poetry from the macaronic lyrics, in which Latin phrases forming part of the rhyme-scheme give resonance and theological depth to the homely vernacular. An example is the well-known Marian song *Of one that is so fair and bright*.[26]

> Al the world it wes furlorn
> thoru *eva peccatrice*   *sinful Eve*
> tofor that Jesu was iborn
> *ex te genitrice*;   *from you his mother*
> thorou *ave*, [h]e wende awei,   '*Hail*'
> the thestri night, and com the dai   *dark*
> *salutis*;   *of salvation*
> the welle springet out of the
> *virtutis*.   *of virtue*

Here the second Latin phrase is virtually free-standing: it adds to the sense, but is not inseparably bound to the preceding syntax. But the others, especially the last two, directly dependent noun-genitives, operate differently, and their effect is one of disclosing hidden truths. The imagery of dawn and spring in the English communicates directly to an uneducated reader (Christ as light of the world and living water). But the abstract nouns in the Latin, for those who can render them, give intellectual precision to the images, making the dawn 'salvation', the night, by implication, sin and death, and the water 'goodness and strength', in the same way as pictorial representations of the Christian faith in the wall-paintings and stained glass of the period. And this they do while not concealing anything from those who cannot translate them, since the English already contains the spiritual sense in a sensuous and affective mode. This lyric's subtle nuances suggest private meditative prayer rather than public worship, and the bold effects of Langland are perhaps more closely paralleled in macaronic processional carols, such as the well-known *Make we joye nowe in this fest*:[27]

A solis ortus cardine,	*from the point of the sun's rising*
So myghty a lord was none as he,	
For to oure kynde he hath yeve gryth,	*given peace*
Adam parens quod polluit.	*which our father Adam defiled*

Here the Latin, untranslated, forms part of a narrative argument, and the carol is accordingly situated midway between English song and Latin hymn. Evidence that Langland learnt from such hymns is Anima's quotation from one of the most famous, the liturgical hymn *Pange lingua*, of a text that comforts the uneducated faithful suffering from negligent priests:

Ac theigh thei overhuppe – as I hope noght – oure bileve suffiseth;
As clerkes in Corpus Christi feeste syngen and reden
That *sola fides sufficit* to save with lewed peple. (XV 386–8)

Langland's macaronic sublime reaches its peak in Vision 6, Passus XVIII being richly veined with expressions from the readings of Holy Week. It is Gospel phrases like those quoted at lines 46–7, 50 and 57 that presumably inspired him with the confidence to execute his interpretative innovations; for we easily forget in the onrush of the poetry how theologically audacious Langland's equation of Piers with Christ is likely to have seemed to his first audience:

This Jesus of his gentries wol juste in Piers armes,
In his helm and in his haubergeon, *humana natura*.
That Crist be noght biknowe here for *consummatus Deus*,
In Piers paltok the Plowman this prikiere shal ryde;
For no dynt shal hym dere as *in deitate Patris*. (XVIII 22–6)

The last phrase uses Latin to express an idea too difficult perhaps
to translate in verse ('the godhead he shares with his Father'). The
first phrase validates the (already familiar) chivalric metaphor
with a Latin that is translucent if not quite transparent. The
second phrase points forward to the unforgettable sentence
quoted in full at 57: ' "*Consummatum est,*" quod Crist': in doing
so it delicately hints that the *summit* of divine goodness was
paradoxically reached in God's *kenosis*, his self-emptying to
assume the humble human shape of the 'ploughman' clad in
'armour' no stouter than a *paltok*.

When we turn to the verse-rhythms of *Piers Plowman*, we find
that they often have the somewhat heavy emphasis characteristic
of the form. But Langland had a particular fondness for alliterating, especially (but not exclusively) in the second half-line, words
of low semantic rank – i.e. words other than nouns, verbs and
main adjectives. This tendency, which from a strict standpoint
could be considered a technical weakness, tends to appear not in
heightened sequences like those discussed above, but in quiet,
relatively undramatic passages. One of these is the forty-line
sentence describing Haukyn the Active Man in XIII 272–311.
Here are six instances where the alliterating stressed syllable in the
b-half of the line is a pronoun, indefinite adjective, adverb, prefix
and the verb *to be*. The stress-effect of vowel-alliterating lines like
282 – 'And inobedient to ben undernome of any lif lyvynge' –
with its subsidiary consonantal stress-patterns of *b* and *l*, is both
thoroughly characteristic of Langland and quite unlike the rest of
alliterative poetry.[28] The labouring movement of a line like XIII
261, 'For er I have breed of mele, ofte moot I swete', may be
compared to that of Shakespeare's late verse, with its preference
for counterpointing speech-stresses against the metrical beat:

> for either thou
> Must as a foreign recreant be led
> With manacles through our streets, or else
> Triumphantly tread on thy country's ruin.
>
> (*Coriolanus* V. iii. 113–16)

The last line shows the canorous monotone of Marlowe's pentameters replaced by a kinetically imitative line of real dramatic power, while in line 115, the 'little' word *our* is pressed into service to enact a sense both precise and rich in poignant ambiguity. It is towards poetic textures of similar emotional density that Langland moves, abandoning the qualities typical of the alliterative form, in his equally dramatic suggestion of the *effort* of Haukyn's work. This he does through placing the full stave-weight on the 'little' word *of* in the a-half, with which *ofte* in the b-half assonates echoically. Another means Langland uses to achieve this effect of powerful bareness is by throwing the stress off the semantically higher and aurally more salient words, the nouns *breed* and *mele* and the verb *moot*, although a secondary, consonantal stave pattern is set up by the *m*-alliteration under the main vowel-alliteration. Lines like this are not uncommon in *Piers Plowman*, and they seem to constitute an adventure into uncharted territory comparable to the Jacobean playwrights' development of Elizabethan lyrical blank verse into a dramatic medium close to heightened speech. It is not impossible that Shakespeare learnt something from reading Langland; the quality of the alliteration in the last line of the passage from *Coriolanus* is highly suggestive.

Another characteristic of Langland's poetry that brings Shakespeare's to mind is his wordplay. He not only puns more frequently than any poet before Shakespeare, he uses the pun in a serious and often vividly illuminating way. Langland's wordplay may sometimes be said to grow out of his metre: the alliterative poet compelled to choose words beginning with the same sound may sometimes seem almost to 'stumble' into homophony, more easily than the writer of rhyming or blank verse. An apparent example of this process at work is XVIII 86, the line describing what happens when Longeus pierces the side of Christ:

The blood sprong doun by the spere and unspered the knyghtes eighen.

But even more striking here than the overt play on *spere* and *unspered* is the almost concealed personification of Christ's *blood* as it opens Longeus' eyes (locked in literal blindness and so in figurative ignorance of the man he has pierced). This is a 'structural' metaphor which anticipates the image, two hundred lines later, of Christ's *soul* as a light that unlocks hell and then goes on to *bynde* Satan *lightliche* (269):

A spirit speketh to helle and bit *unspere* the yates. (XVIII 261)[29]

The intellectual excitement that we feel in Langland's poetry owes much to our sense that he is *exploring* his deepest experience through language. It is an exploration that frequently leads to unexpected discovery, and to appreciate this we need to read the text with closer attention than Hopkins, surprisingly, seems to have brought to it. Under the surface, admittedly often plain, all is agitation and life. Another example, again taken from the Haukyn passage, is the Active Man's account of his slanders:

> Avenged me fele tymes, other frete myselve withinne
> As a shepsteres shere, ysherewed men and cursed. (XIII 330–1)

The two verbs in 331 are near-synonyms; but the homophonic play on *shere* and *ysherewed* draws attention to a meaning latent in the psalm-quotation following, which links *malediccione* 'cursing' with *lingua ... gladius acutus* ('his tongue a sharp sword'), though Langland's creation of a kind of metaphysical identity between the material instrument and the act of cursing one's fellow men is no more than hinted at by the Latin.

A no less serious though much more subtle pun, and one which is sardonically witty as well as just, occurs in Peace's comment on the flattering friar (aptly called Sire *Penetrans-domos*) who 'was my lordes *leche* – and my ladies bothe'. Here the speaker hints at the near-homophone *lecher*, but in the next line he develops the 'physician' part of the image even more tellingly with yet another pun:

> He salved so oure wommen til some were with childe. (XX 348)

Here *salved* plays mainly on 'heal' and 'greet (sexually)' (Latin *salve*); but a still further, and more bitter irony unfolds from the veiled allusion to the Annunciation (perhaps suggested by *my ladies* 347), which resulted in the Virgin Mary's conception of Christ the Saviour. The friar's salutations, by contrast, bring not healing (cf. 373) but 'enchantment' (379), a devilish undoing of the divine works of healing.[30] These examples, although unusually complex, are far from being exceptional. What they point to is the constant presence in Langland's poetry of vigorous and witty thought, as well as the piercing intuition and deep emotion which have long been recognized and admired.

These qualities in rich combination characterize Langland's extended image of the Trinity as a blazing torch in Passus XVII.

The effect here, however, is one not of intense concentration, but of accumulation and extension. It would be a mistake, I think, to approach this, any more than the immediately preceding image of palm, fist and fingers, as a rhetorically suasive analogy. Langland's aim seems to be, rather, to appeal to common experience in order to make ordinary people *feel* what the working of God's grace in the soul might be 'like'. So he relies on our 'kynde knowyng', our direct intuitive awareness, of cold, darkness and the season in which, more than any other, light cheers man's spirit and fire sustains his body. Beginning with a miniature genre-scene from contemporary life of 'werkmen / That werchen and waken in wyntres nyghtes' (218–19), he moves to an equally homely simile for the Father and Son 'frozen' into immobility by man's sin until the Holy Spirit 'flawmeth . . . as fir' and 'melteth hire myght into mercy' (226–7):

> as men may se in wyntre
> Ysekeles in evesynges thorugh hete of the sonne
> Melteth in a mynut while to myst and to watre. (XVII 227–9)

The development of this figure reaches its emotional climax in Langland's description of human *unkyndenesse* or 'unnaturalness' as a wind 'that quencheth, as it were, / The grace of the Holy Goost', an evil exemplified supremely in the murder of a virtuous man, who is seen as a 'torche' ablaze with divine grace:

> And whoso morthereth a good man, me thynketh, by myn inwit,
> He fordooth the levest light that Oure Lord lovyeth. (XVII 280–1)

This passage may bring to mind the famous punning line of Shakespeare's Othello:

> Put out the light, and then put out the light. (*Othello* V.ii.7)

Othello, about to murder Desdemona, thinks of his wife as the 'cunning'st pattern of excelling nature' and does not know 'where is that Promethean heat / That can [her] light relume'. These are, of course, Shakespearean terms, characteristically 'Renaissance' concepts that would have been alien to Langland, whose 'torch' and 'taper' are suggested rather by domestic reality and the immemorial symbolism of the Christian liturgy. But there is surely a genuine connaturality of poetic vision here between Shakespeare, with his 'humanistic' choice of situation and word, and Langland, who sees the 'fordoing' of a gracious human person whether 'with mouth or with hondes', in body or reputation, by slander or murder, as the extinguishing of 'lif and love, the leye of mannes body' (277).

In the foregoing discussion of the structure, thematic development and poetic art of *Piers Plowman*, I have been attempting to offer readers familiar with Shakespeare and Chaucer, and also perhaps with the *Gawain*-poet, some suggestions in support of my claim for the work's standing as the greatest of medieval English poems. The scope of Langland's bold aim – to encompass human experience between the poles of tower and dungeon – has been recognized for generations; but he is still criticized, wrongly I believe, for weak construction, lack of thematic coherence and prosaic style. I have tried to indicate, however summarily, that he possessed poetic genius adequate to his ambitious conception and that in the B-text, the most daring and dynamic of the poem's longer versions, he successfully achieved his aim.[31]

vii *The text of the B-version*

This section contains only a summary account of my basic conclusions about the text of B. A fuller discussion will appear in the Introduction to my forthcoming Longman parallel-text edition (Vol. II).

THE MANUSCRIPTS
The B-text is preserved in the following MSS and early prints:

1	W	Cambridge, Trinity College MS B.15.17
2	Hm	San Marino, Huntington Library MS 128
	Hm[2]	II 209–III 72*a* (in two separate fragments bound with Hm)
3	Cr	Robert Crowley's 3 impressions of 1550 (Cr[1, 2, 3] cited as Cr when agreeing)
4	G	Cambridge, University Library MS Gg. 4.31
5	Y	Cambridge, Newnham College MS 070 (Yates-Thompson MS)
6	O	Oxford, Oriel College MS 79 (defective at XVII 97–344, XIX 283–361)
7	C[2]	Cambridge, University Library MS Ll. 4.14
8	C	Cambridge, University Library MS Dd. 1. 17

9–11	B	London, British Library MS Additional 10574 (Bm); Oxford, Bodleian Library Bodley 814 (Bo); London, British Library MS Cotton Caligula A xi (Cot); (cited as B when agreeing; Bm defective after XX 356). B is a 'conjoint' MS, preceded by C Pr–II 128 + A II 86–198
12	L	Oxford, Bodleian Library MS Laud Misc. 581
13	M	London, British Library MS Additional 35287
14	H	London, British Library MS Harley 3954 (conjoint MS, B Pr–V 125 followed by A V 107–XI = A-MS H³)
15	R	London, British Library MS Lansdowne 398; Oxford, Bodleian Library MS Rawlinson Poetry 38 (contains Pr 125–I 140, II 41–XVIII 412, XX 27–end)
16	F	Oxford, Corpus Christi College MS 201
17	Ht	San Marino, Huntington Library MS 114 (a conflated text of A, B and C)
18	S	Tokyo, MS Takamiya I; formerly Sion College MS Arc. L. 40 2/E. (A modernized text)

The MSS are discussed by Skeat in his EETS edition (1869) (*Sk*), pp. vi–xxxvii and by Kane and Donaldson, *Piers Plowman: The B-Version*, 2nd edn (1989) (K–D), pp. 1–15; see also Doyle, 'Remarks', in Kratzmann and Simpson (1986), esp. pp. 39–44, and Kane, 'Text', in Alford, ed., *Companion* 175–200. I have not collated S or Ht (for an account of the former, see K–D, p. 15; and for the latter, see Russell and Nathan).[32]

The exhaustive classification of the MSS by K–D (pp. 16–69) is fundamental for textual criticism of the poem, and I have relied extensively on it and on their critical apparatus in preparing the text for the present as for the first edition. Like K–D, I think that the text cannot be established by the traditional method of recension, for the following reasons. Firstly, 'none of the medieval copies of *Piers* known to us descends from a surviving copy',[33] so no stemma can be made based solely on the extant copies. Secondly, there is a marked blurring of the genetic relations between MS groups, and members of groups, through the tendency of the *Piers Plowman* scribes to introduce the same errors independently, whether consciously or otherwise. Thirdly, all the surviving copies appear to descend, via nine lost intermediaries, from one of two major lost sources, here called α and β, neither of which derives from the other. Both descend independently from a single archetypal MS, and the unique material in α and β does not represent revision of one by the other, so that neither can be eliminated as part of a process of recension extending beyond extant witnesses to take in hypothetical family originals. Fourthly, many of the extant MSS and, by reliable inference, the lost ones too, have been subjected to deliberate scribal 'correction'. This may be 'normal' correction, aiming to make the reading conform more closely to that of the exemplar, or it may result from readerly enthusiasm to 'improve' or modify the poem's sentiments or style. The latter kind of 'correction' would probably have introduced, as Kane observes, 'readings from another strain of descent', and 'their intrusiveness . . . concealed at the next stage of copying, will have been one source of the random variational groups brought to light in the classification process'.[34] Finally, there are signs that there has been extensive contamination, if not between α and β or from members of both families, then from securely hypothesized lost MSS of the same family, and from MSS of other versions (see pp. lxiv-lxv). Except that it may be in part unconscious, contamination cannot be readily distinguished in practice from 'correction' of the latter kind.

The diagram given below therefore has no claim to be a stemma; but it will serve to indicate broadly the lines of vertical descent that appear secure, and to throw light on at least part of the history of the text. The only indications of lateral transmission (given in broken lines) are those concerning MSS M, Cr^1 and Cr^2. The internal relations between the three components of B, already complex, are further complicated by signs of contamination, from other versions, a feature they appear to share with such MSS as F, G and H (contaminated from the A-version) and Hm (contaminated from C). The outline of genetic relationships provides the background for my attempt to establish the archetypal readings, using the 'direct method' pioneered by Kane in his edition of the A-version. This relies on demonstrating the direction of variation among the attested readings on the basis of a knowledge of 'the scribal tendencies of substitution'. In employing this method, genetic evidence may be, as Kane says, 'only one of a number of available indications of originality'.[35] But it is never to be lightly disregarded; for determination of the 'harder reading' which is 'itself satisfactory' and 'explains the origin of the erroneous alternative'[36] is not a matter on which editors will always agree, as the differences at many points between this text and that of K–D will bear out. Additionally, I am unable to agree with Kane (here following Greg) that 'striking' or what I call 'major' variants are *more* likely to be generated coincidentally by scribes than 'commonplace' ('minor') readings of little lexical, stylistic or metrical significance. It is the latter that principally arise through the various tendencies of scribal substitution; the former are (in my judgement, as a consequence of working on *P–T*), more likely to appear in a MS because they were present in the exemplar of that MS. There are, of course, many exceptions, but I believe that this is true of the A- and C-versions as well as of **B**, and I shall argue this more fully elsewhere.[37] The diagram below therefore

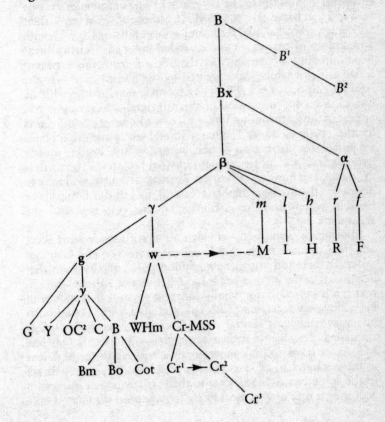

records genetic relationships on the basis of shared 'major' errors *supported* by the evidence from 'minor' ones. But although the latter evidence has not been accorded equal weight, the outcome does not in fact contradict the conclusions K–D reached by Greg's criterion. For many of the 'minor' agreements are also, of course, the result of deriving from the same immediate or proximate original.

TRANSMISSION OF THE TEXT

The reader of *The Prelude*, which Wordsworth worked on for most of his life, can choose between the completed version of 1805, the posthumous 1850 version, and a modern edited text that documents the whole process of composition from the surviving manuscripts. The B-version of *Piers Plowman* may be read in a text based on a single MS (e.g. those of Crowley, Wright and Skeat, who also used R for the passages missing from L), with a minimum of correction and emendation, or in a 'critical' text which attempts to reconstruct the original from the surviving MSS, none of which were written by the author (such are the Athlone editions of A and B). The Everyman text belongs with the latter, and a full discussion of the principles underlying it will appear in the forthcoming Volume II of the Longman parallel text by the present editor.[38] What I offer here is meant to be a simplified reconstruction of the history of the B-text, mostly hypothetical, and a brief account of what the present text offers the reader and how it is to be used. Readers, of course, will have to decide for themselves whether a 'critical' text of B is desirable or feasible when they have considered the evidence and the arguments.

My starting-point is the conviction, which I share with Skeat and the Athlone editors, that Langland wrote A, B and C in that order. To this I add a further assumption, not shared by them, that he also wrote the version known as Z (see section i above). The Z-text is a *complete* if not wholly coherent poem which ends with Piers Plowman receiving Truth's pardon. As a *draft*, even though one surviving in a scribal copy, it cannot have been widely circulated. This would sufficiently explain why there is only one MS. As we have it, Z is connected, by a bridge-passage of A-text in another hand, to a C-text conclusion, a feature it shares with six of the seventeen A-MSS. As with these, it seems that interest in acquiring a text of Z is most likely to have been stimulated only after the poem had been 'published' (i.e. offered by the author for circulation through the production of scribal copies) and had impinged on public consciousness, as we know it did (see p. xx above).[39] 'Publication' presupposes, though it may not, in the period, have strictly necessitated, the existence of at least one fully completed version, and the only indisputable one is B. Few readers during Langland's lifetime were probably aware that there were several distinct 'versions' of the poem; but common-sense suggests that Langland will have written C at least in part for those who knew B directly and not just by repute, though C neither refers nor alludes to the existence of the latter.

The A-version, unlike Z, is neither complete (whether we read to XI or to XII), nor a draft. After revising and clarifying Z in a masterly manner, A adds Piers's tearing of the pardon. It then goes on to an abrupt conclusion at the end of XI, in effect affirming the dangers of learning and the value of a simple faith for salvation. If Passus XII is accepted as genuine, it represents an abortive attempt to continue the poem with a defence of learning, which breaks off after describing how Fever warns Will to live virtuously for whatever days remain to him. This 'ending' John But (see p. xxiii above) rounds off, presumably prompted not by the content of XII but by knowledge that Langland had indeed died after writing 'other works about Piers Plowman', and *finishing* them ('when this work was wrought'). The reference will have been to the long B-version, though But's plural 'works' suggests that he also knew C, whose great differences from B strike anyone reading beyond line 94, where some thirty lines of powerful new material appear. We cannot know if A Pr–XI, incomplete as it was, remained 'unpublished'; but I think it likely that major interest in this version will have dated from a period after the success of B, if not from after Langland's lifetime. Kane thinks the A-text was one of the 'definitive points' in the poem's 'realization', and that copying of it began 'sometime in 1368–75' ('Text' p. 186), i.e. before the B-version. This is possible, but the only evidence for it is that Langland used a scribal copy of A in revising to B, and this is not absolutely certain. We do not know if Langland abandoned A because of the near-fatal illness described in Passus XII or intellectual and artistic dissatisfaction with his treatment of the place of learning in salvation. He came back to both topics in the B-version, but by the time he reached the last two passus of C it seems that the fiction of his approaching death had become the sudden reality to which But refers: 'Death dealt him a blow.'

In re-writing his poem, Langland worked from a copy-text of A; the overlap is too close to assume that he wrote B afresh with no direct reference to the earlier version. He used either his own fair-copy or, lacking this, a scribal copy. Errors could have come into either, since even a careful poet when acting as his own scribe makes errors. A passage such as B XI 303–6 strongly suggests that Langland cared as much for accuracy in a copyist as did Chaucer, who rebuked his scribe Adam for 'negligence and haste'; but whoever copied the A-text from which the *extant* MSS descend, whether during or after Langland's lifetime, introduced some serious corruptions into it. The fate of B was to be no better, and Kane and Donaldson are surely right that one motive for the local changes and revisions in C was Langland's response to major corruptions in the scribal copy of B which he used when revising to C.

THE ARCHETYPE AND THE SUB-ARCHETYPES

How would B have been 'published'? Because of the poem's great length – and for obvious psychological reasons, such as poets' tendency to make further changes even when ostensibly 'copying' – Langland will have given the finished work to a professional scribe for copying. The high cost of this was doubtless defrayed by the prospective purchaser. But, if several copies were to be made, Langland would at this point have lost 'control' of his text. For if he was not able to 'proof-read' the *first* copy against his original, any errors that entered it would thereafter be transmitted to subsequent copies made from it. Langland's fair-copies would have been written on loose sheets of paper, not on bound parchment. Evidence of this is the passage in XV which Kane and Donaldson convincingly argue was misplaced by the scribe who first copied it (see Commentary on XV 503–9, 528–31). This error was very probably in the copy of B Langland used when revising the passage in C XVII (see *P-T*, pp. 602ff). I shall call this 'author's copy', whether or not it was actually the *first* scribal product, '*B¹*'. This seems to have vanished almost as completely as Langland's autograph MS, and its very existence, while more than merely hypothetical, is less assured than that of Bx. However, it may survive in part, as the direct *source* of C XXI–XXII. I incline to think that these passus also include revisions, though minute indeed by comparison with those up to C XX. But this does not amount to disagreement with the view of the Athlone editors, who find no revision, that the substance of these passus is Langland's own B-MS, a scribal copy. What is not clear is whether the *errors* in this text as now preserved (which I call B^2), other than those shared with **Bx**, came in when the C-text up to XX, supplemented by B XIX and XX, was copied after Langland's death, or whether they were already there when he was preparing to revise them. The same reasoning that leads us to posit B^1 also allows the possibility that B^1 could have been little different from **Bx**.

More certain is it that B^1 was not the origin of the B-MSS which did survive. These, as Kane and Donaldson have demonstrated, go back to a single archetype, which I call **Bx**. This can be compared pretty directly with B^1 (i.e. via B^2), in the final two passus. B^1 here both reveals errors not in **Bx** and also lacks some of the errors of **Bx**. This shows that the two are independent B sources of XIX–XX, and the same is antecedently likely to have been true for the preceding Pr–XVIII, of which only the text of **Bx** can (in part) be ascertained. The immediate source of **Bx** is unknown. It was a MS which had perhaps already misplaced the Passus XV passage; but it also contained, or else the scribe of **Bx** introduced in copying, numerous other errors. These include verbal and metrical corruptions (such as misdivisions of lines and massive corruption of the key-stave by substitution of a non-alliterating synonym); eleven spurious lines; and some five omitted lines. Most of these errors were ignored by Skeat, who thereby unintentionally fostered the sense amongst early critics that Langland was careless in matters of stylistic and metrical detail.[40] But the task of the editor of B cannot consist simply in correcting – by reference, where necessary, to the other versions – obvious errors in a uniformly attested archetypal text. For **Bx** itself is securely recoverable in barely more than 40% of the whole, counting only English 'text' lines (with or without embedded Latin phrases), as opposed to 'citation-lines' of appended Latin (numbered as '*a*' lines).[41]

The oldest surviving MSS of the B version cannot be much earlier than *c.* 1400.[42] In the period of not more, or perhaps much less, than twenty years between this date and that of the copying of **Bx**, at least two other independent copies of the latter were made. I call them α and β, and from one or other of these all the extant MSS appear ultimately to descend. Copy β is represented by the MSS WHmCr[1,2,3]GYOC[2]CBmBoCotLMH, and α by the MSS R and F. A comparison of the two traditions, allowing for imperfections in the attestation of α (see below), reveals that each contains a number of major isolative errors which show that α cannot be derived from β nor β from α. Skeat's notion that α might represent a text transitional between B and C fails on close analysis, and Kane–Donaldson's conclusion, implicit also in Skeat's edition, that each is a partial witness to Bx, seems to me almost indisputable. The first difficulty that emerges from the comparison of α and β is fairly easily overcome. This is that α omits about 203 'text lines' and 18 half-lines found in β, while β omits about 165 text lines and 15 half-lines found in α.[43] To include all these lines, as Skeat did, serves in effect to reconstitute the substance of the archetypal text, accepting the proviso that in some 390 lines (aggregating the half-lines) this will have the support of only one of the two 'sub-archetypes', and will therefore be less secure than the rest of the text. Skeat's text could, in principle, be 'improved' somewhat by correcting the manifest errors in this reconstructed archetype and leaving the matter there. Editors of a positivist turn of mind might argue that to go any further would constitute interference with the text comparable to that of the medieval scribes themselves.

However, comparison between α and β proves more problematic. Firstly, the Bx reading is in contestation between them in about 1620 instances. Some 450 are 'major', i.e. involving significant differences of sense, metre or style, or all of these. The editor must judge which alternative reading represents Bx, as well as (though not necessarily before) deciding which is likely to be original. Logically the reading taken to represent Bx will be nearer to the original, but this takes no account of possible 'correction' of one or other sub-archetype, or individual members of its family, from a source outside the Bx tradition, not excluding other versions containing the line(s) in question. Any of these may contain a reading which on intrinsic grounds has a greater claim to originality than that of α or β. Secondly, the α-tradition, though detailed analysis reveals it to be of roughly the same quality as β, is poorly attested in comparison with β. This is firstly because, of the two witnesses R and F, each lacks a number of lines (R about 768, through loss of leaves, and F 62, possibly through loss of a leaf in its exemplar). Where *full* comparison of α and β is possible, i.e.

where both members of α are present along with all or most
members of β, I judge β to preserve the text of **Bx** in some 753
readings, 173 of them major, and α to preserve **Bx** in some 668
readings, of which 168 are major (comparison of the major
readings shows how close the two traditions are in the quality of
their text). Secondly, while α is represented throughout, for nearly
10% of the poem it relies solely on F. This, however, is a heavily
sophisticated MS of little reliability as a witness to α: thus, where
Bx is attested by α alone, with R and F *both* present for
comparison, F appears to err ten times more frequently than R.
Fortunately, for the five lines and three half-lines where F is the
sole witness, parallel lines exist in C which help in establishing the
authenticity of the readings; and for the eighteen B lines with *no*
parallel in other versions, the α witness is not F but R. The MS R,
therefore, though defective, is the single indispensable MS from
either family, being the one unique source of lines not found in
any other version.

No reason appears, other than historical accident, to explain
the paucity of witnesses to the α tradition. Kane and Donaldson
have provided satisfactory mechanical explanations[44] for the
omission of lines and passages from α and β severally. While such
omissions are not unparalleled in the A- and C-versions there is no
real doubt that the material belongs to the B-text, as an integral
version distinct from preceding A and subsequent C. Neither α-
MS is derived from the other, but whereas R is a moderately
accurate copy of its exemplar, F is so sophisticated that much of
the time it virtually rewrites the poem. For this reason, I have not
cited all its readings in the apparatus, even when it stands alone
for α (these appear in full in K–D's corpus of variants); but I
record its readings wherever they seem to represent α reasonably
faithfully or, even when sophisticated, serve to throw light on a
very difficult crux. F exhibits another characteristic which led
Kane–Donaldson to judge it important (Skeat ignored it). Some
instances apparently contain the right reading where R agrees in
error with β. An example is I 73 *halsed* F, supported by ZAC
against *asked* βR (*hasked* R). If R here = α, then α's agreement
with β ought to mean, from the hypothesis of descent from one
archetype, that **Bx** read *(h)asked*, a reading that seems inferior on
grounds of sense and style when compared with ZAC. Other cases
are II 210, where F reads *feerys*, again supported by ZAC, against
felawes βR (=**Bx**); III 145 *She* FZAC against *And* βR (=**Bx**); IV

15 *hym* FZAC (*om* βR); V 32 *He* FZC against *I* βR; VIII 109b–
110*a* FAC (*om* βR). How are these to be explained?

Kane and Donaldson hold that F at some points revises from a
source that embodies corrections from a B-MS superior to both
Bx and B^1. The hypothesis is neither necessary to explain the F
readings Kane and Donaldson judge original nor, without special
pleading, consistent with the pervasive character of F as an α-MS.
It seems barely conceivable that the 'corrector' of F's source
would have made relatively small changes[45] without noticing the
more than 200 lines, many in long sequences, that α lacked but
which must *ex hypothesi* have been in the 'lost' B source. The
hypothesis multiplies entities beyond necessity. A simpler explanation is that of *contamination* from MSS of the other versions of
the poem. The F lines that appear after VIII 49, 80, 101 and 102
are such cases. Absent from β and R (and so presumably from Bx),
they are also absent from revised C. These seem to be little more
than corrupt reflexes of A IX 45, 71, 93 and 95 respectively. Kane
and Donaldson adopt the A form of these lines into their B-text, as
representing lines lost from both B^1 and Bx. Yet in a closely
similar case where, after Pr 94, F adds A Pr 95, which is not in Bx
and has no C parallel, they do not accept the F line as a
'correction' but reject it as (presumably) contamination from A.
But if F's contamination from another version is so clearly
instanced as here, it would seem the simplest explanation also for
the four lines in Passus VIII discussed above. It is much less likely
that F's α-type exemplar was corrected from a lost B-MS of
remarkable purity than that its scribe compared his source with
an A-MS from time to time (as in Passus VIII). This interpretation
would also account for the many minor echoes of A's phrasing
found in variants of F. Elsewhere, as at IV 75, F may be offering an
independent correction that could be the original corrupted in Bx;
but this I judge likely to be a felicitous metrical correction.

The phenomenon of contamination is a factor also to be
reckoned with in a MS of the other family (G)[46] which Kane and
Donaldson believe to be corrected at some points from a superior
lost B-MS. Nor should this cause any surprise; for, as has been
said, MSS of the A-text (especially when 'supplemented' with a C
ending) and of the C-text were unlikely to have been recognized
by contemporaries other than those in Langland's immediate
circle as 'versions' in our sense, successive revisions with autono-
mous status. Rather, they would have been considered 'versions'

in a medieval sense – variously imperfect instances of a supposed single text, to be drawn upon opportunistically according to the capacity and bent of the copyist or compiler. The extreme of such contamination is illustrated by MS Hm 114, a conflated **ABC** text; but different forms of it are found in MS I of the C-text, the **C** portions of the Prologue of A-MS **K**, or the **A** material in BmBoCot between the **C** opening and the B-text proper. Extensive contamination is admittedly not a marked feature of most B- and C-MSS; but it occurs enough to have been a likely cause contributing to the distinctive character of F and certain other B-MSS, and must be taken into account. This becomes especially important when the question arises of turning to the A- and C-versions to seek the correct form of lines judged to have been corrupted in **Bx**. Following Kane and Donaldson here, where Skeat on the whole refrained, has, in my view, made it possible to purge the archetypal B-text of a number of demonstrably wrong readings without, in doing so, incurring the risk of producing a modern 'editorial' text dangerously akin to the 'conflated' ones generated by fifteenth-century scribes.

THE GROUPS

Like α, β seems to descend directly from **Bx**, since its longer omissions, like α's, can be explained as mechanically produced. This would have occurred most easily if its source was a MS in unbound sheets, some of which were lost, as others were when the α scribe received them. Unlike α, β has numerous extant representatives; but these in effect fall into five groups. They are the individual witnesses L, M and H, each separately derived from β; and the two groups w (consisting of WHm and the lost MS sources of Cr) and g (consisting of GYOC²CB), which descend from a common original which I call γ. Thus β displays a more complex history than α, but it is nonetheless better attested, because there are more independent witnesses, they are complete (though five members of g are partly defective), and none suffers from the sophistication of the α-MS F (though G and H, like F, show some contamination from the A-version).

Three *individual* MSS have the status of groups, as none depends on either of the others or on the γ group. Each is descended from β through at least one lost intermediary, which was not influenced by the immediate source of either of the others. Of these H, in some ways the most unusual, is a 'conjoint' MS, a

B-text up to V 125 and thereafter an A-text (= A-MS H³). Among its distinctive errors are about thirty omitted lines. It also omits III 69–72, along with F, perhaps through censorship. It frequently echoes the A-text, diverging from Bx in IV 160, where it has the A reading *meche*; in II 123, where it reads with the A family r; and I 11, where it is close to C but identical with A-MSS RUHE. Its distinctive readings, whether or not the result of contamination, agree with AC in two cases and ZAC in three; in a fourth, I 59, with ZA, its reading is not adopted into the text as Bx is not obviously wrong. In two more cases it also groups with one other B-MS (Cr at IV 94; G at IV 105). In nine cases where H appears to have the right or nearly right reading against Bx (Pr 59, 76; I 186; III 41, 114; IV 47, 90, 145, 190), contamination from A seems likely, given the clear evidence of this at IV 160, II 123 (neither adopted). But in the two readings agreeing with C (Pr 99, IV 90), descent from a B-MS superior to Bx remains a remote possibility. Most probably, though, H is in all these cases a descendant of β showing contamination from the other versions, and the true authority of its readings when adopted is their agreement with AC or, in the case of Pr 99, the intrinsic superiority of the reading, which C supports but which could have been an intelligent guess by the scribe of H (see p. lxiv above on F).

The independent status of M, prior to its extensive visible correction, is only a little more secure than that of H, since it has the right reading uniquely in only three cases. At XII 245 its insertion of necessary *is* and at VIII 49 that of (non-necessary) *þou* (to read *þou þiself* with A) could be intelligent guesses. At VI 119 *her* (supported by AC), which improves but is not strictly necessary to the line, is visibly added, and reference to another version becomes likely. M is more closely related to the group γ than is either L or H. It shares with g the error *þe males* at XI 339, where w, the other sub-group of γ, has smoothed to *þe males ben*. Here *þe* may be simply a coincidental substitution for unintelligible ʒe (for ʒede) in β, as preserved in L. But M cannot derive from L since it has I 37b (omitted by L, though M *adds* by correction I 38a, also missing in L). M also has the (correct) reading *whyes* with g at X 124, where Bx seems to have read *weyes*. Here, though, *weyes* is probably not the noun 'ways' but a spelling variant (paralleled in the Cx tradition) for the word 'whys', and M could have made the correction independently (one member of g, C², actually reads *weyes*). However, M cannot derive from **g**, since it lacks its many distinctive errors (on which see below, on **g**). M is somewhat closer to **w**, sharing its major errors *hunten* X 61, *He pat* XIII 411, *Is* XV 157, and several others by visible correction from a MS of **w**-type (XV 200, 224, XVI 125, XVIII 299, XIX 186). It cannot derive from **w**, however, since it lacks the majority of **w**'s other errors.

L's independent descent from β is shown by seven distinctive readings, three of them major (asterisked). These appear to be original on intrinsic grounds (XIV 181, close to ?α; XIV 258; *XV 611, close to C) or on comparison with C (XVI 27, *XVIII 198, *XIX 38, XX 6). L cannot therefore share an exclusive common ancestor with M or γ, and while contamination from a C source in the postulated *l* cannot be excluded, this is unlikely (e.g. the form of XV 611 both appears original and is not identical with C). L cannot derive from α; but L also agrees with securely attested α against the other β-MSS (i.e. γM, since H is not present) in at least 20 readings, 8 of them major; with ?α (attested only by R but with F present) in at least another 28, of which 6 are major, and possibly another two, more problematic ones (at X 271, XI 339); and with ?α (attested only by F, where R is absent) in six, two of them major. The most important of these agreements with α is XIII 283–4, which is confirmed by revised parallel C VI 36–7. While the loss of 283b, 284a was clearly mechanical, and M could have lost them coincidentally with γ, since L is unlikely to have acquired them from α, and C is here in revised form, L must have preserved the evidently original reading by direct descent from β, where γM have erred. The presumption that when L's independent witness is confirmed by α, it represents β and preserves **Bx**, is strengthened when many of these readings are further confirmed by A or C or both. Of the major readings the most important is XIII 283–4 (discussed above); others include XV 506, XVI 50 (cf. C XVIII 50), XVIII 390, XIX 190, 217 (where R is absent) and XX 287 (where F is corrupt).

However, if L's agreement with α in right readings needs no further explanation, half a dozen cases of agreement with α in certain or probable error against γ (with γ sometimes supported by C) obviously do. For if Lα here represent **Bx**, where has γ acquired its presumptively right reading? The most important of these (V 261) is so significant that it could be a true revision in C of the B reading represented in **Bx** (and preserved in Lα), and the γ reading could be derived from comparison with a C-text, rather than a postulated B source superior to Bx, seemingly the only logical alternative. It is one of several cases where MS M, the β-MS closest to L, erased its original reading and altered to agree with γ, presumably on the basis of a γ-MS (see p. lxvi above); others are V 208, XV 200, IX 98a. To these may be added five cases of clear alteration to the γ reading, with addition to or erasure of a reading like L's (V 441, VI 200, XII 245, XIII 355, XV 63). In all these, the rejected β reading, agreeing with α, may be presumed to be that of Bx; in the first and last, where γ could be right, on the showing of C, the source of γ's right reading becomes a problem. At VI 326, however, M has *altered* its γ-type reading to agree with Lα. In like manner, L in two cases has altered a reading it shared with α to agree with γM. In neither is there a C parallel present as a control. In X 271 the error may be visual (*b* for *l*) and has been corrected in F from the presumed α original *boste* (preserved in R) which was also that of β (corrected by L). In XIII 158 L has altered its (probably β) *sen*, agreeing with α, to read *deme* with γM. Unless *sen* is a visual error for *deme*, this is perhaps another case, like that of *boste*, where L's corrector had recourse to an exemplar of γ type. In addition to these agreements with α, L has six readings shared with R alone, where R may well represent α. Two of these are the same error, omission of *I*, at XIII 385 and XVII 296 (at XVIII 202, a third case of this error, LR are joined by Y). Together with the others, XI 135, XIII 338 (mechanical), XIV 106 and XVIII 39, these readings could faithfully preserve Bx. Correction of these errors by γ, M and (in six of the seven cases) F, was not, however, necessarily by recourse to C or a superior lost B source, since they are all 'commonsense' corrections, which could have been made independently. (Even V 261 *could* be such a case, with γ here anticipating the actual revision later made in C.) Of the many cases of L's agreement with α recorded in the apparatus, only a few major ones are noted in the Commentary, without detailed discussion.

It seems a fair assumption that L, while not a direct copy of β (as speculated in the first edition (1978, p. xxxvii), is removed from it by perhaps only one stage (*l*). But unlike M, which is similarly descended from β (through *m*), it is *virtually* free of influence from γ; and unlike the truncated H, which may derive from β by a single intermediary (*h*), it shows no sign of contamination from A (or, for that matter, from C). L thus represents, within the β family, as faithful a witness of the sub-archetypal readings as does R within the family of α. Skeat's evaluation of the B-text preserved in these two MSS does not appear to have been called in question by further analysis.

With some (limited) help from γ and from F (especially, and necessarily, where R is defective), L and R enable us, through their respective sub-archetypal sources, to reconstruct the common original of all the MSS (**Bx**). Their particular importance is recognized in the present edition in two ways. For β, the reading of L is always cited when the MS variants conflict randomly across the five sub-groups (L, M, H, **g**, **w**). L is not automatically adjudged to be right but, as it usually is, its representative status as the 'best' β witness is accorded due recognition in the form 'L&r' (see section viii below), and this is extended to those cases where β represents **Bx** against α but the base-MS of this edition (W) is itself in error. In the case of α, R is cited habitually as 'α' where it agrees with β, or is confirmed by **A/C/AC**, and F varies, but as '?α' where such agreement or confirmation is lacking. F, however, is not cited as 'α' but as '?α' whether R is present or absent, in testimony to the sophistication which obscures its α character almost continuously throughout the text.

Turning from the individual MSS with group status, we come to γ, the postulated common ancestor of WHmCrGYOC²CB. The existence of a γ group may be inferred from (a) at least 40 distinctive readings (15 of them 'major') and (b) about another 14 (8 of them 'major') in which the MSS that constitute this group are accompanied by M, sometimes showing visible correction of an original that was closer to L (see p. lxviii above). On the assumption that the γM readings are γ readings to which M has varied, the total evidence for γ is some 54 readings, 23 'major', three of them important, supported by another 31 'minor' readings. In the category (a) readings one member of the **w** sub-group of γ (Cr), has varied from the group-reading in two important cases, (i) XVII 184–185a, (ii) XVII 286, and also (here supported by M) in two other major readings, (iii) XVII 304, (iv) XVIII 383, in the latter also with YOCB of sub-group **g**. In (i) and (ii), classic cases of eye-skip, Cr's MS source, of γ type, had been corrected from a MS of *l* type (not of *m*, which omitted 185a and added it from (possibly) the same corrected γ-MS as the Cr source, or from a MS of *l* type). In (iii), Cr shares with M a variant which is either a reflex of the *l* reading (here confirmed by α and C, and so evidently archetypal) or else a correction of the γ original, from a common source of *l* type. In (iv) Cr shares a variant with M, and YOCB have diverged to join Lα in another (erroneous) variant of an evidently difficult phrase. In category (b), the γ readings shared with M, the most important is XIII 283–4 (discussed above under M), where M may have varied with γ coincidentally (through eye-skip). Also important is VI 326, where M's source reads with γ but has been visibly corrected to read with L.

The readings of γ appear throughout the text in the sub-groups **w** and **g**. The γ text is uniformly attested by WHmCrGYOC²CB as far as about V 234, where the sub-groups **w** and **g** begin to be differentiated. The source **w** was an indifferently accurate copy of γ, from which it diverged in some 43 individual cases, 20 of them major, reckoning only those lines where WHmCr read uniformly. The number rises to 55 on including the group WHm (8 readings, 4 major) and WCr (4 minor readings). It expands further to 69 if we add the 14 cases (6 major) where M accompanies **w**, as seems reasonable, since **w** does not derive from M, while M seems to have been corrected from a **w**-type source (see p. lxvii above). The most important readings that serve to identify **w** are the omitted lines XII 103 and XV 373. Group **w** attests what may well be the original reading at X 57, perhaps through correction from A or C or, most probably, as a felicitous guess.

The source of **g** appears to have been a MS which took over from the original exemplar of this group no later than V 234, where it first exhibits a distinctive (minor) variant. Thereafter it is identified by over 130 distinctive readings, about 75 of them major. They fall into three main categories: omitted lines and passages; additional lines; and attempts to modernize or make the sense more explicit, sometimes through evident failure to understand the exemplar's reading. The source of **g** omitted some 16 lines and 4 half-lines, the largest omission being XIX 219b–227a, a classic case of eye-skip. It also added four lines, after XII 154, XV 229, XVIII 259 and 294 (the last of these also included by the lost source of Cr[23], presumably a MS of sub-group g, of *y* type). It made substantial changes in the γ source, re-writing IX 95–6, as prose, XIII 52–6 and XVII 123–4. Finally, and most significantly perhaps, it eliminated cases of rhetorical repetition, often replaced archaic words such as *wye* and *burne* with more modern synonyms, and translated the French in a macaronic line.

The group **g** is independent of **w**, having XII 103 and XV 373 and (here with F) what seems the right reading at IX 11. It is also larger and more complex than **w**, falling into two smaller sub-groups. These are represented respectively by the lost medieval source of the sixteenth-century MS G, and by *y*, the postulated source of YOC²CB. Of these, *y* has in turn four constituents, Y, OC² (which form a genetic pair), C and B (the three members of which, BmBoCot, derive from a single immediate ancestor, B). The sub-group *y* added another five spurious lines, all of which were incorporated by the rejected MS Ht, and three of them by the second and third Crowley prints.[47] MS *y* itself underwent few corrections which might make it worth consideration (one is at VII 56), but B, individual members of B, the ancestor of OC² and C² itself sometimes show readings from other versions. Examples are: OC²B at XIII 411, from C; B at XV 549, from C; Cot at XIX 76, XX 378, from C; C² from C at XVIII 160 and (corruptly) after XX 260. The group **g** is at no point the sole witness of a γ reading which may be taken to stand for β against wLM. However, with the support of ?α and C, it does so stand at XX 147 (joined by Cr²³, here correcting from *y*). It may also preserve γ (and thence β) at XIX 15 (with the support of C and also of Hm, which may here stand for **w**). In another case, Y(OC²) contain a line (IV 10) omitted in Bx, deriving it severally from A or C (Cr²³ joins them, omitting a stave-word). Finally, a number of apparently correct readings are preserved in the sixteenth-century MS G, which I consider to represent a better tradition of **g** than does *y*. K-D see the text of G's lost exemplar as having been corrected at points from a B-MS superior to Bx. But this hypothesis is unnecessary; for many of the cases in which the supposed superiority is diagnosed may be judged as evincing contamination from the A-tradition. In Pr–V, for example, there are some 70 such instances, a number closely comparable to those exhibited by F and H, each of which has about 60.

On the whole, the group γ is of small value as a witness to β, the sub-archetypal ancestor it shares with LMH. But it cannot be eliminated from consideration. Firstly, it cannot derive from L, M or H, because its oldest member (W) is coeval with or older than the oldest of these (L), and because H is defective after V 125, nor from their postulated older originals (*l*, or *m*, or *h*), because it lacks the three characteristic major errors of LM (at VI 322, VIII 127, XIII 265), the seven major errors of L (at XIII 338, 374; XIV 88, 312; XV 461; XVI 145; XIX 367), and those of *h* where its text is present (e.g. the more than 30 missing lines). It is also right against LR(M) at V 232 with F (see also XIII 385, again with F). Secondly, individual members of its sub-groups **w** and **g** have readings which, on being compared with C, seem preferable to the joint witness of the other MSS to the presumed reading of β. To take some examples from **w**: W, the base-MS of this edition, has unique readings at XV 552 and XIX 111, both of which are supported by C. Clearly not archetypal, they may have come in by contamination from C, or else be commonsensical 'corrections' towards a more natural-sounding idiom than that of the exemplar's presumed **Bx** reading; but each requires separate editorial consideration on its own merits. Again, at XI 287, WHm are similarly correct, by contamination from C or from a felicitous guess in their immediate ancestor.

EMENDATION OF THE ARCHETYPAL TEXT

This brief survey of the tradition of the B-text has aimed to show that there is an abundance of evidence for the recovery of the archetypal readings, and that none of the group-readings can be securely eliminated from consideration, for reasons which have been set out above. Where **Bx** is attested unanimously, or nearly so, a body of lines exists which exhibits definite stylistic, linguistic and metrical characteristics. These can serve as criteria for discriminating the archetypal readings where support for variants is divided between the sub-archetypes, or cuts across them, by indicating the likely direction of variation. But a further, and possibly more solid resource exists for determining the latter, and hence the archetypal readings, and to this I now turn.

In attempting to *establish* the readings of **Bx**, before going on to assess their 'originality' or degree of authenticity, the editor cannot refrain from consulting the evidence of the other versions of *Piers Plowman*. The Z-text, and the archetypal texts of A and C, contain between them a small body of lines identical with their parallel lines as preserved in the archetypal text of B. It is the characteristics of style and thought that they display that alone merit the term 'Langlandian'. Empirically established, these core lines also satisfy logically the criteria for 'originality'. The entire process of editorial judgement – discrimination, reconstruction and conjectural emendation – therefore terminates in an appeal to this body of evidence as, at least negatively, final. Thus, to put it simply, any proposed emendation which does not meet, say, the metrical criteria derived from these lines must be considerably less credible than one that does. The correlative of this is that when archetypal B lines which have *no* parallel in ZAC do meet these criteria, they should, in the absence of further evidence to the contrary, *prima facie* be accepted. This is because it is axiomatic that Bx readings are likelier to be nearer to the original than the readings of any later stage of the tradition, allowing only for the possibility of (a) correction from a 'lost source superior to Bx' and (b) contamination from other versions that arguably contain what was also the original B reading. Readings of type (b), which are easier to identify, such as some of those considered above, may well preserve, or be nearer to, the original text in any given instance than Bx itself. But in that case, the authority of these readings will rest solely on their authority in the traditions of the other versions in which they survive.

The witness of the three traditions of ZAC against Bx will offer a strong presumption that B read the same as ZAC. This is because, in my judgement, Langland is unlikely in his final revision to have returned to the readings of his first and second versions after having rejected it in his third version; the possibility, of course, cannot be entirely ruled out. Where Z is absent, the joint witness of AC against B similarly provides a presumption, weaker but still strong, of the same kind, though not one, again, to be acted upon mechanically. Where Z and A agree against B and C, the presumption moves in the other direction; B is likely to have revised A, and the preservation of its reading in C must be taken as a tacit *acceptance* of it by the author, whatever other grounds there might be for questioning a particular archetypal reading in B. The reading of A, or of AZ together, is not sufficient grounds for rejecting the parallel reading in Bx, if it meets the 'Langlandian' criteria mentioned above, even when that reading has *no* support from a parallel reading in C.

It is, of course, debatable how those criteria are to be specified in detail, and how they are to be invoked in given cases; different editors or readers may come to conflicting conclusions even when they start from the same agreed basis. I have myself found this to be so in the course of re-editing the B-text as part of an attempt to establish a parallel text of all four versions. I still hold to the conclusion reached by K–D, that the archetypal text of **B** was seriously corrupt. But I have now reduced the number of emendations from some 750, about the same number as in K-D, to 476 (counting individual readings, of which there may be more than one in a line). If to these are added a number of readings from individual MSS which are likely to be by contamination from either **A** or **C**, the number rises to some 500. Undoubtedly, several more archetypal lines could be put to question than those I have actually judged fit to emend; but the case has not seemed strong enough to warrant editorial intervention, especially in the absence of directly relevant evidence from one or more of the other versions.[48] This is not to deny that reference to the other versions can be of the utmost value, as I found in the first edition, in the process of '*discriminating* B-readings' and in pointing 'to the certainty ["strong probability", I would now say] that many **A** lines were never revised in **B** and many **B** lines never revised in **C**' (1978 edn, p. xxxviii). But the step from discriminating between MS readings to 'reconstructing' the readings of the hypothetical lost sub-archetypes and archetype has been, in many instances, more cautiously taken as a result of subsequent experience of editing both **A** and **C**.

The archetypal text of **B**, when examined in the light of the parallel lines uniformly attested in **ZAC**, **AC**, **C** or, in the case of XIX–XX, of B^2 (see p. lxi above), the possible text of Langland's own B-MS, appears seriously corrupt. To put it in summary form: the **Bx** scribe made about one major error for every twenty lines he copied. Of these errors, the spurious lines he introduced must at least have been deliberate; but there are signs that many others also result from conscious acts: of censorship, objection to features of style and content, and desire to simplify or smooth the difficult sense of the original. No reconstructed text of **Bx** exists, but the reader can get a fair notion of what it must have been like from Skeat's edition of **B**, which is based largely on L and R, with only a few emendations from other B-MSS and barely any from C. However, since L and R are still only imperfect reflexes of β and α respectively, Skeat's edition is necessarily rather more corrupt than **Bx** itself must have been; but many of the further corruptions it contains are relatively minor. What makes Skeat's edition unacceptable as representing 'Langland' is the presence, in the archetypal text it (roughly) transmits, of something like 500 readings which are to be judged 'unoriginal', the product not of the poet but of the archetypal scribe. Of these, perhaps 370 are 'major', and a group of some 22 is important enough to highlight here because it constitutes the most striking evidence that **Bx** was indeed very corrupt. The reader of a 'positivist' turn of mind, who objects in principle to heavily emended texts, should examine these in the first instance before deciding conclusively that editorial responsibility ceases at the restoration of the archetype, where it is securely recoverable, and that further alteration of the text amounts to a form of 'interference' comparable to that of the medieval scribes whom the editor has presumed to criticize.

The important errors to be found in **Bx** fall into three main categories. Firstly, and most obviously, **Bx** *added* twelve lines which appear spurious on grounds of metre, style, thought or a combination of these criteria. They occur after IV 38; V 39*a*, 54, 193, 556; VI 17, 182; VII 59; X 266; XI 67; XIX 373. To these may be added XVIII 82, where this edition substitutes the parallel C line for that of **Bx**, which is wholly scribal in character. Secondly, **Bx** *omitted* about eight lines, which are here supplied from one of the other versions: I 112 (from Z; also in A); V 328; V 338 (from A; also in C); XI 371b; XII 129b; XVIII 161; XIX 373a, 441; XX 261 (from C). Thirdly, **Bx** *mis-divided* a small number of lines which can be re-divided without any or with minimal 'reconstruction' (e.g. XIII 330, XVII 32), and *misplaced* a group of lines, which can be easily re-ordered: e.g. Pr 189–92, II 203, XIV 285–6, XVIII 6–8 and, most important of all, XV 503–9, 528–31, which seem also to have been mis-placed in B^1 (see *K-D*, 178–9). I follow Kane and Donaldson in emending all these errors.

The total number of errors I recognize in **Bx** is, nevertheless, considerably smaller than that diagnosed by the Athlone editors. From the point of view of emendation, they fall into two categories. The first consists of those readings which can be confidently corrected from one or more of the other versions; the second, of those which must be emended by a process of conjectural reconstruction, varying from single restorations of word-order necessary for the scansion of a line, to the pure conjecture of a lost stave-word or half-line. It goes without saying that the emendations of the first group are the more likely to carry conviction. This is because they are based in effect upon the relatively 'objective' procedure of *divinatio* which is fully attested in the apparatus at every point where a parallel line exists in one or more of the other versions. The persuasive force of 'other-version emendation' of **Bx** will thus be in proportion to the persuasive force of the same criterion when it is invoked for discrimination between competing sub-archetypal or group-readings. The procedure is not, of course, without hazards: there are occasionally clashes, as between **ZB** and **AC**, which may seem to call in question the assumption of progressive or 'linear' revision, i.e. revision without reversions to earlier readings; reliance on a special explanation here may seem to weaken the general case for emendation. The sceptical reader will have to consult *P-T*, Vol. II for a fuller justification of my (tentative) judgement that occasional anticipations of **B** or **C** readings in the MS of **Z** probably result from memorial contamination on the part of the scribe of its exemplar, which was not the holograph, and are not themselves necessarily signs of **Z**'s being a total scribal concoction, nor, if its authenticity is *otherwise* accepted, of the doubtful reliability of the 'linear revision' postulated in the revision of **B**. I think it unlikely either that Langland reverted to earlier-version readings in his various revisions, or that his hand is detectable in any stage of the MS tradition from the level of the archetype down. But this may well prove impossible to demonstrate.

Somewhat more than 200 readings have been adopted into the text, in preference to **Bx**, from one or more of the other versions; of these a high proportion (just under 130) are 'major'. The extreme importance of 'parallel-text' editing for the B-text itself will thus be immediately apparent to any reader who accepts these emendations, most of which I follow the Athlone editors in adopting. Given my assumption (not shared by the latter) that the Z-text is also authentic, it will follow that the greatest degree of relative certainty must attach to those emendations supported by the sigils **ZAC**. There are some 53, of which 20 are 'major'. A comparable degree of security may be credited to those supported only by **AC**, about 57, of which 40 are 'major'. Considerably less certain are the more than 80 readings, about 60 of them 'major', in which **Bx** is rejected in favour of **C** alone. Here the 'linear' postulate is necessarily of no use, since there is no possibility of appealing to agreement of a '*pre*-B' with a '*post*-B' version against **Bx**, and in principle any of the C readings in question could be a revision. In practice, however, comparison of **C** with **Bx** of a similar kind to that carried out when attempting to discriminate between B-MS variants in the light of **Z**, **A** and **C**, generally enables us to decide whether revision can be excluded as the possible reason for the differences between the texts. Here, however, I have preferred to proceed with circumspection, especially in XIX–XX, where no attempt has been made to harmonize **Bx** and B^2 in a single uniform emended text, simply because the possibility of revision, however light in character, cannot be securely ruled out. The same reservations apply to those cases, few as they are, where only **A** or **Z** provides the reading preferred to **Bx** (7 for **A**, 6 'major'; one for **Z**, major and important).

Turning to the second and larger class of emendations, the reader will find that slightly more than 260, of which just over 240 are major, are of the type for which evidence in one or more of the other versions is either indirect or entirely wanting. Here, the 'positivist' may well draw the line, regarding such features of **Bx** as defective metre, unless they are demonstrably of mechanical origin, as having to be tolerated, and as possibly having been (as Skeat evidently thought) acceptable on occasion to the author. A very large number of these are indeed diagnosed as corruptions on metrical grounds, the **Bx** scribe having had a particular propensity to introduce a non-alliterating (near-)synonym at the keystave position in the b-half of a line. The main examples are the following 70:

> I 11, 160, 165, 200, 206; II 36, 84, 200; III 71, 260, 298, 319, 346; IV 91; V 47, 128, 165, 194, 400, 405, 412; VI 138, 150, 223; VII 34, 45, 104; VIII 100; IX 15, 33, 39, 188; X 50, 90, 108, 242, 246, 279, 301, 446; XI 127, 343; XII 4, 193; XIII 85, 136, 424, 444; XIV 61, 223; XV 123, 224, 312, 320, 352, 545, 550; XVI 201; XVII 90, 214, 326; XVIII 54, 406; XIX 97, 244, 252, 317, 348, 372, 413.

Another 27, in positions other than that of the key-stave, are the following:

> III 222, 255, 316, 344; IV 86, 158; V 171; VI 123, 242, 272; X 251; XI 289; XIII 8; XIV 8; XV 421, 450, 470, 479, 547; XVII 38; XVIII 154, 280, 392; XIX 90, 183, 230, 409.

Confidence in the emendations adopted here depends on the confidence placed in the understanding of Langland's metre being invoked. This has been set forth in full elsewhere, and the basis for the brief schema given here in the Metrical Appendix is a complete comparative analysis of the lines not only in B but in all four versions. My conclusion from this analysis is that the schema accurately describes all and only the metrical varieties found in the core 'Langlandian' corpus (the archetypally attested A, B and C lines, and the parallel lines in Z, where all agree). As these varieties are exemplified abundantly in the competing B variants at every level below the archetype, providing criteria for discriminating between them, they may be judged to suffice to authorize emendation of archetypal lines that fail to meet those criteria.

The degree of certainty or probability of editorial emendations will vary in strength according to whether they offer themselves as nearer to 'reconstruction' than to pure 'conjecture'. Of these readings in question, about 100, of which about 37 are major, have been adopted from Kane–Donaldson, and a couple were first made by Skeat (XIII 86, 407, both major). I have contributed another 160, of which about 105 can be described as 'major' in type. In this new edition, no deliberate attempt has been made to exercise caution for its own sake: sometimes it is the boldest conjecture that is the best, that is, the one most likely to approximate to what Langland originally wrote. But I have sometimes both proposed new and rejected old conjectures, my own as well as those of the Athlone editors, in the light of an altered understanding both of the text and of the various scribal tendencies at work in the MS tradition. Thus, for example, I have abandoned K-D's bold conjecture *bouste* at XIII 153 (in Patience's riddle); but I have also introduced radical emendations *metri causa* at V 171 (*faste*), where the mechanical probability of the error diagnosed seems high, and at what seems a closely parallel case of haplography, at III 260 (*fel*). The 'boldness' of these editorial 'sins' is, I trust, somewhat 'abought' by the demonstrable existence of this phenomenon within the sub-archetypal traditions of the C-text, viz. at VI 35 (in the passage quoted in full on p. xxii above), where the p tradition of C-MSS reads *yong* for *yong yong*. Here, as so frequently in re-editing the B-text, comparison of the other *Piers Plowman* versions and their total range of variants, together with increased awareness of the need to examine each reading in the context of all the others, has led me to a different conclusion, one not necessarily less radical but, I venture to hope, both safer and more deserving of acceptance.

The reader wishing to assay the results of the present editor's judgements is invited to inspect the following selection of 'major' emendations, all of which are argued for *ad loc.* in the Textual Commentary. Three of the most important types are those which (i) introduce an *idiom* or a *lexeme* instanced in the period, either (a) sometimes or (b) never in one or other version of the poem; and (ii) those involving 'complex reconstructions' of one or more lines:

(i) (a) Pr 11; V 378; X 186, 274, 307, 367, 393; XI 49, 301; XIII 136, 300; XIV 311; XV 123, 312, 320; XIX 186, 241, 244, 348, 372, 409 (*idioms*)
I 160; III 298, 346; IV 86, 91; V 540; VI 123, 148, 150, 223; VII 34; IX 15, 39, 163, 188; X 50, 90, 131, 190, 251, 304; XI 343, 388, 439; XII 60, 131, 203; XIII 85; XIV 8, 196, 300; XV 393, 470, 479; XVI 201; XVII 214; XVIII 281, 392; XIX 413; XX 292, 293 (*lexemes*)

(b) VI 138; X 242, 246, 320; XI 430, 438; XIV 23; XVII 38; XIX 90 (*lexemes*)

(ii) V 456; IX 41–2; X 28, 301; XI 196; XV 126–7; XVIII 159; XIX 255, 306; XX 366, 367.

The detailed reasoning underlying these decisions on the B-text forms part of the comprehensive arguments used for establishing the texts of Z, A and C; these will appear in *P-T*, Vol. II.

Despite the greater length of section vii in this new edition, the textual notes have not been reduced in length, though they have frequently been altered in content to accommodate changes in the text itself. The principles invoked have remained unchanged from those of fifteen years ago. I find it still true, that 'in coming to different conclusions from Kane and Donaldson I have often used their methods and considered possibilities and approaches first suggested by them'. However, the number of differences between my conclusions and theirs has greatly increased. What this indicates about the validity of those 'methods' and 'approaches' must be left to the reader to decide. I certainly hope that this edition will be found to improve on its predecessor, which it is intended to supersede; but if the fate of my author is anything to go by, some of its readers may well conclude otherwise.

viii *Editorial procedure*

The basis of the text in this edition is Cambridge, Trinity College

MS B.15.17 (W), first printed by Thomas Wright in 1842 and used by Kane and Donaldson for their Athlone Press edition. This is the earliest of the B-MSS (*c.* 1400). Despite the fact that its text is substantively inferior to that of Oxford, Bodleian Library MS Laud Misc. 581 (L), it has the advantage of a regular spelling and grammatical system close to that of Langland's day, though the dialect is that of Middlesex, and not the south-west Midlands, the poet's area of origin. It resembles the work of the scribe of the Hengwrt and Ellesmere MSS of *The Canterbury Tales*.

TEXT

1 *Spelling*   The MS is printed as it stands except that:
  i All abbreviations are silently expanded
  ii Small spelling errors (a mere handful) and words damaged by cropping of the MS are silently corrected
  iii Obsolete ME letters are given their appropriate modern equivalent: *gh* or *y* for ȝ, *th* for þ
  iv The letters *v* and *j* are printed for MS *u* and *i* when their values are consonantal and *v* as *u* when a vowel; *s* is printed for *z* after *t* (*servaunts*); the name *Ihesu*(*s*) is printed *Jesu*(*s*)
  v Capitalization is editorial, though I have taken note of the MS practice and sometimes followed its guidance
  vi All readings adopted from other MSS of B or from the A- and C-texts are given in the spelling of W without notice
  vii In a few cases, final *-e* has been added to a word, without square brackets or notice in the Apparatus, in order to provide the feminine ending habitual at the end of the line. This is printed in italics, and may involve minor consequent alteration in the spelling of the base-MS (e.g. 'hymsel*ve*' for 'hymself' at V 279)
  viii The MS symbol *&c* that concludes incomplete Latin quotations is rendered '. . .' in the text; but the lemma in the Apparatus, following the practice adopted for all lemmata, is given in the form it has in the source MS (viz. *&c*)
  ix Square brackets are placed around conjectural readings and readings adopted from the Z-, A- and C-versions, but, in order to make the text easier to read, not around the many readings adopted from other B-MSS in preference to that of W

2 *Punctuation*, *paragraphing* and other *sectional divisions* are editorial, and I have not recorded large capitals in the MS.

APPARATUS

1   I record all departures from the reading of W and all changes
in lineation. Readings from other B-MSS adopted in preference to
W's will be found in the apparatus, followed by the MS sigil(s) in
question.

2   The first entry in the Apparatus, the *lemma*, is given in the
spelling of the MS it comes from. This should cause no difficulty,
as the forms are nearly always easily identifiable and it has the
advantage of giving only authentic spellings, so that the question
of whether a reading is substantive or accidental cannot be
obscured by normalized orthography. When one or more of the
letters of the lemma are *italicized*, MSS cited as supporting the
reading, except only the MS supplying the lemma, contain
different letters to those italicized. When a sigil is italicized, the
MS denoted shares the substantive reading of the sigil it follows
except for a minor difference in word order (e.g. *F* after Cr at I 12).
These are usually only 'accidental' variants; the interested reader
should consult the corpus of variants in Kane and Donaldson for
details. To save space, I frequently *abbreviate* both lemmata and
variants, but not where difficulty in identifying the word(s) in the
text might arise. I have checked all lemmata against the originals.
Lemmata from the Z-text, the A-text and the C-text come from
P-T, in which the base-MS of A is Cambridge, Trinity College MS
R.3.14, that of C San Marino, Huntington Library MS 143 (the
same MSS used by Knott–Fowler for A, by Pearsall for C, and by
the Athlone Press edition), and that of Z the unique Oxford,
Bodleian Library MS Bodley 851.

3   The *sigla* include (i) the B-MSS specified under 'The
Manuscripts' (see pp. liv–lv above) (ii) the symbols for the
archetypal readings of each version, 'Ax', 'Bx' and 'Cx'; (iii) the
sub-archetypal sigla α, β; (iv) the group symbols w, g and *y* (on
which see section vii of the Introduction p. lxxi) and (v) the
symbols Z, A and C, representing the presumed originals of these
versions respectively. The query sign is used where any of these is
uncertain: thus '?AC' or 'A?C' means that a reading is supported
by the C-version and by the A-version but in the case of the
queried sources only *one* of the two sub-archetypes, of A, or of C,
supports the cited reading (for further details, see *P-T*, p. xiii).

4   *Other symbols* used in the Apparatus are (i) *&r* 'all B-MSS other than those (if any) specified elsewhere in the variant-entry', whether immediately after the lemma (e.g. Pr 29 *kairen*) or in later position (e.g. Pr 42); (ii) (C) 'see the Textual Commentary' for discussion of the reading; (iii) '*K-D*', '*Sk*', etc. 'reading first printed by . . .' In referring to Kane and Donaldson's edition I frequently gave a page reference in previous editions of this book. These have been omitted in the present edition in order to restrict the content of the apparatus largely to essential information about the MSS, and because the textual problems will be discussed in full in *P-T*, Vol II. (iv) *cj* is used to mean 'reading conjectured by . . .' and it covers *all* readings, including 'reconstructions', for which there is no direct MS support in any of the B-MSS. (v) *a.h.* = 'another hand'; *l.h.* 'later hand'; *m.h.* 'the main hand of the MS'. (vi) *trs* 'words (in variant) transposed'; *div* 'divided'; *ord* 'ordered'; *canc* 'cancelled'; *arr* 'arranged'; *def* 'defective'; *ins* 'inserted'; *om* 'omitted'; *sg* 'noun in singular in MS'; *pl* 'noun in plural in MS'. (vii) † 'reading seriously corrupt'; + 'word(s) added'; : 'letter obliterated in MS'.

GLOSSES AND TRANSLATIONS

1   The *marginal glosses* of words and phrases are meant to complement the formal Glossary and are supplemented by the *footnote translations*. Problems of syntax are dealt with in the latter, which sometimes become paraphrases. A capital letter is used to signalize the first word in the line. The sign / indicates an alternative rendering. Round brackets enclose words not in the original but needed to fill out the sense. Square brackets enclose elucidation of the meanings of words or phrases that cannot be translated easily, and also Biblical and other quotations which the text cites only in part.

2   Many *individual words* receive further discussion in the Commentary; '(C)' after a gloss or translation refers to this. Most are in the Textual and Lexical Commentary, but a few not arising from or bearing directly on textual problems appear in the Literary and Historical Commentary. Most major problems of meaning have been dealt with, though a number of difficulties of interpretation may require the Textual Commentary to be consulted. (For a full translation and further notes on points of intepretation see the editor's 'World's Classics' translation (1992).)

COMMENTARY

This is divided into two parts for ease of reference. The *first part* presupposes some familiarity with the methods of textual criticism, but is probably not too technical for those interested to enquire into the basis of the edited text. It should be consulted together with section vii above (now much expanded from the first edition). To save space, quotations and references are usually abbreviated, and the Commentary needs to be used in close conjunction with the text, the critical apparatus and, where necessary, the texts of Z, A, and C printed in *P-T*. In the Commentary the symbol // means 'in the parallel part of the text specified' (A, C or Z); and L stands for 'Langland'. Other abbreviation-symbols used are: $\otimes$ = 'contamination'; $\emptyset$ = 'zero-reading'; * = 'lost hypothetical form'; $\Rightarrow$ = 'substituted (for)'. The *second part* provides literary and historical information needed to understand the text, and a small amount of general interpretative comment. Limits of space have required keeping both interpretation and documentation to a minimum; for further details the longer notes of Skeat, Bennett and Pearsall should be consulted, along with the books and articles referred to by short title; and for fuller interpretative commentary, the notes to the World's Classics translation of *Piers Plowman*. For convenience to the reader I have used wherever possible easily accessible standard works of reference and a selection of secondary works many of which are available in paperback. I have cited the Colunga–Turrado edition of the Vulgate Bible (Madrid, 1965) and the Douay–Rheims version for translations of this. Psalms are therefore numbered according to the practice of these versions, as are Biblical books (I and II Kings are I and II Sam in AV). Full details of works cited by short title and a selection of those consulted are given in the Bibliography.

GLOSSARY

Added in the fourth printing of this book (1987), the Glossary, compiled with the assistance of Judith Schmidt, has been brought up to date to accord with the revised text. (A full Glossary of Langland's four versions will appear in *P-T* Vol. II.)

ABBREVIATIONS

The most frequent are AlfG Alford, J. A., *PP: A Glossary of Legal Diction*; AlfQ Alford, J. A., *PP: A Guide to the Quotations*; Bn J.

A. W. Bennett's edition of B Prol and Passus I–VII; *CT The Canterbury Tales*, in *The Riverside Chaucer*, ed. Benson; *Ka* George Kane's edition of the A-text (rev. 1988); *K-D* George Kane and E. Talbot Donaldson's edition of the B-text (rev. 1988); L Langland; *MED Middle English Dictionary*, ed. H. Kurath and S. M. Kuhn (Ann Arbor, Michigan); *OBMLV The Oxford Book of Medieval Latin Verse*, ed. F. J. E. Raby; *OED Oxford English Dictionary*; Pe Derek Pearsall's edition of the C-text; *PL Patrologia Latina*, ed. J.-P. Migne; *P-T* Schmidt, *Parallel-Text* (Vol. I, 1995); *SB Breviarium ad usum insignis ecclesiae Sarum*, ed. F. Procter and C. Wordsworth (3 vols, Cambridge, 1879); Sch Schmidt, A. V. C.; *Sch The Vision of Piers Plowman*, ed. A. V. C. Schmidt (1987 edn); *Sk* W. W. Skeat's Early English Text Society edition of *Piers Plowman*, versions A, B and C, in four parts; *ST* the *Summa theologica* of St Thomas Aquinas (Madrid, 1961); *Wr* Thomas Wright's 1887 edition of the B-text; *YLS Yearbook of Langland Studies* ed. J. Alford and M. T. Tavormina (Michigan, 1987–).

A. V. C. SCHMIDT

References

[References are in abbreviated form; for full details, see Bibliography.]

1. All references to the Z-, A-, B-, and C-texts are to *P-T*, I. The authenticity of Z is maintained by Rigg and Brewer, *Z-Text*, rejected by Kane, ' "Z Version" ', and supported by Schmidt, 'Authenticity', Green, 'Exemplar' and (tentatively) Duggan, 'Authenticity', 40.
2. See the Bibliography under these authors.
3. Sisam, *Verse and Prose*, 160–1.
4. Kane, *Evidence*, pl. 1.
5. Kane, *Autobiographical Fallacy*; see also Burrow, *Fictions*, 83–9 for a subtle discussion of 'fictions of self' in relation to Langland.
6. 'Messenger and Maker'. For a recent discussion of But's conclusion to the A-text, see Middleton, 'But as a Reader of *PP*'.
7. 'The Audience of *PP*', in *Essays*, 102–16 (with Postscript); see also Schmidt, *Clerkly Maker*, 1–20; Middleton, 'Audience and Public'; Schmidt, *Translation*, xii–xvii.
8. 'Date of the A-Text'.
9. Kane, 'The Text', 185.
10. McKisack, *Fourteenth Century*, 436.
11. 'The Text', 186.
12. See Rigg–Brewer, *Z Version*, 12–20.

13. See Bibliography under these authors (Salter (1988), 158–69; Pearsall (1981, 1982)).

14. The first four are edited and discussed by Barr; for a discussion of the last two see Spearing, *Dream-Poetry*, 162–70.

15. For discussion of these, see Schmidt, *Clerkly Maker*, 81–107.

16. *Letters to Bridges*, ed. Abbot, 156.

17. Lewis, *The Allegory of Love* (repr. 1958), 161.

18. Burrow, 'Action', in *Essays*, 79–101; Frank, *Scheme*; Simpson, *Introduction*.

19. See especially Wittig, 'Inward Journey'; Simpson, 'From Reason to Affective Knowledge'.

20. See Lawlor, 'Imaginative Unity'; Alford, 'The Design of the Poem', in Alford, ed., *Companion*, 29–65; Schmidt, *Translation*, xxv–xxxvi.

21. See Schmidt, 'Symbolic Meaning', 162–8, and cf. *idem*, 'Inner Dreams, 35–7.

22. Burrow, 'Action of Langland's Second Vision'.

23. Frank, 'Pardon Scene in *PP*'.

24. Coghill, 'God's Wenches and the Light that Spoke'.

25. See Alford, 'Role of the Quotations'; Schmidt, *Clerkly Maker*, 81–93.

26. In Brown, *Lyrics*, no. 17 (spelling slightly modernized).

27. In Greene, *Carols*, no. 12.

28. For discussion of Langland's verse structure, see Schmidt, *Clerkly Maker*, 27–41.

29. On Langland's wordplay, see Schmidt, *Clerkly Maker*, 108–41; Davlin, *Game of Heuene*.

30. See Schmidt, 'Aspects of Langland's Wordplay', 141–5.

31. See Schmidt, *Clerkly Maker*; 'Structural Imagery'; 'Treatment of the Crucifixion'.

32. Russell and Nathan, 'A *PP* MS'.

33. 'The Text', 186.

34. Ibid., 187.

35. Kane, *A-Version*, 62; 149; 63.

36. Greg, *Calculus*, 20, n. 1.

37. In Vol. II of *P-T*.

38. Volume I, consisting of the parallel texts of Z, A, B and C with critical apparatus, has appeared (1995).

39. A view already expressed in relation to B by Hanna, 'Manuscripts', 19.

40. For examples of such a view, from Thomas Warton to Salter and Pearsall, see Schmidt, *Clerkly Maker*, 23 n. 12.

41. This compares, on my rough estimate, with about 54% for the archetypal text of C, and about 40% for that of A.

42. 'Not earlier than the 1380s or 1390s', with Z 'by 1388' (Doyle, 'Remarks', 36–7); a view disputed by Hanna, who proposes *c.* 1400 for the Z-MS.

43. None occur before Passus X except for VIII 109b–110a (in F only), either mechanically lost by coincidence in R or adopted into F's exemplar from A or C.

44. *K–D, B-Version*, 64–9.

45. Ibid., 171–2.

46. Contamination is well-instanced also in MSS of the A-version (e.g. members of the m-group, EAMH[3] after A V 190, 200) and in MSS of C (such as M, B and I).

47. See *K–D, B-Version*, 224.

48. Some of these lines will be found discussed in the Textual Commentary.

THE VISION OF PIERS PLOWMAN

Prologue

In a somer seson, whan softe was the sonne,   *mild; sun*
I shoop me into shroudes as I a sheep were,   *dressed*
In habite as an heremite unholy of werkes,
Wente wide in this world wondres to here.   *hear*
5 Ac on a May morwenynge on Malverne Hilles   *But; morning*
Me bifel a ferly, of Fairye me thoghte.   *marvel encountered*
I was wery [of]wandred and wente me to reste
Under a brood bank by a bournes syde;   *river*
And as I lay and lenede and loked on the watres,   *leaned (back)*
10 I slombred into a slepyng, it sweyed so murye.   *fell; moved*
   Thanne gan [me] to meten a merveillous swevene—*dream (v. & n.)* *to dream*
That I was in a wildernesse, wiste I nevere where.
    uninhabited place; knew
As I biheeld into the eest an heigh to the sonne,   *east; high*
I seigh a tour on a toft trieliche ymaked,   *knoll; choicely* *tower made*
15 A deep dale bynethe, a dongeon therinne,   *valley; fortress*

---

2 I dressed myself in garments as if I were a sheep (C).
6 I had a strange and marvellous experience, from the land of Fairy (=of a
  supernatural kind), it seemed (C).
7 I was tired, having wandered astray, and turned aside to rest myself.
10 I fell into a sleep, it (the stream) made so sweet a sound (C).
11 Then I proceeded to dream a wonderful dream.
14 I saw a tower upon a hillock, elegantly built.

Collation WHmCrGYOC²CLMHR
(from 125) F.
RUBRIC prologus] *from* A-MS R;
Hic incipit petrus plowman [de
visione liber primus] G[F]; *om*
W&r (C).
2 into] wM(to *ins.* M)F; in gLH.
shroudes] W&r; shroubes Cr; a
shroude H.
3 *In* β; *l. om* F.
4 Wente] W&r; & w. HF.
5 a] β; *om* F.
6 Me bifel; of] β; *trs*; as F.

7 ofwandred] of wandrynge CrHF;
forwandred W&r.
8 Vnder] β; Vpon F.
bournes] W&r; bourne CrGHF.
9 watres] β; wawys F.
10 into] wGHF; in yLM.
-yed] wGMF; -yued yL; -uenyd
H (C).
11 me] I *All MSS* (C).
to] L&r; *om* WHmY.
13 As] L&r; And WCMH (C).
14 ymaked] β; ytymbryd F.

With depe diches and derke and dredfulle of sighte.   *dark*
A fair feeld ful of folk fond I ther bitwene—   *field; found*
Of alle manere of men, the meene and the riche,   *kinds; humble*
Werchynge and wandrynge as the world asketh.   *Working; requires*
20 Somme putten hem to the plough, pleiden ful selde,

                                                        themselves; seldom
In settynge and sowynge swonken ful harde,   *planting; toiled*
And wonnen that thise wastours with glotonye destruyeth.

                                                          obtained what
And somme putten hem to pride, apparailed hem therafter,

                                                       dressed; accordingly
In contenaunce of clothynge comen disgised.
25 In preieres and penaunce putten hem manye,   *prayers*
Al for love of Oure Lord lyveden ful streyte   *strictly, ascetically*
In hope to have heveneriche blisse—
As ancres and heremites that holden hem in hire selles,   *cells*
Coveiten noght in contree to cairen aboute
30 For no likerous liflode hire likame to plese.
    And somme chosen chaffare; they cheveden the bettre—

                                                         trade; succeeded
As it semeth to oure sight that swiche men thryveth;   *prosper*
And somme murthes to make as mynstralles konne,

                                                      entertain; know how
And geten gold with hire glee — synnelees, I leeve.   *singing; believe*

---

20 Some devoted themselves to ploughing, very rarely took a holiday.
24 Came tricked up in an outward show of (fine) array.
27 In the hope of obtaining the blessed happiness of the kingdom of heaven.
28–30 (Such) as anchorites and hermits who keep to their cells And have no
    desire to wander about the land To indulge their bodies with luxurious
    living.

20 þe] W&r; *om* GF.
22 þese] F(?=α) AC; *om* β (C).
24 dis-] L&rA; de- W; di- Z.
25 and] wGHA?C; and in yLMFZ.
    penaunce] L&rA; *pl* WHmFZC.
26 for] OC²CLMZA?C; for þe
    wGYHF.
27 to] wGHFZAC; for to yLM.
    haue] yLMZAC; haue after
    wGH (a.] þera. H); have to hyre F.
29 Coueyten] CZAK–D; And c.
    W&r; that c. Hm.

kairen] L&r(walken C)ZAC; carien
    wYC²H, *many* AC-MSS.
31 chosen] W&rZA?C; chese
    HmCF.
    cheueden] wMZAC; cheuen gL;
    schosyn C²H.
33–4 *Ll. run together* (as . . . glee
    om)F.
34 synne-] W&r (not s. OC²); gilt
    cj Wr (C).
    leeue] W&r; trowe GHA.

35 Ac japeres and jangeleres, Judas children,   *jesters; chatterers*
    Feynen hem fantasies, and fooles hem maketh,   *Devise; fools*
    And han wit at wille to werken if they sholde.
    That Poul precheth of hem I wol nat preve it here: *St Paul; prove*
    Qui loquitur turpiloquium is Luciferes hyne.   *servant*
40   Bidderes and beggeres faste aboute yede   *Beggars; went*
    [Til] hire bely and hire bagge [were] bredful ycrammed;   *belly; brimful*
    Faiteden for hire foode, foughten at the ale.   *Begged falsely; ale house*   °fought
    In glotonye, God woot, go thei to bedde,   *gluttony; knows*
    And risen with ribaudie, tho Roberdes knaves;   robbers:
                                                                                     °lowly·
                                      obscenities; vagabonds (C)   common
45 Sleep and sory sleuthe seweth hem evere.   *wretched sloth; follow*
       Pilgrymes and palmeres plighten hem togidere

                                      vowed, pledged themselves

    To seken Seint Jame and seintes in Rome;   *seek St James* (C)
    Wenten forth in hire wey with many wise tales,   *way; speeches*
    And hadden leve to lyen al hire lif after.   *leave; tell lies; life*
50 I seigh somme that seiden thei hadde ysought seintes: *saw; said*
    To ech a tale that thei tolde hire tonge was tempred to lye
                                                              tongue; tuned   °Fo

---

36–7 Think up grotesque forms of amusement and turn themselves into
      buffoons Though they possess the free use of their intelligence, should they
      wish to work.
38–9 That which St Paul preaches concerning them I will not exemplify here —
      (that) 'He who utters foul speech' is the Devil's serving-man (C).

35   Ac] W&r(butt GHF)A; As
CryM.
37   wit] F (?=α)HACK–D; hire wit
β.
sholde] L&r; wolde WHC; liste
A.
39   *Qui*] L&r (*l. om* F)AC; But *Qui*
W.
loq. turp.] wGMHA; *trs* yLC.
is . . . hyne] W&r(*om* M(*est seruus
diaboli* +M)H)AC; &c Cr¹CL.
41   Til] *so* ZACK–D; Wiþ W&r;
l.om F (C).
bely] L&rZAC; belies wGH.
bagge] LYMZAC; bagges W&r.
were] *so* AZCK–D; of W&r (*om*
H).

42   Faiteden] W&r(fast f. G)ZAC;
Waytyng H; & fele fayted F.
fouȝten] W&r?A; & f. HFZC.
43   *So* W&r(woot) it woot HmyLM)
ZAC; & god w. with g. þey goon
togydre F.
44   risen] W&rZC; r. vp HFA.
46   pliȝten] W&rZAC; plighted ?y
(gedir C)LM; pyghtyn FH.
47   To] L&rZC; For to wGH?A.
in] L&r; of HZC; at wGA.
48   Wenten] *so* ZACK–D; They
wenten W&r; & w. F (C).
49   to] wCLHZAC; for to ?gMF.
50–4 *In* W&r; *ll. om* F (C).

Moore than to seye sooth, it semed bi hire speche.　*truth*
　　Heremytes on an heep with hoked staves　*crowd; crooked*
Wenten to Walsyngham – and hire wenches after:
55　Grete lobies and longe that lothe were to swynke　*lubbers; tall; labour*
Clothed hem in copes to ben knowen from othere,
　　　　　　　　　　　　　　　　　　Dressed; distinguished
And shopen hem heremytes hire ese to have.　*made themselves; comfort*
　　I fond there freres, alle the foure ordres,
Prechynge the peple for profit of [the] womb[e]:　*belly (cf. Phil 3: 19)*
60　Glosed the gospel as hem good liked;　*Expounded; at will*
For coveitise of copes construwed it as thei wolde.　*greed; interpreted*
Manye of thise maistres freres mowe clothen hem at likyng
　　　　　　　　　　　　　　　　　Master-friars; can; as they like
For hire moneie and marchaundise marchen togideres.
　　　　　　　　　　　　　　　　　　　　money; merchandise
For sith charite hath ben chapman and chief to shryve lordes
　　　　　　　　　　　　　　　　　　(a) merchant; confess
65　Manye ferlies han fallen in a fewe yeres.　*strange events*
But Holy Chirche and hii holde bettre togidres　*Unless; they; co-operate*
The mooste meschief on molde is mountynge up faste.
　　　　　　　　　　　　　　　　　　　greatest evil; earth
　　Ther preched a pardoner as he a preest were:　*as if he were a priest*
Broughte forth a bulle with bisshopes seles,　*bull (C); seals*
70　And seide that hymself myghte assoillen hem alle　*absolve*

63　For the money (they obtain) tallies with the wares (they offer in return).
64　Since (those who should stand for) Charity have become sellers of wares
　　and foremost (in wishing) to hear the confessions of noblemen . . .
67　The forces making for a calamitous upheaval are rapidly reaching full
　　strength.

59　Prechynge] WHm(*over erasure*　　63　and] L&rC; and hire wH?A.
　　a.h.)AC; Preched L&r (þat pr. GF)　　　marchen] W&r; macchen Hm;
　　(C).　　　　　　　　　　　　　　　　　mete HA.
　　þe wombe] CA(þe here ?A)K–D;　　66　But] W&r (*l. om* H)A; & but
　　her wombys H; hemselue W&r (C).　　　F?C.
60　Glosed] W&rA; & gl. FG(-ed)　　67　vp] GC?AK–D; vp wel O (w.]
　　-en G)C.　　　　　　　　　　　　　+O)C²; wel W&r (*l. om* H); *om* F.
61　it] W&rA; *om* GHF.　　　　　　69　Brouȝte] W&rA; & browhte
62　maistres] L&rAC; *sg* wOC²MH.　　　FZC; Put H.
　　freres] W&r (*cf.* C); *om* GFA.　　　with] L&rZAC; wiþ many wGH.
　　mowe] L&rA; now W.

Of falshede of fastynge, of avowes ybroken. *deceit; vows*
Lewed men leved hym wel and liked hise wordes,

Uneducated; believed

Comen up knelynge to kissen hise bulles. *Came; on their knees*
He bonched hem with his brevet and blered hire eighen,

struck; dimmed; eyes °document

75 And raughte with his rageman rynges and broches. *got; bull; brooches*
Thus [ye] gyven [youre] gold glotons to helpe, *gluttonous rogues*
And leneth it losels that leccherie haunten!

hand it to wretches; indulge in

Were the bisshop yblessed and worth bothe his eris, *holy; ears*
His seel sholde noght be sent to deceyve the peple.

seal (of authorization)

80 Ac it is noght by the bisshop that the boy precheth— *fellow, rogue*
For the parisshe preest and the pardoner parten the silver *divide*
That the povere [peple] of the parissche sholde have if they ne were.

poor

Persons and parisshe preestes pleyned hem to the bisshop

Rectors; vicars; complained

That hire parisshes weren povere sith the pestilence tyme,

poor; since; plague

85 To have a licence and leve at London to dwelle, *official permission*
And syngen ther for symonie, for silver is swete.

sing (masses) for payment

74–5 He struck them with his letter of indulgence and bedimmed their sight
And obtained by means of his official document rings and brooches [*sc.* in
payment for pardon] (C).
80 It is not in accordance with (the intentions of) the bishop that the rogue
preaches (C).

71 falshede] W&r; falsnes GZAC;
false oþis F.
of³] WLM?C; and of L&r; & fele
F.
72 hym] L&r (hem F); it W.
73 Comen] W&rZA; & kemen
F?C.
hise bulles] W&rC; *sg* HFZA.
74 bonched] W&r (touuchid C²)
ZA?C; blessid FH, *some* AC-MSS.
76 ye] *so* ZACK–D; þei W&r; þe
puple H; men F (C).

youre] *so* ZACK–D; hire W&r;
theym G.
helpe] HZACK–D; kepe W&r.
77 losels] *so* ACK–D; swiche l.
W&r; þo l. F; thys l. ZA-MS M.
78 Were] W&r; But were HF, *some*
A-MSSZ(Ac Z).
82 pouere] Y&r (*l.* om H)ACK–D;
om wCLG.
peple] *so* ACK–D; poraille W&r
(pouerty Cr); parycyoners G; men
F (C).

Bisshopes and bachelers, bothe maistres and doctours—

b., m., d. of divinity

That han cure under Crist, and crownynge in tokene   *duty; token (tonsure)*

And signe that thei sholden shryven hire parisshens,   *parishioners; hear con.*

90 Prechen and praye for hem, and the povere fede—   *feed*

Liggen in Londoun in Lenten and ellis.   *Reside; Lent; other times*

Somme serven the King and his silver tellen,   *keep account of*

In the Cheker and in the Chauncelrie chalangen hise dettes

   make demand for; dues

Of wardes and of wardemotes, weyves and streyves.   *'waifs and strays'; ward-*

95 And somme serven as servaunts lordes and ladies,   *meetings*

And in stede of stywardes sitten and demen.   *(the) position; judge*

Hire messe and hire matyns and many of hire houres   *Mass; offices*

Arn doone undevoutliche; drede is at the laste

   are done undevoutly; dread

Lest Crist in his Consistorie acorse ful manye!   *Court (C); condemn*

100 I parceyved of the power that Peter hadde to kepe—

   comprehended; in his keeping

To bynden and to unbynden, as the Book telleth—   *Bible (Mt 16: 19); bind*

How he it lefte with love as Oure Lorde highte

   commanded (cf. Lk 22: 32)

Amonges foure vertues, most vertuous of alle vertues,   *powerful*

That cardinals ben called and closynge yates   *gates*

105 There Crist is in kyngdom, to close and to shette,   *Where; shut*

And to opene it to hem and hevene blisse shewe.   *i.e. the virtuous*

---

88 Who have responsibility under Christ and the tonsure as a symbol . . .

93–4 In the (courts of) Exchequer and Chancery claim the dues arising to him
  From guardianship-cases [*Bn*] and from ward-meetings and from lost
  property and strayed beasts.

96 And in the position(s) of stewards (in manorial households) sit and pass
  judgement (in the manor courts) (C).

91 in[1]] L&rC; at wGC²H.

93 þe[1,2]] F (?=α)C; *om* β.

94 weyues] W&r; of w.
  HmCrOC²HF.
  After this F *adds* A Pr 95 (C).

98 *So* W&rC; *a spurious l.* F.

99 hys] HC; *om* W&r (*l. om* F) (C).

101 to[2]] LyM; *om* wGHF.

102 it lefte] W&rC; *trs* CrMHF.

103 most vertuous] F (?=α)CK–D;
  þe beste W&r (=β).
  alle vertues] βC(a.] *om* C); hevene
  F.

105 Crist is] L&r(is] *om* Hm)C; *trs*
  W.
  in] L&rC; in his WHmF.

106 shewe] W&r (*l. om* H); hem
  shewe F.

Ac of the Cardinals at court that kaughte of that name   *snatched*
And power presumed in hem a Pope to make   *took for granted*
To han the power that Peter hadde, impugnen I nelle—
                            I don't wish to find fault (with them)
110 For in love and lettrure the eleccion bilongeth;
                          learning; election (of popes)

Forthi I kan and kan naught of court speke moore.   *Therefore*
  Thanne kam ther a Kyng: Knyghthod hym ladde;   *came; led*
Might of the communes made hym to regne.   *common people; reign*
And thanne cam Kynde Wit and clerkes he made,   *Native Intelligence*
115 For to counseillen the Kyng and the Commune save.   *counsel; protect*
The Kyng and Knyghthod and Clergie bothe   *Learning also*
Casten that the Commune sholde hem [communes] fynde
                          Arranged; food

The Commune contreved of Kynde Wit craftes, *devised; through; skills*
And for profit of al the peple plowmen ordeyned   *established*
120 To tilie and to travaille as trewe lif asketh.   *till; labour; honest*
The Kyng and the Commune and Kynde Wit the thridde   *third*
Shopen lawe and leaute – ech lif to knowe his owene.
                          Created; justice; person

108–9 *Either* (a) . . . to make a pope – (that is), assumed they had the power
St Peter possessed *or* (b) to make a pope have [attribute to the papacy] the
power [etc.] (C).

117 Brought it about that the common people should (be obliged to) provide
sustenance for them (cf. 'commons' = 'food').

107 of¹] W&r; *om* HF.
at] W&r; at þe HmCLMF; of H.
þat . . . þat] W&rC; of þat couth þe
H; of hem kawtyn F.

108 And] W&r(Ac O)C; For F.
presumed] W&r; presumeþ FC (C).

109 þe] F (?=α) HCK–D; þat W&r
(?=β).

110 and] L&r?C; and in WCr²³HF.

111 of] W&r (*l. om* Hm); of þe F;
of that GH.

112 hym] W&rC; he F.

114 þanne; made] W&rC; forþ;
hadde F.

115 þe commune] W&r (*pl* Cr); hise
communes F.

116 The] W&r; & þe F.

and¹] W&r; and the HmM; & his
FH.

and²] W&r; and þe MHF.

117 Casten] W&rC; þei casten F.
commune] W&rC; comonys FCr
(*so at* 118, 121).
hem . . . fynde] here comunes fynde
C*K–D*; hemself fynde *All MSS* (*trs*
F) (C).

118 contreued . . . wit] W&r; be k.
wit c. F.

119 al] W&r; *om* HmGMHF.
ordeyned] W&r; þey made F.

120 trewe lif] W&r (l.] skyl F);
trewth H.

122 and] W&r (*om* C²); be F.
lyf] F (?=α) K–D; man W&r (?=β)
(C).

Thanne loked up a lunatik, a leene thyng withalle,   *lean; moreover*
And knelynge to the Kyng clergially he seide,   *learnedly, like a scholar*
125 'Crist kepe thee, sire Kyng, and thi kyngryche,   *protect; kingdom*
And lene thee lede thi lond so leaute thee lovye,

grant; rule; may love you
And for thi rightful rulyng be rewarded in hevene!'   *just; (may you) be*
And sithen in the eyr on heigh an aungel of hevene

thereupon; air on high
Lowed to speke in Latyn – for lewed men ne koude

Came down; did not know how to
130 Jangle ne jugge that justifie hem sholde,   *Argue; judge; that (which)*
But suffren and serven – forthi seide the aungel: *therefore*
' "Sum Rex, sum Princeps"; neutrum fortasse deinceps!
O qui iura regis Christi specialia regis,
Hoc quod agas melius – iustus es, esto pius!
135 Nudum ius a te vestiri vult pietate.
Qualia vis metere, talia grana sere:
Si ius nudatur, nudo de iure metatur;
Si seritur pietas, de pietate metas'.

Thanne greved hym a goliardeis, a gloton of wordes,

grew angry; buffoon (C)
140 And to the aungel an heigh answeres after:
'Dum "rex" a "regere" dicatur nomen habere,

130–1 Dispute and discriminate (the arguments) which should vindicate them,
but (only how to) . . . or *that* may be rel., *suffre* and *serve* indic.

132–5 (You say) 'I am King, I am Ruler'; you may perhaps be neither in
future. O you who administer the sublime laws of Christ the King, in order
to do better what you do, as you are just, be godly! Naked law requires to be
clothed by you with a sense of your duty to God. Sow such grain as you wish
to reap . . .

136–8 If the law is nakedly administered [*lit.* stripped bare] by you, then let
(judgement) be measured out (to you) according to the letter [*lit.* naked law].
If goodness is sown (by you), may you reap goodness (C).

141–2 Inasmuch as a king has his name from (the fact of) being a ruler
[ultimately the word *rex* is from *regere* 'to rule'], he possesses the name
(alone) without the reality unless he is zealous in maintaining the laws (C).

---

124   And knelynge] W&r; he gan
knele F.
clergially he] W&r; & cl. HF.
125   *Here* R *begins;* α= RF; F's
*sophisticated readings not recorded
hereafter.*

126   lene] βR; leue FCrC (leue CrC).
135   ius] βC; vis α.
vestiri] βC; vestire αH.
140   answeres] LR; answerede W&r
(he a. F).
141   Dum] W&r; Cum y.

Nomen habet sine re nisi studet iura tenere'.
  And thanne gan al the commune crye in vers of Latyn
                            proceeded to; verse
To the Kynges counseil – construe whoso wolde—   *whoever wishes*
145 *'Precepta Regis sunt nobis vincula legis!'*
  With that ran ther a route of ratons at ones   *troop; rats; once*
And smale mees with hem: mo than a thousand   *mice; more*
Comen to a counseil for the commune profit;   *the public good*
For a cat of a court cam whan hym liked   *came when he pleased*
150 And overleep hem lightliche and laughte hem at his wille,
                    pounced on; easily; seized
And pleide with hem perillousli and possed hem aboute.
                    played; dashed them
  'For doute of diverse dredes we dar noght wel loke!   *fear*
And if we grucche of his gamen he wol greven us alle,
                complain; game; hurt
Cracchen us or clawen us and in hise clouches holde, *Scratch; clutches*
155 That us lotheth the lif er he late us passe.   *is hateful to us; let*
Mighte we with any wit his wille withstonde,   *ingenious plan; oppose*
We myghte be lordes olofte and lyven at oure ese'.   *above*
  A raton of renoun, moost renable of tonge,   *eloquent/voluble*
Seide for a sovereyn help to [hemselven alle],   *perfect remedy for (C)*
160 'I have yseyen segges', quod he, 'in the Cite of Londoun
                    seen men; said
Beren beighes ful brighte abouten hire nekkes,   *Wear necklaces*
And somme colers of crafty work; uncoupled they wenden
              collars; skilful; unleashed
Bothe in wareyne and in waast where hem leve liketh,
              warren; waste; they please

---

145 The king's bidding has for us the binding force of law (C).
152 For fear of various perils we (scarcely) even dare peep (out).
155 (To the point where) we hate living – before he (will deign to) let us go.

143 And] LCR; om W&r.
vers] β; a vers ?α (o voys F).
144 *In* β; *l. om* α.
147 with] L&rC; myd W (C).
148 Comen] *so* CK–D; And comen
W&r; & wentyn F (C).
149 court] L&rC; contree
WHmCrG+MH.
150 his] βR; *om* FC.
151 hem] yMH?α(vs FC; *om* wGL.

152 dredes] W&r († F); dedes OC²
(C).
153 of] ?β (at CrGY); *om* α.
159 hemseluen alle] hymselue β
(-ue] -uen OC²); hem alle α (C).
162 wenden] L&r; wenten wG;
walke F; were H.
163 leue] L&r; best FH; self wG.
lyketh] L&r; liked WCr¹GMH.

And outher while thei arn elliswhere, as I here telle.   *at other times*

165 Were ther a belle on hire beighe, by Jesu, as me thynketh,

it seems to me

Men myghte witen wher thei wente and awey renne.   *know; run*

And right so', quod that raton, 'reson me sheweth   *teaches*

To bugge a belle of bras or of bright silver   *buy*

And knytten it on a coler for oure commune profit   *fasten*

170 And hangen it upon the cattes hals — thanne here we mowen

neck; can hear

Wher he ryt or rest or rometh to pleye; *Whether; rides; rests; goes forth*

And if hym list for to laike, thanne loke we mowen *he wishes to sport*

And peeren in his presence the while hym pleye liketh,   *appear*

And if hym wratheth, be war and his wey shonye'.

he is angry; path; shun

175   Al this route of ratons to this reson assented;   *line of reasoning*

Ac tho the belle was ybought and on the beighe hanged,   *when*

Ther ne was raton in al the route, for al the reaume of Fraunce,   *realm*

That dorste have bounden the belle aboute the cattes nekke,   *dared*

Ne hangen it aboute his hals al Engelond to wynne,   *neck*

180 And helden hem unhardy and hir counseil feble,   *thought*

And leten hire laboure lost and al hire longe studie.   *considered*

   A mous that muche good kouthe, as me tho thoughte,

had good sense

Strook forth sternely and stood bifore hem alle, *Went sharply forward*

And to the route of ratons rehersed thise wordes: *delivered*

185 'Though we hadde ykilled the cat, yet sholde ther come another

---

180 And believed themselves not bold enough and their plan a poor one.

165 Iesu] βC; Ihesus α.
167 And] βR; *om* F?C.
170 *In* L&rC; *l. om* wG.
     *vp*on] L&r; aboute Cr²,³FC.
171 *In* βC; *l. om* α.
     rom-] YCK–D; renn- W&r; rest- H (C).
172 *In* β (list) lyke HmH) C; *l. om* α.
173 þe] WCrC²FC; þer ?*y*LMR; *om* GH.

175 þis¹] βC; þe α.
     þei] WCrYCLR?C; *om* Hm&r.
176 ybouȝt] L&r?C; ybrouȝt WHmCr¹G.
177 al¹] W&rC; *om* GMHF.
179 his] αCK–D; þe cattes β.
180 And] L&r; Alle W; þei H; But F.
182 tho] GCK–D; *om* W&r.
185 had Iculled] αCK–D; culled ?β (kille*n* wGYH).

To cracchen us and al oure kynde, though we cropen under benches.

crept

Forthi I counseille al the commune to late the cat worthe,   *let ... be*
And be we nevere so bolde the belle hym to shewe.
The while he caccheth conynges he coveiteth noght oure caroyne,

rabbits; carcasses

190 But fedeth hym al with venyson; defame we hym nevere.

feeds; dishonour

For bettre is a litel los than a long sorwe: *loss; long-lasting*
The maze among us alle, theigh we mysse a sherewe!

dismay; though; villain

For I herde my sire seyn, is seven yeer ypassed,   *father say; ago*
"Ther the cat is a kitoun, the court is ful elenge".

Where; kitten; wretched

195 That witnesseth Holy Writ, whoso wole it rede: *whoever; read*
Ve terre ubi puer est rex!
For may no renk ther reste have for ratons by nyghte. *man; because of*
For many mannes malt we mees wolde destruye,   *mice; destroy*
And also ye route of ratons rende mennes clothes,   *tear*

200 Nere the cat of the court that kan yow overlepe;

Were it not for; spring on

For hadde ye rattes youre wille, ye kouthe noght rule yowselve.

way; could

   'I seye it for me', quod the mous, 'I se so muchel after,

such consequences

Shal nevere the cat ne the kiton by my counseil be greved,

advice; offended

Ne carpynge of this coler that costed me nevere.   *talking; cost*

---

192 (It would be) utter confusion among us all, even though we should be free
of (one particular) evil person.
196 Woe to the land where the king is a child (Eccl 10: 16) (C).

186 cracchy] LYOCRC; cacchen
     W&r.
189–92 *Ll. after* 197 *All MSS;
     re-ordered* K–D (C).
193 is] W&r; *om* CrGC.
196 *est rex*] HmOC²RC; *Rex est
     &c.* W&r (*&c*) *om* CrF).
197 þer] W&r (*om* HmF); *no* R.

198 mannus] L&rC; mennes
     wGOF.
200 þe¹] wGFC; þat y (at *erased*
     C)LR.
     the²] HmGC²HαCK–D; þat W&r.
202 it] ?α (þis F)C; *om* β.
204 Ne] L&rC; Thoruȝ W.

205 And though it costned me catel, biknowen it I nolde,

> *wealth; make known*

But suffren as hymself wolde [s]o doon as hym liketh—
Coupled and uncoupled to cacche what thei mowe.   *can*
Forthi ech a wis wight I warne – wite wel his owene!'

> *wise man; know/keep*

(What this metels bymeneth, ye men that ben murye,

> *dream signifies*

210 Devyne ye, for I ne dar, by deere God in hevene)!   *Interpret; dare*
    Yet hoved ther an hundred in howves of selk*e*—   *coifs; silk*
Sergeants, it semed, that serveden at the Barre,   *Barristers-at-law*
Pleteden for penyes and poundes the lawe,   *Pleaded; belabour (C)*
And noght for love of Oure Lord unlose hire lippes ones.

> *(would) unloose*

215 Thow myghtest bettre meete myst on Malverne Hilles

> *more easily measure*

Than get a 'mom' of hire mouth er moneie be shewed!   *murmur*
    Barons and burgeis and bondemen als*e*   *serfs too*
I seigh in this assemblee, as ye shul here after;   *gathering*
Baksteres and brewesteres and bochiers manye,

> *Bakers; brewers; butchers*

220 Wollen webbesters and weveres of lynnen,   *Wool-weavers; linen*
Taillours and tynkers and tollers in markettes,   *Tailors; toll-collectors*
Masons and mynours and many othere craftes: *miners*

205–(6) And even though [the cat's oppressions] *were* to cost me (some of my) wealth, I'd be unwilling to acknowledge it (publicly) But (would rather) let him . . .
208 i.e. mind his own business.
211 Further, there milled about a hundred in coifs of silk.

205 it¹] αGCK–D; it hadde ?β.
206 so] to W&r; †H (C).
    doo*n* as] βR; slen what F.
208 Forþi] β (*l. om* H); For R; & F.
210 Deuyne . . . dar] βR (for . . . dar] ne dar I nouʒt R); I ne dar d. it ʒow F.
212 it] ?βRC; þey FH; theym G.
    semed] L&rC; bisemed w.

213 poundes] βZAC; pountyd H; pownded F; poudres R (C).
215 myst] WGHαAC; þe myste L&r.
216 er] αZ?AC; til wG; but ɣLMH.
    be] W&r (hem by R)A?C; were YCLMZ.
217 burgeis] L&rAC; Burgeises WCrGF.

Of alle lybbynge laborers lopen forth somme—   *living; ran*
As dykeres and delveres that doon hire dedes ille
                                            ditchers; diggers; work
225 And dryveth forth the longe day with *'Dieu vous save Dame Emme!'*
                                                                    pass

Cokes and hire knaves cryden, 'Hote pies, hote!   *Cooks; servants; cried*
Goode gees and grys! Go we dyne, go we!'   *geese; pork; dine*
Taverners until hem tolden the same: *Inn-keepers; unto*
'Whit wyn of Oseye and wyn of Gascoigne,   *Alsace; Gascony*
230 Of the Ryn and of the Rochel, the roost to defie!'
                                    Rhine; La Rochelle; roast; digest
—Al this I seigh slepyng, and sevene sythes more.   *sleeping; times*

---

225 God save you, mistress Emma! (C).

223 alle] αZ; alle kynne β (k.)
     maner of H).
224 dedes] W&rZ?AC; dede H.
225 þe longe day] W&r (l.] dere L;
     fayre F; *om* H)?A; here dayes here
     RC (here²] with C).

vous] L&rC; *om* WCr¹GHZA.
227 gees; grys] W&rAC; *trs* YCLα.
229 wyn²] F (?=α; *om* R) ACK–D;
     reed wyn β.
231 *In* L&rZAC; *l. om* WYF.
     I sagh] GZACK–D; seiȝ I L&r (C).

Passus I

What this mountaigne bymeneth and the merke dale   *signifies; dark*
And the feld ful of folk, I shal yow faire shewe.   *clearly*
A lovely lady of leere in lynnen yclothed   *face*
Cam doun from [the] castel and called me faire,   *graciously*
5 And seide, 'Sone, slepestow? Sestow this peple—   *Do you see*
How bisie they ben aboute the maze?   *(their) vain wanderings*
The mooste partie of this peple that passeth on this erthe,   *majority*
Have thei worship in this world, thei wilne no bettre;   *honour; desire*
Of oother hevene than here holde thei no tale'.   *take no account*
10   I was afered of hire face, theigh she fair weere,
                            afraid; though; might be
And seide, 'Mercy, madame, what [may] this [be] to meene?'
   'The tour up the toft', quod she, 'Truthe is therinne,   *upon; hillock*
And wolde that ye wroughte as his word techeth.
For he is fader of feith, formed yow alle
15 Bothe with fel and with face and yaf yow fyve wittes
                            skin; gave; senses
For to worshipe hym therwith the while that ye ben here.
                            with which to
And therfor he highte the erthe to helpe yow echone
                        commanded; each one
Of wollene, of lynnen, of liflode at nede   *with the necessities of life*
In mesurable manere to make yow at ese;   *moderate degree*

5–6 Son, are you asleep? Do you see these people – how preoccupied they are,
(wandering) about (in) a maze (of worldly concerns)?

Collation WHmCrGYOC²CLMHRF.
RUBRIC *Passus primus de
visione* W&r (*pr.*] *Secundus* F; *de
v.*] *de v. petri le ploughman* BR; *om*
O); *om* GC².
4 þe] *so* Z?A?CK–D; a *All MSS* (C).
6 ben] L&rZAC; ben alle
w GM(alle + M).

8 þei wilne] W&rC; they kepe
GH(*trs* H)A.
11 may . . . meene] *so* C; may þis
bemene H; is þis to m. W&r (C).
12 vp] yLMR; vpon CrFC; on
wGH?A.
14 formed] yLMR; and f.
WCrFZ?AC; that f. HmG.
16 þe] L&r; *om* WHmGHF.

20 And comaunded of his curteisie in commune three thynges:
                                          generosity, grace
        Are none nedfulle but tho, and nempne hem I thynke,
                                          necessary; those; name; intend
        And rekene hem by reson – reherce thow hem after.
                                          enumerate; in order; declare
            'That oon is vesture from chele thee to save,
                                          clothing; the cold; protect
        And mete at meel for mysese of thiselve,
25 And drynke whan thow driest – ac do noght out of reson,
                                          are dry; in excess
        That thow worthe the wers whan thow werche sholdest.
                                          so that; end up; the w. (for it)
        For Lot in hise lifdayes, for likynge of drynke,
                                          love of (the pleasures of) d.
        Dide by hise doughtres that the devel liked: *that which pleased*
        Delited hym in drynke as the devel wolde,   *Had his pleasure*
30 And leccherie hym laughte, and lay by hem bothe——   *took to himself*
        And al he witte it the wyn, that wikked dede: *blamed entirely on*
        Inebriemus eum vino dormiamusque cum eo, ut
        servare possimus de patre nostro semen.   (Gen 19: 32)
        Thorugh wyn and thorugh wommen ther was Loth acombred,
                                          overcome
        And there gat in glotonie gerles that were cherles.   *begot; children*
            'Forthi dred delitable drynke and thow shalt do the bettre.
                                          Therefore; respect; delightful
35 Mesure is medicine, though thow muchel yerne.
                                          Moderation; much; long for
        It is nought al good to the goost that the gut asketh,   *spirit*

---

24 And food at meal (time), to prevent suffering [*not* 'discomfort' (*BnSk*)] to
   yourself.
27 For Lot, during the days of his life, (for love of) the pleasures of drink . . .
31a (Come), let us make him drunk with wine, and let us lie with him, that we
   may preserve seed of our father (Gen 19: 32).
33 And there begot in (his) drunkenness children of base character.

22 þow] WCLRA; ȝe Hm&r (*om* 31 it þe] WHmYCMZ?A; it LGα;
   GY; *l. om* H)Z.   the CrHC; *l. om* OC².
23 chele] L&r; cold WC²H.   31a *Inebriemus*] yHRCK–D;
24 And] βRZ; þe toþir ys FA.   *Inebriamus* W&r.
25 do] W&rZ; do it GHF?A.   36 It . . . al] *All* MSSZ; Al is not
              AC.

Ne liflode to the likame that leef is to the soule.

Leve nought thi likame, for a liere hym techeth—   *Believe, trust; liar*

That is the wrecched world, wolde thee bitraye.   *(that) would like to*

40 For the fend and thi flessh folwen togidere,   *devil; pursue*

And that seeth thi soule and seith it in thin herte.   *sees*

And for thow sholdest ben ywar, I wisse thee the beste.'

          be on guard; advise

'A, madame, mercy,' quod I, 'me liketh wel youre wordes.

          thank you

Ac the moneie of this molde that men so faste holdeth—   *earth; hold(s)*

45 Telleth me to whom that tresour appendeth.'   *treasure belongs*

'Go to the Gospel,' quod she, 'that God seide hymselven,

          Gospel (words)

Tho the poeple hym apposede with a peny in the Temple

          When; questioned

Wheither thei sholde therwith worshipe the kyng Cesar.

          with it; Caesar

And God asked of hem, of whom spak the lettre,   *spoke; inscription*

50 And the ymage ylike that therinne stondeth?   *like(wise); stands*

' "Cesares", thei seiden, "we seen hym wel echone."   *Caesar's; see*

---

37 Nor (is all) that is of value to the soul a benefit to our physical nature.
50 And (asked who) the image that stood within likewise (represented)?

37–8 *So* gMαZACS*k*; *ll. run
  together* WHmCL; *l.* 37 *om* CrH.
37 the[1]] GZACK–*D*; þi W&*r*.
  that . . . soule] gMαZAC; *om*
  WHmCL.
38 Lef . . . licame] Cr&*r* (+ *m.h.*
  M; Lef] Loue; lic.] frele flesch
  H)ZAC; *om* WHmCL; *l. om* GF.
40 folwen] WHmGHZAC; f. þe
  L&*r*.
41 And that] ZACK–*D*; This and
  that W&*r* (*l. om* H); þese three F;
  take thys G (C).
  seeþ] ?β (seiþ C[2]Cr[23]; seest YL;
  sleth(l *over erasure*)Hm)Z
  (seuth)?C; sueth ?α (sewe F); in G;
  shent A*x*.
  and[2]] W&*r* (*om* Y)ZAC; to F.

seiþ . . . herte] ?β (s.] sett G; setth
  C)R; shende it þey casten F.
43 A] F (?=α)ZACK–*D*; *om* βR.
44 holdeþ] βZA; kepeth αC.
45 Telleth] ?α (Tell ȝe F)Z?AC; Tel
  β.
  to whom] FZACK–*D*; to whom;
  madame W&*r* (*trs* HR) (C).
48 þerwiþ worshipe; þe kyng Cesar]
  W&*r*; *trs* GHZA (C).
49 hem] L&*r*ZAC; hym W.
50 ilyke] L&*r*ZA; was lik WF; also
  H.
51 Cesares] wGCMHFZ?AC;
  Cesaris YOC[2]LR.
  hym] L&*r*; it WF; her Cr; *om*
  GHZA.

' "*Reddite Cesari*," quod God, "that *Cesari* bifalleth,   *belongs*
Et que sunt Dei Deo, or ellis ye don ille."   *do evil*
For rightfully Reson sholde rule yow alle,   *in proper manner, justly*
55 And Kynde Wit be wardeyn youre welthe to kepe,   *guardian; protect*
And tutour of youre tresor, and take it yow at nede   *overseer; give*
For housbondrie and he holden togidres.'   *thrifty management*
　　Thanne I frayned hire faire, for Hym that hire made,
　　　　　　　　　　　　　　　　　　　　　　　asked; courteously

'That dongeon in the dale that dredful is of sighte—
60 What may it bemeene, madame, I yow biseche?'   *signify; beseech*
　　'That is the castel of care – whoso comth therinne   *whoever comes*
May banne that he born was to bodi or to soule!   *curse (the fact)*
Therinne wonyeth a wight that Wrong is yhote,   *dwells; being; called*
Fader of falshede, founded it hymselve.   *falsehood*
65 Adam and Eve he egged to ille,   *incited; evil*
Counseilled Kaym to killen his brother,   *Cain*
Judas he japed with Jewen silver,   *deceived; Jews'*
And sithen on an eller hanged hym after.   *then; elder-tree (C)*
He is lettere of love and lieth hem alle: *hinderer; lies to/deceives*
70 That trusten on his tresour bitrayed arn sonnest.'   *Those who; soonest*
　　Thanne hadde I wonder in my wit what womman she weere
　　　　　　　　　　　　　　　　　　　　　　　　mind; might be

That swiche wise wordes of Holy Writ shewed,
And halsede hire on the heighe name, er she thennes yede,
　　　　　　　　　　　　　adjured; (God's) name; went
What she were witterly that wissed me so faire.   *certainly; counselled*
75 'Holi Chirche I am,' quod she, 'thow oughtest me to knowe.
　　　　　　　　　　　　　　　　　　　　　　　　recognize

52–3 'Render to Caesar', said God, 'the things that are Caesar's, and to God,
　　the things that are God's' (Mt 22: 21).
74 To tell me exactly who she, who counselled me thus graciously, might be.

54　riȝtfully] WZAC; riȝtful L&r.
57　he] Cr²³HFZACK–D; heo R; *hij*
　　W&r.
58　hir²] L&rZAC; me wGYH.
59　That] W&r; The HZACK–D;
　　Of þe F.
60　bemene] C²Cr³GHFACZ (mene)
　　K–D; be to meene W&r (C).
64　falshede] *so* ZC; f. he HmFA
　　K–D; f. and W&r (C).
68　after] L&rZA (*cf.* C); selue
　　WHF.
70　bitrayed aren] αGAZK–D;
　　bitrayeþ he ?β (he] he hem WHm;
　　om C²) (*cf.* C); he disseyuyth hem
　　H (C).
71　sche] αHmC; it β.
73　halsede] FZACK–D; asked βR
　　(hasked R) (C).

I underfeng thee first and the feith taughte.   *received; to you*
Thow broughtest me borwes my biddyng to fulfille, *?sponsors, pledges*
And to loven me leelly the while thi lif dureth.'   *loyally; lasts*
   Thanne I courbed on my knees and cried hire of grace,

         bent; for mercy
80 And preide hire pitously to preye for my synnes,
And also kenne me kyndely on Crist to bileve,   *teach; properly*
That I myghte werchen His wille that wroghte me to manne:

         created me a man
'Teche me to no tresor, but tel me this ilke—   *direct; same (thing)*
How I may save my soule, that seint art yholden.' *you who; holy; held*
85   'Whan alle tresors arn tried,' quod she, 'treuthe is the beste. *tested*
I do it on *Deus caritas* to deme the sothe;   *appeal to; judge*
It is as dereworthe a drury as deere God hymselven. *precious; treasure*
[For] whoso is trewe of his tonge and telleth noon oother,

         speaks nought else
And dooth the werkes therwith and wilneth no man ille,

         acts accordingly
90 He is a god by the Gospel, agrounde and olofte,   *according to*
And ylik to Oure Lord, by Seint Lukes wordes.   *(cf. Lk 12: 33–4)*
The clerkes that knowen this sholde kennen it aboute, *make known*
For Cristen and uncristen cleymeth it echone.   *(non)Christian; claim*
   'Kynges and knyghtes sholde kepen it by reson—
95 Riden and rappen doun in reaumes aboute,   *suppress; realms*
And taken *transgressores* and tyen hem faste

         lawbreakers; bind; securely

---

81 And also to instruct me in the right and true way of believing in Christ.
86 I ground my affirmation (that this is) truly to be judged (so) on the text
   God is love (I Jn 4: 8).
90 He is divine, according to the Gospel, (in the estimate of those) on earth
   (and those) in heaven (cf. XVIII 45; and see Jn 10:34, quoting Ps 81:6).

77 Thou] CrGHFACK–D; and thu HmOC²; And WYCLMRZ.
78 me leelly] βA; trs α. þe] W&r; om GHFA.
79 I courbed] W&rZ; knelyd I HAC (trs AC).
80 to] HmGHαZAC; om W&r.
82 In βZA; l. om α.
84–7 In W&r; ll. om H.
85 quod she] W&r; om GOC² CZAC.

87 It] βZAC; þat it α.
88 For] so ZACK–D; om All MSS. whoso] β (-so] om WCr²³)AZC; He R; he þat F; Quod sche he þat H.
91 In W&rZAC; l. om HF. And] W&r; And eke ZA; And also C.
92 The] W&r?A; om HZC. þis] W&rC; it HZA.
96 *transgressores*] W&r; trespacers GAx (C).

Til treuthe hadde ytermyned hire trespas to the ende.

decided; offence; finally

For David in hise dayes dubbed knyghtes,
And dide hem sweren on hir swerd to serven truthe ever.

made; sword(s)

100 And that is the profession apertly that apendeth to knyghtes,

plainly; pertains

And naught to fasten o Friday in fyve score wynter,   *fast on Friday*
But holden with hym and with here that wolden alle truthe,

support; seek

And never leve hem for love ne for lacchynge of silver—   *to get*
And whoso passe[th] that point is apostata in the ordre.   *exceeds*

105 'But Crist, kyngene kyng, knyghted tene—   *king of kings*
Cherubyn and Seraphyn, swiche sevene and another;   *seven such*
And yaf hem myght in his majestee – the murier hem thoughte—

gave; pleasanter; it seemed to

And over his meene meynee made hem archangeles;   *lesser troop(s)*
Taughte hem by the Trinitee treuthe to knowe,

110 To be buxom at his biddyng – he bad hem nought ellis.

obedient; commanded

'Lucifer with legions lerned it in hevene,
[And was the lovelokest of light after Oure Lord selven]   *loveliest*
Til he brak buxomnesse; his blisse gan he tyne,   *broke obedience; lose*
And fel fro that felawshipe in a fendes liknesse   *fiend's likeness*

115 Into a deep derk helle to dwelle there for evere.
And mo thousandes myd hym than man kouthe nombre

more; with; count

---

103 And never abandon them out of partiality [*sc.* towards wrongdoers] nor
for bribes.
104 And whoever infringes (the duties imposed by) that virtue, is/proves
himself an apostate against the order (of knighthood).
105–6 ... made ten (orders) of 'knights', Cherubim and Seraphim, seven
(orders) like these, and one other (order) – [*sc.* making up ten].

98–9 *Ll. after* 103, *and* 100–3
copied after 97 *in All MSS; re-arr.*
K–D (*so* ZA) (C).
100 þe] L&rA(*cf.* C); *om* WHZ.
102 wolden alle] W&r; askeþ þe
GZAK–D.
104 passeth] *so* ZACK–D; passed
All MSS.
is] YOC²MZACK–D; was W&r

(*om* F).
106 anoþre] L&rZAC; oþere WHm
Cr¹G (*canc and corrected*) HR.
108 meene] W&rZ?A; *om* G.
109 treuþe] W&r; the tr. GZA.
110 To] β (*l. om* H); And α.
112 *So* ZA (liȝt) siȝt Ax); *l. om All
MSS* (C).
113 Til] αZAK–D; But for β.

Lopen out with Lucifer in lothliche forme   *Leapt; loathsome*
For thei leveden upon hym that lyed in this manere:

                                                     Because; believed; lied
Ponam pedem in aquilone, et similis ero Altissimo.

120   And alle that hoped it myghte be so, noon hevene myghte hem holde,
But fellen out in fendes liknesse [for] nyne dayes togideres,
Til God of his goodnesse gan stable and stynte   *caused to rest*
And garte [to stekie the hevene], and stonden in quiete.

                                                     made; stick fast
'Whan thise wikkede wenten out, wonderwise thei fellen—

                                                     marvellously
125   Somme in eyr, somme in erthe, somme in helle depe;   *air*
Ac Lucifer lowest lith of hem alle: *lies*
For pride that h[ym] pulte out, his peyne hath noon ende.

                                                     thrust; torment
And alle that werchen with wrong wende thei shulle   *must go*
After hir deth day and dwelle with that sherewe;   *evil one*
130   Ac tho that werche wel as Holy Writ telleth,
And enden as I er seide in truthe, that is the beste,   *end; previously*
Mowe be siker that hire soule shul wende to hevene,   *May be certain*
Ther Treuthe is in Trinitee and troneth hem alle.   *enthrones*
Forthi I seye, as I seyde er, by sighte of thise textes—
135   Whan alle tresors arn tried, Truthe is the beste.

---

119 I shall set my foot in the north, and I shall be like the Most High
     (Augustine) (C).

119   *&* ... *altissimo*] βC; *&c* R; *l.*
      om F.
121   for] *om All MSS* (C).
122   stable] L&r; stablisse W.
123   to stekie; þe heuene] *trs. All*
      MSS (st.] st. ageyn F; spere H) (C).
124   out] L&r; out in w.
125   in¹] L&rZAC; in þe WOC²C
      MHF.
      Eyr] W&rZA; erthe YOC²MαC.
      erþe] W&r (þe e. C)ZA; the eir
      YOC²MαC (the] *om* RC).
      some³] GZACK–D; and somme

W&r.

127   hym] *so* ZC; he *All* BA-*MSS*
      (him A-*MS* W) (C).
      pulte] CrLRZ (*cf.* C); putte W&rA
      (C).
129   and] βZAC; to α.
130   Ac] L&r (*l. om* H; butt G)ZA;
      WCrC²CFC.
132   soule] L&rZA; soules wGH.
133   troneþ] β (coroned G; trowyt
      H)ZA (*cf.* C); for to saue α (for to]
      þat shal F).
134   siȝte of] βZA; *om* α.

Lereth it th[u]s lewed men, for lettred it knoweth—
                              Teach it to; uneducated; educated (men)
That Treuthe is tresor the trieste on erthe.'   *choicest*
    'Yet have I no kynde knowynge,' quod I, 'yet mote ye kenne
        me bettre   *natural; must teach*
By what craft in my cors it comseth, and where.'   *power; body; arises*
140 'Thow doted daffe!' quod she, 'dulle are thi wittes.   *silly fool*
To litel Latyn thow lernedest, leode, in thi youthe: *Too; man*
Heu michi quod sterilem duxi vitam iuvenilem!
It is a kynde knowynge that kenneth in thyn herte   *instructs (you)*
For to loven thi Lord levere than thiselve,   *more dearly*
No dedly synne to do, deye theigh thow sholdest—   *mortal, serious*
145 This I trowe be truthe; who kan teche thee bettre,
                                  believe is; if anyone can
Loke thow suffre hym to seye, and sithen lere it after;
                                  See; allow; then learn
For thus witnesseth his word; werche thow therafter.   *act accordingly*
    'For Truthe telleth that love is triacle of hevene: *the healing remedy*
May no synne be on hym seene that that spice useth.   *visible*
150 And alle his werkes he wroughte with love as hym liste,   *as he wished*
And lered it Moyses for the leveste thyng and moost lik to hevene,
                                                      dearest

---

136 Teach such a lesson to uneducated men, for the educated are familiar with
    it.
139 By (means of) what power in my body it [*sc.* a direct natural knowledge of
    truth] arises, and in what part of it.
141*a* Alas, what a useless life I led in my youth! (proverbial); cf. V 441*a*.

136   it¹] ?β (on HmCr; *l. om* H) C;
      om αG.
      thus] *so* ZACK–D; þise WYOC²;
      þis L&r (thys ye GF); ye M (C).
138   ȝet . . . ȝe] L&r (ȝe] I R)Z?AC;
      ye mote ?w (ȝyt Hm)H; y coueyte
      F.
      kenne me] β (*trs* Cr)ZAC; lerne α.
141   *Defective to* II 40 R; F *collated
      selectively from here* (C).
141*a*   quod] F (?=α)C; quia β (*l. om*
      H).

142   It] βZAC; þat F.
      that] *so* ZACK–D; quod she þat *All
      MSS* (C).
144   No; to] βA (*cf.* Z); & non; *om*
      F.
146   after] β (*l. om* H)ZA; soone F.
147   *In* L&r; *l. om* wGH.
149   that spyce; vseþ] F (?=α); *trs* β.
150–8   *Ll. om* H.
150   And; he] β; *om*; be F.
151   moyses . . . þyng] β; to m. for
      leve F.

And also the plante of pees, moost precious of vertues:

peace; powers, virtues

For hevene myghte nat holden it, so was it hevy of hymself*e*,

Til it hadde of the erthe eten his fille.   *eaten (C)*

155 And whan it hadde of this fold flessh and blood taken,   *earth*

Was nevere leef upon lynde lighter therafter,   *leaf; linden-tree*

And portatif and persaunt as the point of a nedle,

portable; piercing; needle

That myghte noon armure it lette ne none heighe walles.

(So) that; armour; stop

'Forthi is love ledere of the Lordes folk of hevene, *Lord of heaven's*

160 And a meene, as the mair is, [inmiddes] the kyng and the commune;

intermediary; mayor; commons

Right so is love a ledere and the lawe shapeth: *determines*

Upon man for hise mysdedes the mercyment he taxeth. *fine; imposes*

And for to knowen it kyndely – it comseth by myght*e*,

originates; power (of God)

And in the herte, there is the heed and the heighe welle. *chief source*

165 For in kynde knowynge in herte ther [coms]eth a myght*e*—

And that falleth to the Fader that formed us alle,   *pertains*

Loked on us with love and leet his sone dye   *Son; die*

Mekely for oure mysdedes, to amenden us alle.   *Meekly, humbly*

And yet wolde he hem no wo that wroughte hym that peyne,

wished; torment

170 But mekely with mouthe mercy he bisoughte,   *sc. from God*

---

165 For in/through the natural knowledge in the heart, there arises a
power . . .

152 þe] βZA?C; *om* CF.
plant] Cr?AC*SkBn*; planetes Y;
plentee W&rZ (C).
moost] βC; ys moost F.

153 so was it] F (?=α); it was so β.
of] β; *om* F.
hymselue] F; hymself β.

154 eten his fille] W&r (e.] ye- LG;
yhetyn al F); yoten it selue CrC (C).

155 þis fold] β (þis] þe OC²)C;
manhode F.

157 In βC; *l. om* F.

158 That] β; þer F.

159 Forþi] βC; þerfore F; þer H.

160 a . . . is] βC; as þe M. is meene
F.
inmiddes] bitwene *All MSS* (C).
þe commune] W&r; the commons
CrOC²F (þe] *om* F).

162 þe] β (*om* H)C; & F.
taxeþ] βC; askeþ FH.

163–70 *Ll. om* H.

165 in¹] W&rZA; of CrC.
in²] W&rZA; off GC.
comseth; a myght] *so* ZACK–D; a
my3t; bigynneþ *All MSS* (*trs* G) (C).

166 vs] βZAC; faire vs F.

170 he] L&rZA?C; *om* W.

To have pite on that peple that peyned hym to dethe.   *on; tortured*
  'Here myghtow sen ensamples in hymself oone—   *example; alone*
That he was myghtful and meke, and mercy gan graunte   *powerful*
To hem that hengen hym heigh and his herte thirled.   *hung; pierced*
175 'Forthi I rede yow riche, haveth ruthe on the povere,
                                           counsel; pity on; poor

Though ye be myghty to mote, beeth meke in youre werkes,
                                           summon to a law-court; be
For the same mesure that ye mete, amys outher ellis,
                                           mete out; wrongly or otherwise
Ye shulle ben weyen therwith whan ye wenden hennes:
                                           weighed; i.e. die

Eadem mensura qua mensi fueritis remecietur vobis.
For though ye be trewe of youre tonge and treweliche wynne,
                                           honestly earn (profit)
180 And as chaste as a child that in chirche wepeth,
But if ye loven leelly and lene the povere,   *Unless; faithfully; give to*
Of swich good as God yow sent goodliche parteth,
                                           sends; liberally share
Ye ne have na moore merite in masse ne in houres   *the Divine Office*
Than Malkyn of hire maydenhede, that no man desireth.   *virginity*
185 For James the gentile jugged in hise bokes   *noble, good; concluded*

178a For with the same measure that you shall mete withal it shall be
    measured to you again (Lk 6: 38); cf XI 226a.
182 Divide kindly with them such possessions as God sends you.
184 Than (ill-favoured) Molly from her virginity, which no man wants
    (anyway).

171   on] Hm&rZACK–D; of
      WYCL.
172   ensamples] L&rZ?A?C; *sg*
      WCr³GCHF.
174   heye] GZACK–D; on heiʒ
      W&r.
175   yow] βACZ (ye); þe F.
      ruþe] βZAC; pety H; mercy F.
      on] Hm&rZACK–D; of WYOC
      LM.
176   myghty] GCrZACK–D;
      myʒtful W&r (C).
      in] W&rZAC; of G.

177   þe] βZAC; be þe F.
      mesure] HmCrHFACK–D; *pl*
      W&rZ.
180   a] βZAC; þe F.
      in] βA; in þe F.
181   But] βZAC; & but F.
182   Of] F (?=α)ZACK–D; *om* β
      (And H).
      yow sent] W&r (*trs* G)Z?C; hat
      sent H; sent ?A.
183   ne¹] W&rA?C; *om* CrGMHF.
      in¹,²] βZAC; of HF.
184   no man] βZAC; alle men F.

That feith withouten feet is [feblere] than nought,

work(s); weaker, worth less

And as deed as a dorenail but if the dedes folwe:

dead; door-nail; deeds

Fides sine operibus mortua est . . .

  'Forthi chastite withouten charite worth cheyned in helle;

shall be chained

It is as lewed as a lampe that no light is inne.

pointless

190 Manye chapeleyns arn chaste, ac charite is aweye;   *chaplains; absent*

Are none hardere than hii whan [hii] ben avaunced: *they; promoted*

Unkynde to hire kyn and to alle Cristene,   *Unkind, unnatural*

Chewen hire charite and chiden after moore—

Consume; complain (for)

Swiche chastite withouten charite worth cheyned in helle.   *will be*

195 Manye curatours kepen hem clene of hire bodies;   *parish-priests; chaste*

Thei ben acombred with coveitise, thei konne noght out crepe,

weighed down

So harde hath avarice yhasped hem togideres.   *fastened*

And that is no truthe of the Trinite, but tricherie of helle, *faithlessness*

And lernynge to lewed men the latter to deele.   *a lesson; later; give*

200 For [thise ben wordes] writen in the [Euaungelie]:   *Gospel*

187*a* . . . faith without works is dead (Js 2: 26).

199 And (a bad) example to uneducated people to be tardy in giving (alms).

186 -outen] YGHFA?CK–D; -outen þe W&rZ.
feet] ?β (dede GH; werk Hm) Z?AC; fewte, F A-*MSS* EAM (*C*).
febler then nauȝt] *so* ZACK–D; wersse þan nouth H; riȝt noþyng worþi W&r (r.) *om* GF) (*C*).

187 And] βZAC; But F.
nayle] GHZACK–D; tree W&r.
dedes] W&rZ?AC; dede G.

189 as¹] βAC; *om* F.

190 Manye] βZAC; Fele F.

191 Are] βZAC; þere ben F.
non] GFZACK–D; no men W&r.
herder] GZACK–D; Auarouser W&r (*C*).
hij²] *so* A; þei *All MSS* (*C*).

192 Vnkynde; cristene] βZA?C; & vnkynde; cristene peple F.

193 Chewen] βZA?C; they chewen GFH; And schewen C².

195 Manye; hem] β (hem] *om* H); Fele; hemself F.

196 Thei] β; But þey F; ȝet H; ȝe A; and HmZC.
noȝt] βZAC; *om* F.
out crepe] F (?=α)?ZA?C; *trs* H; crye ovte G; doon it from hem ?β (put it away Hm).

198 no] βAC; not F.

199 to²] GHFZAK–D; for to ?β.

200 For] C²ACK–D; Forþi W&r ?Z (Foryth); perfore H.
þise *ben* wordes] *so* ACK–D; ben þese wordys H; þise wordes ben W&r (*C*).
euaungelie] *so* ZACK–D; gospel *All MSS* (*C*).

"*Date, et dabitur vobis* – for I deele yow alle.   *give, distribute to*
And that is the lok of love that leteth out my grace,   *lock*
To conforten the carefulle acombred with synne." *frightened, anxious*
   'Love is leche of lif and next Oure Lord selve,   *physician; closest*
205 And also the graithe gate that goth into hevene.   *direct way*
Forthi I seye as I seide er by sighte of thise textes:
When alle tresors ben tried, Treuthe is the beste.
   'Now have I told thee what truthe is – that no tresor is bettre—
I may no lenger lenge thee with; now loke thee Oure Lord!'

                                          longer remain; protect

---

201 Give; and it shall be given to you (Lk 6: 38). cf. XI 226*a*

201   deele] βZAC; dele with F; ȝeue
       H.
202   And] βC; For HF; *om* CrZA.
       that¹] β; *date* F.
       that²] CrGMHFK–D; and WHm
       YOC²CL.
203   acombred] βZAC; þat is a. F;
       & comeryd H.
204   Loue] βZA; For l. F; So l. C.
       selue] β (hymselue HmGYH); in
       heuene F.
205   also; goþ; heuene] βA; it ys;
       good; blysse F.
206   syght off] GHZACK–D; *om*
       W&r (C).
       thes] HmGZACK–D; þe W&r (þe
       trewe OC²).
207   tresors ben; treuþe] βZAC;
       tresor is; ȝyt t. F.
208   þat . . . bettre] βA; tak it if þou
       lyke F.
209   now] βZA; but G; *om* HF.

Passus II

Yet I courbed on my knees and cried hire of grace,

Still further; bent; favour

And seide, 'Mercy, madame, for Marie love of hevene, *love of Mary in*

That bar that blisful barn that boughte us on the Rode—

bore; blessed child; Cross

Kenne me by som craft to knowe the false.' *skill; recognize*

5   'Loke upon thi left half, and lo where he stondeth— *hand; see*

Bothe Fals and Favel, and hire feeres manye!' *Deceit; their companions*

  I loked on my left half as the lady me taughte, *instructed*

And was war of a womman wonderliche yclothed—

aware; marvellously

Purfiled with pelure, the pureste on erthe, *Trimmed; fur; finest*

10 Ycorouned with a coroune, the Kyng hath noon bettre. *Crown(ed)*

Fetisliche hire fyngres were fretted with gold wyr,

Gracefully; adorned; wire

And thereon rede rubies as rede as any gleede, *red; glowing coal*

And diamaundes of derrest pris and double manere saphires,

highest value

Orientals and ewages envenymes to destroye.

---

9 (Her dress) embroidered with a trimming of fur, the very choicest in the world.

13–14 ... sapphires of two kinds – oriental sapphires and sea-coloured sapphires, (having the power) to act as antidote to poisons (C).

Collation   WHmHm² *(from 209)*
CrGYOC²CLMHR *(from 41)* F.
RUBRIC *Passus secundus de visione
vt supra* W&r *(sec.]* Tercius F; *de
v.]* om O); om GC².

1   Yet; on] βAZ; *om*; ȝyt on F.
courbed] kneled ZAC (C).

3   blisful] W&rZ?A; blessed C²C.

4   Kenne] βZAC; & kenne F.

5   and] β *(om* GH)ZA?C; quod she
& FZ.
lo] βZ?AC; se F.

7   me] βZAC; *om* F.

8   wonders-] G?AC; worþi- ?βZ;
was worchep- F (C).

9   purest on] F (?=α) HZA *(cf.* C);
fyneste vpon β.

10   Ycorouned] βZA; And cr. C; &
crowned she was F.

11   *In* β; *l. om* F.

12   And ... rede] βC; & set
abowhte with F.

13   And] β; & with F.
of ... pris; manere] β; þe derrest;
dyuerse F.

14   enuenymes] β; enemyes F.

15 Hire robe was ful riche, of reed scarlet engreyned, *fast-dyed*
With ribanes of reed gold and of riche stones. *bands*
   Hire array me ravysshed, swich richesse saugh I nevere.
I hadde wonder what she was and whos wif she were. *might be*
'What is this womman,' quod I, 'so worthili atired?' *nobly dressed*
20 'That is Mede the mayde,' quod she, 'hath noyed me ful ofte,
harmed

And ylakked my lemman that Leautee is hoten,
disparaged; lover; called
And bilowen h[ym] to lordes that lawes han to kepe.
told lies about; administer
In the Popes paleis she is pryvee as myselve, *palace; intimate*
But Soothnesse wolde noght so – for she is a bastard, *Truth(fulness)*
25 For Fals was hire fader that hath a fikel tonge, *treacherous*
And nevere sooth seide sithen he com to erthe; *truth; since; came*
And Mede is manered after hym, right as kynde asketh:
takes after; nature requires
Qualis pater, talis filius. Bona arbor bonum fructum facit.
  'I oughte ben hyere than [heo] – I kam of a bettre. *higher; she; from*
My fader the grete God is and ground of alle graces,
source, foundation
30 Oo God withouten gynnyng, and I his goode doughter,
One; beginning

And hath yeven me Mercy to marie with myselve; *to marry me*
And what man be merciful and leelly me love *whoever is; faithfully*
Shal be my lord and I his leef in the heighe hevene; *beloved*
And what man taketh Mede, myn heed dar I legge *head; wager*

---

21 And disparaged my beloved, whose name is Loyal Faithfulness.
27a Like father like son (proverbial); (Every) good tree bringeth forth good
  fruit (Mt 7: 17).

16 of²] β; ful of F.
19 is þis; womman] βZA; *trs* F.
20 That] βZAC; she F.
  quod she] W&rZ?A?C; *om* G.
21 And] βZAC; & often F.
22 bilowen] βC; she is lowly F.
  hym] *so* CK–D; hire β; *om* F (C).
23 In; is] βZAC; & in; is as F.
24 is a] βC; bore F.
27a *Bona*] Hm&rCSk; *Bonus* WL
  MF (*iterum b.* F).

arbor . . . facit] βC; *fructus habet*
  Malus arbor malus fructus profert F.
28 heo] *so* ZAC; she *All MSS* (C).
  kam; bettre] β; am; b. roote F.
29 þe] β; *om* HF.
  and] β; *om* F.
30 Oo; I] β (I] *om* H); he is; y am F.
31 haþ yeuen] β; he gaf F.
32 loue] β; honowre F.
34 heed] W&r; lif YOC²M (*cf.* C).

35   That he shal lese for hire love a lappe of *Caritatis*.

                        lose; portion; Charity

    'How construeth David the Kyng of men that [cacch]eth Mede,

                              explains; take

And men of this moolde that maynteneth truthe,   *earth; support*

And how ye shul save yourself? The Sauter bereth witnesse: *Psalter*

Domine, quis habitabit in tabernaculo tuo. . . ?

40   'And now worth this Mede ymaried to a mansed sherewe,

                              shall be; cursed

To oon Fals Fikel-tonge, a fendes biyete.   *fiend's offspring*

Favel thorugh his faire speche hath this folk enchaunted,

                         Deceit; bewitched

And al is Lieres ledynge that [heo] is thus ywedded.

                    (through) L.'s instigation

Tomorwe worth ymaked the maydenes bridale;

                    will be; wedding (feast)

45   And there myghtow witen if thow wilt whiche thei ben alle

                      might thou know

That longen to that lordshipe, the lasse and the moore.

                  belong; (Mede's) domain

Knowe hem there if thow kanst, and kepe [thee from hem alle],

                Recognize; guard yourself

And lakke hem noght but lat hem worthe, til Leaute be Justice

                 criticize; be; Judge

And have power to punysshe hem – thanne put forth thi reson.

                      argument(s)

50   Now I bikenne thee Crist,' quod she, 'and his clene moder,

                    commit (to); pure

---

39 Lord, who shall dwell in thy tabernacle? (Ps 14: 1) (C).

35 lippe] YCrC*K–D*; lappe W&r;
    lomp G.
36 How . . . kyng] β; See how dauid
    meneþ F.
    caccheþ Mede] *cj K–D*; taketh
    Mede *All MSS* (*trs* F) (C).
37 And] β; & of F.
38 bereþ witnesse] β; ȝow techeþ F.
40 worþ þis; ymaried] βC; shal be
    m. HF.

to] GM (*after erasure*) HFC*K–D*;
vnto w; al to YOC²CL.
41 *Here* R *resumes*; α=RF.
43 heo] she *All MSS*; lady C (*see* 28
    (C)).
45 And] W&r; *om* GHZA.
47 þee . . . alle] *so* ZAC*K–D*; þow
    þi tonge *All MSS* (þow) wel
    YOC²F; *om* CLR) (C).

And that no conscience acombre thee for coveitise of Mede.'

trouble, oppress

   Thus lefte me that lady liggynge aslepe,   *lying*

And how Mede was ymaried in metels me thoughte—   *i.e. I dreamed*

That al the riche retenaunce that regneth with the False

retinue; lords it

55 Were boden to the bridale on bothe two sides,   *bidden*

Of alle manere of men, the meene and the riche. *(Consisting) of; poor*

To marien this mayde was many man assembled,

As of knyghtes and of clerkes and oother commune peple, *clerics*

As sisours and somonours, sherreves and hire clerkes,

assizers (C); sheriffs

60 Bedelles and baillifs and brocours of chaffare,

Beadles (C); brokers of trade

Forgoers and vitaillers and vokettes of the Arches;

Purveyors; advocates

I kan noght rekene the route that ran aboute Mede. *number; throng*

Ac Symonie and Cyvylle and sisours of courtes   *Civil Law*

Were moost pryvee with Mede of any men, me thoughte. *intimate*

65 Ac Favel was the firste that fette hire out of boure

fetched; (her) chamber

And as a brocour broughte hire to be with Fals enjoyned.

broker; united

   Whan Symonye and Cyvylle seighe hir bother wille,

saw; joint, of both

Thei assented for silver to seye as bothe wolde.   *wished*

Thanne leep Liere forth and seide, 'Lo! here a chartre *ran; here is*

70 That Gile with his grete othes gaf hem togidere,'

And preide Cyvylle to see and Symonye to rede it.   *requested*

---

51 And allow no (scruples of) conscience (caused by) any greed for lucre (on
   your part) to weigh you down.

58 ... and other people not of aristocratic or clerical estate.

61 Those who obtain provisions [esp. for the king's itinerant courts etc.], those
   who provide them, and lawyers who practise in the ecclesiastical courts.

51 þat] F (?=α; at R); lat β.

54 þe²] W&rC; sire F; *om* HmC²H
    ZA.

55 þe] βAC; þis ?α (his F)Z; þat H.

56 *In* W&r; *l. om* H.

57 þis] W&r; þe Cr; þat HF.

59 As] W&rC; Of HF.

61 vokates] L&rC; Aduokettes
    WCrGH.

64 me þouȝte] βR (me) *om* R)C;
    þere owte F.

68 Thei] βC; And α.

Thanne Symonye and Cyvylle stonden forth bothe   *stand*
And unfoldeth the feffement that Fals hath ymaked,

deed of endowment

And thus bigynnen thise gomes to greden ful heighe: *men; cry aloud*
'Sciant presentes et futuri, &c.

75 Witeth and witnesseth, that wonieth upon erthe,

know; (you) who dwell

That Mede is ymaried moore for hire goodes
Than for any vertue or fairnesse or any free kynde.   *noble lineage*
Falsnesse is fayn of hire for he woot hire riche;   *desires; knows (to be)*
And Favel with his fikel speche feffeth by this chartre

deceiving; endows

80 To be princes in Pride, and poverte to despise,   *as Princess*
To bakbite and to bosten and bere fals witnesse,   *slander; boast*
To scorne and to scolde and sclaundre to make,   *rail; slander*
Unbuxome and bolde to breke the ten hestes.

Disobedient; commandments

And the erldom of Envye and [Ire] togideres,
85 With the chastilet of cheste and chaterynge out of reson.

little castle; quarrelling

The countee of Coveitise and alle the costes aboute—   *Greed; regions*
That is usure and avarice – al I hem graunte   *usury; miserliness*
In bargaynes and in brocages with al the burghe of thefte,

'deals'; brokerage; borough

[With] al the lordshipe of Leccherie in lengthe and in brede—

domain; breadth

90 As in werkes and in wordes and in waitynges with eighes, *look(ing)s*
And in wenynges and in wisshynges and with ydel thoughtes

hopes; fantasies

Ther as wil wolde and werkmanshipe fayleth.'   *Where; performance*

74a Be it known to all present and to come . . . (legal formula).
75 Know (for certain) and be witness, (all you who) live on the earth.

75 *vp*on] GHFZACK–D; *vp*on þis
     W&r (C).
77 or¹] W&r (cf. C); of HmgH.
83 Vnbuxome; bolde] βC; trs α (b.]
     & to be b. F).
84 Yre] so CK–D; wraþe All MSS
     (C).
85 cheste] β; gestes α; theft H.
     chaterynge . . . reson] βR (r.] tyme

R)C; þe langelynge of synne F.
89 Wyth] so ZACK–D; And All
     MSS (C).
90 and in²] w?C; and L&r; in HF.
91 wenyngis] ?α (wen-] wed- R);
     wendys H; wedes β (C).
92 and] W&r (l. om H ; †F)C; om
     yL.

Glotonye he gaf hem ek and grete othes togidere,
And al day to drynken at diverse tavernes,
95 And there to jangle and jape and jugge hir evencristen,
                              chatter; mock; fellow-Christian
And in fastynge dayes to frete er ful tyme were.   *eat; fully*
And thanne to sitten and soupen til sleep hem assaille,   *sup*
And breden as burgh swyn, and bedden hem esily,
                         breed? grow fat; town pigs; at ease
Til Sleuthe and sleep sliken hise sydes;   *make sleek*
100 And thanne wanhope to awaken hym so with no wil to amende,
                                               despair (at)

For he leveth be lost – this is his laste ende.   *believes he is; final state*
    'And thei to have and to holde, and hire heires after,   *heirs*
A dwellynge with the devel, and dampned be for evere,   *damned*
With alle the appurtinaunces of purgatorie into the pyne of helle;
                                                          torment
105 Yeldynge for this thyng at one yeres ende   *Yielding (up); year's*
Hire soules to Sathan, to suffre with hym peynes,   *pains*
And with hym to wonye with wo while God is in hevene.'   *sorrow*
    In witnesse of which thyng Wrong was the firste,
And Piers the Pardoner of Paulynes doctrine,   *?order of Paulines (C)*
110 Bette the Bedel of Bokynghamshire,
Reynald the Reve of Rutland Sokene,   *the Soke of Rutland*
Munde the Millere – and many mo othere.   *more besides*
'In the date of the devel this dede is asseled   *sealed*
By sighte of Sire Symonie and Cyvyles leeve.'   *In the sight of; and by*
115   Thanne tened hym Theologie whan he this tale herde,
                                               grew angry; speech

---

109 . . . of the order of (Crutched Friars, called) Paulines (*Sk*; but cf. *Bn*) (C).

95   to²] L&rC; *om* WHmHF.
96   *in*] βF; with R.
98   as] β; as a α.
     hem] β; hym α.
100 hym] L&r; hem wGH.
101 his] ?α (þe F; cf. C)K–D; hir β.
104 *ap*purtinaunces] W&r?C; *sg*
     HmyMHZA.
105 ʒeres ende] L&r (*om* H)ZA;
     dayes tyme W.
106 to²] βFZA; and R.

107 with²] wGH (*cf. ZA*); in
     Cr²³&r.
108 which] βZA; þis αHC.
110 Bette] W&rAC; & B. FHZ.
111 Rutland] βZAC; rokeland α.
112 Munde] L&r; Mand (?Maud)
     WCr¹YC.
113 ys *a*seled] HmCHZ?ACK–D; I
     assele L&r (I) we C²; ass-] ens-
     WCrG).
115 te*n*ed] β; teneth R; was teenyd
     F.

And seide to Cyvyle, 'Now sorwe mote thow have—
may you be cursed

Swiche weddynges to werche to wrathe with Truthe!
bring about; anger

And er this weddynge be wroght, wo thee bitide!

For Mede is muliere, of Amendes engendred;   *legitimate; born*

120 And God graunted to gyve Mede to truthe,   *honesty*

And thow hast gyven hire to a gilour – now God gyve thee sorwe!
deceiver

The text telleth thee noght so, Truthe woot the sothe,

For *Dignus est operarius* his hire to have—   *wages*

And thow hast fest hire to Fals; fy on thi lawe!   *joined; fie upon*

125 For al bi lesynges thow lyvest and lecherouse werkes.   *lies*

Symonye and thiself shenden Holi Chirche,   *damage*

The notaries and ye noyen the peple.   *harm*

Ye shul abiggen it bothe, by God that me made!   *pay (for it)*

'Wel ye witen, wernardes, but if youre wit faille,   *deceivers; unless*

130 That Fals is feithlees and fikel in hise werkes

And as a bastarde ybore of Belsabubbes kynne.   *born; the devil's kin*

And Mede is muliere, a maiden of goode,   *noble ancestry*

And myghte kisse the Kyng for cosyn and she wolde.   *as a cousin; if*

Forthi wercheth by wisdom and by wit also,   *work*

135 And ledeth hire to Londoun, there lawe is yshewed,   *where; revealed*

If any lawe wol loke thei ligge togideres.   *provide that they should lie*

And though justices juggen hire to be joyned with False,   *married to*

Yet be war of the weddynge – for witty is Truthe,   *wise*

And Conscience is of his counseil and knoweth yow echone,
intimate with him

---

123 For the labourer is worthy (of his hire) (Lk 10: 7).
135 ... the (process of) law is made manifest (in the courts).

116 to] L&rZAC; vnto W.
117 weddynges] W&rZ; *sg* GC²?AC.
119 engendred] W&r; engendreth YCLR (C).
120 graunted] yFK–D; graunteþ W&r; grant H (C).
122 The] GYHαZAK–D; Thi W&r.
123 *So* W&rZA-MS M; H *has 2 ll. like* T&r *at* A II 87, *apparatus* (C).

124 to] W&r; wyth GFZA.
130 feiþlees] W&rC; feytles HC?A (*cf.* Z) (C).
   fikel] βF; fals R.
131 as] αZACK–D; was β.
133 And] W&r; sche HmZAC.
135 lawe] L&r (þe l. MH)ACZ (lewte Z); it wG.
137 with] L&rZA; to wGH.
138 þe] αGHZACK–D; *om* W&r.

140 And if he fynde yow in defaute and with the False holde,
                                                    at fault; supporting
    It shal bisitte youre soules ful soure at the laste.'   *oppress; bitterly*
        Herto assenteth Cyvyle, ac Symonye ne wolde,   *was unwilling*
    Til he hadde silver for his se[el] and [signes] of notaries.   *seal*
        Thanne fette Favel forth floryns ynowe   *fetched; enough*
145 And bad Gile, 'Go gyve gold al aboute,   *bade*
    And namely to the notaries, that hem noon faille;   *especially; lack*
    And feffe Fals-witnesse with floryns ynowe,   *retain*
    For he may Mede amaistrye and maken at my wille.'
                                                    dominate; persuade
        Tho this gold was ygyve, gret was the thonkyng   *When; thanking*
150 To Fals and to Favel for hire faire yiftes,   *gifts*
    And comen to conforten from care the False,   *(they) came; anxiety*
    And seiden, 'Certes, sire, cessen shul we nevere   *Rest assured; desist*
    Til Mede be thi wedded wif thorugh wittes of us alle;   *(the) ingenuity*
    For we have Mede amaistried thorugh oure murie speche,   *pleasant*
155 That she graunteth to goon with a good wille
    To London, to loken if that the lawe wolde   *see whether*
    Juggen yow joyntly in joie for evere.'   *J. (that) you be married*
        Thanne was Falsnesse fayn and Favel as blithe,   *pleased; happy*
    And leten somone alle the segges in shires aboute,
                                                    had . . . summoned; people
160 And bad hem alle be bown, beggers and othere,   *ready; others*
    To wenden with hym to Westmynstre to witnesse this dede.
                                                    act, deed

        Ac thanne cared thei for caples to cairen hem thider;
                                            wanted horses; convey themselves

---

140 þe] W&rZ?AC; sire F; *om*
     HmCr.
143 his] βZAC; this R; *om* F.
     seel] *so* C; seles ZAK–D; seruice
     W&r; *om* F (C).
     signes of] *so* CK–D (*cf.* ZA); also
     þe β (þe] for H); alle hise F.
145 go] HmCr³GOC²HFACK–D;
     to W&r.
     gyue] L&r; gyuen W.
147 false-witnes] L&r (f.] F. be F.);
     false witnesses WM.
148 he] LαZAC; þei W&r.

149 Tho] βZAC; whan FH;
     cropped R.
153 wittes] W&r; wytt GHFZA.
154 thorȝ] αHZC; wiþ βAx.
155 to] βZAC; for to F; *om* R.
156 that the] yLMF?A; þat RZ; þe
     wGH.
158 -nesse] W&rZ?A(-hed) (*cf.* C);
     om HmF.
159 the] ?αGA; his ?CZ; *om* ?βF.
160 be] L&rZAC; to be WCrG.
161 hym] αCr²³Z?C; hem β?A.
     þis] βZA; þe α.
162 kairen] LMαZ?A; carien wg.

And Favel fette forth thanne foles ynowe   *colts/fools*
And sette Mede upon a sherreve shoed al newe,   *all newly shod*
165 And Fals sat on a sisour that softeli trotted,   *gently*
And Favel on a flaterere fetisly atired.   *elegantly dressed*
Tho hadde notaries none; anoyed thei were   *irritated*
For Symonye and Cyvylle sholde on hire feet gange.   *had to go*
Ac thanne swoor Symonye and Cyvylle bothe   *swore*
170 That somonours sholde be sadeled and serven hem echone.   *saddled*
  'And late apparaille the provisours in palfreyes wise;   *like horses*
Sire Symonye hymself shal sitte upon hir bakkes.   *backs*
Denes and southdenes, drawe yow togideres;   *Deans; sub-deans*
Erchedekenes and officials and alle youre registrers,

                        Archdeacons; presiding officers; registrars

175 Lat sadle hem with silver oure synne to suffre—   *be saddled; permit*
As devoutrye and divorses and derne usurie—

                                    adultery; annulments; secret

To bere bisshopes aboute abroad in visitynge.   *abroad*
Paulynes pryvees for pleintes in the consistorie   *confidential; pleas*
Shul serven myself that Cyvyle is nempned.   *named*
180 And cartsadle the commissarie – oure cart shal he [drawe],   *harness*
And fecchen [oure] vitailles at *fornicatores*;   *from fornicators*
And maketh of Lyere a lang cart to leden alle thise othere,   *long*
As fobberes and faitours that on hire feet rennen.'   *tricksters; run*
  And thus Fals and Favel fareth forth togideres,   *go*
185 And Mede in the middes and alle thise men after.   *midst*
I have no tome to telle the tail that hem folweth,   *leisure; tail/number*
Of many maner man that on this molde libbeth,   *earth; lives*

---

171 And have these provisors got up like riding-horses.
178 Paulines, secret, confidential agents (when it comes to the conduct) of
  pleas in the bishop's court.

163   ynowe] βRZ; sone F; of þe best
  HA.
166   fetis-] W&rZ?A; feyt- G; feete-
  Cr; freys- H(C).
171   þe] ?αZ?A; þise ?β; om GHF.
174   officials] βF; deknes officiales
  R.
176   deuoutrye] RF (?=α)K–D;
  Auoutrye β.
178   the] L&r; om wGC?A.
180   draw] so ZACK–D; lede All
  MSS (C).

181   oure] so ZACK–D; vs All MSS
  (C).
183   fobberes] αA (fobbes ZCK–D);
  Freres β.
185   men] wLRZ?AC; meyny G;
  other yMHF.
186   hem] L&rZAC; hire WCrG.
  folweth] L&r?A?C; folwed WM(d
  over erasure)HZ.
187   In L&rZAC; l. om WCr¹G.

Ac Gyle was forgoer and gyed hem alle.   *harbinger; guided*
    Sothnesse seigh hem wel, and seide but litel,   *Truth(fulness)*
190 And priked his palfrey and passed hem alle,
                                          spurred; (light courier's) horse
    And com to the Kynges court and Conscience it tolde,
    And Conscience to the Kyng carped it after.   *related*
    'Now, by Cryst!' quod the Kyng, 'and I cacche myghte   *if*
Fals or Favel or any of hise feeris,   *companions*
195 I wolde be wroken of tho wrecches that wercheth so ille,
                                            avenged on; evilly
    And doon hem hange by the hals and alle that hem maynteneth.
                                have them hanged; neck; support
    Shal nevere man of this molde meynprise the leeste,   *stand bail (for)*
    But right as the lawe loke[th], lat falle on hem alle!' *determines*
    —And comaunded a constable that com at the firste,   *straight away*
200 'Go attachen tho tyraunts, for any [tresor], I hote,
                           arrest; in spite of; command
    And fettreth [Falsnesse faste], for any kynnes yiftes, *fetter; kind of*
    And girdeth of Gyles heed – lat hym go no ferther;   *smite off*
    And bringeth Mede to me maugree hem alle!   *in spite of*
    And if ye lacche Lyere, lat hym noght ascapen   *capture; escape*
205 Er he be put on the pillory, for any preyere, I hote.'
    Drede at the dore stood and the doom herde,   *judgement*
    And how the Kyng comaunded constables and sergeaunts
Falsnesse and his felawship to fettren and to bynden.   *crew*
Thanne Drede wente wyghtliche and warned the False,   *with alacrity*
210 And bad hym fle for fere, and hise feeris alle.   *fear; cronies*
    Falsnesse for fere thanne fleigh to the freres   *fled; friars*
    And Gyle dooth hym to go, agast for to dye.   *makes him; terrified*
Ac marchaunts metten with hym and made hym abyde,   *stay*
And bishetten hym in hire shoppes to shewen hire ware,
                                          shut him (up); display

---

190 And] βRC; But FAZ(Ac).
191 it] W&r; *om* GZAC.
198 loketh] *so* ZACK–D; wol loke
    W&r; will F (C).
200 Goo] ?α (::oo R; & goo F)C;
    To βZA.
    tresor] *so* ZACK–D; þyng *All MSS*
    (C).
201 Fals*enesse* faste] *so* ZACK–D;

    trs All MSS (C).
202 lat] *so* ZACK–D; and lat *All*
    MSS (C).
203 *After* 204 W&r (*l. om* Y); *so*
    placed ZACK–D (C).
210 feerys] FZACK–D; felawes βR
    (C).
214 shoppes] wGHFA?C; shoppe
    yLMRZ.

215 And apparailed hym as a prentice the peple to serve.   *dressed; apprentice*
    Lightliche Lyere leep awey thenne,   *Smartly; ran; from there*
Lurkynge thorugh lanes, tolugged of manye.   *pulled about by*
He was nowher welcome for his manye tales,   *falsehoods*
Overal yhouted and yhote trusse,
220 Til pardoners hadde pite, and pulled hym into house.   *indoors*
They wesshen hym and wiped hym and wounden hym in cloutes,
                                 washed; patched clothes
And senten hym [on Sondayes with seles] to chirches,   *(bishops') seals*
And gaf pardoun for pens poundemele aboute.
                           pence; by pounds at a time
    Thanne lourede leches, and lettres thei sente   *scowled; physicians*
225 That he sholde wonye with hem watres to loke.   *dwell; inspect urine*
Spycers speken to hym to spien hire ware,   *Spice-merchants; scrutinize*
For he kouthe on hir craft and knew manye gommes.
                         understood; trade; gums
Ac mynstrales and messagers mette with hym ones,   *messengers; once*
And [with]helden hym half a yeer and ellevene dayes.   *harboured*
230   Freres with fair speche fetten hym thennes,
And for knowynge of comeres coped hym as a frere;   *recognition*
Ac he hath leve to lepen out as ofte as hym liketh,   *roam abroad*
And is welcome whan he wile, and woneth with hem ofte.   *dwells*
    Alle fledden for fere and flowen into hernes;   *flew; corners*
235 Save Mede the mayde na mo dorste abide.   *dared remain*
Ac trewely to telle, she trembled for fere,
And ek wepte and wrong when she was attached.   *wrung; taken*

---

219 Everywhere hooted at and ordered to pack up (and be off).
223 And (there he) distributed pardon(s) for pennies, (a number of them, to the value of several) pounds at a time.
231 And to prevent his being recognized by callers, dressed him in a friar's robes.

215 And] L&rC; *om* wHm²GZA.
    a prentice] L&rZAC; Apprentice WHmC².
216 þenne] αZAC; thence GH; þanne ?β.
219 yhouted] L&r?AC; yhonted w Hm²; ?I omyted G.
220 into] W&rZ?AC; to HmHm² MHF.
222 *on* sundais; wiþ selis] *so* ACZK–D; *trs All MSS* (C).

223 gaf] L&rZAC; yeuen W.
226 to¹] αZAC; with β.
227 on] αHmHm²ACK–D; of ?βZ.
228 Ac] L&r (but GH) Z?ACK–D; And WCrC²C; þanne F.
229 wiþ-] *so* ACK–D; *om All MSSZ* (C).
    half a] αCrH; half ZAC; an h. β.
236 fere] αACK–D; drede β.
237 ek] βA; also α.
    whan] βAC; for F; *om* R.

Passus III

Now is Mede the mayde and no mo of hem alle, *no more*
With bedeles and baillies brought bifore the Kyng*e*.
        By; tipstaffs; bailiffs
The Kyng called a clerk – I kan noght his name— *know*
To take Mede the maide and maken hire at ese.
5 'I shal assayen hire myself and soothliche appose *try; truly question*
What man of this world that hire were levest. *would be dearest to her*
And if she werche bi my wit and my wil folwe *wisdom; follow*
I wol forgyven hire this[e] giltes, so me God helpe!' *offences, faults*
 Curteisly the clerk thanne, as the Kyng highte, *Courteously; ordered*
10 Took Mede bi the myddel and broghte hire into chambre.
        waist; private room
Ac ther was murthe and mynstralcie Mede to plese;
        entertainment; music
That wonyeth at Westmynstre worshipeth hire alle.
       (All) those who; honour
Gentilliche with joye the justices somme *Courteously; some, together*
Busked hem to the bour ther the burde dwellede,
       Repaired; lady; was staying
15 Confort[ed]en hire kyndely by Clergies leve, *permission*
And seiden, 'Mourne noght, Mede, ne make thow no sorwe, *weep*

Collation WHmHm²(*to 72a*)Cr GY OC²CBLMHRF.

RUBRIC *Passus tercius de visione vt supra* W&r [*ter.*] *Quartus* F; *de v.*] *de v. petri le ploughman* CotR; *om* M); *om* gC².

1 *Collation of* B (=BmBoCot) *begins*; g = GYOC²CB.

2 and] Cr&rZACK–D; and with WHmYCLR.
bifore] W&rC; to BZA.

3 y can] BHZACK–D; I knowe GF; *trs* W&r.

5 shal] W&rZ?AC; wole BF.
sooþliche] βZAC; softly H; couthliche R; sotilly F.

6 world] αBZACK–D; moolde β.

7 my¹] L&r (*l. om* B); *om* wHm² Z?A.

8 þis gultes] α (þ.] þe F) C (þ.] alle) þis gilt β; þe g. BA; that g. Z.

10 broȝte] βRA; mente F (C).

11 Ac] Bm?αZ?ACK–D; And βF; *om* H.

12 þat] BZACK–D; They þ. W&r; Summe þ. F.
at] BGMHαZAK–D; in wyL.

14 dwellede] W&rZ?AC; dwellyth GBF.

15 Conforteden] *so* ZAK–D; And comforthyd HB (-yd] -eþ B)C; To conforten W&r (C).

For we wol wisse the Kyng and thi wey shape

advise; prepare a way for you

To be wedded at thi wille and wher thee leef liketh   *where you desire*
For al Consciences cast and craft, as I trowe.'   *purpose; skill; believe*

20   Mildely Mede thanne merciede hem alle   *Humbly; thanked*
Of hire grete goodnesse, and gaf hem echone   *For their*
Coupes of clene gold and coppes of silver,   *Bowls; pure; cups*
Rynges with rubies and richesses manye,   *rich gifts*
The leeste man of hire meynee a moton of golde.

followers; 'mutton' (coin)

25   Thanne laughte thei leve thise lordes at Mede.   *took; from*
With that comen clerkes to conforten hire the same,   *learned men*
And beden hire be blithe – 'For we beth thyne owene   *bade; are*
For to werche thi wille the while thow myght laste.'
Hendiliche heo thanne bihighte hem the same—

Graciously; she; promised

30   'To loven yow lelly and lordes to make,   *loyally*
And in the consistorie at the court do callen youre names.

have your names called (C)

Shal no lewednesse lette the clerke that I lovye,   *ignorance; impede*
That he ne worth first avaunced for I am biknowen

will not be advanced; because; acknowledged

Ther konnynge clerkes shul clokke bihynde.'   *learned; limp*

35   Thanne cam ther a confessour coped as a frere;   *dressed*
To Mede the mayde he meled thise wordes,   *addressed, spoke*
And seide ful softely, in shrift as it were,   *confession(al tones)*
'Theigh lewed men and lered men hadde leyen by thee bothe,   *lain*
And Falshede hadde yfolwed thee alle thise fifty wynter,   *Deceit*

---

19   cast; craft] βZAC; *trs* α.
and] Cr?B(a BoCot)?αZACK–D; or βF.

23   rich*esses*] β (Ryches CrCH)ZA; ricch*esse* α.

28   þow my3t] W&rZ?C; we may CrG; thy lyfe HmHm²?A; oure lif B?Ax.

30   3ow] LRZ?A; hem W&r?AxC. to make] W&r?A (to] *om* A); hem to m. F; hem m. H?Ax.

31   þe²] W&r?AC; *om* HmHm²Cr OC²RZ.

3oure] L&rZ?AC; hire wHm² GY?Ax.

32   clerke] Crα (*pl* α)C; leode β; men H; hem Z.

33   ne] β (*l. om* H)ZAC; *om* α.

36   þe] βZAC; þis R; þat F. me*ll*ud] L&r; mened WHmHm²; mouthed G.

37   softely] β (*l. om* H)FA; sotely R.

39   -ede] ?α (*om* F)ACK–D; -nesse β (*om* HmHm²). fifty] βR; fiftene FA; fourty C.

40 I shal assoille thee myself for a seem of whete,   *absolve; horse-load*
    And also be thi bedeman, and bere wel thyn er[ende],

                                            beadsman; messages

   Amonges knyghtes and clerkes, Conscience to torne.'   *obstruct*
    Thanne Mede for hire mysdedes to that man kneled,
    And shrof hire of hire sherewednesse – shamelees, I trowe;

                                      confessed; wickedness

45 Tolde hym a tale and took hym a noble   *gave; noble (coin)*
    For to ben hire bedeman and hire brocour als*e*.   *go-between too*
    Thanne he assoiled hire soone and sithen he seide,   *at once; next*
    'We have a wyndow a-werchynge, wole stonden us ful hye;

                          a-building; cost us a great deal

    Woldestow glaze that gable and grave there thy name,

                               If you would; engrave

50 Sykir sholde thi soule be hevene to have.'   *Certain*
    'Wiste I that,' quod the womman, 'I wolde noght spare

                              If I knew; hold back

    For to be youre frend, frere, and faile yow nevere   *(would) fail*
    While ye love lordes that lecherie haunten   *indulge in*
    And lakketh noght ladies that loven wel the same.   *criticize*
55 It is a freletee of flessh – ye fynden it in bokes—   *frailty*
    And a cours of kynde, wherof we comen alle.   *impulse of nature*
    Who may scape the sclaundre, the scathe is soone amended?

                                escape; slander; harm

    It is synne of the sevene sonnest relessed.   *soonest; remitted*
    Have mercy,' quod Mede, 'of men that it haunteth   *engage in it*
60 And I shal covere youre kirk, youre cloistre do maken,   *roof (vb)*
    Wowes do whiten and wyndowes glazen,   *Walls; have whitewashed*
    Do peynten and portraye [who paied] for the makynge,   *depicted*

---

41   *þin a*rnde] **AC** (þ.] here C)H (a.]
   erdyn H)K–D; þi message **W&r**;
   þyn name F (C).
42   kny3tes; clerkes] βRC; *trs* FA.
46   brocour] **W&r**; baud GA; on
   hand H (C).
   als] **W&r** (also Cr); after GHA.
48   a] YCBLMRC; in **W&r** (*om* F)
   ?Ax.
   stonde] HACK–D; *sitten* **W&r** (C).
49   þere] ?αACK–D; þerInne β (*om*
   Hm²)F.

51–62   So β (*cf.* AC); α *has* 3 *ll.*:
   wist I þat quat3 mede þere nys
   wyndouw no wow3 / þat I ne
   wolde make and amende it with of
   myne / And my name write
   openliche þerInne (*cf.* A) (C).
57   þe¹] L&rC; that HmHm²; *om*
   W.
58   þe] **W&r** (*l. om* BH); that Hm²;
   om CLM.
60   do maken] **W&r**; make
   HmHm²; aboute H.
62   Do] **W&r**?C(And do); And B.

That every segge shall see I am suster of youre house.'   *a sister* (C)
 Ac God to alle good folk swich gravynge defendeth—   *forbids*
65 To writen in wyndowes of hir wel dedes—   *good deeds*
An aventure pride be peynted there, and pomp of the worlde;

         Lest perchance; 'vainglory'
For God knoweth thi conscience and thi kynde wille,   *real motives*
Thi cost and thi coveitise and who the catel oughte.   *owned the money*
Forthi I lere yow lordes, leveth swiche werkes—   *instruct; give up*
70 To writen in wyndowes of youre wel dedes   *good deeds*
Or to greden after Goddes men whan ye [gyve] doles,   *call for; alms*
On aventure ye have youre hire here and youre hevene alse.

         reward; too

Nesciat sinistra quid faciat dextra:
Lat noght thi left half, late ne rathe,   *hand; early*
Wite what thow werchest with thi right syde—   *Know; are doing*
75 For thus [the Gospel bit] goode men doon hir almesse.   *bids; give alms*
 Maires and maceres, that menes ben bitwene   *Mayors; mace-bearers*
The kyng and the comune to kepe the lawes,   *common people*
To punysshe on pillories and on pynynge stooles   *punishment-stools*
Brewesters and baksters, bochiers and cokes—

       Brewers; bakers; butchers; cooks
80 For thise are men on this molde that moost harm wercheth   *earth; do*
To the povere peple that parcelmele buggen.   *buy piecemeal* (sc. *retail*)
For thei poisone the peple pryveliche and ofte,   *Because; secretly*
Thei richen thorugh regratrie and rentes hem biggen   *retail-trade; buy*
With that the povere peple sholde putte in hire wombe.   *belly*

72*a* Let not thy left hand know what thy right hand doth (Mt 6: 3).
76 Mayors and officers of justice [who bear maces], who (act as)
 intermediaries between . . .
83 They become rich through (the profits they make from) selling by retail, and
 buy themselves (properties from which they obtain) incomes.

63 euery] βC; ech a αA.   (C).
 Ise] αACK–D; seye β.   72 alse] also Cr; als W&r.
 of . . . house] βAC (h.] ordre C); to 73 half] W&r; hand HAC.
 ȝow alle α.   75 þe gospel; bit] *trs* L&r (bit] by
64 folk] W&r; men G.   W); *l. om* H (C).
67 god] ?αCK–D; crist βF.   78 on²] HFACK–D; *om* W&r.
68 þi¹] ?α (Boþe þi F)C; And þi β. 80 on] β (of HmCB) A; vpon α.
69–72 *In* W&r; *ll. om* HF.   82 For þei] β (*l. om* Hm)A(*cf.* C);
71 gyue] *so* AK–D; dele *All MSS* and also R; & F.

85 For toke thei on trewely, thei tymbred nought so heighe,   *would build*
   Ne boughte none burgages – be ye ful certeyne!   *would buy; tenements*
   Ac Mede the mayde the mair h[eo] bisought[e]   *beseeched the mayor*
   Of alle swiche selleris silver to take,   *From; (retail) merchants*
   Or presents withouten pens – as pieces of silver,   *non-monetary*
90 Rynges or oother richesse, the regratiers to mayntene.   *retailers; support*
      'For my love,' quod that lady, 'love hem echone,
   And suffre hem to selle somdel ayeins reson.'   *at unreasonable prices*
      Salamon the sage a sermon he made   *wise; discourse*
   For to amenden maires and men that kepen lawes,   *administer*
95 And tolde hem this teme that I telle thynke: *theme*
   Ignis devorabit tabernacula eorum qui libenter accipiunt munera . . .
   Among thise lettrede leodes this Latyn is to mene   *men; means*
   That fir shal falle and [for] brenne al to bloo askes
                                          fire; burn up; pale ashes
   The houses and the homes of hem that desireth
100 Yiftes or yeresyeves because of hire office.   *annual gifts; office*
      The Kyng fro counseil cam, and called after Mede,   *from; for*
   And ofsente hire as swithe with sergeaunts manye   *sent for; at once*
   That broughte hire to boure with blisse and with joye.   *the chamber*
      Curteisly the Kyng thanne comseth to telle;   *begins to speak*
105 To Mede the mayde he melleth this wordes: *utters*
      'Unwittily, womman, wroght hastow ofte;   *Foolishly; hast thou*

85–6 For if they earned their living honestly, they (would be unable to) build
   such tall (imposing) houses Or purchase town-properties [from which to
   derive rents].
92 And allow them to sell to some extent at unreasonable prices.
96 . . . (and) fire shall devour their tabernacles, who love to take bribes (Job
   15: 34).

86 burgages] β (*l. om* H)AC; *sg* R;   99 þe²] L&rAC; *om* wG.
   bargayn F.   100 office] αH; Offices β.
87 *heo* besouȝte] *so* ?ACK–D; haþ   101 fro] L&rAC; fro þe wG.
   bisouȝt W&r; haþ she prayed F (C).   103 That] L&r (*cropped* R); And
91 loue] β (*cf.* C); lord α.   WAC (C).
94 lawes] βR; þe lawes FH(*sg* H)A.   104 cumseth] ?αZAK–D; comsed
96 *accipiunt munera*] βAC; *om* α.   βF; gynneth G; began H.
97 leodes] W&r (*sg* R); men G;   105 melleth] L&r (he m. F)A;
   lordis ?AC.   mouthed G; he meneþ WHmH (he
98 forbrenne] *so* ACK–D; brenne   and Hm; -eþ] -yd H).
   All MSS (C).

Ac worse wroghtest thow nevere than tho thow Fals toke.   *took*

But I forgyve thee that gilt, and graunte thee my grace;   *favour*

Hennes to thi deeth day do so na moore!   *From henceforth*

110 I have a knyght, Conscience, cam late fro biyonde;

(who) has come lately

If he wilneth thee to wif, wiltow hym have?'   *desires; as a w.; will you*

'Ye, lord,' quod that lady, 'Lord it me forbede!   *forbid*

But I be holly at youre heste, lat hange me [ellis]!'

Unless; wholly; bidding; otherwise

Thanne was Conscience called to come and appere   *appear*

115 Bifore the Kyng and his conseil, as clerkes and othere.   *others*

Knelynge, Conscience to the Kyng louted,   *bowed*

What his wille were and what he do sholde?   *know; might be*

'Woltow wedde this womman,' quod the Kyng, 'if I wole assente?

Will you

For she is fayn of thi felaweshipe, for to be thi make.'

desirous; company; spouse

120 Quod Conscience to the Kyng, 'Crist it me forbede!

Er I wedde swich a wif, wo me bitide!

For she is frele of hire feith and fikel of hire speche,   *weak; deceitful*

And maketh men mysdo many score tymes.   *do wrong*

In trust of hire tresor she t[en]eth ful manye;   *hurts*

125 Wyves and widewes wantounnesse she techeth,   *unchastity*

And lereth hem lecherie that loveth hire yiftes.   *teaches; gifts*

Youre fader she felled thorugh false biheste,   *brought down; promise(s)*

---

107   wr. thu] Cr&rACK–D; wroʒtestow WYCLR (C). þo] W&r (*om* H)?AC; whan HmGFZ (C).

109   do] ?β; do thow GHZA; to do R; yf þou do F.

112   it me forbede] ?αZC; forbede ellis β (f.] f. it WHmBM)F.

113   ell*u*s] *so* ZACK–D; soone *All MSS* (C).

114   þan] HG(& *added* G)ZA CK–D; And þanne W&r (C).

115   as] W&rC; of Z; *om* GHA.

117   What] *so* A?CZ(And w.) K–D; To wite what *All MSS* (C). sh*u*lde] L&rZAC; wolde W.

118   quod þe kyng] W&r; *om* GZACK–D.

119   fayn . . . fel.] βR (fayn *om* R) ZAC; of faire shap F.

122   and] HmHαC; *om* ?βZA.

124   In . . . tresor] & þo þat tristne on trewþe F (C). In] GZACK–D; *om* βR. she] FZACK–D; *om* βR. teneth] *so* CAZK–D; treieþ L&r (bitrayeþ WCrGC²B); dysseyuyt H. ful manye] βRZAC; hem ofte F.

125   wantounnesse] Y&rZACK–D; wantounes WCrGLMH; and wantowne wenches F.

127   false] β (*l. om* H)ZA (*cf.* C); faire ?α (hire f. F).

And hath apoisoned popes and apeireth Holy Chirche.   *damages*
Is noght a bettre baude, by Hym that me made,   *?harlot, bawd*
130 Bitwene hevene and helle, and erthe though men soghte!
                                          even if; were to search
For she is tikel of hire tail, talewis of tonge,   *loose; sex; garrulous*
As commune as the cartwey to [knaves and to alle]—   *servants*
To monkes, to mynstrales, to meseles in hegges.   *lepers; hedges*
    Sisours and somonours, swiche men hire preiseth,   *praise*
135 'Sherreves of shires were shent if she nere—   *would be ruined*
For she dooth men lese hire lond and hire lif bothe.   *makes; lose*
She leteth passe prisoners and paieth for hem ofte,   *go free; pays*
And gyveth the gailers gold and grotes togidres   *gaolers; groats*
To unfettre the Fals — fle where hym liketh;   *to flee; he wishes*
140 And taketh Trewthe bi the top and tieth hym faste,   *hair; firmly*
And hangeth hym for hatrede that harm[e]de nevere.   *did harm*
    'To be cursed in consistorie she counteth noght a russhe,
                                    condemned; 'cares nothing'
For she copeth the commissarie and coteth hise clerkes.
                                    provides copes and coats for
She is assoiled as soone as hireself liketh;   *absolved; pleases*
145 She may neigh as muche do in a monthe ones   *nearly; at one time*
As youre secret seel in sixe score dayes!
She is pryvee with the Pope — provisours it knoweth,   *provisors (C)*
For Sire Symonie and hirselve seleth hire bulles.   *seal; mandates*

---

128 And[1]] βR; & she F; Sche HC.
a-] L&r (y- F; en- W)AC; *om*
HmCrGH.
and[2]] W&r (+M); *om* CBLZA;
heo C.
appayreth] ?αZAC; þeired βF.
130 and[2]] ?α (al F)HZ?A?CK–D; in
β.
131 of[2]] αHZ?ACK–D; of hire β.
132 þe] GHZACK–D; a W&r (*om*
HmF).
knaues . . . alle] *so* ZACK–D; ech a
knaue þat walkeþ *All MSS* (ech a]
euery H; þat w.] of towhne F) (C).
133 to[2]] ?βZAC; and to
?α(&F)CrY.
135 nere] L&rZ?AC; ne were WHm
GBH; w. not Cr.

140 taketh trewthe] ?α (trewþe ys
take F)HZAC; t. þe trewe β.
hym] L&rZAC; hem WCr[2][3]G
YM; fy3n F.
141 hym] L&r (*om* F); WCrGYM.
harmed] *so* ZACK–D; harm dide
All MSS (C).
142 russhe] L&rZAC; bene
wGH.
145 She] F (?=α)ZACK–D; And
βR.
ones] Hm&rZACK–D; one
WCrCLM.
147 She] *so* ACK–D; For she *All
MSSZ.*
148 hire] W&rZAC; the
HmCrGHF.

She blesseth thise bisshopes, theigh thei be lewed;   *though; ignorant*
150 Provendreth persones and preestes she maynteneth

provides (prebends) for

To h[old]e lemmans and lotebies alle hire lif daies

mistresses; concubines

And bryngeth forth barnes ayein forbode lawes.

children; laws that forbid

'Ther she is wel with the kyng, wo is the reaume—

in favour with; realm

For she is favourable to Fals and fouleth Truthe ofte.   *injures Fidelity*
155 By Jesus! with hire jeweles the justices she shendeth,   *corrupts*
And lith ayein the lawe and letteth hym the gate,   *lies; blocks his way*
That feith may noght have his forth, hire floryns go so thikke.

course

She ledeth the lawe as hire list and lovedaies maketh,

likes; love-days (C)

And doth men lese thorugh hire love that lawe myghte wynne—

makes; that which legal proceedings

160 The maze for a mene man, though he mote evere!   *confusion; litigate*
Lawe is so lordlich, and looth to maken ende: *reluctant*
Withouten presents or pens he pleseth ful fewe.   *satisfies very*
'Barons and burgeis she bryngeth in sorwe,   *burgesses; into trouble*
And al the comune in care that coveiten lyve in truthe,   *desire to*
165 For clergie and coveitise she coupleth togidres.
This is the lif of that lady – now Lord yyve hire sorwe,   *life; give*
And alle that maynteneth hire men, meschaunce hem bitide!

misfortune

149–50 *So* βZACK(F); *run together* R(?=α).
149 þeiȝ . . . lewed] β; *om* R; & beggerys she hateþ F.
150 Prouendreþ persones] β (-eþ) -es C); *om* α.
she] α (a R)ZACK–D; *om* β.
151 holde] *so* ACK–D; haue *All MSSZ* (C).
lemmans] βF; lotebies R.
lot.] β; lemmanes R; *om* F.
152 bryngeþ] wBHZ?AC; bryngen L&r?Ax; so ben browht F.

154 to] wGHFZA?C; to þe L&r.
fouleth] L&r (folweþ CB; sowleth Y)A (*cf.* Z); defouleþ WF (*cf.* C).
155 þe] αC; youre βZ?A.
Iustices] W&rZ?AC; *sg* H.
160 moote] GFCK–D; mote hire W&r (h.] *erased* Bm; with hyr H) (C).
162 he] ?α (it F)?Z(a)?A?CK–D; she β.
ful] R (?=α)CrZ?AC; wel β; but HF.
163 burgeys] L&rZA (*cf.* C); Burgeises WCrGOC²F.

For povere men may have no power to pleyne hem though thei
    smerte,   *complain; hurt*
Swich a maister is Mede among men of goode.'   *master; property*

170   Thanne mournede Mede and mened hire to the Kynge *complained*
To have space to speke, spede if she myghte.   *opportunity; succeed*
The Kyng graunted hire grace with a good wille: *leave*
'Excuse thee if thow kanst; I kan namoore seggen,   *say*
For Conscience accuseth thee, to congeien thee for evere.' *dismiss*

175   'Nay, lord,' quod that lady, 'leveth hym the werse   *believe*
Whan ye witen witterly wher the wrong liggeth.   *certainly; lies*
Ther that meschief is gret, Mede may helpe.   *mishap, ill luck*
And that thow knowest, Conscience — I kam noght to chide, *quarrel*
Ne to deprave thi persone with a proud herte.   *revile; disdain*

180   Wel thow woost, wernard, but if thow wolt gabbe,   *deceiver; lie*
Thow hast hanged on myn half ellevene tymes, *taken my side;i.e. many*
And also griped my gold, and gyve it where thee liked.   *clutched*
Whi thow wrathest thee now, wonder me thynketh!

                                      are angry; strange
Yet I may, as I myghte, menske thee with yiftes   *could; honour*
185   And mayntene thi manhode moore than thow knowest.   *support*
    'Ac thow hast famed me foule bifore the Kyng here;

                                      foully slandered
For killed I nevere no kyng, ne counseiled therafter,   *accordingly*
Ne dide as thow demest — I do it on the Kynge.   *claim; appeal to*
In Normandie was he noght noyed for my sake—   *vexed, troubled*
190   Ac thow thiself, soothly, shamedest hym ofte: *brought disgrace on*
Crope into a cabane for cold of thi nayles, *Crept; shelter; to prevent*
Wendest that wynter wolde han ylasted evere,   *Thought; lasted*
And dreddest to be ded for a dym cloude,   *dreaded; dark*
And hyedest homward for hunger of thi wombe.   *hurried; belly*
195   Withouten pite, pilour, povere men thow robbedest   *pity; pillager*
And bere hire bras at thi bak to Caleis to selle,   *bore; Calais*
Ther I lafte with my lord his lif for to save. *Whereas; remained; protect*
I made his men murye and mournynge lette;   *cheerful; prevented*
I batred hem on the bak and boldede hire hertes, *slapped; emboldened*

---

168 hem] W&r(*l.* om H)Z; *om*
    BoCotMFAx.
175 leueþ] β?AC; leue αCrZ?Ax.
178 þat] αC; *om* βZA.
179 to] HmHZACK–D; *om* W&r.
182 &²] GBF?AC; *om* W&r.

183 Whi] *so* ACK–D; And whi βR;
    But why FZ (Ac wy).
187 kyng] β (k. ne pope H)ZAC;
    kniȝt α.
198 men] W&r (*om* Cot)Z?A;
    meene H.

200 And dide hem hoppe for hope to have me at wille.   *made; dance*
    Hadde I ben marchal of his men, by Marie of hevene!   *marshal (C)*
    I dorste have leyd my lif and no lasse wedde,   *pledged; surety*
    He sholde have be lord of that lond in lengthe and in brede,   *breadth*
    And also kyng of that kith his kyn for to helpe—   *country; kindred*
205 The leeste brol of his blood a barones piere!   *brat; equal*
    Cowardly thow, Conscience, conseiledest hym thennes—

    (to go from) thence
    To leven his lordshipe for a litel silver,   *abandon; domain*
    That is the richeste reaume that reyn overhoveth.   *rain; hovers over*
    'It bicometh to a kyng that kepeth a reaume   *rules; kingdom*
210 To yeve [men mede] that mekely hym serveth—   *obediently serve*
    To aliens and to alle men, to honouren hem with yiftes;   *foreigners*
    Mede maketh hym biloved and for a man holden.   *held a 'real' man*
    Emperours and erles and alle manere lordes   *earls*
    Thorough yiftes han yomen to yerne and to ryde.

    attendants; run (on errands)
215 The Pope and alle prelates presents underfongen   *receive*
    And medeth men hemselven to mayntene hir lawes,

    reward; administer
    Servaunts for hire servyce, we seeth wel the sothe,   *see; truth*
    Taken mede of hir maistres, as thei mowe acorde.   *payment; can agree*
    Beggeres for hir biddynge bidden men mede.

    in return for their prayers ask
220 Mynstrales for hir myrthe mede thei aske.   *entertainment*
    The Kyng hath mede of his men to make pees in londe.   *from, ?for*
    Men that [kenne clerkes] craven of hem mede.

    teach students; request a fee
    Preestes that prechen the peple to goode   *to good conduct*
    Asken mede and massepens and hire mete [alse].   *mass-pence; food*

---

205   blood] ?β (kynne CB; *l. om* H); lond α.
210   men mede] *so* CA (men) hise m. AK–D); mede to men *All MSS.*
211   and to] βRC?A; & F; to H.
214   þorghʒ] α (:::urʒ R)ACK–D; For β (*l. om* H).
      ʒoumen] αC; yonge men βA. ʒernen] α?C; renne βAx.
215   and alle] L&r (alle) a. þe WCrGCot; a. his Hm)C; also of F.

217   Seruauntʒ] L&rAC; Sergeauntʒ WHmCr¹GC²MH.
219   bidd-] β (*l. om* H); begg- α.
222   kenne clerkis] *so* ACK–D; teche children *All MSS* (C).
223–4 *So div.* A (cf. C)K–D; *after* Mede *All MSS.*
224   alse] *so* ?AK–D (*cf.* bothe C); at þe meel tymes *All MSS* (þe] *om* R; here F) (C).

225 Alle kynne crafty men craven mede for hir prentis.

craftsmen; for (training)

Marchaundise and mede mote nede go togideres: *Trade; must needs*
No wight, as I wene, withouten Mede may libbe!'   *suppose; can live*
   Quod the Kyng to Conscience, 'By Crist, as me thynketh,

it seems to me

Mede is worthi the maistrie to have!'   *sway, victory*
230   'Nay,' quod Conscience to the Kyng and kneled to the erthe,
'Ther are two manere of medes, my lord, by youre leve.   *kinds*
That oon God of his grace graunteth in his blisse   *The one; goodness*
To tho that wel werchen while thei ben here.   *those; work; sc. on earth*
The Prophete precheth therof and putte it in the Sauter: *Psalter*
Domine, quis habitabit in tabernaculo tuo? . . .
235 Lord, who shal wonye in thi wones with thyne holy seintes

dwelling(s)

Or resten on thyne holy hilles? – This asketh David.   *David asks this*
And David assoileth it hymself, as the Sauter telleth: *resolves*
Qui ingreditur sine macula et operatur iusticiam.
Tho that entren of o colour and of one wille,   *in one; single, undivided*
And han ywroght werkes with right and with reson,   *done works*
240 And he that ne useth noght the lyf of usurie   *engages in; usury*
And enformeth povere men and pursueth truthe: *instructs; honesty*
*Qui pecuniam suam non dedit ad usuram, et
   munera super innocentem . . .*
And alle that helpen the innocent and holden with the rightfulle,

just

Withouten mede doth hem good and the truthe helpeth—

234a Lord, who shall dwell in thy tabernacle? (Ps 14: 1).
237a He that walketh without blemish, and worketh justice (Ps 14: 2).
241a He that hath not put out his money to usury, nor [taken] bribes against
   the innocent (Ps 25: 10).

225 crafty] L&r; craftes WCr.
   prentis] L&rA?C; Prentices
   WCrOC²R.
226 Marchandyse] HC (*cf.* A)K–D;
   Marchaunt3 W&r (C).
229 is] αACK–D; is wel β.
231 by] αK–D; wiþ β.
234a &c] Hm&r; *om* WYCBLMH;
   *atque quis requiescet in monte
   sancto eius innocens manibus et*

mundo corde F.
235 with] αHK–D; and with β (and
   erased Hm).
236 on] LMα; *in* wgH.
   askeþ] β; asked αCot.
240 ne] L&r; *om* wGHF.
243 truþe] β; trewe α.

Swiche manere men, my lord, shul have this firste mede
245 Of God at a gret nede, whan thei gon hennes.   *From; (sc. at death)*
    'Ther is another mede mesurelees, that maistres desireth:

immoderate; lords, rulers

To mayntene mysdoers mede thei take,   *support; evil-doers*
And therof seith the Sauter in a salmes ende—   *psalm's conclusion*
In quorum manibus iniquitates sunt; dextra eorum repleta est
muneribus;
250 And he that gripeth hir gold, so me God helpe,
    Shal abien it ful bittre, or the Book lieth!   *pay for it grievously; Bible*
    Preestes and persons that plesynge desireth,   *parsons; pleasure*
    That taken mede and moneie for masses that thei syngeth,   *money*
    Taken hire mede here as Mathew us techeth: *in this world*
    Amen, Amen, receperunt mercedem suam.
255 That laborers and lowe [lewede] folk taken of hire maistres,
    It is no manere mede but a mesurable hire.   *moderate, appropriate wage*
    In marchaundise is no mede, I may it wel avowe: *commerce; declare*
    It is a permutacion apertly – a penyworth for another.

exchange; manifestly

    'Ac reddestow nevere *Regum*, thow recrayed Mede,   *Kings; recreant*
260 Whi the vengeaunce fel [fel] on Saul and on his children?   *terrible*
    God sente to Saul by Samuel the prophete   *sent (word)*
    That Agag of Amalec and al his peple after   *as well*
    Sholden deye for a dede that doon hadde hire eldres.   *ancestors*
    "Forthi," seide Samuel to Saul, "God hymself hoteth   *Therefore*
265 To be buxom at his biddynge, his wil to fulfille.   *obedient; will, wishes*
    Weend to Amalec with thyn oost, and what thow fynst there – sle it:

Go: host; find; slay, destroy

---

249 In whose hands are iniquities: their right hand is filled with gifts (Ps 25:
10).

254a Amen, I say to you, they have received their reward (Mt 6: 5).

244 þis] W&r; the HmCr²³
    YOC²HF.
251 ful]BHRA; *om* W&r.
253 syngeþ] W&rA; songen R.
254a -erunt] HmOC²H(*over
    erasure*)FAK–D; -iebant W&r.
255 lowe lewede] *cj* K–D ; lowe
    WCr¹?gL; lewed HmC²Hα; mene
    M; pore Cr²³ (C).

256 is] βF; nis R.
258 a¹] βAC; *om* α.
260 fel²] *om All MSS* (C).
262 al] βFAC; *om* R.
264 hoteþ] W&rAC; þe hotethe
    GF.
265 To] *so* AC; Thee W&r (þe to
    HmOC²); þou HF.
266 fynst] α; fyndest β.

Burnes and beestes – bren hem to dethe!	*Men; burn*
Widwes and wyves, wommen and children,	*Widows*
Moebles and unmoebles, and al that thow myght fynde—	
	Movables; immovables
270 Bren it, bere it noght awey, be it never so riche;	*carry; valuable*
For mede ne for monee, loke thow destruye it!	*In spite of; be sure to*
Spille it and spare it noght – thow shalt spede the bettre."	
	Destroy; prosper
And for he coveited hir catel and the kyng spared,	*because; goods*
Forbar hym and his beestes bothe as the Bible witnesseth	
	Allowed to live
275 Otherwise than he was warned of the prophete,	*by*
God seide to Samuel that Saul sholde deye,	*must die*
And al his seed for that synne shenfulliche ende.	*ignominiously*
Swich a meschief Mede made Saul the kyng to have	*misfortune*
That God hated hym for evere and alle his heires after.	*heirs*
280 'The *culorum* of this cas kepe I noght to shewe;	*conclusion; care*
On aventure it noyed me, noon ende wol I make,	*Lest it should harm*
For so is this world went with hem that han power	*turned*
That whoso seith hem sothest is sonnest yblamed!	*most truly; soonest*
'I, Conscience, knowe this, for Kynde Wit me taughte—	
285 That Reson shal regne and reaumes governe,	*reign; realms*
And right as Agag hadde, happe shul somme:	*it shall happen to*
Samuel shal sleen hym and Saul shal be blamed,	
And David shal be diademed and daunten hem alle,	*subdue*
And oon Cristene kyng kepen [us] echone.	*rule*
290 Shal na moore Mede be maister as she is nouthe,	*at present*
Ac love and lowenesse and leautee togideres—	*humility; right*

271 Take care (not to fail to) destroy it, for (any) bribe or monetary payment (you may be offered).
280 The full implications of this event I have no wish to spell out (C).

267 deþe] W&r (*over erasure* M)?A; dede yLR.
269 þat] L&r; *om* WBoCotF.
277 ende] βAC; endede αHm.
278 Saul þe kyng] βR; kyng s. F.
280 shewe] L&rAC; telle wGH; expowne F.
281 On] β (*l. om* H)AC; For F; *om* R.
me] *so* ACK–D; men W&r (*l. om* H).
283 soþest] WG; sonest soth H; sothes L&r (*sg* Cr) (C).
284 me tauʒte] *so* ?ACK–D; me t. it OC²; it me tauʒte WCr¹GH; me it t. L&r (it *erased* M).
289 vs ichone] *so* ?ACK–D; hem echone MCrBm; hem alle W&r (*l. om* H); al þe frape F.

Thise shul ben maistres on moolde [trewe men] to save.   *protect*

And whoso trespaseth ayein truthe or taketh ayein his wille,   *against*

Leaute shal don hym lawe, and no lif ellis.

                       execute the law upon; nobody

295   Shal no sergeant for [that] service were a silk howve,   *lawyer; coif*

Ne no pelure in his cloke for pledynge at the barre.   *fur*

    'Mede of mysdoeres maketh manye lordes,   *out of criminals*

And over lordes lawes [lord]eth the reaumes.   *holds sway over*

Ac kynde love shal come yit and Conscience togideres   *with (him)*

300   And make of lawe a laborer; swich love shal arise

And swich pees among the peple and a parfit truthe

                       perfect uprightness

That Jewes shul wene in hire wit, and wexen wonder glade,

                       suppose; grow

That Moyses or Messie be come into this erthe,   *Moses; the Messiah*

And have wonder in hire hertes that men beth so trewe.   *righteous*

305   'Alle that beren baselard, brood swerd or launce,   *dagger; broad*

Ax outher hachet or any wepene ellis,   *or; hatchet*

Shal be demed to the deeth but if he do it smythye

                       condemned; have it hammered

Into sikel or to sithe, to shaar or to kultour—   *(plough)share; coulter*

Conflabunt gladios suos in vomeres . . .

Ech man to pleye with a plow, pykoise or spade,   *be active; pick-axe*

310   Spynne, or sprede donge, or spille hymself with sleuthe;

                       manure; destroy

Preestes and persons with *Placebo* to hunte,   *psalm(s)*

And dyngen upon David eche day til eve.   *pound away upon*

Huntynge or haukynge if any of hem use,   *hawking; practise*

---

298 And exercises control of kingdoms over (and above) the king's laws.

308*a* . . . and they shall turn their swords into ploughshares (Is 2: 4).

311–12 . . . to 'hunt' (only) with (the psalm) *I will please (the Lord)* [Ps 114: 9] And keep pounding away all day at the psalms in his Psalter . . .

314 His boast in his/that he will obtain a benefice will be stripped away from him as a result (of it).

292   trewe men] *so* C*K–D*; tru├e *All MSS* (C).

293   ayein¹] W&rC; to GA.

295   ├at] *so* AC*K–D*; his WCrGMH; here L&r; no F.

298   lordeth) rule├ *All MSS* (*over erasure* M) (C).

301   pees] αC*K–D*; a pees β (*l. om* H).

310   spille] β (*l. om* B) (*cf.* C); lese α.

312   eche] WHmGC²B; eche a L&r; euery CrF.

His boost of his benefice worth bynomen hym after.   *taken away*
315 'Shal neither kyng ne knyght, constable ne meire   *mayor*
Over[carke] the commune ne to the court sompne,
                                          over-burden; summon
Ne putte hem in panel to doon hem plighte hir truthe;
                                          empanel them as jurors; swear
But after the dede that is doon oon doom shal rewarde
                                          judgement; apportion
Mercy or no mercy as Truthe [moot] acorde.   *must agree*
320 'Kynges court and commune court, consistorie and chapitle—
                                          chapter(-court)
Al shal be but oon court, and oon baron be justice: *lord; judge*
That worth Trewe-tonge, a tidy man that tened me nevere.
                                          will be; good; grieved
Batailles shul none be, ne no man bere wepene,   *carry*
And what smyth that any smytheth be smyte therwith to dethe!
                                          forges; struck
Non levabit gens contra gentem gladium ...
325 'And er this fortune falle, fynde men shul the worste,   *befall*
By sixe sonnes and a ship and half a shef of arwes;   *quiverful; arrows*
And the myddel of a moone shal make the Jewes torne,   *be converted*
And Sarsynes for that sighte shul synge *Gloria in excelsis*— Moslems
For Makometh and Mede myshappe shul that tyme;   *come to grief*
330 For *Melius est bonum nomen quam divicie multe*.'
Also wroth as the wynd weex Mede in a while.
                                          angry; became; moment
'I kan no Latyn?' quod she. 'Clerkes wite the sothe!   *know*
Se what Salomon seith in Sapience bokes:
That thei that yyven yiftes the victorie wynneth,   *give gifts*
335 And muche worshipe have[th] therwith, as Holy Writ telleth—
                                          honour; obtain

324*a* Nation shall not lift up sword against nation (Is 2: 4).
330 A good name is better than great riches (Prov 22: 1).

316 Ouerkarke] *so* CK–D;   328 þat siȝte] β; þe syghte þerof α.
    Ouerlede *All MSS* (C).   excelsis] Hm&r; *e. &c* WBoL; *e.*
319 moot] wole *All MSS* (C).   *deo &c* Cr (*&c*) *om* Cr²³)Y.
322 That] Bm (*alt. from* Thanne)   332 I . . . she] W&r (no] *om* Cr³R);
    ?CK–D; Thanne W&r (*l. om* H)   Quod she y can lytyl latyn F.
    (C).   335 moche] L&r; moost wGH.
324 smyþeþ] β (*cf.* C); smithie α.   haueþ] haue HmCr¹F; hath Cr²³;
327 torne] αGCK–D; to torne β.   hadde W&r.

Honorem adquiret qui dat munera.'
   'I leve wel, lady,' quod Conscience, 'that thi Latyn be trewe.

believe

Ac thow art lik a lady that radde a lesson ones,   *read*
Was *omnia probate*, and that plesed hire herte—
340 For that lyne was no lenger at the leves ende.   *line; page's*
Hadde she loked that other half and the leef torned, *examined; leaf*
She sholde have founden fel[l]e wordes folwynge therafter: *severe*
Quod bonum est tenete – Truthe that text made.
And so, [madame, ferde ye] – ye kouthe na moore fynde *you fared*
345 Tho ye [on Sapience loked], sittynge in youre studie. *When*
This text that ye han told were [tidy] for lordes, *would be; useful*
Ac yow failed a konnynge clerk that kouthe the leef han torned.

lacked; skilful; could . . . have

And if ye seche Sapience eft, fynde shul ye that folweth, *examine; again*
A ful teneful text to hem that taketh mede: *painful*
350 And that is *Animam autem aufert accipientium.*
And that is the tail of the text of that that ye shewed—

end; which; quoted

That theigh we wynne worshipe and with mede have victorie,

though; obtain honour

The soule that the soude taketh by so muche is bounde.' *payment*

---

336 He that maketh presents shall purchase victory and honour . . . (Prov 22: 9).
339 But prove [*sc.* put to the test] all things (I Thess 5: 21).
343 . . . hold fast that which is good (I Thess 5: 21).
350 . . . but he carrieth away the souls of the receivers (Prov 22: 9).

336 *munera*] αCrH; *m. &c* β.
338 radde . . . ones] βR; a lessoun redde FC.
342 fel*l*] GCr (fel)?CK–D; fele W&r (C).
344 madame; ferde ye] *trs All MSS* (C).
345 on Sapience; loked] *trs All MSS* (loked] sey3e F)(C).
346 were . . . lordes] were good for

lordes W&r; 3ee takyn nout þe ende F (C).
350 *accipientium*] ?α(*l.* om F)C; *acc. &c.* β (*a bono munera* H).
351 þat³] W&r(*om* HmGBm; at H); tale þat F.
  3e] L&r; she WHmCr¹GM(*over erasure*)H.
  shewed] β (schewyt H); schede R; to me pitte F.
352 Mede] β; me α.

Passus IV

'Cesseth!' seide the Kyng, 'I suffre yow no lenger.   *Stop; will allow*
Ye shul saughtne, forsothe, and serve me bothe.   *be reconciled*
Kis hire,' quod the Kyng, 'Conscience, I hote!'   *command*
    'Nay, by Crist!' quod Conscience, 'congeye me rather!

                                                            dismiss; sooner
5 But Reson rede me therto, rather wol I deye.'   *Unless; advise*
    'And I comaunde thee,' quod the Kyng to Conscience thanne,
    'Rape thee to ryde, and Reson that thow fecche.   *Make haste; fetch*
Comaunde hym that he come my counseil to here,   *inner thoughts*
For he shal rule my reaume and rede me the beste   *realm; counsel*
10 Of Mede and of mo othere, what man shal hire wedde,

                                                            other matters too
And acounte with thee, Conscience, so me Crist helpe,   *settle*
How thow lernest the peple, lered and lewed!'   *teach*
    'I am fayn of that foreward,' seide the freke thanne,

                                                    content; agreement; man
And ryt right to Reson and rouneth in his ere,   *rides straight; whispers*
15 And seide hym as the Kyng seide, and sithen took his leve.   *then*
    'I shal arraye me to ryde,' quod Reson, 'reste thee a while,'

                                                            prepare
And called Caton his knave, curteis of speche,   *servant; courteous*
And also Tomme Trewe-tonge – tel-me-no-tales   *true-tongue; lies*
Ne-lesynge-to-laughen-of-for-I-loved-hem-nevere.   *lies; at*
20 'And set my sadel upon Suffre-til-I-se-my-tyme,   *saddle*
And lat warroke hym wel with witty-wordes gerthes.   *fasten; girths*
Hange on hym the hevy brydel to holde his heed lowe,   *bridle; head*

Collation WHmCrGYOC²CBLMHRF.

RUBRIC *Passus quartus de visione vt supra* W&r (*de v.*] *de v. petri plowman* R; *om* OF); *om* GC².

1 seyde] HmCr²³BmHα ZACK–D; seiþ W&r.

4 rather] Cr²³gHF(r. sone F)?A?C; for euere W&r (er for e. W) (C).

7 þat þou] F (?=α)ZACK–D; þow β(to Cr¹H)R.

10 *In* YOC²Cr²³ (mo] *om* Cr²³) ZACK–D; *l. om* W&r (C).

12 lered; lewed] R (?=α)Z?AC; þe l.; þe l. βF(þe¹] boþe F).

15 hym] FZACK–D; *om* β (*l. om* Hm)R.

seide²] FC; sente Z?A; bad βR (C).

20 and] βRC; he bad go F; *om* MZA.

For he wol make "wehee" twies er he be there.'   *neigh twice; before*
   Thanne Conscience upon his capul caireth forth faste,   *horse; proceeds*
25 And Reson with hym ryt, rownynge togideres   *rides; whispering*
Whiche maistries Mede maketh on this erthe.   *displays of (her) power*
   Oon Waryn Wisdom and Witty his fere   *One; companion*
Folwed hem faste, for thei hadde to doone   *Followed; business*
In the Cheker and in the Chauncerye, to ben descharged of thynges,
   Exchequer
30 And riden faste for Reson sholde rede hem the beste   *in order that*
For to save hem for silver from shame and from harmes.

   disgrace; trouble
A[c] Conscience knew hem wel, thei loved coveitise,   *(that) they*
And bad Reson ryde faste and recche of hir neither:

   care about; of them
'Ther are wiles in hire wordes, and with Mede thei dwelleth—
35 Ther as wrathe and wranglynge is, ther wynne thei silver;   *Where*
Ac there is love and leautee, thei wol noght come there:
Contricio et infelicitas in viis eorum . . .
Thei ne gyveth noght of God one goose wynge: *care not for*
Non est timor Dei ante oculos eorum . . .
For thei wolde do moore for a dozeyne c[apo]nes   *dozen capons*

---

29 In the (courts of) Exchequer and Chancery, (where they intended) to be
  released from various legal liabilities.
36a; 37a Destruction and unhappiness [are] in their ways; [and the way of
  peace they have not known:] there is no fear of God before their eyes (Ps 13:
  3).

24 kaireþ] L&rZA; carieþ WGC²B;
    rydyth H.
26 Mede . . . erþe] β; on eerth mede
    þe mayde maketh α.
28 hem] L&rZAC; hym wGCot.
    for þei] W&r (þ.] he M)ZA; *om*
    LR.
29 þe cheker] L&r (þe] *om* H)ZA
    (þe] *om* A); thescheker w.
    and] βFZA; *om* R.
    in²] W&r (*om* GMHF)ZA; at
    LCr²³R.
    þe²] W&r; *om* HmMHFZA.
31 hem for siluer] βR(for]fro R);
    here syluer & hem F; hem selue
    YZA.

32 Ac] *so* ZACK–D; And *All MSS.*
    þei . . . coueitise] βR; þat k. þey l. F.
33 Reson] β (*l. om* CB)F; *om* R.
36 Ac] ?β (but G)C; And CrC²CHF;
    om R.
    þere] L&rC; where wHF.
    wol] βR; leete F.
37a dei] W&rC; *Domini* Cry.
    eorum] L&r (*l. om* H)C; *eorum &c*
    wGYOC²Bm.
38 capones] *cj* K–D (*cf.* C); chiknes
    All MSS (C). *After this another*
    line: Or as manye capons or for a
    seem of Otes *All MSS; rej. as*
    spurious K–D (C).

Than for love of Oure Lord or alle hise leeve seintes!   *dear*
40 Forthi, Reson, lat hem ride, tho riche by hemselve—   *those rich men*
For Conscience knoweth hem noght, ne Crist, as I trowe.'   *reckon*
   And thanne Reson rood faste the righte heighe gate,
                                                      direct high way
As Conscience hym kenned, til thei come to the Kynge.   *instructed*
Curteisly the Kyng thanne com ayeins Reson,   *to meet*
45 And bitwene hymself and his sone sette hym on benche,
And wordeden wel wisely a gret while togideres.   *they talked*
   And thanne com Pees into parlement and putte up a bille—
                                                     Peace; petition

How Wrong ayeins his wille hadde his wif taken,   *against*
And how he ravysshede Rose, Reignaldes love,   *carried off; sweetheart*
50 And Margrete of hir maydenhede maugree hire chekes.   *i.e. by force*
'Bothe my gees and my grys hise gadelynges feccheth;   *pigs; fellows*
I dar noght for fere of hym fighte ne chide.   *fear; complain*
He borwed of me bayard and broughte hym hom nevere,
                                                   (my) bay horse; home
Ne no ferthyng therfore, for nought I koude plede.   *farthing*
55 He maynteneth hise men to murthere myne hewen,   *murder; servants*
Forstalleth my feires and fighteth in my chepyng,
                                          Forestalls (C); fairs; market
And breketh up my bernes dores and bereth awey my whete,   *barn*
And taketh me but a taille for ten quarters otes.   *gives; tally-stick (C)*
And yet he beteth me therto and lyth by my mayde;
                                        further; lies; maid-servant

---

54-6 Nor any farthing (in payment) for it, in spite of any pleading of mine. He
    aids and abets his retainers to murder my workmen, makes forced purchases
    in advance (of the goods I intend to sell) at fairs and causes brawls in my
    market.

39 for] L&r; for þe WHmGHF.
40 Reson] β; *om* α.
41 hem] W&r; þei HF.
47 And] W&r?C; *om* HZA.
    vp] HZACK–D; forþ W&r (C).
49 loue] L&r; looue WBo; leve
    dowhter F.
52 hym] L&r (*l. om* F); hem
    WHmG.
53 and] HmCrαZA?CK–D; he
    WglLM.
    hom neuere] W&r (*trs* Cr)C; me

neuere ?A; n. aȝen HmHF(*trs* F)
    some A–MSSZ.
54 nauȝte] LMαAC; ouȝt W&r (*l.*
    om CBH)Z.
55 hewen] βZAC; hennes α.
56 Forstalleþ] βZA; He for. R; & to
    for. F; And for. C.
57 bernes] WHmLRZC; berne
    Cr&r (*l. om* CB)A.
58 otys] HmCrGMFZACK–D; of
    Otes W&r (*l. om* H).

60 I am noght hardy for hym unnethe to loke!'   *bold; because of; scarcely*
        The Kyng knew he seide sooth, for Conscience hym tolde   *truth*
    That Wrong was a wikked luft and muche sorwe wroghte.

                                        rascal; trouble
    Wrong was afered thanne, and Wisdom he soughte   *afraid*
    To maken pees with hise pens, and profred hym manye,   *pence*
65 And seide, 'Hadde I love of my lord the Kyng, litel wolde I recche
    Theigh Pees and his power pleyned hem evere!'   *Though; supporters*
        Tho wan Wisdom and Sire Waryn the Witty,   *strove*
    For that Wrong hadde ywroght so wikked a dede,   *Because*
    And warnede Wrong tho with swich a wis tale—

                                such prudent words as these
70 'Whoso wercheth by wille, wrathe maketh ofte.   *wilfully; arouses*
    I seye it by thyself – thow shalt it wel fynde;   *concerning*
    But if Mede it make, thi meschief is uppe;   *make (good); at its peak*
    For bothe thi lif and thi lond lyth in his grace.'   *at his disposal*
        Thanne wowede Wrong Wisdom ful yerne   *solicited; eagerly*
75 To maken his pees with his pens, handy-dandy payed.

                                    by secret bribery (C)
    Wisdom and Wit thanne wenten togidres,
    And token Mede myd hem mercy to wynne.   *took; with; obtain*
        Pees putte forth his heed and his panne blody: *brain-pan, skull*
    'Withouten gilt, God it woot, gat I this scathe.'   *received; injury*
80   Conscience and the commune knowen wel the sothe,   *know; truth*
    Ac Wisdom and Wit were aboute faste   *busily set about*
    To overcomen the Kyng with catel, if thei myghte.   *through wealth*
        The Kyng swor by Crist and by his crowne bothe   *too*
    That Wrong for hise werkes sholde wo tholie,   *endure suffering*
85 And comaundede a constable to casten hym in irens,

---

60 Because of him, I am scarcely bold enough to show my face!

62   muche sorwe; wrou3te] ?αH(*cf.*
    C); *trs* βF.
65   my lord] ?βZAC; *om* CrHα.
66   hem] HmCr²³GHRZAK–D;
    hym W&r.
67   wan] LRCB (whan CB)ZA;
    wente W&r (*om* H; *l. om* F).
71   þi-] LYOC²αZA my- W&r (*over
    erasure* M).

75   handy dandy; payed] βRZAC;
    trs F (C).
76   Wisdom . . . þanne] βRC; þ. wit
    & w. FZA.
79   it] W&r; *om* CrHZ?AC.
80   knowen] W&rC; knewen HmB
    HZA.
    wel] F (?=α)ZA(*cf.* C)K–D; *om*
    βR.

'And [suffre] hym noght thise seven yer seen his feet ones.'   *let*
  'God woot,' quod Wisdom, 'that were noght the beste!
And he amendes mowe make, lat Maynprise hym have   *If; can; Bail*
And be borgh for his bale, and buggen hym boote,

                                                        evil acts; buy; remedy

90 And so amenden that is mysdo, and everemoore the bettre.'   *ill-done*
     Wit acorded therwith, and [with]seide the same,   *agreed; objected*
  'Bettre is that boote bale adoun brynge   *reparation; evil; defeat*
Than bale be ybet, and boote nevere the bettre!'   *beaten, punished*
     Thanne gan Mede to meken hire, and mercy she bisoughte,

                                                                act humble

95 And profrede Pees a present al of pure golde.
  'Have this, man, of me,' quod she, 'to amenden thi scathe,   *injury*
For I wol wage for Wrong, he wol do so na moore.'   *guarantee*
     Pitously Pees thanne preyde to the Kynge   *Forgivingly*
To have mercy on that man that mysdide hym ofte: *wronged; injured*
100 'For he hath waged me wel, as Wisdom hym taughte,   *paid*
And I forgyve hym that gilt with a good wille.
So that the Kyng assente, I kan seye no bettre,   *Provided*
For Mede hath maad myne amendes — I may na moore axe.'   *ask*
  'Nay', quod the Kyng tho, 'so me Crist helpe!   *then*
105 Wrong wendeth noght so awey er I wite more.

---

88 If he can make monetary compensation, let Bail assume responsibility for
   him and stand surety for the wrongs he has done, and purchase a remedy for
   (Peace).
91 . . . and put forward a counter-argument likewise.
92–3 (It is better) that compensation should extinguish wrong done than that
   wrongs should be punished and still no compensation be forthcoming.

86   suffre hym] lete hym W&r (hym)
     om Cot); *om* F; A schal ZAK–D;
     Ther he sholde C (*C*).
90   And] HC; And so W&r; *om* ZA.
     eueremoore] β (m.) *om* Cr¹) ZAC;
     euere be R; he shal do euere F; so
     hym H.
91   wiþseide] seide *All MSSZA*;
     witnessede C (*C*).
94   Than] CrHZACK–D; And þanne
     W&r.
     meken] αZACK–D; mengen ?β
     (meue*n* CrG); medel H.

she] W&rZ?C; *om* HmGCB
HFA.
99   oft] GMZAK–D; so ofte W&r.
103 made myn amendes]
     αZACK–D; made me am. L&r
     (?=β; *l. om* H); me am. maad w
     (me] *om* Hm) G.
104 þo] W&rZ?A; *om* Hm (*cf.* C).
     crist] β (*cf.* C); god αH (*cf.* ZA).
105 er I] HGZACK–D; erst wole I
     W&r (erst) furst HmF; wole I] *trs*
     CrF) (*C*).

Lope he so lightly, laughen he wolde,   *If he ran away; easily*
And eft the boldere be to bete myne hewen.   *next time; servants*
But Reson have ruthe on hym, he shal reste in my stokkes   *pity*
As longe as [I lyve], but lowenesse hym borwe.' *humility; stand bail for*
110   Som men radde Reson tho to have ruthe on that shrewe,

                                                     advised; villain
And for to counseille the Kyng and Conscience after: *as well*
That Mede moste be maynpernour, Reson thei bisoughte.

                                                     might; surety
  'Reed me noght,' quod Reson, 'no ruthe to have   *Advise; mercy*
Til lordes and ladies loven alle truthe   *all love honest living*
115   And haten alle harlotrie, to heren it or to mouthen it; *obscenity; utter*
Til Pernelles purfill be put in hire hucche,   *trimming; trunk*
And childrene cherissynge be chastised with yerdes,   *spoiling; rods*
And harlottes holynesse be holden for an hyne; *ribalds'; held worthless*
Til clerkene coveitise be to clothe the povere and fede, *clerks' avarice*
120   And religiouse romeris *Recordare* in hir cloistres *wandering religious*
As Seynt Beneyt hem bad, Bernard and Fraunceis;   *Benedict; Francis*
And til prechours prechynge be preved on hemselve; *demonstrated in*
Til the Kynges counseil be the commune profit;   *public good*
Til bisshopes bayardes ben beggeris chaumbres,   *horses; dwellings*
125   Hire haukes and hire houndes help to povere religious;
And til Seint James be sought there I shal assigne—   *indicate*
That no man go to Galis but if he go for evere;   *Galicia (C)*

---

109   . . . unless (his own future) humility should act as a surety for him.
117   And children, instead of being over-indulged, be disciplined with beating.
118   *Lit.* valued as a farm-labourer – i.e. very cheaply.
120   And members of religious orders who go travelling about sing the
      offertory 'Remember, Lord' [*sc.* recall their duties in their cloisters; 'meditate
      upon the Scriptures' (AlfQ)].

106   Lope] *so* ZACK–D; For lope   115   it¹] L&r (*erased* M)Z; *om*
      All MSS.   wGA.
      liȝtly] βRC; l. awey FZA.   117   chastysed] HmHFZACK–D;
107   eft] W&rZ?AC; ofter G.   chastynge W&r.
108   my] W&r(*om* F)Z?AC; þe GH,   118   an hyne] ?β (vnhende YOC²; *l.*
      some A-*MSS.*   *om* H)ZA; nauȝte R; vanyte F.
109   I lyue] *so* AZCK–D; he lyueþ   119   and] W&r; & to yLR.
      All MSS.   125   Religious] β; religiouses ?α
110   Som men] W&r (Fele F)?A?C;   (relygyous howsys F).
      Summe HmHZ.

And alle Rome renneres for robberes of biyonde   *runners; from abroad*
Bere no silver over see that signe of kyng sheweth—   *sea; stamp*
130 Neither grave ne ungrave, gold neither silver—   *stamped, unstamped*
Upon forfeture of that fee, whoso fynt hym at Dovere,
  money; if anyone finds
But if it be marchaunt or his man, or messager with lettres,   *warrants*
Provysour or preest, or penaunt for hise synnes.   *Provisor; penitent*
  'And yet,' quod Reson, 'by the Rode! I shal no ruthe have   *Cross*
135 While Mede hath the maistrie in this moot-halle.
  sway; council-chamber
Ac I may shewe ensamples as I se outher.   *can; others*
I seye it by myself,' quod he, 'and it so were   *for; if*
That I were kyng with coroune to kepen a reaume,   *rule*
Sholde nevere Wrong in this world that I wite myghte   *know (about)*
140 Ben unpunysshed in my power, for peril of my soule,   *if I could help it*
Ne gete my grace thorugh giftes, so me God save!   *mercy, indulgence*
Ne for no mede have mercy, but mekenesse it made;   *brought it about*
For "*Nullum malum* the man mette with *inpunitum*
  innocence; unpunished
And bad *Nullum bonum* be *irremuneratum*."   *wickedness; unrewarded*
145 Late thi confessour, sire Kyng, construe this [on] Englissh,   *in*
And if ye werchen it in werk, I wedde myne eris   *practise; bet*
That Lawe shal ben a laborer and lede afeld donge,   *carry afield*
And Love shal lede thi lond as the leef liketh.'   *rule; you would desire*
  Clerkes that were confessours coupled hem togideres   *joined in pairs*
150 Al to construe this clause, and for the Kynges profit,   *interpret*
Ac noght for confort of the commune, ne for the Kynges soule,
  (the) benefit

---

128 And until no (more) hasty travellers to Rome [carry sterling abroad] for
the benefit of foreign thieves.

128 of] L&r; *om* WHmCr¹GCotF.
131 Vpon] W&r (on G); Vp
HZAC.
  -so] W&rZ?A?C; *om* GF.
  hym] L&rZAC; it w.
132 if] W&r; *om* HmBmHFZAC.
  it] W&rZA?C; he CrgF.
136 othur] *so* ZACK–D;
ouþerwhile β (othere o. R); somme
tyme H.
137 quod he] W&rC (he) Resoun

C); *om* GZA.
141 þoruȝ] αZACK–D; for β (*l. om*
H).
  saue] W&r; helpe G.
142 made] HmCrHαZAK–D; make
WgLM.
145 on Englissh] *so* ACK–D; englys
HZ; vnglosed W&r (vn-] en- C²)
(C).
150 and] W&r; al F; as H; *om*
CrGYOC²M.

For I seigh Mede in the moot-halle on men of lawe wynke,   *saw*
And thei laughynge lope to hire and lefte Reson manye.   *ran*
    Waryn Wisdom wynked upon Mede
155 And seide, 'Madame, I am youre man, what so my mouth jangleth;
                           patters out
I falle in floryns,' quod that freke, 'and faile speche ofte.'   *lose*
    Alle rightfulle recorded that Reson truthe tolde.   *just men opined*
[Kynde] Wit acorded therwith and comendede hise wordes,
And the mooste peple in the halle and manye of the grete,   *most*
160 And leten Mekenesse a maister and Mede a mansed sherewe.
                           held; cursed
Love leet of hire light, and Leaute yet lasse,   *held in low esteem*
And seide it so heighe that all the halle it herde: *loudly*
'Whoso wilneth hire to wif, for welthe of hire goodes – *wants to marry*
But he be knowe for a cokewold, kut of my nose!' *recognized; cuckold*
165   Mede mornede tho, and made hevy chere,   *looked miserable*
For the mooste commune of that court called hire an hore.   *whore*
Ac a sisour and a somonour sued hire faste,   *followed; firmly*
And a sherreves clerk bisherewed al the route: *cursed; crowd*
'For ofte have I,' quod he, 'holpen yow at the barre,   *helped; in court*
170 And yet yeve ye me nevere the worth of a risshe!'   *value; rush*
    The Kyng callede Conscience and afterward Reson,
And recordede that Reson hadde rightfully shewed;
                  stated; justly expounded
And modiliche upon Mede with myght the Kyng loked,   *wrathfully*
And gan wexe wroth with Lawe, for Mede almoost hadde shent it,
                          angry; destroyed
175 And seide, 'Thorugh youre lawe, as I leve, I lese manye chetes;
                       escheats, reversions
Mede overmaistreth Lawe and muche truthe letteth.
                            overcomes; impedes
Ac Reson shal rekene with yow, if I regne any while,   *settle; reign*

---

155 iangleth] L&r (tellythe G);
    Iangle WHmHF.
156 þat] β (om C²; *l.* om H); þe
    αCr²³.
158 Kynde] *cj* K–D (*cf.* C); And
    W&r; I H.
159 þe²] β (om H)F; þis R.
160 mansed] W&r; meche H (*cf.*
    ZA).

161 yet] βC; wel αHm; meche H.
162 seide] L&rZA; seiden W.
164 kut] βFZAC; bitte R.
168 a] βR; also a F.
173 wiþ; loked] β(*cf.* C); om; loke α.
175 ʒoure] L&rC; om WCr¹.
    chetes] L&rC; eschetes wB.

And deme yow, bi this day, as ye han deserved.   *judge*

Mede shal noght maynprise yow, by the Marie of hevene!

                                                     stand surety for

180 I wole have leaute in law, and lete be al youre janglyng, *protestation*

And as moost folk witnesseth wel, Wrong shal be demed.'

    Quod Conscience to the Kyng, 'But the commune wole assente,

It is ful hard, by myn heed, herto to brynge it,   *to this point*

[And] alle youre lige leodes to lede thus evene.'

                                      loyal subjects; unswervingly

185 'By Hym that raughte on the rode!' quod Reson to the Kynge,

                                             stretched

But if I rule thus youre reaume, rende out my guttes—   *Unless*

If ye bidden buxomnesse be of myn assente.'   *Provided; obedience*

    'And I assente,' seith the Kyng, 'by Seinte Marie my lady,

Be my counseil comen of clerkes and of erles.   *As soon as . . . is*

190 Ac redily, Reson, thow shalt noght ride hennes;   *quickly; hence*

For as longe as I lyve, lete thee I nelle.'   *abandon; shall not*

    'I am aredy,' quod Reson, 'to reste with yow ever;

So Conscience be of oure counseil, I kepe no bettre.'

                                      Provided that; require

    'And I graunte,' quod the Kyng, 'Goddes forbode he faile!

                                            God forbid

195 Als longe as oure lyf lasteth, lyve we togideres!'   *lasts; let us live*

---

181 moost] β; alle α.
    folk] βR; wyȝes F.
    wel] ?β; *om* CrGHα.
183 -to] L&r (*om* Hm); -too W.
184 And] *so* ZACK–D; *om* All
    MSS.
186 if] W&r; *om* HmBHZAC.
189 Be] L&r (*l. om* C)ZA; By
    wGBm; To F.

190 hens] HZACK–D; fro me W&r
    (*trs* G).
192 a-] L&rZ; al WHmGCBHF;
    om Cr?Ax.
193 oure] W&r (*om* G; *l. om*
    F)Z?A; youre MC², *most* A-*MSS*;
    my H.
194 he faile] ?α (he] þou F)ZAK–D;
    it faile β (ellis W).

Passus V

The Kyng and hise knyghtes to the kirke wente   *church*
To here matyns of the day and the masse after.
Thanne waked I of my wynkyng and wo was withalle   *sleep; sorry*
That I ne hadde slept sadder and yseighen moore.   *more deeply; seen*
5 Ac er I hadde faren a furlong, feyntise me hente,   *faintness; seized*
That I ne myghte ferther a foot for defaute of slepynge,   *further; lack*
And sat softely adoun and seide my bileve;   *carefully; Creed*
And so I bablede on my bedes, thei broughte me aslepe.

                   as; mumbled; prayers

    And thanne saugh I muche moore than I bifore tolde—   *described*
10 For I seigh the feld ful of folk that I before of seide,
And how Reson gan arayen hym al the reaume to preche,   *prepare*
And with a cros afore the Kyng comsede thus to techen.   *began*
    He preved that thise pestilences was for pure synne,   *showed; solely*
And the south-west wynd on Saterday at even   *evening*
15 Was pertliche for pride and for no point ellis.   *manifestly; other reason*
Pyries and plum-trees were puffed to the erthe   *Pear-trees*
In ensample, [segges, that ye] sholden do the bettre.   *As a sign; men*
Beches and brode okes were blowen to the grounde   *Beeches; broad*
And turned upward here tail in tokenynge of drede

                   roots; as a fearful portent

---

13 He showed by arguments that the recent outbreaks of the plague were the
direct consequence of (the people's) sin(s) (C).

Collation WHmCrGYOC²CBLMH(*to*
125)RF.
RUBRIC *Passus quintus de visione
vt supra* W&r (*de v.*] *de v. petri
plowman* R; *om* OF); *om* GC².
7 And sat] W&r (and] and y Hm);
þan sat y F; I sat HZA.
8 so bablede] β; y.b. so F; bab. R; b.
I H.
9 tolde] L&rAZ(telle)C; of tolde
WCr+M.
10 seide] W&r; tolde HZA.
13 was] L&rZ?AC; were wGCotF.

14 -west] L&rZAC; -westrene
wGH.
15 pruyde] αZACK–D; pure p. β;
synne H.
17 In] β (*l. om* H)AC; And in RZ;
& al þese was F.
segges that ye] *so* ZAC (ye] we)
K–D; þat ye s. WHm; th*e* s. ye Cr;
ȝe s. ȝe L&r(ȝe²]*om* B); þat we F).
19 And; taile] αACZ (And] *om* Z);
om; tailes β.
in] βZAC; *om* α.

20 That dedly synne er domesday shal fordoon hem alle. *destroy*
　　Of this matere I myghte mamelen ful longe, *mumble, ramble on*
　　Ac I shal seye as I saugh, so me God helpe, *saw*
　　How pertly afore the peple [to] preche gan Reson. *forthrightly*
　　He bad Wastour go werche what he best kouthe *do; knew how to*
25 And wynnen his wastyng with som maner crafte; *earn what he spent; skill*
　　And preide Pernele hir purfil to le[v]e, *trimmings; put aside*
　　And kepe it in hire cofre for catel at hire nede. *chest; money*
　　Tomme Stowue he taughte to take two staves
　　And fecche Felice hom fro wyvene pyne. *punishment* (C)
30 He warnede Watte his wif was to blame *open to reproach*
　　That hire heed was worth half marc and his hood noght worth a grote. *a mark; groat* (C)
　　He bad Bette kutte a bough outher tweye *or two*
　　And bete Beton therwith but if she wolde werche. *Betty; unless; work*
　　He chargede chapmen to chasten hir children: *merchants*
35 'Late no wynnyng forwanye hem while thei be yonge, *profit; weaken*

---

20 That before the (actual) Day of Judgement (itself), (their) mortal sins shall prove the destruction of all of them.
29 And bring (his wife) Felice home [to receive a beating there with the two staves] from the punishment meted out to shrewish wives [the cucking or ducking-stool].
31 Because the (cloth of the) head (dress) she wore was worth half a mark (£⅓) and his hood not fourpence (cf. Chaucer, *GP* (*CT* I.435–5).
35–6 Do not let your prosperity cause a weakening (of their moral character) during their childhood, and do not, (to make up) for (the hardship and suffering caused by) the plague, pander excessively to their every wish.

20 hem] W&rZA?C; vs HF.
23 to . . . Reson] prechen gan resoun FK–D; r. gan to preche β (*l.* om H;
gan] bigan wGB)R (C).
24 go] βF?A?C; to RZ.
25 crafte] βZA; pl ?α (of werkys F).
26 And] L&rZA; He WCrGFC. leue] *so* ZACK–D; lete *All MSS.*
27 hire²] W&rC; om GHFA.
29 wyuene] αZACK–D; wyuen β.
31 Pat] L&rZA; For WC.
half] WHmOBαZC; half a L&r; a Ax.
&] wB+(*and erased*)MFZAC; om ?gLR.
worþ²] W&r; om HmGCotHRC.
32 He] F (?=α)ZCK–D; And β (And he Cr)R (C).
34 He] *so* ACK–D; And þanne he W&r; & namely he F; om Z.
chasten] CrGCLRZC; chastiȝen W&r?A.
35 forwanyen hem] α (h.] þe R)ZACK–D; *trs* β (*l.* om H).

Ne for no poustee of pestilence plese hem noght out of reson.

to excess

My sire seide so to me, and so dide my dame,   *father; mother*
That the levere child the moore loore bihoveth; *dearer; teaching; needs*
And Salamon seide the same, that Sapience made—

the Wisdom writings

"*Qui parcit virge odit filium*:

40 Whoso spareth the spryng spilleth hise children." '   *switch; ruins*
    And sithen he preide prelates and preestes togideres,

then

'That ye prechen to the peple, preve it on yowselve,   *What; practise*
And dooth it in dede – it shal drawe yow to goode.   *do*
If ye leven as ye leren us, we shul leve yow the bettre.'

live; teach; believe

45 And sithen he radde religion hir rule to holde—   *advised; abide by*
    'Lest the Kyng and his Conseil youre comunes apeire

reduce your provisions

And be stywardes of youre stedes til ye be [stew]ed bettre.'

places; established

    And sithen he counseiled the Kyng his commune to lovye: *subjects*
    'It is thi tresor, if treson ne were, and tryacle at thy nede.'

treason; remedy

50 And sithen he preide the Pope have pite on Holy Chirche,
    And er he gyve any grace, governe first hymselve. *(spiritual) favour(s)*
    'And ye that han lawes to kepe, lat Truthe be youre coveitise

administer; desire

Moore than golde or outher giftes, if ye wol God plese;   *or*

39*a* He that spareth the rod hateth his son (Prov 13: 24).
49 . . . were it not for (the possibility of) treason, and (it is) a source of
    (strength and) healing when you need (it).

39*a* *After this a line*: The englissh of   (C).
    þis latyn (is) whoso wole (it) knowe   47 stewed] *so* CZAK–D; ruled
    All MSS; *rej. as spurious* K–D.   W&r (*om* F) (C).
40 spilleþ] βC; he spilleth α.   48 his] wHC; þe L&r.
41 he preyed] β (pr.] prechede W)   49 tresore . . . were] L&r (tresoun]
    ZAC; he preued ?α (parled he to F).   resoun Hm; ne] *om* R); trewe
42 to] W&rC; *om* HFZA.   tresor W.
    it on] W&rZ; on CrG; it HAC.   53 or] L&r (& OC², *canc* O); *om*
44 leuen] WC²CH; lyuen L&rCZA   WCrGMH.

For whoso contrarieth Truthe, He telleth in the Gospel,

acts contrary to

55 *Amen dico vobis, nescio vos.*

And ye that seke Seynt James and seyntes of Rome,   *seek, go to visit*

Seketh Seynt Truthe, for he may save yow alle.   *Seek*

Qui cum Patre et Filio – that faire hem bifalle   *may it go well with*

That seweth my sermon' – and thus seyde Reson.   *follow*

60   Thanne ran Repentaunce and reherced his teme   *repeated; theme*

And gart Wille to wepe water with hise eighen.   *made; eyes*

   Pernele Proud-herte platte hire to the erthe   *threw herself flat*

And lay longe er she loked, and 'Lord, mercy!' cryde,   *looked (up)*

And bihighte to Hym that us alle made   *promised*

65 She sholde unsowen hir serk and sette there an heyre

shift; hair-shirt (C)

To affaiten hire flessh that fiers was to synne.   *subdue; bold/fierce (C)*

'Shal nevere heigh herte me hente, but holde me lowe

pride; seize; (I shall) hold

And suffre to be mysseyd – and so dide I nevere.   *put up with reproach*

But now wole I meke me and mercy bieseche   *humble myself; beseech*

70 For al that I have hated in myn herte.'

   Thanne Lechour seide 'Allas!' and on Oure Lady he cryde

Lecher; cried

To maken mercy for hise mysdedes bitwene God and his soule

bring about

With that he sholde the Saterday seven yer therafter *Provided; on Sat.*

---

55 Amen, I say to you, I know you not (Mt 25: 12).

58 Who with the Father and the Son . . . (formula ending of a prayer or
blessing).

67 Feelings of pride shall never take possession of me, but I shall humble
myself . . .

73–4 (Giving assurance) that on every Saturday for the next seven years he
would drink nothing but water and eat only one meal a day [i.e. as a
penance].

54 *After this a line:* That god
knoweþ hym noȝt ne no Seynt of
heuene *All MSS; rej. as spurious*
K–D.

61 gart] W&rZ; made HmHFAC.

63 she; cryde] βFZAC; he; he cr. R.

67 holde] L&rZAC; holde I wole
W.

69 wil I] L&rZAC; I wole W.

70 For al þat] For al þis β; For þis
?α (þis] þat F); Of alle þat ACZ (þ.]
hem Z) (C).

71 he] W&r; *om* HmGOC²HZAC.

73 þe Saterday] βZA (*cf.* C); on þe
day R; euery day F.

Drynke but myd the doke and dyne but ones.   *only with; duck; once*

75 Envye with hevy herte asked after shrifte   *for confession*
And carefully *mea culpa* he comsed to shrewe.

sorrowfully; (his sins); began

He was as pale as a pelet, in the palsy he semed,   *(stone) ball*
And clothed in a kaurymaury – I kouthe it nought discryve—

coarse cloth; describe

In a kirtel and courtepy, and a knyf by his syde;

under-jacket; short coat

80 Of a freres frokke were the foresleves.   *friar's gown; fore-part of s.*
And as a leek that hadde yleye longe in the sonne,   *lain*
So loked he with lene chekes, lourynge foule.   *lean; grimacing hideously*
His body was to-bollen for wrathe, that he boot hise lippes,

all swollen; bit

And wryngyede with the fust – to wreke hymself he thoughte

twisted; fist; avenge

85 With werkes or with wordes whan he seyghe his tyme.   *should see*
Ech a word that he warp was of a neddres tonge;   *flung out; an adder's*
Of chidynge and of chalangynge was his chief liflode.

accusing; sustenance

With bakbitynge and bismere and berynge of fals witnesse: *calumny*
This was al his curteisie where that evere he shewed hym.   *appeared*

90 'I wolde ben yshryve,' quod this sherewe, 'and I for shame dorste.
I wolde be gladder, by God! that Gybbe hadde meschaunce

misfortune

Than though I hadde this wouke ywonne a weye of Essex chese.

week; 3 cwt

---

76 And wretchedly with 'through my fault' began to curse (his sins) (C).

74 myd] ?βZ; wyth HmC²CαAC.
76 schrewe] ?α (shryve F) (*cf.* C);
    shewe βA; cry3e H (C).
78 And] βR; He was FA.
79 In a] B (a +Cot)H?α; In ?β; he
    hadde on F.
80 þe] β?A; his αH.
81 And] βR; *om* FA.
    hadde] L&r; þat hadde wA.
84 wryng3ed . . . fist] R (?=α; hise
    hondis he wrong F) (*cf.* AC);
    wryngynge he yede β (he y.] *om* Cr;

he went G).
hymself] W&r (*om* F); hym
HmBHA.
86 Ech a] W&r; Ech CrGHR; &
    euery F.
87 chalangynge] W&r?C; ianglynge
    HmHF.
88 and¹] βF; and with R.
89 *In* L&r (shewed hym] went H);
    Swiche manerys he made to ech
    man he medled with F; *l. om* W.

I have a neghebore neigh me, I have anoyed hym ofte,   *troubled*
And lowen on hym to lordes to doon hym lese his silver,   *lied; lose*
95 And maad his frendes be his foon thorugh my false tonge.   *foes*
His grace and his goode happes greven me ful soore.   *success; luck*
Bitwene mayné and mayné I make debate ofte,   *household; quarrel(s)*
That bothe lif and lyme is lost thorugh my speche.   *limb*
And whan I mete hym in market that I moost hate,   *meet*
100 I hailse hym hendely, as I his frend were;   *greet; courteously*
For he is doughtier than I, I dar do noon oother;   *Since; braver; dare*
Ac hadde I maistrie and myght – God woot my wille!   *advantage*
    'And whan I come to the kirk and sholde knele to the Roode
And preye for the peple as the preest techeth—
105 For pilgrymes and for palmeres, for al the peple after—
Thanne I crye on my knees that Crist yyve hem sorwe   *give*
That baren awey my bolle and my broke shete.   *carried; bowl; torn*
Awey fro the auter thanne turne I myne eighen   *altar; eyes*
And biholde how Eleyne hath a newe cote;   *coat*
110 I wisshe thanne it were myn, and al the web after.   *all the cloth too*
And of his lesynge I laughe – that li[th]eth myn herte;   *loss; cheers*
Ac for his wynnynge I wepe and waille the tyme;   *profit; bewail*
And deme men that thei doon ille, there I do wel werse: *where; much*
Whoso undernymeth me herof, I hate hym dedly after.

                              reproves for this
115 I wolde that ech a wight were my knave,   *everybody; servant*
For whoso hath moore than I, that angreth me soore.   *vexes sorely*
    'And thus I lyve lovelees like a luther dogge   *fierce, vicious*
That al my body bolneth for bitter of my galle.   *swells; bitterness*
I myghte noght ete many yeres as a man oughte,   *eat*
120 For envye and yvel wil is yvel to defie.   *ill-will; hard to digest*
May no sugre ne swete thyng aswage my swellyng,   *assuage, lessen*

---

93 ney3e] L&rA; by WH.
95 ma*ad*] βF; doon A; also R.
97 mayne[1,2]] ?α (hym; manye men F) K–D; manye; manye β (man; man Hm).
100 hailse] W&r; haylsed GHA.
103 sholde] βR; *om* FA.
105 and] W&r; *om* HFA.
107 baren] OC²B; bar L&r; beren W.
109 Eleyne] βR(El-] hel- R); hervy

F; Heyne A.
ha[th] β?A; hath on ?α (h.] hadde F).
111 his] ?αAK–D; mennes βF. li[th]eth] liketh W&r; aketh y (werkes C)MCr[23] (C).
112 Ac; his] α (Ac] But F)A; And; hir β (h.] his Y).
113 And] βR; I FA. men] ?α (hem F); *om* β.
116 For] β (*l. om* H)R; & FA.
118 of] βA; in R; ys F.

Ne no diapenidion dryve it fro myn herte,   *cough-medicine (C)*
Ne neither shrifte ne shame, but whoso shrape my mawe?'
             unless someone scrape; stomach
  'Yis, redily!' quod Repentaunce, and radde hym to the beste,
             counselled
125 'Sorwe of synnes is savacion of soules.'   *salvation*
    'I am evere sory,' quod [Envye], 'I am but selde oother,
             seldom anything else
And that maketh me thus megre, for I ne may me venge.
             thin; avenge myself
Amonges burgeis have I be, [bigg]yng at Londoun,   *burgesses; living*
And gart bakbityng be a brocour to blame mennes ware.
             made; agent; goods
130 Whan he solde and I nought, thanne was I aredy   *sold (his goods)*
To lye and to loure on my neghebore and to lakke his chaffare.
             scowl; disparage; trade
I wole amende this if I may, thorugh myght of God Almyghty.'   *can*
    Now awaketh Wrathe, with two white eighen,
And nevelynge with the nose, and his nekke hangyng.   *running at*
135 'I am Wrathe,' quod he, 'I was som tyme a frere,   *friar*
And the coventes gardyner for to graffen impes.   *friary's; graft shoots*
On lymitours and listres lesynges I ymped,   *lectors; grafted*
Til thei beere leves of lowe speche, lordes to plese,   *produced; servile*
And sithen thei blosmede abrood in boure to here shriftes.
             blossomed; bedroom(s)
140 And now is fallen therof a fruyt – that folk han wel levere
             result; prefer
Shewen hire shriftes to hem than shryve hem to hir persons.
             parish-priests

---

123 . . . unless my stomach is scraped (clean of it)?
129 And used slander to disparage men's merchandise (for my own gain).
136 And the friary gardener, (whose job was) to graft scions on trees.
137 Upon friars mendicant and preaching friars I grafted mendacity.
141 To make their confessions to the friars than to their own parish priests.

125 of[1]] W&r; for HmCrHFA.   W&r.
   Here H *ceases as a* B-MS.   biggyng] *cj* K–D; dwellyng *All*
126 euere] αC; *om* βA.   *MSS* (C).
   enuye] *so* ACK–D; þat segge βR;   130 aredy] ?α (ful redy F)C; redy β.
   he F.   131 chaffare] β; ware α.
128 burgeys] HmYCBα; burgeises   139 abrood] β (a-] *so* M); *om* α.

And now persons han parceyved that freres parte with hem,

are sharing

Thise possessioners preche and deprave freres; *beneficed priests; revile*
And freres fyndeth hem in defaute, as folk bereth witnesse,

find fault (with)

145 That whan thei preche the peple in many places aboute,
I, Wrathe, walke with hem and wisse hem of my bokes. *teach (from)*
Thus thei speken of spiritualte, that either despiseth oother,

spirituality (C)

Til thei be bothe beggers and by spiritualte libben,   *live*
Or ellis al riche and ryden aboute; I, Wrathe, reste nevere
150 That I ne moste folwe this wikked folk, for swich is my grace.

fortune

'I have an aunte to nonne and an abbesse: *nun; abbess*
Hir were levere swowe or swelte than suffre any peyne.

she'd rather faint; die

I have be cook in hir kichene and the covent served   *convent*
Manye monthes with hem, and with monkes bothe.   *too*
155 I was the prioresse potager and other povere ladies,   *stew-maker*
And maad hem joutes of janglyng – that Dame Jone was a bastard,

stews of squabbling

And Dame Clarice a knyghtes doughter – ac a cokewold was hir sire,

cuckold; father

And Dame Pernele a preestes fyle – Prioresse worth she nevere,

concubine; will be

For she hadde child in chirie-tyme, al oure Chapitre it wiste!

cherry-time; knew

160 Of wikkede wordes I Wrathe hire wortes made,   *vegetables*
Til "Thow lixt!" and "Thow lixt!" lopen out at ones

liest; leapt; once

---

151 ... who is both a nun and an abbess ...

142 persons han] wGL+M; *trs* yα.
144 freres] β; *om* α.
147 of] L&r; of my
      wGM(my]+M)R.
148 by] αHmC; by my β.
149–50 *So div.* Cr²³K–D (*cf.* C); *as*
      3 *ll. after* aboute, folwe W&r; *as* 2
      ll. after aboute Cr¹, folwe B (149a

om B; wikked] *om* Cr¹).
151 abbesse] αC; Abbesse boþe β.
152 were] L&r; hadde WCrG.
154 boþe] βC; alse ? α (*l.* †F).
156 Ione] CrOC²CotMαC; Iohane
      W&r.
160 made] W&r (*l.* †F); I made
      OC²LR.

And either hitte oother under the cheke;
Hadde thei had knyves, by Crist! hir either hadde kild oother.

each of them

Seint Gregory was a good pope, and hadde a good forwit   *foresight*
165   That no Prioresse were preest – for that he [purveiede]:

should be; provided/foresaw

Thei hadde thanne ben *infamis* the firste day, thei kan so yvele hele
    counseil.

  'Among monkes I myghte be, ac manye tyme I shonye,

avoid doing so

For ther ben manye felle frekes my feeris to aspie—   *severe; doings*
Bothe Priour and Suppriour and oure *Pater Abbas*;

Sub-Prior; Father Abbot

170   And if I telle any tales, thei taken hem togideres,   *get together*
And doon me faste [faste] Frydayes to breed and to watre;   *steadily*
And [yet am I] chalanged in the Chapitrehous as I a child were,

charged

And baleised on the bare ers – and no brech bitwene!

beaten; arse; breeches

Forthi [no likyng have I] with tho leodes to wonye;   *people; dwell*
175   I ete there unthende fissh and feble ale drynke.   *small; weak*
Ac outher while whan wyn cometh [and whan] I drynke wel at eve,

at other times; evening

I have a flux of a foul mouth wel fyve dayes after.   *discharge; a good*
Al the wikkednesse that I woot by any of oure bretheren,   *evil; about*

164–6 . . . had a sound anticipation (in providing) that no prioress be a priest
    (*or* because he foresaw that (if they had been ordained . . .)): they would then
    have been of ill-repute from the start, so badly can they conceal secrets (*C*).

162 hitte] L; hite W.
163 hir] WLMR; *om* Hm&r.
165 purueiede] *cj K–D*; prouided
    Cr; ordeyned W&r (*C*).
166 þe . . . day] W&r (*l.* †Cr); *om*
    GYOC²M.
167 shonye] L&r; shonye it W.
171 faste²] *om All MSS* (*C*).
172 ȝut am I] *so* C; ȝeet am R
    (?=α); y am F; am β (*om* HmG)

    (*C*).
173 ers] βR (*canc for* bak *a.h.*); bak
    F.
174 no likyng; haue I] *trs All MSS*
    (*l. om* OC²; h. I] *trs* GCotF) (*C*).
176 and whan] *so* C; and Hm&r
    (*om* Cr¹F); whan GLMR; þanne W
    (*C*).
    wel] α; wyn ?β (it Cr²³yHm).
177 I] L&r (þat y F)C; And W.

I cou[gh]e it in oure cloistre, that al the covent woot it.'   *knows*

180 'Now repente thee,' quod Repentaunce, 'and reherce thow nevere
                                                                   declare

Counseil that thow knowest, by contenaunce ne by speche;
                                              Private matters; expression

And drynk nat over delicatly, ne to depe neither,   *daintily; too deeply*

That thi wille by cause therof to wrathe myghte turne.

Esto sobrius!' he seide, and assoiled me after,   *Be sober (1 Pet 5: 8)*

185 And bad me wilne to wepe my wikkednesse to amende.   *desire*

     And thanne cam Coveitise, I kan hym naght discryve—   *describe*

So hungrily and holwe Sire Hervy hym loked.   *hollowly*

He was bitelbrowed and baberlipped, with two blered eighen, *eyes*

And as a letheren purs lolled hise chekes—   *leather; hung down*

190 Wel sidder than his chyn thei chyveled for elde;
                                                lower; trembled; old age

And as a bondeman of his bacon his berd was bidraveled;
                                    labourer; with; covered with grease

With an hood on his heed, a lousy hat above,   *lice-infested; on top of it*

In a [torn] tabard of twelf wynter age;   *coat*

But if a lous couthe lepe, [leve I], the bettre.   *Unless; louse; leap*

---

188 He had beetling brows, thick lips and inflamed eyes.

179   couȝe] *so* CK–D; couþe W&r
(kiþe B; make knowe it C²) (C).
the] Hm&r (*om* R) K–D; oure
WCrLM; your G.
180   þee] W&r?C; *om* GF.
181   speche] αCK–D; riȝt ?β (r-] s-
Cr²³OC²; n- G).
184   and] βF; and so he R.
me] W&r; hym CrM (*over erasure*)
C.
185   me; my] W&r; hym; his CrM
(*by correction*).
186   And] *so* All MSS; *om* ZAC.
I can] αOC²ACK–D; trs ?β.
188   So ?ACK–D; *as* 2 ll. div. before
Wiþ All MSS (C).
wiþ] *so* ?ACK–D; also Wiþ W&r
(a.] boþe CB).
eiȝen] *so* ?ACK–D; e. as a blynd

hagge *All MSS*.
192   Wiþ an hood] W&r; His hood
he hadde F.
his] ?αC; an β.
lousy; ab.] βR; heyȝ; þer vppe F.
193   In] *so* ACK–D; And in W&r
(in) *om* Cr¹); He hadde on F.
torn] *so* ACK–D; tawny W&r;
tanne HmB.
After this a line: Al torn and baudy
and ful of lys crepyng (ful . . . cr.]
lappe syȝd it semede F) *All MSS;
rej. as spurious* K–D (C).
194   if] αGCotACK–D; if þat ?β
(that Hm).
lepe] αACK–D; han lopen β.
leue I] I leue *cj* K–D; *om* All MSS
(C).

195 She ne sholde noght wa[ndr]e on that Welche, so was it thredbare!

                Welsh flannel

  'I have ben coveitous,' quod this caytif, 'I biknowe it here;

              wretch; acknowledge

  For som tyme I served Symme-atte-Style,   *at the Style*

  And was his prentice yplight his profit to wayte. *contracted; look after*

  First I lerned to lye a leef outher tweyne: *a leaf or two (C)*

200 Wikkedly to weye was my firste lesson.   *Dishonestly; weigh*

  To Wy and to Wynchestre I wente to the feyre *Weyhill (C); fair*

  With many manere marchaundise, as my maister me highte. *ordered*

  Ne hadde the grace of gyle ygo amonges my ware, *luck; guile*

  It hadde ben unsold this seven yer, so me God helpe!

205 'Thanne drough I me among drapiers, my Donet to lerne,

             betook; grammar (C)

  To drawe the liser along – the lenger it semed; *selvage (C); (so that) it*

  Among the riche rayes I rendred a lesson— *striped clothes; memorized*

  To broche hem with a bat-nedle, and playted hem togideres,

       sew; needle (for sewing) packages; folded

  And putte hem in a press[our] and pyned hem therinne

               press; tortured

210 Til ten yerdes or twelve tolled out thrittene. *yards; stretched . . . to*

  'My wif was a webbe and wollen cloth made;   *weaver*

  She spak to spynnesteres to spynnen it oute.   *spinners*

  The pound that she paied by peised a quarter moore *weighed*

  Than myn owene auncer wh[an I] weyed truthe. *steelyard (C); honestly*

215 'I boughte hire barly – she brew it to selle.   *brewed*

  Peny ale and puddyng ale she poured togideres; *thick ale; at one time*

---

195   ne] ?αC; *om* βF.
  wandre] *so* ACK–D; walke α; han
  walked β.
  on . . . welche] L&r (w.) welþe
  WCrM; web F); ther*on* gHm (on)
  om HmCB).
203   ware] LMαAC; chaffare wg.
206   liser] W&r?A?C; lyst GF.
208   bat] Lα?AC; pak W&r (*over
  erasure* M).
  plaited] L&r?A; *play*te wGM.
209   pressour] *so* AC (*pl*) K–D;
  presse *All MSS.*

pyned] Lα?A; pynne*d* Cr&r
(pynnen Cr²³; pyne W)C.
210   tolled] LMαAC; hadde tolled
  wg.
212   spynnesteres] β?AC (þe s. AC);
  a sp. α.
213   pe] *so* ACK–D; Ac þe W&r
  (Ac) but GF); And the CrC²C.
  quarter] αAC; quartron β.
214   whan I] *so* ACK–D; whoso
  W&r (*so*) þat F).
215   barly] ?αACK–D; barly malt
  βF.

For laborers and for lowe folk, that lay by hymselve.
The beste ale lay in my bour or in my bedchambre,   *inner room (C)*
And whoso bummed therof, he boughte it therafter—
                                    tasted; accordingly
220 A galon for a grote, God woot, no lesse,   *groat*
[Whan] it cam in cuppemele – this craft my wif used!   *by cupfuls*
Rose the Regrater was hir righte name;   *Retailer*
She hath holden hukkerye [this ellevene wynter].   *practised retail trade*
Ac I swere now (so thee Ik!) that synne wol I lete,
                                    may I prosper; abandon
225 And nevere wikkedly weye ne wikked chaffare use,
                                    dishonestly; sharp practice
But wenden to Walsyngham, and my wif alse,   *go (on pilgrimage); too*
And bidde the Roode of Bromholm bryng me out of dette.'   *pray*
  'Repentedestow evere?' quod Repentaunce, 'ne restitucion
    madest?'   *Did you ever repent or make r.*
  'Yis: ones I was yherberwed', quod he, 'with an heep of chapmen;
                                    once; lodged; crowd
230 I roos when thei were a-reste and riflede hire males!'   *rose; rifled; bags*
  'That was no restitucion,' quod Repentaunce, 'but a robberis
    thefte;
Thow haddest be bettre worthi ben hanged therfore   *for it*
Than for al that that thow hast here shewed!'   *confessed to*
  'I wende riflynge were restitucion,' quod he, 'for I lerned never rede
    on boke,   *thought; read*
235 And I kan no Frenssh, in feith, but of the fertheste ende of Northfolk.'
                                    know; Norfolk

---

217 (The ale intended) for labourers, etc., stood apart by itself.

217 for²] WHmGLRC; *om* Cr&rA.
  hym-] w (it Cr)LCotα?AC; hem
  gM; þe F.
218 ale] βFC; of alle; *om* A.
219 he] ?y (*l. om* B)α; *om* wGLM.
221 Whan*ne*] *so* ACK–D; And yet
  All MSS.
  vsed] βAC; vseth α.
222 was] βAC; is α.
223 þis . . . wynter] *so* ACK–D (þis]
  om K–D); al hire lif tyme *All MSS*
  (C).

224 thee ik] β?A(*cf.* Z); theich α.
225 wikked] Y&rA; wikke WLM;
  fals G.
228 Repentedest-] WHmRC;
  Repentest- L&r.
  ne] LM?α(&F)C; or wg.
232 be] Hm&r (be þe W; +M); *om*
  LR.
233 shewed] W&r; now sh. yHm.
234 quod he] W&r; *om* HmGMF.
  for] W&r; *so* F; *om* g.

'Usedestow evere usurie,' quod Repentaunce, 'in al thi life tyme?'

            Did you practise

'Nay, sothly,' he seide, 'save in my youthe;   *except*

I lerned among Lumbardes a lesson, and of Jewes— *Lombards; from*

To weye pens with a peis, and pare the hevyeste, *pence; weight; clip*

240 And lene it for love of the cros, to legge a wed and lese it.

           lend; lay; pledge; lose (C)

Swiche dedes I dide write if he his day breke;

         bonds; had written; in case

I have mo manoirs thorugh rerages than thorugh

 Miseretur et commodat.   *arrears*

I have lent lordes and ladies my chaffare,   *goods*

And ben hire brocour after, and bought it myselve. *agent; later*

245 Eschaunges and chevysaunces – with swich chaffare I dele,

          loans; business; deal

And lene folk that lese wole a lippe at every noble. *portion; coin (=£⅓)*

And with Lumbardes lettres I ladde gold to Rome,

        bills of exchange; carried

And took it by taille here and told hem there lasse.' *tally; counted; less*

 'Lentestow evere lordes for love of hire mayntenaunce?'

          protection (C)

250 'Ye, I have lent lordes, loved me nevere after, *(who) loved*

And have ymaad many a knyght bothe mercer and draper

        silk-, cloth-dealer

That payed nevere for his prentishode noght a peire of gloves!'

        apprenticeship

 'Hastow pite on povere men that [borwe mote nedes]?' *needs must*

 'I have as muche pite of povere men as pedlere hath of cattes,

---

242 I have (got possession of) more properties through (my debtors' failure to
 pay what they owed me in time) than through (the gratitude felt by them
 towards me) for compassionately lending to them in their time of need
 '[Acceptable is the man that] sheweth mercy and lendeth' (Ps 111: 5).

238 a . . . iewes] α (of i.] be herte
  F)CK–D; and Iewes a lesson β.

242 comm-] CrCotK–D; com-
  W&r.

244 bouȝt] βF; brouȝt RCot.

248 taille] L&r (i *erased* Cot); tale
  WCrM (*over erasure*)F.
  here] β; þere R;*om* F.

250 lordes] β (to l. W)C; to l. quod
  heo α (heo] þat F).

251 a] W&rC; *om* YOC²CR.

253 borwe; mote nedes] *trs All MSS*
  (n.] for nede F) (C).

254 pouere men] W&r; þe pore
  CrF; hem y.
  as²] β; as þe α.

255   That wolde kille hem, if he cacche hem myghte, for coveitise of hir
        skynnes!'
        'Artow manlich among thi neghebores of thi mete and drynke?'
                                             charitable
        'I am holden,' quod he, 'as hende as hounde is in kichene;
                                       courteous; a dog
        Amonges my neghebores namely swich a name ich have.' *particularly*
        'Now [but thow repente the rather,' quod Repentaunce, 'God lene
        thee nevere]   *unless; sooner; grant*
260   The grace on this grounde thi good wel to bisette,
                              bestow (in charitable acts)
        Ne thyne heires after thee have joie of that thow wynnest,   *earn*
        Ne thyne executours wel bisette the silver that thow hem levest;
                                         employ
        And that was wonne with wrong, with wikked men be despended.
                             that (which); by, among; spent
        For were I a frere of that hous ther good feith and charite is,
265   I nolde cope us with thi catel, ne oure kirk amende,
                             clothe; money; improve
        Ne have a peny to my pitaunce of thyne, bi my soule hele,
                                  allowance; health
        For the beste book in oure hous, theigh brent gold were the leves,
                                    burnished
        And I wiste witterly thow were swich as thow tellest!   *If; for certain*
        Servus es alterius, cum fercula pinguia queris;
        Pane tuo pocius vescere, liber eris.
        'Thow art an unkynde creature – I kan thee noght assoille
                                   unnatural; absolve

268a Seek costly foods, another's slave you'll be;
       But eat your own plain bread and you'll stay free (source unknown).

255   if he] β; and he R; all F.
     cacche hem] β (*trs* HmCr); *om* gF.
256   þi²] W&r; *om* gF.
     and] W&r; & of y.
257   is] W&r; *om* CrGR.
     in] β; in his R; in the GF.
259   but . . . neuere] god lene þee
     neuere quod Rep. but þow repente
     þe raþer W&r (lene; neuere] gyve;
     grace F; þee] w; *om* gLMα) (C).

260   The] W&r (*om* HmCr);
     Grawnte þe F.
261   heires] ?β (*over erasure* M)C;
     ysue LR; houswif F.
265   nolde; kirk] β; wolde nouȝt;
     cherche α.
266   of . . . hele] L&r; so mote
     pyȝghne in helle F; so god my soule
     helpe w (h.] saue W)G (C).
268a *cum*] L&rC; *dum* W.

270 Til thow make restitucion' quod Repentaunce, 'and rekene with hem
      alle.   *settle up what you owe to*
      And sithen that Reson rolle it in the Registre of hevene
                                               (until) after; record
      That thow hast maad ech man good, I may thee noght assoille. *can*
      Non dimittitur peccatum donec restituatur ablatum.
      For alle that han of thi good, have God my trouthe,
      Is haldyng at the heighe doom to helpe thee to restitue;
                                               obliged; make restitution
275 And who so leveth noght this be sooth, loke in the Sauter glose,
                                                    Psalter gloss
      In *Miserere mei, Deus,* wher I mene truthe: *speak of*
      Ecce enim veritatem dilexisti . . .   (Ps 50: 8)
      Shal nevere werkman in this world thryve with that thow wynnest.
      Cum sancto sanctus eris: construwe me that on Englissh.' *interpret*
         Thanne weex the sherewe in wanhope and wolde han hanged
         hymselve   *rogue; fell into; despair*
280 Ne hadde Repentaunce the rather reconforted hym in this manere:
                                               soon; again comforted
      'Have mercy in thi mynde, and with thi mouth biseche it,
      For [His] mercy is moore than alle Hise othere werkes— *greater*
      Misericordia eius super omnia opera eius . . .

272a The sin is not forgiven until the stolen goods are returned (St Augustine,
     Epistle 153, Sect. 20 (*PL* 2: 662); cf. XVIII 306a.
276, 276a In 'Have mercy on me, O God' (Ps 50: 3); 'For, behold, thou hast
     loved truth' (ibid., verse 8).
278 'With the holy thou wilt be holy' (Ps 17: 26; ['. . . and with the perverse
     thou wilt be perverted', ibid., 27]).
282a His tender mercies [*miserationes,* Vulg.] are over all his works (Ps 144:
     9).

270   quod repentance] ?αK–D; *om* β   þat knoweth peres þe plowman α
      (*l. om* Y)F.   (*replacing* 276a F) (C).
272   assoille] βF (*cf.* C); saue R.   277 Shal] β; For schal α.
272a donec] β; *nisi* αCr.   278 þat] L&r; þis WCF.
      abl-] L&r; *obl-* WYCBmBo.   279 þe] αK–D; þat β.
274   Is] LMαCK–D; Ben wg.   -selve] self L&r; *cropped* W.
      haldynge] ?α?C; holden βF.   280 re-] W&r; *om* HmGR.
      þee] ?α (†F)C; þee to β.   282 His] goddes *All MSS* (C).
275   *Four spurious ll.* F.   alle] W&r; manye of F.
      þe] βC; a ?α.   282a *In* LYOC²MR (*eius*¹] *domini*
276a *So* βRC; *after it the line:* þere   R).
      is no laborere wolde leue with hem

And al the wikkednesse in this world that man myghte werche or
   thynke   *do*
Nis na moore to the mercy of God than in[middes] the see a gleede:
                                 (compared) to; glowing ember
Omnis iniquitas quantum ad misericordiam Dei est
quasi scintilla in medio maris.
285 Forthi have mercy in thy mynde – and marchaundise, leve it!
                                    goods, wealth
For thow hast no good ground to gete thee with a wastel   *cake*
But if it were with thi tonge or ellis with thi two hondes.
                               sc. by begging or working
For the good that thow hast geten bigan al with falshede,
                                 wealth; originated
And as longe as thow lyvest therwith, thow yeldest noght but
   borwest.   *pay (back)*
290 And if thow wite nevere to whiche ne whom to restitue,   *know*
Ber it to the Bisshop, and bid hym of his grace   *Bear; beg*
Bisette it hymself as best is for thi soule.   *Dispose of*
For he shal answere for thee at the heighe dome,   *Last Judgement*
For thee and for many mo that man shal yeve a rekenyng: *account*
295 What he lerned yow in Lente, leve thow noon oother, *taught; believe*
And what he lente yow of Oure Lordes good, to lette yow fro synne'.
                                sc. grace, forgiveness; keep

   Now bigynneth Gloton for to go to shrifte,
And kaireth hym to kirkewarde his coupe to shewe.
                                 goes to church; sin

Ac Beton the Brewestere bad hym good morwe   *ale-wife*
300 And [with that asked of hym], whiderward he wolde,
                                which way he was going

284*a* Compared to God's mercy all wickedness is like a spark of fire in the
   midst of the sea (thought from St Augustine; see AlfG, p. 47).
286 For you have no good claim for trying to obtain even the smallest luxury.

283 werche] W&r (*om* G); do *y*.
284 inmiddes] amyd *cj* K–D; in *All*
   MSS (C).
284*a* maris] L&r (*m. &c* YB); m
   (*cropped*)W.
292 is] W&r; be HmC.
296 oure lordes; lette] W&r (*l. om*
   F; lette] kepe Cr²³); his; wite *y*.

298 kaires] L&rAC; karieþ wB;
   wendis F.
299 Ac] L&r (but G)A; An C; Anon
   F; And WCrC².
300 wiþ þat; asked of hym] *trs All*
   MSS (w. þ] w. þ. word M; whens
   he cam & F; of] L&r; at W; *om*
   Cr²³MF) (C).

'To holy chirche,' quod he, 'for to here masse,
And sithen I wole be shryven, and synne na moore.'   *then*
    'I have good ale, gossib,' quod she, 'Gloton, woltow assaye?'

                                                            friend; try

'Hastow,' quod he, 'any hote spices?'
305 'I have pepir and pioné,' quod she, 'and a pound of garleek,

                                                            peony seeds
A ferthyngworth of fenelseed for fastynge dayes.'   *farthing's worth*
    Thanne goth Gloton in, and grete othes after.   *oaths*
    Cesse the Souteresse sat on the benche,   *?female shoemaker*
    Watte the Warner and his wif bothe,   *warren-keeper*
310 Tymme the Tynkere and tweyne of his [knav]es,   *lads*
    Hikke the Hakeneyman and Hugh the Nedlere,

                                          horse-hirer; needle-seller
    Clarice of Cokkeslane and the Clerk of the chirche,   *Cock's Lane*
    Sire Piers of Pridie and Pernele of Flaundres,   *Sir P. the priest*
    Dawe the Dykere, and a dozeyne othere—   *Davy the ditcher*
315 A Ribibour, a Ratoner, a Rakiere of Chepe,

                            fiddler; rat-catcher; scavenger; Cheapside
    A Ropere, a Redyngkyng, and Rose the Dysshere,   *?lackey; dish-seller*
    Godefray of Garlekhithe and Griffyth the Walshe   *Welshman*
    And [of] upholderes an heep, erly by the morwe,

                                          old-clothes men; a number
Geve Gloton with glad chere good ale to hanselle.

                                          (Who) gave; as a treat
320 Clement the Cobelere caste of his cloke,   *cloak*
    And to the newe faire nempned it to selle.   *put it up for barter (C)*
    Hikke the Hakeneyman hitte his hood after,   *flung down*
    And bad Bette the Bocher ben on his syde.   *asked; butcher*

---

304 Hastow] so CAK–D; H. ouȝt
     in þi purs *All MSS* (o.] *om* F) (C).
     quod he] WFAC; *om* L&r.
305 pioyne] ?αACK–D; piones βF.
     and²] HmACK–D; quod she and
     W&r (and] *om* G).
306 A] L&rAC; And a WCrC²F.
308 Souteresse] W&r?C; sowestere
     BA.
310 Tymme] WCrOL?C; Tomme
     MGC²BmF?A; symme HmYCBo
     CotR.
     knaues] so ACK–D; prentices *All*

MSS.
313, 314 *So* αACK–D; *ll. trs* β
     (Sire] βAC; And s. α).
316 dyschere] HmOC²BACK–D;
     dyssheres WCrGYCLM; dissheres
     douȝter α.
317 grifyth] ?α (Geffrey F)?C;
     Griffyn βA.
318 And of] *so* C?A; And *All MSS*.
321 to¹] ?α (in F)C; at βA.
     feyre] ?αACK–D; feire he βF.
323 ben] βAC; to ben α.

Ther were chapmen ychose this chaffare to preise: *bargain; evaluate*
325 Whoso hadde the hood sholde han amendes of the cloke.

                                                        compensation

    Tho risen up in rape and rouned togideres,   *They; haste; whispered*
And preised the penyworthes apart by hemselve.

                                                valued; bargains; privately
[And there were othes an heep, for oon sholde have the werse];
Thei kouthe noght by hir conscience acorden in truthe,   *agree*
330 Til Robyn the Ropere arise the[i by]sou[ght]e,   *begged to get up*
And nempned hym for a nounpere, that no debat were.

                                            umpire; dispute should occur

Hikke the Hostiler hadde the cloke   *ostler*
In covenaunt that Clement sholde the cuppe fille   *On condition*
And have Hikkes hood the Hostiler, and holden hym yserved;

                                            H. the H.'s hood; satisfied
335 And whoso repented rathest shoulde aryse after   *had regrets soonest*
And greten Sire Gloton with a galon ale.   *treat G. to …*
    There was laughynge and lourynge and 'Lat go the cuppe!'

                                                            scowling

[Bargaynes and beverages bigonne to arise;]   *Barterings; drinking*
And seten so til evensong, and songen umwhile,   *(they) sat; at times*
340 Til Gloton hadde yglubbed a galon and a gille.   *gulped down; ¼ pint*

---

328 There was much swearing, for one or the other had to come off worse (C).
331 And nominated him umpire, so that there should be no dispute (C).
334 And have Hick the Ostler's hood, and consider himself fairly done by.
338 Bargains were made and drinks (to seal the bargains) bought.

324   were] βFAC; *om* R.
325   Who so] L&rA; That whoso
WC; which of hem sholde F.
hadde] WHmYOC²AC; haueth
GLMRCr; haue CBF(sholde h. F).
326   þo] ?α (þan F)Bm?A?CK–D;
Two β.
vp] βAC; þey F; *om* R.
327   þe] αACK–D; þise β.
hem-] βAC; hym αHm.
328   So CA (for … werse] ouer þe
hood and þe cloke ?A)K–D; *l. om*
All MSS (C).
330   aryse they bisouhte] *so* C (*cf.*

A)K–D; arise þe southe R; was
reysed fram his sete F; aroos by þe
Southe β (C).
331   were] HmGBRAC; nere W&r;
þere fylle F.
After this a spurious line Cr²³y.
334   the] HmCr²³YBMACK–D; *om*
W&r.
338   So AC (arise] awake C)K–D; *l.
om* All MSS (C).
339   seten] W&rAC; sytten CrGR.
songen] βFAC; syngen R.

His guttes gonne to gothelen as two gredy sowes;   *rumble; greedy*
He pissed a potel in a *Paternoster*-while,
And blew his rounde ruwet at his ruggebones ende,

trumpet; backbone's

That alle that herde that horn helde hir nose after
345 And wisshed it hadde ben wexed with a wispe of firses!

wax-polished; furze

He myghte neither steppe ne stonde er he his staf hadde,
And thanne gan he to go like a glemannes bicche,   *minstrel's bitch*
Som tyme aside and som tyme arere,   *backwards*
As whoso leith lynes for to lacche foweles.   *lays; catch birds*

350   And whan he drough to the dore, thanne dymmed hise eighen;   *drew*
He [thr]umbled on the thresshfold and threw to the erthe.   *jostled; fell*
Clement the Cobelere kaughte hym by the myddel   *caught; waist*
For to liften hym olofte, and leyde hym on his knowes.   *up; knees*
Ac Gloton was a gret cherl and a grym in the liftyng,   *terrible*
355 And koughed up a cawdel in Clementes lappe.   *coughed, vomited; mess*
Is noon so hungry hound in Hertfordshire
Dorste lape of that levynge, so unlovely it smaughte!   *lap up; smelled*
    With al the wo of this world, his wif and his wenche   *servant-girl*
Baren hym to his bed and broughte hym therinne;   *Carried*
360 And after al this excesse he had an accidie,   *attack of sloth*
That he sleep Saterday and Sonday, till sonne yede to reste.   *went*
Thanne waked he of his wynkyng and wiped hise eighen;   *slumbers*
The first word that he warp was – 'Where is the bolle?'   *uttered; bowl*
    His wif [and his wit] gan edwyte hym tho how wikkedly he lyvede,

reproach

---

342 He pissed ½ gallon in the time (it takes to say) an 'Our Father' (C).
345 . . . polished with a handful of furze (C).

341   gunne] LMBαC; bigonne
    W&r.
344   þat¹ . . . horn] βAC; þat
    horn R; þe folk in þe houws F.
    nose] L&rAC; noses WHm
    GCotM.
347   go]YCLMα?ACK–D; to go
    W&r.
350   And] βF?C; Ac R.
351   thromblede] so CK–D;
    tremblede L?α (tripplid F);
    stumbled wgM (over

    erasure)?Ax (C).
357   leuyng] ?α (þerof F)C;
    leuynges β.
    it] HmBMαK–D; þei W&r.
359   to] αACK–D; hom to β.
363   warp] W&r; spak
    HmACK–D (C).
364   wif . . . wit] wif and his
    inwit C; wif WCr¹M (f over
    erasure M); witte L&r (C).

365 And Repentaunce right so rebuked hym that tyme:
   'As thow with wordes and werkes hast wroght yvele in thi lyve,
                                                      evil; life
   Shryve thee and be shamed therof, and shewe it with thi mouthe.'
                                                      reveal
      'I, Gloton,' quod the gome, 'gilty me yelde—
                                   yield, admit myself (to be)
   Of that I have trespased with my tonge, I kan noght telle how ofte,
370 Sworen "Goddes soule and his sydes!" and "So helpe me God and
      halidome!"   *Sworn; sides; relics*
   Ther no nede ne was nyne hyndred tymes;
   And overseyen me at my soper and som tyme at nones, *forgot myself*
   That I, Gloton, girte it up er I hadde gon a myle,   *vomited*
   And yspilt that myghte be spared and spended on som hungry;
375 Over delicatly on f[ee]styng dayes dronken and eten bothe,
                                                  Over-luxuriously
   And sat som tyme so long there that I sleep and eet at ones.
   For love of tales in tavernes, to drynke the moore I dyned;
   And hyed to the mete er noon whan [it] fastyng dayes were.'
                                         hastened; food; before
   'This shewynge shrift,' quod Repentaunce, 'shal be meryt to the.'
                                                open confession
380   And thanne gan Gloton greete, and gret doel to make
                                                   weep; lament
   For his luther lif that he lyved hadde,   *evil life*
   And avowed faste – 'For hunger or for thurste,   *In spite of*

---

372 And forgot myself (so far as to over-eat) at my evening meal and
      sometimes at my midday meal (too) (C).
374 And wasted what could have been saved and spent on some hungry
      person.

368   gome] L&r; grome   fastyng *All MSS* (C).
WHmCr¹G.   376 þat I] β; at y F; and R.
369   Of] ?α (*l. om* F)C; *om* β.   377 to drynke] L&r (to) and for
370   and his sydes] ?α (and side   W); to ete R.
F)CK–D; *om* β.   moore . . . dyned] βR; sunnere y
*h*elp me god] αMC; god me   wente F.
helpe ?β (god me] *trs* W; me h.   378 it] *om All MSS* (C).
trs Hm).   were] βR; felle F.
371   ne] L&r?C; *om* wGYF.   380 greete] W&r; to grete HmBR.
373   it] WHmGL?α; *om* CryMF.   382 faste] GLRZ; to f. W&r (to
375   feestyng] feeste *cj K–D*;   +M)A.

Shal never fyssh on the Fryday defyen in my wombe   *digest; stomach*
Til Abstinence myn aunte have yyve me leeve—   *given; permission*
385 And yet have I hated hire al my lif tyme!'
    Thanne cam Sleuthe al bislabered, with two slymed eighen.   *soiled*
'I moste sitte,' seide the segge, 'or ellis sholde I nappe.   *fall asleep*
I may noght stonde ne stoupe ne withoute stool knele.   *stoop*
Were I brought abedde, but if my tailende it made,   *tail-end; caused*
390 Sholde no ryngynge do me ryse er I were ripe to dyne.'   *(of bells); ready*
    He bigan *Benedicite* with a bolk, and his brest knokked,

Bless me (C); belch

And raxed and rored – and rutte at the laste.   *stretched; snored*
    'What, awake, renk!' quod Repentaunce, 'and rape thee to shryfte!'   *man; hurry*
    'If I sholde deye bi this day,' quod he, 'me list nought to loke.   *
395 I kan noght parfitly my *Paternoster* as the preest it syngeth,

do not know properly

But I kan rymes of Robyn Hood and Randolf Erl of Chestre,   *about*
Ac neither of Oure Lord ne of Oure Lady the leeste that evere was maked.   *composed*
I have maad avowes fourty, and foryete hem on morwe;

vows; forgotten

I parfournede nevere penaunce as the preest me highte,   *carried out*
400 Ne right sory for my synnes [sithenes] was I nevere.   *afterwards*
And if I bidde any bedes, but if it be in wrathe,   *say; prayers; unless*
That I telle with my tonge is two myle fro myn herte.   *say; miles*
I am ocupied ech a day, halyday and oother,
With ydel tales at the ale and outherwhile in chirches;

gossip; other times

389–90 If I were put to bed, unless (the needs of) my bowels caused it The
    ringing (of no church bells) would make me get up until I were ready to eat.
394 Even if I should die, (by) this day, I have no wish to open my eyes (C).
400 And I say still further – I was never even genuinely sorry for my sins! (C).

383   þe] LBRZ?A?C; *om* W&r.   W&r (þe *erased* M).
386   slymed] αC; slymy β.   400   sithenes] yet W&r; yet soþly F
388   stool] αHmG?CK–D; a stool ?β   (C).
    (a] mi Cr).   403   ech a] Hm?αC; eche W&r;
394   quod he] α?C; *om* β.   euery CrF.
398   morwe] OCBαC; þe morwe   404   cherches] L&rC; *sg* WHmCr¹α.

05 Goddes peyne and his passion, [pure] selde thenke I thereon;   *very*
   'I visited nevere feble men ne fettred folk in puttes;   *sick; prisons*
I hadde levere here an harlotrye or a somer game of souters,

obscene story

Or lesynges to laughen of and bilye my neghebores,   *tell lies (against)*
Than al that evere Marc made, Mathew, Johan and Lucas.   *wrote*
10 And vigilies and fastyng dayes – alle thise I late;   *vigils; neglect*
And ligge abedde in Lenten and my lemman in myne armes

lie with; lover

Til matyns and masse be do, and thanne [mengen I of] the Freres;

remember

Come I to *Ite, missa est* I holde me yserved.   *i.e. at; satisfied*
I am noght shryven som tyme, but if siknesse it make,   *unless; cause*
15 Noght twyes in two yer, and thanne [telle I up gesse].   *without thinking*
   'I have be preest and person passynge thritty wynter,   *more than*
Yet kan I neyther solve ne synge ne seintes lyves rede,

'sol-fa', sing by note

But I kan fynden in a feld or in a furlang an hare   *ten-acre area*
Bettre than in *Beatus vir* or in *Beati omnes*   *the Psalms*
20 Construe clausemele and kenne it to my parisshens.   *clause by clause*
I kan holde lovedayes and here a reves rekenyng,   *settlement-days*
Ac in Canoun ne in the Decretals I kan noght rede a lyne.   *canon law*

---

407 I prefer to hear a bawdy tale or a shoemakers' summer game [a play?].
413 If I turn up at (the priest's words of dismissal), 'Go, mass is finished', I
    consider that I have fulfilled my obligations satisfactorily.
419–20 Better than I can interpret the clauses that make up (the psalms)
    'Blessed is the man' (Ps 1 *or* Ps 111) and 'Blessed are all they . . .' (Ps 127)
    and teach (their meaning) to my parishioners (C).

405 pure] *cj* K–D (*cf.* C); ful W&r;
    om G (C).
   þereon] L&r (*om* F); on OC²C; on
    it WM (it) +M).
406 feble] βC; seke α.
    folk]W&r; men HmGMC(man).
    puttes] βR; prisoun FC.
407 hadde] αC; haue β.
408 lesynges] L&r; lesynge W.
    of] α (*cf.* C)K–D; at β.
409 Than] βC; & F; *om* R.
410 And] W&r; *om* MC.
    I late] ?α (y leet hem F); late I passe
    β.

412 mengen I of] haue I a memorie
    at C; go to W&r; y muste to F (C).
414 am] Hm&rCK–D; nam
    WOCBLM.
415 telle . . . gesse] *cj* K–D (*cf.* C);
    vp gesse shryue me βR; me þynkþ
    to sone F (C).
417 ȝete] L&rC; And yet WF.
420 clausemele] *cj* K–D; it
    clausemel α; oon clause wel β (C).
421 and] β; or α.
422 ne] L&r (*l. om* CB); *nor* ?w (or
    Cr¹; and Cr²³).
    þe] GLMR; *om* W&r.

'If I bigge and borwe aught, but if it be ytailed,   *buy; recorded*
I foryete it as yerne, and yif men me it axe   *quickly; ask for*
425 Sixe sithes or sevene, I forsake it with othes;   *times; deny (the debt)*
And thus tene I trewe men ten hundred tymes.   *injure; honest*
And my servaunts som tyme, hir salarie is bihynde: *overdue*
Ruthe is to here rekenyng whan we shal rede acountes,   *Pitiful*
So with wikked wil and wrathe my werkmen I paye!   *such ill-will*
430   'If any man dooth me a bienfait or helpeth me at nede,   *good turn*
I am unkynde ayeins his curteisie and kan nought understonden it;
                                                           in return for
For I have and have had somdel haukes maneres—
                                                           somewhat hawklike
I am noght lured with love but ther ligge aught under the thombe. *lie*
The kyndenesse that myn evenecristene kidde me fernyere
                                                           showed; in times past
435 Sixty sithes I, Sleuthe, have foryete it siththe   *since*
In speche and in sparynge of speche; yspilt many a tyme
                                                           failure; wasted
Bothe flessh and fissh and manye othere vitailles,   *foodstuffs*
Bothe bred and ale, buttre, melk and chese   *milk; cheese*
Forsleuthed in my service til it myghte serve no man.
                                                           Spoilt for lack of use
440 I [yarn] aboute in youthe, and yaf me naught to lerne   *ran; dedicated*
And evere sitthe [beggere be be] my foule sleuthe: *through; sloth*
Heu michi quod sterilem vitam duxi iuvenilem!'

423–5 If I buy (anything), and borrow any money, unless it is scored upon a
   tally-stick (to record the loan), I forget it as soon (as I have obtained the
   sum), and if I am asked (to repay) . . . I deny the existence of the loan with
   oaths.
436 In what I said and in what I failed to say.
441a Alas what a fruitless life I have led! (proverbial); cf. I 141a above.

423 auȝt] wGC; it L&r; *om* F.
424 ȝif] HmLR?C; if W&r; *om* M.
426 tene I] ?W&r; *trs* αB.
428 is] L&rC; it is WB.
  here] LMα?C; here þe wg.
430 dooþ] W&r; do CrgC.
  helpeþ] W&rC; helpe Crg.
431 his] L&r (†F)C; þis Bm; *om* W.
433 lured] wBLMαC; lered ?g.
  þe] β?C; *om* α.

435 siþes] βF?C; sithe R.
437 manye] β; myn R; fele F.
438 Bothe] L&r; Boþ W; As F.
440 yarn] *cj K–D*; ran *All MSS* (C).
441 beggere be] be beggere LRK–D;
  haue I be b. W&r (haue I] *trs* GB;
  haue] +M; I] *om* CrY); I am þe F
  (C).
  be²] for W&r; þorghȝ F (C).
441a quod] αBoCotC; quia β.

'Repentest the noght?' quod Repentaunce – and right with that
he swowned,   *(Sloth) fainted*
Til *Vigilate* the veille fette water at hise eighen   *'Keep-watch Wakeful'*
And flatte it on his face and faste on hym cryde   *dashed; earnestly*
445 And seide, 'Ware thee fro Wanhope, wolde thee bitraye.
                                    Guard against; Despair
"I am sory for my synnes", seye to thiselve,
And beet thiself on the brest, and bidde Hym of grace,   *beat; ask*
For is no gilt here so gret that His goodnesse is moore.'   *is not greater*
   Thanne sat Sleuthe up and seyned hym swithe,   *crossed himself often*
450 And made avow tofore God for his foule sleuthe: *before*
'Shal no Sonday be this seven yer, but siknesse it [make],
That I ne shal do me er day to the deere chirche   *betake myself*
And here matyns and masse as I a monk were.
Shal noon ale after mete holde me thennes   *food; keep; from there*
455 Til I have evensong herd – I bihote to the Roode!   *promise*
And yet [what I nam] wole I yelde ayein, if I so muche have—
                                    further; took; give back
Al that I wikkedly wan sithen I wit hadde;   *obtained; reason*
And though my liflode lakke, leten I nelle   *sustenance; give up*
That ech man shal have his er I hennes wende;   *go hence (i.e. die)*
460 And with the residue and the remenaunt, bi the Rode of Chestre,
I shal seken truthe erst er I see Rome!'   *first before*
   Roberd the robbere on *Reddite* loked,   *'Give back' (C)*
And for ther was noght wher[with], he wepte swithe soore.
And yet the synfulle sherewe seide to hymselve:
465 'Crist, that on Calvarie upon the cros deidest,

---

442 Repentest] αC; Repentestow ?β
   (-estow] -edestow WHmY).
   þe] BLMαC; *om* W&r.
445 fram] L&r?C; for WCrYOC².
446 to] w?g (þou to B)ZAC; so to
   LMα.
448 is²] Hm&rCK–D; nys WLM.
451 but] W&r (*l. om* F)?C; but ȝif
   HmMR.
   it make] *so* ACK–D; it lette W&r

456 And ... I²] And yet wole I β;
   what I nam ?α (& what y have take
   to F) (C).
459 man]
   HmGOC²BoCotαZAK–D;
   man ne W&r.
461 erst] W&r; *om* HmA; tryst F.
463 -with] *so* AZCK–D; -of *All
   MSS.*

(it] me R).

Tho Dysmas my brother bisoughte thee of grace,   *At that time; begged*
And haddest mercy on that man for *Memento* sake,   *you had*
So rewe on this Rober[d] that *Reddere* ne have,

                                                                        pity; means to restore (C)
Ne nevere wene to wynne with craft that I knowe;   *expect; earn; skill*
470 But for thi muchel mercy mitigacion I biseche: *great; compassion*
Dampne me noght at Domesday for that I dide so ille!'   *Damn*
        What bifel of this feloun I kan noght faire shewe.   *properly*
Wel I woot he wepte faste water with hise eighen,
And knoweliched his [coupe] to Crist yet eftsoones,   *guilt; again*
475 That *Penitencia* his pik he sholde polshe newe   *pikestaff; polish afresh*
And lepe with hym over lond al his lif tyme,   *go with it*
For he hadde leyen by *Latro*, Luciferis Aunte.   *Robber(y)*

        And thanne hadde Repentaunce ruthe and redde hem alle to knele.

                                                                        instructed
'For I shal biseche for alle synfulle Oure Saveour of grace   *for grace*
480 To amenden us of oure mysdedes and do mercy to us alle.
Now God,' quod he, 'that of Thi goodnesse gonne the world make,
And of naught madest aught and man moost lik to Thiselve,

                                                                        everything
And sithen suffredest hym to synne, a siknesse to us alle—   *permitted*
And al for the beste, as I bileve, whatevere the Book telleth:

                                                                        Bible; 'the authorities' (Bn)
O *felix culpa! O necessarium peccatum Ade!*

---

467 . . . for (his words to you, 'Lord), remember [me when thou shalt come
    into thy kingdom'] (Lk 23: 42) (C).
484a O happy fault! O necessary sin of Adam! (*Exultet*, from the liturgy of
    Easter Saturday; see *Bn ad loc.*).

466 Dysmas] β (*l. om* B)FZAC;   473 his] CrGFZACK–D; boþe hise
    bysmas R (C).   W&r.
    the] Hm(*over erasure*)AC?ZK–D;   474 coupe] *so* Z?ACK–D; gilt β; *l.*
    yow W&r; crist F.   *om* α.
468 þis] βRA; me Hm(*over eras-   477 hadde] βAC; hath ?α (*om* F).
    ure*)FZC.   481 þat . . . gonne] L&r (þat;
    Roberd] Robert ZAC; Robbere *All*   gonne] *om*; þat gonne yF (þ.] þou
    MSS (C).   F); g.] bigonne W; coud Cr[1]).
469 knowe] αCrZAC; owe ?β (sewe   483 hym] αCK–D; for β (*om*
    G; vse Hm).   HmG).
471 Dampne] *so* ACK–D; Ne   484a Ade] αCr[23]GC; Ade *&c* ?β
    dampne W&r (*l. om* F).   (*&c* Cr[1]).

485 For thorugh that synne Thi sone sent was to this erthe
And bicam man of a maide mankynde to save—
And madest Thiself with Thi sone us synfulle yliche: *through; like*
Faciamus hominem ad imaginem et similitudinem nostram; Et alibi,
Qui manet in caritate, in Deo manet, et Deus in eo;
And siththe with Thi selve sone in oure sute deidest   *through; guise*
On Good Fryday for mannes sake at ful tyme of the day;   *noon (C)*
490 Ther Thiself ne Thi sone no sorwe in deeth feledest,   *felt*
But in oure secte was that sorwe, and Thi sone it ladde: *bore away*
Captivam duxit captivitatem.
The sonne for sorwe therof lees sight for a tyme   *became sightless*
Aboute myddday whan moost light is and meel-tyme of seintes—
Feddest tho with Thi fresshe blood oure forefadres in derknesse:
     You fed at that time
Populus qui ambulabat in tenebris vidit lucem magnam.
495 And the light that lepe out of Thee, Lucifer it blente,   *leapt; blinded*
And blewe alle Thi blessed thennes into the blisse of Paradys!
  'The thridde day [ther]after Thow yedest in oure sute:
     went; (human) form
A synful Marie The seigh er Seynte Marie Thi dame,   *saw; mother*
And al to solace synfulle Thow suffredest it so were—
     comfort; allowed that
Non veni vocare iustos set peccatores ad penitenciam.

487a Let us make man to our image and likeness (Gen 1: 26); And elsewhere,
  he that abideth in charity abideth in God, and God in him (I Jn 4: 16) (C).
488 And then through the person of your Son himself died in our (human)
  form.
491a [Ascending on high], he led captivity captive (Eph 4: 8) (C).
494a The people that walked in darkness have seen a great light (Is 9: 2) (C).
499a I came not to call the just, but sinners to penance (Lk 5: 32) (C).

485 þis] W&r; the CrGM; *om* FC.
487 vs] *cj* K–D; and vs *All MSS*
  (C).
488 þi] βF; þe R.
  sute] L&r; secte W (*cf.* C) (C).
491 þat] α; þe β.
492 siȝte] L&r; liȝt WCrYOC²M(l
  alt. from s) (C).
494 þo] RF (?=α)C; *om* β.
  fresshe] W&r?C;

flessche & GB.
495 And] And þoruȝ W&r; And by
  Cr (C).
  it blent] ?α (it) *om* F)C; was blent
  β.
496 þennes] α (þ. boldly F)C; *om* β.
497 þeraftur] *so* CK–D; after W&r;
  a. ȝit F (C).

500   'And al that Marc hath ymaad, Mathew, Johan and Lucas
                                                         set down

Of Thyne doughtiest dedes were doon in oure armes: *arms, form (C)*
Verbum caro factum est et habitavit in nobis.
And by so muche it semeth the sikerer we mowe   *more surely; can*
Bidde and biseche, if it be Thi wille   *Pray*
That art oure fader and oure brother – be merciable to us, *merciful*
505   And have ruthe on thise ribaudes that repenten hem soore

                                                   sinners; earnestly

That evere thei wrathed Thee in this world, in word, thought or
       dede!'

Thanne hente Hope an horn of *Deus tu conversus vivificabis nos*
                                                         seized

And blew it with *Beati quorum remisse sunt iniquitates,*
That alle Seintes in hevene songen at ones
'*Homines et iumenta salvabis, quemadmodum multiplicasti
misericordiam tuam, Deus!*'
510   A thousand of men tho thrungen togideres,   *thronged*
Cride upward to Crist and to his clene moder   *Cried; pure*
To have grace to go [to] Truthe – [God leve that they moten!]

                                                     grant; might

Ac there was wight noon so wys, the wey thider kouthe, *(who) knew*
But blustreden forth as beestes over ba[ch]es and hilles,

                                                   strayed; valleys

---

501*a* And the Word was made flesh, and dwelt among us (Jn 1: 14).
507 O God, you will turn and bring us back to life (from the mass, after Ps 70:
     20) (C).
508 Blessed are they whose iniquities are forgiven (Ps 31: 1).
509*a* Men and beasts thou wilt preserve, O Lord: How hast thou multiplied
     thy mercy, O God! (Ps 35: 7–8).

501   douȝtiest] LMαC; douȝty wg.
      were] L&r (þat w. B); was WC.
502   it] αCK–D; me β.
505   ruþe] βC; mercy α.
      sore] αGCotCK–D; here soore ?β
      (h.] so M; selfs Cr).
506   dede] Hm&rC; dedes WLR.
507   *nos*] αCrGCSk; *om* ?β.

509*a* *deus*] WCrYαC; *deus &c*
      L&r.
512   To . . . go] βC (*cf.* ZA); Grace
      to god R; To graunte swich gr. to
      go F.
      to³] *so* CK–D; wiþ hem βR; *om* F.
      God . . . mote] *so* ZACK–D; to
      seke *All MSS* (C).
514   baches] *so* Z?ACK–D; bankes
      W&r; balkys F (C).

515 Til late was and longe, that thei a leode mette   *man*
　　Apparailled as a paynym in pilgrymes wise.

　　　　　　　　　　　　　　　　　　　　　'outlandishly', like a Saracen

　　He bar a burdoun ybounde with a brood liste   *staff; strip of cloth*
　　In a withwynde wise ywounden aboute.   *woodbine-fashion*
　　A bolle and a bagge he bar by his syde.   *bowl*
520 An hundred of ampulles on his hat seten,   *phials; sat*
　　Signes of Syse and shelles of Galice,   *Emblems of Assisi (C)*
　　And many a crouch on his cloke, and keyes of Rome,   *cross-ornament*
　　And the vernicle bifore, for men sholde knowe   *in front; so that*
　　And se bi hise signes whom he sought hadde.

525 　　This folk frayned hym first fro whennes he come.   *inquired of*
　　'Fram Synay,' he seide, 'and fram [the] sepulcre.   *Sinai*
　　In Bethlem and in Babiloyne, I have ben in bothe,   *Babylon (C)*
　　In Armonye, in Alisaundre, in manye othere places.

　　　　　　　　　　　　　　　　　　　Armenia; Alexandria (C)

　　Ye may se by my signes that sitten on myn hatte
530 That I have walked ful wide in weet and in drye   *wet*
　　And sought goode seintes for my soule helthe.   *soul's*
　　　'Knowestow aught a corsaint,' [quod thei], 'that men calle Truthe?

　　　　　　　　　　　　　　　　　　　　　　　(saint's) shrine

　　Koudestow wissen us the wey wher that wye dwelleth?'

　　　　　　　　　　　　　　　　　　　　　　　direct; person

　　　'Nay, so me God helpe!' seide the gome thanne.   *man*
535 'I seigh nevere palmere with pyk ne with scrippe   *pilgrim; pike staff*
　　Asken after hym er now in this place.'
　　　'Peter!' quod a Plowman, and putte forth his heved,
　　'I knowe hym as kyndely as clerc doth hise bokes.   *intimately; scholar*
　　Conscience and Kynde Wit kenned me to his place   *directed*

---

519 bolle] βZAC; bulle α.
521 Syse] ?α (asise R; seyntys F) ZAC; Synay β.
522 a] W&r(+M)ZAC; *om* YCR. keyes] βZAC; þe cayes α.
526 Synay] βRZAC; þe sepulcre F. þe sepulcre] *so* A?CK–D; oure lordes sepulcre βR; synay hyȝe hilles F (C).
528 in²] W&rZAC; and in R; and Cr.
531 soule] HmGCotMαACK–D; soules W&r.

532 quod they] *so* CAK–D; *om All MSSZ*(C).
533 wissen] gFZACK–D; auȝt wissen W&r (a.] not Cr). wher] βF?A (*cf.* C); þere RZ. wye] ?wLMFZA; wyȝte RCr¹³; he g.
536 er] yZA?CK–D; er til wGLR; til MF.
537 heued] *so* CZ?A; hed W&r; face F.

540 And diden me suren hym [siththen] sikerly to serven hym for evere,
                                                              give my word

Bothe to sowe and to sette the while I swynke myghte.   *plant; toil*
I have ben his folwere al this fourty wynter—   *follower*
Bothe ysowen his seed and suwed hise beestes,   *followed, tended*
Withinne and withouten waited his profit.   *looked to, after*
545 I dyke and I delve, I do that he hoteth.   *ditch; dig; orders*
Som tyme I sowe and som tyme I thresshe,
In taillours craft, in tynkeris craft, what Truthe kan devyse,
I weve and I wynde and do what Truthe hoteth.   *weave; wind (yarn)*
For though I seye it myself, I serve hym to paye;   *to (his) satisfaction*
550 I have myn hire of hym wel and outherwhiles moore.   *pay; from him*
He is the presteste paiere that povere men knoweth:

                                                           promptest paymaster
He withhalt noon hewe his hire that he ne hath it at even.

                                                           withholds from; workman
He is as lowe as a lomb and lovelich of speche.   *humble; loving*
And if ye wilneth to wite where that he dwelleth,   *desire to know*
555 I shal wisse yow [the wey wel right] to his place.'   *direct; straight*
     'Ye, leve Piers!' quod thise pilgrimes, and profred hym huyre.

                                                           dear; payment
     'Nay, by [the peril of] my soule!' quod Piers and gan to swere,
'I nolde fange a ferthyng, for Seint Thomas shryne!   *accept; by*
Truthe wolde love me the lasse a long tyme after.
560 Ac if ye wilneth to wende wel, this is the wey thider: *journey aright*
Ye moten go thorugh Mekenesse, bothe men and wyves,   *must*

---

540 hym¹] βC; hem α.
    siththen] *om All MSS; cf.* ZAC (C).
542 fourty] LMαZAC; fifty wg.
545 I¹ . . . do] W&r (I³] and
    CrGOC²B); & boþe diggid and
    deluyd & dyde F.
    he] αZAK–D; truþe β.
547 in²] ?α (*l. om* F); and β.
550 of hym] αZAC; *om* β.
552 he¹] gαZACK–D; He ne wLM.
    hewe] ?β (hyne HmGBoCot; helk
    Cr) Z?AC; men ?α (man F).
    his] βFZAC; hire CotR.
    he; haþ; at euen] βZA; þei; haue;
    anone α (a.] soone F).

555 þe wey wel riȝt] *so* Z; witterly
    þe wey *All MSS* (þe] the hye Cr)
    (C).
556 *After this a line:* For to wende
    wiþ hem to truþes dwellyng place
    W&r (to . . . place] þere tr. gan
    dwelle F); *rej. as spurious* K–D (C).
557 þe . . . soule] *so* ACZK–D; þe
    soule perel R (?=α); my soules
    helþe wGLM; my soule yF.
    to] *so* ACK–D; for to W&r; *om* F.
559 after] g MFZACK–D; þerafter
    wLR.
560 ȝe] L&rZA; yow WCr¹.

Til ye come into Conscience, that Crist wite the sothe,
'*that C. may know the truth*' (Bn)

That ye loven Oure Lord God levest of alle thynges,   *most dearly*
And thanne youre neghebores next in none wise apeire   *no way harm*
565 Otherwise than thow woldest h[ii] wroughte to thiselve.
they did, acted towards

'And so boweth forth by a brook, "Beth-buxom-of-speche",
proceed; mild

[Forto] ye fynden a ford, "Youre-fadres-honoureth":   *Till; honour*
Honora patrem et matrem.

Wadeth in that water and wassheth yow wel there,
And ye shul lepe the lightloker al youre lif tyme.   *run; more nimbly*
570 And so shaltow se "Swere-noght-but-if-it-be-for-nede-
And-nameliche-on-ydel-the-name-of-God-almyghty."
particularly; in vain

'Thanne shaltow come by a croft, but come thow noght therinne:
field

The croft hatte "Coveite-noght-mennes-catel-ne-hire-wyves- *is called*
Ne-noon-of-hire-servaunts-that-noyen-hem-myghte."
(so as) to trouble

575 Loke thow breke no bowes there but if it be [thyn] owene.   *boughs*
'Two stokkes ther stondeth, ac stynte [thow] noght there:
stumps; pause

Thei highte "Stele-noght" and "Sle-noght" – strik forth by bothe,
Slay; press on

And leve hem on thi lift half and loke noght therafter,   *left hand side*
And hold wel thyn haliday heighe til even.   *observe; holy day(s)*
580 'Thanne shaltow blenche at a bergh, "Bere-no-fals-witnesse",
turn aside; hill

---

579 Observe your holy days properly till the late evening (of them).

562 into] w LMRZAC; to gF.

565 hii] they C; a Z; he *All MSS* (be G); men Ax (C).

566 of] βA; of þi α.

567 Forto] *so* ZACK–D; Til *All MSS* (C).

567a matrem] αC; matrem &c β.

568 wascheth] LHmBmBoRAC; wasshe W&rZ.
þere] L&rZAC; þerInne WFM (I.] +M).

572 þow] W&r ZAC; *om* g.

573 þe] αGZACK–D; That β.
catel] βZAC; maydins F; *om* R.

575 þow] ?α (*l.*†F)CotACK–D; ye β.
be] β (*om* Bm); be on R.
thyn] *so* ZACK–D; youre βR.

576 þow] *so* ZACK–D; þe C; ye W&r (*om* Cot).

578 half] W&r?A; hende CrFZC.

Is frythed in with floryns and othere fees manye: *hedged; payments*
Loke thow plukke no plaunte there, for peril of thi soule.
'Thanne shalt thow see "Seye-sooth-so-it-be-to-doone-
In-no-manere-ellis-noght-for-no-mannes-biddyng."
585 'Thanne shaltow come to a court as cler as the sonne.

                                                          castle; bright
The moot is of Mercy the manoir aboute,   *moat*
And alle the walles ben of Wit to holden Wil oute,   *Wisdom*
[The kerneles ben of] Cristendom that kynde to save,

                                     battlements; (human) nature
Botrased with "Bileef-so-or-thow-beest-noght-saved."

                                              Buttressed; Believe
590 And alle the houses ben hiled, halles and chambres,   *covered*
With no leed but with love and lowe speche, as bretheren [of o
     wombe].   *lead; gentle; one*
The brugge is of "Bidde-wel-the-bet-may-thow-spede;"

                                        (draw)bridge; Pray; prosper
Ech piler is of penaunce, of preieres to seyntes;   *pillar*
Of almesdedes are the hokes that the gates hangen on.   *hooks*
595 'Grace hatte the gateward, a good man for sothe;   *porter*
His man hatte "Amende-yow" – many man hym knoweth.
Telleth hym this tokene: "Truthe w[oot] the sothe—   *sign; knows*
I parfourned the penaunce that the preest me enjoyned   *carried out*
And am ful sory of my synnes and so I shal evere
600 Whan I thynke theron, theigh I were a pope."
'Biddeth Amende-yow meke hym to his maister ones

                                              humbly approach
To wayven up the wiket that the womman shette   *open; wicket; shut*

---

581 is] ?α (It is F)ZC; He is β?Ax.
582 þow] βACZ; ȝe α.
     þi soule] β; ȝoure soules ?α (†F).
583 shall þou] GZAC*K–D*; shul ye
     W&r; *l.* om F.
584 no[1]] L&r (*l.* om F); good W.
588 The . . . of] *so* ZAC*K–D*; And
     kerneled wiþ *All MSS.*
     þat] ?αAC*K–D*; man βF.
591 of o wombe] *so* A (*cf.* C) *K–D*;
     om All MSS (C).

592 brugge] L&r; brugg W.
596 many] αZ?AC; for many β.
     man] LMαZAC; men wg.
597 trewþe] F (?=α)ZAC*K–D*; in þat
     truþe βR.
     wot] *so* ZAC*K–D*; wite βR;
     knowith F (C).
599 ful] βRZ; *om* FAC.
     of] βZ?C; for βA.
601 to] GYOC²MαZAC; til w
     CBLM.

Tho Adam and Eve eten apples unrosted:
Per Evam cunctis clausa est et per Mariam virginem iterum
patefacta est;
For he hath the keye and the cliket, though the kyng slepe.   *latch-key*
605   And if Grace graunte thee to go in in this wise
Thow shalt see in thiselve Truthe sitte in thyn herte
In a cheyne of charite, as thow a child were,   *chain*
To suffren hym and segge noght ayein thi sires wille.

Suffering; against; father's

'Ac be war thanne of Wrathe-thee, that wikked sherewe:

'Get-angry'

610   [For] he hath envye to hym that in thyn herte sitteth,   *enmity towards*
And poketh forth pride to preise thiselven.   *praise*
The boldnesse of thi bienfetes maketh thee blynd thanne   *good deeds*
And [so] worstow dryven out as dew, and the dore closed,   *you'll be*
Keyed and cliketted to kepe thee withouten   *outside*
615   Happily an hundred wynter er thow eft entre!   *Perhaps; again*
Thus myght thow lesen his love, to lete wel by thiselve,

by thinking well of

And [gete it ayein thorugh] grace, [ac thorugh no gifte ellis].
'Ac ther are seven sustren that serven Truthe evere   *sisters*
And arn porters over the posternes that to the place longeth.

side-doors; belong

603*a* Through Eve (the gate of paradise) was closed to all and through the
Virgin Mary it was made open once again (From the Lauds Antiphon of the
BVM said in the Monday of the week within the Octave of Easter to the Vigil
of the Ascension (*Bn, q.v.*)).

603*a* *cunctis*] Hm&r (*l.* om Y)*Sk*;
  cuntis WGOC²LF.
  iterum] α*CSk*; om β.
  patefacta est] βC; *&c* α.
605   in¹] LMAC; om W&r (*l.* om F).
606   *sitte*] L&rZAC; om
  WHmCr¹G.
608   no3t] βF; om R.
609   Ac] L&r (But F)ZAC; And
  WCrC²C; om G.
  þee] WHmGLα; the nat Z?A; om
  CryMC (C).
  that] *so* ZACK–D; þat is a W&r;

he is a F.
610   For] *so* ZACK–D; om *All MSS.*
611   Forþ] βZAC; om α.
613   so] *so* ZACK–D; þanne W&r;
  om OC²F.
616   myght thow] L&rZAC;
  my3testow wGOC².
617   geten . . . elles] *so* ZACK–D;
  neuere happily eft entre but grace
  þow haue *All MSS* (C).
618   Ac] L&r (but GF)A?C; and
  WCrC²C.
619   ouer] ?α(at F)C; of β(to Cr²³)A.

620 That oon hatte Abstinence, and Umblete another;

one is called; Humility

Charite and Chastite ben hise chief maydenes;
Pacience and Pees, muche peple thei helpeth;
Largenesse the lady, she let in ful manye—   *Generosity; lets*
Heo hath holpe a thousand out of the develes punfolde.   *pinfold*
625 And who is sib to thise sevene, so me God helpe,   *related to*
He is wonderly welcome and faire underfongen. *marvellously; received*
And but if ye be sibbe to some of thise sevene,
It is ful hard, by myn heed, any of yow alle
To geten ingong at any gate but grace be the moore!'   *entrance; unless*
630   'Now, by Crist!' quod a kuttepurs, 'I have no kyn there.'   *cutpurse*
'Ne I,' quod an apeward, 'by aught that I knowe.'   *ape-keeper*
'Wite God,' quod a wafrestere, 'wiste I this for sothe,   *wafer-seller*
Sholde I never ferther a foot for no freres prechyng.'   *(go) further*
'Yis,' quod Piers the Plowman, and poked hem alle to goode,

urged

635 'Mercy is a maiden there, hath myght over hem alle;   *who has power*
And she is sib to alle synfulle, and hire sone also,   *kins(woman)*
And thorugh the help of hem two – hope thow noon oother—

expect nothing else

Thow myght gete grace there – so thow go bityme.'   *provided; early*
'Bi Seint Poul!' quod a pardoner, 'paraventure I be noght knowe there;

perhaps I shan't be known

640 I wol go fecche my box with my brevettes and a bulle with bisshopes lettres.'

indulgences

'By Crist!' quod a commune womman, 'thi compaignie wol I folwe.

prostitute

Thow shalt seye I am thi suster.' I ne woot where thei bicome.

they went

---

620   vmblete] ?α?C; humilite βFA.
625   who] W&rC; whoso Hmy?A; she F.
627   if] ?β?A; if þat R; *om* CrMF.
628   any] *so* ACK–D; for any GF; quod Piers for any W&r (C).
629   ingonge] L&rAC; ingoing WC²B; in passage F.

631   Ne] LMC²αAC; Nor wg. I²] L&rAC; I kan wY.
632   for] βAC; þe F; *om* R.
634   alle] W&rC; *om* GFA.
635   hem] LMCrαAC; *om* WHmg.
638   so] WGAC; bi so L&r.
639   knowe þere] β; welcome α.

Passus VI

'This were a wikkede wey but whoso hadde a gyde
very difficult; unless one
That [myghte] folwen us ech a foot' — thus this folk hem mened.
complained

Quod Perkyn the Plowman, 'By Seint Peter of Rome!
I have an half acre to erie by the heighe weye;
plough; near
5 Hadde I eryed this half acre and sowen it after,
sown
I wolde wende with yow and the wey teche.'
   'This were a long lettyng,' quod a lady in a scleyre;
delay; veil (C)
'What sholde we wommen werche the while?'
do meanwhile
   'Somme shul sowe the sak,' quod Piers, 'for shedyng of the whete;
to prevent; falling through
10 And ye lovely ladies with youre longe fyngres,
That ye have silk and sandel to sowe whan tyme is
(See) that; cendal (C)
Chesibles for chapeleyns chirches to honoure.
Chasubles; priests
Wyves and widewes, wolle and flex spynneth:
flax; spin
Maketh cloth, I counseille yow, and kenneth so youre doughtres.
15 The nedy and the naked, nymeth hede how thei liggeth,
take
And casteth hem clothes, for so comaundeth Truthe.
make
For I shal lenen hem liflode, but if the lond faille,
provide
As longe as I lyve, for the Lordes love of hevene.
Lord of heaven's love
And alle manere of men that thorugh mete and drynke libbeth,
live

---

1 This would be a very difficult journey for anyone who did not have a guide.
15 . . . take heed of the conditions in which they live.

Collation WHmCrGYOC²CBLMRF.
RUBRIC *Passus sextus de visione vt supra* W&r (*de v.*] *de v. petri le ploughman* Cot; *om* O); *om* GBm C²F.
2 myght] *so* ZACK–D; wolde *All MSS.*
6 wolde] W&rAC; wol YCLR.
8 þe] W&r (*l. om* CB)ZAC; þere

LMα; *to* G; *in the meane* Cr.
9 quod Piers] W&r (P.] he G) (*cf.* C); *om* MZA.
17 *After this a line:* Flessh and breed boþe to riche and to poore *All MSS*; *om* ZAC; *rej. as spurious* K–D (C).
19 þoruȝ] W&r; *with* F; *by* HmZAC.

20 Helpeth hym to werche wightliche that wynneth youre foode.'
vigorously

'By Crist!' quod a knyght thoo, 'he kenneth us the beste;
Ac on the teme, trewely, taught was I nevere. *plough-team (?theme)*
Ac kenne me,' quod the knyght, 'and by Crist I wole assaye!' *try*
'By Seint Poul!' quod Perkyn, 'ye profre yow so faire *graciously*
25 That I shal swynke and swete and sowe for us bothe, *toil*
And othere labours do for thi love al my lif tyme, *for love of you*
In covenaunt that thow kepe Holy Kirke and myselve *condition*
Fro wastours and fro wikked men that this world destruyeth;
And go hunte hardiliche to hares and to foxes, *boldly after*
30 To bores and to bukkes that breken down myne hegges, *boars; deer*
And go affaite thi faucons wilde foweles to kille, *train; falcons*
For swiche cometh to my croft and croppeth my whete.' *such (birds)*
Curteisly the knyght thanne co[nseyved] thise wordes: *uttered (C)*
'By my power, Piers, I plighte thee my trouthe *pledge; solemn word*
35 To fulfille this forward, though I fighte sholde; *agreement; have to*
Als longe as I lyve I shal thee mayntene.' *support*
'Ye, and yet a point,' quod Piers, 'I preye yow of moore:
one more thing
Loke ye tene no tenaunt but Truthe wole assente; *trouble; unless*
And though ye mowe amercy men, lat mercy be taxour *fine; assessor*
40 And mekenesse thi maister, maugree Medes chekes. *in despite of M.*
And though povere men profre yow presentes and yiftes,
Nyme it noght, an aventure thow mowe it noght deserve; *in case*
For thow shalt yelde it ayein at one yeres ende *give it back*

38–40 Take care that you trouble no tenant (of yours) unless you have a just
cause for doing so/Truth agrees (to your course of action); And even when
you are fully justified in fining them, let mercy assess the amount (you exact)
and gentle moderation be your governing principle, in spite of desire for gain.

23 Ac] L&r; But WGF; And
CrC²C.
by crist] W&rZ (*cf.* C); *om* ?g
(*cropped* G)?Ax.
26 labours] β; laboreres αHm.
28 fro²] W&r?AC; *om* γMZ.
30 bukkes] ?α (boores F) ACZ;
brokkes β.
31 go] L&r; so W.
32 swiche] βR; þei FC; these Z?A.
33 conseyued] *so* ?A?CK–D;
comsed *All* MSSZ, *most* C-MSS

(C).
34 I] *so* ZACK–D; quod he I *All*
MSS.
35 þis] βFZA; þi R.
37 ʒow] βRC; þe FZA (C).
38 ye] βRC; þou FZA.
39 men] α (*cf.* C); hem β (*om* CB).
40 þi] β (þe CB)FC; ʒoure R.
41 yow] βRZC; þe FA.
42 þow] αZACK–D; ye β.
43 ende] L&rZA; tyme W.

In a ful perilous place – Purgatorie it hatte.   *is called*
45   And mysbede noght thi bondeman – the bettre may thow spede;
                                                    injure; prosper

Though he be thyn underlyng here, wel may happe in hevene
                                                    inferior; happen

That he worth worthier set and with moore blisse: *placed higher*
Amice, ascende superius.   *Friend, go up higher* (Lk 14: 10)
For in a charnel at chirche cherles ben yvel to knowe,   *hard; make out*
Or a knyght from a knave there – knowe this in thyn herte.
                                                    serving-lad

50   And that thow be trewe of thi tonge, and tales that thow hatie,   *hate*
But if thei ben of wisdom or of wit, thi werkmen to chaste.   *correct*
Hold noght with none harlotes ne here noght hir tales,
                                            associate; vulgar buffoons

And namely at the mete swiche men eschuwe—   *especially; avoid*
For it ben the develes disours, I do the to understonde.'
                                            they are; story-tellers; I'd have you

55   'I assente, by Seint Jame,' seide the knyght thanne,   *agree*
'For to werche by thi wordes the while my lif dureth.'   *lasts*

'And I shal apparaille me,' quod Perkyn, 'in pilgrymes wise *clothe*
And wende with yow I wile til we fynde Truthe.'
[He] caste on [hise] clothes, yclouted and hole,   *patched; whole*
60   [Hise] cokeres and [hise] coffes for cold of [hise] nailes,
                                                    leggings; mittens

---

47–8a That he will be seated in a more honourable position and (invested)
   with greater glory: 'Friend, go up higher' (Lk 14: 10). For in the
   charnel-house (beneath) the church, (the bones of peasants) are hard to
   distinguish [*sc.* from those of nobles] (C).
51 Unless they contain some moral lesson with which to correct your
   labourers.
52 Do not patronize tellers of obscene stories . . .

45   And] W&rA; Ne F; *om* yZC.   þat²] wBLMαZ; *om* ?gA.
   -man] αHmCK–D; -men βZA.   51   þei ben] W&rC; it be yZA.
   may] W&rC; shalt FZA.   of²] wLMR?A; by F; *om* Cr²³gZ.
47   worþ] W&r(were Cr)C; *om*   52   nauȝt¹] αC; *om* βA.
   Hmg.   56   wordes þe] W&r (þe] *om* G);
48   a] αHm; þe Cr¹C; *om* β.   word FZA.
   at] W&rC; & in Cr²³y; or in a F. 59   He; hise] *so* ZACK–D; And (I
   cherles] βC; clerkes ?α (a clerk F).   wil F); me (me my LR) *All MSS*
49   þere] wLMR; *om* gFC.   (C).
50   þat þow¹] W&r; *om* g.   60   Hise¹,²,³] *so* ZAC(¹,²C)K–D; My
   þi] β (*cf.* C); *om* α.   *All MSS.*

And [heng his] hoper at [his] hals in stede of a scryppe:

seed-basket; neck

'A busshel of bred corn brynge me therinne,   *seed-corn*
For I wol sowe it myself, and sithenes wol I wende   *afterwards*
To pilgrymage as palmeres doon, pardon for to have.

Jerusalem pilgrims

65 And whoso helpeth me to erie or sowen here er I wende,   *plough*
Shal have leve, by Oure Lord, to lese here in hervest   *glean; harvest*
And make hym murie thermyd, maugree whoso bigrucche it.

therewith; complain who will

And alle kynne crafty men that konne lyven in truthe,

craftsmen; know how to

I shal fynden hem fode that feithfulliche libbeth—   *provide; honestly*
70 Save Jakke the Jogelour and Jonette of the Stuwes,   *buffoon; brothel*
And Danyel the Dees-pleyere and Denote the Baude,   *dice-player*
And Frere the Faitour, and folk of his ordre,   *Deceiver*
And Robyn the Ribaudour, for hise rusty wordes.   *Ribald; foul*
Truthe tolde me ones and bad me telle it forth[er]:
75 *Deleantur de libro vivencium* – I sholde noght dele with hem,   *deal*
For Holy Chirche is hote, of hem no tithe to aske,   *bidden; demand*
Quia cum iustis non scribantur.
Thei ben ascaped good aventure – now God hem amende!'

by good luck

Dame Werch-whan-tyme-is Piers wif highte;   *was called*
His doughter highte Do-right-so-or-thi-dame-shal-thee-bete;   *beat*
80 His sone highte Suffre-thi-Sovereyns-have-hir-wille-:   *Superiors*
Deme-hem-noght-for-if-thow-doost-thow-shalt-it-deere-abugge-;

Judge; pay for it dearly

75, 76a 'Let them be blotted out of the book of the living: and with the just let
    them not be written' (Ps 68: 29).

61 heng; his[1,2]] *so* ACK–D; hange;
    myn *All MSS.*
64 for] W&r; *om* GOC[2]FC.
65 And] WCrC[2]CBoCotZAC; Ac
    L&r (but GF).
    or] L&rZAC; and WCr.
    here] WHmLMR; *om* CrgF.
67 hym] αACK–D; hem β (*om* y).
    -so] βA; -so it R; *om* FC.
    -grucche] αCr?AC; -gruccheþ β.
    it] WCrLMCA; *om* Hmgα.

70 Iakke] L&rAC; Iagge W.
72 þe] W&r; *om* CrFC.
    his] L&r; hire W.
74 forthere] *so* CA; forþ after B;
    after W&r (*l. om* Hm).
76 hote] βR?AC; holde F(C).
    aske] ?αACK–D; take βF.
77 now] LMαAC; *om* wg (but
    OC[2]).
80 haue] αOC[2]C; to hauen βA.
81 doost] W&rAC; do g.

Lat-God-yworthe-with-al-for-so-His-word-techeth.   *be*

'For now I am old and hoor and have of myn owene,   *grey*

To penaunce and to pilgrimage I wol passe with thise othere;

85 Forthi I wole er I wende do write my biqueste.   *have written; will*

'*In Dei nomine, Amen*; I make it myselve. *In the name of God; draw up*

He shal have my soule that best hath deserved it,

And [defende it fro the fend], for so I bileve,

Til I come to hise acountes as my crede telleth,   *reckoning; Creed*

90 To have a relees and a remission – on that rental I leve.

                                        release; record; believe

'The kirke shal have my caroyne, and kepe my bones,   *corpse*

For of my corn and [my] catel he craved the tithe. *i.e. the priest; asked*

I paide it hym prestly, for peril of my soule;   *promptly*

He is holden, I hope, to have me in his masse   *obliged; think; include*

95 And mengen me in his memorie amonges alle Cristene.

                                        remember me (by name)

'My wif shal have of that I wan with truthe, and namoore,

                                        earned honestly

And dele among my doughtres and my deere children;   *divide*

For though I deye today, my dette is yquyted: *paid in full*

I bar hom that I borwed er I to bedde yede.   *returned; went*

100 And with the residue and the remenaunt, by the Rode of Lukes!

                                        Lucca (C)

I wol worshipe therwith Truthe by my lyve,

And ben His pilgrym atte plow for povere mennes sake.   *at the*

---

95 And remember to mention me by name in his commemorative prayer.

83   old] β?AC; holde αZ.

85   bi] βZAC; en- F; *om* R.

86-8 *So* βZAC; *as* 2 *ll. div. after*
      soule α.

88   defenden . . . fend] *so* ZAC*K*–D;
     fro þe f. it defende B; fro þe f.
     Ikeped it R; weyvid fram yt þe
     fendis F) (C).
     for . . . bileue] βZAC; *om* α.

89   to] βFA; til RC.
     crede] αZ?AC; *Credo* me ?β (*Cr.*]
     crede HmCr³C²B).

92   my²] *so* ZA?C*K*–D; *om All
     MSS.*

he] L&rACZ (a); she WCrBoCot;
þe kirke F.

93   it hym] L&r (hym] hem BmBo;
     hire Cot) Z?A; him ful M; it ful W;
     it FC.

94   He is] *so* ACZ (He] And he Z)
     K–D; Forþi is he W&r (F.]
     Therfore Cr; is he] *trs* GF; he] *om*
     Hm).

95   me] F (?=α) AC*K*–D; *om* βRZ.

97   dele] βRZA; dele it FC.

98   deye] βZAC; deyede α.
     dette is Iquited] ?αZC; dettes are
     quyte βF (are] ben all F).

My plowpote shal be my pikstaf and picche atwo the rotes,

plough-pusher; separate

And helpe my cultour to kerve and clense the furwes.'   *cut; furrows*

105   Now is Perkyn and thise pilgrimes to the plow faren.   *gone*

To erie this half-acre holpen hym manye: *plough; helped*

Dikeres and delveres digged up the balkes;   *ridges (?left unploughed)*

Therwith was Perkyn apayed and preised hem faste.   *pleased; highly*

Othere werkmen ther were that wroghten ful yerne: *eagerly*

110   Ech man in his manere made hymself to doone,

And somme to plese Perkyn piked up the wedes.   *hoed*

At heigh prime Piers leet the plough stonde,   *(=) 9 a.m.*

To oversen hem hymself; whoso best wroghte,   *oversee; whoever*

He sholde be hired therafter, whan hervest tyme come.   *accordingly*

115   And thanne seten somme and songen atte nale,   *sat; over drink, at ale*

And holpen ere his half acre with 'How trolly lolly!'   *helped plough*

'Now, by the peril of my soule!' quod Piers al in pure tene,   *anger*

'But ye arise the rather and rape yow to werche,   *hasten*

Shal no greyn that here groweth glade yow at nede,   *grain (of wheat)*

120   And though ye deye for doel, the devel have that recche!'

pain; should care

Tho were faitours afered, and feyned hem blynde;

impostors; pretended to be

Somme leide hir legges aliry, as swiche losels konneth,   *wastrels*

And made hir [pleynt] to Piers and preide hym of grace: *to be let off*

'For we have no lymes to laboure with, lord, ygraced be ye!   *thanked*

125   Ac we preie for yow, Piers, and for youre plowgh bothe,

---

103 My plough-pusher shall be my pikestaff and separate the roots.
120 And even though you should die of starvation-pangs, the Devil take the man who should regret it!
122 Some laid their legs in such a way as to seem maimed, as such rascally vagabonds know how to (C).

103 -pote] αZAK–D; -foot β.
atwo] βZ; at R?Ax; awey F.
105 þese] ?αC; þe FZA; hise β.
109 yerne] W&rZC; faste CMAx.
113 To o.] βA; And ȝeed to o. ?α
(ȝ.] wente F); And ouersey CZ.
whoso] BZACK–D; and w. W&r
(l. †F).
115 and] W&r?A?C; om HmZ.
116 his] L&r; þis WC; the ZA.

119 her] + M, so ZACK–D; om
W&r (C).
120 deye] βFZAC; deyede R.
recche] αHmCrZACK–D; reccheþ
β.
123 pleynt] mone All MSS (C).
124 For] W&r (& seyd F); om
GZA.
ȝe] L&rA; þe WHmZ.

That God of his grace youre greyn multiplie,
And yelde yow of youre almesse that ye yyve us here;   *pay for; alms*
For we may neither swynke ne swete, swich siknesse us eyleth.'   *ails*
'If it be sooth,' quod Piers, 'that ye seyn, I shal it soone aspie.
                                                                  discover

130 Ye ben wastours, I woot wel, and Truthe woot the sothe;   *the facts*
And I am his olde hyne and highte hym to warne   *servant; bidden*
Whiche thei were in this world hise werkmen apeireth.   *(who) harm*
Ye wasten that men wynnen with travaille and with tene;   *effort; pain*
Ac Truthe shal teche yow his teme to dryve,   *(plough)-team*
135 Or ye shul eten barly breed and of the broke drynke;   *(=plain water)*
But if he be blynd or brokelegged or bolted with irens,   *shackled*
He shal ete whete breed and drynke with myselve
Til God of his goodnesse [garisoun] hym sende.   *deliverance*
Ac ye myghte travaille as Truthe wolde and take mete and hyre
                                                                  food; wages
140 To kepe kyen in the feld, the corn fro the bestes,   *For keeping cows*
Diken or delven or dyngen upon sheves,   *(For threshing) corn*
Or helpe make morter or bere muk afelde.   *spread dung on fields*
In lecherie and in losengerie ye lyven, and in sleuthe,   *deceitfulness*
And al is thorugh suffraunce that vengeaunce yow ne taketh!
                                                      (God's) long-suffering

145   'Ac ancres and heremites that eten but at nones   *'Nones', noon-tide*
And na moore er morwe — myn almesse shul thei have,
And of my catel to cope hem with that han cloistres and chirches.
Ac Robert Renaboute shal noght [recey]ve of myne,
Ne postles, but thei preche konne and have power of the bisshop:
                                                      (wandering) preachers
150 Thei shul have payn and potage and [putte] hemself at ese—
                                                      bread; soup

127 of] L&rAC; for wG; *om* FZ.
128 neiþer] ?B (*l. om* Cot)Cr
     ZACK–D; noȝt W&r (C).
130 Ye] β; þat ȝee F; þo R.
     and] βFAC; *om* RZ.
     woot²] βFZA; wot wel R.
132 apayreth] αG; apeired β.
136 be] βAC; is F; *om* R.
138 garisoun] amendement *All MSS*
     (C).
143 in²] W&r; *om* g.

145 but] CrLMα; noȝt but ?wg.
146 er] L&r (er þe W); til on FHm
     (on) on the Hm).
147 of my] LMα; of wG; *om* Cr³y.
     cope] L&r (kouere F); kepe wG.
148 receyue of myne] haue of myne
     βR; rewle my goodis F (C).
149 and] βF; and ȝut R.
150 putte . . . ese] make hemself at
     ese β (self] *om* g)R; a pytawnce
     bysyde F (C).

For it is an unresonable Religion that hath right noght of certein.'
Thanne gan Wastour to wrathen hym and wolde have yfoughte,

get angry

And to Piers the Plowman he profrede his glove.   *(i.e. in challenge)*
A Bretoner, a braggere, abosted Piers alse   *Breton; boastingly defied*
155 And bad hym go pissen with his plowgh, forpynede sherewe!

damned

'Wiltow or neltow, we wol have oure wille,   *Like it or not*
And of thi flour and of thi flesshe fecche whanne us liketh,
And maken us murye thermyde, maugree thi chekes.' *have fun with it*
Thanne Piers the Plowman pleyned hym to the knyghte
160 To kepen hym as covenaunt was fro cursede sherewes

protect; as agreed

And fro thise wastours wolveskynnes that maketh this world deere:

wolfish destroyers

'For tho wasten and wynnen noght, and that [while ilke]

as long as they do

Worth nevere plentee among the peple the while my plowgh liggeth.'

lies (idle)

Curteisly the knyght thanne, as his kynde wolde,   *nature required*
165 Warnede Wastour and wissed hym bettre: *counselled*
'Or thow shalt abigge by the lawe, by the ordre that I bere!'

pay the penalty; my rank

'I was noght wont to werche,' quod Wastour, 'and now wol I noght
bigynne!'—
And leet light of the lawe, and lasse of the knyghte,

set small store by; less

And sette Piers at a pese, and his plowgh bothe,   *valued; pea*

---

151 For it would be against reason for a religious order to have absolutely no source of sure sustenance.

151 riȝt . . . of] W&r (r.) *om* G); no
þinge in y; rentys none F.
152 Thanne] yFZACK–D; And þ.
wGLMR.
gan] WZAC; gan a L&r.
154 alse] *so* Z?A; also CrBFC; als
W&r (C).
155 with] β (hym w. GOC²)ACZ;
on α.
157 And of] ?α (& F); And ZC; Of

βA.
161 þis] ?α (*l. om* F)GC; þe β.
162 þat . . . ilke] þat ilke while βR;
wete wel for soþe F (C).
163 þe¹] βF; *om* R.
166 by¹] βFZAC; with R.
167 wol I noȝt] W&rZAC; I nill
Cr³g.
168 liȝt] βZAC; liȝtly αHm.

170   And manaced Piers and his men if thei mette eftsoone.
                                                    threatened; again
         'Now, by the peril of my soule!' quod Piers, 'I shal apeire yow
       alle'—   *hurt*
       And houped after Hunger, that herde hym at the firste.
                                                    shouted; straightaway
       'Awreke me of thise wastours,' quod he, 'that this world shendeth!'
                                                    Avenge; harm
         Hunger in haste thoo hente Wastour by the mawe   *then; stomach*
175   And wrong hym so by the wombe that al watrede hise eighen.
                                                    wrung; belly
       He buffetted the Bretoner aboute the chekes
       That he loked lik a lanterne al his lif after.
       He bette hem so bothe, he brast ner hire guttes;   *beat; nearly burst*
       Ne hadde Piers with a pese loof preyed [hym bileve],
                                                    pease-loaf; leave off
180   They hadde be dolven bothe – ne deme thow noon oother.
                                                    (dead and) buried
         'Suffre hem lyve,' he seide 'and lat hem ete with hogges,   *Allow*
       Or ellis benes and bren ybaken togideres.'   *beans; bran; baked*
         Faitours for fere herof flowen into berns   *fled; barns*
       And flapten on with flailes fro morwe til even,   *threshed; evening*
185   That Hunger was noght hardy on hem for to loke   *(so) bold (as to)*
       For a potful of peses that Piers hadde ymaked.   *Because of*
       An heep of heremytes henten hem spades   *crowd; got hold of*
       And kitten hir copes and courtepies hem made,   *cut; short coats*
       And wenten as werkmen with spades and with shoveles,
190   And dolven and dikeden to dryve awey Hunger.   *dug; ditched*
         Blynde and bedreden were bootned a thousand,   *bedridden; cured*

---

171   Now] βZAC; *om* αG.
174   mawe] L&rZAC; wombe W.
175   al . . . ey3es] ?αZACK–D; boþe
      hise ei3en watrede β (b.) *om* G
      Cr¹²)F.
179   hym byleue] *so* ZACK–D;
      hunger to cesse *All MSS* (to] *om* α)
      (C).
180   boþe ne] L&r (ne] *om* BMF);
      depe +G; ne w.
182   and] L&r; or W.
      After this a line: Or ellis melk and

mene ale þus preied Piers for hem
All MSS (þus . . . hem] to meyntene
here lyvis F); *rej. as spurious K–D*
(C).
183   herof] W&r; þerof g (-of] *om*
      G); tho Z?A (*cf.* C); *om* F?Ax.
185   hardy] αGZACK–D; so hardy
      β.
188   made] L&rC; maked W.
189   wenten] L&rC; wente WG.
      wiþ¹ . . . shoueles] β (wiþ²] *om* y)R;
      to swynkyn abowtyn F.

That seten to begge silver, soone were thei heeled;   *sat; healed*
For that was bake for Bayard was boote for many hungry;   *i.e. horses*
And many a beggere for benes buxum was to swynke,   *willing; toil*
195 And ech a povere man wel apaied to have pesen for his hyre,
          satisfied; pay
And what Piers preide hem to do as prest as a sperhauk.
          prompt; sparrow-hawk
And therof was Piers proud, and putte hem to werke
And yaf hem mete [and money as thei] myghte [deserve]
   Thanne hadde Piers pite, and preide Hunger to wende
200 Hoom into his owene erd and holden hym there [evere]: *land; remain*
'For I am wel awroke of wastours thorugh thy myghte. *avenged upon*
Ac I preie thee, er thow passe,' quod Piers tho to Hunger,
'Of beggeris and of bidderis what best be to doone?
For I woot wel, be thow went, thei wol werche ful ille;   *once you go*
205 Meschief it maketh thei be so meke nouthe,   *Distress (alone); now*
And for defaute of hire foode this folk is at my wille.   *lack; obedient*
[And] it are my blody bretheren, for God boughte us alle.
          by blood; redeemed

Truthe taughte me ones to loven hem ech one
And to helpen hem of alle thyng, ay as hem nedeth.   *always*
210 Now wolde I wite of thee, what were the beste,   *know from*
And how I myghte amaistren hem and make hem to werche.' *govern*
   'Here now,' quod Hunger, 'and hoold it for a wisdom:
Bolde beggeris and bigge that mowe hir breed biswynke,
          strong; labour for

---

193   for³] βC; to R; *om* F.
194   buxum] β (*l. om* Cr²³; ful b.
    M); ful bown F; fayne R.
196   to] β; for to R; *om* GF.
198   and . . . *deserue*] *so* ZACK–D;
    as he myȝte aforþe and *mesurable*
    hyre *All MSS* (af.] mete F; mesur-]
    reason- Cr³OC²) (C).
200   in-] L&r (*om* GYF)ZAC; vn-
    WCr.
    erde] LRZ?A?C; erthe y; yerd wG;
    hold F.
    there euere] *so* ZACK–D; styll þere
    F; þere βR (C).
201   of] wGC; now *of* L&r.
202   þo] α; *om* β.
203   best be to] ?β (be to] *trs* Cr; to]

    om L)ZAC; best is to ?α (is best to
    F)Y.
204   ful] W&r (*erased* M)Z?AC; *om*
    G.
205   Meschief] *so* ZACK–D; For
    meschief *All MSS*.
206   hire] βR; *om* FZA.
207   And it] *so* ZACK–D; It R; Thei
    β (& yet they YOC²)F.
    for] YZACK–D; quod Piers for
    W&r.
210   Now] *so* ZACK–D; And now
    All MSS.
212   Here now] W&r (H.] I h. R)
    AZ; *trs* FC.

With houndes breed and horse breed hoold up hir hertes—   sustain
215 Aba[v]e hem with benes, for bollynge of hir wombe;

                                Confound; to stop; swelling

And if the gromes grucche, bidde hem go and swynke,   complain; toil
And he shal soupe swetter whan he it hath deserved.   more pleasantly
'Ac if thow fynde any freke that Fortune hath apeired   person; injured
O[the]r any manere false men, fonde thow swiche to knowe: Or; try
220 Conforte hem with thi catel for Cristes love of hevene;   possessions
Love hem and lene hem, for so lawe of [kynde wolde]:   give to; nature
Alter alterius onera portate.
And alle manere of men that thow myght aspie   discover
That nedy ben and noughty, [norisse] hem with thi goodes.

                                destitute; sustain

Love hem and lakke hem noght — lat God take the vengeaunce;

                                blame

225 Theigh thei doon yvele, lat thow God yworthe: be (?settle it)
Michi vindictam et ego retribuam.
And if thow wilt be gracious to God, do as the Gospel techeth,

                                pleasing

---

215 Discomfort them with [the food we give animals] beans, to prevent their
bellies from swelling (with hunger) (C).
221a Bear ye one another's burdens; [and . . . fulfil the law of Christ] (Gal 6: 2
(C); cf. XI 210a.
225a Revenge is mine and I will repay [them in due time] (Deut 32: 35, quoted
in Rom 12: 19, Heb 10: 30) (C).

215 Abaue] so Z?A; And abaue
CK–D; Abate All MSS (& a. F)
(C).
wombe] L&r (wombes WF)
ZAC; herte Hm.
216 þe gromes] MZAC; þe gomes
W&r (þe] her Cr¹²); they y.
and] αZA?CK–D; om β.
217 In βZAC; l. om α.
218 Ac] ?αACZ(But)K–D; And βF.
Fortune] βZA; falshed R; False FC
(fals men C) (C).
219 Other] Or W&r; l. om CB (C).

220 hem] Cr²³&r (l. om CB)ACSk;
hym wLZ.
221 so] wLMR?A?C; for so yCr³;
for F.
lawe . . . wolde] so ZACK–D; l. of
god techeþ β (l.] the l. Cr¹²GY; of
god] om Cr³OC²CB)R; goddes law
so techiþ F (C).
222 men] ?αBC; of men βFA.
223 nouȝty] W&r; noȝt han B.
norisse] help All MSS (C).
225 þow] LR; om W&r.

And bilowe thee amonges lowe men – so shaltow lacche grace: *get*
Facite vobis amicos de mammona iniquitatis.'

'I wolde noght greve God,' quod Piers, 'for al the good on
grounde!'   *wealth on earth*
Mighte I synnelees do as thow seist?' seide Piers thanne.

230   'Ye, I bihote thee,' quod Hunger, 'or ellis the Bible lieth.   *promise*
Go to Genesis the geaunt, the engendrour of us alle: *giant; procreator*
"*In sudore* and swynke thow shalt thi mete tilie,   *food; earn by tilling*
And laboure for thi liflode," and so Oure Lord highte.   *living*
And Sapience seith the same – I seigh it in the Bible:

                                                  (the) Wisdom (writings); saw
235   "*Piger pro frigore* no feeld wolde tilie—   *till*
And therfore he shal begge and bidde, and no man bete his hunger."

                                                                 relieve
'Mathew with mannes face moutheth thise wordes—   *utters*
That *servus nequam* hadde a mnam, and for he wolde noght chaffare,

                                                          pound; trade
He hadde maugree of his maister for everemoore after   *the disfavour*
240   And bynam hym his mnam for he ne wolde werche,   *took away from*
And yaf that mnam to hym that ten mnames hadde,
And [after] that he seide, that Holy Chirche it herde:
"He that hath shal have and helpe there it nedeth;   *is necessary*

227–7a And humble yourself amongst humble people – that way you will
  obtain God's favour (for yourself): 'Make unto you friends of the mammon
  of iniquity' [worldly riches] (Lk 16: 9) (C).
232 'In the sweat [of thy face shalt thou eat bread]' (Gen 3: 19).
235 'Because of the cold, the sluggard [would not plough]' (Prov 20:4).
238 That 'a wicked servant' had a *mina* [=£1], and because he was unwilling
  to do business (with it) (cf. Lk 19: 12ff. esp. verse 22).

227   bilow] LMα (bi-] *om* F); biloue   wolde] WGLMα; nolde HmCry ZA.
  wg.   239   for] L&crZ?A; and Cr¹²; *om*
230   þee] βAC; god ?α (to god F)Z.   WHmGYCB.
231   þe²] βR; *om* FZA.   240   ne wolde] W&r (ne] *om* C);
232   and] WCr¹²YLZA (*cf.* C); & in   wold not Cr¹²F; nolde CotGMZA.
  Hm (*over erasure*)&r.   241   þat ... hym] W&r (mnam¹,²]
234   it] βZA; *om* ?α (†F).   besant(es) G); it to anoþer man F.
235   wolde] HmCrMαAK–D; nolde   242   after that] wiþ þat *All MSS*;
  WgLZ.   siþen ZA (C).
237   mouteth] αZAK–D; mouþed   þat²; holy chirche] βR; þat dede; all
  β.   men F.
238   Mnam] β (*glossed* besaunt
  WHmLM; besaunt Cr¹²G)ZA; man
  αBoCot.

And he that noght hath shal noght have, and no man hym helpe,
245 And that he weneth wel to have, I wole it hym bireve.'
that which he thinks; take from

'Kynde Wit wolde that ech a wight wroghte,   *should work*
Or in dichynge or in delvynge or travaillynge in preieres—
Either; digging

Contemplatif lif or actif lif, Crist wolde men wroghte.
The Sauter seith in the psalme of *Beati omnes*,
250 The freke that fedeth hymself with his feithful labour,   *honest*
He is blessed by the book in body and in soule:
Labores manuum tuarum . . .'

'Yet I preie yow,' quod Piers, '*pur charite*, and ye konne
for charity; if

Any leef of lechecraft, lere it me, my deere;   *leaf; medicine; teach*
For some of my servaunts and myself bothe
255 Of al a wike werche noght, so oure wombe aketh.'   *For a whole week*
'I woot wel,' quod Hunger, 'what siknesse yow eyleth;   *afflicts*
Ye han manged over muche – that maketh yow grone.   *eaten*
Ac I hote thee,' quod Hunger, 'as thow thyn hele wilnest,
health; desire

That thow drynke no day er thow dyne somwhat.
260 Ete noght, I hote thee, er Hunger thee take   *come upon you*
And sende thee of his sauce to savore with thi lippes;
make food tasty to

And keep som til soper tyme and sitte noght to longe;
Arys up er appetit have eten his fille.
Lat noght Sire Surfet sitten at thi borde—   *table*
265 Leve hym noght, for he is lecherous and likerous of tonge,
Believe; dainty

---

249 'Blessed are all they [that fear the Lord] . . .' (Ps 127: 1).
251a 'For [thou shalt eat] the labours of thy hands . . .' (Ps 127: 2).

245 wel] βZAC; for α.
247 dichyng] R; dikynge β (dik-]
  digg- Cr²³)F.
248 men] YLMR; we F; þei w?g.
249 þe²] β; a α.
252 yow; ye] βR (*cf.* C); þe; þou F.
  pur] HmCr³OC²BFZACK–D; *par*
  W&r; praye Cr¹².

257 þat] BZACK–D; and þat W&r.
261 wiþ] W&rZ?AC; *om* MF.
262 til] W&rC; to YOC²R; for CB;
  forto Z?A.
263 Arise] LMRZA; But a. F; And
  rys wg (r.] aryse Cot).
265 Leue] W&rZ?A: Loue MCot.

And after many maner metes his mawe is afyngred.

kinds of food; hungry

'And if thow diete thee thus, I dar legge myn eris   *wager; ears*
That Phisik shal hise furred hodes for his fode selle,

the medical profession

And his cloke of Calabre with alle the knappes of golde,

Calabrian fur; buttons

270 And be fayn, by my feith, his phisik to lete,   *give up the practice of p.*
And lerne to laboure with lond [lest] liflode [hym faille].
Ther are mo [li]eres than leches – Lord hem amende!

impostors; physicians

They do men deye thorugh hir drynkes er destynee it wolde.' *potions*
'By Seint Poul,' quod Piers, 'thise arn profitable wordes!
275 For this is a lovely lesson, Lord it thee foryelde!   *reward*
Wend now, Hunger, whan thow wolt, that wel be thow evere.'

'I bihote God,' quod Hunger, 'hennes ne wole I wende   *promise*
[Er] I have dyned bi this day and ydronke bothe.'

'I have no peny,' quod Piers, 'pulettes for to bugge,   *pullets; buy*
280 Ne neither gees ne grys, but two grene cheses,   *pigs; fresh, unmatured*
A fewe cruddes and creme and [ek] an haver cake,   *curds; oat-cake*
And two loves of benes and bran ybake for my fauntes.   *children*
And yet I seye, by my soule, I have no salt bacon   *further still*
Ne no cokeney, by Crist, coloppes to maken! *egg; fried eggs and bacon*
285 Ac I have percile and porett and manye [plaunte coles],

parsley; leeks; greens

---

266 afyngred] βRZ; alustyd F;
     alongid A.
268 hodes] W&rZC; *sg* CrOC²
     BFAx.
269 alle] βR; *om* FZA.
     þe] β (his Cr¹²G); *om* α.
271 lest . . . faille] *so* ACK–D; for
     liflode is swete *All MSSZ* (C).
272 Ther . . . leches] *so* AK–D (*cf.*
     C); þer aren mo morareres þan α
     (þer] Now; mor.] moraynerys F);
     For murþereris are manye β (For
     many lechys ben m. B) (C).
273 it] W&rAC; *om* g.
275–6 *So* ZACK–D; *ll. trs All MSS.*
276 be þow] β (þow] þe HmOC²
     BmBo)A?C; yow yow R; þe F.

277 I] GBFZACK–D; *om* W&r.
     god] W&r?A; the CotZC.
278 Er] *so* ACK–D; Til *All MSSZ*
     (C).
279 for] L&rC; þe F; *om* WHmG
     MZA.
280 Ne] W&r (*l. om* CB)C; *om*
     HmYZA.
281 ek] *om All MSS* (C).
284 to] OC²ZACK–D; for to W&r;
     of to Hm; þe to F.
285 porett] ?αBZA (*cf.* C)K–D;
     porettes βF.
     plaunte coles] *so* ?AZK–D; cole
     plauntes β; queynte herbes R;
     propre herbys F (C).

And ek a cow and a calf, and a cart mare
To drawe afeld my donge the while the droghte lasteth.
And by this liflode we mote lyve til Lammesse tyme,

sustenance; Lammas (C)

And by that I hope to have hervest in my crofte;   *by then; field*

290 Thanne may I dighte thi dyner as me deere liketh.'   *prepare; I really like*
Al the povere peple tho pescoddes fetten;   *pea-pods; fetched*
Benes and baken apples thei broghte in hir lappe,
Chibolles and chervelles and ripe chiries manye,   *Spring-onions; chervil*
And profrede Piers this present to plese with Hunger.   *please H. with*

295 Al Hunger eet in haste and axed after moore.   *asked*
Thanne povere folk for fere fedden Hunger yerne;   *anxiously*
With grene poret and pesen to poisone hym thei thoghte!   *cabbage*
By that it neghed neer hervest and newe corn cam to chepyng;

then; market

Thanne was folk fayn, and fedde Hunger with the beste—   *pleased*
300 With good ale, as Gloton taghte – and garte Hunger go slepe.

taught; made

And tho wolde Wastour noght werche, but wandren aboute,
Ne no beggere ete breed that benes inne were,   *containing beans*
But of coket or clermatyn or ellis of clene whete,

breads of fine white flour; other kinds (of fine wheat)

Ne noon halfpenny ale in none wise drynke,   *in no way*
305 But of the beste and of the brunneste that [brewesteres] selle.

darkest, strongest

Laborers that have no land to lyve on but hire handes

---

303 But only loaves made of fine white flour, or at least only out of wheat
unmixed [with other grains, beans, etc.].

287 þe¹] W&rC; *om* GBFZA.
289 And] W&rZC; For F; *om* CrA.
290 Thenne] *so* ZACK–D; And þ.
All MSS.
me] W&rZ?AC; þe F.
292 lappe] ?αZ?AC; lappes βF.
298 and] WBFC; *om* L&r; that ZA.
300 go] W&r (*l. om* CB; go to F);
to HmCr³GC²; a Cr¹².
301 þo . . . noȝt] βACZ (wolde]
nolde Z); þo ne wolde no w. α (þo
ne] þan F).

wandren] W&rZ?A?C; wandred
HmyF.
303 or¹] L&r (or of R; *om* CB)Z?A;
and WCrGYC.
ellis] W&r; *om* CBZAC.
305 of þe²] wLR?C; the ?g (*om* CB)
MZA; *om* F.
breusteris] *so* ACK–D; in Burgh is
to *All MSSZ* (C).
306 to; on but] W&r?AC; but; with
?y (*l. om* CB)FZ (w.] on Z).

Deyned noght to dyne aday nyght-olde wortes   *Deigned; eat; greens*

May no peny ale hem paie, ne no pece of bacoun,   *satisfy; piece*

But if it be fressh flessh outher fissh fryed outher ybake—   *or; baked*

310   And that *chaud* and *plus chaud*, for chillynge of his mawe.   *to prevent*

And but if he be heighliche hyred, ellis wole he chide—

highly paid; complain

And that he was werkmen wroght wa[ri]e the tyme.   *curse*

Ayeins Catons counseil comseth he to jangle: *begins; dispute*

Paupertatis onus pacienter ferre memento.

He greveth hym ageyn God and gruccheth ageyn Reson,

gets angry; grumbles against

315   And thanne corseth he the Kyng and al his Counseil after   *curses*

Swiche lawes to loke, laborers to greve.   *For decreeing such...; grieve*

Ac whiles Hunger was hir maister, ther wolde noon of hem chide,

Ne stryven ayeins his statut, so sterneliche he loked!   *fiercely, sternly*

  Ac I warne yow werkmen – wynneth whil ye mowe,

obtain (food); are able

320   For Hunger hiderward hasteth hym faste!   *is hastening*

He shal awake [thorugh] water, wastours to chaste,

by means of; chastise (C)

---

307   Would not deign to eat on the morrow last night's greens.

310   And that (to be served) 'hot' and 'piping hot', to prevent their stomachs catching chill.

313*a* [Since nature created you a naked child], remember to bear patiently the burden of poverty (*Distichs of Cato* ed. M. Boas (Amsterdam, 1952), I, 21) (C).

307   Deyne*d* . . . day] W&r (no3t] β; *om* ααCr²³; aday] or suppe F; *om* M)ZAC; wolde ete no ?*y* (*l. om* CB).

309   *So* βZAC; *run together with* 310 α.
if it be] W&rZAC (if] *om* MF ZC); *om y.*
fryed . . . ybake] β (fr.] rosted M (*over erasure*)ZA (yb.] rostid ?A)C; *om* α.

310   And . . . *chaud²*] β (or] and WHm)ZAC; *om* α.
his] ?αZ?A?C; hir βF.

312   warie] *so* AZCK–D; waille W&r; *l. om y* (C).

315   And] βFZAC; *om* R.
þanne] W&rZAC; þus F; *om* Hmg.
corseþ he] W&r; *trs y* FC; c. *also* Hm.

317   þer . . . noon] W&rZAC (þer] þanne F; *om* CrGZA); wolde they nat *y.*
of hem] W&r; *om* yFZAC (C).

318   his] W&rZ?A?C; þe BF; þis G.

320   faste] β; ful faste α.

321   thorw] *so* CAK–D; wiþ W&rZ; sum F(C).

Er fyve yer be fulfilled swich famyn shal aryse:
Thorough flodes and thorugh foule wedres, fruytes shul faille—

weather; crops

And so sei[th] Saturne and sent yow to warne:

sends as a warning to you

325 Whan ye [merke] the sonne amys and two monkes heddes,   *observe*
And a mayde have the maistrie, and multiplied by eighte,
Thanne shal deeth withdrawe and derthe be justice,   *scarcity; judge*
And Dawe the Dykere deye for hunger—
But if God of his goodnesse graunte us a trewe.   *truce*

---

322 fyue] W&rZA; fewe BC.
ʒere] Hm&rZACS*k*; om WCr¹²
GCLM.
323 flodes] βFC; flod RZA.
þoruʒ²] WHmLZ?A?C; om
CrgMα.

324 seyth] *so* ZACK–D; seide βR; *l.*
†F.
325 merke] se *All MSS* (C).
326 multiplied] LM (d +M)α;
multiplie wg.
329 But if] L&rC; But WF; nd R.

Passus VII

Treuthe herde telle herof, and to Piers sente   sc. *a message*
To taken his teme and tilien the erthe,
And purchaced hym a pardoun *a pena et a culpa*

                         obtained an absolute pardon (C)

For hym and for hise heires for everemoore after;
5   And bad hym holde hym at home and erien hise leyes,   *fallow lands*
And alle that holpen hym to erye, to sette or to sowe,   *plant*
Or any [man]er mestier that myghte Piers availe—   *occupation*
Pardon with Piers the Plowman Truthe hath ygraunted.

Kynges and knyghtes that kepen Holy Chirche   *protect*
10   And rightfully in remes rulen the peple,   *justly; (their) kingdoms*
Han pardon thorugh purgatorie to passen ful lightly,   *easily*
With patriarkes and prophetes in paradis to be felawes.   *companions*

Bysshopes yblessed, if thei ben as thei sholde   *holy*
Legistres of bothe lawes, the lewed therwith to preche,

                         Expert in canon, civil law

15   And in as muche as thei mowe amenden alle synfulle,
Arn peres with the apostles – thus pardon Piers sheweth—   *equals of*
And at the day of dome at heighe deys to sitte.   *judgement; daïs*

Marchaunts in the margyne hadde manye yeres,   *(added) in*
Ac noon *a pena et a culpa* the Pope nolde hem graunte,

                         absolute pardon (C)

20   For thei holde noght hir haliday as Holy Chirche techeth,   *holy days*

---

18 ... had remission of many years of temporal punishment *or, more probably*, of punishment in purgatory after death.

Collation WHmCrGYOC²CBLMRF.
RUBRIC *Passus vij^{us} de visione vt supra* W&r (*de. v.*] om YO); om GF.
1   sente] HmCrGOC²ZAK–D; he sente WYCLMα; he wente B.
7   manere] *so* ZACK–D; ooþer *All MSS.*
8   þe plowman] ?α (*om* F)BC; Plowman β.
9   chirche] βFZAC; cherches R.

12   felawes] LMGα; felawe wy.
14   lawes] wBα; the lawes ?gLM.
16   þus] LMαK–D; þis ?w(such Cr)g.
17   heie] αMZA; þe heiȝe ?β.
19   A¹] βA?C; om α.
     nolde] ?βZ?A?C; wolde αGBCrF. hem] β (*om* G); hem nauȝt ?α (h.] *om* F).
20   -day] αMC; -dayes βZ?A.

And for thei swere 'by hir soule' and 'so God moste hem helpe'
Ayein clene Conscience, hir catel to selle.   *(the dictates of) C.; goods*
Ac under his secret seel Truthe sente hem a lettre,   *private seal*
[And bad hem] buggen boldely what hem best liked   *buy*
25 And sithenes selle it ayein and save the wynnynges,   *then; profit*
And amende mesondieux therwith and myseisé folk helpe;

        hospitals; sick
And wikkede weyes, wightly hem amende,   *bad roads; actively*
And do boote to brugges that tobroke were;   *repair; broken down*
Marien maydenes or maken hem nonnes;   *nuns*
30 Povere peple and prisons, fynden hem hir foode,   *prisoners; provide*
And sette scolers to scole or to som othere craftes;   *schoolboys*
Releve religion and renten hem bettre.   *Support; endow*
'And I shal sende yow myselve Seynt Michel myn angel,   *St Michael*
That no devel shal yow dere ne [drede] in your deying,   *harm; terror*
35 And witen yow fro wanhope, if ye wol thus werche,   *preserve; despair*
And sende youre soules in saufte to my Seintes in joye.'   *safety*

    Thanne were marchaunts murie – manye wepten for joye
And preiseden Piers the Plowman, that purchaced this bulle.

    Men of lawe leest pardon hadde that pleteden for mede,   *pleaded*
40 For the Sauter saveth hem noght, swiche as take yiftes,
And nameliche of innocents that noon yvel ne konneth: *especially*
Super innocentem munera non accipies.

---

32 Aid religious orders and provide them with a more adequate source of income.

41–1a And particularly from simple people who suspect no guile: '. . . nor take bribes against the innocent . . .' (Ps 14: 5).

21 by . . . and] βZAC; ofte α.
moste] ?βAC; om αGMZ.
24 And bad hem] *so* ACK–D; That þei sholde *All* MSSZ (C).
what] BZACK–D; þat W&r.
liked] βZAC; liketh α.
25 it] βFACZ; it vs R.
wynnynges] αZC; wynnyng β?Ax.
26 -with] αGCB?AC; -myd ?βZ.
27 hem] L&r (*l.* om CB); om WCrG; to ZA.
30 and] βF; or R.
31 som] βZA; om α.
33 Aungel] HmFZACK–D;

Archangel W&r (C).
34 drede] fere yow *All MSS* (C).
37 murie . . . manye] ?β (manye] and YOC²M)ZAC; manye marchauntz þat α.
39 *So* β; *as* 2 *ll. div. after* hadde α. But m. of l. of pardoun þe leest part þey h./ for þey for meede pletyn moore þan mychil for goddes helpe F(C).
mede] β; m. for þat craft is schrewed R.
41 ne] WCrGLα; om HmyM.
41a *In* βZA; *l.* om α.

Pledours sholde peynen hem to plede for swiche and helpe;

Barristers; take trouble

Princes and prelates sholde paie for hire travaille: *efforts*
A regibus et principibus erit merces eorum.

Ac many a justice and jurour wolde for Johan do moore
45 Than *pro Dei pietate* – [pr]eve thow noon oother!

for love of God; experience (C)

Ac he that speneth his speche and speketh for the povere
That is innocent and nedy and no man apeireth,   *injures*
Conforteth hym in that caas, coveit[eth noght hise] yiftes, *payments*
And [for Oure Lordes love lawe for hym sheweth]—

exercises his legal skill

50 Shal no devel at his deeth day deren hym a myte   *harm; in the least*
That he ne worth saaf and his soule, the Sauter bereth witnesse:

saved

Domine, quis habitabit in tabernaculo tuo? . . .

Ac to bugge water, ne wynd, ne wit, ne fir the ferthe— *fire; fourth*
Thise foure the Fader of Hevene made to this foold in commune:

earth

Thise ben Truthes tresores trewe folk to helpe,   *honest*
55 That nevere shul wex ne wanye withouten God hymselve.   *wane*
Whan thei drawen on to the deth, and indulgences wolde have,
His pardon is ful petit at his partyng hennes   *small; hence*
That any mede of mene men for hir motyng taketh.

poor; legal services

43*a* Their payment shall be from kings and princes.
51*a* Lord, who shall dwell in thy tabernacle? (Ps 14: 1).
55 (Commodities) that shall never come into being or cease to be except
   through (the power of) God himself.

45   preve] *leue All MSS* (beleve F)
(C).
46   speneth] *?αZC*; spendeþ βF.
48   Conforteþ] βZA; And c. α; That
c. C.
coueitiþ . . . h*i*s] *so* AZCK–D;
wiþouten coueitise of *All MSS* (of]
om F).
49   for[1] . . . shewith] *so* ZA (*cf.* C)
K–D; sheweþ lawe for o. l. loue as
he it haþ ylerned *All MSS* (C).

51   and his soule] W&r (and] *om*
C[2]); *om* G.
51*a* &c] L&r; *om* WCrOC[2]CB.
56   on] WCrLM; vn- Hmy; in R; *om*
GFC.
þe deþ] *?y*K–D; deth Hmα; deye
WCrLMG; þe day C (C).
57   His[1]] *y?*αCZAK–D; Hir
wGLMF.
his[2]] *?*αCK–D; hir βF.
58   hir] W&rC; his *y*Z; *om* A.

Ye legistres and lawieres, [if I lye witeth Mathew]:   *M. knows if (C)*
Quodcumque vultis ut faciant vobis homines, facite eis.

60   Alle libbynge laborers that lyven with hir hondes,   *living*
That treweliche taken and treweliche wynnen,   *obtain (wealth); gain*
And lyven in love and in lawe, for hir lowe herte   *humble*
Haveth the same absolucion that sent was to Piers.
      Beggeres ne bidderes ne beth noght in the bulle
65 But if the suggestion be sooth that shapeth hem to begge:
                                                                 reason; genuine; causes
For he that beggeth or bit, but if he have nede,   *begs; unless*
He is fals with the feend and defraudeth the nedy,
And also he gileth the gyvere ageynes his wille;   *cheats; against*
For if he wiste he were noght nedy he wolde yyve that another
                                                                                         give . . . (to)
70 That were moore nedyer than he – so the nedieste sholde be holpe.
Caton kenneth men thus, and the Clerc of the Stories;
                                                                 Cato; Peter Comestor (C)

Cui des, videto is Catons techyng;
And in the Stories he techeth to bistowe thyn almesse: *i.e. Comestor*
Sit elemosina tua in manu tua donec studes cui des.
      Ac Gregory was a good man, and bad us gyven alle

59a All things (therefore) whatsoever you would that men should do to you,
    do you also to them (Mt 7: 12).
72 Take heed whom you give [alms] to (*Distichs of Cato, brev. sent.* 17).
73a Let your alms remain in your hand until you have taken pains to find out
    whom you should give to (C).

59   Ye . . . Mathew] *cj* K–D; *cf.* leiȝe
     I ouȝt trowe ye ?AZ (o.] now Z);
     as 3 ll.: Ye l. and l. holdeþ þis for
     truþe/ That if þat I lye M. is to
     blame/ For he bad me make ȝow
     þis and þis prouerbe me tolde *All
     MSS* (and¹] and ye R; For . . . tolde
     om F) (C).
60   wiþ] βRC; by FZA.
62   herte] αZAK–D; hertes β.
68   he gyleth] ?αZAC [he] *om*
     ZAC); he bigileþ W&r [he] *om*
     GC²F).

69   *Div. from* 70 *before* Anoþer *All
     MSS* (C).
     ȝyue þat] W&r; gyue yt GF; it gyue
     y.
70   nedyer] αM (-ere *erased* M);
     nedy β.
     þan he] βF (he] & he F); and
     nauȝtier R.
71   men] L&r; me wGOC².
     þe²] LMα; *om* wg.
73a in] LMα; tua in wg.
74   was a] β; is a R; þat F.

75 That asketh for His love that us al leneth: *for love of Him; gives*
    Non eligas cui miserearis, ne forte pretereas illum qui meretur
        accipere; quia incertum est pro quo Deo magis placeas.
    For wite ye nevere who is worthi – ac God woot who hath nede.
    In hym that taketh is the trecherie, if any treson walke—   *deceit*
    For he that yeveth, yeldeth, and yarketh hym to reste,

                                              gives; pays; prepares
    And he that biddeth, borweth, and bryngeth hymself in dette.

                                                   (i.e. to sin)
80 For beggeres borwen everemo, and hir borgh is God Almyghty—

                                                   surety
    To yelden hem that yeveth hem, and yet usure moore: *interest also*
    Quare non dedisti pecuniam meam ad mensam, ut
    ego veniens cum usuris exigissem utique illam?
    Forthi biddeth noght, ye beggeres, but if ye have gret nede.
    For whoso hath to buggen hym breed – the Book bereth witnesse—
    He hath ynough that hath breed ynough, though he have noght ellis:
    Satis dives est qui non indiget pane.
85 Lat usage be youre solas of seintes lyves redyng;

75*a* Do not choose (for yourself) whom to take mercy upon, for it may be that
       you will pass over someone who deserves to receive (your alms): for it is not
       certain for which (act) you may please God more [*sc.* giving to the deserving
       or the undeserving] (Jerome) (C).
78   He who gives renders payment [*sc.* to God for his own sins] and (in doing
     so) procures relief for himself [*sc.* from the punishment otherwise due for
     these].
81–1*a* Who will pay their almsgivers with interest [*sc.* for the 'use' of their
     money]: 'And why then didst thou not give my money into the bank, that at
     my coming I might have exacted it with usury [*sc.* interest]?' (Lk 19: 23).
84*a* He is rich enough, who does not lack bread (Jerome) (C).
85   Let the practice of reading saints' lives be your comfort.

75*a* *misere-*] L&r; *miseri-*
       WHmYCBmBo.
       deo] wGCotM; *deum* L&r.
76   wite ye] W&r; *trs* CryF.
77   In; þe] β; Alle in (A.] For F); *om*
     α.
78   þat] βF; *om* R.
80   For] β; Forthi α.
81*a*   *veniens*] L&r; *v. meum* Cr²³;

meum Cr¹; *veniam* WHm.
exigissem] ?yα (*ex.*] & *ex.* α; *-ig-*]
-eg- CotFSk); *exigerem* CrL;
exigere WHmGOC².
vtique illam] F; *illam &c* Cot; *&c*
Hm&r; *om* WCrYLR (C).
82   gret] wLMR; *om* gF.
84*a*   *non*] βF; *om* R.

The Book banneth beggerie, and blameth hem in his manere;   *forbids*
Iunior fui etenim senui, et non vidi iustum derelictum, nec
   semen eius querens panem.

   For [thei] lyve in no love, ne no lawe holde: *observe*
[Thei] ne wedde [no] wommen that [thei] with deele,

                                             have intercourse with

90 But as wilde bestes with 'wehee' worthen uppe and werchen,

                                             mount; go to it

   And bryngen forth barnes that bastardes men calleth.   *children*
   Or the bak or som boon thei breketh in his youthe,   *Either; bone*
   And goon [and] faiten with hire fauntes for everemoore after.

                                             beg falsely; children

   Ther is moore mysshapen amonges thise beggeres   *deformed people*
95 Than of alle [othere] manere men that on this moolde walketh.
   Tho that lyve thus hir lif mowe lothe the tyme
   That evere he was man wroght, whan he shal hennes fare.   *made*
      Ac olde men and hore that helplees ben of strengthe,   *grey*
   And wommen with childe that werche ne mowe,
100 Blynde and bedreden and broken in hire membres,   *bedridden*
   That taken this myschief mekeliche, as mesels and othere,   *lepers*
   Han as pleyn pardon as the Plowman hymselve.   *full*
   For love of hir lowe hertes Oure Lord hath hem graunted   *humble*

---

87 I have been young, and now am old: and I have not seen the just forsaken,
   nor his seed seeking bread (Ps 36: 25).

86 hem] wLMR; *om* gF.
87 *derelictum . . . panem*] β (*q. p.*]
   q. p. &c HmOC²B; *&c* WGL)F;
   om R?C.
88 they] *so* ZACK–D; ȝe W&r;
   beggeres F.
89 They¹] *so* AZCK–D; Manye of
   yow βR; Many man F.
   no] *so* ZACK–D; noȝt þe *All MSS.*
   wommen] L&rZ?AC; womman
   WHmYOCBF.
   þat] wBLMα; *om* ?g.
   they²] *so* ZACK–D; he F; ye βR.
92 som] βFC; þe R.
   þei] αZACK–D; he β.
   his] βZA; here αCot (*cf.* C); þe G.
93 And¹] *so* AZCK–D; And siþþe

W&r; & *so* F.
   and²] *so* ZACK–D; þey F; *om* βR.
   here] αOC²ZACK–D; youre ?β.
94 mysshapen] *so* AZCK–D; m.
   peple *All MSS.*
95 oþer] *so* AZCK–D; *om All MSS.*
   walkeþ] βRC; wandreþ FZA;
   reignyn Hm.
96 þo] ?α (For þo F)ZA?CK–D;
   And þei β.
97 he was man] L&r (he was] *trs*
   F);
   þei were men wZ.
   he²] L&rA; þei WHmCr²³.
100 in] ?α (*l. om* F)Z?AC; *om* β.
101 þis mischief] LMαZA; þise
   myschiefs wg (þ.] the Cr; *om* GC.

Hir penaunce and hir purgatorie upon this [pure] erthe.   *very*
105   'Piers,' quod a preest thoo, 'thi pardon moste I rede;
      For I shal construe ech clause and kenne it thee on Englissh.' *explain*
          And Piers at his preiere the pardon unfoldeth—   *request*
      And I bihynde hem bothe biheld al the bulle.
      In two lynes it lay, and noght a le[ttre] moore,
110   And was ywriten right thus in witnesse of Truthe:
      Et qui bona egerunt ibunt in vitam eternam;
      Qui vero mala, in ignem eternum.
          'Peter!' quod the preest thoo, 'I kan no pardon fynde
      But "Do wel and have wel, and God shal have thi soule,"
      And "Do yvel and have yvel, and hope thow noon oother   *expect*
      That after thi deeth day the devel shal have thi soule!" ' *But that*
115   And Piers for pure tene pulled it atweyne   *sheer anger, vexation*
      And seide, '*Si ambulavero in medio umbre mortis*
      Non timebo mala, quoniam tu mecum es.
          'I shal cessen of my sowyng,' quod Piers, 'and swynke noght so
      harde,   *leave off; labour*
      Ne aboute my bely joye so bisy be na moore;   *pleasure in food*
120   Of preieres and of penaunce my plough shal ben herafter, *In; consist*
      And wepen whan I sholde slepe, though whete breed me faille.
          'The prophete his payn eet in penaunce and in sorwe, *bread*
      By that the Sauter seith – so dide othere manye.
      That loveth God lelly, his liflode is ful esy: *He who loves; faithfully*
      Fuerunt michi lacrime mee panes die ac nocte.

110*a* And those who have done well shall go into eternal life; but those who
      (have done) evil (will go) into eternal fire (40th clause of Athanasian Creed)
      (C).
116–17 (For) though I should walk in the midst of the shadow of death, I will
      fear no evils: for thou art with me (Ps 22: 4); cf. XII 291.
124*a* My tears have been my bread day and night (Ps 41: 4).

104   Vpon ... puyr] *so* ZACK–D;
      here vpon þis ?α (here is open F);
      here on þis β.
      (*Z ceases here*) (C).
106   shal] αAK–D; wol β.
107   vnfoldeþ] W&r (eþ) -ed Cr²³F)
      AC; he v. R.
109   In] GACK–D; Al in L&r (& al
      in F); And in W.
      lettre] *so* ACK–D; leef *All MSS*

      (C).
110   Iwriten] αAC; writen β.
113   &³] F (?=α) ACK–D; *om* W&r
      (*l. om* Cot).
114   þat] LMαA; But wg (And Y; *l.*
      om Cot)C.
120   of²] W&rA; *om* Hmg.
      penaunce] βA; *pl* α.
123   othere manye] W&r?A; *trs* y.

125 And but if Luc lye, he lereth us be fooles: *teaches; fools*
    We sholde noght be to bisy aboute the worldes blisse:
    Ne soliciti sitis, he seith in the Gospel,
    And sheweth us by ensamples us selve to wisse.   *parables; conduct*
    The foweles in the feld, who fynt hem mete at wynter? *provides; food*
130 Have thei no gerner to go to, but God fynt hem alle.'   *granary*
        'What!' quod the preest to Perkyn, 'Peter! as me thynketh,
    Thow art lettred a litel – who lerned thee on boke?'
                                        educated; taught to read

        'Abstynence the Abbesse,' quod Piers, 'myn a.b.c. me taughte,
    And Conscience cam afterward and kenned me muche moore.'
135 'Were thow a preest, Piers,' quod he, 'thow myghtest preche where
        thow woldest
    As divinour in divinite, with *Dixit insipiens* to thi teme.'   *expositor*
        'Lewed lorel!' quod Piers, 'litel lokestow on the Bible;
                                        Ignorant wastrel
    On Salomons sawes selden thow biholdest—   *sayings; seldom; look*
    Eice derisores et iurgia cum eis ne crescant . . .'
    The preest and Perkyn apposeden either oother—
                                        disputed with each other
140 And I thorugh hir wordes awook, and waited aboute,   *looked*
    And seigh the sonne in the south sitte that tyme.
    Metelees and moneilees on Malverne hulles,   *Without food and money*
    Musynge on this metels a my[le] wey ich yede.   *dream; went*

---

127 Be not solicitous (for your life etc.) (Mt 6: 25; also in Lk 12: 22).
136 The fool hath said [in his heart: There is no God] (Ps 13: 1) (C).
138a Cast out the scoffer, and contention shall go with him: and quarrels and
     reproaches shall cease (Prov 22: 10).

125 he] β (*om* Hm); or α.
    be foles] α?A; by foweles β (by] be
    C²) (C).
129 in] wgFA; on LM; of R.
133 þe Abbesse] βA; *om* α.
134 -ward] ?A; *om* M.
    muche moore] W&r (mu.] wil F);
    better GA.
135 where . . . *w*oldest] W&r (w.]
    wold ::: R; sholdest β); abowte F.
136 in] β; of αG.
137 þe] βF; þi C²CotR.
138 On] ?β (Vppon B; Or on OC²;
    And on Y)A; and R; þere F.

138a Eice] OC²BmCotMαASk;
     Ecce W&r.
     & . . . &c] βA; & exibit cum eo
     iurgium cessabitque cause &
     contumelie F; *om* R.
139 apposeden] L&rAC; opposeden
    WBmBoC.
140 I . . . awook] W&r?A; þorgh
    here wordes y awook FY (y] *om* Y).
143 þis] W&rAC; thise HmCr²³g.
    a myle] *so* ACK–D; a my R; on my
    M; as y my F; my G; many Y; and
    my ?β.

Many tyme this metels hath maked me to studie   *ponder (upon)*
145 Of that I seigh slepynge – if it so be myghte;
And for Piers the Plowman ful pencif in herte,   *(to be) pensive*
And which a pardon Piers hadde, al the peple to conforte,

                                                      what sort of
And how the preest inpugned it with two propre wordes.

                                                      impugned; fine (C)
Ac I have no savour in songewarie, for I se it ofte faille;

                                                      taste for interpreting dreams
150 Caton and canonistres counseillen us to leve   *canonists; refrain from*
To sette sadnesse in songewarie – for *sompnia ne cures.*

                                                      Taking seriously
Ac for the book Bible bereth witnesse   *However, since*
How Daniel divined the dremes of a kynge   *interpreted, expounded*
That was Nabugodonosor nempned of clerkes . . .

                                                      named N. by scholars (C)
155 Daniel seide, 'Sire Kyng, thi dremels bitokneth   *dream signifies*
That unkouthe knyghtes shul come thi kyngdom to cleyme;

                                                      strange soldiers; claim
Amonges lower lordes thi lond shal be departed.'   *divided*
And as Daniel divined, in dede it fel after: *it actually turned out*
The kyng lees his lordshipe, and lower men it hadde.   *lost*
160   And Joseph mette merveillously how the moone and the sonne

                                                      dreamed
And the ellevene sterres hailsed hym alle.   *stars; did obeisance to*
Thanne Jacob jugged Josephes swevene: *interpreted; dream*
'*Beau fitz,*' quod his fader, 'for defaute we shullen—

                                                      Fair son; lack; famine
I myself and my sones – seche thee for nede.'   *seek (cf. Gen 37: 9–10)*
165 It bifel as his fader seide, in Pharaoes tyme,
That Joseph was Justice Egipte to loke: *Judge; govern*

---

151 Take no account of dreams, [for while asleep the human mind sees what it
hopes and wishes for] (*Distichs of Cato* II, 31).

144 þis] W&r (*om* F)AC; thise Hm
Cr²³g.
146 And] GACK–D; And also
W&r.
147 al] W&r; *om* GFC.
152 book] W&rC; b. of þe Hm?g

(of] *om* G); *om* ?Ax.
153 dremes] L&rAC; dreem
WHmR.
155 -els] W&r; -es HmCrC²CBF.
156 cleyme] ?β (cleue GOC²LM)A;
reue α.

It bifel as his fader tolde – hise frendes there hym soughte.   *family*

   Al this maketh me on metels to thynke—

And how the preest preved no pardon to Dowel,   *(belonged) to*

170 And demed that Dowel indulgences passed,   *(I) judged that D. excelled*

Biennals and triennals and bisshopes lettres,

                                     Biennial, triennial masses (C)

And how Dowel at the day of dome is digneliche underfongen,

                                    honourably received

And passeth al the pardon of Seint Petres cherche.

                               is superior to papal pardons

   Now hath the Pope power pardon to graunte   *the Pope has (C)*

175 The peple, withouten penaunce to passen into [joye];

This is oure bileve, as lettred men us techeth: *faith*

Quodcumque ligaveris super terram erit ligatum et in celis . . .

And so I leve leelly (Lordes forbode ellis!) *believe faithfully; Lord forbid*

That pardon and penaunce and preieres doon save

Soules that have synned seven sithes dedly.   *times; mortally*

180 Ac to trust to thise triennals – trewely, me thynketh,

It is noght so siker for the soule, certes, as is Dowel.   *sure, certain*

   Forthi I rede yow renkes that riche ben on this erthe: *advise; men*

Upon trust of youre tresor triennals to have,

                         Trusting in your wealth to have

Be ye never the bolder to breke the ten hestes;   *Commandments*

185 And namely ye maistres, meires and jugges,   *rulers; mayors*

That have the welthe of this world and wise men ben holden,   *held*

176a [And] whatsoever thou shalt bind upon earth, it shall be bound also in heaven . . . (Mt 16: 19) (C).

167 frendes . . . souȝte] βR (þ. h.] trs R); fawntys sowtyn þere F.
168 Al; on] *so* ACK–D; and al; on þis *All MSS* (þ.] my F).
170 Indulgences] W&rC; *sg* Cr²³Y CBRA.
173 þe] βFA; *om* R.
174–81 *Ll. om* OC².
174–5 *So div.* F (?=α)ACK–D; *after* peple βR(C).
175 Ioye] *so* ACK–D; heuene *All MSS*.

176a *&c*] W&r (*l. om* F)C; *om* CrCotRA.
177 lordes forbode] W&r (l.] oure l. B, -is *erased* Cot); our l. forbede Hm (-bede] -bode Hm)GFA?C.
180 to²] W&r; on GFA; *vp* C.
181 It] αACK–D; *om* β.
182 renkes] βAC; thenke RB (to þ. B); all F.
186 and] g (þat Y)αACK–D; and for wLM.

To purchace yow pardon and the Popes bulles.

(Do not rely on it) to ...

At the dredful dome, whan dede shulle rise   *judgement; the dead*
And comen alle bifore Crist acountes to yelde—

190   How thow laddest thi lif here and hise lawes keptest,   *you led*
And how thow didest day by day the doom wole reherce.   *declare*
A pokeful of pardon there, ne provincials lettres,   *Neither a bagful*
Theigh ye be founde in the fraternite of alle the fyve ordres

'as an associate member' (C)

And have indulgences doublefold – but Dowel yow helpe,   *unless*
195   I sette youre patentes and youre pardon at one pies hele!

value; licences; crust

Forthi I counseille alle Cristene to crie God mercy,
And Marie his moder be oure meene bitwene,   *intermediary*
That God gyve us grace here, er we go hennes,
Swiche werkes to werche, the while we ben here,
200   That after oure deth day, Dowel reherce   *might declare*
At the day of dome, we dide as he highte.   *commanded.*

---

188   rise] WLαC; aryse HmCrgMA.
189   bi-] L&rAC; to w; a- G.
191   þow didest] βR (d.] dost R)A;
      3e don F.
193   fyue] ?αC; foure βF(C).
194   but] αGACK–D; but if β.
      Dowel] βFAC; d. wil R.

199   þe] αC; om βA.
RUBRIC   *Explicit octavus passus de
visione* G; *Explicit Passus Quintus*
F; *Explicit visio Willelmi de petro
plowman et sequitur vita de dowel
Dobett et Do beste secundum wytt
et reson* + *l. h.* C²ACSk; *om* W&r.

Passus VIII

Thus yrobed in russet I romed aboute   *coarse woollen cloth*
Al a somer seson for to seke Dowel,
And frayned ful ofte of folk that I mette   *inquired*
If any wight wiste wher Dowel was at inne,   *dwelling*
5 And what man he myghte be of many man I asked.   *what (sort of)*
    Was nevere wight as I wente that me wisse kouthe *could direct me*
Where this leode lenged, lasse ne moore—   *man lived; humble or great*
Til it bifel on a Friday two freres I mette,
Maistres of the Menours, men of grete witte.   *Friars Minor (C)*
10 I hailsed hem hendely, as I hadde ylerned,   *greeted; courteously*
And preide hem, *pur charite*, er thei passed ferther, *for charity's sake*
If they knewe any contree or costes [aboute]   *regions*
Where that Dowel dwelleth – 'Dooth me to witene'— *Let me know*
For thei be men of this moolde that moost wide walken, *world*
15 And knowen contrees and courtes and many kynnes places—
Bothe princes paleises and povere mennes cotes,   *cottages*
And Dowel and Do-yvele, wher thei dwelle bothe.   *Do-ill, evil*
    'Amonges us', quod the Menours, 'that man is dwellynge,
And evere hath, as I hope, and evere shal herafter.'
20   '*Contra!*' quod I as a clerc, and comsed to disputen, *'I dispute that'*
And seide, 'Soothly, *Sepcies in die cadit iustus.*
Sevene sithes, seith the Book, synneth the rightfulle,   *times; just*

---

21 For a just man shall fall seven times [and shall rise again] . . . (Prov 24: 16).

Collation WHmCrGYOC²CBLMRF.
RUBRIC *Passus viij^us de visione et
primus de dowel* W&r (*v.*] *v. petri
plowhman incipit dowel dobet et
dobest* R; *pr.*] *incipit inquisicio
prima* M); *Incipit Passus Sextus* F.
4 was] βAC; were α.
6 Was] βAC; And was R; But þere
was F.
wiȝt . . . wente] βFA; in þis worlde
RC (C).
9 Maistres] βAC; And m. ?α (m.]

weryn M. F).
11 *pur*] HmOC²BFAC; *par* WGY
LM; for CrCR.
12 contree] βAC; courte αCr²³.
aboute] *so* ACK–D; *as* þei wente
All MSS (as] þer α).
14–17 *In* βC; *ll. om* α.
18 *So* βR (þe] a R); Marye quod þo
m. amongys vs he dwellyþ FA (C).
20 a] βFAC; *om* YR.
21 sothli] ?β (hem s. wg)C; *om* ?α
(*l. om* F).

And whoso synneth,' I seide, 'dooth yvele, as me thynketh,
And Dowel and Do-yvele mowe noght dwelle togideres.
25 *Ergo* he nys noght alwey at hoom amonges yow freres: *Therefore*
He is outherwhile elliswhere to wisse the peple.'   *sometimes; guide*
    'I shal seye thee, my sone,' seide the frere thanne,
'How seven sithes the sadde man synneth on the day*e*.   *virtuous; daily*
By a forbisne,' quod the frere, 'I shal thee faire shewe.   *parable; aptly*
30 'Lat brynge a man in a boot amydde a brode watre: *Put; boat; wide*
The wynd and the water and the [waggyng of the boote]   *rocking*
Maketh the man many tyme to falle and to stonde.   *rise again*
For stonde he never so stif, he stumbleth if he meve—
                                            firmly; loses footing; move
Ac yet is he saaf and sound, and so hym bihoveth;   *needs must be*
35 For if he ne arise the rather and raughte to the steere,
                                            sooner; grasp; helm
The wynd wolde with the water the boot overthrowe,   *capsize*
And thanne were his lif lost thorugh lachesse of hymselve.   *fault*
    'And thus it fareth,' quod the frere, 'by folk here on erthe.
The water is likned to the world, that wanyeth and wexeth;
40 The goodes of this grounde arn lik to the grete wawes   *earth; waves*
That as wyndes and wedres walweth aboute;   *storms; toss*
The boot is likned to oure body that brotel is of kynde,   *fragile; nature*
That thorugh the fend and thi flessh and this frele worlde   *changeable*
Synneth the sadde man [seven sithes a day*e*].
45 'Ac dedly synne doth he noght, for Dowel hym kepeth,   *protects*
And that is charite the champion, chief help ayein synne;   *against*
For he strengtheth man to stonde, and steereth mannes soule
                                            strengthens

---

23   seide] *All MSS*; s. sertis **AC** (C).
25   at hoom] **FACK–D**; om βR(C).
28   synneþ; on þe day] **F** (d.] day
     ty3de **F**)**ACK–D**; *trs* βR (þe] a wg)
     (C).
30   a³] **LRAC**; þe **W&r**.
31   waggyng . . . boote] *so* **ACK–D**;
     boot waggyng *All MSS* (bote] **L**;
     boot **W**).
32   tyme] **CrOC²R?ACK–D**; a tyme
     W&r.
34   Ac] **WOLMR?C**; and **Hm&rA**.
35   steere] βA; sterne α**HmC²**.

36   wiþ] βA; and **R**; on **F**.
38   And] βR; Ryght **FA**.
     ytt farethe] **GF** (*trs* **F**)**ACK–D**; it
     falleþ **W&r** (C).
41   walweth] **LMAC**; walkeþ **W&r**
     (*l. om* **Hm**).
43   þi] **LR**; þe **wgMA**; oure **FC**.
     þis] ?α**C**; þe β**FA**.
     frele] β**RC**; false **FA**.
44   seuen siþes; a day] *so* **A** (a] in þe
     A)**K–D**; *trs All MSS*.
45   kepeþ] βR; helpiþ **FA**.
47   man] **L&r**; men **W**.

That, though thi body bowe as boot dooth in the watre, *So that; sink*
Ay is thi soule saaf but thow thiselve wole   *Always; unless*
50 Do a deedly synne and drenche so thiselve.   *drown*
God wole suffre wel thi sleuthe, if thiself liketh;
For he yaf thee to yeresyyve to yeme wel thiselve—

                                        a New Year's gift; govern
And that is wit and free will, to every wight a porcion,

                                            intelligence; creature
To fleynge foweles, to fisshes and to beestes;   *'birds of the air'*
55 Ac man hath moost therof, and moost is to blame
But if he werche wel therwith, as Dowel hym techeth.'
    'I have no kynde knowyng,' quod I, 'to conceyve alle thi wordes,
                                                          take in
Ac if I may lyve and loke, I shal go lerne bettre.'
    'I bikenne thee Crist,' quod he, 'that on the cros deyde.'

                                            commend you to
60 And I seide, 'The same save yow from myschaunce,   *misfortune*
And yyve yow grace on this grounde goode men to worthe!'

    And thus I wente widewher, walkyng myn one,

                                    far and wide; on my own
By a wilde wildernesse and by a wode side;   *edge of a wood*

51–2 God is quite willing to put up with your backsliding, if that's the way
    you must have it; For he gave you as a pure gift (the power) to govern
    yourself properly . . .

57–8 I cannot understand by my native wit alone the full import of what you
    say, But if I can [learn by] experience and observation, I shall learn better
    how to do so/learn a better lesson [than you teach].

48 þat] αAK–D; And β (*om* G).   53 and²] W&r; a LM.
    þi] L&rA; þe WHmG.   54 and] W&r; & also g.
49 but] LMRA; but if W&r.   57 conceyue] L&r; conceyuen W.
    þiself wole] L&r (þi.] þou þi. M);   alle þi] ?αC (þi] þis C); a. youre β;
    þou w. þi WCr.   þi FA.
    After this a line: If þou folwe þy   59 quod he] WHm?α (he] þat on
    fowle flesh3 & þe feend þereafter   Hm; þei R)C; *om* CrgLMA.
    FA (Folewe þi flesshis wil & þe   þe] L&rAC; *om* WGM.
    fendis aftir A) (C).   61 men to worþe] βR; ende to make
50 so] W&r (þanne F); *om* g.   F(C).
    -selue] ?αAK–D; soule βF.   63 wode] L&rC; wodes WCr
51 sleuþe] β; soule αHm.   (brookes Cr¹) GYC²CB.
52 to¹] L&r (two CrF); a WG.

Blisse of the briddes abide me made,   *The joyful sound; birds; stop*
65 And under lynde upon a launde lened I a stounde
          linden; clearing; reclined; time
To lythe the layes that the lovely foweles made.   *listen to; songs*
Murthe of hire mouthes made me ther to slepe;   *(The) merry sound*
The merveillouseste metels mette me thanne   *dream*
That ever [wight dremed] in world, as I wene.   *man*
70   A muche man, as me thoughte, lik to myselve,   *tall*
Cam and called me by my kynde name.   *right, very own*
  'What art thow,' quod I tho, 'that thow my name knowest?' *then*
  'That thow woost wel,' quod he, 'and no wight bettre.'
  'Woot I,' [quod I], 'who art thow?' 'Thought,' seide he thanne.
75 'I have sued thee this seven yeer; seye thow me no rather?'
          followed; saw; earlier
  'Art thow Thought?' quod I thoo; 'thow koudest me wisse *inform*
Where that Dowel dwelleth, and do me to knowe.'
  'Dowel,' quod he, 'and Dobet and Dobest the thridde
         Do-better; third
Arn thre faire vertues, and ben noght fer to fynde.   *far*
80 Whoso is trewe of his tunge and of his two handes,
And thorugh his labour or thorugh his land his liflode wynneth,
And is trusty of his tailende, taketh but his owene,   *reckoning*
And is noght dronkelewe ne deynous, Dowel hym folweth.
        given to drink; arrogant

---

64 þe] W&rAC; þo HmLR.
  abyde me made] αCASk; brou3te
  me aslepe β.
65 vnder] BoCotRC; v. a W&rA.
66 þat þe] ?αB (þe) þo BmBo)?A; the
  HmCMF; þo W&r.
68 The] βF (& þe F)A; om R.
69 wi3t . . . wene] dremed w. in
  world as I wene βR; w. in þis w. as
  y wene dremede F (C).
70 lik] so ACK–D; and lik βR; he
  was mychil l. F.
72 art þow] R&rACK–D; artow
  WYCLM.
  I] ?α?AC; I þo βF.
  þow²] W&rC; om MA.
74 quod y] so CAK–D; om All
  MSS.

who art þou] FACK–D; what þow
art βR (C).
76 So div. from 77 βFCA; after
  where R.
  Art þow] L&rAC; Artow WGYC.
  wisse] βRC; telle FA.
77 to] so ACK–D; þat to β; hym to
  α.
78 So FA (cf. C)K–D; Do. and do.
  and do. þe þridde quod he βR (C).
80 After this a line: & meeke in his
  herte & my3lde of his speche F (cf.
  A) (C).
81 or þoru3] W&r; or Cr²³OC²CA;
  and YCr¹B; of FG.
  land] W&r (pl y); hand FG (pl G).
83 deygnous] CB?αA?CK–D;
  dedeynous βR (de- canc R).

'Dobet dooth right thus, ac he dooth muche moore;

85 He is as lowe as a lomb and lovelich of speche, *humble; pleasing, kind*
And helpeth alle men after that hem nedeth. *according to their needs*
The bagges and the bigirdles, he hath tobroke hem alle

purses; destroyed

That the Erl Avarous heeld, and hise heires;
And with Mammonaes moneie he hath maad hym frendes,

Mammon's (cf. Lk 16: 9)

90 And is ronne into religion, and hath rendred the Bible,

the religious life; expounded

And precheth to the peple Seint Poules wordes—
Libenter suffertis insipientes cum sitis ipsi sapientes:
[Ye wise], suffreth the unwise with yow for to libbe, *allow; live*
And with glad wille dooth hem good, for so God yow hoteth.

commands

95 'Dobest is above bothe and bereth a bisshopes cro[c]e, *crosier*
Is hoked on that oon ende to halie men fro helle. *hooked; draw*
A pik is on that potente, to pulte adown the wikked

spike; staff; thrust

That waiten any wikkednesse Dowel to tene. *contrive; injure*
And Dowel and Dobet [ordeyned hem amonges]
100 To crowne oon to be kyng to [kepen] hem bothe, *govern*
That if Dowel or Dobet dide ayein Dobest, *(So) that; acted against*

---

90 And has entered the ministry *(Sk)* / a religious order.
92 [For] you gladly suffer the foolish; whereas yourselves are wise (II Cor 11: 19).

87 to-] W&rC; *om* HmGBFA.
89 and] αACK–D; And þus β.
90 into] LMα?AC; to wg.
91 -eþ] wBLM?αAC; -ed ?gR. to] βRC; *om* FA.
92 *insip-; sitis ipsi]* β; *incip-; trs* α.
93 ʒe wise] *so* AC (w.] worldliche w. C)K–D; And βR; he seyþ ʒee sholde gladly F (C).
95 croce] *so* AC; crosse *All MSS.*
96 hoked] βFA; an hoke R. on] βR; at FA.
97 is] βFA; *om* R. pulte] L&r (pul CrY) *(cf.* C); *pulte* WHmGCBMF.

99–108 *In the order* 104–7, 101–2, 108 F.
99 ordeyned hem amonges] am. hem ord. L&r (ord.] han ord. w); *l. om* F (C).
100 *So* β *(cf.* AC); *run together with* 105 R (oon] β; and R); *l. om* F (C). kepe] *so* AK–D; rulen β; 100b *om* R.
101 That if] βA; For if þat ?α (*l. om* R).
or] W&r?A; and Cr.
After this a line: & weren vnbuxum to don his byddyngge & bown to do ille FA (C).

Thanne sholde the kyng come and casten hem in prisoun,
And but if Dobest bede for hem, thei to be ther for evere.

intercede; they (were) to be

'Thus Dowel and Dobet and Dobest the thridde

105 Crowned oon to be kyng to kepen hem alle
And rule the reme by hire thre wittes,   *the wisdom of those three*
And ootherwise [ne ellis noght], but as thei thre assented.'
   I thonked Thoght tho that he me [so] taughte.
'Ac yet savoreth me noght thi seying, so me Crist helpe!

appeals to me

110 For more kynde knowynge I coveite to lerne—

a more direct understanding

How Dowel, Dobet and Dobest doon among the peple.'
   'But Wit konne wisse thee.' quod Thoght, 'where tho thre dwelle;
Ellis woot I noon that kan, that now is alyve.'   *Apart (from him)*

   Thoght and I thus thre daies we yeden   *went (about)*
115 Disputyng upon Dowel day after oother—   *each day in succession*
And er we war were, with Wit gonne we mete.   *aware*
He was long and lene, lik to noon oother;   *tall; lean*
Was no pride on his apparaille, ne poverte neither;
Sad of his semblaunt and of [a] softe [speche].   *Grave; countenance*
120 I dorste meve no matere to maken hym to jangle   *urge; dispute, argue*

---

107 And not in any other manner else, except in so far as those three should
agree.

102   sholde; presoun] ?α (*l. om* R)
AK–D; shal; irens β.
After this a line: & pitte hem þere
in penawnce withoute pite or grace
FA (C).

103   *In* βA; *l. om* α.

104   thus] βAC; And þus ?α (*l. om*
R).

105   Crowned ... kyng] βF (Cr.)
haue crowne F)AC; *om* R.
to ... alle] βRC (hem] vs C); & be
here conseyl wirche FA (C).

106   hire ... wittes] βRC; reed of
hem alle FA (C).

107   oþere ... nouȝt] *so* ACK–D;
noon ooþer wise *All MSS* (n.] in n.
BM; be n. F) (C).

108   me so] *so* ACK–D; me þus β
(þus] *om* B)R; so faire me F.

109–10   So FACK–D; *run together*
βR(C).

109   so ... helpe] FCA (crist] god
AK–D); *om* βR.

110   For ... knowynge] FCA (For]
A C; *om* A); *om* βR.

113   woot] βR?Ax; knowe FC.

114   we] W&rAC; *om* g.

115   vpon] βRC; on FA.

116   war were] ?αAC; *trs* βF.

119   of ... speche] *so* AC (of] with
C)K–D; of softe chere βR; softe he
was of chere F.

But as I bad Thoght thoo be mene bitwene   *asked; intermediary*
And pute forth som purpos to preven hise wittes,   *line of argument*
What was Dowel fro Dobet, and Dobest from hem bothe.

Thanne Thoght in that tyme seide thise wordes:
125 'Wher Dowel and Dobet and Dobest ben in londe   *Where; on earth*
Here is Wil wolde wite if Wit koude teche hym;
And wheither he be man or no man this man fayn wolde aspie,
And werchen as thei thre wolde – this is his entente.'   *act; aim*

122–3 And propose some line of discussion with which to put his intellect to
the test And distinguish between . . .

121 be] βFA?C; to be BoCotR.
122 And] βRC; To FA.
125 Wher] βAC; Whether CrR;
where dwellyþ F.
and¹] BFACK–D; *om* ?βR.
ben] β (was CB) AC; *om* α.
126 Here . . . wite] βR (is) *om* R);
Fayn wold y wete witt F.

teche hym] β (*trs* G)RAC (hym) *om*
AC); me telle F.
127 no man] ?α (noon F)CBSk; man
L; womman W&r.
fayn wolde] WCrLM (f.) *erased*
M)α(*trs* F); wolde Hmg.
128 þis] L&r; thus WHmCr¹.

Passus IX

'Sire Dowel dwelleth,' quod Wit, 'noght a day hennes   *day('s journey)*
In a castel that Kynde made of foure kynnes thynges.

           Nature (=God); kinds of
Of erthe and eyr is it maad, medled togideres,   *air; mixed*
With wynd and with water wittily enjoyned.   *ingeniously joined*
5 Kynde hath closed therinne craftily withalle   *skilfully*
A lemman that he loveth lik to hymselve.   *beloved*
Anima she hatte; [to hir hath envye]   *Soul; is called; hostility*
A proud prikere of Fraunce, *Princeps huius mundi,*   *horseman*
And wolde wynne hire awey with wiles and he myghte.   *if*
10   'Ac Kynde knoweth this wel and kepeth hire the bettre,   *guards*
And hath doon hire with Sire Dowel, duc of thise marches.

           placed; duke; borderlands
Dobet is hire damyselle, Sire Doweles doughter,   *handmaid*
To serven this lady leelly bothe late and rathe.   *loyally; early*
Dobest is above bothe, a bisshopes peere;   *equal*
15 That he bit moot be do – he [bidd]eth hem alle.   *commands; directs (C)*
[By his leryng] is lad [that lady *Anima*].   *teaching; guided*
  'Ac the Constable of that castel, that kepeth [hem alle],   *looks after*

---

8 The Prince of this world [= the Devil] (Jn 16: 11).

Collation WHmCrGYOC²CBLMRF.
RUBRIC *Passus ix^{us} de visione vt
supra et primus de Dobet* W&r (*de
... Do.*] *om* YOC²; *vt ... Do*] *om*
LM; *et ... Do.*] *om* CR; *primus
... Do.*] *secundus de do weel*
HmB; *om* GF.
2 kynnes] βAC; maner α (m of F).
3 and] L&rAC; and of WB.
is it] W&r?A?C; *trs* HmOC²F.
4 wittili] OC²AC; witterly W&r
(C).
6 loueþ lik] βR; l. wel she is lych F.
7 to ... enuye] *so* ACK–D; ac
enuye hir hateþ *All MSS* (ac) but
GF; and CrC²C) (C).

9 and²] βR?C; yff GFA.
10 Ac] ?βA; And CrC²αC.
11 hath do] L&rAC; dooþ wCBF.
sire] βAC; *om* α.
duke] GYOC²FACK–D; is duc
W&r.
þise] βAC; þe R; þat F.
14 aboue] βC; ab. hem F; aboute R.
15 biddeþ] ruleþ *All MSS* (C).
16 By ... *Anima*] *so* C (By; þat]
And by; þat ilke C) K–D; *Anima
þat l. is lad by his leryng All MSS*
(An.] & An. F) (C).
17 þat¹] W&rC; þe Cr²³FA.
hem alle] *so* ACK–D; al þe wacche
All MSS.

Is a wis knyght withalle – Sir Inwit he hatte,   *'Conscience' (C); is called*
And hath fyve faire sones by his firste wyve: *wife*
20 Sire Se-wel, and Sey-wel, and Sire Here-wel the hende,   *courteous*
Sire Werch-wel-with-thyn-hand, a wight man of strengthe,   *powerful*
And Sire Godefray Go-wel – grete lordes [alle].
Thise fyve ben set to save this lady *Anima*   *preserve, keep safe*
Til Kynde come or sende to kepen hire hymselve.'
25 'What kynnes thyng is Kynde?' quod I, 'kanstow me telle?'
'Kynde,' quod Wit, 'is creatour of alle kynnes thynges,
Fader and formour of al that evere was maked—   *creator, former*
And that is the grete God that gynnyng hadde nevere,   *beginning*
Lord of lif and of light, of lisse and of peyne.   *delight*
30 Aungeles and alle thyng arn at his wille,
Ac man is hym moost lik of marc and of shafte.   *feature; form*
For thorugh the word that he spak woxen forth beestes:

                                                    were produced

Dixit et facta sunt.
'And made man [moost lik] to hymself one   *alone*
And Eve of his ryb bon withouten any mene.   *rib-bone; intermediary*
35 For he was synguler hymself seide *Faciamus*—   *singular, quite alone*
As who seith, "Moore moot herto than my word oone:
My myght moot helpe now with my speche."   *power must*
Right as a lord sholde make lettres, and hym [ne] lakked parchemyn,

                                                    Just as if; parchment

---

32*a* [For] he spoke, and they were made (Ps 148: 5).
35 Let us make (Gen 1: 26 *or* 2: 18) (C).
36 As if to say, 'More is needed to (bring) this about than my word alone'.

20   sire²] α?C; *om* βA.
22   grete lordes] βAC; a grete lord α.
 alle] *so* ACK–D; forsoþe *All MSS*
 (C).
23   fyue] βR?AC; sixe F (C).
24   kepen; hymselue] FACK–D;
 sauen (haue Hm); for euere βR.
25   kynnes] W&rA?C; *om* g.
26   is] MRACK–D; is a W&r (a
 Hm).
27   þat . . . maked] βR; þynge on
 erthe F.
28   that is] βA; He is F; *om* R.
29   lisse] W&r?AC; blisse CrGBMα.

31   hym moost] βAC; *trs* α.
 shafte] W&r?A; shape CrGC.
32   *After this* 2 *spurious ll. and
 another:* & al was maad þorgh his
 word as his will wolde F (*cf.* A) (C).
33   And] βR; But he F.
 man] βR (+ *a.h.* R; *glossed* i. adam
 LM); Adam Cr; furst Adam man
 Hm; Adam a man F.
 moost lik] likkest *All MSS* (C).
 -self one] W&r; selue F; one M.
35   seide] ?α (he s. F); and s. β.
37   now] L&r; forþ WF.
38   ne] *om All MSS* (C).

Though he koude write never so wel, if he [wel]de no penne,

knew how to

40   The lettre, for al the lordshipe, I leve were nevere ymaked!

would never be

'And so it semeth by him, as the Bible telleth, there he seide—
[*Dixit*, "*Faciamus*"]—
He moste werche with his word and his wit shewe.
And in this manere was man maad thorugh myght of God almyghty,

45   With his word and werkmanshipe and with lif to laste.

action; lasting life

And thus God gaf hym a goost, of the godhede of hevene,

spirit(ual soul); from

And of his grete grace graunted hym blisse—
And that is lif that ay shal laste to al his lynage after.   *descendants*
And that is the castel that Kynde made, *Caro* it hatte,

Flesh, living body

50   And is as muche to mene as "man with a soule."
And that he wroghte with werk and with word bothe:
Thorgh myght of the mageste man was ymaked.   *the (divine) majesty*
'Inwit and alle wittes yclosed ben therinne   *'Mind' (C); senses*
For love of the lady *Anima*, that lif is ynempned.   *named*

55   Over al in mannes body he[o] walketh and wandreth,
Ac in the herte is hir hoom and hir mooste reste.

'special dwelling-place' (C)

Ac Inwit is in the heed, and to the herte he loketh
What *Anima* is leef or looth – he lat hire at his wille;

pleasing or displeasing to A.; leads

---

43   He had to act as well as speak, and manifest (the power of his) mind.

39   if] βR; & F.
welde] hadde βR; lakked F (*C*).
no] W&r; a CBF.

41   *Div from* 42 *after* telle *All MSS*
(*C*).
semeþ] β (bis. M)F; semed R.
bible] W&r; boke g.
he seide] β (he] it CB)R; god seyde
þis sawe F.

42   *Dixit Faciamus*] *Dixit & facta*
sunt βR; *faciamus hominem ad*
ymaginem &c F (*C*).

46   of] L&r; þoru3 W.

48   his] αW; our Cr; *om* ?β.

49   þat[1]] βFA; þis R.

51   word] βA; his word*is* ?α (w.]
word F).

53   yclosed] ?α (Iclothed R)A; closed
βCx.

55   heo] *cj* K–D; 3he Hm; she Cr; he
W&r(*C*).

56   Ac] L&r (but GF)A; Ay M; And
wC[2]C.

57   he] βF; *om* CrR.

For after the grace of God, the gretteste is Inwit.

60 'Muche wo worth that wight that mysruleth his Inwit,

(will) befall; abuses

And that ben glotons glubberes – hir God is hire wombe:

gluttonous gulpers; belly

Quorum deus venter est.

For thei serven Sathan, hir soule shal he have:

That lyven synful lif here, hir soule is lich the devel.   *like*

And alle that lyven good lif are lik God almyghty:

Qui manet in caritate, in Deo manet . . .

65 'Allas! that drynke shal fordo that God deere boughte,

destroy; redeemed at such a cost

And dooth God forsaken hem that he shoop to his liknesse: *created*

Amen dico vobis, nescio vos. Et alibi, Et dimisi eos

secundum desideria eorum.

'Fooles that fauten Inwit, I fynde that Holy Chirche

lack; find (in books)

Sholde fynden hem that hem fauteth, and faderlese children,

provide what

And widewes that han noght wherwith to wynnen hem hir foode,

obtain

70 Madde men and maydenes that helplese were—

Alle thise lakken Inwit, and loore bihoveth.   *teaching*

'Of this matere I myghte make a long tale   *discourse*

And fynde fele witnesses among the foure doctours,   *many*

And that I lye noght of that I lere thee, Luc bereth witnesse.   *teach*

75 'Godfader and godmoder that seen hire godchildren

61a . . . whose god is their belly (Phil 3: 19).
64a He that abideth in charity abideth in God (I Jn 4: 16).
66a Amen, I say to you, I know you not (Mt 25: 12); And elsewhere, So I let
    them go according to the desires of their heart (Ps 80: 13).
71 All these lack the power to exercise rational control (over their own lives),
    and (so) they require guidance and instruction.

60 wiȝt] α; man β.   fauted WLM; faylen Hm); Ne
62 soule] LMR; pl W&r.   knowe non defawhte of F.
64 like] LR; lik to W&r; l. after F.   71 loore] βR; l. hem F.
66 he shoop] β; schope hem α.   73 witnesses] wBLMF; sg ?gR.
68 sholde . . . and] W&r (hem²]   74 of þat] β; om α.
    they Hm; om CrR; fauteth gRCr;   75 -fader; -moder] L&r; pl WCr.

At myseise and at myschief and mowe hem amende   *illness; distress*
Shul have penaunce in purgatorie, but yif thei hem helpe.
For moore bilongeth to the litel barn er he the lawe knowe   *is due*
Than nempnynge of a name, and he never the wiser!   *conferring*
80 Sholde no Cristene creature cryen at the yate   *Would; gate*
Ne faille payn ne potage, and prelates dide as thei sholden.

    lack bread or stew; if
A Jew wolde noght se a Jew go janglyng for defaute   *crying out; lack*
For alle the mebles on this moolde, and he amende it myghte. *goods*
   'Allas that a Cristene creature shal be unkynde til another!   *to*
85 Syn Jewes, that we jugge Judas felawes,   *Since; deem; companions*
Eyther helpeth oother of hem of that that hym nedeth.   *that which he*
Whi nel we Cristene [be of Cristes good as kynde]   *with Christ's goods*
As Jewes, that ben oure loresmen? Shame to us alle!   *teachers*
The commune for hir unkyndenesse, I drede me, shul abye.

    common people; pay

90   'Bisshopes shul be blamed for beggeres sake;
[Than Judas he is wors] that yyveth a japer silver   *buffoon (C)*
And biddeth the beggere go, for his broke clothes: *because of; torn*
Proditor est prelatus cum Iuda qui patrimonium Christi
minus distribuit. Et alibi, Perniciosus dispensator est
qui res pauperum Christi inutiliter consumit.
He dooth noght wel that dooth thus, ne drat noght God almyghty,

    fears

92a A traitor along with Judas is the prelate who falls short in distributing
   Christ's goods; And elsewhere, A ruinous giver is he who uselessly consumes
   what is due to Christ's poor (acc. to *Sk*, perhaps from Peter Cantor's
   Compendium (= his *Verbum abbreviatum*), chs 43, 47 (*PL* 205: 135, 150).

76 At[1]] β (& G); In F; þat is R.   of[2]] βF; *om* R.
   at[2]] wLR; *om* gMF.   hym] L&r; hem wGF.
77 ʒif] L&r; *om* WCrG.   87 nel] ?β; ne wol HmBR; wil Cr[1]F.
81 Ne[1]] β; And α.   be . . . kynde] of Cristes good be as
   ne[2]] β; and αHmG.   kynde *All MSS* (k.] k. willed (w.]
83 mebles] β; nobles ?α(mone   *added*)M) (C).
   F)Hm.   88 shame] β; to shame R; It is s. F.
   on] β (in G)F; of BR.   91 Than Iudas; he is wors] *trs All*
84 be] W&r; be so YOC[2]BM; so   *MSS* (C).
   ben F.   a Iaper] W&r; Iapers Cr[23]g.
86 Eyþer] β; þat ayther α (ay.] ech F).   92a christi[2]] W&r; *om* g.
   helpeth o.; of hem] α; *trs* β.

Ne loveth noght Salomons sawes, that Sapience taughte:
                                    sayings; wisdom

Inicium sapiencie timor Domini.

95 'That dredeth God, he dooth wel; that dredeth hym for love
And drad hym noght for drede of vengeaunce, dooth therfore the
    bettre.
He dooth best that withdraweth hym by daye and by nyghte
                            refrains constantly (from)
To spille any speche or any space of tyme: *Wasting (idly)*
Qui offendit in verbo, in omnibus est reus.

    '[Tyn]ynge of tyme, Truthe woot the sothe,   *Losing*
00 Is moost yhated upon erthe of hem that ben in hevene;   *by*
And siththe to spille speche, that spire is of grace, *next; shoot, sprout*
And Goddes gleman and a game of hevene.   *minstrel; delight*
Wolde nevere the feithful fader his fithele were untempred,
                                    fiddle; untuned
Ne his gleman a gedelyng, a goere to tavernes.   *scoundrel*

05 'To alle trewe tidy men that travaille desiren, *honest upright; labour*
Oure Lord loveth hem and lent, loude outher stille, *grants at all times*
Grace to go to hem and ofgon hir liflode: *obtain*
Inquirentes autem Dominum non minuentur omni bono.

94a The fear of the Lord is the beginning of wisdom (Ecclus 1: 16, Ps 110: 10).
98a [And] whosoever [shall keep the whole law, but] offend in one point, is
    become guilty of all (Js 2: 10). cf. XI 308a.
100 Is the earthly fault most repugnant to those who are in heaven.
106–8 ... under all circumstances permits Grace to go to them and (enable
    them) to procure their livelihood: '. . . but they that seek the Lord shall not
    be deprived of any good' (Ps 33: 11). In secular society, Dowel is the life of
    faithfully married people.

94 Ne] L&r; He wF.
95–6 *So W&r; as one line:* Drede
    god for loue & þou dost wel but
    noȝt for vengeaunce & þou dost
    bet ?g (*so y;* & þou¹] *om* G).
96 And drad hym] ?α (he dredyþ
    F)K–D; And wLM(?=β).
    drede] β; loue α.
    dooþ þerfore] β; to do α (to] for to
    F).
97 He ... hym] W&r; thow doest
    best yff þou withdrawe g.

98a verbo] L?α (*vno verbo* F); *vno*
    wgM (*-no over erasure*) (C).
99 Tynynge] *cj* K–D; Lesynge *All
    MSS* (C).
101 siþþe] β; seche R; all swiche F.
    þat ... of] L&r (spyre] enspired
    CrM; spicerie WHm); her spiryȝt
    haþ no F.
103 his] L&r; þis W.
    -tempred] βF; -tymbred R.
107 to hem] β; to h. tille R; h. to F.

'Trewe wedded libbynge folk in this world is Dowel,

For thei mote werche and wynne and the world sustene.   *support*

110 For of hir kynde thei come that confessours ben nempned,   *stock*

Kynges and knyghtes, kaysers and cherles   *emperors; serfs*

Maidenes and martires – out of o man come.   *one*

The wif was maad the w[y]e for to helpe werche,   *man*

And thus was wedlok ywroght with a mene persone—   *intermediary*

115 First by the fadres wille and the frendes conseille,   *family's advice*

And sithenes by assent of hemself, as thei two myghte acorde;   *agree*

And thus was wedlok ywroght, and God hymself it made;

In erthe the heven is – hymself was the witnesse.   *(it) is; (He) himself*

'Ac fals folk and feithlees, theves and lyeres,

120 Wastours and wrecches out of wedlok, I trowe,

Conceyved ben in yvel tyme, as Caym was on Eve.   *Cain (C)*

Of swiche synfulle sherewes the Sauter maketh mynde: *mention*

Concepit dolorem et peperit iniquitatem.

And alle that come of that Caym come to yvel ende.

'For God sente to Seem and seide by an aungel,   *Seth (C)*

125 "Thyn issue in thyn issue, I wol that thei be wedded,

And noght thi kynde with Caymes ycoupled ne yspoused."   *stock*

'Yet some, ayein the sonde of Oure Saveour of hevene,   *bidding*

Caymes kynde and his kynde coupled togideres—

Til God wrathed for hir werkes, and swich a word seide,   *grew angry*

122*a* . . . he [=the sinner] hath conceived sorrow, and brought forth iniquity (Ps 7: 15).

110 þei] βC; he α.
111 cherles] W&r; clerkes CotBoF(C).
113 wye] *so K–D*; weyʒ F; weye βR (C).
114 *So* β; *run together with* 117, 114b–117a *om* α.
118 þe . . . is] L&r (þe] þere R; here F; *in* C²; *and in* WCrM; is] *erased* M; *om* WCr).
was þe] L&r; bereþ WCBF.
119 and] α; *om* β.
121 in] βFA; *om* R.

122*a* dolorem] αHm (*over erasure*)K–D; *in dolore* β.
iniquitatem] CrGBαACK–D; *in. &c* W&r.
124 For] L&r (*om* C²)A (Forþi A); And W.
seem] W&r; seyn F (C).
126 Caymes] β; Caym α.
ne] L&r; *nor* w (ner Hm).
127 some] W&r; Sem CrM (*over erasure*).
129 for] wLR; with ?g (129b *om* CB)F (*cf.* A).

130 "That I makede man, now it me forthynketh: *I am sorry*
      Penitet me fecisse hominem."
         'And com to Noe anon and bad hym noght lette: *delay*
      "Swithe go shape a ship of shides and of bordes.   *Quickly; planks*
      Thyself and thi sones thre and sithen youre wyves,
      Busketh yow to that boot and bideth ye therinne   *Hurry; remain*
135 Til fourty daies be fulfild, that flood have ywasshen
      Clene awey the corsed blood that Caym hath ymaked.   *accursed race*
         ' "Beestes that now ben shul banne the tyme   *curse*
      That evere that cursed Caym coom on this erthe.   *came*
      Alle shul deye for hise dedes by dales and hulles,   *hills*
140 And the foweles that fleen forth with othere beestes,   *along with*
      Excepte oonliche of ech kynde a couple   *species*
      That in thi shyngled ship shul ben ysaved."   *tiled, 'clinker-built'*
         'Here aboughte the barn the belsires giltes,   *paid for; ancestor's sins*
      And alle for hir forefadres thei ferden the werse.   *on account of; fared*
145 The Gospel is heragein in o degre, I fynde: *against this; read*
      Filius non portabit iniquitatem patris et pater
      non portabit iniquitatem filii . . .
      Ac I fynde, if the fader be fals and a sherewe,   sc. *by experience; wicked*
      That somdel the sone shal have the sires tacches.

                                              somewhat; (bad) qualities

      Impe on an ellere, and if thyn appul be swete,   *Graft; elder-tree* (C)
150 Muchel merveille me thynketh; and moore of a sherewe   *great*
      That bryngeth forth any barn, but if he be the same

130a [for] it repenteth me that I have made them [*sc.* man] (Gen 6: 7).
145–6 The Gospel is against this view in one ?respect/passage, I read: 'the son
    shall not bear the iniquity of the father, and the father shall not bear the
    iniquity of the son' (Ezech 18: 20; 'Gospel': cf. Jn 9: 1–3).

130 it me] wLαA; trs ?g (it] *om*
     CB)M.
     for-] wGFAC; a-] yLM; *om* R.
133 sones þre] W&rAC; *trs* g (þre]
     om β).
134 ye] βR; *om* FAC.
135 þat] L&r (þat þe WCr³Y)A;
     and MF (& þe F)C.
     ywasshen] βAC; Iwasted α.

138 þat²] W&r?AC; *om* HmG.
141 ech] βAC; euery CrF; on R.
142 þi] βC; þis ?α (*l. om* F); þe A.
144 forfadres] L&r (*over erasure*
     Hm)C; fadres WCr¹; sake B.
145 -ageine] L&rC; -ayein WOC²
     BM.
146 &c] βC; *om* αCr.
149 on] β (in C; off G); vpon αHm.

And have a savour after the sire – selde sestow oother: *taste like*
Numquam colligitur de spinis uva nec de tribulis ficus.

  'And thus thorugh cursed Caym cam care upon erthe,   *trouble, woe*
And al for thei wroghte wedlokes [Goddes wille ayeines];

155 Forthi have thei maugre for hir mariages, [men that marie so now] hir
    children.   *ill-luck, misfortune*

For some, as I se now, soothe for to telle,
For coveitise of catel unkyndely ben wedded.   *wealth; unnaturally*
As careful concepcion cometh of swiche mariages   *sorrowful*
As bifel of the folk that I bifore of tolde.

160 For goode sholde wedde goode, though thei no good hadde;

                                good (men/women); goods

"I am *via et veritas*," seith Crist, "I may avaunce alle."   *prosper*

  'It is an uncomly couple, by Crist! as me thynketh—

                                unbecoming match

To yeven a yong wenche to an[y] olde feble,   *girl; tired old man (C)*
Or wedden any wodewe for welthe of hir goodes   *widow*

165 That nevere shal barn bere but if it be in armes!   *(i.e. by carrying it)*
In jelousie joyelees and janglynge on bedde,   *quarrelling*
Many a peire sithen the pestilence han plight hem togideres.

                                plague (C); joined

The fruyt that thei brynge forth arn [manye] foule wordes;

152a Men never gather grapes of thorns, or figs of thistles (Mt 7: 16).
161 'I am the way, and the truth, [and the life]' (Jn 14: 6).

152a   *colligitur*] wLMR; *colligimus*
  g; *coligunt* FC.
  vua] w; *vuas* L&r (s *erased* M)C
  (C).
154   wedlokes] W&r; *sg* Cr²³g.
  Goddes . . . ayeines] ayein goddes
  wille W&r; *l. om* Cr¹ (C).
155   So β (for . . . mariages] *om* g)R;
  as 2 ll. F.
  for] LMα; of w.
  mariages] βR; m. vnkende/ & on þe
  same maner F.
  men . . . now] as men m. now ?α
  (now men m. F); þat marie so β (m.
  so] *trs* g (so] *om* B)) (C).
158   As] WCr¹LMR;Ac YOB; and

HmCr²³C²C; a GF (þan a F)A.
  of] βFA; to R.
  swiche mariages] β; þat m. α (m.]
  pl R).
159   þe] β; þat α.
160–1   *In* βC (For; alle] L&rC;
  Therfore; yow alle W); *ll. om* α.
162   crist] βA; Ihesus α.
163   any] an *All MSS* A (C).
165   in] L&r (*om* Y)?A; in hir W; in
  two F.
166   So ACK–D; *after* 168 β; *l. om*
  α (C).
168   manye] *so* ACK–D; but F; *om*
  βR.

Have thei no children but cheeste and chopp[es] hem bitwene.

fighting; blows

170 Though thei do hem to Dunmowe, but if the devel helpe   *set off*
    To folwen after the flicche, fecche thei it nevere;   *side (of bacon) (C)*
    But thei bothe be forswore, that bacon thei tyne.   *forsworn; lose*
     'Forthi I counseille alle Cristene coveite noght be wedded

desire . . . (to)

    For coveitise of catel ne of kynrede riche;   *wealth; kindred*
175 Ac maidenes and maydenes macche yow togideres;

virgins (male and female)

    Wideweres and wodewes, wercheth the same;   *do*
    For no londes, but for love, loke ye be wedded,
    And thanne gete ye grace of God, and good ynough to live with.
     'And every maner seculer that may noght continue,

layman; persevere

180 Wisely go wedde, and ware hym fro synne;   *(let him) guard himself*
    For lecherie in likynge is lymeyerd of helle.   *pleasure; lime-rod (C)*
    Whiles thow art yong, and thi wepene kene,   *sharp, strong*
    Wreke thee with wyvyng, if thow wolt ben excused: *Vent yourself*
    Dum sis vir fortis, ne des tua robora scortis.
    Scribitur in portis, meretrix est ianua mortis.
     'Whan ye han wyved, beth war, and wercheth in tyme—

have intercourse at the right time

185 Noght as Adam and Eve whan Caym was engendred.   *begotten*
    For in untyme, trewely, bitwene man and womman   *wrong time (C)*

183–3a Find an outlet for your (sexual desires) by marrying, if you wish to
    avoid guilt: 'While young and strong, give not your strength to whores;
    "Harlot is Death's Gate" is written on (her) doors' (traditional Leonine
    verses; cf. Prov 7: 27).

169 cheeste] β (chydes C)AC;
    iangelynge R; *om* F.
    choppes] *so* ACK–D; choppyng ?β
    (chopp-] chid- M; carp- Hm; clapp-
    WCrY); gaying R; langlyng F.
170–2 *So* βAC; 3 *spurious ll.* α.
170 Thogh] CAK–D; And þouȝ β.
172 But] BACK–D; And but W&r.
173 be] W&r?AC; to be CrMR.
175 macche] βA; make R; marye
    FC.

176 Wydeweres] α (& w. F)A?C;
    Wodewes β.
    -es] αHmCrA?C; -eres β.
177 ye] βF; þat ȝe R.
178 ȝe] α (*cf.* A)K–D; ye þe β.
179–85 *In* βC; *ll. om* α.
180 hym] W&r; þe GC.
181 lik-] wLM (*cf.* C); lok- Cr²³g.
183a *Dum*] wLMC; *cum* g.
186 For] βFA (*cf.* C); And R.

Ne sholde no [bedbourde] be: but if thei bothe were clene

intercourse; unless; pure

Of lif and of soule, and in [leel] charite,
That ilke derne dede do no man ne sholde.   *intimate act*
190 And if thei ledden thus hir lif, it liked God almyghty,   *pleased*
For he made wedlok first and hymself it seide:
Bonum est ut unusquisque uxorem suam habeat propter
    fornicacionem.
'That othergates ben geten, for gedelynges arn holden
And fals folk, fondlynges, faitours and lieres,   *bastards, rogues*
195 Ungracious to gete good or love of the peple;   *Without grace to*
Wandren and wasten what thei cacche mowe.   *destroy; get hold of*
Ayeins Dowel thei doon yvel and the devel serve,
And after hir deeth day shul dwelle with the same
But God gyve hem grace here hemself to amende.   *Unless*
200 'Dowel, my frend, is to doon as law techeth.
To love thi frend and thi foo — leve me, that is Dobet.
To yyven and to yemen bothe yonge and olde,   *care for*
To helen and to helpen, is Dobest of alle.   *heal*
'And thus Dowel is to drede God, and Dobet to suffre,
205 And so cometh Dobest of bothe, and bryngeth adoun the mody—
                                                    from; the proud one
And that is wikked wille that many werk shendeth,   *harms*
And dryveth awey Dowel thorugh dedliche synnes.'

---

192 It is good that for fear of fornication every man have his own wife (I Cor
   7: 1–2).
193 Those who are begotten in any other way are considered to be worthless
   creatures.
201 To love (both) your friend and your foe — believe me, that is Do-better.

187   bedbourde] *so* ACK–D; bourde   it seyde] β (*om*Cr¹)R; seyde FCr²³.
      on bedde W&r (bo.] berde HmR);   191a   *propter forn.*] βC; *om* α.
      liggyn In b. F.   193   That] *so* CAK–D; And þei þat
      if] βRC; *om* FA.   *All MSS* (þat] *om* Cot).
188   Of] R (?=α)A (*cf.* C); Boþe of   194   And] αBAC; As β.
      βF(of] in F).   198   same] β; devel R; Mayster R.
      leel] parfit *All MSS* (C).   200–3   *In* β (*cf.* AC); *ll. om* α.
189   sholde] RFC; ne sholde β.   200   as] wLC; as the gM.
190   And] wC²LMα; Ac ?g (but   204   And . . . dowel] ?α (And] *om*
      GCB).   F); And dowel is β.
      ledden] αC²; leden β.   to²] W&rA; ys to g.
      liked] L?α (wold lyke F); likeþ   206   werke] β (a werk WCot)A;
      wgM.   werkes α.
191   and] βR; and þus F.   207   synnes] W&r; synne gF.

Passus X

Thanne hadde Wit a wif, was hote Dame Studie,   *who was called*
That lene was of lere and of liche bothe.   *lean; face; body*
She was wonderly wroth that Wit me thus taughte,   *extraordinarily*
And al starynge Dame Studie sterneliche seide.   *glaring; spoke*
5 'Wel artow wis,' quod she to Wit, 'any wisdomes to telle
To flatereres or to fooles that frenetike ben of wittes!'—   *crazed in*
And blamed hym and banned hym and bad hym be stille—

reproached

'With swiche wise wordes to wissen any sottes!'   *counsel; fools*
And seide, '*Noli mittere*, man, margery perles

Do not cast pearls (Mt 7: 6)

10 Among hogges that han hawes at wille.   *pigs; hawthorn berries*
Thei doon but dryvele theron – draf were hem levere

hog's-wash; preferable

Than al the precious perree that in paradis wexeth.   *jewels* (C)
I seye it by swiche,' quod she, 'that sheweth by hir werkes   *of*
That hem were levere lond and lordshipe on erthe,   *they would rather*
15 Or richesse or rentes and reste at hir wille   *income; leisure*
Than alle the sooth sawes that Salamon seide evere.   *true sayings*
     'Wisdom and wit now is noght worth a kerse   *cress*
But if it be carded with coveitise as clotheres kemben hir wolle.

combed; comb; wool

Whoso can contreve deceites and conspire wronges   *contrive* (C)
20 And lede forth a loveday to lette the truthe—

manage; confound honesty

---

11 They do nothing but slobber over them – they would prefer husks/swill.

Collation WHmCrGYOC²CBLMRF.
RUBRIC *Passus X^us de visione et ii^us de dowel (de . . . dowel] &c* Y; *om* OC²; *et . . . do.] vt supra* CR; *ii^us] iij^us* HmB); *Incipit Passus Septimus* F; *om* G.
1 hote] β?AC; called R; klepid F.
3 me þus] β (*trs* Hm)RA; me F; me so CrC.

4 seyde] L&r (she s. GF)AC; loked W.
5 to wit] βR?AC; *om* F.
11 dryuele] W&rC; drauele YOC² MF?A.
14 on erþe] βA; here α.
18 if] W&r; *om* GMF?AC. hir] wLMAC; *om* gα.
20 to] βA; and α. þe] ?α (euere F)AK–D; wiþ β.

That swiche craftes kan to counseil [are] cleped;   *who know arts*
Thei lede lordes with lesynges and bilieth truthe.   *tell lies against*
   'Job the gentile in hise gestes witnesseth   *good; story*
That wikked men, thei welden the welthe of this worlde,   *control*
25 And that thei ben lordes of ech a lond, that out of lawe libbeth:
                                                            live lawlessly

*Quare impii vivunt? Bene est omnibus qui prevaricantur
et inique agunt?*

   'The Sauter seith the same by swiche that doon ille: *concerning*
Ecce ipsi peccatores habundantes in seculo obtinuerunt divicias.
"Lo!" seith holy lettrure, "whiche lordes beth thise sherewes!"
                                                      scripture; what; rogues

Thilke that God [moost good gyveth, God moost greveth] – leest
   good thei deleth,   *Those; distribute*
And moost unkynde to the commune, that moost catel weldeth:
                                                      wealth; possess

Que perfecisti destruxerunt; iustus autem . . .

30   'Harlotes for hir harlotrie may have of hir goodes,   *Ribald minstrels*
And japeris and jogelours and jangleris of gestes;   *jesters; tellers; tales*
Ac he that hath Holy Writ ay in his mouthe   *always*
And kan telle of Tobye and of the twelve Apostles   *Tobias*
Or prechen of the penaunce that Pilat wroghte   *suffering; caused*
35 To Jesu the gentile, that Jewes todrowe—   *noble, ?gentle; mutilated*
Litel is he loved [or lete by] that swich a lesson sheweth,
                                                      loved/?praised; esteemed

---

25*a* Why then do the wicked live. . . ? (Job 21: 7); Why is it well with all them
   that transgress and do wickedly? (Jer 12: 1).
26*a* Behold these are sinners; and yet abounding in the world they have
   obtained riches (Ps 72: 12).
29*a* For they have destroyed the things which thou hast made; but what (has)
   the just man (done)? (Ps 10: 4).

21   That; are] *so* CAK–D; He þat; is
   W&r (*l. om* F).
23   witnesseþ] W&rC; gretly w.
   Cr²³g.
24   þei] WCr¹LMR; *om* Cr²³&r.
25   of¹] W&r; in HmR.
   a] W&r; *om* Crg.
25*a   omnibus*] W&r; *hominibus* g.
26*a   diuicias*] β; *om* α.
27   lordes] L&rC; woordes Hm; *om*

WCr¹.
28   Thilke] βR; þo FC.
   God¹ . . . greueþ] god moost good
   gyueþ OC²; m. good god yeueþ M;
   god moost gyueth GYBL; god
   gyueþ m. w; most greue*th* αC (C).
33   þe] L&rAC; *om* WY.
34   þe] W&rA; *om* g.
36   or . . . by] *so* AC (by] *her*fore
   C)K–D; *om All MSS* (C).

Or daunted or drawe forth – I do it on God hymselve!

flattered; advanced; declare

'But thoo that feynen hem foolis and with faityng libbeth

pose as; fraud

Ayein the lawe of Oure Lord, and lyen on hemselve, against; lie about

40 Spitten and spuen and speke foule wordes,   spew up

Drynken and drevelen and do men for to gape,   slobber; make

Likne men and lye on hem that leneth hem no yiftes—

Compare (satirically); slander

Thei konne na moore mynstralcie ne musik men to glade

musical entertainment

Than Munde the Millere of Multa fecit Deus.

45 Ne were hir vile harlotrye, have God my trouthe,   Were it not for

Sholde nevere kyng ne knyght ne canon of Seint Poules

Yyve hem to hir yeresyyve the worth of a grote!   New Year's gift

Ac murthe and mynstralcie amonges men is nouthe   now

Lecherie and losengerye and losels tales—

Debauchery; flattery; wastrels'

50 Glotonye and grete othes, this [game] they lovyeth.   amusement

'Ac if thei carpen of Crist, thise clerkes and thise lewed, talk about

Atte mete in hir murthes whan mynstrals beth stille,   feasts, dinners

Thanne telleth thei of the Trinite [how two slowe the thridde], slew

And bryngen forth a balled reson, taken Bernard to witnesse,

crafty argument (MED s.v.)

55 And puten forth presumpcion to preve the sothe.   supposition; try

Thus thei dryvele at hir deys the deitee to knowe,

daïs; the divine nature

And gnawen God with the gorge whanne hir guttes fullen.

revile; throat; grow full (C)

---

44 God has done great things (Ps 39: 6).

46   canoun] ?α (þe comoun
F)?AK–D; Chanon β.

47   worth] α; value ?gA; ȝifte
wCBLM.

49   and¹] Hmg?α(†F)A; om
WCrLM.

50   game] cf. A; glee M; murþe
W&r (pl OC²) (C).

52   Atte] LHmCr¹BMR?A; At W&r;
And they Cr²³.

murthes] L&r; murþe w.

53   how . . . þridde] so ACK–D; a
tale ouþer tweye All MSS (C).

54   taken] so C?AK–D; and taken
All MSS.

55   forth] so C?A; forþ a All MSS.

57   guttes fullen] w (f.] fallen Cr);
guttes been fulle O&r (g.] gutte
YLR; been] is YCLR).

'Ac the carefulle may crie and carpen at the yate,   *distressed; wail*
Bothe afyngred and afurst, and for chele quake;   *hungry; thirsty; cold*
60 Is non to nyme hym in, nor his noy amende,   *take in (C); trouble*
But hoen on hym as an hound and hoten hym go thennes.   *shout at*
Litel loveth he that Lord that lent hym al that blisse,   *grants*
That thus parteth with the povere a parcell whan hym nedeth!

    shares; portion

Ne were mercy in meene men moore than in riche,   *humble*
65 Mendinaunts metelees myghte go to bedde.   *Beggars; without food*
God is muche in the gorge of thise grete maistres, *'masters of theology'*
Ac amonges meene men his mercy and hise werkes.
And so seith the Sauter – I have seighen it [in *Memento*]:

    Remember (Ps 131)

Ecce audivimus eam in Effrata; invenimus eam in campis silve.
Clerkes and othere kynnes men carpen of God faste,
70 And have hym muche in hire mouth, ac meene men in herte.   *humble*
    'Freres and faitours han founde [up] swiche questions   *thought up*
To plese with proude men syn the pestilence tyme,   *since*
And prechen at Seint Poules, for pure envye of clerkes,

    St Paul's Cross; hostility (C)

That folk is noght fermed in the feith, ne free of hire goodes,

    strengthened; generous

75 Ne sory for hire synnes; so is pride woxen   *grown*
In religion and in al the reme amonges riche and povere

    religious orders; realm

That preieres have no power thise pestilences to lette.   *prevent, stop*

---

67 i.e. but it is among humble people that Christian mercy and Christian acts
    are to be found.
68a Behold, we have heard of it [*sc.* God's tabernacle] in Ephrata: we have
    found it in the fields of the wood (Ps 131: 6) (C).

60 Is] L&rC?A; Is þer WBF (*trs*).   69 kynnes] β; *om* αG(C).
    in n*o*r] M?AK–D; neer W&r (C).   70 here] FGACK–D; þe W&r; *om*
    nuye] ?αAK–D; noy to β (n.] anoy   BM (C).
    W)F.   71 vp] soACK–D; *om All MSS.*
61 hoen on] R&r; howlen on B;   72 tyme] βA; *om* αC (C).
    hunten wM.   75 so is pride] βC; so p. is R; p. so
62 lent] wGLRA; lente yMFC.   hyȝe is F.
66 gorge] βA; gorges α.   77 þis pestilences] αCK–D; þe
68 in *Memento*] so ACK–D; ofte   pestilence β.
    All MSS (C).

For God is deef nowadayes and deyneth noght us to here,
That girles for hire giltes he forgrynt hem alle. *children; sins; destroys*
80 And yet the wrecches of this world is noon ywar by oother,
Ne for drede of the deeth withdrawe noght hir pride,   *the plague*
Ne beth plentevouse to the povere as pure charite wolde,   *bountiful*
But in gaynesse and in glotonye forglutten hir good hemselve,

extravagance; greedily eat up

And breketh noght to the beggere as the Book techeth: *break bread*
Frange esurienti panem tuum . . .
85 And the moore he wynneth and welt welthes and richesse   *possesses*
And lordeth in londes, the lasse good he deleth.   *servants; distributes*
   'Tobye techeth yow noght so! Taketh hede, ye riche,   *Tobias*
How the book Bible of hym bereth witnesse:
Si tibi sit copia, habundanter tribue; si autem exiguum,
illud impertiri libenter stude.
Whoso hath muche, spende manliche – so meneth Tobye—

generously (cf. V 256)

90 And whoso litel weldeth, [loke] hym therafter,   *behave accordingly*
For we have no lettre of oure lif, how longe it shal dure.

written assurance; last

Swiche lessons lordes sholde lovye to here,

---

80 No worldly wretch, however, takes warning from (what he sees happening
   to) another.
83 But greedily consume their property in extravagance (esp. of dress) and
   luxury.
84a Deal thy bread to the hungry (Is 58: 7).
86 And (the more) land he is lord of, the less of his goods he gives [probably as
   alms].
88a If thou have much, give abundantly: if thou have little, take care even so
   to bestow willingly a little (Tob 4: 9).

78 *In* αCK–D; *l. om* β (C).
nowa-] RCK–D; on þese F.
not . . . here] FCK–D; his heres to
opne R.
79 *In* α (That g.] þe gystys F)CK–D;
l. om β (C).
83 in²] wLRC; *om* gMF.
good] W&r; goods CrGC; *om* F.
85 richesse] W&r; *pl* YOC²BR.
86 And] βC; Euere as he α.
londes] W&r; leedis and l. B; ledes

C.
87 techeth ȝow] ?αC (ȝ.] *om* FC);
telleþ yow β.
88 book bible] WLMR; *trs* CrF;
book of þe bible Hmg.
88a *sit cop.; ill.*] W&rC; *trs; om* g.
-tiri] W&rC; *-tire* GC²Mα.
libenter stude] αC; *trs* β.
89 manliche] W&r; moche g.
90 loke] rule *All MSS* (C).

And how he myghte moost meynee manliche fynde—   *provide for*
Noght to fare as a fithelere or a frere to seke festes,   *dinner-parties*
95 Homliche at othere mennes houses, and hatien hir ownene.

At home; hate, shun

'Elenge is the halle, ech day in the wike,   *Wretched; week*
Ther the lord ne the lady liketh noght to sitte.
Now hath ech riche a rule – to eten by hymselve   *rich person*
In a pryvee parlour for povere mennes sake,   *private; so as to avoid*
100 Or in a chambre with a chymenee, and leve the chief halle   *fireplace*
That was maad for meles, men to eten inne,   *meals*
And al to spare to spille that spende shal another.   *avoid wasting*
'I have yherd heighe men etynge at the table   *noble*
Carpen as thei clerkes were of Crist and of hise myghtes,   *powers*
105 And leyden fautes upon the fader that formede us alle,   *laid blame*
And carpen ayein clerkes crabbede wordes;   *ill-tempered*
"Why wolde Oure Saveour suffre swich a worm in his blisse,

tolerate; serpent

That bi[w]iled the womman and the [wye] after,   *deceived; man*
Thorugh whiche wiles and wordes thei wente to helle,
110 And al hir seed for hir synne the same deeth suffrede?
' "Here lyeth youre lore," thise lordes gynneth dispute,   *teaching*
"Of that ye clerkes us kenneth of Crist by the Gospel:
Filius non portabit iniquitatem patris ...
Why sholde we that now ben, for the werkes of Adam   *exist*

---

93 And how he might hospitably provide (employment) for the largest (possible) number of household retainers.

102 And entirely in order to avoid 'letting go to waste' what another [*sc.* his heir] shall consume.

111–12 At this point your doctrine goes astray, when it comes to what you learned men inform us, on the basis of the Gospel, was the teaching of Christ.

94 or a] β; or as a R; *om* F.
to] HmCrGRK–D; for to W&r.

97 ne] W&r; & g.

100 wiþ] βF; by R.

102 to² . . . spende] L&r (to sp.] þe powndes F); to spende þat spille WCr.

105 vpon] W&r; on gF.

108 -wiled] *cj* K–D; -giled *All MSS*

(C).

wye] *so* AK–D; man *All MSS* (C).

112 ȝe] L&r; þe WHmCr¹GCBF.

112a *patris*] βF; *om* R.

Roten and torende? Reson wolde it nevere!   *Rot and be torn apart*
Unusquisque onus suum portabit."

115 'Swiche motyves they meve, thise maistres in hir glorie,
   motions; (vain) glory
And maken men in mysbileve that muse muche on hire wordes.
   bring men into
Ymaginatif herafterward shal answere to youre purpos.
   Imaginative (C)
   'Austyn to swiche argueres, he telleth hem this teme: *proposition*
Non plus sapere quam oportet . . .
Wilneth nevere to wite why that God wolde   *Desire*
120 Suffre Sathan his seed to bigile;   *i.e. Adam's seed*
Ac bileve lelly in the loore of Holy Chirche,   *faithfully*
And preie hym of pardon and penaunce in thi lyve,
And for his muche mercy to amende yow here.   *great*
For alle that wilneth to wite the whyes of God almyghty,   *'whys'*
125 I wolde his eighe were in his ers and his fynger after
That evere wilneth to wite why that God wolde
Suffre Sathan his seed to bigile,
Or Judas the Jew Jesu bitraye.
Al was as he wolde – Lord, yworshiped be thow—
130 And al worth as thow wolt whatso we dispute!   *will be; argue about*
   'And tho that useth thise havylons to [a]blende mennes wittes
   tricks (C); blind
What is Dowel fro Dobet, now deef mote he worthe—   *(As to) what*
Siththe he wilneth to wite whiche thei ben alle—
But if he lyve in the lif that longeth to Dowel;   *Unless; appertains*

114a [For] every one shall bear his own burden (Gal 6: 5).
118a . . . not to be more wise than it behoveth to be wise (Rom 12: 3) (C).
122 and (the opportunity to make reparation for sin by) penance . . .

114 torende] W&r (to-] *om* gF);
   toreue R.
114a honus . . . portabit] α; *trs* (s.]
   s. &c) β.
116 muche] W&r; *om* CrFA.
118 he . . . hem] HmLMα; telleþ
   WCr(he t. Cr¹)g.
118a &c] HmgR; *sapere* FA; *om*
   WCrLM.
121 byleue] HmCrLRA; bileueþ
   WgF.

124 whyes] ?g (the . . . almyghty *om*
   CB)M?AK–D; weyes wC²Lα.
125 fynger] W&r (l. *om* CB);
   elbowe F.
128 þe Iew] αK–D; to þe Iewes β.
129 he wolde] αAK–D; þow
   woldest β (w.] wolde L).
   þow] L&rA; þe W; euere F.
131 ablende] blende *All MSS* (C).
132 now] L&rA; & Cr; *erasure*
   Hm; þat W.
133 alle] αAK–D; boþe β.

135   For I dar ben his bolde borgh that Dobet wole he nevere,

                                                  strong surety

     Theigh Dobest drawe on hym day after oother.'   *pull him along*

        And whan that Wit was ywar how Dame Studie tolde,

     He bicom so confus he kouthe noght loke,

     And as doumb as deeth, and drough hym arere.   *drew himself back*

140   And for no carpyng I kouthe after, ne knelyng to the grounde,

                                    for nothing further I could say

     I myghte gete no greyn of his grete wittes,   *grain, morsel*

     But al laughynge he louted and loked upon Studie   *bowed*

     In signe that I sholde bisechen hire of grace.

        And whan I was war of his wille, to his wif gan I loute,   *bow, kneel*

145   And seide, 'Mercy, madame; youre man shal I worthe   *Thanks*

     As longe as I lyve, bothe late and rathe,   *early*

     And for to werche youre wille the while my lif dureth,   *lasts*

     With that ye kenne me kyndely to knowe what is Dowel.'   *Provided*

        'For thi mekenesse, man,' quod she, 'and for thi mylde speche,

150   I shal kenne thee to my cosyn that Clergie is hoten.   *direct; called*

     He hath wedded a wif withinne thise six monthes,

     Is sib to the sevene arts — Scripture is hir name.   *(Who) is kin to*

     They two, as I hope, after my techyng,

     Shullen wissen thee to Dowel, I dar wel undertake.'   *direct; affirm*

155   Thanne was I as fayn as fowel of fair morwe, *pleased; bird; morning*

     Gladder than the gleman that gold hath to yifte,   *minstrel; as a gift*

     And asked hire the heighe wey where that Clergie dwelte,   *direct*

     'And tel me som tokene,' quod I, 'for tyme is that I wende.'

                              'word of introduction' (to Clergie)

        'Aske the heighe wey,' quod she, 'hennes to Suffre-

160   Bothe-wele-and-wo, if that thow wolt lerne;

---

135   For] β (?*erased* Cot)R; *om* FA.
    bolde] β; *om* α.

137   how] αAK–D; what βC.

139   deeþ and] W&r (d.] deaffe GB;
    and] he B); a dore nail & FC²
    (*above, a.h.*; &] *om* C²)A (n.] *om*
    A).
    arere] W&r; *on* syʒde FC²
    (*above, a.h.*)A (C).

140   after] βR; *om* FA.

147   And] αC; *om* βA.
    þe] βRC; *om* HmFA.

151   monþes] βR; wykis FA.

153   techyng] *All MSS*; bysekynge
    above, a.h. C²(*so AK–D*).

154   wel] ?αAK–D; it β (*om* Cr).

155   as¹] CrGMRAC; also W&r;
    om F.

156   Gladder] *so* ACK–D; And
    gladder *All MSS*.

157   þat] W&rC; *om* GFA.

159   she] W&rAC; stodye g.

And ryd forth by richesse, ac rest thow noght therinne,
For if thow couplest thee therwith, to Clergie comestow nevere.
  'And also the likerouse launde that Lecherie hatte—   *lascivious*
Leve hym on thi left half a large myle or moore,   *hand; good*
165 Til thow come to a court, Kepe-wel-thi-tunge-
Fro-lesynges-and-lither-speche-and-likerouse-drynkes.   *evil; delicious*
Thanne shaltow se Sobretee and Sympletee-of-speche,
                                    Soberness; simplicity
That ech wight be in wille his wit thee to shewe;
And thus shaltow come to Clergie, that kan manye thynges.   *knows*
170 'Seye hym this signe: I sette hym to scole,
And that I grette wel his wif, for I wroot hire [the Bible],
And sette hire to Sapience and to the Sauter glosed.   *glossed*
Logyk I lerned hire, and [al the Lawe after],
And alle the musons in Musik I made hire to knowe.   *measures (C)*
175 'Plato the poete, I putte hym first to boke;   *to learn (to write)*
Aristotle and othere mo to argue I taughte.
Grammer for girles I garte first write,   *children; had written*
And bette hem with a baleys but if thei wolde lerne.   *beat; birch*
Of alle kynne craftes I contreved tooles—   *invented*
180 Of carpentrie, of kerveres, and compased masons, *carvers; established*
And lerned hem level and lyne, though I loke dymme.   *weak-sightedly*
  'Ac Theologie hath tened me ten score tymes: *vexed, troubled*
The moore I muse therinne, the mystier it semeth,   *mistier, obscurer*
And the depper I devyne, the derker me it thynketh.   *deeper; ponder*

---

168 (So) that (as a result) everyone may be willing to reveal his knowledge (to you).
170 Tell him this (as a) sign (of whom you have come from).
177 I first caused grammar(s) for children to be written.
181 And taught them the use of the builder's level (?T-square) and (plumb-) line . . .

161 þow] W&rA; om gFC.
162 clergie] βAC; cherche R; crist F.
163 hatte] βAC; is hote α.
164 hym] HmLMRA; it W&r.
167 speche] β; berynge α.
171 grette] OC²LMRC; grete W&rA.
  þe bible] so AC (þe) a C)K–D; manye bokes W&r; bokes MF (C).
172 glosed] BHmACK–D; glose W&r (C).

173 al . . . aftir] so ACK–D; manye opere lawes βR; þe lawys manye F.
174; 175 þe; hym] L&rAC; om W.
176 mo] βA; om αC.
177 write] L&rC?A; to write wM.
180 Carpentrie] W&rC; carpenters Cr³GF.
  of²] W&rC; & GFA.
182 Ac] ?w (And Cr)YLMα (But F); om ?g.
184 it] βRC; om FA.

185 It is no science, forsothe, for to sotile inne.   *argue subtly*
     A ful lethi thyng it were if that love [therinne] nere;   *empty, vain*
     Ac for it leteth best by love, I love it the bettre,   *esteems; love, ?praise*
     For there that love is ledere, ne lakked nevere grace.
     Loke thow love lelly, if thee liketh Dowel,   *you wish to*
190 For Dobet and Dobest ben of loves k[e]nn[yng].   *discipline*
       'In oother science it seith – I seigh it in Catoun—   *philosophy*
     Qui simulat verbis, nec corde est fidus amicus,
     Tu quoque fac simile; sic ars deluditur arte:
     Whoso gloseth as gylours doon, go me to the same,

                           speaks flatteringly; deceivers; you do
195 And so shaltow fals folk and feithlees bigile—
     This is Catons kennyng to clerkes that he lereth.   *instruction; teaches*
     Ac Theologie techeth noght so, whoso taketh yeme;   *heed*
     He kenneth us the contrarie ayein Catons wordes,   *the opposite of*
     For he biddeth us be as bretheren, and bidde for oure enemys,

                           bids; pray
200 And loven hem that lyen on us, and lene hem whan hem nedeth,

                           against; give to
     And do good ayein yvel – God hymself it hoteth: *in return for*
     Dum tempus habemus, operemur bonum ad omnes,
     maxime autem ad domesticos fidei.
       'Poul preched the peple, that parfitnesse lovede,   *Paul, (who loved)*
     To do good for Goddes love, and gyven men that asked,

---

186 If love were not contained within it, theology would be a vain pursuit.
192–3 Who simulates in his words, but is no true friend at heart—
     Imitate him yourself – thus art is beguiled by art (*Distichs of Cato* 1,
    26).
201*a* [Therefore], whilst we have time, let us work good to all men, but
  especially to those who are of the household of the faith (Gal 6: 10).

185 sotile] βA; sauȝtele α.
186 therinne] *om All MSS* (C).
187 Ac] W&r (But F)?AC; and Crg.
188 ne] L&r; þer WG.
     lakked] W&r?A; lakkeþ Crg.
189 Loke . . . likeþ] β; Loue þow
     loue l. if þow thenke ?α (L.] þerfore
     l.; loue l.] *trs* F).
190 kennyng] kynne *All MSS* (C).
192 -ulat] W&r; -ilat Cr²³CotLα.
     nec] Hm&r (*over erasure* M)*Sk*; *vel*

WLR.
    corde] βF; *in corde* HmR.
194 go me to] W&r(†F); do hem g.
197 yeme] βR (them Cr¹; gome R);
     hede Cr²³FA.
198 He] W&rA; & g.
201 ay-] W&rA; ag- CrFG.
201*a* *habemus*] β; *est* α.
203 asked] WCr¹YLM; asken
     Cr²³&r (aske it F).

And [to swiche, nameliche], that suwen oure bileve;

especially; follow; faith

205   And alle that lakketh us or lyeth us, Oure Lord techeth us to lovye,

disparage; slander

And noght to greven hem that greveth us – God hymself forbad it:

injure

Michi vindictam et ego retribuam.

Forthi loke thow lovye as longe as thow durest,   *live, last*

For is no science under sonne so sovereyn for the soule. *health-giving*

   'Ac Astronomye is hard thyng, and yvel for to knowe;

difficult, ?evil

210   Geometry and Geomesie is gynful of speche;   *geomancy; treacherous*

Whoso thynketh werche with tho two thryveth ful late—

meddle; will prosper

For sorcerie is the sovereyn book that to the science longeth.

chief; pertains.

   'Yet ar ther fibicches in forceres of fele mennes makynge,

tricks; boxes

Experiments of Alkenamye the peple to deceyve;   *alchemy*

215   If thow thynke to dowel, deel therwith nevere!

Alle thise sciences I myself sotilede and ordeynede,   *subtly planned*

And founded hem formest folk to deceyve.   *first of all*

   'Tel Clergie thise tokenes, and to Scripture after,   *cf. 158*

To counseille thee kyndely to knowe what is Dowel.'

206*a* Revenge is mine, and I will repay [them in due time] (Deut 32: 35, quoted in Rom 12: 19).

210 . . . full of terms which deceive (those who profess or study them).

204 to swiche; nameliche] *trs* All MSS (C).
   þat] L&rA; as WG.
   suwen] βA; sh*eweth* αG (showen G) (C).
205 vs¹] β; *om* αCr.
   or] W&r; and *y*M.
   vs²] L&r; *om* w.
206 God . . . it] wLMR; god þat forbed*eth* g; It is not goddes will F.
208 science] wBoCotLMR;
   conscience ?g (*corrected, m.h.* GBm); salue F.

209 is] αAK–D; is an β.
210 is] L&rA; so w.
212 þe²] L&r; that GBA; þo WHmα.
   science] L&rA; sciences WHm(s+Hm)F.
   longeth] L&rA; bilongeþ WCr²³.
217 founded] βA; fond ?α (byf. R).
218 þise tokenes] L&r; þis tokene WCr¹.
   to] αK–D; *om* β.
219 To] wLMR; þat þey F; I g.
   to . . . is] β; for to knowe α.

220   I seide, 'Graunt mercy, madame,' and mekely hir grette,
       And went wightly my wey withoute moore lettyng—   *quickly; delay*
       And til I com to Clergie I koude nevere stynte.   *stop*
       I grette the goode man as the goode wif me taughte,   *greeted*
       And afterwardes the wif, and worshiped hem bothe,
                                                       bowed respectfully to
225   And tolde hem the tokenes that me taught were.
       Was nevere gome upon this ground, sith God made the worlde,
       Fairer underfongen ne frendloker at ese   *More courteously received*
       Than myself, soothly, soone so he wiste   *as soon as*
       That I was of Wittes hous and with his wif Dame Studie.
230   I seide to hem soothly that sent was I thider
       Dowel and Dobet and Dobest to lerne.
          'It is a commune lyf,' quod Clergie, 'on Holy Chirche to bileve,
                                                   'a way of life common to all'
       With alle the articles of the feith that falleth to be knowe: *are proper*
       And that is to bileve lelly, bothe lered and lewed,
235   On the grete God that gynnyng hadde nevere,   *beginning*
       And on the soothfast Sone that saved mankynde
       Fro the dedly deeth and the develes power
       Thorugh the help of the Holy Goost, the which goost is of bothe—
                                                   which spirit proceeds from
       Thre propre persones, ac noght in plurel nombre,   *individual*
240   For al is but oon God and ech is God hymselve:
       Deus Pater, Deus Filius, Deus Spiritus Sanctus—
       God the Fader, God the Sone, God Holy Goost of bothe,
                                                       (proceeding) from
       Maker of mankynde and of [animal]es bothe.   *too*
          'Austyn the olde herof made bokes,   *St Augustine (C)*

---

220 I said, 'Many thanks, my lady', and humbly took my leave of her.

221 wight-] β; miȝte- ?α (*l. om* F).
     my wey] ?αK–D; awey β.
222 til] βF; *om* R.
     I koude] β; *trs* HmF.
223 I] ?αACK–D; And βF.
     as] W&r; well as ?g (ac Y); wel
     Cr²³.
     þe gode wif] ?α (þe lentel lady F)
     AK–D; Studie β.
224 þe wif and] βR; his wif y F (*cf.*
     A).
230 hem] wLα; hym gM.
     sent was I] β; sent I was R; y was
     sent F.
237 þe²] L&r; *om* W.
238 goost²] βR; *om* F.
239 propre] ?αSk; *om* βF.
242 animales] beestes βR; al þe
     Mounde F (C).
243 made] ?βC; he made αL.

And hymself ordeyned to sadde us in bileve.   *set about; confirm; faith*
245 Who was his auctour? Alle the foure Evaungelistes;   *authority, source*
And Crist cleped hymself so, the [Gospelleres] bereth witness:

i.e. claimed divinity

Ego in Patre et Pater in me est; et qui videt me
videt et Patrem meum.

'Alle the clerkes under Crist ne koude this assoille,   *unravel, explain*
But thus it bilongeth to bileve to lewed that willen dowel.

uneducated people

For hadde nevere freke fyn wit the feith to dispute,

subtle understanding

250 Ne man hadde no merite, myghte it ben ypreved:
Fides non habet meritum ubi humana racio prebet experimentum.

'[Siththe] is Dobet to suffre for thi soules helthe   *after this*
Al that the Book bit bi Holi Cherche techyng—   *commands*
And that is, man, bi thy myght, for mercies sake,   *according to*
Loke thow werche it in werk that thi word sheweth;   *professes*
255 Swich as thow semest in sighte be in assay yfounde: *trial*
Appare quod es vel esto quod appares.
And lat no body be by thi beryng bigiled,   *manner, outward; deceived*
But be swich in thi soule as thow semest withoute.

246–6a And Christ referred to himself in such terms [*sc.* as divine] . . . 'I am in
  the Father and the Father in me' (Jn 14: 10 *or* 11); '[and] he that seeth me
  seeth the Father also' (Jn 14: 9).
249 No man ever had an intellect so excellent that 'he could demonstrate the
  truths of faith by argument (C).
250a No merit attaches to believing (only) those things that human reason can
  put to the test of experience (Gregory, *Homilies on the Gospels* II, 26 [*PL* 76
  1197]).
255a Seem what you are; be what you seem (pseudo-Chrysostom, Homily 45
  on Matthew [*PG* 56: 885]).

246 Gospelleres] Euang*elistes All*
  MSS (-istes) -yst g; -ieʒ R; -ye F)
  (C).
246a *In* L&rC; *l. om* w.
  est; *videt*[1]] β; *om* α.
  et[3]] βF; *om* R.
248 bilongeþ] ?βC; longeth αGOC[2].
  lewed] W&r; men g (C).
250 merite] β; mercy α.
251 Siþþe] Thanne *All MSS* (C).

þi] L&r; þe WHmCr[1].
soules] ?β; soule αCB.
252 cherche] L&r; cherches w.
254 þi] β; þis ?α (þe F).
255a *vel*] β; *aut* α.
256 by . . . bigiled] β; by þi b. be bi.
  ?α (by] *om*; be] here be F)Hm.
257 be] W&r; *om* g.

'Thanne is Dobest to be boold to blame the gilty,
Sythenes thow seest thiself as in soule clene;   *Since, inasmuch as*

260 Ac blame thow nevere body and thow be blameworthy: *if*
Si culpare velis culpabilis esse cavebis;
Dogma tuum sordet cum te tua culpa remordet.
God in the Gospel grymly repreveth   *fiercely rebukes*
Alle that lakketh any lif and lakkes han hemselve: *blame; faults*
Quid consideras festucam in oculo fratris tui, trabem in
oculo tuo non vides?
Why mevestow thi mood for a mote in thi brotheres eighe, *get angry*
Sithen a beem in thyn owene ablyndeth thiselve?   *beam, plank; blinds*
Eice primo trabem de oculo tuo! . . .

265 Which letteth thee to loke, lasse outher moore?   *obstructs your vision*
  'I rede ech a blynd bosard do boote to hymselve—

dim-sighted oaf; heal

As persons and parissh preestes, that preche sholde and teche

parsons (C)

Alle maner men to amenden, bi hire myghte.   *according to their power*
This text was told yow to ben war, er ye taughte,

270 That ye were swiche as ye seyde to salve with othere.

in order to heal others

For Goddes word wolde noght be lost – for that wercheth evere;
If it availled noght the commune, it myghte availle yowselve.   *Though*

260a If to blame others thou desire / Take care blameworthy not to be. / Thy
    teaching flaunts a foul attire / When thine own vices snap at thee (anon).
262a [And] why seest thou the mote that is in thy brother's eye, and [seest not]
    the beam that is in thy own eye? (Mt 7: 3).
265 *Either* less or more (adverbial) *or, more likely,* (the) smaller or (the)
    greater.
270 That you yourselves were following the ideal you held up to others as the
    means to salvation.

260a esse] L&r (*te e.* F); *esto* WHm.
261 grymly] L&r; greuously wF.
262a Quid] L&r; *Qui* WHmCot.
  in² . . . *vides*] αSk; *in oculo tuo &c*
  ?β (*in . . . tuo*) *om* g; *&c*] *om* M).
263 broþeres] β; brother α.
264 in] βR; is in F.
264a de] L&r; *in* w.
265 Which] β; þe wiche F; witt R.
266 *After this a line:* For Abbotes

and for Priours and for alle manere
prelates β (for¹,²] *om* g; maner] m.
of y)R; Boþe prelatis & prioures
sholde punshe here sogettis F; *rej.
as spurious* K–D (C).
268 men] WCrGLR; of men
HmyMF.
my3te] L&r (†F); *pl* WHm.
271 lost] β (*alt. from* boste L)F;
boste R (C).

'Ac it semeth now soothly, to [sighte of the worlde],
That Goddes word wercheth no [wi]ght on lered ne on lewed

not at all

275 But in swich a manere as Marc meneth in the Gospel: *declares*
Dum cecus ducit cecum, ambo in foveam cadunt.

'Lewed men may likne yow thus – that the beem lith in youre
eighen,   *compare; lies*
And the festu is fallen, for youre defaute,   *mote; fallen (in the eyes)*
In alle manere men thorugh mansede preestes.   *cursed, wicked*
The Bible bereth witnesse that alle the [barnes] of Israel   *people*
280 Bittre aboughte the giltes of two badde preestes,   *Grievously paid for*
Offyn and Fynes – for hir coveitise   *Ophni; Phinees (C)*
Archa Dei myshapped and Ely brak his nekke.   *The Ark of God; Heli*

'Forthi, ye correctours, claweth heron, and correcteth first
yowselve,   *grasp this (moral)*
And thanne mowe ye manliche seye, as David made the Sauter:

courageously; wrote (in)

285 *Existimasti inique quod ero tui similis: Arguam te,*
et statuam contra faciem tuam.

'And thanne shul burel clerkes ben abasshed to blame yow or to
greve,   *half-educated; trouble*
And carpen noght as thei carpe now, and calle yow doumbe
houndes—
Canes non valentes latrare—

275a [And if] the blind lead the blind, both fall into the pit (Mt 15: 14).
282 The Ark of God came to grief [i.e. was captured] (1 Kg 4: 11, 18).
283 Therefore you men with authority to correct others, take a firm hold on this (lesson) . . .
285 Thou thoughtest unjustly that I should be like to thee: but I will reprove thee, and set before thy face (Ps 49: 21).
287a [dumb] dogs not able to bark (Is 56: 10).

273 sizte . . . worlde] *cj K–D;* þe worldes sizte *All MSS* (C).
274 word] β; wordes ?α (*om* F). no wizt] nozt W&r; owt F.
275 a] WHmLMR; *om* CrgF.
276 þus] wLMR; *om* gF.
279 alle] OCotLMR; al W&r; *l. om* F.
barnes] *cj K–D;* folk *All MSS* (C).

280 a-] W&r (*l. om* F); *om* Cr²³g.
283 ye] ?wLMα+Bm; *om* Cr¹g.
284 manliche] ?α (soþly F)K–D; saufly β.
þe] L&r; in þe WF.
286 And] WHmLMα; *om* Crg. or to greue] β; *om* α.
287 carpen] W&r; do g. and] L&r; ne W; to F.

And drede to wrathe yow in any word, youre werkmanshipe to lette,   *actions; impede*

And be prester at youre preiere than for a pound of nobles,   *prompter (to act); request*

290 And al for youre holynesse – have ye this in herte.   *entirely*

   'Amonges rightful religious this rule sholde be holde.   *worthy*

Gregorie, the grete clerk and the goode pope,   *scholar*

Of religioun the rule reherseth in his *Morales*   *declares;* Moralia *(C)*

And seith it in ensample for thei sholde do therafter: *in order that*

295 "Whan fisshes faillen the flood or the fresshe water,   *lack; sea*

Thei deyen for droughte, whan thei drie ligge;   *lie dry*

Right so religion ro[i]leth [and] sterveth   *strays about; dies, decays*

That out of covent and cloistre coveiten to libbe."   *desire*

For if hevene be on this erthe, and ese to any soule,   *peace, tranquillity*

300 It is in cloistre or in scole, by manye skiles I fynde.   *arguments; note*

For in cloistre cometh no man to [querele] ne to fighte,

But al is buxomnesse there and bokes, to rede and to lerne.

                      co-operativeness

   'In scole there is skile, and scorn but if he lerne,   *university; reason*

And gret love and likyng, for ech of hem l[er]eth oother.

                    affection; teaches the other

305 Ac now is Religion a rydere, a romere by stretes,   *wanderer about*

A ledere of lovedayes and a lond buggere,   *presider at; land-purchaser*

A prikere [up]on a palfrey fro manere to manere,   *rider; manor, estate*

An heep of houndes at his ers as he a lord were;   *pack; behind him*

291–302 *In* αACSk; *ll. om* β(C).

292 Gregorie] RAC; Seynt G. F.

293 religioun þe r.; morales] RA;
Relygyonys rewle he; bookis F.

294 it; for] RA; *om*; þat F.

295 or] RA; & F.

297 *So div* ACK–D; *as* 2 *ll. div after*
rolleth α.
so] *so* C; so be AK–D; so quod
Gregorie α.
roileþ] *cj Sk*; rolleth R; trollyþ F.
and sterueþ] *cj* K–D; St. and
stynketh and steleth lordes almesses
α (St.; alm.] It st.; *sg* F) (C).

299 on þis] RC; in F.
any] R (*cf.* C); þe F.

300 many] RC; fele F.

301 no] FCSk; *om* R.
querele] chide RFCx; carpe *cj* K–D
(C).

302 þere] R; *om* F.

303 þere . . . he] ?α (is anoþer skyle
for skorn but he F); þere is scorn
but if a clerk wol β (is] ys a g) (C).

304 of hem] βR; man F.
lereth] loueþ *All MSS* (C).

305 Ac] WHmLMα (But F); And
Crg.
Romere] βR; rennere F.

306 a[2]] βF; *om* R.

307 upon] *on All MSS* (of Cr[1]) (C).

And but if his knave knele, that shal his coppe brynge,   *servant; cup*
310 He loureth on hym and asketh hym who taughte hym curteisie?
Litel hadde lordes to doon to yyve lond from hire heires
                                  had no business alienating
To religiouse that han no routhe though it reyne on hir auters!
                                     care; rain; altars
   'In many places ther thei persons ben, be hemself at ese,
                                     incumbents
Of the povere have thei no pite – and that is hir pure charite,   *entire*
315 Ac thei leten hem as lordes, hir lond lith so brode.
                             consider themselves; extensive
   'Ac ther shal come a kyng and confesse yow religiouses,
                               hear the confessions of
And bete yow, as the Bible telleth, for brekynge of youre rule,
And amende monyals, monkes and chanons,   *nuns; (secular) canons*
And puten hem to hir penaunce – *Ad pristinum statum ire*,
                               return to their first state
320 And barons with erles b[iy]eten, thorugh *Beatus vir*res techyng,
                                    Take over
That hir barnes claymen, and blame yow foule: *That which; children*
Hii in curribus et hii in equis ipsi obligati sunt . . .
   'And thanne freres in hir fraytour shul fynden a keye   *refectory*
Of Costantyns cofres, [which the catel is inne]
That Gregories godchildren han yvele despended.   *wickedly spent (C)*
325   'And thanne shal the Abbot of Abyngdoun and al his issue for evere
Have a knok of a kyng, and incurable the wounde.   *blow from*

---

320 Blessed is the man (opening of Ps 1; see verse 6).
321*a* Some [trust] in chariots, and some in horses . . . They are bound [and
  have fallen] . . . (Ps 19: 8–9) (C).

309 his²] W&rC; hym þe ?g (þe) *om*
  GYC).
314 pure] αCK–D; *om* β.
  charite] βR; charge F; chartre C.
315 lond lith] L&rC; londes lyen
  wF.

316 -ouses] WLMR; -*ous* HmCrgF.
320 biyeten] biten hem ?α; beten
  hem β (*om* G)F (C).
323 which . . . inne] in which is þe
  catel *All MSS* (C).

That this worth sooth, seke ye that ofte overse the Bible: *look at*
Quomodo cessavit exactor, quievit tributum? Contrivit Dominus
baculum impiorum, et virgam dominancium cedencium plaga
insanabili.

'Ac er that kyng come Caym shal awake,
Ac Dowel shal dyngen hym adoun and destruye his myghte.'   *strike*
330   'Thanne is Dowel and Dobet,' quod I, '*dominus* and knyghthode?'
                                           lord(ship), the nobility
'I nel noght scorne,' quod Scripture; 'but if scryveynes lye,
                                           jeer; scribes
Kynghod ne knyghthod, by noght I kan awayte,   *see, find out*
Helpeth noght to heveneward oone heeris ende,   *a hair's end (=at all)*
Ne richesse right noght, ne reautee of lordes.   *royalty, noble blood*
335   'Poul preveth it impossible – riche men have hevene.   (I Tim 6: 9)
Salamon seith also that silver is worst to lovye:
Nichil iniquius quam amare pecuniam;
And Caton kenneth us to coveiten it naught but at [nede];
Dilige denarium set parce dilige formam.
And patriarkes and prophetes and poetes bothe
Writen to wissen us to wilne no richesse,   *Wrote; counsel; desire*
340   And preiseden poverte with pacience; the Apostles bereth witnesse
That thei han eritage in hevene – and by trewe righte,
                                           i.e. the poor; inheritance
Ther riche men no right may cleyme, but of ruthe and grace.'
                                           Whereas; except by mercy
   '*Contra*,' quod I, 'by Crist! That kan I repreve,   *refute*
And preven it by Peter and by Poul bothe:

327*a* How is the oppressor come to nothing, the tribute hath ceased? The Lord
   hath broken the staff of the wicked, the rod of the rulers, [That struck the
   people in wrath] with an incurable wound . . . Is 14:4-6 (C).
336*a* There is not a more wicked thing than to love money (Ecclus 10: 10).
337*a* Money esteem, but not for its own sake (*Distichs of Cato* IV, 4).

327*a* *cedencium*] W&r; *credencium*
   gM.
329   Ac] HmLMR; But WF; And
   Crg.
331   if] βR; *om* FA.
332   ne] wLMRA; and gF.
   no3t] W&r?A; aught Cr²³CotM.
335   haue] L&r; to haue WCrOC²B.

337   it] W&r; *om* g.
   at nede] at pure nede R; in gret n.
   F; as n. techeþ wLM; as it nedeth g
   (it] vs G) (C).
342   ruþe and] β (and) off G); ri3t
   (*canc for* reuth *a.h.*) and R; goddes
   F.

345 That is baptized beth saaf, be he riche or povere.'   *He who; saved*
　　 'That is *in extremis*,' quod Scripture, 'amonges Sarsens and
　　 Jewes—   *pagans*
　　 They mowen be saved so, and that is oure bileve:
　　 That an uncristene in that caas may cristen an hethen,   *pagan; baptize*
　　 And for his lele bileve, whan he the lif tyneth,   *true; loses*
350 Have the heritage of hevene as any man Cristene.

　　 'Ac Cristene men withoute moore maye noght come to hevene,
　　 For that Crist for Cristene men deide, and confermed the lawe
　　 That whoso wolde and wilneth with Crist to arise—
　　 Si cum Christo surrexistis . . .
　　 He sholde lovye and lene and the lawe fulfille.   *give*
355 That is, love thi Lord God levest above alle,   *most dearly*
　　 And after, alle Cristene creatures in commune, ech man oother;
                                                         universally
　　 And thus bilongeth to lovye, that leveth to be saved.   *believes*
　　 And but we do thus in dede er the day of dome,   *unless; before*
　　 It shal bisitten us ful soure, the silver that we kepen,   *afflict; bitterly*
360 And oure bakkes that mothe-eten be, and seen beggeris go naked,
                                                    cloaks; whilst (we)
　　 Or delit in wyn and wildefowel, and wite any in defaute. *know; need*
　　 For every Cristene creature sholde be kynde til oother,
　　 And sithen hethen to helpe in hope of amendement.   *next; conversion*
　　 'God hoteth bothe heighe and lowe that no man hurte oother,
365 And seith, "Slee noght that semblable is to myn owene liknesse,
                                                              resembles

---

353*a* . . . if you be risen with Christ, [seek the things that are above . . .] (Col
　　 3: 1).
357 The man that trusts to be saved has a duty to love.

345 is] wLα; ben Cr²³?g (*l. om* CB)
　　 MF.
　　 saaf] ?wLα; saue*d* Cr²³Hm?g.
　　 he] wLR; þei ?gMF.
348 an¹] *All MSS; alt. to* arn C²
　　 (C).
353*a* surr-] L&r (*l. om* F); sur-
　　 WM; resur- CB.
355 aboue] L&r (*l. om* F); abouen

Hm; of CB.
　　 alle] W&r; al þyng Crg (*pl* CB).
357 to²] L&r; *om* W.
358 ar] L&r; at W.
360 mothe eten be] β; mote eten be
　　 ?α (e. be] be betyn F).
361 and¹] W&r; & in R; or GCot.
364 bothe] L&r (*l. om* B); *om*
　　 WHmF.

But if I sende thee som tokene," and seith "*Non mecaberis*—
Is slee noght but suffre, and al[so] for the beste,
For *Michi vindictam et ego retribuam*:   see VI 225a
"For I shal punysshe in purgatorie or in the put of helle   pit
370 Ech man for hise mysdedes, but mercy it lette." '   prevent

    'This is a long lesson,' quod I, 'and litel am I the wiser!
Where Dowel is or Dobet derkliche ye shewen.   obscurely
Manye tales ye tellen that Theologie lerneth,   speeches; teaches
And that I man maad was, and my name yentred
375 In the legende of lif longe er I were,   Book of Life (Rev 20: 12)
Or ellis unwriten for som wikkednesse, as Holy Writ witnesseth:
                                                                         not written down

Nemo ascendit ad celum nisi qui de celo descendit.

    'And I leve it wel, by Oure Lord, and on no letrure bettre.
For Salomon the Sage that Sapience [made]   wrote
God gaf hym grace of wit and alle goodes after   gift of mind, wisdom
380 To rule his reume and riche to make;   make it rich
He demed wel and wisely, as Holy Writ telleth.   judged
Aristotle and he — who wissed men bettre?   instructed

---

366 Thou shalt not kill (Lk 18: 20) *is intended*; *lit*. Thou shalt not commit
    adultery (C).
376a [And] no man hath ascended into heaven, but he that descended from
    heaven (Jn 3: 13).
377 *Possibly* On Our Lord's own authority and not that of any better (written
    authority) *or else* There is no written text I believe more firmly.

366 *mecaberis*] W&r (*alt. to*
    nechaberis GL) (*cf.* A); necaberis
    Cr²³Y; *necabis* Cr¹OC²; *occides*
    (*over erasure, a.h.*) M (C).
367 Is] wGLR; I Cr²³M (?s *erased*
    M); God seiþ y F.
    also] al W&r; al is F; so *cj* K–D
    (C).
368 *In* αASk; *l. om* β.
369 For] W&r; *om* HmA.
    in¹] αAK–D; hem in β.
376 som] wLMRC; *om* gF (*cf.* A).

witnesseþ] β (manaceth Cr) (*cf.* A);
    telleth α.
377 And¹] ?α (For F)AC; *om* β.
    be oure lorde] α (be] on F)
    ACK–D; quod I; by o. l. ?β (*trs*
    Cr²³g; by o. l.] *om* M).
378 made] *so* ACK–D; tauȝte *All*
    MSS.
379 alle] R (?=α)K–D; of all FC;
    alle hise β.
380 *In* α (his] þe R; and] wel &
    hym F) CASk; *l. om* β.

Maistres that of Goddes mercy techen men and prechen,
Of hir wordes thei wissen us for wisest in hir tyme—
385 And al Holy Chirche holdeth hem bothe [in helle]!   *considers*
And if I sholde werche by hir werkes to wynne me hevene,
That for hir werkes and wit now wonyeth in pyne—   *dwell; torment*
Thanne wroughte I unwisly, whatsoevere ye preche!
      'Ac of fele witty, in feith, litel ferly I have   *many; wonder*
390 Though hir goost be ungracious God for to plese. *spirit be unpleasing*
For many men on this moolde moore sette hir herte   *earth*
In good than in God – forthi hem grace failleth   *(material) goods*
At hir mooste meschief, whan [men] shal lif lete, *supreme need; leave*
As Salamon dide and swiche othere, that shewed grete wittes,
395 Ac hir werkes, as Holy Writ seith, was evere the contrarie.
Forthi wise witted men and wel ylettred clerkes   *educated*
As thei seyen hemself selde doon therafter: *seldom practise*
Super cathedram Moysi . . .
      'Ac I wene it worth of manye as was in Noes tyme   *will become*
Tho he shoop that ship of shides and of bordes: *When; made; planks*
400 Was nevere wrighte saved that wroghte theron, ne oother werkman
      ellis,   *craftsman*
But briddes and beestes and the blissed Noe
And his wif with hise sones and also hire wyves;
Of wrightes that it wroghte was noon of hem ysaved.
      'God lene it fare noght so bi folk that the feith techeth   *grant*
405 Of Holi Chirche, that herberwe is and Goddes hous to save   *shelter*

---

384 *Either* Theologians inform us that (as far as) their words (went), A. & S.
were the wisest etc *or* Theologians instruct us, drawing upon their words, as
those of the wisest etc.
397a [The scribes and the Pharisees have sitten] on the chair of Moses (Mt 23:
2).

384 in] αGMC; as in ?β.
385 in helle] *so* ACK–D; ydampned
     All MSS (C).
387 and] βC?A; and here α.
389 Ac] W&r (But F); And Crg.
391 men] β (beene G)C; man α.
     sette] L&r; setten wOC²CB.
     herte] αCK–D; hertes β.
393 At; hir] W&r; Ac (but G; and
     C²C); þe g.
     men] þei *All MSS* (C).
394 dide . . . oþere] β; and othere
     dede α.
395 holy . . . seiþ] β; h. w. R; s. þe
     book F.
     was] L&r; were w.
396 and] βFC; ne R.
397a -dram] Hm&r (*l. om* F)?CSk;
     -dra WYCBLM.
398 it] W&rC; I R.
399 of²] WCrα?C; *om* L&r.
403 In W&r (wri-] wi- w)C; *l. om*
     g.

And shilden us from shame therinne, as Noes ship dide beestes,

shield

And men that maden it amydde the flood adreynten. *Whilst; drowned*

The *culorum* of this clause curatours is to mene,   *conclusion; priests*

That ben carpenters Holy Kirk to make for Cristes owene beestes:

Homines et iumenta salvabis, Domine . . .

410 At domesday the deluvye worth of deth and fir at ones;   *deluge*

Forthi I counseille yow clerkes, of Holy [Kirke] the wrightes,

Wercheth ye werkes as ye sen ywrite, lest ye worthe noght therinne!

'A Good Friday, I fynde, a felon was ysaved *On; read* (Lk 23: 39–43)

That hadde lyved al his lif with lesynges and with thefte;   *lies*

415 And for he beknew on the cros and to Crist shrof hym,

acknowledged; confessed

He was sonner ysaved than Seint Johan the Baptist   *sooner*

And or Adam or Ysaye or any of the prophetes,   *before; Isaiah*

That hadde yleyen with Lucifer many longe yeres.   *remained in hell*

A robbere was yraunsoned rather than thei alle   *ransomed; sooner*

420 Withouten any penaunce of purgatorie to perpetuel blisse.

'Than Marie Maudeleyne wh[o myghte do] werse?   *Magdalen* (C)

Or who worse dide than David, that Uries deeth conspired?

Uriah's (II Kg 11)

Or Poul the Apostle that no pite hadde

Cristene kynde to kille to dethe?   *people* (Ac 9)

425 And now ben thise as sovereyns with seintes in hevene—   *princes*

Tho that wroughte wikkedlokest in world tho thei were;   *most evilly*

409a Men and beasts thou wilt preserve, O Lord (Ps 35: 7).

408 clause] βC; cl. in R; cl. of F.
409 holy kirk] WCrLM (*cf.* C); h.
     cherche Hm&r; *om* F.
410–12 *In* αCSk; *ll. om* β.
410 deluye; deth] RC; flood; water
     F.
411 kirke] *cj* K–D; cherche α.
     þe] R; *om* F.
412 werkes; nauȝt þerinne] R; *om*;
     ydrenklid F.
413 A] *so* AC; On β; For a R; For
     on F.
414 with²] βR; *om* HmFA.

415 biknewe on] L&r (on] it on F)
     AC; beknede to WHmCr¹.
417 And] βRC; *om* FA.
420 any] W&r; *om* FGA (*cf.* C).
421 Than] W&rAC; & g; & also F.
     who . . . do] *so* ACK–D; what
     womman dide *All MSS* (C).
422 worse . . . þan] ?α(þan dyde
     F)A; worse þan β.
424 *In* βAC (Cr.) *so* ACK–D;
     Muche Cr. β); *l. om* α (C).
425 now] W&rC; ȝit Hm (*over
     erasure*); *om* LR.
     wiþ] W&r (*om* B); & Cr²³?g.

And tho that wisely wordeden and writen manye bokes   *spoke; wrote*
Of wit and of wisedom, with dampned soules wonye.   *dwell*

   'That Salomon seith I trowe be sooth and certein of us alle: *about*
Sunt iusti atque sapientes, et opera eorum in manu Dei sunt.

430 Ther are witty and wel libbynge, ac hire werkes ben yhudde

                                     wise; upright; hidden

In the hondes of almyghty God, and he woot the sothe—
Wher for love a man worth allowed there and hise lele werkes,
Or ellis for his yvel wille and envye of herte,   *malignity*
And be allowed as he lyved so, for by luthere men knoweth the goode.

                                       judged; evil

435   'And wherby wote men which is whit, if alle thyng blak were,
And who were a good man but if ther were som sherewe?   *evil-doer*
Forthi lyve we forth with lithere men – I leve fewe ben goode—

                                       evil; believe

For "*quant OPORTET vient en place il ny ad que PATI;*"
And he that may al amende, have mercy on us alle!
440 For sothest word that ever God seide was tho he seide *Nemo bonus.*

                            No man is good (Lk 18: 19)

   'Clergie tho of Cristes mouth comended was it litel,   *Learning*
For he seide to Seint Peter and to swiche as he lovede,
"*Dum steteritis ante reges et presides . . .*
Though ye come bifore kynges and clerkes of the lawe,

                           men learned in the law

429*a* There are just men and wise men, and their works are in the hand of God (Eccl 9: 1).

432 Whether in heaven a man will be assessed for his love and just actions . . .

438 For 'when *must* comes on the scene, there's nought but *to endure*' (prov.).

443 When you shall stand before governors and kings [for my sake . . . be not thoughtful beforehand what you shall speak . . .] (Mk 13: 9, 11).

429*a* Sunt[1]] αCr[23]Sk; Sint B; Siue (?Sine) β.
   sunt[2]] CrGOC[2]CotαC; s. &c W&r.
430 ac] W&r (but F); & Crg.
432 for . . . man] L&r (for) fore wGYCB; loue] *om* WCr); he F.
433 and] gM?α (þoruh F); and for w; or L.
434 as he lyued] βR (as] for R); of his lyf F.
   bi] L&r (by þe W); *om* OC[2]CBF.

435 wote] LR; wite ?gHm; wiste WCrBm(*over erasure*)M *over erasure*; l. *om* F (C).
   is] L&r; were W.
436 And] β; Or R; For F.
437 lither] L&r; oþere w.
438 vient en] W&r; cometh in g.
441 þo] W&r; *om* OC[2].
442*a* Dum] L&r; Cum w.
   &c] W&r (*om* G)C; *nolite cogitare* FA.

445 Beth noght abasshed, for I shal be in youre mouthes,
And yyve yow wit at wille [with] konnyng to conclude hem

intelligence; knowledge; confute

Alle that ayeins yow of Cristendom disputen." *about*

'David maketh mencion, he spak amonges kynges,
And myghte no kyng overcomen hym as by konnynge of speche.

through skill in

450 But wit ne wisedom wan nevere the maistrie *victory, upper hand*
When man was at meschief withoute the moore grace. *in peril*

'The doughtieste doctour and devinour of the Trinitee, *theologian*
Was Austyn the olde, and heighest of the foure, *(Who) was; greatest*
Seide thus in a sermon – I seigh it writen ones— *discourse*

455 *"Ecce ipsi idiote rapiunt celum ubi nos sapientes in inferno
mergimur"*—

And is to mene to Englissh men, moore ne lesse,
Arn none rather yravysshed fro the righte bileve *orthodox faith*
Than are thise konnynge clerkes that knowe manye bokes, *clever*
Ne none sonner ysaved, ne sadder of bileve *more constant in*

460 Than plowmen and pastours and povere commune laborers,

herdsmen

Souteres and shepherdes – swiche lewed juttes *unimportant*
Percen with a *Paternoster* the paleys of hevene *penetrate*
And passen purgatorie penauncelees at hir hennes partyng

without punishment; death

Into the blisse of paradis for hir pure bileve, *sheer faith*

---

451 i.e. without grace playing the greater role in saving him.
455 Lo, the unlearned themselves take heaven by force while we wise ones are
drowned in hell (St Augustine, *Confessions* VIII, 8).

446 *Div from* 447 *after* conclude
All MSS (C).
at] αL; and W&r.
wiþ] and βF; *om* R (C).
447 of cristendom] βR (of] *om* R);
goddes lawe F.
449 And] βC; Al R; þere F.
450 ne] L&r; and wF.
453 þe²] βFA; hem R.
455 ydiote] CrgFC; ydioti WHm
LMR?Ax.

456 to²]W&r; on g (In G).
englisshe] L&r (*om* W); meene F.
men] w (men to Cr²³) LMα (m.
neyþer F); to g.
ne] wLMR (no HmR); and to
Cr²³g.
458 knowe] α (*cf.* C); konne βA.
459 Isaued] αAC; saued β (*l. om* G).
460 pore] L&rC (*cf.* A); oþere Wg.
461 suche] Cr¹LRA; and s. w (s.]
oþere W)g (*l. om* B).

465 That inparfitly here knewe and ek lyvede.   *?incompletely*
        'Ye, men knowe clerkes that han corsed the tyme   *learned men*
     That evere thei kouthe or knewe moore than *Credo in Deum patrem*
                                                                learnt

     And principally hir *Paternoster* – many a persone hath wisshed.
        'I se ensamples myself and so may many an other,
470 That servaunts that serven lordes selde fallen in arerage   *debt*
     But tho that kepen the lordes catel – clerkes and reves.
                                      (own) property; reeves

     Right so lewed men and of litel kunnyng
     Selden falle thei so foule and so fer in synne   *badly, grievously*
     As clerkes of Holy Kirke that kepen Cristes tresor— *guard, look after*
475 The which is mannes soule to save, as God seith in the Gospel:
     "*Ite vos in vineam meam.*" '

---

465 That possessed and existed in only an imperfect state of knowledge here
     on earth.
467 I believe in God the Father (Almighty) (opening of Apostles' Creed).
475*a* Go you [also] into my vineyard (Mt 20: 4).

465   here] βF; *om* R.   468   hir] β; þe α.
466   þat . . . corsed] β (han] *om* Cr)F   469   many another] HmCr¹Lα;
      (þ.] þ. þey F); cursen R.   manye oþere W&r.
467   or knewe] w (knowe Hm)LMα   471   þe] β (my Hm); *om* α.
      (or] *om* F); on þe boke g (þe] *om* 472   kunnyng] α; knowyng β.
      Cot).   473   so¹] αCK–D; þei so β.
      patrem] W&r; *om* HmCrg (&c   474   kirke] L&r; chirche wGCotR.
      YC).

Passus XI

Thanne Scripture scorned me and a skile tolde,   *derided; statement*
And lakked me in Latyn and light by me she sette,   *disparaged*
And seide, '*Multi multa sciunt et seipsos nesciunt.*'
   Tho wepte I for wo and wrathe of hir speche   *resentment at*
5 And in a wynkynge w[o]rth til I was aslepe.   *fell into a drowse*
A merveillous metels mette me thanne,   *dream*
For I was ravysshed right there – for Fortune me fette   *carried off*
And into the lond of longynge and love she me broughte,
And in a mirour that highte Middelerthe she made me to beholde.
                                      'the World', Middle Earth (C)
10 Sithen she seide to me, 'Here myghtow se wondres,
And knowe that thow coveitest, and come therto, peraunter.'
                                      obtain it perchance
   Thanne hadde Fortune folwynge hire two faire damyseles:
                              young ladies (-in-waiting)
Concupiscencia Carnis men called the elder mayde,
                           Lust of the Flesh (1 Jn 2: 16)
And Coveitise of Eighes ycalled was that oother.
15 Pride of Parfit Lyvynge pursued hem bothe,   *the Pride of Life*
And bad me for my contenaunce acounten Clergie lighte.
                                    ?for the sake of my looks

---

3 Many know many things yet do not know themselves (pseudo-Bernard) (C).
16 *Apparently* bade me set small store by learning, lest I damage my looks by excessive study.

Collation WHmCrGYOC²CBLMRF.
RUBRIC *Passus vndecimus* W&r (*v.*] *v. de visione* CrMR (*v. de v. vt supra* R); *xjᵘˢ de v. et iiiiᵘˢ de do weel* HmB); *Incipit Passus Octauus* F; *om* G.
2 she] W&r (he α); *om* gC.
4 wo] βC; sorwe RF.
5 *So* W&rC; *6 spurious ll.* F. wynkynge] wLMR; wyndyng g. warth] *so* CK–D; wraþe W&r (C). til I was] ?α; weex I β.

6 metels] W&r; sweuene g.
mette me þanne] β (me] I me YOC²) (*cf.* C); me tydde to dreme α (C).
7 For¹] ?αCK–D; that β. for²] ?αC; and β.
8 & loue] ?αCK–D; allone β (alone B)F (C).
9 to] wLM?α (in F)C; *om* g.
10 Sitthen] L&rC; & afterward F; Sone W.

Concupiscencia Carnis colled me aboute the nekke   *embraced*
And seide, 'Thow art yong and yeep and hast yeres ynowe   *lusty*
For to lyve longe and ladies to lovye;
20 And in this mirour thow might se myrthes ful manye   *delights*
That leden thee wole to likynge al thi lif tyme.'   *pleasure*
    The secounde seide the same: 'I shal sewe thi wille;   *follow*
Til thow be a lord and have lond, leten thee I nelle   *abandon*
That I ne shal folwe thi felawship, if Fortune it like.'   *company*
25 'He shal fynde me his frend,' quod Fortune therafter;
'The freke that folweth my wille failled nevere blisse.'   *missed*
    Thanne was ther oon that highte Elde, that hevy was of chere,
                      Old Age; gloomy of face
'Man,' quod he, 'if I mete with thee, by Marie of hevene,
Thow shalt fynde Fortune thee faille at thi mooste nede,   *greatest*
30 And *Concupiscencia Carnis* clene thee forsake.
Bittrely shaltow banne thanne, bothe dayes and nyghtes,   *curse*
Coveitise of Eighe, that evere thow hir knewe;
And Pride of Parfit Lyvynge to muche peril thee brynge.'
    'Ye? Recche thee nevere!' quod Rechelesnesse, stood forth in
    raggede clothes,   *Recklessness, (who)*
35 'Folwe forth that Fortune wole – thow hast wel fer to Elde.
                      a long way to go till
A man may stoupe tyme ynogh whan he shal tyne the crowne.'
                      lose (hair)
    '*Homo proponit*,' quod a poete tho, and Plato he highte,
                      Man proposes
    'And *Deus disponit*,' quod he, 'lat God doon his wille.
                God disposes (proverbial, cf. Prov 16: 9)
If Truthe wol witnesse it be wel do, Fortune to folwe,   *well done*
40 *Concupiscencia Carnis* ne Coveitise of Eighes
Ne shal noght greve thee graithly, ne bigile thee but thow wole.'
                      quickly

---

20 in] βFC; *om* R.
    myrthes] L&rC; myȝtes WHmCr[1].
21 wole] βC; wel R; *om* F.
26 folweþ] αCr[23]YCB (*cf.* C);
    folwede ?β.
32 hir] W&rC; *it* g.
33 of] βFC; of þi R.

35 to] Hm&r C; til WCrL.
36 tyme] W&rC; tymes HmLMR.
37 þo] αC; *om* β.
41 graythly] αK–D; gretly βC (C).
    þe[2]] L&r; *om* W.
    wolle] MC; wolt L&r (w. þi selue
    W); knowe F.

'Ye, farewel Phippe!' quod Faunteltee, and forth gan me drawe,
                                                        Childishness

Til *Concupiscencia Carnis* acorded til alle my werkes.

'Allas, eighe!' quod Elde and Holynesse bothe,   *Oh!*

45 'That wit shal torne to wrecchednesse for wil to have his likyng!'

   Coveitise of Eighes conforted me anoon after

And folwed me fourty wynter and a fifte moore,   *fifth (winter)*

That of Dowel ne Dobet no deyntee me ne thoughte.

                                            I took no pleasure in

I hadde no likyng, leve me, [o]f the leste of hem ought to knowe.

                                            least (C); anything

50 Coveitise of Eighes com ofter in my mynde   *into (my) thoughts*

Than Dowel or Dobet among my dedes alle.

   Coveitise of Eighes conforted me ofte,

And seide, 'Have no conscience how thow come to goode.

                                        scruples; achieve wealth

Go confesse thee to som frere and shewe hym thi synnes.

55 For whiles Fortune is thi frend freres wol thee lovye,

And fecche thee to hir fraternitee and for thee biseke

To hir Priour Provincial a pardon for to have,

And preien for thee pol by pol if thow be *pecuniosus*.'

                                        head (C); rich, moneyed

—*Pena pecuniaria non sufficit pro spiritualibus delictis.*

By wissynge of this wenche I dide, hir wordes were so swete,

60 Til I foryat youthe and yarn into elde.   *lost recollection of; ran*

---

42 Off with you, (Philip) Sparrow! (contemptuous dismissal).
58a [However], pecuniary penance does not suffice for spiritual faults [i.e.
   sins]. A maxim of canon law; see the ref. in *Pe*, p. 210n.

43   til alle] ?α (with F)C; alle ?β   L&r.
   (with alle B).
46   *In* βC; *l. om* α.   55   freres] βFC; sum frere R.
   anon] wLM; sone g.   56   fecche . . . to] βR (f.] fette R);
47–9 *In* β; *ll. om* αC.   sette þee in F.
47   and a fifte] wLM; or fifty and   58   *pecuniosus*] β?C; pecunious α (p.
   Cr²³?g (and] or GOC²).   holde F)B.
48   ne] LM; *om* wg.   58a   *Pena*] αCK–D; *Set pena* β.
49   leue me] wLM; *om* Cr²³ g.   -niaria] βFC; -laria R.
   of the leste] if þe leste LM?w (þe]   59   By . . . dide] ?αCK–D; By . . .
   þee W; þu Hm; ye Cr¹; l.] list w);   wrouȝte β; þanne wrowhte y after
   ne no luste Cr²³g [no] *om* OC²] (C).   þat w. F.
50   my] Cr²³GOC²?α (l. *om* F); *om*   60   yarn] W&rC; ran HmR; ȝeede
                                                    F; then G.

And thanne was Fortune my foo, for al hir faire biheste,   *promise(s)*
And poverte pursued me and putte me lowe.   *brought me down*
And tho fond I the frere afered and flittynge bothe   *changeable*
Ayeins oure firste forward, for I seide I nolde   *agreement*
65 Be buried at hire hous but at my parisshe chirche
(For I herde ones how Conscience it tolde
That there a man [cristned were], by kynde he sholde be buryed).

                                                                 rights

And for I seide thus to freres, a fool thei me helden,   *considered*
And loved me the lasse for my lele speche.   *honest*
70   Ac yet I cryde on my confessour that heeld hymself so konnyng.
'By my feith, frere!' quod I, 'ye faren lik thise woweris *behave; suitors*
That wedde none widwes but for to welden hir goodes.   *control*
Right so, by the roode, roughte ye nevere   *you would care*
Where my body were buryed, by so ye hadde my silver!   *provided*
75 Ich have muche merveille of yow, and so hath many another,

                                                          greatly wonder at

Whi youre covent coveiteth to confesse and to burye
Rather than to baptize barnes that ben catecumelynges.

                                                          catechumens (C)

Baptizynge and buryinge bothe beth ful nedefulle;
Ac muche moore meritorie me thynketh it is to baptize;   *meritorious*
80 For a baptized man may, as maistres telleth,   *theologians*
Thorugh contricion come to the heighe hevene—
Sola contricio delet peccatum—

63–4 ... and not to be relied upon when it came to fulfilling [with pun on
  'arguing against'] Our original agreement [i.e. absolution for my sins].
81a Contrition alone (can) blot out sin (theological maxim).

61 biheste] L&rC; speche W.   74 my²] W&rC; þe g.
67 cristned were] *trs All MSS* (C). 75 an-] WHmLMF; *om* CrgR.
    After this a line: Or where he were   G.
    (were) w. a R; a F) parisshen riȝt   79 it is] W&r; is HmYOC²C; *om*
    þere he sholde be grauen *All MSS*;   WLMR; *om* CrF.
    rej. as spurious K–D (C).   80 as] L&r; as þise w; as grete F; as
70 Ac] WHmLMα(But F); And Crg.   wel as B.
    heeld ... konnyng] βR; Con.   81 to] β; til R; into F.
    hyghte hymselue F (C).   81a *delet peccatum*] HmgSk; &c
72 goodes] βF; goed R.   WLMR; *om* CrF.

Ac a barn withouten bapteme may noght [be so] saved—   *baptism*
Nisi quis renatus fuerit.
Loke, ye lettred men, wheither I lye or do noght.'
And Lewte tho lo[ugh] on me, and I loured after.   *Equity; lowered*
85 'Wherfore lourestow?' quod Lewtee and loked on me harde.
   'If I dorste [amonges men,' quod I], 'this metels avowe!'

                                                            dream; declare
   'Ye, by Peter and by Poul!' quod he, 'and take hem bothe to
   witnesse: *Yes indeed*
   Non oderis fratres secrete in corde tuo set publice argue illos.'
   'They wole aleggen also,' quod I, 'and by the Gospel preven:

                                                        adduce (texts); prove
90 *Nolite iudicare quemquam.'*
   'And wherof serveth lawe,' quod Lewtee, 'if no lif undertoke it—
                                                            rebuked
   Falsnesse ne faiterie? For somwhat the Apostle seide   *(good) reason*
   Non oderis fratrem.
   And in the Sauter also seith David the prophete
95 *Existimasti inique quod ero tui similis . . .*   *See X 285 above, note.*
   It is *licitum* for lewed men to segge the sothe   *lawful; declare*
   If hem liketh and lest – ech a lawe it graunteth;   *canon and civil law*
   Except persons and preestes and prelates of Holy Chirche:
   It falleth noght for that folk no tales to telle—   *befits; make comments*

82*a* Unless a man be born again [of water and the Holy Ghost . . .] (Jn 3: 5).
88 Thou shalt not hate thy brothers [secretly] in thy heart: but reprove him [*lit.*
   them] openly (Lev 19: 17; cf. Gal 2: 11, I Tim 5: 20).
90 Judge not, [that you may not be judged] (Mt 7: 1).

82 be so] so be W&r (so) so sone
    F); be Crg (C).
82*a* *fuerit*] W&r (*f. &c* Hm); *f. ex
    aqua &c* g (*&c*] *om* C²; *& spiritu
    sancto &c* Cot).
83 Loke . . . no3t] βR (L.] *om* R);
    þis resoun y radde sone F.
    do] W&r; *om* g.
84 þo] α (*cf.* C); *om* β.
    lou3] *cj* K–D *after* C; loked W&r;
    lok C (C).
    and] βR; for F (*cf.* C) (C).

86 amonges men; quod I] *trs All
    MSS* (q. I] *om* G) (C).
    þis] W&r; þise g (þes G).
87 3e] L&r (*om* CB); 3is w.
    take] GLMR; took W&r.
90 *quemquam*] W&rC; *q. &c*
    HmGR.
91 if] βF; þanne if R.
93 *So div from* 94 FCSk; *as one l.
    with* 94 βR.
96 segge] L&r; sigge W; synge Hm.
98 chirche] βF; *pl* R.

100 Though the tale were trewe – and it touched synne. *if; concerned (C)*
       'Thyng that al the world woot, wherfore sholdestow spare *refrain*
    To reden it in retorik to arate dedly synne?   *teach it poetry; reprove*
    Ac be neveremoore the firste the defaute to blame;
    Though thow se yvel, seye it noght first – be sory it nere amended.
105 No thyng that is pryvé, publice thow it nevere;   *private; make public*
    Neither for love laude it noght, ne lakke it for envye: *praise; hatred*
    Parum lauda; vitupera parcius.'
       'He seith sooth,' quod Scripture tho, and skipte an heigh and
          preched;   *rose up hurriedly*
    Ac the matere that she meved, if lewed men it knewe,   *put forward*
    The lasse, as I leve, lovyen it thei wolde—   *less; believe; love*
110 The bileve [of Oure] Lord that lettred men techeth.   *faith*
       This was hir teme and hir text – I took ful good hede:
                                                      theme; heed, note
    '*Multi* to a mangerie and to the mete were sompned;
                                                  Many; feast; summoned
    And whan the peple was plener comen, the porter unpynned the yate
                                                   fully; unlocked; gate
    And plukked in *Pauci* pryveliche and leet the remenaunt go rome.'
                                                      A few; wander off
115   Al for tene of hir text trembled myn herte,   *distress at*
    And in a weer gan I wexe, and with myself to dispute
                                                   became perplexed

---

106a Praise little; blame less (attrib. to Seneca in Vincent of Beauvais,
     Speculum doctrinale v, 69).
112, 114 [For] many [are called, but] few [are chosen] (Mt 22: 14).

100   were] L&r; be W.
      touched] L&r (t. to F); touche
      WHm.
101   pyng] βC; Ac þ. ?α (Ac) A F).
102   To] WHmC; And L&r (C).
103   be] W&r?C; be thu HmFK–D
      (C).
105   No] wLMR; & ony F; And
      OC²C; a GYB.
106   loue . . . noȝt] leef ne for looþ
      F.
      laude] L&r; looue G; preise W; lab

      BC; lakke R (C).
107   sooþ] β (om G)F; þe sothe R.
108   she] wLMRC; he gF.
      if] βC; om α.
      it knewe] βC; it knowe R; not
      knowe F.
109   it] βR; om FC.
110   *In* αCK–D; *l. om* β (C).
      The . . . oure] *so* CK–D; The b. þat
      R; But þey beleven on þe F.
      men] RC; men hem F.
116   to] WCrLMαC; om HmgF.

Wheither I were chose or noght chose; on Holy Chirche I thoughte,

                                         elect

That underfonged me atte font for oon of Goddes chosene.

                               received (cf. I 76)

For Crist cleped us alle, come if we wolde—   *called*

120 Sarsens and scismatikes, and so he dide the Jewes: *Pagans; schismatics*

    O vos omnes sicientes, venite . . .

And bad hem souke for synne save at his breste   *suck; a remedy (C)*

And drynke boote for bale, brouke it whoso myghte. *cure; evil; enjoy*

    'Thanne may alle Cristene come,' quod I, 'and cleyme there entree

By the blood that he boughte us with and thorugh bapteme after:

    Qui crediderit et baptizatus fuerit . . .

125 For though a Cristen man coveited his Cristendom to reneye, *abjure*

Rightfully to reneye no reson it wolde.

    'For may no cherl chartre make, ne his c[h]atel selle   *property*

Withouten leve of his lord – no lawe wol it graunte.   *leave; allow*

Ac he may renne in arerage and rome fro home, *run into debt; wander*

130 And as a reneyed caytif recchelesly aboute.   *wretch forsworn*

Ac Reson shal rekene with hym and rebuken hym at the laste,

And Conscience acounte with hym and casten hym in arerage,

                                      settle accounts

And putten hym after in prison in purgatorie to brenne,   *burn*

For hise arerages rewarden hym there right to the day of dome,

                                      debts, sins

120*a* All you that thirst, come to the waters (Is 55: 1).

124*a* He that believeth and is baptized shall be saved . . . (Mk 16: 16).

125–6 For even if a Christian *wanted* to renounce his Christianity, Reason would not allow that he could legitimately do so.

117 chose[1,2]] αC; chosen β ([2]] *om* Crg).

121 saue] α?C; safly β.

124 þat] βC; *om* αG. wiþ] βFC; *om* R.

125 reneye] β (forsake C)C; receyue α.

127 chatel] *so* ?CK–D; catel *All MSS* (C).

128 no] βFC; ne R.

129 rome] βC; renne ?α (rayke F)Cr. fro] αGCK–D; so fro β.

130 a reneyed] β (*cf.* C); he renneth α. aboute] gL (gon a., gon +L)MR; rennen ab. w; or romeþ ab. F.

131–2 *So* αC; *run together* β.

131 Ac] L&r (but G); ʒit F; and wC²C. and . . . laste] αCSk; *om* β.

132 And . . . hym] α (ac.] shal ac. F)CSk; *om* β.

133 in[1]] g?α (in strong F)CK–D; in a wBmBoLM.

134 arerages] W&r; sg g. riʒte] ?αCK–D; *om* βF.

135 But if contricion wol come and crye by his lyve   *life*
Mercy for hise mysdedes with mouthe or with herte.'
   'That is sooth,' seide Scripture; 'may no synne lette   *prevent*
Mercy, may al amende, and mekenesse hir folwe;   *that can amend; if*
For thei beth, as oure bokes telleth, above Goddes werkes: *are*
Misericordia eius super omnia opera eius.'
140   'Ye, baw for bokes!' quod oon was broken out of helle   *bah!*
Highte Troianus, a trewe knyght, took witnesse at a pope
                                  called; Trajan; just
How he was ded and dampned to dwellen in pyne   *torment*
For an uncristene creature: 'Clerkes wite the sothe— *As; unchristened*
That al the clergie under Crist ne myghte me cracche fro helle
                                    snatch
145 But oonliche love and leautee of my lawful domes. *upright judgements*
Gregorie wiste this wel, and wilned to my soule   *desired for*
Savacion for the soothnesse that he seigh in my werkes.
And after that he wepte and wilned me were graunted grace,
                                according as
Withouten any bede biddyng his boone was underfongen, *praying*
150 And I saved, as ye may see, withouten syngynge of masses,
By love and by lernyng of my lyvynge in truthe,
Broughte me fro bitter peyne ther no biddyng myghte. *praying*
   'Lo! ye lordes, what leautee dide by an Emperour of Rome

139a His tender mercies are over all his works (Ps 144: 9).
149 Without any saying prayers, his request for favour was accepted.
151–2 Through (his) love and through (his) learning of my just life, which
  brought . . .

135 wol] W&r (*om* F); wel LR.
136 or] L&r; and WHmFC (C).
137 seide] W&rC; quod Hmg.
138 may al] α (*cf.* C); al to β.
  and] βC; if F; þat R.
  hir] β (*om* G); hym F; he R.
141 Hiȝte] W&r (That h. B); I CrC;
  he was F (C).
  hadde ben] W&r (h.] that h. Hm;
  & h. B); was G; *om* CrC.
  took] W&r (he t. F); take Cr¹C.
  a²] W&r; the gF.
142 he] W&r; I CrC.
  pyne] W&r; paine CrgF.
144 ne] wC; *om* L&r.

145 and] βFC; and my R.
  of] α (*cf.* C); and β.
146 wilned] W&rC; wilneth g.
147 þe] αC; *om* β.
  in] β (*om* CB)C; of α.
148 *Div from* 149 *before* Grace *All*
  MSS (C).
149 any bede] W&r (any) *om* G);
  more F.
150 may] ?β (mowen OC²; *om* w)
  FC; now R.
151 By¹] β; þoru F; *om* R.
153 dide] βC; doþ F; *om* R.

That was an uncristene creature, as clerkes fyndeth in bokes.
155 Nought thorugh preiere of a pope but for his pure truthe
                                                simply for his upright life
Was that Sarsen saved, as Seint Gregorie bereth witnesse.   *pagan*
Wel oughte ye lordes that lawes kepe this lesson to have in mynde,
And on Troianus truthe to thenke, and do truthe to the peple.
                                            administer (true) justice to
   'This matere is merk for many of yow – ac, men of Holy Chirche,
                                                            obscure
160 The legende *sanctorum* yow lereth more largere than I yow telle.
                                                    teaches; amply
   Ac thus leel love and lyvyng in truthe   *faithful*
   Pulte out of peyne a paynym of Rome.   *Took out by force; pagan*
   Yblissed be truthe that so brak helle yates   *burst (open); hell's gates*
   And saved the Sarsyn from Sathanas and his power,
165 Ther no clergie ne kouthe, ne konnyng of lawes!   *learning; knowledge*
   Love and leautee is a leel science,   *trustworthy, true*
   For that is the book blissed of blisse and of joye:
   God wroughte it and wroot it with his on fynger
   And took it Moises upon the mount, alle men to lere.   *gave; teach*
170   'Lawe withouten love,' quod Troianus, 'ley ther a bene—
                                            bean (i.e. is worthless)
   Or any science under sonne, the sevene arts and alle!
   —But thei ben lerned for Oure Lordes love, lost is al the tyme,
   For no cause to cacche silver therby, ne to be called a maister,   *get*
   But al for love of Oure Lord and the bet to love the peple.   *better*
175   'For Seint Johan seide it, and sothe arn hise wordes:
   Qui non diligit manet in morte.
   Whoso loveth noght, leve me, he lyveth in deeth deyinge;
                                                'is spiritually dead'

---

173 i.e. likewise if the motive is to obtain money or titles of respect.
175a He that loveth not abideth in death (I Jn 3: 14).

157 ye] β (*om* CrG)C; þise B; þe α.   163 so brak] R; *trs* F.
    to] WHmLMRC; *om* CrgF.   164 sath. and his] R; sathenases F.
159–69 *In* α (*cf.* C)*Sk; ll. om* β.   166 Loue . . . is] R; þan is l. and l.
159 of ȝow ac] R; save F.   ryght F.
160 ȝow lereth] R; lerneþ ȝow F.   167 *In* R (*cf.* C); *l. om* F.
161 Ac; lyuynge] R; &; leel l. F.   168 on] R; owne F.
162 Pulte] R; Pytten F.   169 vpon; to] R; on; it to F.
    peyȝne] F; pyne R.

And that alle manere men, enemyes and frendes,   *(he says) that . . .*
Love hir eyther oother, and lene hem as hemselve.   *love; give (to)*
Whoso leneth noght, he loveth noght, Oure Lord woot the sothe,
180 And comaundeth ech creature to conformen hym to lovye   *be willing*
And [principally] povere peple, and hir enemyes after.
For hem that haten us is oure merite to lovye,   *(it) is*
And povere peple to plese – hir preieres maye us helpe.
For oure joy and oure [ju]ele, Jesu Crist of hevene,   *jewel, treasure*
185 In a povere mannes apparaille pursueth us evere,   *guise, clothing*
And loketh on us in hir liknesse and that with lovely chere,
                                                                      expression

To knowen us by oure kynde herte and castynge of oure eighen,
                                                         'where we choose to look'
Wheither we love the lordes here bifore oure Lord of blisse;
And exciteth us by the Evaungelie that whan we maken festes,
                                                         urges; Gospel; feasts
190 We sholde noght clepe oure kyn therto, ne none kynnes riche:
                                                         invite; no kind of rich men
Cum facitis convivia, nolite invitare amicos.
"Ac calleth the carefulle therto, the croked and the povere;
                                                         distressed; crippled
For youre frendes wol feden yow, and fonde yow to quyte   *try; repay*
Youre festynge and youre faire yiftes – ech frend quyt so oother.
Ac for the povere I shal paie, and pure wel quyte hir travaille
                                                         thoroughly; pains
195 That yyveth hem mete or moneie and loveth hem for my sake."

190*a* When thou makest a dinner . . . call not thy friends [nor thy brethren nor
thy kinsmen nor thy neighbours who are rich] (Lk 14 : 12; see also verses
13–14).

178   hem²] W&r (hym F; hys G); hir
      YCBLMR.
179   Who-] β; For ho- α.
      oure lorde] ?α; god βF.
180   And] L&r; he F; Crist W.
181   principally . . . peple]
      souereynly pouere peple β (pou.] þe
      pou. W
      Cr)R; his neyȝhebore as hymselue
      F (C).
      hir enemyes] βR; hise enemyȝe F.

184   For] L&r; And w.
      Iuel] *cj* K–D; euel R (?=α); heele
      W&r (helthe FCr) (C).
      Iesu] β; is Iesu α.
185   -eth] L&r; -ed wG.
187   eiȝen] W&r; eyghe g.
188   owre] L&r; þe wGF.
193   yiftes] gα; yifte wML.
      quit] ?α (ȝeldith F); quyteþ β.
195   and] L&r; or WF.

'Almighty God [myghte have maad riche alle] men, if he wolde,
Ac for the beste ben som riche and some beggeres and povere.
For alle are we Cristes creatures, and of his cofres riche,   *from*
And bretheren as of oo blood, as wel beggeres as erles.   *one; earls*
200 For at Calvarie, of Cristes blood Cristendom gan sprynge,
                                                from; Christianity
And blody bretheren we bicome there, of o body ywonne,   *redeemed*
As *quasi modo geniti* gentil men echone—   *noble*
No beggere ne boye amonges us but if it synne made: *knave; caused*
Qui facit peccatum servus est peccati.
In the olde lawe, as the lettre telleth, "mennes sones" men called us,
205 Of Adames issue and Eve, ay til God-Man deide;   *God-(made)-man*
And after his resurexcion *Redemptor* was his name,   *Redeemer*
And we hise bretheren thorugh hym ybought, bothe riche and povere.
Forthi love we as leve children shal, and ech man laughe up oother,
                                                affectionate; rejoice at
And of that ech man may forbere, amende there it nedeth,
                                                from, with; spare; make good
210 And every man helpe oother – for hennes shul we alle:
                                                must we (go) – i.e. die
Alter alterius onera portate.
And be we noght unkynde of oure catel, ne of oure konnyng neither,
                                                goods; knowledge

---

201–2 And we became brethren-by-blood (or brethren *through* Christ's blood)
there, delivered from/redeemed by one body, 'As newborn babes' (I Pet 2: 2).
203a Whosoever committeth sin is the servant of sin (Jn 8: 34).
208 And so let us love each other as loving children do and each man take joy
in his fellows.
210a Bear ye one another's burdens . . . (Gal 6: 2); cf. VI 221a (C).

196 *In* αK–D; *l. om* β.
Almi3ty . . . riche] A. god hath
made r. R; God myghte ryche a
maad all F (C).
197 Ac] α (But F)K–D; *om* β.
199 And] βF; As R.
oo] W&r; *om* gF.
200 at] αCK–D; on β.
202 gentil] *so* CK–D; and g. *All
MSS* (C).
203a *peccati*] Cr&rCK–D; *p. &c*
WHmGYLM.
204 *So div* CK–D; *as* 2 *ll. div before*

mennes *All MSS* (C).
þe²] αCK–D; holy β.
vs] *so* CK–D; vs echone W&r (vs]
om CotF).
208 childern] αCK–D; breþeren β.
shal] L&r; *om* WCrFC.
vp] LMR; vpon YCB; on GOC²F;
of WHm; *om* Cr.
209 of] W&r; if g.
210 ooþer] βC; oþer here α.
210a *portate*] WCrLMα; *p. &c*
Hmg.

For noot no man how neigh it is to ben ynome fro bothe.

knows not; taken (away)

Forthi lakke no lif oother, though he moore Latyn knowe,

criticize; person

Ne undernyme noght foule, for is noon withoute defaute.

rebuke; bitterly

215 For whatevere clerkes carpe of Cristendom or ellis,

Crist to a commune womman seide in commune at a feste

prostitute; openly (C)

That *Fides sua* sholde saven hire and salven hire of alle synnes.

Her faith (Lk 7: 50); cure (C)

'Thanne is bileve a lele help, above logyk or lawe.   *faith; trusty*

Of logyk ne of lawe in *Legenda Sanctorum*

220 Is litel alowaunce maad, but if bileve hem helpe;   *approval*

For it is overlonge er logyk any lesson assoille,   *explain*

And lawe is looth to lovye but if he lacche silver.   *obtain s. (thereby)*

Bothe logyk and lawe, that loveth noght to lye,   *(you) who love*

I conseille alle Cristene, clyve noght theron to soore,   *stick; closely*

225 For some wordes I fynde writen, were of Feithes techyng,

That saved synful men, as Seint Johan bereth witnesse:

Eadem mensura qua mensi fueritis remecietur vobis.

Forthi lerne we the lawe of love as Oure Lord taughte;

And as Seint Gregorie seide, for mannes soule helthe,

Melius est scrutari scelera nostra quam naturas rerum.

230   'Why I meve this matere is moost for the povere; *introduce; subject*

For in hir liknesse Oure Lord ofte hath ben yknowe.   *encountered*

Witnesse in the Pask wyke whan he yede to Emaus—

Easter week; went; Emmaus

226a With what measure you mete, it shall be measured to you again (Mt 7: 2).

229 It is better to examine our sins than the natures of things (C); cf. I 178a.

212 noet] L&r; woot wGCotF.
     neiȝ] W&r; om g.
214 defaute] WHmC²α; faute
     Cr?gLM.
216 commune²] W&r; come G;
     conen Y.
217 alle] LHmCrR; hyr GYCBM;
     om WOC²F.
219 ne] L&r; or w.

220 Is . . . maad] β; Is l. alowed þei
     both R; Been but l. alowed F.
     if] ?β; om αGCot.
223 to] βF; for to R.
224 cristene] WCrLMR; cr. men
     HmgF (m.] men ȝee F).
225 were] L&r; þat were WGC²B.
231 hir] W&r; hys g; pore F.

Cleophas ne knew hym noght, that he Crist were,

For his povere apparaille and pilgrymes wedes,   *dress*

235 Til he blessede and brak the breed that thei eten.   (Lk 24: 30)

So bi hise werkes thei wisten that he was Jesus,   *actions; knew*

Ac by clothyng thei knewe hym noght, ne by carpynge of tonge.

the way he spoke

And al was ensample, for sooth, to us synfulle here,   *an example*

That we sholde [lowe be] and loveliche of speche,   *humble; gracious*

240 And apparaille us noght over proudly – for pilgrymes are we alle.

And in the apparaille of a povere man and pilgrymes liknesse

Many tyme God hath ben met among nedy peple,

Ther nevere segge hym seigh in secte of the riche.

Whereas; man; class/clothes

'Seint Johan and othere seintes were seyen in poore clothyng,

i.e. the Baptist; seen

245 And as povere pilgrymes preyed mennes goodes.   *asked for alms*

Jesu Crist on a Jewes doghter lighte: gentil womman though she were,

descended, was born of

Was a pure povere maide and to a povere man ywedded.   *truly poor*

'Martha on Marie Maudelayne an huge pleynt she made,

And to Oure Saveour self seide thise wordes:

250 *Domine, non est tibi cure quod soror mea reliquit me solam*
     ministrare?

And hastily God answerde, and eitheres wille folwed,   *concurred with*

Bothe Marthaes and Maries, as Mathew bereth witnesse;

Ac poverte God putte bifore, and preised it the bettre:

Maria optimam partem elegit, que non auferetur ab ea.

---

250 Lord, hast thou no care that my sister hath left me alone to serve? (Lk 10:
40).

253*a* Mary hath chosen the best part which shall not be taken away from her
(Lk 10: 42).

233   ne] W&r; *om* gM.
238   was] BMαCK–D; was in w?gL.
      for sothe] ?α (*cf.* C); *om* βF.
239   lowe be] *trs All MSS* (C).
240   ouer] WHmLMR; to YCB; *om*
      CrGOC²F.
245   mennes] β; men R; men of here
      F.
247   was] ?β; A was ?α (*l. om* F)
      HmY (Yet was she Y).

248   she] L&r(†F)C; *om* WCot.
250   quod . . . ministrare] W&r
      (*solam*) sola LMF; min.] m. *&c*
      HmLM; *&c* y; *om* G)C; *&c* R.
251   folwed] βR; fulfylde F.
252   Boþe; and] W&r; b. in; & in g.
253   it] L&r; þat w.
253*a*   que . . . ea] β (*auf. ab ea*) auf
      &c Cot; *&c* WCrLM)F?CSk; *&c*
      R.

'And alle the wise that evere were, by aught I kan aspye,
as far as I can discover

255 Preisen poverte for best lif, if pacience it folwe,   *accompany*
And bothe bettre and blesseder by many fold than richesse.   *time(s)*
Although it be sour to suffre, ther cometh swete after;
As on a walnote – withoute is a bitter barke,   *on the outside; husk, shell*
And after that bitter bark, be the shelle aweye,   *removed*

260 Is a kernel of confort kynde to restore.   *strength; nourish, refresh*
So is after poverte or penaunce paciently ytake,
Maketh a man to have mynde in God and a gret wille   *thought(s) of*
To wepe and to wel bidde, wherof wexeth mercy,   *pray; grows, arises*
Of which Crist is a kernell to conforte the soule.

265 And wel sikerer he slepeth, the segge that is povere,   *more securely*
And lasse he dredeth deeth and in derke to ben yrobbed   *(the) dark*
Than he that is right riche – Reson bereth witnesse: *it stands to reason*
Pauper ego ludo dum tu dives meditaris.

'Although Salomon seide, as folk seeth in the Bible,
Divicias nec paupertates . . .

270 Wiser than Salomon was bereth witnesse and taughte   *(One) wiser*
That parfit poverte was no possession to have,
And lif moost likynge to God, as Luc bereth witnesse: *pleasing*
Si vis perfectus esse, vade et vende . . .
And is to mene to men that on this moolde lyven,   *earth*
Whoso wole be pure parfit moot possession forsake,   *completely; must*

275 Or selle it, as seith the Book, and the silver dele   *give away*
To beggeris that goon and begge and bidden good for Goddes love.
ask alms

---

260 i.e. a kernel with the power of building up one's natural strength.
267a Poor, I relax, while you, being wealthy, brood (Alexander of Ville-Dieu,
    Doctrinale, ed. D. Reichling (Berlin, 1893), verse 1091).
269 Give me neither beggary [*mendicitatem,* Vulg.] nor riches (Prov 30: 8).
272 If thou wilt be perfect, go sell [. . . and give to the poor] (Mt 19: 21).

255 -sen] L&r; -seden WMC.   262 Maketh] αCK–D; For it m. β.
     folwe] β (folwed W); wolde ?α   a¹] W&r; *om* gC.
     (welde F).   265 segge] αCK–D; man β.
257 Al-] LMαC; and HmCrg; For   268 folk] β; men α.
     W.   272a &c] L&r; *om* W.
     þere . . . after] L&rC; þerafter   273 þis] βF; *om* R.
     comeþ swete w.   276 good] W&r; syluer Hm; *om*
261 is] W&r; *om* CBC.   GF.

For failed nevere man mete that myghtful God serveth,   *lacked*
As David seith in the Sauter; to swiche that ben in wille   (Ps 36: 25)
To serve God goodliche, ne greveth hem no penaunce—   *privation*
Nichil inpossibile volenti—
280 Ne lakketh nevere liflode, lynnen ne wollen: *lack necessaries*
Inquirentes autem Dominum non minuentur omni bono.
  'If preestes weren wise, thei wolde no silver take
For masses ne for matyns, noght hir mete of usureres,
Ne neither kirtel ne cote, theigh thei for cold sholde deye,   *tunic*
And thei hir devoir dide, as David seith in the Sauter: *If; duty*
Iudica me, Deus, et discerne causam meam.
285   'Spera in Deo speketh of preestes that have no spendyng silver
That if thei travaille truweliche and truste in God almyghty,   *honestly*
Hem sholde lakke no liflode, neyther lynnen ne wollen.
And the title that ye take ordres by telleth ye ben avaunced;
Thanne nedeth yow noght to [nyme] silver for masses that ye syngen.
290 For he that took yow youre title sholde take yow youre wages,

                                                    gave; give
Or the bisshop that blessed yow, if that ye ben worthi.
  'For made nevere kyng no knyght but he hadde catel to spende
As bifel for a knyght, or foond hym for his strengthe.   *provided*

279a Nothing is impossible to him who wills it (cf. Mt 17: 19).
280a [The rich have wanted, and have suffered hunger:] but they that seek the
    Lord shall not be deprived of any good (Ps 33: 11).
284 *Either* And they would be doing . . . *or, more likely* If they were doing . . .
284a Judge me, O God, and distinguish my cause [from the nation that is not
    holy] (Ps 42: 1).
285 Trust in God . . . the salvation of my countenance (Ps 42:6) (C).
288 And the claim to financial solvency, on the basis of which you receive
    ordination, guarantees your position.

277 serueþ] WHmCr[1]αK–D; serued   284 dide] β; *om* α.
    L&r.   287 lynnen; wollen] WHmC; *trs*
278 So β; *as 2 ll. div after* wille R,   L&r (C).
    after soþe F.   288 þat] W&r († F); *om* Crg?C.
    to] & hise sawis ben soþe to F.   ye[1]] WαC; þei ?β.
    wille] w. With eny wel or wo R;   289 yow noȝt] WBM?α (n.] *om* F);
    will to suffre wo for welthe F.   *trs* L&r.
279 hem] CrMα; hym W&r; *om*   to] wBLMR; *om*?gF.
    Cot.   nyme] *so* CK–D; take *All MSS* (C).
279a inpossibile] β; difficile α.   290 yow[1]] βF; *om* R.
    volenti] W&r; v. &c HmGYR.   291 Or] wBLMα; Of ?g.
281 wise] ?α (all wise men F)K–D;
    parfite β (C).

It is a careful knyght, and of a caytif kynges makyng,   *wretched*
295 That hath nother lond ne lynage riche ne good loos of hise handes.

                                                            reputation

The same I segge for sothe by alle swiche preestes   *about*
That han neither konnynge ne kyn, but a crowne one   *tonsure only*
And a title, a tale of noght, to his liflode at meschief.

                                                    empty name; trouble

He hath moore bileve, as I leve, to lacche thorugh his croune *obtain*
300 Cure than for konnynge or "knowen for clene of berynge."

                                              (A) benefice; good repute

I have wonder [at] why and wherfore the bisshop
Maketh swiche preestes, that lewed men bitrayen!
  'A chartre is chalangeable bifore a chief justice:

                                             document; open to dispute

If fals Latyn be in that lettre, the lawe it impugneth,   *calls in question*
305 Or peynted parentrelynarie, parcelles overskipped.

                                             interlined; portions left out

The gome that gloseth so chartres for a goky is holden.   *glosses; fool*
So is it a goky, by God! that in his gospel failleth   *makes mistakes*
Or in masse or in matyns maketh any defaute: *omission(s)*
Qui offendit in uno, in omnibus est reus.
And also in the Sauter seith David to overskipperis,
310 *Psallite Deo nostro, psallite; quoniam rex terrae Deus Israel, psallite
    sapienter.*
  'The bisshop shal be blamed bifore God, as I leve,

---

298 And the mere empty name of 'Sir Priest' [*or* mere verbal guarantee of
     support (*OED s.v. title* sb., 8)] to earn a living with in time of distress.
299–300 He actually has more hope of getting a benefice through (the mere
     fact of) being ordained than through any (claim) to learning or reputation for
     piety (C).
303 The validity of a legal document can be questioned . . .
308a [*And*] whosoever [*shall keep the whole law but*] offend in one point, is
     become guilty of all (Js 2: 10); cf. IX 98a.
310 Sing praises to our God, sing ye; . . . for [the] God [of Israel] is the king of
     all the earth: sing ye wisely (Ps 46: 7–8).

294 a²] wBLMα; *om* g.
295 noþer] αBC; no β.
     riche] βC; *om* α.
298 at] L&r; at his w; in F.
300 knowen] W&r; knowing Cr²³g.
     of] L&r; *om* WCrBF (C).

301 at] and L&r; for W; þat G; *om*
     CrB (C).
305 parceles] L&rC; or p. wF.
308 in²] wBLMRC; *om* Cr?gF.
308a *est reus*] βF; *&c* R.

That crouneth swiche Goddes knyghtes that konneth noght *sapienter*

tonsures, i.e. ordains; wisely

Synge, ne psalmes rede, ne seye a masse of the day.

Ac never neither is blamelees, the bisshop ne the chapeleyn;   *priest*

315 For hir either is endited, and that of "*Ignorancia*

each of them; accused

Non excusat episcopos nec ydiotes preestes."   *unlearned*

'This lokynge on lewed preestes hath doon me lepe from poverte—

considering; made me digress

The which I preise, ther pacience is, moore parfit than richesse.'

esteem; where; perfect

Ac muche moore in metynge thus with me gan oon dispute—

320 And slepynge I seigh al this; and sithen cam Kynde

And nempned me by my name, and bad me nymen hede,   *take note*

And thorugh the wondres of this world wit for to take.   *understanding*

And on a mountaigne that Myddelerthe highte, as me tho thoughte,

I was fet forth by ensaumples to knowe,   *led, brought*

325 Thorugh ech a creature, Kynde my creatour to lovye.

I seigh the sonne and the see and the sond after,   *sand*

And where that briddes and beestes by hir make thei yeden,   *mate(s)*

Wilde wormes in wodes, and wonderful foweles   *serpents*

With fleckede fetheres and of fele colours.   *many*

330 Man and his make I myghte se bothe;

Poverte and plentee, bothe pees and werre,   *war*

Blisse and bale – bothe I seigh at ones,   *misery; at one time*

And how men token Mede and Mercy refused.

Reson I seigh soothly sewen alle beestes   *follow*

335 In etynge, in drynkynge and in engendrynge of kynde.   *offspring*

315–16 Ignorance [*sc.* of ordinands' deficiencies] does not excuse bishops (C).

314   Ac] L&r (but G); And
    WCrC²C; For F.
315   of] L&r; is of Y; ys be F; is w.
318   The] W&r; *om* Crg.
321   my] W&r; *om* g.
322   wondres] β; wordis BR;
    worchynge F (C).
    þis] βF; þe R.
323   -erþe] wGC; -erd L&r.
    þo] L&r; *om* wCotF.

325   creature] *so* K–D (*cf.* C); cr.
    and W&r (*pl* F).
327   make] L&rC; makes WCrGF.
    þei] L&rC; *om* WGOC²F.
328   in] βFC; and R.
330   se bothe] ?α (seyʒ y þere F)
    CK–D; boþe biholde β.
332   at ones] L&rC; al atones w.

And after cours of concepcion noon took kepe of oother
the process; notice

As whan thei hadde ryde in rotey tyme; anoonright therafter
copulated; rutting-time

Males drowen hem to males amorwenynges by hemselve,
withdrew; in the mornings (C)

And in evenynges also yede males fro femelles.   *went*

340 Ther ne was cow ne cowkynde that conceyved hadde   *cattle*

That wolde belwe after boles, ne boor after sowe.   *bellow; boar*

Bothe hors and houndes and alle othere beestes   *horses*

Medled noght with hir makes that [mid] fole were.
Coupled; with foal, pregnant

Briddes I biheld that in buskes made nestes;   *bushes*

345 Hadde nevere wye wit to werche the leeste.   *a human being; build*

I hadde wonder at whom and wher the pye   *from; magpie*

Lerned to legge the stikkes in whiche she leyeth and bredeth.
lay; lays (eggs)

Ther is no wrighte, as I wene, sholde werche hir nest to paye;
satisfactorily

If any mason made a molde therto, muche wonder it were.
mould, pattern; ?comparable to

350 And yet me merveilled moore: many othere briddes

Hidden and hileden hir egges ful derne   *covered; secretly*

In mareys and moores for men sholde hem noght fynde,   *marsh; that*

And hidden hir egges whan thei therfro wente,

For fere of othere foweles and for wilde beestes.

355 And some treden hir makes and on trees bredden
copulated with; mated

---

336 of²] βC; til R; to C².

337 As] W&r (*l. om* F); and Hmg.

338 a-] W&r (*l. om* F)C; all Hm.
morwenynges] W&r; *sg* HmCr³
C²C (C).

339 ȝede males] ?α (*l. om* F)
?L(ȝe)Sk; þe males ben w; þe males
gM (C).

340 ne was] W&rC; was non F; was
g.

341 boles] βR; bole FC.

343 þat . . . were] þat wiþ f. w. βR;
save man oone F (C).

346 *So div from* 347 CK–D; *after*
lerned *All MSS.*

347 she] W&r (a R) (*cf.* C); he g.

348 is no] αC; nys β.
wriȝte] W&rC; wiȝt OC²; wit R.

350 And] L&r (*om* F)C; Ac W.
many] ?αC; how many β; of m.
FG.

355 treden] αCr²³C; troden β.

And broughten forth hir briddes so al above the grounde.   *young*
And some briddes at the bile thorugh brethyng conceyved,   *bill*
And some caukede; I took kepe how pecokkes bredden.   *trod*
Muche merveilled me what maister thei hadde,   *teacher*
360   And who taughte hem on trees to tymbre so heighe   *build*
That neither burn ne beest may hir briddes rechen.   *man; reach*
      And sithen I loked upon the see and so forth upon the sterres;
Manye selkouthes I seigh, ben noght to seye nouthe.

wonders; mention

I seigh floures in the fryth and hir faire colours,   *wood*
365   And how among the grene gras grewe so manye hewes,
And some soure and some swete – selkouth me thoughte: *wonderful*
Of hir kynde and of hir colour to carpe it were to longe.
      Ac that moost meved me and my mood chaunged—

perturbed my heart

That Reson rewarded and ruled alle beestes   *watched over*
370   Save man and his make: many tymes and ofte
No Reson hem folwede, [neither riche ne povere].
And thanne I rebukede Reson, and right til hymselven I seyde.
      'I have wonder of thee, that witty art holden,   *wise; considered*
Why thow ne sewest man and his make, that no mysfeet hem folwe.'

misdeed

375   And Reson arated me, and seide, 'Recche thee nevere

corrected; Trouble yourself

Why I suffre or noght suffre – thiself hast noght to doone.

'It's no concern of yours'

Amende thow it if thow myght, for my tyme is to abide.   *Improve*

---

356   brouȝten] βC; brynge F; bredde R.
       so] W&r; *om* HmYFC.
358   caukede] W&r; kakeled g.
       bredden] W&r; breden CrGR; wirche F.
359   þei hadde] L&r; hem made W.
361   burn] W&r; barne Crg.
       may] βF; ne may R.
362   vpon[1]] WHmLMR; on CrgFC.
       forþ] W&rC; *om* gF.
       vpon[2]] WCrLMR; yn Hm; on gFC.
364   in] βF; of R.
365   grewe] L&rC; growed wB.

367   of here[2]] ?α (*om* F)CrCotC; hir β.
370   tymes] αC; tyme β (*l. om* CB).
371   *So div from* 372 *K–D* (*cf.* C);
       after reb. βR; *after* þanne F (C).
       hem folwede] βR; rewlyþ hem F (*cf.* C).
       neiþer . . . pouere] *so* CK–D; *om All MSS* (C).
372   I[2]] W&rC; *om* gM.
374   sewest] βR (s-) sch- R); makst F.
       -feet] ?β; -faut C; -faiþ BoCotR; -chef F.
377   þow it] w (*trs* Hm)LR; it F; þou gM.

Suffraunce is a soverayn vertue, and a swift vengeaunce.

Patience (cf. Lk 18: 1–8)

Who suffreth moore than God?' quod he; 'no gome, as I leeve.   *man*
380 He myghte amende in a minute while al that mysstandeth,

moment; is amiss

Ac he suffreth for som mannes goode, and so is oure bettre.

   'Holy Writ,' quod that wye, 'wisseth men to suffre: *counsels*
Propter Deum subiecti estote omni creature.

Frenche men and fre men affaiteth thus hire children: *train*
Bele vertue est suffraunce; mal dire est petite vengeance.
Bien dire et bien suffrir fait lui suffrant a bien venir.

385 Forthi I rede [the],' quod Reson, 'thow rule thi tonge bettre,   *control*
And er thow lakke my lif, loke if [thyn] be to preise.   *criticize*
For is no creature under Crist can formen hymselven,   *form, create*
And if a man myghte make hymself [Cristen],
Ech a lif wolde be laklees – leeve thow non other.   *without fault*
390 Ne thow shalt fynde but fewe fayne for to here   *willing*
Of here defautes foule bifore hem reherced.   *vile faults; declared*

   'The wise and the witty wroot thus in the Bible:
De re que te non molestat noli certare.

For be a man fair or foul, it falleth noght for to lakke   *is not right*
395 The shap ne the shaft that God shoop hymselve;   *form; figure*

---

381 But he tolerates (evil) for the benefit of particular individuals, and (in doing so, shows himself) to be superior to our human notions.
382a Be ye subject to every creature for God's sake (I Pet 2: 13).
384 Patience is a fair virtue, say-evil is a poor vengeance:
   Say-well and suffer-well dispose a man to come through well.
393 Strive not in a matter which doth not concern thee (Ecclus 11: 9).

378 a¹] W&r; om g.
382–91 *In* αCSk; *ll. om* β.
382 wye] *so* K–D; weye α.
  wisseth] R (*cf.* C); wyssheþ F.
383 *So* R; *preceded by a line:* Now will ȝe leere tale was told me in towne F.
  Frenche . . . men²] R; How Frensshe in France F.
  þus] *om* F.
384 *Beele*] FCSk; *Vele* R.
  petite] *so* CSk; *pety* α.
  suffrir] *so* CSk; *soffrer* R; *suffre* F.

385 þe quod] þe F; quod R (C).
  rewle] R; þou r. FC.
  þi tonge; bettere] R (*cf.* C); *trs* F.
386 if þyn] if þow R; þyn F.
387 is] R; þere is F.
388 hymself cristen] h. good to þe poeple R; lakles hymselue F (C).
389 a lif] R; man F.
390 þow; for to] R; *om;* wolde F.
391 defautes foule; hem] R; *trs;* here face F.
393 que te] βFC; quiete R.
  noli] βC; nolite ?α (*non* F).
394 for] W&r; hym F; *om* GOC².

For al that he wroughte was wel ydo, as Holy Writ witnesseth:
Et vidit Deus cuncta que fecerat, et erant valde bona.
And bad every creature in his kynde encreesse,   *species; increase*
Al to murthe with man that most wo tholieth   *gratify; endures grief*
In fondynge of the flessh and of the fend bothe.   *temptation from*
400   For man was maad of swich a matere he may noght wel asterte

                                                            escape
That som tyme hym bitit to folwen his kynde.   *it befalls him; nature*
Caton acordeth therwith – *Nemo sine crimine vivit!'*   *agrees*

        Tho caught I colour anoon and comsed to ben ashamed,   *blushed*
And awaked therwith. Wo was me thanne
405   That I in metels ne myghte moore have yknowen.   *dream*
And thanne seide I to myself, and chydde that tyme,   *spoke; cursed*
'Now I woot what Dowel is,' quod I, 'by deere God, as me thynketh!'
And as I caste up myne eighen, oon loked on me and asked
Of me, what thyng it were? 'Ywis, sire,' I seyde,
410   'To se muche and suffre moore, certes,' quod I, 'is Dowel.'
        'Haddestow suffred,' he seide, 'slepynge tho thow were,

                                                    'waited patiently'; when
Thow sholdest have knowen that Clergie kan and conceyved moore
        thorugh Reson;   *what Cl. knows; grasped*
For Reson wolde have reherced thee right as Clergie seide.   *declared*
Ac for thyn entremetynge here artow forsake: *interfering; abandoned*
Philosophus esses, si tacuisses.
415   'Adam, the whiles he spak noght, hadde paradis at wille;

396a And God saw all the things that he had made, and they were very good
    (Gen 1: 31).
402 No man lives free of fault (*Distichs of Cato* 1, 5).
414a You would have been a philosopher if you had held your peace (John
    Bromyard, *Summa Praedicantium* 1:450/2, *adapted from* Boethius, *De
    consolatione Philosophiae* II, pr. vii, 74–6).

396 wrou3t] αK–D; dide β.   406 And] wLMRC; *om* gF.
397 euery] β; to vch a R; ech F.   seide I to; chidde . . . tyme] βR;
398 most] L&r; moste WHmBmM.   chydd y; seyd þese woordes F (C).
    tholieþ] αOC²; þolie ?β.   412 conceiued] L&r; contreued
401 þat] αCK–D; That ne β.   WHm; kend Cr.
    tyme] W&r?C; tymes LR.   414 Ac] W&r (*l. om* F)C; And Crg.
402 þerwiþ] βC; þerto F; with al R.   415 þe] ?αC; *om* βF.

Ac whan he mamelede aboute mete and entremeted to knowe
prated; food
The wisedom and the wit of God, he was put fram blisse.   *expelled*
And right so ferde Reson bi thee – thow with thi rude speche   *dealt*
Lakkedest and losedest thyng that longed noght the to doone.
praised; was not fitting to
420 Tho [no likyng hadde he] for to lere the moore.   *wish; teach you*
'Pryde now and presumpcion paraventure wol thee appele, *accuse*
That Clergie thi compaignye ne kepeth noght to suwe.
(Saying) that; cares; keep
For shal nevere chalangynge ne chidynge chaste a man so soone
scolding; chasten
As shal shame, and shenden hym, and shape hym to amende.
mortify; dispose
425 For lat a dronken daffe in a dyk falle,   *fool; ditch*
Lat hym ligge, loke noght on hym til hym liste to ryse.
lie; feel like rising
For though Reson rebuked hym thanne, reccheth he nevere;   *cares*
Of Clergie ne of his counseil he counteth noght a risshe.   *values; rush*
[To blame] or for to bete hym thanne, it were but pure synne.
beat; sheer malice
430 Ac whan nede nymeth hym up, for [noye] lest he sterve,
picks; to avoid mortal harm
And shame shrapeth hise clothes and hise shynes wassheth,
scrapes; shins
Thanne woot the dronken daffe wherfore he is to blame.'

---

419 Damned and praised what there was no call to.

416 to] W&rC; hym to gM.
417 and . . . of] W&r; of þe w. of g;
    of his F.
    blisse] βF; þe blisse R.
418 þee . . . wiþ] β (w.] wiþ þi wCB)
    R; þyn F.
419 noght þe to] ?α; þe noȝt to WF;
    n. to OC²; n. to be L&r.
420 no likyng; hadde he] *trs All
    MSS* (C).
422 þi] β (to thy Hm); in þi α.
    ne] L&r; *om* WHmF.
    to] β; efte to α.
    suwe] β; sawe G; shew CrC; sitte
    α.

423 For] αC; *om* β.
424 As] β; he R; þan F.
426 to ryse] L&r (r.] aryse Cr);
    aryse WG.
427 *So* αCSk; *as one l. with* 429b β.
    reccheth he neuere] α (he] FSk;
    hym R)C; *om* β.
428 *In* αCSk; *l. om* β.
429 To blame] *so* CSk; *om* α (C).
    or . . . þanne] α (or] *om* F); *om* β.
430 noye] doute *All MSS* (C).

'Ye siggen sooth, by my soule,' quod I, 'Ich have yseyen it often.
say truly; seen

Ther smyt no thyng so smerte, ne smelleth so foule   *strikes; sharply*
435 As Shame, there he sheweth hym – for every man [shonyeth] his
felaweshipe.   *where; shuns; company*
Why ye wisse me thus,' quod I, 'was for I rebuked Reson.'
'Certes,' quod he, 'that is sooth,' and shoop hym for to walken.
got ready

And I aroos up right with that and [raughte] hym after,   *set off (C)*
And [craved] hym of his curteisie to [kenne] me his name.
begged; inform me of

---

433   by my soule; quod I] α (*trs* F)C;
quod I β.

434   no þyng] βC; non R; no man F.
foule] ?αCK–D; so*u*re βF (sore
GBmBoF).

435   euery] β; ech CrC; no α.
shonyeth his felaweshipe] sh. his
companye C; hym shonyeþ β (sh.]
shendethe G); loueth his felachipp
α (C).

437   he] βFC; I R.
walken] βFC; waken RCr¹.

438   I . . . and] βRC; gan faren on
hys weyȝ & y F.
raughte] folwed *All MSS* (C).

439   craved; kenne] preyde; telle *All
MSS* (C).

Passus XII

'I am Ymaginatif,' quod he, 'ydel was I nevere,   *idle, inactive*
Though I sitte by myself, in siknesse ne in helthe.
I have folwed thee, in feith, thise fyve and fourty wynter,
And manye tymes have meved thee to [m]yn[n]e on thyn ende,
                                              reflect
5 And how fele fernyeres are faren, and so fewe to come   *past years*
And of thi wilde wantownesse tho thow yong were,   *recklessness*
To amende it in thi myddel age, lest myght the faille *power (to do so)*
In thyn olde elde, that yvele kan suffre   *poorly; endure*
Poverte or penaunce, or preyeres bidde: *say*
Si non in prima vigilia nec in secunda . . .
10 'Amende thee while thow myght; thow hast ben warned ofte
With poustees of pestilences, with poverte and with angres—
                           violence; sorrows, afflictions
And with thise bittre baleises God beteth his deere children: *rods*
Quem diligo, castigo.
And David in the Sauter seith, of swiche that loveth Jesus,
"*Virga tua et baculus tuus, ipsa me consolata sunt:*
Although thow strike me with thi staf, with stikke or with yerde, *rod*
15 It is but murthe as for me to amende my soule."
And thow medlest thee with makynge – and myghtest go seye thi
   Sauter,   *dabble in verse-making*

9*a* If not in the first watch or the second . . . (cf. Lk 12: 38).
12*a* Such as I love I [rebuke and] chastise (Apoc 3: 19; cf. Prov 3: 12).
13*a* Thy rod and thy staff: they have comforted me (Ps 22: 4).

Collation WHmCrGYOC²CBLMRF.
RUBRIC *Passus xii^{us}* W&r (*xii^{us}*]
duodecimus de visione Cr; *xij^{us} de
v. et v^{us} de do weel* Hm; *duo de v.
et quintus de dowel* B (*de v.*] *om* Bm
Bo)); *P. xj. de v. vt supra* R; *om* GF.
1 was] βRC; am F.
2 ne] LMR; nor W; or F; and HmCrg.

4 mynne] *cj K–D*; þynke *All MSS*
(C).
7 faille] Y&r (f. after F)*K–D*; failled
wL.
9 bidde] L&r; to bidde WF.
11 pestilences] β (*sg* YC) penaunce
α (*pl* F).
13–13*a* *In* β; *ll. om* α.
16 makynge] αM; *pl* wL; mastryes
g.

And bidde for hem that yyveth thee breed; for ther are bokes ynowe
To telle men what Dowel is, Dobet and Dobest bothe,
And prechours to preve what it is, of many a peire freres.'   *pair (of)(C)*

20   I seigh wel he seide me sooth and, somwhat me to excuse,
Seide, 'Caton conforted his sone that, clerk though he were,
To solacen hym som tyme – as I do whan I make;   *amuse; versify*
Interpone tuis interdum gaudia curis.

'And of holy men I herde,' quod I, 'how thei outherwhile   *at times*
Pleyden, the parfiter to ben, in [places manye].

25   Ac if ther were any wight that wolde me telle
What were Dowel and Dobet and Dobest at the laste,
Wolde I nevere do werk, but wende to holi chirche
And there bidde my bedes but whan ich ete or slepe.'   *prayers; except*

'Poul in his pistle,' quod he, 'preveth what is Dowel: *epistle*
Fides, spes, caritas, et maior horum . . .

30   Feith, hope and charitee – alle ben goode,
And saven men sondry tymes, ac noon so soone as charite.
For he dooth wel, withouten doute, that dooth as lewte techeth;
That is, if thow be man maryed, thi make thow lovye,

married; spouse

And lyve forth as lawe wole the while ye lyven bothe.   *i.e. in chastity*

35   'Right so, if thow be religious, ren thow nevere ferther

'a monk or nun'; run

To Rome ne to Rochemador, but as thi rule techeth,

Rocamadour (C)

And holde thee under obedience, that heigh wey is to hevene.

22a Give a place sometimes to pleasures amid your pressing cares (*Distichs of Cato* III, 6).

29a . . . faith, hope, charity . . . [but] the greatest of these [is charity] (I Cor 13: 13).

17 ynowe] L&r (*om* OC²);yknowe W.
19 preue] L&r; preuen W.
20 and] βF; ac R.
21 Seide] β (I s. Cr²³); and seide α.
    his] L&r; me his WHmCr¹.
22 as] β; and ?α (*l.* †F).
23 I herde] β; I here α (*trs* F).
24 places manye] *trs* βR (pl.] a place R); here prayeres after F (C).

25 Ac] W&r (butt G); and CrC²C; Nou F; *om* R.
29 Poul . . . pistle] β; with p. in his pistles R; See Poulis p. F.
29a *et*] β; *om* αCr²³.
    horum &c] β; h. est Karitas F; &c R.
30 alle] α; and alle β.
34 þe] α; *om* β.
    boþe] W&r; here g.

'And if thow be maiden to marye, and myght wel continue,

i.e. as a virgin

Seke thow nevere seint ferther for no soule helthe!   *health of soul*

40 For what made Lucifer to lese the heighe hevene,   *lose*

Or Salomon his sapience, or Sampson his strengthe?

Job the Jew his joye deere he it aboughte;   *dearly paid for it*

Aristotle and othere mo, Ypocras and Virgile,   *Hippocrates*

Alisaundre that al wan, elengliche ended.   *won, conquered; wretchedly*

45 Catel and kynde wit was combraunce to hem alle.

native intelligence; trouble

'Felice hir fairnesse fel hire al to sclaundre,   *became a disgrace to her*

And Rosamounde right so reufulliche bisette   *pitiably bestowed, used*

The beaute of hir body; in baddenesse she despended.   *spent it*

Of manye swiche may I rede – of men and of wommen—

50 That wise wordes wolde shewe and werche the contrarie:

do; opposite

Sunt homines nequam bene de virtute loquentes.

'And riche renkes right so gaderen and sparen,   *men; gather; save*

And tho men that thei moost haten mynistren it at the laste;

have the use of

And for thei suffren and see so manye nedy folkes   *allow (to exist)*

And love hem noght as Oure Lord bit, lesen hir soules: *commands*

Date et dabitur vobis.

55 So catel and kynde wit acombreth ful manye;   *hinder, cause trouble to*

Wo is hym that hem weldeth but he hem wel despende: *possesses*

Scient[es] et non facient[es] variis flagellis vapulab[un]t.

50a They are evil men, who *speak* well of virtue (Godfrey of Winchester,
   epigram 169) (C).

54a Give; and it shall be given to you (Lk 6: 38).

56a Those who know [God's will] and do not act [according to it] shall be
   beaten with many whips (cf. Lk 12: 47).

38   to marye] β; & to m. R; meeke
   F.

42   dere he it] L&r (*l. om* C; he it]
   trs OC²; he B; ytt G); ful deere W.

47   bysette] L&r (she b. F); to bileue
   w.

48   -nesse she] β; vse α.

49   may y] ?α (m.] men may R); *trs*
   β.

50   wolde shewe] W&r; can sey g.

50a *bene; de virtute*] W&r; *trs* g.

54   hir] βF (h. owen F); ʒoure R.

54a *vobis*] WCrα; *v. &c* ?β.

55–7a *In* αCSk; *ll. om* β.

55   so] R; & þerfore F.
   kynde] RC; vnkynde F.

56   he; wel] FCK–DSk; if he; wil R.

56a -tes¹˒²; -bunt] so CSk; -ti; -bit
   α.

Sapience, seith the Bok, swelleth a mannes soule:
Sapiencia inflat . . .
And richesse right so, but if the roote be trewe.   *its origin; honest*
   'Ac grace is a gras therfore, tho grevaunces to abate.   *healing herb*
60 Ac grace ne groweth noght but amonges [gomes] lowe:

                                                             humble people
Pacience and poverte the place is ther it groweth,   *where*
And in lele lyvynge men and in lif holy,   *men of holy life*
And thorugh the gifte of the Holy Goost, as the Gospel telleth:
Spiritus ubi vult spirat . . .
   'Clergie and kynde wit cometh of sighte and techyng,   *observation*
65 As the Book bereth witnesse to burnes that kan rede: *men*
Quod scimus loquimur, quod vidimus testamur.
Of *quod scimus* cometh clergie, a konnynge of hevene,

                                               From 'what we know'; from
And of *quod vidimus* cometh kynde wit, of sighte of diverse peple.

                                            From 'what we have seen'; from
Ac grace is a gifte of God, and of greet love spryngeth;
Knew nevere clerk how it cometh forth, ne kynde wit the weyes:
Nescit aliquis unde venit aut quo vadit.
70   'Ac yet is clergie to comende, and kynde wit bothe,   *be commended*
And namely clergie for Cristes love, that of clergie is roote.
For Moyses witnesseth that God wroot for to wisse the peple
In the Olde Lawe, as the lettre telleth, was the lawe of Jewes,   *Bible*

57a Knowledge puffeth up; [but charity edifieth] (I Cor 8: 1).
63a The Spirit breatheth where he will . . . (Jn 3: 8).
65a . . . we speak what we know and we testify what we have seen (Jn 3: 11).
69a But thou knowest [*lit.* he knows] not whence he [*sc.* the Spirit] cometh and whither he goeth (Jn 3: 8).
71 And particularly learning (acquired) for the love of Christ, who is the source of [all true] learning.

57a *&c*] R; *om* F.
59 gras] β (graffe Cr²³); grace R; grate F.
   -fore] αCK–D; of β.
   þo] wLα; þe gM.
   greuaunces] W&r; *sg* Cr¹g.
60 gomes] þe OC²; *om* W&r (C).
61 Pacience] β; Of p. ?α (*l. om* F).
   is] L&r; hiȝte W.

63 þe¹] β; þat F; *om* R.
63a *&c*] L&r; *om* WCrOC²FC.
65 burnes] WGLMF; barnes Cr&r.
66 a] αK–D; and β.
68 Ac] wLMα (But F); and Crg.
69 wit þe] β; wit his ?α (witys F).
69a *vadit*] αCrCB; *v. &c* ?β.
73 was . . . of] ?αG (of] off þe G); þe l. so was to þe F; þat was þe l. of β.

That what womman were in avoutrye taken, were she riche or poore,
adultery

75 With stones men sholde hir strike, and stone hire to dethe.
(Lev 20: 10)

A womman, as we fynden, was gilty of that dede;   *read*
Ac Crist of his curteisie thorugh clergie hir saved.   *graciousness*
For thorugh Cristes caractes, the Jewes knewe hemselve
characters; recognized

Giltier as afore God and gretter in synne   (Jn 8: 3–9)
80 Than the womman that there was, and wenten awey for shame.
The clergie that there was conforted the womman.
Holy Kirke knoweth this – that Cristes writyng saved;
So clergie is confort to creatures that repenten,
And to mansede men meschief at hire ende.   *cursed (C); disaster*

85   'For Goddes body myghte noght ben of breed withouten clergie,
i.e. in the Eucharist

The which body is bothe boote to the rightfulle,   *remedy; virtuous*
And deeth and dampnacion to hem that deyeth yvele;
As Cristes caracte confortede and bothe coupable shewed   *guilty*
The womman that the Jewes broughte, that Jesus thoughte to save:
Nolite iudicare et non iudicabimini.

90 Right so Goddes body, bretheren, but it be worthili taken,
Dampneth us at the day of dome as dide the caracte the Jewes.
    'Forthi I counseille thee for Cristes sake, clergie that thow lovye,
For kynde wit is of his kyn and neighe cosynes bothe
To Oure Lord, leve me – forthi love hem, I rede.
95 For bothe [as mirours ben] to amenden oure defautes,
And lederes for lewed men and for lettred bothe.

89a Judge not, that you may not be judged (Mt 7: 1).

74 were she] L&r (w.] where WF);
    om Crg.
75 deþe] βF; dede R.
76 *In* β (we f.] I fynde W); *l. om* α.
77 þoruȝ] β; and þ. ?α (†F).
78 For] L&r; And w.
    cristes carectus] α; car. þat crist
    wroot β (wr.] wrought Cr¹GOC²C;
    om Y).
81 The . . . was] βR; þus þoruh
    clergye þere con. was þe F.

82 kirke] β; cherche αHmB.
    saued] L&r; s. hire wMF(*trs*).
88 As] β (And Cr); Ac ?α (But F).
    caracte] WHmLMα; *pl* Crg.
89 þe²; brouȝte] βF; *om*; bouȝte R.
89a *&c*] L&r; *om* WCrOC²F.
90 but] L&r; but if WHmC².
91 dede . . . carecte] α; þe caractes
    dide β (þe] *om* M).
92 þat þow] W&r; to g.
95 as . . . ben] ben as mirours *All
    MSS* (C).

'Forthi lakke thow nevere logik, lawe ne hise custumes,   *criticize*
Ne countreplede clerkes – I counseille thee for evere!   *argue against*
For as a man may noght see that mysseth hise eighen,   *lacks*
100 Na moore kan no clerk but if he caughte it first thorugh bokes.
can (know); obtained
Although men made bokes, God was the maister,   *teacher*
And Seint Spirit the samplarie, and seide what men sholde write.
exemplar
And right as sight serveth a man to se the heighe strete,
Right so lereth lettrure lewed men to reson.   *literacy; uneducated*
105 And as a blynd man in bataille bereth wepne to fighte,
And hath noon hap with his ax his enemy to hitte,   *luck*
Na moore kan a kynde witted man, but clerkes hym teche,   *unless*
Come, for al his kynde wit, to Cristendom and be saved—
Which is the cofre of Cristes tresor, and clerkes kepe the keys,
110 To unloken it at hir likyng, and to the lewed peple   *unlock; ignorant*
Yyve mercy for hire mysdedes, if men it wole aske
Buxomliche and benigneliche, and bidden it of grace.
    '*Archa Dei*, in the Olde Lawe, Levites it kepten;   *The Ark of God*
Hadde nevere lewed man leve to leggen hond on that cheste   *layman*
115 But he were preest or preestes sone, patriark or prophete.   *Unless*
Saul, for he sacrificed, sorwe hym bitidde,   *because; befell (I Sam 13:12)*
And his sones also for that synne mischeved,   *came to grief*
And manye mo other men that were no Levites,   *(II Sam 6: 7)*
That with *archa Dei* yeden, in reverence and in worship,   *went*
120 And leiden hond theron to liften it up – and loren hir lif after.   *lost*
    'Forthi I conseille alle creatures no clergie to dispise,
Ne sette short by hir science, whatso thei don hemselve.   *little store*

107–8 No more can a man equipped only with the knowledge derived from
common experience . . . Arrive at [the truths of] Christianity.
112 In a spirit of humble obedience and good will, and pray for it through the
grace of God.

99   ei3en] βC; si3te α.
102   þe] W&r; hys g.
103   *In* L&r; *l. om* w.
104   lereth] αCK–D; ledeþ β.
107   kynde witt*ed*] βC; k. wedded
      R; lewid F.
111   3yue] βC; & graunteþ F; For R.
112   of] βFC; as R.
114   on . . . cheste] β (þat] þe

gM)RC; þeronne F.
116–25a *In* αCSk; *ll. om* β.
116   he sacrifised] RC; his
      myssacrifyse F.
119   3eden in worchippe] R; wenten
      with worchepeful reuerencis F.
120   hond . . . to] R; on hond & F.
121   to] RC; 3ee F.
122   sette schort] RC; settiþ lyght F.

Take we hir wordes at worth, for hire witnesses be trewe,
And medle we noght muche with hem to meven any wrathe,   *stir up*
125 Lest cheste cha[f]en us to choppe ech man other: *argument; inflame*
Nolite tangere christos meos . . .
'For clergie is kepere under Crist of hevene;
[Com] ther nevere no knyght but clergie hym made.
Ac kynde wit cometh of alle kynnes sightes—   *natural understanding*
Of briddes and of beestes, [of blisse and of sorwe],
130 Of tastes of truthe and of deceites.   *From experiences; deceptions*
'[Olde] lyveris toforn us useden to marke   *Men of old; used to note*
The selkouthes that thei seighen, hir sones for to teche,   *strange sights*
And helden it an heigh science hir wittes to knowe.   *minds, ?meanings*
Ac thorugh hir science soothly was nevere no soule ysaved,
135 Ne broght by hir bokes to blisse ne to joye;
For alle hir kynde knowynges come but of diverse sightes.

'Patriarkes and prophetes repreveden hir science,   *condemned*
And seiden hir wordes ne hir wisdomes was but a folye;   *foolishness*
As to the clergie of Crist, counted it but a trufle: *Compared with; trifle*
Sapiencia huius mundi stulticia est apud Deum.
140 'For the heighe Holy Goost hevene shal tocleve,   *cleave asunder*
And love shal lepe out after into this lowe erthe,

125a Touch ye not my anointed (Ps 104: 15).
139–9a Considered it trivial when compared with Christian learning
[=knowledge of Christ and the Scriptures]: '[For] the wisdom of this world is
foolishness with God' (I Cor 3: 19) (C).

123   we; for] RC; *om* F.
      wytnesses] F?C; *sg* R.
124   medle we] *so* C; ne medle we
      R; medle F(C).
125   cheste . . . vs] *so* CR (chafen]
      CSk; chasen R); Charyte be chased
      owt F (C).
125a   *&c*] R; *om* FC.
126   kepere] β; kynge and k. R; keye
       & k. F.
127   Com] Was *All MSS* (C).
129–30   *As one line All MSS* (C).
129   of³ . . . sorwe] *so* C; *om All
      MSS* (C).
131   Olde] *om All MSS* (C).
      marke] β (*cf.* C); make αCr.

132   þe] L&r (*om* Cr); For WHm.
134   no] wLMR; *om* gFC.
135   broȝt] βC; bouȝte α.
136   knowynges] wLMR; *sg* gFC.
      come] β; cam αB(com)C.
137   repreueden] βC; repreueth αB.
138   ne] L&rC; and W.
      wisdomes] β (counsell Cr)C; *sg* R;
      scyence F.
      was] α (was al F)CrCSk; nas β
      (were not G).
139   As] L&r (& as G)C; And W.
      it] W&rC; *om* g.
140–7a   *In* βC; *ll. om* α.
141   lepe] L&rC; lepen WCr.
      þis] L&rC; his OC²; þe W.

And clennesse shal cacchen it and clerkes shullen it fynde: *purity*
Pastores loquebantur ad invicem.
He speketh there of riche men right noght, ne of right witty,   *clever*
Ne of lordes that were lewed men, but of the hexte lettred oute:

most learned men of all

Ibant magi ab oriente . . .
145 (If any frere were founde there, I yyve thee fyve shillynges!)
Ne in none beggers cote was that barn born,   *cottage; child*
But in a burgeis place, of Bethlem the beste: *burgess's house*
Set non erat locus in diversorio – et pauper non habet
  diversorium.

To pastours and to poetes appeared the aungel,   *shepherds*
And bad hem go to Bethlem Goddes burthe to honoure,
150 And songe a song of solas, *Gloria in excelsis Deo!*   *joy, comfort*
Riche men rutte tho and in hir reste were,   *were snoring (in sleep)*
Tho it shon to shepherdes, a shewer of blisse.   *(i.e. the star); image*
Clerkes knewen it wel and comen with hir presents,
And diden hir homage honurably to hym that was almyghty.
155 'Why I have told thee al this – I took ful good hede
How thow contrariedest clergie with crabbede wordes,

opposed; peevish

How that lewed men lightloker than lettrede were saved,   *more easily*
Than clerkes or kynde witted men, of Cristene peple.
And thow seidest sooth of somme – ac se in what manere.   *about*
160 'Tak two stronge men and in Themese cast hem,   *the Thames*

142*a* . . . the shepherds said to one another . . . (Lk 2: 15).
144*a* . . . there came wise men from the east (Mt 2: 1).
147*a* But there was no room for them [*lit.* him] in the inn (Lk 2: 7); and a
  beggar does not use an inn!
150 Glory to God in the highest! (Lk 2: 14).

143 ri3t¹] W&r; *om* g.
144 hexte] LM; hyeste wg (C).
144*a* &c] L&r; *om* WCrOC²C.
146 beggares] L&r; burgeises W.
147 burgeys] L&rC; Burgeises
  WOM.
147*a* *locus*] L&r (*om* CB); *ei l.* w.
148 þe] ?β (þat LM)C; an α.
151–2 *In* αCSk; *ll. om* β.
151 and] RC; þat F.

152 þo . . . schepherdes] RC; whan
  to sh. a sterre shon F.
153 Clerkes] βC; And clerkes α.
154 *After this a spurious line* g.
155 þee] gRSk; *om* wLMF.
159 se] W&rC; se ytt ?g (ytt] 3it
  OC²CB).
in . . . manere] βC; in whanere R;
  an ensample F.

And bothe naked as a nedle, hir noon sikerer than other;

> *neither of them safer*

That oon hath konnynge and kan swymmen and dyven,

> *One; knows how to*

That oother is lewed of that labour, lerned nevere swymme. *ignorant*
Which trowestow of tho two in Themese is in moost drede—
165 He that nevere ne dyved ne noght kan of swymmyng,
Or the swymmere that is saaf by so hymself like,   *safe if he please*
Ther his felawe flet forth as the flood liketh,   *Whereas;companion;floats*
And is in drede to drenche, that nevere dide swymme?'   *terror of*
'That swymme kan noght,' I seide, 'it semeth to my wittes.'

> *The one who*

170 'Right so,' quod the renk, 'reson it sheweth,   *man; it stands to reason*
That he that knoweth clergie kan sonner arise   *sooner*
Out of synne and be saaf, though he synne ofte,
If hym liketh and lest, than any lewed, leelly. *wants; ignorant man; truly*
For if the clerk be konnynge, he knoweth what is synne,   *instructed*
175 And how contricion withoute confession conforteth the soule,
As thow seest in the Sauter in salmes oon or tweyne,   *psalms; two*
How contricion is comended for it cacheth awey synne: *chases*
Beati quorum remisse sunt iniquitates et quorum tecta sunt peccata.
And this conforteth ech a clerk and kevereth hym fro wanhope,

> *protects; despair*

In which flood the fend fondeth a man hardest; *tempts, puts to the test*
180 Ther the lewed lith stille and loketh after Lente,   *lies; waits for*
And hath no contricion er he come to shrifte – and thanne kan he litel telle,

> *confession*

But as his loresman lereth hym bileveth and troweth,   *teacher; thinks*

177a Blessed are they whose iniquities are forgiven: and whose sins are covered (Ps 31: 1).

161 sikerer] W&r; syker LM (-er² +M) R(C).
162 haþ . . . and²] βRC; can wel swymme & konynge to F.
163 swymme] WLR?C; to s. Hm&r (*om* F).
164 in Themese] L&rC; þat W.
165 ne¹] W&r; *om* HmCrGCotMα.
167 flet] L&r (*l. om* CotF); fleteþ WHmGBm.

169 *In* βC; *l. om* α.
172 be] βFC; he be CrR.
176 As] W&rC; and Hmy; *om* G. þe] W&rC; thy y. Salmes] ?βC; psalme αL.
177a peccata] αHm (*p. &c* Hm)Sk; *&c* β (*om* Y).
178 keuereth] β (couereþ W); kenneth α.
181 þanne] βC; þereof ne F; *om* R.
182 But] WHmFC; And L&r.

And that is after person or parissh preest, and paraventure bothe
   unkonnynge.   *both of them perhaps unskilled*
To lere lewed men, as Luc bereth witnesse:
Dum cecus ducit cecum . . .

185   'Wo was hym marked that wade moot with the lewed!
                                    allotted; must go with
Wel may the barn blesse that hym to book sette,   *the one who*
That lyvynge after lettrure saved hym lif and soule.
                            an educated (way of) life
Dominus pars hereditatis mee is a murye verset
                            heartening little text (C)
That hath take fro Tybourne twenty strong theves,
                        saved from hanging; confirmed
190   Ther lewed theves ben lolled up – loke how thei be saved!
                          Whereas; set swinging
   'The thef that hadde grace of God on Good Fryday as thow speke,
Was for he yald hym creaunt to Crist on the cros, and knewliched
   hym gilty,
And grace asked of God, that [graith is hem evere]   *ready to (grant)*
That buxomliche biddeth it, and ben in wille to amenden hem.
                          humbly pray for; desire

184a . . . if the blind lead the blind, both fall into the pit (Mt 15: 14; cf. Lk 6:
   39).
185 Misery was allotted to the man whose fate it is to be one of the ignorant.
188 The Lord is the portion of my inheritance . . . (Ps 15: 5).
192 *Either* That was because . . . [*anacoluthon*] *or* Was saved [*ellipsis*] because
   he submitted in faith . . . and acknowledged his sin.

183 *So div from* 184 *K–D (after* C);
   before vnkonnynge *All MSS* (C).
   and] L&r(*om* F)C; þe whiche ben
   W.
   bothe] ?α (þey be F)C; *om* ?β (he
   Cr²OC²; he is Cr³).
185 *In* βC; *l. om* α.
186 þat] L&rC; þat man þat W.
   hym . . . sette] βC; hym sette to
   scole ?α (h. s.] *trs*; to] fyrst to F).
187 saued] L&rC; saueþ WCr.
191 speke] L&r; spekest WHm.

192 creaunt] βC; recreant ?α (*om*
   F)M.
   on . . . &] β (þe] *om* OC²); & vpon
   a cros R (?=α); & FC.
   knewliched] W&r; knew g.
   hym²] βF; *om* R.
193 *In* β (*cf.* C); *l. om* α.
   þat . . . euere] *cj* K–D; þat to
   graunten it is redy W; and he is
   euer redy L&r (?=β) (C).
194 *So* β (þat] þam BoCot; To hem
   þat W)R; & buxum was in meende
   his Mercy was to crave F.

195 Ac though that theef hadde hevene, he hadde noon heigh blisse,
                                        exalted (state of) glory
    As Seint Johan and othere seintes that asserved hadde bettre.
                                                        deserved
    Right as som man yeve me mete and sette me amydde the floore:
                                        Just as if; were to give
    I have mete moore than ynough, ac noght so muche worshipe
                                            I (would) have; honour
    As tho that sitten at the syde table or with the sovereynes of the halle,
                                            sit; lords, high ones
200 But sete as a beggere bordlees by myself on the grounde.
                                    would sit; without a table
    So it fareth by that felon that a Good Friday was saved: *with; on*
    He sit neither with Seint Johan, ne Symond ne Jude,
    Ne with maydenes ne with martires ne [mid] confessours ne
        wydewes,   *with*
    But by hymself as a soleyn, and served on the erthe.   *solitary; ground*
205 For he that is ones a thef is everemoore in daunger,
    And as lawe liketh to lyve or to deye:
    De peccato propiciato noli esse sine metu.
    And for to serven a seint and swich a thef togideres—
    It were neither reson ne right to rewarde both yliche.   *equally, alike*
       'And right as Troianus the trewe knyght tilde noght depe in helle
                                                dwelt; (so) deep
210 That Oure Lord ne hadde hym lightly out, so leve I [by] the thef in
        hevene: *easily; concerning*
    For he is in the loweste of hevene, if oure bileve be trewe,   *sc. part*

206a Be not without fear about sin forgiven (Ecclus 5: 5).

195   Ac] W&r (But F)C; and Crg.
196   asserued] LRC; deserued W&r.
197   man] W&rC; men HmgM.
      sette . . . flore] L&r (þe fl.] his hall
      F)C; am. þe floor s. me W.
198   Ich haue] L&rC; And hadde W.
199   sytte] Hm&rC; seten WL.
      syde] W&rC; om gF.
      þe²] W&rC; om Crg.
200   a beggere] W&rC; beggers g.
202   wiþ] W&rC; by gM.
      Seint . . . ne¹] *so* ?C; seint Iohan β

(Io.] Io nether G); Io. ne α.
203   with²] wBLMαC; om ?g.
      ne³] αC; om β.
      mid] with FC; om βR (C).
204   þe] L&rC; om w.
208   rewarde] ?αCK–D; r. hem βF.
209   tilde] L&rC; dwelte w.
210   by þe þef] cj K–D(cf. C); þe þef
      be β (be] om G); þe be R; it be F
      (C).
211   of] WHmL?α (in F)C; om
      CrgM.

And wel losely he lolleth there, by the lawe of Holy Chirche,

loosely, at ease; rests, relaxes

Quia reddit unicuique iuxta opera sua.

'Ac why that oon theef upon the cros creaunt hym yelde   *yielded*
Rather than that oother theef, though thow woldest appose,

question, inquire

215 Alle the clerkes under Crist ne kouthe the skile assoille:

reason; explain

Quare placuit? Quia voluit.   *'Why? Because!'*
And so I seye by thee, that sekest after the whyes,   *'why's', reasons*
And aresonedest Reson, a rebukynge as it were,

argued with; upbraiding

And willest of briddes and of beestes and of hir bredyng knowe,
Why some be alough and some aloft, thi likyng it were;

low down; high up

220 And of the floures in the fryth and of hire faire hewes—
Whereof thei cacche hir colours so clere and so brighte, *From where*
And of the stones and of the sterres – thow studiest, as I leve,
How evere beest outher brid hath so breme wittes . . .   *powerful*
'Clergie ne Kynde Wit ne knew nevere the cause,
225 Ac Kynde knoweth the cause hymself, no creature ellis.
He is the pies patron and putteth it in hir ere   *magpie's; ear*
That there the thorn is thikkest to buylden and brede. *where; build*
And Kynde kenned the pecok to cauken in swich a kynde,

taught; couple; manner

212a For he renders to every man according to his works (Ps 61: 13).
215a Why did it seem good to him? Because he willed it (cf. Ps 134: 6, 113b:
      3, Job 23: 13).

212 lose-] L&rC; losel- wCot;
     lowse- GC.
212a *Quia reddit*] ?β (Q.] *Qui*
     wBM; *omnia* G); And *reddite* ?α
     (And] þere þe byble seyþ F).
     sua] CrOC²CBαCK–D; *sua &c*
     WHmGYLM.
213 Ac] α (But F)CK–D; And β.
     vpon] ?αC; on βF.
     hym ȝelde] R&r (yald W)C; gan
     hym yeld CrF; gylty C.
214 woldest] W&rC (-est] -e gL);
     þynkst me to F.

215 assoille] βC; telle α.
218–21 *So ordered* αK–D; 218 *and*
     219, 220 *and* 221 *trs* β.
218 of²] W&r (+L); om Crg.
221 colours] β; colour α.
222 þe¹] βF; om R.
225 no] L&rK–D; and no Wg.
226 it] W&r; om g.
227 þat þere] L&r (þere] om CB);
     There W.
     to] β; þere to α.
228 kenned] WLMR; kenneþ
     Hm&r.

And Kynde kenned Adam to knowe hise pryvé membres,

sexual organs

230 And taughte hym and Eve to helien hem with leves. *cover themselves*

'Lewed men many tymes maistres thei apposen, *teachers; question*

Whi Adam ne hiled noght first his mouth that eet the appul, *covered*

Rather than his likame alogh? – lewed asken thus clerkes. *body*

Kynde knoweth whi he dide so, ac no clerk ellis!

235 'Ac of briddes and of beestes men by olde tyme

Ensamples token and termes, as telleth thise poetes, *similitudes*

And that the faireste fowel foulest engendreth, *breeds in the ugliest way*

And feblest fowel of flight is that fleeth or swymmeth. *weakest; flies*

And that is the pecok and the pehen – proude riche men thei bitokneth.

symbolize

240 For the pecok and men pursue hym may noght flee heighe: *if*

For the trailynge of his tail overtaken is he soone.

And his flessh is foul flessh, and his feet bothe,

And unlovelich of ledene and looth for to here. *cry; hateful*

'Right so the riche, if he is richesse kepeth

245 And deleth it noght til his deeth day, the taille of alle is sorwe.

end/?tally (C)

Right as the pennes of the pecok peyneth hym in his flighte,

feathers; hamper

So is possession peyne of pens and of nobles *burden, affliction; pence*

To alle hem that it holdeth til hir tail be plukked.

And though the riche repente thanne and birewe the tyme *rue*

250 That evere he gadered so grete and gaf therof so litel,

Though he crye to Crist thanne with kene wille, *ardent desire*

I leve his ledene be in Oure Lordes ere lik a pies. *cry will be; magpie's*

And whan his caroyne shal come in cave to be buryed. *corpse; tomb*

I leve it flawme ful foule the fold al aboute, *will smell; earth*

---

229 Kynde] so K–D; kende α; om β.

231 þei] W&r; om gF.

232 ne] W&r; om HmgF.

234 ac] W&r; & Crg.

236 þis] L&r; þe wOC²F.

239 is] L&r; om w.
    þei] L&r (he F); om WHm.

240 may] β; ne may ?α; he may CrF.

244 kepeth] α; kepe β.

245 taille] LM (-le *erased*)R; tail W&r (taile CrG)(C).
    is] M; om W&r.

246 as] L&r; so as WCot; so C BmBo.

251 *Div from* 252 *after* leue *All MSS* (C).
    wille] L; wil W (C).

252 be] W&r; ys g (om C²).
    pyes] L&r (*l.* †F); pies chiterynge w (C).

255 And alle the othere ther it lith envenymed thorugh his attre.

poisoned; venom

By the po feet is understande, as I have lerned in Avynet,

peacock's; meant; Avianus (C)

Executours — false frendes that fulfille noght his wille

That was writen, and thei witnesse to werche right as it wolde.

(even though); act

Thus the poete preveth that the pecok for his fetheres is reverenced;

260 Right so is the riche by reson of hise goodes.

'The larke, that is a lasse fowel, is moore loveliche of ledene,

smaller; pleasant; voice

And wel awey of wynge swifter than the pecok,

And of flessh by felefold fatter and swetter; *many times; tastier*

To lowe libbynge men the larke is resembled. *likened*

265 Aristotle the grete clerk, swiche tales he telleth;

Thus he likneth in his logik the leeste fowel oute.

compares; smallest; in existence

And wheither he be saaf or noght saaf, the sothe woot no clergie,

saved; no learned men

Ne of Sortes ne of Salamon no scripture kan telle.

Socrates; written authority

Ac God is so good, I hope that siththe he gaf hem wittes

270 To wissen us weyes therwith, that wisshen to be saved, *guide; men*

(And the bettre for hir bokes) to bidden we ben holden

That God for his grace gyve hir soules reste;

For lettred men were lewed yet, ne were loore of hir bokes.'

were it not for

'Alle thise clerkes,' quod I tho, 'that on Crist leven *believe*

275 Seyen in hir sermons that neither Sarsens ne Jewes *pagans*

---

271 We are obliged to pray (for them) because of the benefit to us of the books
they wrote.

255 -imed] CrLR; -ymeþ W&r.
256 haue] W&r; *om* gF.
258 witnesse] β (*om* C)F; *pl* R.
riȝt as] WHmLMR; as gF; al þat
Cr.
it] β; he α.
265 Aristotle] β; For aristotel α.
he] W&r; *om* g.
266 logik] β; glos*ing* α (glose F).
267 saaf²] WHmLMRC; *om* CrgF.

268 of²] W&rC; *om* g.
270 weyes] β (wey C²)RC; wyȝen F
(C).
wisshen] *cj* K–D; wishen vs Cr³;
wissen vs W&r (C).
272 soules] βC; soule α.
273 men²] W&rC; *om* Cr²³g.
hir] β; þe R; *om* F.
274 on] L&rC; in W.
275 neiþer] W&rC; no g.

Ne no creature of Cristes liknesse withouten Cristendom worth
   saved.'   *human being; will be*
  '*Contra!*' quod Ymaginatif thoo, and comsed for to loure,
                                              'Not so!'; frown

And seide, '*Salvabitur vix iustus in die iudicii;*
Ergo – salvabitur!' quod he, and seide no moore Latyn.
280   'Troianus was a trewe knyght and took nevere Cristendom,
                                      Christian baptism

And he is saaf, so seith the book, and his soule in hevene.   *saved*
Ac ther is fullynge of font and fullynge in blood shedyng,   *baptism*
And thorugh fir is fullyng, and that is ferme bileve: *firm (Mt 3: 11)*
Advenit ignis divinus, non comburens set illuminans . . .
  'Ac truthe that trespased nevere ne traversed ayeins his lawe,
285 But lyvede as his lawe taughte and leveth ther be no bettre,   *believes*
  (And if ther were, he wolde amende) and in swich wille deieth—
Ne wolde nevere trewe God but trewe truthe were allowed.
                                          approved

And wher it worth or worth noght, the bileve is gret of truthe,
                                          whether

And an hope hangynge therinne to have a mede for his truthe;

278–9 'The just man shall scarcely be saved' (I Pet 4: 18) on the day of
   judgement; therefore – he *shall* be saved! Cf. XIII 19.
283*a* There came a divine fire, not burning but illuminating (*sc.* at Pentecost,
   Acts 2: 3; from Sarum Breviary, Pentecost Antiphon (Hort)).
284 But a just man who never sinned or acted against his principles . . .
287 Righteous God would never/Would that righteous God should never
   permit such genuine righteousness to go uncommended.
288–9 And whether it will (actually) turn out (so) or not, the faith (found) in a
   just (pagan) is great (*or* great trust can be put in truth) And (there is) a hope
   depending on it (also) that he will have a reward for his righteousness.

277   quod] βFC; quod I R.
   for] W&r; *om* GC.
281   is] W&rC; *om* C²R.
   so] W&r; as *y*F; *om* CrC.
282   Ac] α (But F)CK–D; For β.
283*a* &c] ?βC; *om* OC²Cotα.
284   þat] βC; *om* α.
   trauersed] ?βC; transuersed αCrL.
285   lyued] ?α (beleved F)C; lyueþ β.
   his . . . be] βRC (tau3te] RC; techeþ
   β); was tawht hym for he ne knew
   F.

287   trewe treuthe] ?α (his wil F)
   CK–D; truþe β.
288   wher] HmCr¹LC²C; were Cr²³
   &r (*l. om* Y); wheiþer W.
   worth¹] L&rC; be worþ WHm.
   worth nou3t þe] L&r (w. n.] *trs*
   WF)C; not þe ?g (þe] *om* G).
   is . . . truþe] W&r (of] in F)C; of it
   is gret Cr (C).
289   a] wLα; *om* Crg (*l. om* Cot)M.

290 For *Deus dicitur quasi dans* [*eternam vitam*] *suis, hoc est fidelibus.*
    Et alibi, Si ambulavero in medio umbre mortis . . .
    The glose graunteth upon that vers a greet mede to truthe.   *gloss (C)*
    And wit and wisdom,' quod that wye, 'was som tyme tresor
    To kepe with a commune – no catel was holde bettre—   *rule; wealth*
295 And muche murthe and manhod' – and right myd that he vanysshed.

290–1 For God is spoken of as giving eternal life to his own – that is to the
    faithful (cf. Jn 17: 2); and elsewhere, For though I should walk in the midst
    of the shadow of death [I will fear no evils] (Ps 22: 4); cf. VII 116.
292 *Either* The gloss upon that verse grants *or* The gloss grants, on the
    strength of that verse.
295 And (a source of) much happiness and human value.

290   For] W&r; *Quia* g.   *timebo mala quoniam tu mecum es*
    eternam vitam] *cj* K–D; *trs* All   *domine* F.
    MSS (C).   292 tru þe] βF; trewe R.
291   *&c*] Hm&r; *om* WCrL; *non*   295 myd] ?α; wiþ βF.

Passus XIII

And I awaked therwith, witlees nerhande,   *almost out of my mind*
And as a freke that fey were, forth gan I walke *man; doomed, luckless*
In manere of a mendynaunt many yer after,   *mendicant*
And of this metyng many tymes muche thought I hadde: *dream*
5 First how Fortune me failed at my mooste nede,   *greatest*
And how that Elde manaced me, myghte we evere mete; *threatened*
And how that freres folwede folk that was riche,
And [peple] that was povere at litel pris thei sette,   *value*
And no corps in hir kirkyerd ne in hir kirk was buryed *churchyard*
10 But quik he biquethe hem aught or sholde helpe quyte hir dettes;
                                              Unless (when) alive
And how this coveitise overcom clerkes and preestes;
And how that lewed men ben lad, but Oure Lord hem helpe, *led*
Thorugh unkonnynge curatours to incurable peynes; *parish priests*
And how that Ymaginatif in dremels me tolde   *dream*
15 Of Kynde and of his konnynge, and how curteis he is to bestes,
                                              gracious
And how lovynge he is to bestes on londe and on watre:
Leneth he no lif lasse ne moore;   *He gives no living creature*
The creatures that crepen of Kynde ben engendred; *by; produced*
And sithen how Ymaginatif seid, 'Vix iustus salvabitur,'
20 And whan he hadde seid so, how sodeynliche he passed.

---

10 Unless while still alive he bequeathes something to them or helps pay their
    debts.

Collation WHmCrGYOC²CBLMRF.
RUBRIC *Passus xiij^us &c* W&r
(*xiij^us de visione et vj^us de do weel*
HmB); *duodecimus de v. vt supra*
R; *Incipit Passus Decimus* F; *om* G.
2 fey] ?B (*over erasure* Bm; faynt
Cot)CK–D; fere R; afeerd F; fre ?β.
3 yere] g (*pl* G)MRCK–D; a yer
wLF.
4 tymes] αHmGC; tyme ?β.
6 my3te we euere] W&r; we m.
neuere g.

8 peple] *so* CK–D; folk *All MSS*
(poore f. F) (C).
9 ne] L&r (*om* F); nor WCr.
10 hem] L&r; *om* WG.
11 þis] ?β (that Cr)LMR (þus)C; *om*
gF.
14–20 *In* βC; *ll. om* α.
15 his] wLMC; *om* g.
16 bestes] L&r; briddes W.
19 vix . . . saluabitur] L&r (ius.;
sal.] *trs* HmCr²³OC²); vix sal.
WCr¹.

I lay down longe in this thoght, and at the laste I slepte;
And as Crist wolde ther com Conscience to conforte me that tyme,
And bad me come to his court – with Clergie sholde I dyne.
                                                              manor-house
And for Conscience of Clergie spak, I com wel the rather; *the sooner*
25 And there I seigh a maister – what man he was I nyste— *did not know*
That lowe louted and loveliche to Scripture.   *bowed; graciously*
    Conscience knew hym wel and welcomed hym faire;   *courteously*
Thei wesshen and wipeden and wenten to the dyner.   *washed*
Ac Pacience in the paleis stood in pilgrymes clothes,   *?courtyard*
30 And preyde mete *pur charite* for a povere heremyte.   *for charity*
    Conscience called hym in, and curteisliche seide,
'Welcome, wye, go and wassh; thow shalt sitte soone.'
    This maister was maad sitte as for the mooste worthi, *honoured*
And thanne Clergie and Conscience and Pacience cam after.
35 Pacience and I were put to be mettes,   *dinner-companions*
And seten bi oureselve at a side borde.   *sat; side-table*
    Conscience called after mete, and thanne cam Scripture
And served hem thus soone of sondry metes manye—
Of Austyn, of Ambrose, of alle the foure Evaungelistes:
Edentes et bibentes que apud eos sunt.
40 Ac this maister ne his man no maner flessh eten,
Ac thei eten mete of moore cost, mortrews and potages: *stews; soups*
Of that men myswonne thei made hem wel at ese. *wrongfully obtained*
Ac hir sauce was over sour and unsavourly grounde   *ill-tastingly*
In a morter, *Post mortem*, of many bitter peyne—   *after death*

39a Eating and drinking such things as they have (Lk 10: 7).

22 þat] βF; in þat R.
28 þe] W&rC; *om* gF.
29 Ac] W&r (but GF); And
    WCrC²C.
30 *pur*] BFCK–D; por C²; *par* W?g;
    for Hm&r.
33 as] W&rC; and Hmg.
34 And] W&rC; *om* g.
35 mettes] αK–D; macches β.

36 a] L&r; þe w.
38 hem] W&rC; hym HmBR.
39 of alle] L&r (& of a. G); and of
    w; & with F.
40 ne] L&r; nor W; and Cr.
41 eten mete] β; hadde metes α.
43 ouer] W&rC; euer g.
44 many] L&rC; many a WBM (a
    + M).

45 But if thei synge for tho soules and wepe salte teris:
Vos qui peccata hominum comeditis, nisi pro eis lacrimas et
oraciones effuderitis, ea que in deliciis comeditis, in tormentis
    evometis.
Conscience ful curteisly tho commaunded Scripture
Bifore Pacience breed to brynge and me that was his mette.
He sette a sour loof toforn us and seide, 'Agite penitenciam,'
                                           loaf; 'Do penance' (Mt 3: 2)
And siththe he drough us drynke: 'Dia perseverans—
50 As longe,' quod he, 'as lif and lycame may dure.'   body; last, endure
    'Here is propre service,' quod Pacience, 'ther fareth no prince
    bettre!'   excellent
And he brought us of Beati quorum of Beatus virres makyng,
And thanne he broughte us forth a mees of oother mete, of   dish
    Miserere mei, Deus,
    Et quorum tecta sunt peccata
In a dissh of derne shrifte, Dixi and Confitebor tibi.   secret confession
55 'Bryng Pacience som pitaunce,' pryveliche quod Conscience;
                                                      portion; quietly

---

45a You who feast upon men's sins — unless you pour out tears and prayers for
   them, you will vomit forth in torment what you eat with pleasure (source
   unknown, derived perhaps from Osee 4: 8 (AlfQ)).
49 Long-persevering (cf. Mt 10: 22) (C).
52 Blessed are they whose [iniquities are forgiven: and whose sins are covered];
   Blessed is the man [to whom the Lord hath not imputed sins] (Ps 31: 1–2).
53 Have mercy on me, O God (Ps 50: 1); for 53a, see 52 above.
54 I said: I will confess [against myself my injustice to the Lord] (Ps 31: 5).

45   and wepe] βC; with many R;
     many F.
45a effud-] ?gCK–D; effund-
     wBmBoLM (n erased HmM) α.
46   ful] W&r; om gF.
47   mete] αC; macche wLM; make
     g.
49   drough] L&rC; brouȝte w.
     Dia] W&r?C; diu GOC²BMF (C).
50   quod he; as lif] α (trs F)CK–D;
     quod I as I lyue β (I¹) he OC²).
52, 53   So arr. K–D; trs All MSS
     (C).

he ... us] W&r (vs] om R; l. †F);
om g.
of²] W&r; and of R.
-res] wLM; his CotR; om g.
53   vs] WLMR; anoþer F; om HmCr
     g.
     a ... of] WCrLMR; mees F; om
     Hmg.
     deus] βF; om CrR.
53a Div from 54 after dissh W&r;
     after loo F (dissh] plater a loo &
     F)(C).
54   and] L&r; & WF.

And thanne hadde Pacience a pitaunce, *Pro hac orabit*
Omnis sanctus in tempore oportuno.
And Conscience conforted us, and carped us murye tales:

         entertained; cheerful words

Cor contritum et humiliatum, Deus, non despicies.
    Pacience was proude of that propre service,   *delighted with*
60 And made hym murthe with his mete; ac I mornede evere,

         sulked constantly

For this doctour on the heighe dees drank wyn so faste—

         daïs; continuously

Ve vobis qui potentes estis ad bibendum vinum!—
And eet manye sondry metes, mortrews and puddynges,
Wombe cloutes and wilde brawen and egges [with grece yfryed].

         Tripes; brawn; fat

    Thanne seide I to myself so Pacience it herde,
65 'It is noght foure dayes that this freke, bifore the deen of Poules,

         dean of St Paul's

Preched of penaunces that Paul the Apostle suffrede—
In fame et frigore and flappes of scourges: *blows from*
Ter cesus sum et a Iudeis quinquies quadragenas . . .
Ac o word thei overhuppen at ech a tyme that thei preche *one; skip*
That Poul in his Pistle to al the peple tolde—
70 *Periculum est in falsis fratribus!*'
    (Holi Writ bit men be war – I wol noght write it here   *bids*

56–56a For this [*sc.* forgiveness] shall every one that is holy pray to thee in a
    seasonable time (Ps 31: 6).
58 A contrite and humbled heart, O God, thou wilt not despise (Ps 50: 19).
61a Woe to you that are mighty to drink wine (Is 5: 22).
67–67a, 70 In hunger and thirst . . .; Thrice was I beaten [with rods] . . . Of
    the Jews five times did I receive forty stripes [save one] . . .; [In] peril[s from]
    false brethren (II Cor 11: 27, 25, 24, 26).

56   *As one l. with* 56a wLM; *div*
    before Of g; *before Pro* α.
    hadde] wLMR; come to g (to) þer
    to B); was brouht to F.
    Pro] wLMRC; Ibroughte Of *Pro* g;
    ful soone *Pro* F.
    orabit] αC; *o. ad te* β.
60   mete] βC; mene R; mowht F.
61   þe] βFC; þis HmR.

62   And] ?α (þey F)C; He β.
63   egges . . . yfried] bacoun with e.
    fryed F; egges yfr. with gr. βR(C).
65   of] βF; of seynt R.
67a *&c*] ?β; *om* CrOC²α.
68   a] WLMR; *om* HmCrgF.
70   *So* βC; *Et in periculo falsis
    fratribus* R; *Per. in f. fratribus* was
    neuere ʒit no teeme F.

In Englissh, on aventure it sholde be reherced to ofte

lest perchance; spoken

And greve therwith that goode men ben – ac gramariens shul rede:

scholars

Unusquisque a fratre se custodiat, quia, ut dicitur,
periculum est in falsis fratribus.

Ac I wiste nevere freke that as a frere yede bifore men on Englissh

75 Taken it for hir teme, and telle it withouten glosyng!   *theme*
They prechen that penaunce is profitable to the soule,
And what meschief and maleese Crist for man tholede).   *pain; suffered*
  'Ac this Goddes gloton,' quod I, 'with hise grete chekes,
Hath no pite on us povere; he parfourneth yvele   *acts badly*
80 That he precheth, and preveth noght,' to Pacience I tolde,   *lives out*
And wisshed witterly, with wille ful egre,   *truly; fierce*
That disshes and doublers [this ilke doctour bifore]   *platters*
Were molten leed in his mawe, and Mahoun amyddes!

stomach; the Devil (C)

'I shal jangle to this jurdan with his juste wombe   *jordan; bottle-belly*
85 To [preve] me what penaunce is, of which he preched rather!'

earlier, before

  Pacience parceyved what I thoughte, and [preynte] on me to be stille,

winked at

And seide, 'Thow shalt see thus soone, whan he may na moore,

is capable of (eating)

73–73a And thereby offend those (friars *suggested K–D*) who *are* good men –
    but those who understand Latin are to read (it): 'Let every man guard himself
    from a *brother* [=friar], because, as they say, there is danger in false
    brethren.'
84 I shall argue with this chamber-pot, with his bottle-like belly (*Sk*).

72 In] WCrGBR; On L&r.
73 þat . . . ben] L&r (men] *om* gM);
      goode men w.
      rede] L&r; redde W.
74 Ac] ?β (And CrC²C; For Hm)C;
      om αG.
      freke . . . a] βR (a) *om* R); ȝit F.
75 her] L&r; his WHmGM (*over
      erasure*)FC.
76 They] βC; Ac þei α (Ac) But F).
79 pouere] W&rC; p. men g.

80 and] ?α (þus & F)CK–D; he β
      (C).
      noȝt] βC; yt F; *om* R.
81 witterly] L&rC; ful w. w.
82 this . . . bifore] b. þis ilke d. βR
      (ilke] *om* R); on dees b. þe d. F(C).
83 his] βF; here R.
84 Iuste] β; iuysty α.
85 preve] telle *All MSS* (C).
86 preynte . . . be] *cj K–D after Sk*;
      wynked on me to be β; bad me be
      ?α (bad holde me F) (C).

He shal have a penaunce in his paunche and puffe at ech a worde,

penance/pain; belch

And thanne shullen his guttes gothele, and he shal galpen after;

rumble; yawn

90 For now he hath dronken so depe he wole devyne soone   *expound*

And preven it by hir Pocalips and passion of Seint Avereys

Apocalypse; ?St Greed (C)

That neither bacon ne braun ne blancmanger ne mortrews

chicken stew

Is neither fissh ne flessh but fode for penaunts.

And thanne shal he testifie of a trinite, and take his felawe to witnesse

triad

95 What he fond in a f[or]el after a freres lyvyng;   *box concerning*

And but if the first leef be lesyng, leve me nevere after!   *lies; believe*

And thanne is tyme to take and to appose this doctour

Of Dowel and of Dobet and if Dobest be any penaunce.'

    And I sat stille as Pacience seide, and thus soone this doctour,

100 As rody as a rose rubbede hise chekes,   *red*

Coughed and carped; and Conscience hym herde,   *spoke*

And tolde hym of a trinite, and toward us he loked.

    'What is Dowel, sire doctour?' quod I; 'is Dobest any penaunce?'

    'Dowel?' quod this doctour – and drank after—

105 'Do noon yvel to thyn evencristen – nought by thi power.'

    'By this day, sire doctour,' quod I, 'thanne be ye noght in Dowel!

Today (or an oath)

For ye han harmed us two in that ye eten the puddyng,

Mortrews and oother mete – and we no morsel hadde.

---

88 a²] WOC²LMRC; *om* HmCr?gF.
91 by] βC; in F; *om* R.
92 ne²] αC; *om* β.
93 ne] Cr&rCSk; no L; nor WHm; neþer Bm.
    penauntes] ?α (þe p. R)C); a penaunt β.
94 a] L&rC; þe w (*om* Cr¹)F.
    felawe] wCotLMαC; *pl* g.
95 forel] *so* CK–D; frayel W&r; sell F (C).
    a²] W&rC; *om* g.
96 if] L&r; *om* wCotFC.
    þe] L&rC; he w.

leef] ?g (leyeffe G; lif CBmBo; life Y)C; lyue w; lyne LMα (C).
97 take] W&rC; talke OC²R; aposen F.
98 of²] CrCBLMRC; *om* W&r.
    dobest] L&r?C; dowel W.
100 rubbede] βR; ruddud HmC; gan rodye F (C).
103 dobest] αCK–D; dowel β (it W).
104 dronk after] α (a.] anon þere-F)CK–D; took þe cuppe and dr. β.
105 Do] L&rC; Is do WCr.

And if ye fare so in youre fermerye, ferly me thynketh   *infirmary*
110 But cheeste be ther charite sholde be, and yonge children dorste
    pleyne!   *strife; if*
  I wolde permute my penaunce with youre – for I am in point to
    dowel.'   *exchange; yours; ready*
  Thanne Conscience ful curteisly a contenaunce he made,
                                      gave a look

And preynte upon Pacience to preie me to be stille,
And seide hymself, 'Sire doctour, and it be youre wille,
115 What is Dowel and Dobet? Ye dyvynours knoweth.'   *theologians*
  'Dowel?' quod this doctour; 'do as clerkes techeth;
And Dobet is he that techeth and travailleth to teche othere;
And Dobest doth hymself so as he seith and precheth:
  Qui facit et docuerit magnus vocabitur in regno celorum.'
  'Now thow, Clergie,' quod Conscience, 'carpest what is Dowel?'
                                      will you say

120 'I have sevene sones,' he seide, 'serven in a castel
Ther the lord of lif wonyeth, to leren hym what is Dowel.   *learn*
Til I se tho sevene and myself acorden
I am unhardy,' quod he, 'to any wight to preven it.   *lack confidence*
For oon Piers the Plowman hath impugned us alle,
125 And set alle sciences at a sop save love one;   *morsel; only*
And no text ne taketh to mayntene his cause   *support his position*
But *Dilige Deum* and *Domine quis habitabit* . . .
And seith that Dowel and Dobet arn two infinites,
Whiche infinites with a feith fynden out Dobest,
130 Which shal save mannes soule – thus seith Piers the Plowman.'

118a [But] he that shall do and teach, he shall be called great in the kingdom
    of heaven (Mt 5: 19).
127 [Thou shalt] love [the Lord thy] God . . . (Mt 22: 37); Lord, who shall
    dwell [in thy tabernacle]? (Ps 14: 1) (C).

109   And if] β; And RC; If F.
110   yonge] WHmLMR; *om* CrgF.
112   ful] αC; *om* β.
        he] HmLαC; *om* WCrgF.
113   to²] wLMR; *om* gFC.
116   do] β (is do Cr)C; dos R; ys to
        doon F.
119   *carpest*] W&r (þou c. F);
        carpethe G; carpe vs Cot.

120   seuene] W&r (+L); *om* R.
      in] W&r; at g.
121   hym] LMR; hem Hm&r; *om*
      WCrOC² (C).
123   to²] β; *om* α.
125   sciences] W&r; *sg* OC²R.
127   *&c*] L&r; *om* wBFC.
130   þe] WLMR; *om* HmCrgF.

'I kan noght heron,' quod Conscience, 'ac I knowe wel Piers.

don't know about this

He wol noght ayein Holy Writ speken, I dar wel undertake.
Thanne passe we over til Piers come and preve this in dede.

demonstrate; in action

Pacience hath be in many place, and paraunter knoweth   *perhaps*
135 That no clerk ne kan, as Crist bereth witnesse:
Pacientes vincunt . . .'
      'At your preiere,' quod Pacience tho, '[by] so no man displese hym:
Disce,' quod he, '*doce; dilige inimicos.*
Disce, and Dowel; *doce*, and Dobet;
Dilige, and Dobest – thus taughte me ones
140 A lemman that I lovede – Love was hir name.
"With wordes and with werkes," quod she, "and wil of thyn herte
Thow love leelly thi soule al thi lif tyme.
And so thow lere the to lovye, for the Lordes love of hevene,
Thyn enemy in alle wise eveneforth with thiselve.   *equally*
145 Cast coles on his heed of alle kynde speche; (Prov 25: 22; Rom 12: 20)
Bothe with werkes and with wordes fonde his love to wynne,   *try*
And leye on him thus with love til he laughe on the;   *belabour*
And but he bowe for this betyng, blynd mote he worthe!"   *submit*
      'Ac for to fare thus with thi frend – folie it were;   *behave, act*
150 For he that loveth thee leelly, lite of thyne coveiteth.   *little*
Kynde love coveiteth noght no catel but speche.

135*a* The patient overcome (*Testament of Job* xxvii, 10) (C).
137 Learn, teach, love your enemies (?school maxim; and cf. Lk 6: 27).
151 True affection desires nothing of yours but your conversation.
152 From the power of transitivity (C).

131 wel] wLα; *om* gM.
132 wel] wLMα; *om* g.
134 place] WHmLα (a pl. R); *pl*
     CrgM.
     cnoweth] L&r (he k. F); mouþed w
     (-ed) -eþ M).
135 ne] β; *om* αOC².
136 At] gMαSk; Ac ?w (And Cr)
     CotL.
     by] *om All MSS* (C).
137 doce] WLMRC; *Doce and*
     Cr&r (*D.*] *& d.* HmOC²F).

141 wiþ²] W&r; *om* g.
142 Thow] βF; *om* R.
143 þow . . . þe¹] β; to *l*ere and α
     (and] *om* F).
145 of] wM?α·(þat ys F); and
     Cr²³gL.
146 werkes . . . wordes] wLMα;
     werk & word g.
150 lyte] LR; litel W&r.
     coueiteþ] αC; desireth α.

With half a laumpe lyne in Latyn, *Ex vi transicionis,*

> *inscription (on a) lamp*

I bere therinne aboute faste ybounde Dowel,
In a signe of the Saterday that sette first the kalender,

> *tokening; established*

155 And al the wit of the Wodnesday of the nexte wike after;

> *?meaning; week*

The myddel of the moone is the myght of bothe.   *full; power*
And herwith am I welcome ther I have it with me.
    'Undo it – lat this doctour se if Dowel be therinne;
For, by hym that me made, myghte nevere poverte,
160 Misese ne mischief ne man with his tonge,   *Illness; pain, suffering*
Coold, ne care, ne compaignye of theves,
Ne neither hete, ne hayl, ne noon helle pouke,   *fiend of hell*
Ne neither fuyr, ne flood, ne feere of thyn enemy,   *fire; fear*
Tene thee any tyme, and thow take it with the:
Caritas nichil timet.
165   'And ek, have God my soule! and thow wilt it crave,   *if; demand*
Ther nys neither emperour ne emperesse, erl, kyng ne baroun,
Pope ne patriark, that pure reson ne shal make thee
Maister of alle tho men thorugh myght of this redels—   *power; riddle*
Nought thorugh wicchecraft but thorugh wit; and thow wilt thiselve
170 Do kyng and quene and alle the comune after   *Make*
Yyve thee al that thei may yyve, as thee for best yemere,   *guardian (C)*
And as thow demest wil thei do alle hir dayes after: *judge, pronounce*
Pacientes vincunt.'

164a Fear is not in charity (I Jn 4: 18) (C).
173 It's just the tale of Dido – an old romancer's yarn!

153 -Inne] W&r; in Cr.
    aboute] ?w LMα; aboute Hm (nte
    + *over erasure*)Y; a beaute ?g (C).
156 is] L&r; as w.
    mi3te] L&r; nyght WHmCB.
158 it] β (þis M); it and α.
    se if] se where ?α (wh.] it wh. F);
    deme if β (*alt. from* sen if L) (C).
160 ne²] L&r; ne no W.
163 noither] L&r; *om* W.
164a timet] L&r; t. *&c* WHmGYB.
165–72a In α (*cf.* C)Sk; *ll. om* β.

165 eek; it] R; eek so; lore F.
166 neyther] R; *om* F.
    erl kynge] R; neyþer Erl F.
167 *Div from* 167 *after* make ?α
    (m. þe] R; *trs* F) (C).
168 þo; þis red.] R; *om*; his reede F.
169 wicche-; & . . . þi-]R; no ryche;
    of hem- F.
170 *In* R; *l. om* F.
171 3yue; þe for] R; To 3.; þou F.
172 *In* R; *l. om* F.
172a *vincunt*] FK–D; *v. &c* R.

'It is but a dido,' quod this doctour, 'a disours tale!

old story; minstrel's

Al the wit of this world and wight mennes strengthe *wisdom; energetic*
175 Kan noght [par]formen a pees bitwene the Pope and hise enemys,

establish (C)

Ne bitwene two Cristene kynges kan no wight pees make
Profitable to either peple' – and putte the table fro hym, *(he) pushed*
And took Clergie and Conscience to conseil, as it were,

privately apart

That Pacience tho most passe – 'for pilgrymes konne wel lye.'

(Saying) that; should go away

180   Ac Conscience carped loude and curteisliche seide,   *spoke up*
'Frendes, fareth wel,' and faire spak to Clergie,   *fare well; pleasantly*
'For I wol go with this gome, if God wol gyve me grace,
And be pilgrym with Pacience til I have preved moore.' *experienced*
   'What!' quod Clergie to Conscience, 'are ye coveitous nouthe
185 After yeresyeves or yiftes, or yernen to rede redels?

presents; long; interpret

I shal brynge yow a Bible, a book of the olde lawe,
And lere yow, if yow like, the leeste point to knowe, *teach; minutest*
That Pacience the pilgrym parfitly knew nevere.'   *thoroughly*
   'Nay, by Crist!' quod Conscience to Clergie, 'God thee foryelde.

repay

190 For al that Pacience me profreth, proud am I litel;
Ac the wil of the wye and the wil of folk here   *will, attitude*
Hath meved my mood to moorne for my synnes.   *stirred my heart*
The goode wil of a wight was nevere bought to the fulle:

'is beyond price'

For ther nys no tresour therto to a trewe wille.   *(compared) to*
195   'Hadde noght Marie Maudeleyne moore for a box of salve

ointment

---

174 and] β?C; ne α.
175 par-] *so* CK–D; con- *All MSS*
   (C).
   þe pope] L&rC; *om* W.
179 þo] L&r (*om* F); þow WCr¹M
   (*over erasure*).
182 gyue] Hm&r; yeue WYBL.
185 or¹] wYLMR; and ?gF.
187 yow like] β; ȝe liken α.

leeste] wYLα; best ?g.
188 That] βF; *om* R.
   neuere] βF; euere RHm.
191 þe³] W&r (*om* F); ye y.
   of²] W&r (+M); *om* CBLR.
193 a] β; vch a ?α (euery F).
194 nys] WLR; is HmCrgMF.
   þerto] L&r; forsoþe W.
195 marie] αGK–D; *om* β.

Than Zacheus for he seide, "*Dimidium bonorum meorum do
    pauperibus*,"
And the poore widewe for a peire of mytes   *couple of farthings*
Than alle tho that offrede into *gazophilacium*?'

the treasury (Lk 21: 1–4)

    Thus curteisliche Conscience congeyed first the frere, *took leave of*
200 And sithen softeliche he seide in Clergies ere,
'Me were levere, by Oure Lord, and I lyve sholde,   *I'd prefer; if*
Have pacience parfitliche than half thi pak of bokes!'
    Clergie to Conscience no congie wolde take,   *farewell; give*
But seide ful sobreliche, 'Thow shalt se the tyme   *gravely*
205 Whan thow art wery forwalked, wilne me to counseille.'

tired with walking (and) want

    'That is sooth,' seide Conscience, 'so me God helpe!
If Pacience be oure partyng felawe and pryvé with us bothe,

partner, sharer; intimate

Ther nys wo in this world that we ne sholde amende,
And conformen kynges to pees, and alle kynnes londes— *dispose*
210 Sarsens and Surre, and so forth alle the Jewes— *Moslems; ?pagans* (C)
Turne into the trewe feith and intil oon bileve.' *convert; one religion*
    'That is sooth,' quod Clergie, 'I se what thow menest.
I shal dwelle as I do, my devoir to shewe,   *duty*
And confermen fauntekyns and oother folk ylered

children; instructed

215 Til Pacience have preved thee and parfit thee maked.' *tried, tested*
    Conscience tho with Pacience passed, pilgrymes as it were.
Thanne hadde Pacience, as pilgrymes han, in his poke vitailles: *bag*
Sobretee and symple speche and soothfast bileve,   *humble; genuine*
To conforte hym and Conscience if thei come in place

strengthen; came

220 There unkyndenesse and coveitise is, hungry contrees bothe.

---

196 The half of my goods I give to the poor (Lk 19: 8).

203 to] HmyL; of WCrGM (*over
    erasure*); and R; ne F (C).
205 for-] L&r; of- W.
    wilne] L&r; wille w.
206 seide] HmCrLMR; quod WgF.

208 nys] WCrLMR (ne is R); is no
    HmgF.
209 and²] β; of α.
210 Sarsens] β; And s. α.
214 confermen] β; confourmen α
    (con-] en- F)G.

And as thei wente by the weye, and of Dowel carped,   *talked*
Thei mette with a mynstral, as me tho thoughte.
Pacience apposed hym first and preyde hym he sholde telle *questioned*
To Conscience what craft he kouthe, and to what contree he wolde.

trade; was going

225 'I am a mynstrall,' quod that man, 'my name is *Activa Vita*.

Active Life

Al ydel ich hatie, for of Actif is my name,   *idle people; hate; from A.*
A wafrer, wol ye wite, and serve manye lordes—   *wafer-seller*
And fewe robes I fonge or furrede gownes.   *obtain; furred*
Couthe I lye and do men laughe, thanne lacchen I sholde *make; get*
230 Outher mantel or moneie amonges lordes mynstrals.   *Either*
Ac for I kan neither taboure ne trompe ne telle no gestes, *stories*
Farten ne fithelen at festes, ne harpen,   *fiddle; play the harp*
Jape ne jogele ne gentilliche pipe,   *Jest; juggle; expertly*
Ne neither saille ne saute ne synge with the gyterne,

dance; tumble; gittern

235 I have no goode giftes of thise grete lordes   *from*
For no breed that I brynge forth – save a benyson on the Sonday,

except; blessing

Whan the preest preieth the peple hir *Paternoster* to bidde *asks; say*
For Piers the Plowman and that hym profit waiten—

those (who); look to (his)

And that am I, Actif, that ydelnesse hatie;
240 For alle trewe travaillours and tiliers of the erthe,   *labourers; tillers*
From Mighelmesse to Mighelmesse I fynde hem with wafres.

Michaelmas (29 Sept); provide

Beggeris and bidderis of my breed craven,   *desire*
Faitours and freres and folk with brode crounes.   *i.e. tonsured clerics*
'I fynde payn for the Pope and provendre for his palfrey, *fodder*
245 And I hadde nevere of hym, have God my trouthe,

---

221   and of dowel] α; of d. þei β.
223   first] W&r; þoo OC²; *om* FC.
      hym²] LMα; *om* wgC.
      tel] CrFCK–D; *h*em telle W&r
      (hem) hym HmC²CotM(*erased*).
226   ydel] L&r; ydelnesse WHmF.
228   And] W&rC; A B; But F; I C.
229   and] αCK–D; to β.

230   lordes] L&r (*om* Y); l. or
      WCr¹; oþere F.
233   logele] β?C; iangele α.
234   saille] W&rC; sawtrye F.
      saute] W&r; sautre CC; saylen F.
236   brynge] β (*cf.* C); brouȝt α.
239   þat am I] wLM; þ. I am gR; for
      me F.
240   For] β; & for F; Of R.
241   with] L&r; wiþ my WCr+M.

Neither provendre ne personage yet of the Popes yifte,
Save a pardon with a peis of leed and two polles amyddes!

Only; lump; heads (C)

Hadde Ich a clerc that couthe write I wolde caste hym a bille

draw up; note

That he sente me under his seel a salve for the pestilence,
250 And that his blessynge and hise bulles bocches myghte destruye:

plague-sores (C)

*In nomine meo demonia eicient et super egros manus imponent et
bene habebunt.*

And thanne wolde I be prest to the peple, paast for to make, *pastry*
And buxom and busy aboute breed and drynke *willing*
For hym and for alle hise, founde I that his pardoun *if I were to find*
Mighte lechen a man – as I bileve it sholde. *heal*
255 For sith he hath the power that Peter hymself hadde, he hath the pot
with the salve:

*Argentum et aurum non est michi: quod autem habeo, hoc
tibi do: In nomine Domini surge et ambula.*

'Ac if myght of myracle hym faille, it is for men ben noght worthi
To have the grace of God, and no gilt of the Pope. *fault*
For may no blessynge doon us boote but if we wile amende,
Ne mannes masse make pees among Cristene peple,
260 Til pride be pureliche fordo, and that thorugh payn defaute.

destroyed; lack of bread

For er I have breed of mele, ofte moot I swete, *from grain; sweat*
And er the commune have corn ynough many a cold morwenyng;
So, er my wafres be ywroght, muche wo I tholye. *hardship; endure*

---

246 Neither a clerical living nor a parsonage that lies in the Pope's gift.
250a In my name they shall cast out devils; . . . they shall lay their hands upon
the sick; and they shall recover (Mk 16: 17, 18).
255a 'Silver and gold I have none; but what I have, I give thee. In the name of
the Lord, arise and walk' (Acts 3: 6).

246 þe] L&r; *om* WG.
  ȝifte] W&r; *pl* RY.
250 And¹] β; *om* α.
255 *So* CK–D; *as* 2 *ll. div after*
  hadde W&r; *after* selfe Cr²³;
  hymself hadde] *trs* Cr²³; hadde FC.
  salue] *so* CK–D; s. sooþly as me
  þynkeþ W&r (so.] truly Cr²³) (C).

255a hoc] αOC²Cot?C; *om* ?β.
257 þe¹] β (*om* Cr)C; no α.
258 For] βC; þere F; *om* R.
260 pureliche] βC; priueliche α.
  þat] L&rC; *om* WCrMF; alle R.
261 ofte] W&r (*l. om* B); erst g.
262 a] ?wLMα; *om* Crg.

'Al Londoun, I leve, liketh wel my wafres,
265 And louren whan thei lakken hem; it is noght longe ypassed

> scowl; lack

There was a careful commune whan no cart com to towne *distressed*
With bake breed fro Stratford; tho gonnen beggeris wepe,
And werkmen were agast a lite – this wole be thought longe;

> afraid; remembered

In the date of Oure Drighte, in a drye Aprill,   *year; Lord*
270 ·A thousand and thre hundred, twies thritty and tene,   *i.e. 1370*
My wafres there were gesene, whan Chichestre was maire.'

> scarce; mayor

I took greet kepe, by Crist, and Conscience bothe,   *careful note*
Of Haukyn the Actif Man, and how he was yclothed.
He hadde a cote of Cristendom as Holy Kirke bileveth;
275 Ac it was moled in many places with manye sondry plottes—

> stained; patches

Of pride here a plot, and there a plot of unbuxom speche, *rebellious*
Of scornyng and of scoffyng and of unskilful berynge;

> unreasonable conduct

As in apparaill and in porte proud amonges the peple;   *demeanour*
Ootherwise than he hath with herte or sighte shewynge;
280 Hym wilnyng that alle men wende he were that he is noght,
Forwhy he bosteth and braggeth with manye bolde othes;

> For which reason

And inobedient to ben undernome of any lif lyvynge;   *criticized by*
And so singuler by hymself as to sighte of the peple

---

279 Pretending to be, inwardly and outwardly, something that he isn't.

265 hem] W&r (*om* OC²); it Hm
GYLM.
267 bake] αSk; *om* β.
268 wole] β; wel R; *om* F.
270 twies . . . ten] W&r (tw.] thries
(*over erasure*) M; ʒeer & two & F;
thr.] LR; twenty W&r); syxty and
nyne Hm (Cw).
271 þere w.] W&r (*trs* HmF); were
g.
272 grete] αK–D; good β.
274 kirke] WCrLMR; cherche
HmgF.

275 places] βF; place R.
276 here] βR (he R); was þere F.
279 or] β (*cf.* C); and R; *om* F.
siʒte] W&r; eyghe g.
280 wilnynge] ?α (wil-] wen- F)C;
Willyng β.
283 *So* LαC; *run together with* 284
wgM.
so] L&r; goo F; noon so WCr.
as . . . poeple] Lα (as to] *in* F)C; *om*
wgM.

Was noon swich as hymself, ne noon so pope holy;
285 Yhabited as an heremyte, an ordre by hymselve—   *Dressed*
Religion saunz rule and resonable obedience;   *without*
Lakkynge lettrede men and lewed men bothe; *Reproaching, criticizing*
In likynge of lele lif and a liere in soule;
With inwit and with outwit ymagynen and studie
290 As best for his body be to have a bold name;
And entremetten hym over al ther he hath noght to doone;
                                    interfere; has no business
Wilnynge that men wende his wit were the beste,   *thought*
Or for his crafty konnynge or of clerkes the wisest,
Or strengest on stede, or styvest under girdel, *horse; most potent, virile*
295 And lovelokest to loken on and lelest of werkes,   *handsomest*
And noon so holy as he ne of lif clennere,   *more chaste*
Or feirest of feitures, of forme and of shafte,   *features; figure*
And most sotil of song other sleyest of hondes,   *skilled in; most deft*
And large to lene lo[o]s therby to cacche;   *praise; obtain*
300 And if he gyveth ought to povere gomes, [go] telle what he deleth;
Povere of possession in purs and in cofre,   *coffer, chest*
And as a lyoun on to loke and lordlich of speche;   *lion; haughty*
Boldest of beggeris, a bostere that noght hath,
In towne and in tavernes tales to telle

285–6 . . . a religious order composed of only one member, Without any rule
or rationally ordained obedience to superiors.
288 [Giving the impression] of desiring to live honestly . . .
289–90 With his faculties of intelligence and sense given over to imagining and
brooding over How best to acquire a reputation for sexual prowess.
299 Generous in giving, as a means of winning praise.

284 Was . . . hymself] Lα (Was) þat
þere is F)C; *om* wgM.
none²] L&r; *om* WCr.
pope] Cr&rCSk; pomp WHmL
(C).
286 and] L&r; or W.
289 wiþ²] β; *om* αCr.
290 bolde] αK–D; badde β.
292 -nyng] L&rC; -ynge WYBF.
293–9 *In* α (*cf.* C)Sk; *ll. om* β.
293 or of clerkes] R; of cl. he were
F.
294 vnder] RC; gyrt with F.
295 louelokest] RC; lowlyest F.

296 ne] R; ne non F.
297 fourme . . . shafte] R; face ne of
forme F.
298 And] R; Or F.
299 *So* R (loos] *cj* K–D; losse R);
Or looþ for to leene & large for to
cacche F(C).
300 ouȝte] LR; o. the CB; o. to
W&r (to] to þe G); *om* F.
go] *om All MSS* (C).
301 coffre] Lʔα(*l. om* F); cofre
bothe wg (c.] *pl* g).
302 on] β; *om* α.

305 And segge thyng that he nevere seigh and for sooth sweren it,   *saw*
    Of dedes that he nevere dide demen and bosten,

About; pronounce; boast

    And of werkes that he wel dide witnesse and siggen,   *testify; declare*
    'Lo! if ye leve me noght, or that I lye wenen,   *believe; suppose*
    Asketh at hym or at hym, and he yow kan telle
310 What I suffrede and seigh and somtymes hadde,
    And what I kouthe and knew, and what kyn I com of.'
    Al he wolde that men wiste of werkes and of wordes
    Which myghte plese the peple and preisen hymselve:

redound to his credit

    Si hominibus placerem, Christi servus non essem. Et alibi:
    Nemo potest duobus dominis servire.

    'By Crist!' quod Conscience tho, 'thi beste cote, Haukyn,
315 Hath manye moles and spottes – it moste ben ywasshe!'   *stains*
    'Ye, whoso toke hede,' quod Haukyn, 'bihynde and bifore,

observed; in front

    What on bak and what on body half and by the two sides—   *front*
    Men sholde fynde manye frounces and manye foule plottes.'

creases; patches

    And he torned hym as tyd, and thanne took I hede;   *quickly*
320 It was fouler bi fele fold than it first semed.   *many times*
    It was bidropped with wrathe and wikkede wille,   *spattered; evil intent*
    With envye and yvel speche entisynge to fighte,   *hostility; provoking*
    Lying and lakkynge and leve tonge to chide;   *tongue willing to quarrel*
    Al that he wiste wikked by any wight, tellen it,   *bad about*
325 And blame men bihynde hir bak and bidden hem meschaunce;

pray for; bad luck

    And that he wiste by Wille, [to Watte tellen it],
    And that Watte wiste, Wille wiste it after,
    And made of frendes foes thorugh a fals tonge:

313a If I yet pleased men, I should not be the servant of Christ (Gal 1: 10);
    And in another place: No man can serve two masters (Mt 6: 24).

308   ye] W&rC; þou g.
312   of²] β; *om* α.
313   hym-] W&r; hem- OC²CR.
317   what²] ?β; om GOC²α.
     half] W&r.
323   lakkynge] αK–D; laughynge β.

and¹] βF; or R.
and²] β; a R; & with a F.
326   to . . . it] *cj* K–D (*cf.* C); tellen
it watte *All MSS* (it] it to HmCrOC²
    BR) (C).
327   watte] βR; he of walter F.

'Or with myght of mouth or thorugh mannes strengthe
Either; slander; violence

330 Avenged me fele tymes, other frete myselve withinne   *gnawed, fretted*
As a shepsteres shere, ysherewed men and cursed hem.'
tailor's scissors

Cuius malediccione os plenum est et amaritudine; sub lingua
eius labor et dolor. Et alibi: Filii hominum dentes eorum
arma et sagitte et lingua eorum gladius acutus.

  'Ther is no lif that I lovye lastynge any while;
person; for any length of time

For tales that I telle no man trusteth to me.
And whan I may noght have the maistrie, swich malencolie I take
come out on top

335 That I cacche the crampe, the cardiacle som tyme,   *heart-pains*
Or an ague in swich an angre, and som tyme a fevere   *violent access*
That taketh me al a twelvemonthe, til that I despise   *afflicts*
Lechecraft of Oure Lord and leve on a wicche,   *Medicine; believe in*
And seye that no clerc ne kan – ne Crist, as I leve—   *has knowledge*

340 To the Soutere of Southwerk, or of Shordych Dame Emme,
(Compared) to; Cobbler (C)

And seye that [God ne] Goddes word gaf me nevere boote,
But thorugh a charme hadde I chaunce and my chief heele.'
luck; recovery

  I waitede wisloker, and thanne was it soilled   *looked more carefully*

---

331 As with [*lit*. like] a tailor's scissors, and damned men and cursed them.
331*a* His mouth is full of cursing, and of bitterness: under his tongue are
  labour and sorrow (Ps 9B(10): 7). And in another place: The sons of men,
  whose teeth are weapons and arrows: and their tongue a sharp sword (Ps 56:
  5).

329 of] L&rC; or G; or with W.
330 *So div from* 331 CK–D; *after*
  selue *All MSS* (C).
  Auenged] ?αC; Auenge βF (& but y
  avenge F).
331 ysherewed . . . cursed] W&r
  (men] man W; cursed] W&r; c.
  hem Hm); so shrewidly y grynte F.
331*a labor et dolor*] W&r; *&c* g.
  Et alibi . . . acutus] βC; *om* α.

332 I lo*uye*] L&r (l.] leve F); me
  loueþ WCr.
334 swich] wM(*over erasure*
  HmM)?α(which R)C; with gL.
335 þe²] L&r; and þe WBF.
338 of] W&rC; or LR; be F.
341 God ne] *so* C; no W&r; none
  of B (C).
343 wisloker] W&r; bisiloker g
  (more busyly G).
  it] β; I R; he F.

With likynge of lecherie as by lokynge of his eighe.
345 For ech a maide that he mette, he made hire a signe
Semynge to synneward, and somtyme he gan taste *suggesting s.; touch*
Aboute the mouth or bynethe bigynneth to grope,
Til eitheres wille wexeth kene, and to the werke yeden, *act; they went*
As wel fastyng dayes and Fridaies and forboden nyghtes,

forbidden (C)

350 And as lef in Lente as out of Lente, alle tymes yliche— *willingly; alike*
Swiche werkes with hem were nevere out of seson—   *season*
Til thei myghte na moore, and thanne hadde murye tales, *sexy talk*
And how that lecchours lovye laughen and japen,   *jest*
And of hir harlotrye and horedom in hir elde tellen.   *old age*

355   Thanne Pacience parceyved, of pointes his cote   *with specks*
Was colomy thorugh coveitise and unkynde desiryng.   *grimy*
Moore to good than to God the gome his love caste,

possessions; directed

And ymagynede how he it myghte have
With false mesures and met, and with fals witnesse   *measure*
360 Lened for love of the wed and looth to do truthe,   *pledge*
And awaited thorugh wittes wyes to bigile, ·
And menged his marchaundise and made a good moustre:

adulterated; show

'The worste withinne was – a greet wit I let it! *splendid device; thought*
And if my neghebore hadde an hyne, or any beest ellis,   *servant*
365 Moore profitable than myn, manye sleightes I made   *tricks*
How I myghte have it – al my wit I caste;   *exercised*

355–6 . . . that his coat was grimy with specks (of sin) . . .
360–1 Lent (money simply out of) desire (to gain) the security (deposited by
    the borrower), and through no love of honest dealing (for its own sake), And
    sought with cunning ingenuity opportunities for cheating people.

344   likynge . . . as] W&r (as] and   354   And of; in] βF; Or; and in R.
    HmgR); lykyngery3e F.   hir[1]] β; om α.
345   he[1,2]] βR; y FC.   355   his] LRK–D; off hys gM
346   -tyme] βR; om FC.   (of+)F; of þis w.
349   wel] αCK–D; wel in β.   356   Was] L&r; were (*over erasure*)
    and[1]] W&rC; as g.   M; That were W.
    and[2]] L&r; as W.   361   whitus weys] ?α (his wit fele
350   lef] αCK–D; wel β.   wy3es F)K–D; which wey β.
352   had] L&r; helde it F; om w.   364   if] wBLMα; om ?g.
353   lecchours] wOBoLMα;   an] αCK–D; any β.
    lecherous ?gF (l. men F).

And but I it hadde by oother wey, at the laste I stale it,   *stole*
Or pryveliche his purs shook, unpikede hise lokes;   *picked; locks*
Or by nyghte or by daye, aboute was Ich evere   *Either*
370 Thorugh gile to gaderen the good that Ich have.   *amass; wealth*
  'If I yede to the plowgh, I pynched so narwe   *encroached*
That a foot lond or a forow fecchen I wolde   *foot of land; furrow*
Of my nexte neghebore, nymen of his erthe;   *From; take*
And if I rope, overreche, or yaf hem reed that ropen
                                                              reaped; advised those
375 To seise to me with hir sikel that I ne sew nevere.   *appropriate; sowed*
  'And whoso borwed of me aboughte the tyme   *had to pay for*
With presentes pryvely, or paide som certeyn—   *secretly; definite sum*
So wolde he or noght wolde he, wynnen I wolde;   *make a profit*
And bothe to kith and to kyn unkynde of that Ich hadde.
380 'And whoso cheped my chaffare, chiden I wolde   *bought my wares*
But he profrede to paie a peny or tweyne
Moore than it was worth, and yet wolde I swere   *further still*
That it coste me muche moore — swoor manye othes.
  'In haly daies at holy chirche, whan Ich herde masse   *holy days*
385 Hadde I nevere wille, woot God, witterly to biseche   *truly*
Mercy for my mysdedes, that I ne moornede moore   *lamented*
For losse of good, leve me, than for likames giltes;   *sins of my body*

371–5 If I went ploughing, I encroached so closely that I would obtain for
  myself a foot or a furrow's width of land (from my neighbour's adjacent
  strip) and take from him his (very) earth; and if I was reaping, I would reach
  across (to my neighbour's corn) or give instructions to the reapers to
  appropriate to me with their sickles corn I had never sown.

367 but] βFC; but if RCr.
  it hadde] WLM; *trs* HmY; hadde
  Cr?gR; gete yt F.
368 vn.] L&r; and vn. W; or y vn.
  F.
373 *So* βC; *run together with* 374
  α.
  nymen ... erþe] β (n.] and n. W)C;
  om α.
374 And ... ouerreche] β (rope]
  LM C; repe w?g)C; *om* α.
  ropen] W&r; repen CrYBoCotα.
375 To] WHmLαC; And CrgMF.
  hir] W&r; my g.

ne] W&rC; *om* CrGOC²BF.
376 borwed] WCrM?α; borweþ
  Hmg L; borwe F.
378 walde ... he²] L&r (w. he¹] *trs*
  W; he²] *om* WR); w. he or he nolde
  g (he n.] *trs* Cot)F (w. he] *trs* F).
381 to] W&r; me to Hmg.
383 me] β; *om* α.
  swore] L&r; y sw. HmF; sw. I M;
  & sw. OC²B; and so swoor W.
384 In] L&rC; On W.
  at] W&rC; yn GOC²F; and YCB.
385 I] W&rC; *om* LR.
387 fore²] ?αCK–D; for my βF.

As, if I hadde dedly synne doon, I dredde noght that so soore
As whan I lened and leved it lost or longe er it were paied.   *lent*
390 So if I kidde any kyndenesse myn evencristen to helpe,   *showed*
Upon a cruwel coveitise my conscience gan hange.

'And if I sente over see my servaunts to Brugges,   *Bruges (C)*
Or into Prucelond my prentis my profit to waiten,   *Prussia; see to*
To marchaunden with moneie and maken here eschaunges,

do business; monetary exchanges

395 Mighte nevere me conforte in the mene tyme   *meanwhile*
Neither masse ne matynes, ne none maner sightes;   *no kind of*
Ne nevere penaunce parfournede ne *Paternoster* seide   *performed*
That my mynde ne was moore in my good in a doute   *in (my) anxiety*
Than in the grace of God and hise grete helpes.'
Ubi thesaurus tuus, ibi et cor tuum.

400   Yet that glotoun with grete othes his garnement hadde soiled

Further; garment

And foule beflobered it, as with fals speche,   *foully muddied*
As, there no nede ne was, Goddes name an idel—   *in vain*
Swoor therby swithe ofte and al biswatte his cote;   *covered with sweat*
And moore mete eet and dronk than kynde myghte defie—   *digest*
405 'And kaughte siknesse somtyme for my surfetes ofte;   *over-indulgence*
And thanne I dradde to deye in dedlich synne'—   *dreaded; mortal*
That into wanhope he w[orth] and wende nought to be saved,

despair; fell; thought

---

391 'Inwardly I clung to pitiless greed' (C).
399a [For], where thy treasure is, there is thy heart also (Mt 6: 21).

388 dredde] WL (dred L)MαC;
  drede HmCrg.
391 my conscience] αK–D; myn
  herte β (C).
394 wiþ] βR; my F.
  here] ?α (om F)BmBoC; hire ?β
  (her HmCrOC²L); þer G.
395 tyme] L&rC; while w.
398 in¹] ?αC; on βF.
399a Vbi] βFC; Vbi est RCot.
400–9 In αSk; ll. om β.
400 þat glotoun] glotoun R; þat
  goome F.
  gar-] FSk; gra- R.
  hadde] R; was F.

401 as] R; al F.
402 As; ne; godes . . . Idel] R; &;
  om; nempnede god ydellyche F.
403 Swore] R; & swoor F.
  and . . . cote] R; abowte þe ale
  cuppe F.
404 And; mete] R; & ofte; om F.
405 for my] R; þoruh F.
  surfetys] FSk; forfetes R.
406 And þanne] R; þat for dowhte
  F.
407 þat; he] R; &; y F.
  worthe] cj Sk; wrathe R; wente F
  (C).
  and; nauȝt] R; y; neuere F.

The whiche is sleuthe, so slow that may no sleightes helpe it,

sluggish; devices

Ne no mercy amenden the man that so deieth.   *i.e. in despair*

410   Ac whiche ben the braunches that bryngen a man to sleuthe?

Is whan a man moorneth noght for hise mysdedes, ne maketh no
sorwe,   *(It) is when*

Ac penaunce that the preest enjoyneth parfourneth yvele, *does badly*

Dooth non almesdede, dred hym of no synne, *has no fear for his sin*

Lyveth ayein the bileve and no lawe holdeth.   *faith; keeps*

415   Ech day is halyday with hym or an heigh ferye,   *festival*

And if he aught wol here, it is an harlotes tonge.   *ribald jester's*

Whan men carpen of Crist, or of clennesse of soule,   *speak*

He wexeth wroth and wol noght here but wordes of murthe.   *angry*

Penaunce and povere men and the passion of seintes—

420   He hateth to here therof and alle that it telleth.

Thise ben the braunches, beth war! that bryngen a man to wanhope.

    Ye lordes and ladies and legates of Holy Chirche

That fedeth fool-sages, flatereris and lieris, *maintain licensed jesters (C)*

And han likynge to lithen hem [in hope] to do yow laughe—

listen to; make

Ve vobis qui ridetis—

425   And yyveth hem mete and mede, and povere men refuse,   *rewards*

In youre deeth deyinge, I drede me soore

Lest tho thre maner men to muche sorwe yow brynge: *kinds of*

Consencientes et agentes pari pena punientur.

424*a* Woe to you that [now] laugh; [for you shall mourn and weep] (Lk 6: 25).

427*a* Those who consent [*sc.* to evil] and those who do [it] will be punished
with the same penalty (*maxim of canon law*; see AlfQ p. 86).

408 is . . . it] R; slewþe is so sl. þere
    m. no sleyghte it helpe F.
409 amenden; so deyeth] R; am. it;
    d. þereInne F.
410 Ac] ?αCK–D; *om* β (þe Hm)F.
411 Is . . . man] OC²B (a) *om*
    B)CSk; hys woman GYCLR; He
    þat wM; þat F (C).
412 Ac] L?g (but G); And wC²CM
    (nd *over erasure*, þe +M)R; Ne F.
413 almesdede] L&r (*pl* CrM)C;
    almesse W.
415 is] wLα; is an ?GM; or eche
    BC.

417 of²] wLMRC; *om* gF.
    soule] L&rC; soules WCr.
419 and¹] L&rC; of WF.
422 chirche] βFC; *pl* R.
423 fole] ?αC; fooles βF.
424 in hope] *so* CK–D; *om All MSS*
    (C).
    you] GRCK–D; yow to W&r.
424*a* ridetis] αCr¹C; r. *&c* β.
426 me] ?α (*om* F)CK–D; me ful β.
427 þo þre] wBLMRC; þe thre ?g;
    swiche F.
    yow] βFC; *om* R.
427*a* -entur] βC; -endi sunt α.

Patriarkes and prophetes, and prechours of Goddes wordes,
Saven thorugh hir sermon mannes soule fro helle; *speech, preaching*
430 Right so flatereris and fools arn the fendes disciples   *devil's*
To entice men thorugh hir tales to synne and harlotrie.   *obscenity*
Ac clerkes, that knowen Holy Writ, sholde kenne lordes   *teach*
What David seith of swiche men, as the Sauter telleth:
Non habitabit in medio domus mee qui facit superbiam; qui loquitur
    iniqua . . .
Sholde noon harlot have audience in halle ne in chambre
435 Ther wise men were – witnesseth Goddes wordes—   *take to witness*
Ne no mysproud man amonges lordes ben allowed.

                                                        arrogant; approved

Clerkes and knyghtes welcometh kynges minstrales,
And for love of hir lord litheth hem at festes;   *listen to*
Muche moore, me thynketh, riche men sholde
440 Have beggeres bifore hem, the whiche ben Goddes minstrales,
As he seith hymself – Seynt Johan bereth witnesse:
Qui vos spernit me spernit.
Forthi I rede yow riche [th]at reveles whan ye maketh,   *give feasts*
For to solace youre soules, swiche minstrales to have—
The povere for a fool sage sittynge at th[i] table,   *in place of, as*
445 And a lered man to lere thee what Oure Lord suffred   *teach*
For to save thi soule fram Sathan thyn enemy,
And fithele thee, withoute flaterynge, of Good Friday the storye,

                                                                perform

---

433*a* He that worketh pride shall not dwell in the midst of my house: he that
    speaketh unjust things [did not prosper before my eyes] (Ps 100: 7–8).
441*a* He that despiseth you despiseth me (Lk 10: 16; cf. Jn 5: 23).

429 sarmoun] L&rC; sermons w.
430 arn] wBLMαC; & ?g.
431 and] L&r; and to WGM (to
    +M)C.
433*a* *qui²*] ?α (*qui . . . in.*] *om* F)C;
    & *qui* β.
434 ne] L&rC; nor W.
    Chambre] WCrGBFC; *pl* L&r.
437–54 *In* αCSk; *ll. om* β.
437 Cl.; kn.] RC; Boþe kn.; cl. F.
438 for] RC; for þe F.
    here] FCK–D; þe R.

likeþ] RC; þey lyghten F.
439 ryche] RC; þan ryche F.
440 þe] RC; *om* F.
442 Forthi] RC; þerfore F.
    þat] at R; men at F; *om* C.
443 to²] RC; ȝee F.
444 sittynge] RC; ȝee sette F.
    thy] *so* CK–D; þe F; þe heyȝ R (C).
447 fithel þe; without flaterynge]
    RC; *trs* (þe] *om*)F.
    friday þe] RC; frydaes F.

And a blynd man for a bourdeour, or a bedrede womman

jester; bedridden

To crie a largesse tofore Oure Lord, your good loos to shewe.

bounty; fame; declare

450   Thise thre maner minstrales maketh a man to laughe,
And in his deeth deyinge thei don hym gret confort
That bi his lyve lithed hem and loved hem to here.   *while alive*
Thise solaceth the soule til hymself be falle
In a welhope, [for he wroghte so], amonges worthi seyntes,

good hope

455   There flateres and fooles thorugh hir foule wordes
Leden tho that loved hem to Luciferis feste
With *turpiloquio*, a lay of sorwe, and Luciferis fithele.   *(cf. Pr 39)*

Thus Haukyn the actif man hadde ysoiled his cote,
Til Conscience acouped hym therof in a curteis manere,

accused, found guilty

460   Why he ne hadde wasshen it or wiped it with a brusshe. *(Asking) why*

---

449 *Either* 'To ask for bounty for you before Our Lord [*sc.* at Judgement
   Day], to make manifest your good deserts' *or* 'To ask for bounty / proclaim
   "a bounty!" on Our Lord's (abiding) presence, to make known your good
   reputation'.

448   And; for a] RC; & tak; þy F.
449   tofore] *so* C; to F; byfor R.
      ȝoure] RC; þyn F.
450   maner; a man] RC; m. of; pl F.
452   lythed] RꝣC; he lystned F.
453   þise . . . hymselue] RC; þey
      solace þy s. til þyself F.
454   wel-] RC; wol good F.
      for . . . so] *so* CSk; *om* α (C).

worthi] RC; goode F.
455   þere] αCK–D; Ac ꝣβ (but G;
      And CrC²C).
      flateres] WC²LMα; flaterers
      HmCrꝣgC.
456   loued] α; louen β.
457   lay] L&rC; lady W.
460   wasshen] L&r; whasshen WG.

Passus XIV

'I have but oon hater,' quod Haukyn, 'I am the lasse to blame   *cloak*
Though it be soiled and selde clene – I slepe therinne o nyghtes;   *at*
And also I have an houswif, hewen and children—   *wife; servants*
Uxorem duxi, et ideo non possum venire—
That wollen bymolen it many tyme, maugree my chekes.

                         stain; for all I can do

5 It hath be laved in Lente and out of Lente bothe   *washed*
  With the sope of siknesse, that seketh wonder depe,   *soap; penetrates*
  And with the losse of catel, that [me was] looth forto agulte

                      so that; hateful; offend

  God or any good [gome], by aught that I wiste;   *man*
  And was shryven of the preest, that [for my synnes gaf me]
10 To penaunce, pacience, and povere men to fede,   *As a penance*
  Al for coveitise of my Cristendom in clennesse to kepen it.   *concern*
  And kouthe I nevere, by Crist! kepen it clene an houre,
  That I ne soiled it with sighte or som ydel speche,
  Or thorugh werk or thorugh word, or wille of myn herte,   *intention*
15 That I ne flobre it foule fro morwe til even.'   *sully; foully*
    'And I shal kenne thee,' quod Conscience, 'of Contricion to make

                      sc. make something

  That shal clawe thi cote of alle kynnes filthe—   *scrape (free) of*
  Cordis contricio . . .   *Contrition of heart (C)*

3*a* I have married a wife; and therefore I cannot come (Lk 14: 20).
7–8 . . . so that I would be unwilling Wittingly to offend God etc.

Collation WHmCrGYOC²CBLMRF.

RUBRIC *Passus xiiij^us &c* W&r
  (*&c*] *de visione ut supra* C; *de vis.*
  et vij^us de do weel HmB); *P. xiij^us*
  de v. vt supra R; *om* FG.
1 on] αL; oon hool wgM.
2 selde clene] W&r; fowle g.
3 hous-] W&r; *om* g.
3*a* *venire*] βF; *&c* R.
4 wollen] W&r; wolden g.
  tyme] β; *pl* αCr²³; adayes Cr.

7 þat . . . agulte] þat looþ me was to
  leese F; looþ for to agulte βR (C).
8 *So* βR (gome] man); & grucched
  ageyn god whan grevis he me sente
  F.
9 for my synnes; gaf me] *cj* K–D; *trs*
  All MSS (C).
12 neuere] β; nouȝt α.
14 þoruȝ²] wLM; *om* Cr³gα.
  word] β; thouȝt α (elles þ. F).
  or³] β; or þoruh F; and other R.
15 That] wBLMα; but ?g.

Dowel shal wasshen it and wryngen it thorugh a wis confessour—
Oris confessio ...   *Confession of mouth*
Dobet shal beten it and bouken it as bright as any scarlet,   *'buck'*
20   And engreynen it with good wille and Goddes grace to amende the,
                                                dye fast
And sithen sende thee to Satisfaccion for to sonnen it after:
                                                dry in the sun
Satisfaccio – Dobest.
Shal nevere my[te] bymolen it, ne mothe after biten it,   *defile, blemish*
Ne fend ne fals man defoulen it in thi lyve.   *dirty, sully*
25   Shal noon heraud ne harpour have a fairer garnement
                                                herald; garment
Than Haukyn the Actif man, and thow do by my techyng,   *if*
Ne no mynstrall be moore worth amonges povere and riche
Than Haukyn wi[l] the wafrer, which is *Activa Vita.'*   *Than will H.*
     'And I shal purveie thee paast,' quod Pacience, 'though no plough
erye,   *provide; dough; till*
30   And flour to fede folk with as best be for the soule;
Though nevere greyn growed, ne grape upon vyne,
Alle that lyveth and loketh liflode wolde I fynde,   *sustenance; provide*
And that ynogh – shal noon faille of thyng that hem nedeth.
We sholde noght be to bisy abouten oure liflode:
Ne *soliciti sitis ... Volucres celi Deus pascit ... Pacientes*
vincunt ...'
35   Thanne laughed Haukyn a litel, and lightly gan swerye,   *mildly*
'Whoso leveth yow [either], by Oure Lord, I leve noght he be blessed!'

---

19   and steep in a solution of lye ('buck') – *sc.* to restore its original colour.
34a ... Be not solicitous for your life ... [Behold] the birds of the air ... your
     heavenly Father feedeth them (Mt 6: 25, 26) The patient are victorious ...
     (see XIII 135a (C)).

18   shal] wOC²+M; *om* ?gLα.
19   shal] β; þat schal R; *om* F.
     it¹] βF; *om* R.
21   to¹] W&r; *om* g.
22   *Satisfaccio* Dobest] wLMR; S.
     &c g (*as one l. with* 23 W&r; *l. om*
     F).
     After this 2 *ll:* & Dobest & keep þe
     cleene fram vnkyȝnde werkis/ &
     þey þou slyde or stumble soore

soone vp þou ryȝse F(C).

23   myte] myste L&r; cheeste w (C).
28   Haukyn wil] *cj* K–D; Haukyn F;
     Haukyns wif βR.
     which is] αK–D; with his β.
29   no] β; þow no α.
30   þe] wYLMα; þi ?g.
32   Alle] L&r; To all W; For all F.
36   yow eiþer] y. nother R; eyþer of
     yow F; yow β (C).

'No?' quod Pacience paciently, and out of his poke hente   *took*
Vitailles of grete vertues for alle manere beestes,
And seide, 'Lo! here liflode ynogh, if oure bileve be trewe.
40 For lent nevere was there lif but liflode were shapen,
                                        means of sustenance; created
Whereof or wherfore and wherby to libbe.
  'First the wilde worm under weet erthe,
Fissh to lyve in the flood, and in the fir the criket,
The corlew by kynde of the eyr, moost clennest flessh of briddes,
                                                the natural vigour
45 And bestes by gras and by greyn and by grene rootes,
In menynge that alle men myghte the same   *As a sign*
Lyve thorugh leel bileve and love, as God witnesseth: *true faith*
Quodcumque pecieritis a patre in nomine meo ... Et alibi, Non
in solo pane vivit homo, set in omni verbo quod procedit de ore Dei.'
  But I lokede what liflode it was that Pacience so preisede;
And thanne was it a pece of the *Paternoster – Fiat voluntas tua.*
                                        piece; Thy will be done
50 'Have, Haukyn,' quod Pacience, 'and et this whan the hungreth,
Or whan thow clomsest for cold or clyngest for droughte;
                                        are benumbed; parch; drought
And shul nevere gyves thee greve ne gret lordes wrathe, *fetters; afflict*
Prison ne peyne – for *pacientes vincunt.*
By so that thow be sobre of sighte and of tonge,   *Provided*
55 In etynge and in handlynge and in alle thi fyve wittes,   *touching*
Tharstow nevere care for corn ne lynnen cloth ne wollen, *You need*
Ne for drynke, ne deeth drede, but deye as God liketh,
Or thorugh hunger or thorugh hete – at his wille be it.   *?heat, ? fever*

---

40 Life was never given without means of living also being provided.
47a Whatsoever you shall ask the Father in my name, [that will I do] (Jn 14:
    13); And in another place, Not in bread alone doth man live, but in every
    word that proceedeth from the mouth of God (Mt 4: 4).

40   þere] ?α (*cf.* C); *om* βF.
41   and] ?α (*l. om* F)OC²C; or β.
45   by²] W&rC; *om* g.
46   þe] wLRC; do the ?g {do] see
     BC; þe] *om* C)MF.
47   Lyue] βC; Lif R; & lyve F.
47a a patre] βC; *om* α.
48   liflode it] β (*cf.* C); þat l. α.

49   it] β; *om* αHmCr.
51   drouȝthe] ?α(*pl* F)C; drye β.
52   And] ?α (þere F)C; *om* β.
     gyues] β (gomes OC²; synne
     BoCot)C; feytoures α (*sg* F).
55   in³] W&rC; *om* g.
56   tharst] HmgαC; Darst-
     WCrCotLM.

For if thow lyvest after his loore, the shorter lif the bettre:
Si quis amat Christum mundum non diligit istum.

60   'For thorugh his breeth beestes woxen and abrood yeden:

came into being

Dixit et facta sunt . . .
Ergo thorugh his breeth mowen [bothe] men and beestes lyven,
As Holy Writ witnesseth whan men seye hir graces: *grace (at meals)*
Aperis tu manum tuam, et imples omne animal benediccione.

     'It is founden that fourty wynter folk lyvede withouten tulying,

tilling

And out of the flynt sprong the flood that folk and beestes dronken;

(Num 20: 11)

65   And in Elyes tyme hevene was yclosed,   *Elias' time*
That no reyn ne roon – thus ret men in bokes,

rained; read (III Kg 17: 1, Js 5: 17)

That manye wynter men lyveden and no mete ne tulieden.

food; cultivated

     'Sevene slepe, as seith the book, sevene hundred wynter,   *slept (C)*
And lyveden withouten liflode – and at the laste thei woken.   *food*
70   And if men lyvede as mesure wolde, sholde never moore be defaute

lack

Amonges Cristene creatures, if Cristes wordes ben trewe.
Ac unkyndenesse *caristia* maketh amonges Cristes peple,   *dearth*
And over-plentee maketh pryde amonges poore and riche; *superfluity*
Ac mesure is so muche worth it may noght be to deere;

expensive, precious

59*a* If a man cares for Christ, he will not cleave to this world (*Cartula* (C)).
60*a* [For] he spoke, and they were made (Ps 148: 5).
62*a* Thou openest thy hand: and fillest with blessing every living creature (Ps
     144: 16).

59   lyuest] L&rC; lyue WCrG.   72   Ac . . . makeþ] βR (*caristia*]
     bettre] βC; leuere α.   L&r; *caristiam* WCr); But welthe is
60   woxen] βC; wexeth R; weren F.   so mych a maister F.
61   bothe] *cj* K–D (*cf.* C); *om All*   cristes] R (?=α); cristen βF.
     MSS (C).   73   ouer] W&r; oþer B.
66   rett; on] ?αC; rede; in βF.   74   Ac] L&r (but G); and HmC²CF;
67   many wynter] ?α(*om* F)Cr;   Therfore WCr.
     manye wyntres β.   so] L&r; *om* W.
70   moore] wLMR; *om* gFC.

75 For the meschief and the meschaunce amonges men of Sodome

disaster

Weex thorugh plentee of payn and of pure sleuthe: *Arose from; bread*
Ociositas et habundancia panis peccatum turpissimum nutrivit.
For thei mesured noght hemself of that thei ete and dronke,

moderated

Diden dedly synne that the devel liked, *(But) did . . .*
So vengeaunce fil upon hem for hir vile synnes; *fell*
80 Thei sonken into helle, the citees echone.
   'Forthi mesure we us wel and make oure feith oure sheltrom;

defence (C)

And thorugh feith cometh contricion, conscience woot wel,
Which dryveth awey dedly synne and dooth it to be venial.
And though a man myghte noght speke, contricion myghte hym save,
85 And brynge his soule to blisse, by so that feith bere witnesse *provided*
That whiles he lyvede he bilevede in the loore of Holy Chirche.
Ergo contricion, feith and conscience is kyndeliche Dowel, *essentially*
And surgiens for dedly synne whan shrift of mouthe failleth. *oral*
Ac shrift of mouth moore worthi is, if man be ynliche contrit,

inwardly

90 For shrift of mouthe sleeth synne be it never so dedly— *mortal*
Per confessionem to a preest *peccata occiduntur*—
Ther contricion dooth but dryveth it doun into a venial synne,

reduces

As David seith in the Sauter, *et quorum tecta sunt peccata.*
Ac satisfaccion seketh out the roote, and bothe sleeth and voideth,

removes

95 And as it nevere hadde ybe, to noghte bryngeth dedly synne,
That it nevere eft is sene ne soor, but semeth a wounde yheeled.'

visible; sore; healed/covered

76a Sloth and abundance of bread nourished the basest sin (after Peter Cantor,
   PL 205: 331).
91 Through sacramental confession sins are slain.
93 . . . and whose sins are covered (Ps 31: 1).

76a *peccatum . . . nutriuit*] β; *om* ?α
   (*l. om* F).
78 Diden] L&r; & d. F; Thei d.
   WCr.
80 Thei] βR; þat þei F.
   þe] W&r; tho Cr²YLMF.
85 by] LCrα; for WM; *om* Hmg.

86 in] W&r; *om* g.
88 synne] HmCrBα; *pl* W&r.
89 Inlich] YOMRSk; yliche W&r
   (*om* Cr²³); veryliche G; with F.
93 As] W&r; and Cr²³g.
96 it . . . is] ?wLMα; ytt ys neuer
   efte g (ytt) *om* Y); eft it is not Cr.

'Where wonyeth Charite?' quod Haukyn. 'I wiste nevere in my lyve
Man that with hym spak, as wide as I have passed.'
'Ther parfit truthe and poore herte is, and pacience of tonge—
100 There is Charite the chief, chaumbrere for God hymselve.'

                                              confidant

'Wheither paciente poverte,' quod Haukyn, 'be moore plesaunt to
Oure Drighte   *Our Lord*
Than richesse rightfulliche wonne and resonably yspended?' *honestly*
'Ye – *quis est ille?*' quod Pacience, 'quik – *laudabimus eum!*
Though men rede of richesse right to the worldes ende,
105 I wiste nevere renk that riche was, that whan he rekene sholde,
                                 had to settle accounts
Whan he drogh to his deeth day, that he ne dredde hym soore,
                                 drew near
And that at the rekenyng in arrerage fel, rather than out of dette,
                                 arrears
Ther the poore dar plede, and preve by pure reson
To have allowaunce of his lord; by the lawe he it cleymeth:
                                 re-imbursement
110 Joye, that nevere joye hadde, of rightful jugge he asketh,   *a just judge*
And seith, "Lo! briddes and beestes, that no blisse ne knoweth,
And wilde wormes in wodes, thorugh wyntres thow hem grevest,
                                 you afflict
And makest hem wel neigh meke and mylde for defaute,   *tame; lack*
And after thow sendest hem somer, that is hir sovereyn joye,
115 And blisse to alle that ben, bothe wilde and tame."
'Thanne may beggeris, as beestes, after boote waiten,
                               expect recompense
That al hir lif han lyved in langour and in defaute.   *pain; want*
But God sente hem som tyme som manere joye   *Unless*

---

103 *Is there such a man?* [*lit.* Yes – who is that man?] Quick, we'll praise *him!*
(C).

97 Where] β; ʒe where α.
100 chaumbrere] WCrYOC²L;
    chambre Hm&r.
101 oure driʒte] L&r (o.d
    (*cropped*)W); o. sight CB; o.
    saueoure C²; o. lorde GR; god
    more F.

102 y-] LMR; de- w; *om* gF.
106 Whan he] wgMC; Whan it LR;
    & F.
107 þat] W&r; *om* GMR.
111 knoweþ] W&r; couthe g.
116 as] WCrLMC; and Hmgα.
117 in²] W&r; *om* BGC.

Outher here or elliswhere, kynde wolde it nere;   *never*
120 For to wrotherhele was he wroght that nevere was joye shapen!
                                                                  misfortune

'Aungeles that in helle now ben hadden joye som tyme,
And Dives in deyntees lyvede and in *douce vie*;   *pleasure; luxury*
Right so reson sheweth that tho men that [riche were]
And hir makes also lyvede hir lif in murthe.   *wives; pleasure*
125 'Ac God is of a wonder wille, by that kynde wit sheweth,
To yyve many men his mercymonye er he it have deserved.   *reward*
Right so fareth God by some riche: ruthe me it thynketh—
                                              acts; in the case of; pity
For thei han hir hire heer, and hevene, as it were   *payment*
(And is greet likynge to lyve withouten labour of bodye)
130 And whan he dyeth, ben disalowed, as David seith in the Sauter:
                                                                  barred
Dormierunt et nichil invenerunt.
And in another stede also, *Velud sompnum surgencium,*
Domine, in civitate tua, ad nichilum [*eorum rediges ymaginem*].
Allas, that richesse shal reve and robbe mannes soule   *deprive*
Fram the love of Oure Lord at his laste ende!
'Hewen that han hir hire afore arn everemoore nedy;   *in advance*

119–20 . . . it would be a contradiction to their very nature; for he who was
made never to experience joy was created for an evil destiny indeed!
125 But God's purpose is a strange one, to judge by the criteria of
commonsense.
130a They have slept [their sleep]: and [all the men of riches] have found
nothing [in their hands] (Ps 75: 6). And in another place, As the dream of
them that awake, O Lord; so in thy city thou shalt bring [their image] to
nothing (Ps 72: 20).

119 it nere] ?α (so be keende F); it
neuere β (*l. om* G).
120 wroþerhele] W&rC; wo other
wel CB; ouermuch wo Cr²³?g.
was Ioye] βC; *trs* αHmY.
123 þo] L&r; þe w; no Y.
þat . . . were] þat were r. β;
shull redyly acounte F; *om* R (C).
125 a] L&r; *om* W.
126 men] L&r; man WCrGF.
mercymonye] L&r (-monye] -ment
F); mede W.

129 is] L&r (his BoCot); ek YOC²;
om wF.
to lyue] β; to þe lif R; of lyf F.
131 And . . . also] βR; *et alibi* FC
(C).
131a ad] αOC²; *et ad* ?β.
eorum . . . ymaginem] e. rediges R;
rediges ym. F; *rediges* β (*r. &c*
WHmB) (C).
134 afore] β (a-] be- Cr³G); tofore
α.

135   And selden deyeth out of dette that dyneth er he deserve it
      And til he have doon his devoir and his dayes journee.   *duty; stint*
      For whan a werkman hath wroght, than may men se the sothe—
      What he were worthi for his werk, and what he hath deserved,
      And noght to fonge bifore, for drede of disalowyng.
                                          receive (pay); disfavour
140   'So I seye by yow riche: it semeth noght that ye shulle   *concerning*
      Have two hevenes – for youre here-beyng, and hevene herafter,
                                                  existence here
      Right as a servaunt taketh his salarie bifore, and siththe wolde clayme
          moore,
      As he that noon hadde, and hath hire at the laste.   *wages; end*
      It may noght be, ye riche men, or Mathew on God lyeth:
      De deliciis ad delicias difficile est transire!
145   'Ac if ye riche have ruthe, and rewarde wel the poore,   *look after*
      And lyven as lawe techeth, doon leaute to alle,   *justice*
      Crist of his curteisie shal conforte yow at the laste   *mercy, grace*
      And rewarden alle double richesse that rewful hertes habbeth.
                                              reward (with); pitiful
      And as an hyne that hadde his hire er he bigonne,   *labourer; began*
150   And whan he hath doon his devoir wel, men dooth hym oother
          bountee—   *a further reward*
      Yyveth hym a cote above his covenaunt – right so Crist yyveth hevene
                                                      agreed wages

---

139 And [it is not proper for him] to receive his payment in advance, in case
     his work should be found unsatisfactory.
144a From delights to delights is a difficult crossing (St Jerome, *Epistola ad
     Julianum (PL* 22: 965)) (cf. Mt 19: 23).

135 deyeth] ?α (þei suppe F)C;
     deyeþ he β.
     þat dyneþ] βR; & dyȝhgne F.
     he] βC; þei α.
139 noȝt] β; *om* R; ryght soo þe
     same F.
141 haue . . . for] ?α (haue] Clayme;
     for] oon here F)C; H. heuene in β
     (in] here yn HmG).
     here-[1]] W&r (*om* HmG); hee C;
     hiȝe B.
     -beyng] L&r (-berynge HmCr[1]
     GYCB); dwelling W; & anoþer F.
     her-[2]] L&r; ther- GR; also þer W.

142 So β; *as 2 ll. div before* & α
     (&] his terme & F)Hm.
     as] L&r; so as W.
     moore] β (m. ȝif hy mygth Hm);
     huire α (his heere eft soones F).
143 noon] β; n. ne R; n. hevene F.
     hire] β; heuene α.
144a *transire*] β; *ascendere* α.
146 done] L&r; & doon WBF.
     alle] L?α; hem alle wgM; his
     brothir F.

Bothe to riche and to noght riche that rewfulliche libbeth;

compassionately

And alle that doon hir devoir wel han double hire for hir travaille—

pay; effort

Here foryifnesse of hir synnes, and hevene blisse after.

155   'Ac it nys but selde yseien, as by holy seintes bokes,   *seldom seen*

That God rewarded double reste to any riche wye.

For muche murthe is amonges riche, as in mete and clothyng,

pleasure

And muche murthe in May is amonges wilde beestes,

And so forth while somer lasteth hir solace dureth.   *joy continues*

160   Ac beggeris aboute midsomer bredlees thei soupe,   *sup*

And yet is wynter for hem worse, for weetshoed thei gange,

even; wet-shod; go

Afurst soore and afyngred, and foule yrebuked   *Thirsty; hungry*

And arated of riche men, that ruthe is to here.   *scolded by*

Now, Lord, sende hem somer, and som maner joye,

165   Hevene after hir hennes goyng, that here han swich defaute!

For alle myghtestow have maad noon mener than oother,   *poorer*

And yliche witty and wise, if thee wel hadde liked.   *equally*

And have ruthe on thise riche men that rewarde noght thi prisones;

care for; prisoners

Of the good that thow hem gyvest *ingrati* ben manye;

For; ungrateful (cf. Lk 6: 35)

170   Ac God, of thi goodnesse, gyve hem grace to amende.

For may no derthe be hem deere, droghte ne weete,   *injurious to them*

Ne neither hete ne hayll, have thei hir heele;   *health*

Of that thei wilne and wolde wanteth hem noght here.   *desire*

'Ac poore peple, thi prisoners, Lord, in the put of meschief—

175   Conforte tho creatures that muche care suffren   *pit; distress*

---

162 Afflicted grievously by thirst and hunger, and ignominiously abused.

152   rewfulliche] β; riȝtfullich α (r. here F).
155-9   *In* β (*cf.* C); *ll. om* α.
155   nys] L&r; is WCrG.
160   soupe] L&r; slepe W.
161   gange] L&r?C; gone W; wandre F.
162   foule] W&r; fouliche g.
167   þee wel] wYLR; thy wyll ?gMF.

168   -ones] R; -oners β; porayle F.
171   be] W&r; *om* Cr²³OC².
weet] L&r; w. hem greue WCr.
174   peple] βR; in F.
prisoners lord] β; prisones lore R; prisoun lyȝn F.

Thorugh derthe, thorugh droghte, alle hir dayes here,
Wo in wynter tyme for wantynge of clothes,
And in somer tyme selde soupen to the fulle;   *eat their fill*
Conforte thi carefulle, Crist, in thi riche—   *wretched; kingdom*
180 For how thow confortest alle creatures clerkes bereth witnesse:
Convertimini ad me et salvi eritis.

'Thus *in genere* of his gentries Jesu Crist seide *in the nature; nobility*
To robberis, to reveris, to riche and to poore,   *thieves*
To hores, to harlotes, to alle maner peple.
Thou taughtest hem in the Trinite to taken bapteme
in (the name of) the T.
185 And be clene thorugh that cristnyng of alle kynnes synnes,
And if us fille thorugh folie to falle in synne after,   *it befell us*
Confession and knowlichynge and cravynge thi mercy
acknowledging (sin)
Shulde amenden us as manye sithes as man wolde desire.   *times*
Ac if the pouke wolde plede herayein, and punysshe us in conscience,
devil; against this
190 He sholde take the acquitaunce as quyk and to the queed shewen it—
evil one

Pateat &c: Per passionem Domini—
And putten of so the pouke, and preven us under borwe.
repel;pledge
Ac the parchemyn of this patente of poverte be moste, *deed; must be*
And of pure pacience and parfit bileve.   *faith*
Of pompe and of pride and parchemyn decourreth, *From; departs*

180a If you return . . . you shall be saved (Is 45: 22).
190–90a He should take the document of acquittal immediately and produce
    it before the Devil (our accuser) – 'Let it be manifest &c [opening words of
    the deed] through the passion of Our Lord' . . . and thereby repel the fiend
    and prove us secure under the pledge [of Christ's redemptive death] (C).

177 wynter tyme] w. tymes β;
     wyntres tyme α.
179 riche] L&r; richesse wM (esse
     after erasure M).
181 his] L; alle his R; alle F; om
     wgM.
182 to²] ?α; and to βF.
183 *In* αK–D; *om* β.
     hores . . . maner] R; harlotys & to
     hoorys & to all oþer F.
185 be] L&r; to be WF.

sinnes] Cr&r (*om* L)Sk; synne WB.
186 if] WCrα; *om* HmgLM.
187 Conf.; knowl.] β; *trs* R; &
     beknowleche it; In confessioun F.
     and²] L&r; in W.
189 Ac] L?g (but)M; And wC²Cα.
     pouke] αSk; pope β.
     vs] βF; on vs R.
190 He] β; Ho R; We F (C).
191 so] W&r; *om* g.

195 And principalliche of alle peple, but thei be poore of herte.
     Ellis is al on ydel, al that evere we wr[ogh]ten—   *In vain; did*
     Paternostres and penaunce and pilgrimage to Rome,
     But oure spences and oure spendynge sprynge of a trewe welle;

                                                             expenses

     Ellis is al oure labour lost – lo, how men writeth
200 In fenestres at the freres! – if fals be the foundement.

                                     windows; foundation

     Forthi Cristene sholde be in commune riche, noon coveitous for
       hymselve.
     'For sevene synnes that ther ben assaillen us evere;
     The fend folweth hem alle and fondeth hem to helpe,   *tries*
     Ac with richesse tho ribaudes rathest men bigileth.

                                    evil ones; most quickly

205 For ther that richesse regneth, reverences folweth,
     And that is plesaunt to Pride, in poore and in riche.   *pleasing*
     And the riche is reverenced by reson of his richesse
     Ther the poore is put bihynde, and paraventure kan moore

                           Where; though perhaps he knows

     Of wit and of wisdom, that fer awey is bettre
210 Than richesse or reautee, and rather yherd in hevene. *royalty; sooner*
     For the riche hath muche to rekene, and right softe walketh; *gingerly*

194–5 The document (of release from sin through confession) in no way
    applies to the proud, and utterly leaves out any but the humble.
198 Unless what we spend comes from an honest source [sincere repentance].

195 alle] L&r; *al* þe WM; þe F.
196 we wroghten] *we* writen *All*
    MSS (we] þey F; *om* W) (C).
197 Paternostres] WHmLMF; *sg*
    Cr&r.
    penaunce] β; *pl* α (penauntis
    F)HmC.
    pilgrimage] L&r; *pl* WCrG;
    pilgrimes F.
198 But] βC; And ?α (with F).
    and oure] ?α (of F)B?C; and β.
    welle] L&r?C; wille WCrOC²C
    (C).

201 coueitous] W&r (*l. om* F);
    coueyte g.
202 þat] HmCrLMRC; *om* WgF.
    assaillen] L&r; þat a. WCBFC (C).
204 þo ribaudes] αCK–D; þat
    Ribaude β (R.] R. he WCr¹).
205 reuerences] αCK–D; *sg* β.
207 And] βC; Ac α (But F).
209 awey] β; wei ?α (*l. om* F)C.
211 riȝte softe] L&rC; ofte hym þat
    Cr; many tyme hym þat W.

The heighe wey to heveneward ofte riche letteth—   *obstructs*
Ita possibile diviti . . .
Ther the poore preesseth bifore, with a pak at his rugge—   *back*
Opera enim illorum sequuntur illos—
Batauntliche as beggeris doon, and boldeliche he craveth
                                        With noisy eagerness; confidently
215 For his poverte and his pacience a perpetuel blisse:
Beati pauperes: quoniam ipsorum est regnum celorum.

   'And Pride in richesse regneth rather than in poverte: *holds sway*
Or in the maister or in the man som mansion he haveth.   *dwelling*
Ac in poverte ther pacience is, Pride hath no myghte,
Ne none of the seven synnes sitten ne mowe ther longe,
220 Ne have power in poverte, if pacience it folwe.
For the poore is ay prest to plese the riche,   *always prompt*
And buxom at his biddyng for his broke loves;   *obedient; scraps*
And buxomnesse and boost [ben] everemoore at werre,   *arrogance*
And either hateth oother in alle maner werkes.
225 If Wrathe wrastle with the poore he hath the worse ende,
                                        gets the worse of it
For if thei bothe pleyne, the poore is but feble,   *plead; weak*
And if he chide or chatre, hym cheveth the worse.   *he succeeds*
For lowliche he loketh and lovelich is his speche
That mete or money of othere men moot asken.
230   'And if Glotonie greve poverte, he gadereth the lasse, *vex; collects*

212a Thus it is (im)possible for a rich man [to enter into the kingdom of
    heaven] (cf. Mt 19: 23–4).
213a . . . for their works follow them (Rev 14: 13) (C).
215a Blessed are the poor [in spirit]; for theirs is the kingdom of heaven (Mt 5:
    3; but cf. Lk 6: 20, which omits 'in spirit') (C).
225 And if (Wrath) scolds or argues with (a poor man) he gets the worst of it.

212 heiȝe] βC; riȝt αG.   217 Or[1,2]] αCK–D; Arst; þan β (þ.]
    oft] L&r; *om* WCr.   or Cr).
    riche] α; Richesse β.   he] βFC; *om* R.
    letteth] L&r; hym l. WCr; is lettyd   220 it] L&r (*l. om* Cr[3]); hem F; *om*
    F.   W.
212a *possibile*] L&r (*l. om* F);   222 his biddyng] L&rC; *pl* W.
    inpossibile WCot.   223 ben] *cj* K–D; þey been F; arn
213 preesseth] β (praiseth CrBo);   βRCx (C).
    precheth ?α (procheth F).   226 For] L&rC; And w.
213a *sequu-*] C[2]CSk; *sequ-* W&r.   228–38 *In* αCSk; *ll. om* β.
215 his[2]] wL?α (*l. om* F)C; *om* gM.   229 mete] RC; ony meete F.
216 And] βC; Ac α (But F).

For his rentes wol naught reche no riche metes to bigge;

income; foods; buy

And though his glotonye be to good ale, he goth to cold beddyng,
And his heved unheled, unesiliche ywrye—

uncovered; uncomfortably twisted

For whan he streyneth hym to strecche, the strawe is his shetes.

tries; sheets

235 So for his Glotonie and his greete Sleuthe he hath a grevous penaunce,
That is welawo whan he waketh and wepeth for colde—   *misery*
And som tyme for his synnes – so he is nevere murie   *content*
Withoute mournynge amonge and meschief to bote.

an admixture of sadness; suffering

'And theigh Coveitise wolde cacche the poore, thei may noght
come togideres,

240 And by the nekke, namely, hir noon may hente oother.

especially; neither of them; grip

For men knowen wel that Coveitise is of a kene wille,   *fierce*
And hath hondes and armes of a long lengthe,
And Poverte nys but a petit thyng, apereth noght to his navele—

little; that reaches; navel, middle

And lovely layk was it nevere bitwene the longe and the shorte.

good sport (i.e. wrestling)

245 And though Avarice wolde angre the poore, he hath but litel myghte,

afflict

For Poverte hath but pokes to putten in hise goodes,   *his goods in*
Ther Avarice hath almaries and yren-bounden cofres.

cupboards; iron-bound chests

And wheither be lighter to breke? Lasse boost it maketh—

which is easier; cause of boasting (C)

A beggeris bagge than an yren-bounde cofre!

250 'Lecherie loveth hym noght, for he yyveth but litel silver,

---

231   wol] FC; ne wol R.
232   glotonye; to . . . beddynge] RC;
         glut be in; acold to bedde F.
233   vnheled] RC; euele yheled & F.
234   schetes] RC; schete F.
235   his[1]; and . . . scleuthe] RC; his
         grete; om F.
236   wepeth] RC; w. sore F.
238   and] R; and myche F.

239   þou3] αC; if β.
         wolde] LαC; om wgM.
241   a] L&rC; om WCr.
242   a longe] L&r (a) om R)C; an
         huge F; ful greet W.
243   nys] ?wCBLM; ne is R; is
         Cr?gF.
244   it] W&r (yet Cr)C.
248   it] L&r (erased M)C; he F; om
         WCr.

Ne dooth hym noght dyne delicatly ne drynke wyn ofte.   *choicely*
A straw for the stuwes! It stoode noght, I trowe,   *brothels*
Hadde thei noon but of poore men – hir houses were untyled!

untiled, roofless

'And though Sleuthe suwe Poverte, and serve noght God to paie,

follow; satisfactorily

255   Meschief is his maister, and maketh hym to thynke

Misfortune; teacher

That God is his grettest help and no gome ellis,   *nobody*
And he is servaunt, as he seith, and of his sute bothe.   *retinue*
And wher he be or be noght, he bereth the signe of poverte,

whether

And in that secte Oure Saveour saved al mankynde.

garb, character (C)

260   Forthi al poore that pacient is, may [asken and cleymen],
After hir endynge here, heveneriche blisse.
   'Muche hardier may he asken, that here myghte have his wille

boldly

In lond and in lordshipe and likynge of bodie,   *bodily pleasure*
And for Goddes love leveth al and lyveth as a beggere.   *abandons*
265   And as a mayde for a mannes love hire moder forsaketh,   *leaves*
Hir fader and alle hire frendes, and folweth hir make—   *spouse*
Muche is swich a maide to love of hym that swich oon taketh,
Moore than a maiden is that is maried thorugh brocage,   *arrangement*
As by assent of sondry parties and silver to boote,
270   Moore for coveitise of good than kynde love of bothe—

252–3 Fie upon the brothels! They could not continue to exist/would not have
existed Had they been frequented only by the poor.

267–8 A girl greatly deserves love from a man who takes her on those terms –
More than does one whose marriage is arranged like a business transaction.

252–3 *In* βC; *ll. om* α.
252 it] L&rC; þei W.
253 none; were] L; no þyng (noght G); stoode W&r (C).
256 his] βC; *om* αB.
257 he[1]] WCr+MαC; *om* HmgL. is] ?αCBC; his ?βF.
258 where] LRC; wheiþer W&r.
260 al] L&rC; euery W. asken; cleymen] *trs All MSS* (C).
263 In . . . in] βC; In lorde and in R; As a lord of F.
265 a[2]] ?αC; *om* βF.
266 folweþ] βF; folwed R.
267 Moche] L&rC; Muche moore WCr. *su*che a mayde] ?β (a G; *om* WCr)C; þat mayde α.
268 More] L&rC; *om* WCr. a mayden is] β (is þat maiden W)R; þat m. is FC.
269 As] W&rC; and g.

So it fareth by ech a persone that possession forsaketh   *property*
And put hym to be pacient, and poverte weddeth,
The which is sib to God hymself, and so neigh is poverte.'
    'Have God my trouthe,' quod Haukyn, 'that here faste preise
poverte—   *constantly*
275 What is poverte, Pacience,' quod he, 'proprely to mene?'   *precisely*
    '*Paupertas*,' quod Pacience, '*est odibile bonum—*
Remocio curarum, possessio sine calumpnia; donum Dei,
sanitatis mater, absque sollicitudine semita; sapiencie
temperatrix, negocium sine dampno; incerta fortuna,
absque sollicitudine felicitas.'
    'I kan noght construe al this,' quod Haukyn, 'ye moste kenne me this
on Englissh.'   *teach*
    'In Englissh,' quod Pacience, 'it is wel hard, wel to expounen,
        expound
Ac somdeel I shal seyen it, by so thow understonde.
        provided you (try to) understand
280 Poverte is the firste point that Pride moost hateth;   *quality, virtue (C)*
Thanne is it good by good skile – al that agasteth pride.
        reason; scares off
Right as contricion is confortable thyng, conscience woot wel,
        a comforting thing
And a sorwe of hymself, and a solace to the soule,   *pain in itself; comfort*
So poverte propreliche penaunce [is to the body
285 And joye also to the soule], pure spiritual helthe,

---

276 Poverty is a good – yet a hateful one: – the removal of anxieties;
possession without calumny; a gift of God; the mother of (good) health; a
path free from worry; mistress of wisdom; business without losses; amidst
fortune's uncertainty, happiness without worry (Vincent of Beauvais) (C).

273 The which] W&r; which R;
Such Cr.
  neyȝ is pouerte] ?α (p.] þat persone
F)*K–D*; to hise seintes β.
274 þat huyre faste preyse] ?α (þ.] y;
f.] *om* F); ye preise faste β.
275 pac.] ?α (*om* F)C*K–D*; wiþ p. β.
276a *sanitatis*] L&rC; *sanitas* WCr[1]
YCB; *semita* R.
sollicitudine[1]] ?βC; *solitudine* α
Cr[2]OC[2]B.
277 So βF; *as 2 ll. div before* ye R.
al] WCrLMαC; *om* Hmg.

kenne] W&r; telle Hm; seyn g.
me] WR; þis HmCrLM; it OC[2]
BF; *om* GYC.
278 wel[2]] W&r; *om* HmCrGF.
279 Ac] W&r (but GF)C; And
CrC[2]R.
283 and a[2]] WHmLMR; & Crg; it
is F.
284 is . . . body] *cj K–D*; and Ioye
All MSS (C).
285 And . . . soule] Is to þe body
W&r; & to þe body ys F; Is the
bodyes Cr[23].

And contricion confort, and *cura animarum*:   *guardian of souls*
Ergo paupertas est odibile bonum.

 'Selde sit Poverte the sothe to declare, *sits the poor man (sc. on juries)*
Or as justice to jugge men enjoyned is no poore,
Ne to be a mair overe men, ne mynystre under kynges;   *mayor*
290 Selde is any poore yput to punysshen any peple;
Remocio curarum.
Ergo Poverte and poore men parfournen the comaundement—

               carry out

Nolite iudicare quemquam.   *'Judge not'* (Mt 7: 1)
 'Selde is poore right riche but of his rightful heritage:
Wynneth he noght with wightes false ne with unseled mesures,

              weights; unsealed (C)

Ne borweth of hise neighebores but that he may wel paie:
Possessio sine calumpnia.
295 'The ferthe it is a fortune that florissheth the soule   *prospers*
With sobretee fram alle synne and also yit moore;   *(away) from*
It afaiteth the flessh fram folies ful manye—   *restrains*
A collateral confort, Cristes owene yifte: *accompanying*
Donum Dei.
 'The fifte it is moder of helthe, a frend in alle fondynges,

              temptations

---

292 A poor man seldom gets rich except through lawful inheritance (i.e. not crime).

286 *So ord* K–D; *trs with* 286a All MSS (C).
animarum] W&r; *an.* þe seconde Cr²³g.
288 Or] L&r?C; for WCr¹M; As sytt a F.
enioyned . . . poore] β; of gyltys F; *om* R.
289 to be] W&r (to) for to R)C; as a F.
a] L&rC; *om* wGC².
ouere] ?α (on F)C; aboue β.

290 any¹] β?C; enemye R; þe F.
291a *quemquam*] CotCK–D; q. þe þridde W&r.
292 pore riȝt] αCK–D; any poore β.
his] ?αC; *om* β (any G)F.
293 wiȝtes] β?C; wittes R; wyȝles F.
294 neighebores] βR; *sg* FC.
295 it] ?αC; *om* βF.
299 it is] is hit C; it is þe ?α (it] *om* F); is β.
moder] βC; þe moder α.

300 And for the l[owe] evere a leche, a lemman of alle clennesse:

humble; physician; chaste lover

Sanitatis mater.

'The sixte it is a path of pees – ye, thorugh the paas of Aultoun

pass; Alton (C)

Poverte myghte passe withouten peril of robbyng!
For ther that Poverte passeth pees folweth after,
And ever the lasse that he bereth, the [light]er he is of herte—
Cantabit paupertas coram latrone viator—

305 And an hardy man of herte among an heep of theves;
Forthi seith Seneca *Paupertas est absque sollicitudine semita.*

'The seventhe it is welle of wisedom and fewe wordes sheweth,
For lordes alloweth hym litel or listneth to his reson.

approve; speech, arguments

He trempreth the tonge to trutheward, that no tresor coveiteth:
Sapiencie temperatrix.

310 'The eightethe it is a lele labour and looth to take moore   *honest*
Than he may [so] wel deserve, in somer or in wynter,
And if he chaffareth, he chargeth no losse, mowe he charite wynne:

does business; accounts it

Negocium sine dampno.

'The nynthe it is swete to the soule, no sugre is swetter;
For pacience is payn for poverte hymselve,   *bread, food*

---

300 And a perpetual attraction to purity of life for all humble men [*sc.* who
   might turn to lechery if they were rich].
304*a* A traveller with an empty purse / Will sing when he shall meet a thief
   (Juvenal, *Sat.* x, 22; *paup.*] *vacuus* orig.).
309 The man who does not long for riches tunes his tongue to tell the truth.

300   lowe] lawe F; lawde YCR;
   lewde GOC²B; land wLM(C).
   a leche] βR (a liche R) (*cf.* C);
   ylyche F.
300*a*   sanitatis] L&rC; *sanitas* WCr¹
   YCB.
301   it] ?αC; *om* βF.
304   lighter] *so* CK–D; hardier W&r
   (*l. om* F) (C).
304*a*   *So ordered* K–D; *trs with* 306
   All MSS (C).
   Cantabit] βF; *Cantabat* CrCotR.
   viator] L&r (*v. &c* Hm; *&c* Y);

viatore WCrM.
306   *sollicitudine*] ?βC; *solitudine*
   αOC²B.
307   it] ?αC; *om* βF.
308   For] L&rC; Therfore WCr.
309   He] L&rC; For he WCr.
   þat] αCK–D; and β.
309*a*   *In* β; *l. om* α.
310   it] ?αC; *om* βF.
311   so] *om All MSS* (C).
313   it] ?αC; *om* βF.
   is²] W&r; *om* gC.

315 And sobretee swete drynke and good leche in siknesse.
Thus lered me a lered man for Oure Lordes love, Seint Austyn—
A blessed lif withouten bisynesse for body and for soule:
Absque sollicitudine felicitas.
Now God, that alle good gyveth, graunte his soule reste
That thus first wroot to wissen men what Poverte was to mene!'

320 'Allas,' quod Haukyn the Actif Man tho, 'that after my cristendom
I ne hadde be deed and dolven for Dowelis sake!   *buried*
So hard it is,' quod Haukyn, 'to lyve and to do synne. *miserable, cruel*
Synne seweth us evere,' quod he, and sory gan wexe,
                                  follows; sorrowful
And wepte water with hise eighen and weyled the tyme   *bewailed*

325 That evere he dide dede that deere God displesed—
Swouned and sobbed and siked ful ofte   *sighed*
That evere he hadde lond or lordshipe, lasse other moore,
Or maistrie over any man mo than of hymselve.   *power; more*
  'I were noght worthi, woot God,' quod Haukyn, 'to werien any
    clothes,   *wear*

330 Ne neither sherte ne shoon, save for shame one
                            shirt; shoes; modesty alone
To covere my careyne,' quod he, and cride mercy faste,
                            carcass; constantly
And wepte and wailede – and therwith I awakede.

---

328 ... over any man other than (*or*, more than) (he had) over himself.

316–17a *So div* CK–D; *div after*
  loue, bysynesse L&r; *after* loue,
  ladde M; *after* heuene, bis. F; *after*
  heu., ladde WCr (C).
316 lered²] αC; lettred β.
  loue] L&rC; l. of heuene WCrF.
317 bys.] L&rC; b. ladde WCrM.
  for²] W&r; *om* g.
317a *Absque*] βFC; *om* R.

319 þus] L&rC; þis w.
320 þe ... þo] β; þanne F; *om* R.
323 seweþ] β; scheweth α.
325 euere he] L&r; *trs* W.
327 or] L&r (*om* Cr); ouþer W.
329 woot god] W&r (w.] wite R);
  om gF.
331 mercy faste] W&r; *trs* g.

Passus XV

Ac after my wakynge it was wonder longe
Er I koude kyndely knowe what was Dowel.
And so my wit weex and wanyed til I a fool weere;   *waxed; waned*
And some lakkede my lif – allowed it fewe—   *blamed; approved*
5 And leten me for a lorel and looth to reverencen   *held; wastrel*
Lordes or ladies or any lif ellis—   *person*
As persons in pelure with pendaunts of silver;   *fur; pendants*
To sergeaunts ne to swiche seide noght ones,   *serjeants-at-law*
'God loke yow, lordes!' – ne loutede faire,   *watch over; bowed*
10 That folk helden me a fool; and in that folie I raved,
Til Reson hadde ruthe on me and rokked me aslepe,
Til I seigh, as it sorcerie were, a sotil thyng withalle—

magic; subtle, fine-drawn

Oon withouten tonge and teeth, tolde me whider I sholde   *(who) told*
And wherof I cam and of what kynde. I conjured hym at the laste,
15 If he were Cristes creature for Cristes love me to tellen.
    'I am Cristes creature,' quod he, 'and Cristene in many a place,
In Cristes court yknowe wel, and of his kyn a party.   *?partly (C)*
Is neither Peter the Porter, ne Poul with the fauchon,   *sword*
That wole defende me the dore, dynge I never so late.   *forbid; knock*
20 At mydnyght, at mydday, my vois is so yknowe   *familiar*
That ech a creature of his court welcometh me faire.'

Collation WHmCrGYOC²CBLMRF
(428a–91 om).
RUBRIC *Passus xv^{us} &c finit dowel
et incipit dobet* W&r; *P. xv^{us}de
dowel Et incipit primus de dobet* B;
Incipit primus passus de dobett G;
Passus xiiij^{us} de visione vt supra R;
Passus xv M; *Incipit Passus xij^{us}* F.
1 wakynge] βF; walkyng BmBoR.
5 leten] L&r; lete W.
me] WCrB+Mα; *om* Hm?gL.
8 ne] β; and α.
swiche] β; s. and R; s. men F.
seyde] L&r; s. I wM (I+M).

12 Til . . . were] βR (it] it of R); þan
sey3 y a syght of sorsery3e F.
13 whider] βF; wonder R.
14 *So* βF; *as* 2 *ll. div after* shulde R.
of²] wLM; *om* gα.
what kynde] β; kendely F; whider I
schulde R.
15 for . . . loue] L&rC; leue Hm;
anoon WCr.
16 a] W&r?C; *om* GCotR.
18 þe²] ?α?CK–D; his βF.
20 is so] HmCrYαC; *trs* W?g (ys
G)LM.
y-] L&rC; *om* WCrYOC².

'What are ye called?' quod I, 'in that court among Cristes peple?'
'The whiles I quykke the cors,' quod he, 'called am I *Anima*;
give life to, animate; body
And whan I wilne and wolde, *Animus* ich hatte;   *am called*
25 And for that I kan and knowe, called am I *Mens*, "Thoughte";
And whan I make mone to God, *Memoria* is my name; *pray, recollect*
And whan I deme domes and do as truthe techeth,
make (moral) judgements
Thanne is *Racio* my righte name, "Reson" on Englissh;
And whan I feele that folk telleth, my firste name is *Sensus*— *perceive*
30 And that is wit and wisdom, the welle of alle craftes;
source; skills, activities
And whan I chalange or chalange noght, chepe or refuse,
claim; buy, choose
Thanne am I Conscience ycalled, Goddes clerk and his notarie;
scribe
And whan I love leelly Oure Lord and alle othere,   *faithfully*
Thanne is "Lele Love" my name, and in Latyn *Amor*;
35 And whan I flee fro the flessh and forsake the careyne,   *corpse*
Thanne am I spirit spechelees – and *Spiritus* thanne ich hatte.
    'Austyn and Ysodorus, either of hem bothe   *Isidore of Seville (C)*
Nempnede me thus to name – now thow myght chese *named; choose*
How thow coveitest to calle me, now thow knowest alle my names.
Anima pro diversis accionibus diversa nomina sortitur; dum
vivificat corpus, Anima est; dum vult, Animus est; dum scit,
Mens est; dum recolit, Memoria est; dum iudicat, Racio est;
dum sentit, Sensus est; dum amat, Amor est; dum negat vel
consentit, Consciencia est; dum spirat, Spiritus est.'

39a The Soul selects different names according to its different modes of
    operation. As (the power which) gives life to the body, it is (called) 'soul'; as
    (that which) wills, 'intention'; knows, 'mind'; reflects (on things past, *or*,
    prays), 'memory'; judges, 'reason'; perceives sensations 'sense'; loves, 'love';
    denies or consents, 'conscience'; breathes (the breath of life), 'spirit' (Isidore
    of Seville, *Etymologiae* XI, i 13) (*PL* 82).

22   quod I; in þat court] WCrLα; *trs*
     HmgM.
23   quykke] LMα(q. in F)C; quykne
     WCr; quyk was in Hmg.
25   and²] L&rC; y F; *om* W.
     am . . . thouȝte] ?α (*mens* y am ofte
     F)?C; am I *mens* β (C).
36   and] αLC; *om* wgM.
     spirit] L&rC; a spirit WF.
38   now] L&rC; and now W.
39   now] L&r (*om* F)C; for now W.
     þow knowest] W&rC; *trs* g.
     alle] L&rC; *om* WG.

40   'Ye ben as a bisshop,' quod I, al bourdynge that tyme,   *jesting*
'For bisshopes yblessed, thei bereth manye names—
Presul and *Pontifex* and *Metropolitanus*,   *Prelate; Pontiff; Metropolitan*
And othere names an heep, *Episcopus* and *Pastor*.'   *Bishop; Shepherd*
'That is sooth,' seide he, 'now I se thi wille!   *purpose, intent*
45   Thow woldest knowe and konne the cause of alle hire names,
And of myne, if thow myghtest, me thynketh by thi speche!'
'Ye, sire,' I seide, 'by so no man were greved,   *provided; offended*
Alle the sciences under sonne and alle the sotile craftes
I wolde I knewe and kouthe kyndely in myn herte!'   *intimately*
50   'Thanne artow inparfit,' quod he, 'and oon of Prides knyghtes!
For swich a lust and likyng Lucifer fel from hevene:
Ponam pedem meum in aquilone et similis ero Altissimo.
'It were ayeins kynde,' quod he, 'and alle kynnes reson
That any creature sholde konne al, except Crist oone.   *alone*
Ayein swiche Salomon speketh, and despiseth hir wittes,   *scorns*
55   And seith, *Sicut qui mel comedit multum, non est ei bonum,*
Sic qui scrutator est maiestatis opprimatur a gloria.
'To Englisshe men this is to mene, that mowen speke and here,
The man that muche hony eet, his mawe it engleymeth,

    stomach; cloys

And the moore that a man of good matere hereth,
But he do therafter it dooth hym double scathe.   *act accordingly; harm*
60   "*Beatus est*," seith Seint Bernard, "*qui scripturas legit*
Et verba vertit in opera fulliche to his power."
Coveitise to konne and to knowe science

51a   I shall place my foot in the north, and be like the Most High
(Augustine; cf. Is 14: 13–14); cf. I 119 (C).
55–5a   As it is not good for a man to eat much honey, so he that is a
searcher of majesty [*sc.* God's] shall be [*lit.* let him be] overwhelmed by
[his] glory (Prov 25: 27).
60–1   Blessed is the man who reads the Scriptures And turns (its) words
into works as far as he is capable (St Bernard, *Tractatus de ordine vitae*
(PL 184: 566)).

41   þei] wLαC;*om* gM.
42   *Metropolitanus*] βC;
    metropolitanus α.
48   sciences] W&rC; science yR.
49   I knewe] wYLMαC; knowe ?g.
50   inparfit] W&rC; vnparfytt g.
53   konne] βC; kenne αCr. oone β
    (alone G)C; hym oone F; *om* R.

55a   -atur] ?α(-etur F)C; -itur β.
57   eet] αC; eteþ β. it engleymeþ]
    βC; is engleymed ?α (mote be e.
    F)Cr23B.
61   *verba vertit*] βC; *trs* αHm.
62   science] L&r (*l. om* C); *pl.*
    WFC.

Pulte out of Paradis Adam and Eve:
Sciencie appetitus hominem inmortalitatis gloriam spoliavit.
　'And right as hony is yvel to defie and engleymeth the mawe,

hard; digest

65　Right so that thorugh reson wolde the roote knowe
　Of God and of hise grete myghtes – hise graces it letteth.　obstructs
　For in the likynge lith a pride and a licames coveitise
　Ayein Cristes counseil and alle clerkes techynge—
　That is *Non plus sapere quam oportet sapere.*

70　'Freres and fele othere maistres that to the lewed men prechen,
　Ye moeven materes unmesurables to tellen of the Trinite,

adduce; unfathomable

　That oftetymes the lewed peple of hir bileve doute.　doubt their faith
　Bettre bileven were, by manye doctours, swich techyng,

in the case of; abandon (C)

　And tellen men the ten comaundementes, and touchen the sevene
　synnes,

deal with

75　And of the braunches that burjoneth of hem and bryngen men to
　helle,

shoot

　And how that folk in folies mysspenden hir fyve wittes—　misuse
　As wel freres as oother folk, foliliche spenen　　(who) foolishly

---

63a The longing for knowledge deprived man of the glory of immortality (St
　Bernard, Sermon 4 *in ascensione Domini* (PL 183: 311)).
67 For in the desire of knowledge [with pun on 'licking'?] lies a (form of pride)
　and fleshly greed . . .
69 . . . not to be more wise than it behoveth to be wise (Rom 12: 3).

63　Pulte] LM (*alt. to* Putte)R;
　Pullede OC²; Putte w?gC; was pyt
　F.
63a　*gloriam*] L&r (m *del.* O)C;
　gloria w.
64　riȝt] βFC; ȝet R.
65　so] L&r; so he WCr.
66　grete] W&r; *om* g.
　graces] W&r; *sg* HmgF.
67　a²] OC²LMR; In a GYCB (in
　Cot); *om* wF.
70　fele] β (*cf.* C); *om* αG.
　þe] L&r; *om* WOC²CotF.
71　Ye] W&r; *om* Cr²³gC.
　-ables] L&r; -able WCrYCotF.
72　*In* βC; *l. om* α.

73　So L&r (Bettre] B. to Cr²³g; by-]
　om Cr²³GYCB; byleuen . . .
　doctours] it were to manye d. to
　leuen WM (*over erasure l. h.* M; l.]
　bileuen M); by] R; *om* β (to W);
　swich] β; *om* R); B. it were to
　beleve on as d. vs techeþ F (C).
74　þe¹] ?αG(*cf.* C); of þe ?β (þe] *om*
　CrYC)F.
75　burioneþ] β (*l. om* GCB)F;
　bourgeleth R.
77　spenen] CrCLR; spenden
　W&rC; speken B.

In housynge, in haterynge, in to heigh clergie shewynge   *clothing*
Moore for pompe than for pure charite – the peple woot the sothe!
80 That I lye noght, loo! – for lordes ye plesen,   *flatter*
And reverencen the riche the rather for hir silver:
Confundantur omnes qui adorant sculptilia; Et alibi,
Ut quid diligitis vanitatem, et queritis mendacium?
  'Gooth to the glose of the vers, ye grete clerkes;   *gloss on (C)*
If I lye on yow to my lewed wit, ledeth me to brennyng!   *burning*
For as it semeth ye forsaketh no mannes almesse—   *turn down; alms*
85 Of usurers, of hoores, of avarouse chapmen—   *greedy merchants*
And louten to thise lordes that mowen lene yow nobles   *bow; give*
Ayein youre rule and religion. I take record at Jesus,   *witness from*
That seide to hise disciples, "*Ne sitis acceptores personarum.*"
Of this matere I myghte make a muche bible;   *vast tome*
90 Ac of curatours over Cristen peple, as clerkes bereth witnesse,
                                                        about priests
I shal tellen it for truthe sake – take hede whoso liketh!
  'As holynesse and honeste out of Holy Chirche spredeth
Thorugh lele libbynge men that Goddes lawe techen,   *upright*
Right so out of Holy Chirche alle yveles spredeth
95 There inparfit preesthode is, prechours and techeris. *imperfect, faulty*
And se it by ensaumple in somer tyme on trowes: *trees*
Ther some bowes ben leved and some bereth none,   *leafy*
Ther is a meschief in the more of swiche manere bowes. *disease; root*
Right so persons and preestes and prechours of Holi Chirche
100 Is the roote of the right feith to rule the peple;   *orthodox*

81*a* Let them all be confounded that adore graven things (Ps 96: 7); And in
   another place, Why do you love vanity, and seek after lying? (Ps 4: 3).
88 Do not be respecters of persons (cf. Js 2: 1, also Deut 1: 17) (C).

78 in to] into α; and into ?β (and   91 treuth] LMα; truþes wg.
  ?g); in GC.   92 spredeþ] W&r; spryngeth (+
81 þe²] βC; men þe F; *om* R.   *over erasure* M; *cf.* C).
81*a sculptilia*] W&r; *s. &c* g.   93 lawe] β; lawes α.
  mendacium] βF; *&c* R.   94 spredeth] L&rC; spryngeþ W.
82 þe²] L&r; þise WHm.   95 is] βC; is and α.
85 of³] β; & of F; and R.   96 And] L&r (*om* F)C; I w.
87 and] βF; & ʒoure R.   99 so] L&rC; so bi W; so of Cr.
  at] W&r; of g.   100 Is þe] ?α (þey sholde been F)
88 *acc. personarum*] αC; *trs* β.   CK–D; That aren β.
89 mychil] ?α (grete R); long β.
90 ouer] ?α; of βF.

Ac ther the roote is roten, reson woot the sothe,
Shal nevere flour ne fruyt, ne fair leef be grene.   *f. or f. (grow)*
   'Forthi wolde ye lettrede leve the lecherie of clothyng,
And be kynde as bifel for clerkes and curteise of Cristes goodes,

                                              generous

105 Trewe of youre tonge and of youre tail bothe,   *sex(ual organs)*
And hatien to here harlotrie, and aught to underfonge   *receive at all*
Tithes of untrewe thyng ytilied or chaffared—
Lothe were lewed men but thei youre loore folwede
And amenden hem that thei mysdoon, moore for youre ensaumples
110 Than for to prechen and preven it noght – ypocrisie it semeth!

                                              practice

For [in Latyn ypocrisie] is likned to a dongehill   *dunghill*
That were bisnewed with snow, and snakes withinne,   *snowed over*
Or to a wal that were whitlymed and were foul withinne.

                         washed with white lime (Mt 23: 27)

Right so manye preestes, prechours and prelates—
115 Ye [b]en enblaunched with *bele paroles* and with clothes,

                             whitened; fine words

Ac youre werkes and wordes therunder aren ful w[o]lveliche.

                             wolf-like (C)

   'Johannes Crisostomus of clerkes speketh and preestes:

---

107 Tithe-offerings of produce obtained from dishonest farming or trade.
108–9 The uneducated would be reluctant [*or, possibly*, wicked] to do
   anything other than follow your teaching And would amend their evil
   ways . . .
115 You are made fair with fine words and with the finery you wear . . .

103 ye] βC; þe αB.
106 auȝt] ?α (looþ wrong F)K–D;
   noȝt β.
107 of vntrewe] ?β; of trewe αG;
   but of t. WCr.
109 amenden] L&rC; amendeden
   WHmBF.
   þei] ?αK–D (cf. C); om βF.

111 For . . . ypocrisie] For yp. in l.
   L&r (For yp.] The which W) (C).
   dongehill] βC; dongoun α.
115 Ye] wLMR; om Cr²³gF.
   ben] so C; aren W&r; were Cr¹
   (C).
   clothes] αC; c. also β.
116 wlueliche] ?α (foxly F) (cf. C)
   K–D; vnloueliche (vnlyche G).

Sicut de templo omne bonum progreditur, sic de templo omne
malum procedit. Si sacerdocium integrum fuerit, tota floret
ecclesia; si autem corruptum fuerit, omnium fides marcida est.
Si sacerdocium fuerit in peccatis, totus populus convertitur
ad peccandum. Sicut cum videris arborem pallidam et marcidam,
intelligis quod vicium habet in radice, ita cum videris
populum indisciplinatum et irreligiosum, sine dubio
sacerdocium eius non est sanum.

    'If lewed men wiste what this Latyn meneth,

120 And who was myn auctour, muche wonder me thinketh   *authority*

    But if many preest beere, for hir baselardes and hir broches, *swords*

    A peire of bedes in hir hand and a book under his arme.

                      set of rosary-beads; prayer-book

    Sire Johan and Sir Geffrey, [ech] hath a girdel of silver,

    A baselard or a ballok-knyf with botons overgilte.

125 Ac a porthors that sholde be his plow, *Placebo* to sigge, *breviary; say*

    Hadde he nevere, [his] service to [h]ave,

    [And save he have] silver therto, seith it with yvel wille.

    'Allas, ye lewed men, muche lese ye on preestes!

---

118 Just as all good comes out of the temple, so does all evil. If the priesthood
  has integrity, the whole Church flourishes; but if it is corrupt, the faith(ful) as
  a whole wither up. If the priests live in sin, the whole people turns to sin. Just
  as, when you see a tree pale and drooping, you know it has a diseased root,
  so when you see a people undisciplined and irreligious, you can be sure their
  priests are diseased (pseudo-Chrysostom, Homily 38 on St Matthew (*PL* 56:
  839)).

120–1 . . . it (would) amaze me If many a priest did not carry instead of
  swords and brooch-ornaments . . .

125–7 But a breviary that might be his working equipment, with which to say
  the psalm 'I will please the Lord [in the land of the living (Ps 114: 9, Vespers,
  Office of the Dead)]' He has never possessed, with which to provide his
  service, And unless sure of payment for doing so, says it with a bad grace (C).

118   *progreditur* (*pro-*) *e-* **g**);
    corruptum; sacerdocium²] βC;
    procedit; corupta; sacerdos α.
    -andum] βC; *-atum* αCr²³.
    pallidam; marcidam] wYLMαC; *trs*
    ?**g**.
121   preest] αMK–D; a p. β; *pl* Cr.
    baselardes . . . brooches] β; br.
    (brode br. F) and for (*om* F) hir
    bas. α.
122   peyre] L&r (*spurious l.* OC²);

    p. of wMF.
123   ech] *om All MSS* (C).
124   or] W&r; and **g**.
126–7 *As one line All MSS* (C).
126   his . . . haue²] seruice to saue β;
    s. to haue R; s. ne F.
127   seiþ . . . wille] W&r (yvel) LR;
    ydel w?**g**M); with evil will he will
    synge F; for spendyng at ale OC²
    (C).

Ac thing that wikkedly is wonne, and with false sleightes,   *tricks*
130 Wolde nevere wit of witty God but wikkede men it hadde—   *wise*
The whiche arn preestes inparfite and prechours after silver,
Secutours and sodenes, somonours and hir lemmannes.

Executors; sub-deans; mistresses

This that with gile was geten, ungraciousliche is spened.

got; scandalously mis-spent

So harlotes and hores arn holpe with swiche goodes,
135 Ac Goddes folk for defaute therof forfaren and spillen.

come to grief; die

'Curatours of Holy Kirke, and clerkes that ben avarouse,

avaricious

Lightliche that thei leven, losels it habbeth,

Quickly; leave behind; wastrels

Or deieth intestate, and thanne [entreth the bisshop]
And maketh murthe therwith, and hise men bothe,   *regales himself*
140 And seyen, "He was a nygard, that no good myghte aspare

miser; spare

To frend ne to fremmed – the fend have his soule!   *stranger*
For a wrecchede hous he held al his lif tyme,
And that he spared and bispered, spene we in murthe!"

hoarded; locked up; amusement

'By lered, by lewed, that looth is to spene—
145 Thus goon hire goodes, be the goost faren.   *when the spirit is gone*
Ac for goode men, God woot, greet doel men maken,   *sorrow*
And bymeneth goode meteyyveres, and in mynde hem haveth

lament; food providers

In preieres and in penaunces and in parfit charite.'

---

130 witte . . . god] L&r (w.] þe wit
    WHm); of w. god the wit g.
132 Sectoures] L&rC; Executours
    wM.
133 þis] L&r; That WCr; Al F.
    spened] ?αC; spended β (despended
    W)F.
135 Ac] ?α (But F)K–D; And β.
136 kirke] WCrLM; cherche
    Hmgα?C.
    and] αC; as β.

138 entreþ; þe bisshop] cj K–D; trs
    All MSS (C).
139 -with] L&r; -myd WCr.
    men] W&r; meyne HmF.
142 he helde] L&r; trs W.
143 spene] LMR; spende Hm&r
    (dispende W).
144 spene] ?α; spende β (desp. W)F.
147 hem] αB; om ?β.
148 penaunces] W&r; sg Crg.

'What is charite?' quod I tho. 'A childissh thyng,' he seide—
                                                    childlike

'*Nisi efficiamini sicut parvuli, non intrabitis in regnum celorum*—
150 Withouten fauntelte or folie a fre liberal wille.' *childishness; generous*
    'Where sholde men fynde swich a frend with so fre an herte?
    I have lyved in londe,' quod I, 'my name is Longe Wille—
    And fond I nevere ful charite, bifore ne bihynde. *perfect; 'anywhere'*
    Men beth merciable to mendinaunts and to poore, *compassionate*
155 And wollen lene ther thei leve lelly to ben paied. *give; believe; honestly*
    Ac charite that Poul preiseth best and moost plesaunt to Oure
        Saveour— *pleasing*
    As *Non inflatur, non est ambiciosa, non querit que sua sunt*—
    I seigh nevere swich a man, so me God helpe,
    That he ne wolde aske after his, and outherwhile coveite *sometimes*
160 Thyng that neded hym noght – and nyme it, if he myghte! *he needed*
    'Clerkes kenne me that Crist is in alle places;
    Ac I seigh hym nevere soothly but as myself in a mirour: *teach*
    Hic in enigmate, tunc facie ad faciem.
    And so I trowe trewely, by that men telleth of charite,
    It is noght chaumpions fight, ne chaffare, as I trowe.'
                        (a matter of) prize-fighting; trade
165   'Charite,' quod he, 'ne chaffareth noght, ne chalangeth, ne craveth;
    As proud of a peny as of a pound of golde,
    And is as glad of a gowne of a gray russet *(a rough woollen material)*

149*a* Unless [you be converted and] become as little children, you shall not
    enter into the kingdom of heaven (Mt 18: 3).
152 I have lived in this world, my name is Tall Will / 'Perseverance itself',
    [*longanimitas*].
157 ... is not puffed up, Is not ambitious, seeketh not her own (I Cor 13:
    4–5).
162*a* [We see] here [through a glass] in a dark manner; but then face to face (I
    Cor 13: 12).
165 Charity does not engage in trade, lay claims, make demands.

152 I²] L&r; he WHmCr¹.   . sunt] L&r; sunt &c W.
    my ... wille] W&r (l. w.] *om* Y);   160 neded hym] β (-ed] -eþ g)C; *trs*
    & l. w. is my name F.   α.
154 and] β; ne F; *om* R.   162 a] β; *om* α.
156 plesau*nt*] W&r; pleseþ gF.   162*a* *Hic*] αMCK–D; *Ita* gL (*It* L);
    saueoure] β (lord WCr¹); god ?α   *om* w.
    (god in heuene F)Cr²³.   165 ne²] βF; noþer R.
157 As] L&r; Is wM; *om* GCBC.

As of a tunycle of Tarse or of trie scarlet.   *jacket; silk; choice*
He is glad with alle glade and good til alle wikkede,
170   And leneth and loveth alle that Oure Lord made.
Corseth he no creature, ne he kan bere no wrathe,   *curses; feel*
Ne no likynge hath to lye ne laughe men to scorne.
Al that men seyn, he leet it sooth, and in solace taketh,
                                                          considers; content
And alle manere meschiefs in myldenesse he suffreth.
175   Coveiteth he noon erthely good but heveneriche blisse.'
'Hath he anye rentes or richesse, or any riche frendes?'
'Of rentes ne of richesse ne rekketh he nevere,   *cares*
For a frend that fynt hym, failed hym nevere at nede: *provides for*
Fiat-voluntas-tua fynt hym everemoore.   *'Thy will be done'* (Mt 6: 10)
180   And if he soupeth, eet but a sop of *Spera in Deo*.
                                        sups; 'Hope in God' (Ps 41: 6)
He kan portreye wel the *Paternoster* and peynte it with *Aves*,
                                        draw; i.e. say his rosary
And outherwhile is his wone to wende on pilgrymages   *custom*
Ther poore men and prisons liggeth, hir pardon to have;
Though he bere hem no breed, he bereth hem swetter liflode,
185   Loveth hem as Oure Lord bit and loketh how thei fare.   *commands*
'And whan he is wery of that werk than wole he som tyme
Labouren in a lavendrye wel the lengthe of a mile,   *laundry*
And yerne into youthe, and yepeliche seche   *run; eagerly seek (out)*
Pride, with al the appurtenaunce, and pakken hem togideres,
190   And bouken hem at his brest and beten hem clene,   *cleanse with lye*

---

187 Work away for twenty minutes [the time taken to walk a mile] at the
(inward) cleansing of his soul (see *Sk ad loc.*).

170   And] β; He αY.
172   haþ to] βF; haue R.
      men] β; me R; non F.
175   good] β; godes α.
177   ne[2]] WCrLMα; *om* Hmg.
178   fynt] ?αC; fyndeþ βF.
180   eet] ?α(*om* F)L; eteþ WCr[1]; he
      eteþ HmCr[23]g (e.] ete YC).
181   Aues] βC; aue α.
182   is his] HmLM; is R; he is W&r.
      wone] L&rC; woned WGC

BoCot.
wende] L&rC; wenden WHmF.
pilgr.] WGYCBFC; *sg* L&r.
183   prisons] WHmLMRC;
      prisoners CrgF.
185   bit] α; biddeþ β (bade Cr).
187   a[1]] LR (*cf.* C); *om* W&r.
188   seche] ?α (þere seken F)K–D;
      speke β.
189   *ap*purtenaunce] L&r; *pl* WCr
      GMFC.

And leggen on longe with *Laboravi in gemitu meo*,

lay on (i.e. labour at)

And with warm water at hise eighen wasshen hem after.

Thanne he syngeth whan he doth so, and som tyme seith wepynge,

Cor contritum et humiliatum, Deus, non despicies.'

195 'By Crist! I wolde that I knewe hym,' quod I, 'no creature levere!'

more dear

'Withouten help of Piers the Plowman,' quod he, 'his persone

sestow nevere.'

will you see

'Where clerkes knowen hym,' quod I, 'that kepen Holi Kirke?' *Do*

'Clerkes have no knowyng,' quod he, 'but by werkes and by

wordes.

Ac Piers the Plowman parceyveth moore depper   *perceives; deeply*

200 What is the wille, and wherfore that many wight suffreth:

Et vidit Deus cogitaciones eorum.

For ther are ful proude herted men, pacient of tonge

restrained in speech

And buxome as of berynge to burgeis and to lordes,   *deferential*

And to poore peple han pepir in the nose,   *act superciliously*

And as a lyoun he loketh ther men lakken hise werkes.   *criticize*

205 'For ther are beggeris and bidderis, bedemen as it were,   *beadsmen*

Loken as lambren and semen lif-holy—   *(Who) look; lambs*

Ac it is moore to have hir mete on swich an esy manere

Than for penaunce and parfitnesse, the poverte that swiche taketh.

assume

'Therfore by colour ne by clergie knowe shaltow hym nevere,

appearances

---

191 'I have laboured in my groanings, [every night I will wash my bed: I will water my couch with my tears]' (Ps 6: 7).

194 ... a contrite and humbled heart, O God, thou wilt not despise (Ps 50: 19).

200a And God saw their thoughts (after Lk 11: 17) (C).

192 at] βR; of FC.

193 þanne] αCK–D; And þ. β.

195 quod I] W&r (*cf.* C); *om* g.

196 þe plowman] ?α (*om* F)M; Plowman β.

197 Where] L&r; Wheiþer WHm Cot.

198 knowyng] βF; knowlechynge R. by²] W&r; *om* Cr²³gF.

200 þat] Lα; What wM(wh *over erasure*); where g.

201 herted] βF; herte R.

202 -eys] L&r; -eises WCr²³GF.

206 semen] β; seme of F; semed R. lyf] L&r; ful W.

207 on] αK–D; yn Hmg; wiþ WCr LM. an] W&r; *om* gF.

208 and] W&r; or Crg.

209 hym] L&r (hem C); *om* WCr.

210 Neither thorugh wordes ne werkes, but thorugh wil oone, *will alone*
    And that knoweth no clerk ne creature on erthe
    But Piers the Plowman – *Petrus, id est, Christus.*
    For he nys noght in lolleris ne in londleperis heremytes. *vagabond*
    Ne at ancres there a box hangeth – alle swiche thei faiten.

                                                        on whom; cheat
215 Fy on faitours and *in fautores suos*!   *on their patrons*
    For Charite is Goddes champion, and as a good child hende,
                                                        well-behaved
    And the murieste of mouth at mete where he sitteth.

                                                        most cheerful; words
    The love that lith in his herte maketh hym light of speche,
    And is compaignable and confortatif, as Crist bit hymselve: *sociable*
    Nolite fieri sicut ypocrite tristes.
220 For I have seyen hym in silk and som tyme in russet,
    Bothe in grey, and in grys, and in gilt harneis—   *fur; gilded armour*
    And as gladliche he it gaf to gomes that it neded. *equally gladly; men*
       'Edmond and Edward, either were kynges   *both*
    And seintes yset – [stille] charite hem folwede. *considered; constantly*
225   'I have yseyen Charite also syngen and reden,   *(sc. as a priest)*
    Riden, and rennen in raggede wedes;
    Ac biddynge as beggeris biheld I hym nevere.
    Ac in riche robes rathest he walketh,   *soonest*
    Ycalled and ycrymyled and his crowne yshave.   *Wearing a cap*
230 And in a frere frokke he was yfounden ones—   *once*
    Ac it is fern ago, in Seint Fraunceis tyme;   *a long while*
    In that secte siththe to selde hath he ben knowen.   *order; since then*

---

212 Peter, that is, Christ; *cf.* and the rock [*petra*] was Christ (I Cor 10: 4), *also*
    Thou art Peter, and upon this rock . . . (Mt 16: 18). See Huppé, '*Petrus*'.
219–19a And is good company and cheering (to be with), as Christ himself
    tells (us to be): '[And, when you fast], be not as the hypocrites, sad . . .' (Mt
    6: 16).
229 Wearing a cap, and with his head anointed / his hair curling (round it),
    and with his head tonsured (C).

211 on] wα; in gLM.
213 nys] WHmLMR; is Crg; loveþ
     F.
218 The] β; To ?α (*l.* om F).
219a *tristes . . . ypocrite*] RC; *fieri
     sicut ypocrites tristes &c* βF (*&c*]
     om CrGYOC²F).

223 eyther] L&rC; *om* WCr.
224 stille] *cj* K–D; tyl Lg; for
     wM(*over erasure*); so α (C).
230 frere] RC; freres βF.
232 In] W&rC; and In g.
     knowen] L&r; founde WC.

'Riche men he recomendeth, and of hir robes taketh   *commends*
That withouten wiles ledeth hir lyves:
Beatus est dives qui . . .

235   'In kynges court he cometh ofte, ther the counseil is trewe;   *honest*
Ac if coveitise be of the counseil he wol noght come therinne.
In court amonges japeris he cometh but selde,
For braulynge and bakbitynge and berynge of fals witnesse.

'In the constorie bifore the commissarie he cometh noght ful ofte,
                                                        bishop's officer

240   For hir lawe dureth overlonge but if thei lacchen silver,   *lasts*
And matrimoyne for moneie maken and unmaken,
                                        marriage(s); (they) make

And that conscience and Crist hath yknyt faste,   *what; bound firmly*
Thei undoon it unworthily, tho doctours of lawe.

'Amonges erchebisshopes and other bisshopes and prelates of Holy
     Chirche,

245   For to wonye with hem his wone was som tyme,   *dwell; habit; once*
And Cristes patrimonye to the poore parcelmele dele.
                                        divide by portions

Ac avarice hath the keyes now and kepeth for his kynnesmen
And for his seketoures and his servaunts, and som for hir children.

'Ac I ne lakke no lif, but, Lord, amende us alle.   *disparage no person*
250   And gyve us grace, goode God, charite to folwe!
For whoso myghte meete with hym, swiche maneres hym eileth—
                                                        afflict

Neither he blameth ne banneth, bosteth ne preiseth,   *curses*
Lakketh, ne loseth, ne loketh up sterne,   *praises; sternly*

234*a* Blessed is the rich man [that is found without blemish] (Ecclus 31: 8).
240 For their legal proceedings drag on interminably unless they receive bribes.

234   ledeþ] βR; heere lowly ledyn F.
237   but] GML?α (*om* F)C; noȝt but
      W&r.
239   constorye] HmBLαC;
      Consistorie WCr?gM.
244–8   *In* α (*cf.* C)Sk; *ll. om* β.
244   *So* Sk; *as* 2 *ll. div after*
      bisshopes² R.
      Amonges . . . bischopes] R; with

Bisshopis & abbotys F.
246   patry-; dele] R; parsy-; þey
      deltyn F.
247   Ac; now] R; But; *om* F.
248   his²; here] R; *om*; his F.
251   with] L&r; myd W.
252   blameþ; banneþ] W&r; *trs* g.
253   *So* W&r; *l. trs with* 254 g.

Craveth, ne coveiteth, ne crieth after moore:
In pace in idipsum dormiam . . .
255 The mooste liflode that he lyveth by is love in Goddes passion;
    Neither he ne biddeth, ne beggeth, ne borweth to yelde;   *pay (back)*
    Misdooth he no man, ne with his mouth greveth.   *Harms; offends*
        'Amonges Cristene men this myldenesse sholde laste,
    In alle manere angres have this at herte—   *troubles; (they should) have*
260 That theigh thei suffrede al this, God suffrede for us moore
    In ensample we sholde do so, and take no vengeaunce
    Of oure foes that dooth us falsnesse – that is oure fadres wille.
    For wel may every man wite, if God hadde wold hymselve,
    Sholde nevere Judas ne Jew have Jesu doon on roode,   *crucified*
265 Ne han martired Peter ne Poul, ne in prison holden.
    Ac he suffrede in ensample that we sholde suffren also,
    And seide to swiche that suffre wolde that *Pacientes vincunt.*
        '*Verbi gratia,*' quod he – and verray ensamples manye.
                                                For example; true

    'In *Legenda Sanctorum*, the lif of holy seintes,
270 What penaunce and poverte and passion thei suffrede—   *pain*
    In hunger, in hete, in alle manere angres.   *afflictions*
        'Antony and Egidie and othere holy fadres   *Egidius*
    Woneden in wildernesse among wilde beestes;   *Dwelt*
    Monkes and mendinaunts, men by hemselve
275 In spekes and in spelonkes, selde speken togideres.   *hollows; caves*
    Ac neither Antony ne Egidie ne heremyte that tyme
    Of leons ne of leopardes no liflode ne toke,   *From; sustenance*
    But of foweles that fleeth – thus fynt men in bokes—   *fly; read*
    Except that Egidie after an hynde cride,   *doe; called*
280 And thorugh the mylk of that mylde beest the man was sustened;

254a In peace in the selfsame I will sleep, [and I will rest] (Ps 4: 9).
255 His chief sustenance is love (nourished by) Christ's sufferings.

254a *In* β (*&c*) W&r; *et requiescam*
      &c HmCrG (*&c*] *om* CrG)); *l. om*
      α.
255 þat] WHmLR; *om* CrgMF.
     by] βF; *om* R.
256 ne¹] ?α?C; *om* βF.
261 no] βF; *om* R.
263 wel . . . man] β; euery man may
     wel α.

264 ne] β; þe ?α (þat F)B.
268 verray] βR; verred F (C).
271 in²] W&r; & in g; & F.
273 wildernesse] βF; *pl* R.
275 in²] WHmYLF; *om* Cr?gMR.
278 of] β; of þe α.
     fynt] LR; fynde HmGB; fyndeþ
     W&r; is fownde F.
280 mylde] β (hynde B); meke ?α
     (*om* F).

Ac day bi day hadde he hire noght his hunger for to slake,
But selden and sondry tyme, as seith the book and techeth.
Antony on a day aboute noon tyme   *daily; midday*
Hadde a brid that broughte hym breed that he by lyvede;   *bird*
285 And though the gome hadde a gest, God fond hem bothe.

                                        guest; provided for

   'Poul *primus heremita* hadde parroked hymselve,

                                   the first hermit; enclosed

That no man myghte hym se for mosse and for leves.
Foweles hym fedde fele wyntres with alle   *many; moreover*
Til he foundede freres of Austynes ordre.   *(Augustinian canons)*
290 Poul, after his prechyng, paniers he made,   *i.e. the Apostle; baskets*
And wan with hise hondes that his wombe neded.   *earned; stomach*
Peter fisshed for his foode, and his felawe Andrew: *companion*
Som thei solde and som thei soden, and so thei lyved bothe.   *cooked*
And also Marie Maudeleyne by mores lyvede and dewes,   *roots*
295 Ac moost thorugh devocion and mynde of God Almyghty.

                                        contemplating

I sholde noght thise seven daies siggen hem alle

                                   could not in seven days

That lyveden thus for Oure Lordes love many longe yeres.
   'Ac ther ne was leoun ne leopard that on laundes wenten,   *glades*
Neither bere, ne boor, ne oother beest wilde
300 That ne fil to hir feet and fawned with the tailles;   *fell; tails*
And if thei kouthe han ycarped, by Crist, as I trowe,   *spoken*
Thei wolde have yfed that folk bifore wilde foweles.
For al the curteisie that beestes konne, thei kidde that folk ofte,

                                   are capable of; showed to

In likkyng and in lowynge, there thei on laundes yede.

                                   submitting (themselves); went

305 Ac God sente hem foode by foweles, and by no fierse beestes,

---

281 Ac] ?α (*om* F); And β.
282 tyme] α; tymes β.
283 on a day] α; adayes β.
184 hym] β; hym his R; hym to F.
285 fond] β; fedde α.
286 hym-] β; in hym- α.
289 ordre] W&r; o. or ellis frerys
     lyen B(+Bm) (*cf.* C) (C).
291 hise] W&r; *om* RC.
293 soden] βC; eeten α.

294 lyuede and] β; and by α.
297 many longe yeres] βC; amonges
     wilde bestes α.
298; 300 leo.; tailles] βF; *pl*; *sg* R.
303-4 *In* α (*cf.* C)*Sk*; *ll. om* β.
303 curteisie . . . kunne] R;
     ky3ndenesse þat þey cowde F.
304 in lowynge; laundes 3ede] R;
     lovynge; londis wentyn F.

In menynge that meke thyng mylde thyng sholde fede.

As a sign; creature

As who seith religious rightfulle men sholde fynde,

As if to say; upright; provide for

And lawefulle men to lif-holy men liflode brynge;

men who keep (God's) law

And thanne wolde lordes and ladies be looth to agulte,   *commit sin*

310 And to taken of hir tenaunts moore than trouthe wolde,

their honest due

Founde thei that freres wolde forsake hir almesse

Were they to find; give up

And bidden hem bere it there it [hath ben] yborwed.

For we ben Goddes foweles and abiden alwey,

Til briddes brynge us that we sholde [by lyve].   *live by*

315 For hadde ye potage and payn ynogh, and peny-ale to drynke,

stew; bread; cheap ale

And a mees thermyd of o maner kynde,   *dish; one*

Ye hadde right ynogh, ye religiouse – and so youre rule me tolde.

would have

"Numquam," dicit Job, "rugiet onager cum habuerit herbam?
Aut mugiet bos cum ante plenum presepe steterit?" Brutorum
animalium natura te condempnat, quia cum eis pabulum commune
sufficiat; ex adipe prodiit iniquitas tua.

  'If lewed men knewe this Latyn, thei wolde loke whom thei yeve,

take care whom they gave to

And avisen hem bifore a fyve dayes or sixe

And take advice well in advance

317a Will the wild ass [lit. never] bray, says Job, when he hath grass? Or will
the ox low when he standeth before a full manger? (Job 6: 5). The (very)
nature of brute beasts is a condemnation of you, since with them common
(?shared/ordinary) food suffices; your evil has originated from excess (exact
source unknown).

307 -ous] L&r (-ouns Hm); -ouses
W.
fynde] L&r (*cf.* C); fede WF.
308 brynge] L&r; sholde br. WF.
311 almesse] O&r; *pl* WHmLC.
312 hath ben] was *All MSS* (C).
313 foweles] W&r; foles Cr²³ (C).
314 þat] W&r; mete þat g.

by lyue] *trs All MSS* (C).
316 o] W&r; any g.
317 rule] β; ordre α.
317a -quam] W&rC; -quid Cr²³F.
rugiet] αCSk; rugit β.
hab. herbam] αOC; *trs* β.
brutorum . . . suffic.] βC; *om* α.
319 a] β; *om* αGOC².

320 Er thei [moore] amortisede to monkes or chanons hir rentes.

                                         conveyed; incomes from land

    Allas! lordes and ladies, lewed counseil have ye   *ill-advised are you*

    To yyve from youre heires that youre aiels you lefte,   *forefathers*

    And yyveth to bidde for yow to swiche as ben riche,   *pray*

    And ben founded and feffed ek to bidde for othere!   *enfeoffed*

325   'Who parfourneth this prophecie, of the peple that now libbeth—

                                        fulfils; among; live

    Dispersit, dedit pauperibus?

    If any peple parfourne that text, it are thise poore freres: *fulfil*

    For that thei beggen aboute, in buyldynge thei spene,

    And on hemself som, and swiche as ben hir laborers;

330 And of hem that habbeth thei taken, and yyveth hem that ne habbeth!

    'Ac clerkes and knyghtes, and communers that ben riche,

                                        common people

    Fele of yow fareth as if I a forest hadde   *Many; behave*

    That were ful of faire trees, and I fondede and caste   *tried; contrived*

    How I myghte mo therinne amonges hem sette.   *more; plant*

335 Right so ye riche – ye robeth that ben riche,   *clothe those who are*

    And helpeth hem that helpeth yow, and yyveth ther no nede is;

    As whoso filled a tonne ful of a fressh ryver,   *one who; tun; from*

    And wente forth with that water to woke with Themese.   *moisten*

    Right so ye riche, ye robeth and fedeth

340 Hem that han as ye han – hem ye make at ese.

---

320 Before alienating any more of their (income-yielding) properties in
    mortmain to (corporations of) monks and canons (regular).

323–4 And give (away your patrimony), in order that they should pray for
    you, to those who are wealthy And, moreover, have been established and
    (already) endowed with lands for the purpose, precisely, of praying for
    others.

326 He hath distributed, he hath given to the poor (Ps 111: 9); cf. II Cor 9: 9
    (C).

320 moore] *om All MSS*; *cf.* C (C).
    to ... Chanons] βR; sikirly vnto
    monkes F.
    rentes] L&r; rente W.
323 to[1]] L&r; it to WCrBF.
    as] αCrM; þat WHmgL.
326 *pauperibus*] W&r; *p. &c*
    HmYBLMR.
327 þat] wLMR; þis gF; þe Cr[23].

328 spene] LYO; spende GC[2]BR;
    spende it wCF (*trs* HmF).
329 as] ?β; þat BF; *om* R.
330 ne] L&r; nede BF; *om* w.
335 robeþ] WYCLM; robbeþ
    Hm&r.
337 ful] αK–D; *om* β.
    fressh] β; ful R; *om* F.
339 robeþ] WCLM; robbeth Y&r.

'Ac religiouse that riche ben sholde rather feeste beggeris *entertain*
Than burgeis that riche ben, as the book techeth:
Quia sacrilegium est res pauperum non pauperibus dare.
Item idem: peccatoribus dare est demonibus immolare.
Item: monache, si indiges et accipis, pocius das quam accipis;
Si autem non eges et accipis, rapis.
Porro non indiget monachus, si habeat quod nature sufficit.

'Forthi I counseille alle Cristene to conformen hem to charite—
For charite withouten chalangynge unchargeth the soule,
                                          undeniably; frees

345 And many a prison fram purgatorie thorugh hise preieres he
       delivereth.
Ac ther is a defaute in the folk that the feith kepeth,   *sc. the clergy*
Wherfore folk is the febler, and noght ferm of bileve.   *firm in faith*
As in lussheburwes is a luther alay, and yet loketh he lik a sterlyng:
                                          bad alloy
The merk of that monee is good, ac the metal is feble.   *imprint on*
350 And so it fareth by som folk now: thei han a fair speche,
Crowne and Cristendom, the kynges mark of hevene,
Ac the metal, that is mannes soule, [myd] synne is foule alayed:
                                          debased
Bothe lettred and lewed beth alayed now with synne,
That no lif loveth oother, ne Oure Lord, as it semeth.

342a For it is sacrilege not to give to the poor what is theirs (Peter Cantor, ch.
47, quoting St Jerome, Epist 66, sect. 8). Also, to give to sinners is to sacrifice
to devils (Peter Cantor, ch. 47, after Jerome). Also, monk, if you are in need
and receive, you are giving rather than receiving: but if you do not need and
(yet) accept, you are stealing (Peter Cantor, ch. 48, after Jerome) (*PL* 205:
147, 149, 152). Further, a monk is not in need if he has what suffices for
nature (cf. I Tim 6: 8).
348 As Luxembourg coins [light coins of poor quality] are alloyed with base
metal, and yet they look like (genuine) sterling (silver).
351 Tonsure and Christianity, the mark of the King of Heaven [*sc.* the sign of
the cross made in baptism (*Sk*)].

341 feeste] β; fede α.
342 -eys] L&r; -eises WCrG.
342a idem] α; *om* β.
       Item² ... rapis] β; *om* α.
345 he deliuereþ] β (he] *om* g); is
       deliuered ?α (is] ben F).

347 -fore] βF; *om* RCot.
348 As] wLMR; Ryght as F; and ?g
       (*om* Y).
352 myd] *cj* K–D; with *All MSS*
       (C).
353 alayed now] wL?α; *trs* ?gM; *l.*
       om GCBF.

355 For what thorugh werre and wikkede werkes and wederes
        unresonable,
    Wederwise shipmen and witty clerkes also   *Weather-wise, experienced*
    Han no bileve to the lifte, ne to the loore of philosophres.   *in; sky*
        'Astronomiens alday in hir art faillen,   *Astronomers*
    That whilom warned bifore what sholde bifalle after;
360 Shipmen and shepherdes, that with ship and sheep wenten,
    Wisten by the walkne what sholde bitide;   *sky; happen*
    As of wedres and of wyndes thei warned men ofte.
    Tilieris that tiled the erthe tolden hir maistres
    By the seed that thei sewe what thei selle myghte,   *sowed*
365 And what to leve and to lyve by, the lond was so trewe;   *reliable*
    Now failleth the folk of the flood and of the lond bothe—
    Shepherdes and shipmen, and so do thise tilieris:
    Neither thei konneth ne knoweth oon cours bifore another.
                                                skill, procedure
        'Astronomyens also aren at hir wittes ende:
370 Of that was calculed of the clem[a]t, the contrarie thei fynde.
                                        calculated concerning
    Grammer, the ground of al, bigileth now children: *basis; perplexes*
    For is noon of thise newe clerkes – whoso nymeth hede—
                                                    takes notice
    That kan versifie faire ne formaliche enditen,
    Ne naught oon among an hundred that an auctour kan construwe,
375 Ne rede a lettre in any language but in Latyn or in Englissh.
        'Go now to any degree, and but if Gile be maister,

---

365 And what (or, how much) to leave [? for seed-corn] (or, part with) and
    what (or, how much) to keep for their own food, the earth yielded so reliably
    and consistently.

370 *clemat* 'a region of the earth often considered with respect to its weather'
    (*MED s.v.*) (C).

373 Who can write good verses or compose (letters/ poetry) correctly.

355 what] αC; *om* β.
    vnresonable] W&r (res-] seas-
    Cr²³); vnstable F (C).
358 Astrono-] W&rC; Astro-
    OC²BLR.
359 byfalle] ?αC; falle βF.
360 ship and] βR; *om* F.
362 of²] α; *om* β.
365 to²] LMαK–D; what to wg.

369 Astrono-] W&r; Astro- C²BLR.
370 clemat] *so* C; clement α;
    element β (*pl* g) (C).
373 *In* L&r (-diten] -denten R)C; *l.
    om* w.
374 Ne] L&r (no Hm); Is OC²; *om*
    WCr.
375 in²; or in] W&r (in²] *om* Cr³F);
    om; & g.

And Flaterere his felawe [to fourmen hym under],   *teach*
Muche wonder me thynketh amonges us alle!
Doctours of decrees and of divinite maistres,   *canon law*
380 That sholde konne and knowe alle kynnes clergie,   *learning*
And answere to arguments and also to a *quodlibet*—
                                   general intellectual problem (C)
I dar noght siggen it for shame – if swiche were apposed, *questioned*
Thei sholde faillen in hir philosophie, and in phisik bothe.
    'Wherfore I am afered of folk of Holy Kirke,   *frightened by*
385 Lest thei overhuppen, as oothere doon, in Offices and in Houres.
                                            skip over parts
Ac theigh thei overhuppe – as I hope noght – oure bileve suffiseth;
As clerkes in Corpus Christi feeste syngen and reden   *feast of C. C.*
That *sola fides sufficit* to save with lewed peple—
And so may Sarsens be saved, scribes and Jewes.   *Moslems*
390   'Allas thanne! but oure looresmen lyve as thei leren us,
                           but (that); teachers; should live
And for hir lyvynge that lewed men be the lother God agulten.
For Sarsens han somwhat semynge to oure bileve,   *resembling*
For thei love and bileve in o [Lede] almyghty, *one (divine) person, lord*
And we, lered and lewed, [bileveth in oon God]—
395 Cristene and uncristene on oon God bileveth.
Ac oon Makometh, a man, in mysbileve   *into infidelity*
Broughte Sarsens of Surree – and see in what manere.

---

388 That 'Faith alone suffices' to save uneducated people with (*Pange lingua*, stanza 4) (C).
390–1 Alas, then, that our teachers should not live as they teach us to, And the laity as a consequence of *their* (holy) lives be all the more reluctant to offend God.

377 to . . . vnder] vnder hym to fourmen βR; to formen his speche & F (C).
378 Muche] βF; And muche R (*cf.* F at 377 *above*).
383 yn] GLMαC; of W&r.
385 offices] L&r; *sg* WGMF.
386 Ac] L&r (*om* Hm; but GF); And WCrC²C.
þouȝ] ?α (*om* F); if β.
suffiseth] β; *sufficit* α.

393 Lede] persone W&r; god Cr (C).
394 bileueþ . . . god] *cj* K–D; in on god bileueth L&r; in oon god almyȝty WCot (C).
395 *In* α (Cristene; bil.] R; & so cr; ben leven F)K–D; *l. om* β.
396 *So div from* 397 L&r; *after* brouȝte WCr.
Ac] BL?α (But F); And wgM.

'This Makometh was Cristene man, and for he moste noght ben a
pope,　*because; might*
Into Surrie he soughte, and thorugh hise sotile wittes　*went*
400　Daunted a dowve, and day and nyght hire fedde.　*Tamed; dove*
The corn that she croppede, he caste it in his ere;　*ate; put*
And if he among the peple preched, or in places come,
Thanne wolde the colvere come to the clerkes ere　*dove*
Menynge as after mete – thus Makometh hire enchauntede,
Seeking food; charmed
405　And dide folk thanne falle on knees, for he swoor in his prechyng
That the colvere that com so com from God of hevene
As messager to Makometh, men for to teche.
And thus thorugh wiles of his wit and a whit dowve
Makometh in mysbileve men and wommen broughte,　*false belief*
410　That lered there and lewed yit leeven on hise lawes.　*still believe*
'And siththe Oure Saveour suffred the Sarsens so bigiled
allowed; (to be) thus deceived
Thorugh a Cristene clerk acorsed in his soule—
Ac for drede of the deeth I dar noght telle truthe,
How Englisshe clerkes a colvere fede that Coveitise highte,
415　And ben manered after Makometh, that no man useth trouthe.
'Ancres and heremytes, and monkes and freres
Peeren to Apostles thorugh hire parfit lyvynge.　*Are as equals*
Wolde nevere the feithful Fader that hise ministres sholde
Of tiraunts that teneth trewe men taken any almesse,　*From; harm*
420　But doon as Antony dide, Dominyk and Fraunceys,　*(should) do*
Beneit and Bernard [bothe], the whiche hem first taughte
To lyve by litel and in lowe houses by lele mennes fyndynge.　*support*
Grace sholde growe and be grene thorugh hir goode lyvynge,

398　was] CrgK–D; was a
　　WHmLM.
　　man] Lα; *om* W&r.
　　a] W&r; *om* HmCrGCotMF.
400　Daunted] L&r; He d. WHmGF.
402–3　*In* βC; *ll. om* α.
402　places] wLMC; *sg* g.
404　en-] βC; *om* α.
407　As] β; And α.
410　lered . . . lewed] L&r (ler.]
　　leernede men F; ler.; lew.] *trs* Hm;
　　þere] *om* gF) (*cf.* C); lyued þo þere

and lyue WCrM (lyved *over
erasure,* þo +M).
413　Ac] L?α (But F); and HmgM;
　　om WCr.
417　Peeren] β; Peeres R; Been p. F.
420　and] β; or α.
421　and] β; or α.
　　bothe] *om All MSS* (C).
422　houses] βF; house R.
　　fyndynge] α; almesse β.
423　Grace] βF; Grasse RCot.
　　goode] β; lele α.

And folkes sholden fynde, that ben in diverse siknesse,

> *feel (v. MED s.v. 6c)*

425 The bettre for hir biddynges in body and in soule.   *prayers*
Hir preieres and hir penaunces to pees sholde brynge
Alle that ben at debaat, and bedemen were trewe: *strife; if*
Petite et accipietis . . .
"Salt saveth catel," siggen thise wyves;   *preserves; (here=) meat, fish*
Vos estis sal terre . . .
The hevedes of Holy Chirche — and thei holy were—   *heads; if*
430 Crist calleth hem salt for Cristene soules,
Et si sal evanuerit, in quo salietur?
Ac fressh flessh outher fissh, whan it salt failleth,   *lacks*
It is unsavory, for sothe, ysoden or ybake;   *ill-tasting; boiled*
So is mannes soule, soothly, that seeth no good ensample
Of hem of Holi Chirche that the heighe way sholde teche
435 And be gide, and go bifore as a good banyer,   *guide; standard-bearer*
And hardie hem that bihynde ben, and yyve hem good evidence.

> *embolden; example*

'Ellevene holy men al the world tornede   *converted*
Into lele bileve; the lightloker, me thynketh,   *more easily*
Sholde alle maner men, we han so manye maistres—
440 Preestes and prechours, and a pope above,
That Goddes salt sholde be, to save mannes soule.   *preserve/save*
'Al was hethynesse som tyme Engelond and Walis,

> *entirely pagan; Wales*

Til Gregory garte clerkes to go here and preche.   *made*
Austyn at Caunterbury cristnede the kyng there,

427a ... seek, and you shall find (Mt 7: 73).
428a, 430a You are the salt of the earth. [But], if the salt lose its savour,
  wherewith shall it be salted? (Mt 5: 13).

424 folkes] ?β; *sg* αHmCCot.
   fynde] L&r; fare WHm (*over
   erasure*).
426 brynge] β; hem bringe α.
428 catel] L&r; þe c. wYBF.
428a–91 *In* βR; *ll. om* F.
430 calleþ] β; called ?α.
430a *salietur*] L&r; s. *&c* WHm
   YBoCot.

431 Ac] L&r (but G); and C²C; for
   WCr.
433 good ensample] L&r; goode
   ensamples W.
435 a] β; *om* ?α.
443 garte] β (made G); and grete
   ?αB.
   here] w (hyder Hm)LM; *om* g?α.
   and] wBLM; & to ?g?α.
444 þere] ?α; *om* β.

445 And thorugh miracles, as men mow rede, al that marche he tornede
                                                         may; district, territory
     To Crist and to Cristendom, and cros to honoure,
     And follede folk faste, and the feith taughte   *baptized*
     Moore thorugh miracles than thorugh muche prechyng,
     As wel thorugh hise werkes as with hise holy wordes,
450 And [fourmed] what fullynge and feith was to mene.   *taught; baptism*
        'Clooth that cometh fro the wevyng is noght comly to were   *fit*
     Til it is fulled under foot or in fullyng stokkes,   *cleansing-frames*
     Wasshen wel with water and with taseles cracched,   *teazles; teased*
     Ytouked and yteynted and under taillours hande;   *tucked; stretched*
455 And so it fareth by a barn that born is of wombe: *child*
     Til it be cristned in Cristes name and confermed of the bisshop,
     It is hethene as to heveneward, and helplees to the soule.

                                          in respect of heaven, the soul
     "Hethen" is to mene after heeth and untiled erthe—

                                             derives from; unploughed
     As in wilde wildernesse wexeth wilde beestes,   *spring up*
460 Rude and unresonable, rennynge withouten keperes.

                                                   Untrained; keepers
        'Ye mynnen wel how Mathew seith, how a man made a feste:
     He fedde hem with no venyson, ne fesaunts ybake,   *pheasants*
     But with foweles that fram hym nolde, but folwede his whistlyng:
     Ecce altilia mea et omnia parata sunt . . .
     And with calves flessh he fedde the folk that he lovede.
465   'The calf bitokneth clennesse in hem that kepeth lawes;

                                                 stands for purity
     For as the cow thorugh kynde mylk the calf norisseth til an oxe,

                                       its own; feeds; until (it is) an oxe
     So love and leaute lele men susteneth;

463a Behold . . . my [beeves and] fatlings [are killed] and all things are ready
      (Mt 22: 4).

447 faste] β; *om* ?α.
450 And fourmed] Enformed *cj*
     K–D; And seide *All MSS* (C).
452 is] LM?α; be wg.
454 hande] β; *pl* ?αHm.
455 And] L&r; Right W.
     of] L&r; of a wM.
460 keperes] ?αK–D; cropers β
     (cro-] cre- GYOC²L; -ers] -iers W).

461 mynnen] ?β (menen CrHmOC²
     Cot; nymmen LGYBmBo);
     take ?αC.
     wel] β; wel hede α.
     how¹] β; whate ?αG.
463a &c] L&r; *om* WCrYBm.
467 So; leaute] β; So doth; l. and
     ?α.

And maidenes and mylde men mercy desiren
Right as the cow-calf coveiteth swete melke—
470 So [mowen] rightfulle men mercy and truthe.
And by the hond-fedde foweles [i]s folk understonde
That looth ben to lovye withouten lernynge of ensaumples. *unwilling*
Right as capons in a court cometh to mennes whistlynge—

chickens; yard

In menynge after mete folweth men that whistlen—   *Seeking food*
475 Right so rude men that litel reson konneth
Loven and bileven by lettred mennes doynges,   *actions*
And by hire wordes and werkes wenen and trowen;

form opinions; believe

And as tho foweles to fynde foode after whistlynge,
So hope thei to have hevene thorugh hir [wiss]ynge.   *instruction (C)*
480 And the man that made the feste the mageste bymeneth—   *signifies*
That is God, of his grace gyveth alle men blisse.   *(who) out of*
With wederes and with wondres he warneth us with a whistlere

tempests; portents

Where that his wil is, to worshipen us alle,   *do honour to*
And feden us and festen us for everemoore at oones.

485 'Ac who beth that excuseth hem that arn persons and preestes

(those) who

(That hevedes of Holy Chirche ben) that han hir wil here
Withouten travaille the tithe deel that trewe men biswynken—

the tenth part of the labour

Thei wol be wrooth for I write thus – ac to witnesse I take
Bothe Mathew and Mark and *Memento Domine David:*
Ecce audivimus e[a]m in Effrata . . .

---

487 Without doing a tenth part [with pun on *tithe(s)*] of the hard labour that
honest men have to engage in.
489–9a Both Matthew [28: 19] and Mark [16: 15; see 489a] and 'O Lord,
remember David'; 'Behold, we have heard of it [God's tabernacle] in
Ephrata' (Ps 131: 1, 6).

469 swete mylke] L&r; melk sw. W.   480 þe¹] by þe R.
470 mowen] don *All MSS* (C).   485 þat²] β; *om* ?α.
471–84 *In* R (=α)Sk; *ll. om* β.   aren] L&r; ben W.
471 is] *cj* K–D; his R.   486 chirche] β; cherches ?α.
479 wissynge] techynge *cj* Sk;   489a *In* ?αSk (*eam*) Sk; *eum* R); *l.*
whistlynge R (C).   *om* β.

490 What pope or prelate now parfourneth that Crist highte—
      Ite in universum mundum et predicate. . . ?
          'Allas, that men so longe on Makometh sholde bileve!
      So manye prelates to preche as the Pope maketh—*(There are) so many*
      Of Nazareth, of Nynyve, of Neptalym and Damaske.
      That thei ne wente as Crist wisseth – sithen thei wilne a name—
                                                    (Alas) that; title

495 To be pastours and preche the passion of Jesus,
      And as hymself seide, so to lyve and dye:
      Bonus pastor animam suam ponit . . .
      And seide it in salvacion of Sarsens and othere—
      For Cristene and uncristene, Crist seide to prechours,
      Ite vos in vineam meam . . .

500   'And sith that thise Sarsens, scribes and Jewes
      Han a lippe of oure bileve, the lightloker, me thynketh,   *portion*
      Thei sholde turne, whoso travaile wolde and teche hem of the Trinite:
                                      be converted; if anyone would work

      Querite et invenietis . . .
      For alle paynymes preieth and parfitly bileveth   *(here=) Moslems*
      In the [grete holy] God, and his grace asken,
505   And make hir mone to Makometh, hir message to shewe.   *pray*
      Thus in a feith lyveth that folk, and in a fals mene,
                                      a single faith; mediator

---

490*a* Go ye into the whole world and preach [the Gospel to every creature] (Mk 16: 15).
496*a* The good shepherd giveth his life [for his sheep] (Jn 10: 11).
499 Go you also into my vineyard (Mt 20: 4).
502*a* Seek, and you shall find (Mt 7: 7).
505 And pray to M. to make known their entreaty to God [*sc.* as mediator].

491 sholde] β; schullen ?α.
492 F *resumes here.*
494 wilne] αC; wille β.
     a] LR; þe FC; haue wgM.
496 so] L&r; go Cot; *om* WGYF.
498 For; and] β; To(& to F); and to
     α.
499 &c] ?β; *om* αCrCot L.
501 liʒtloker] L&r; lightlier
     WCrGC²C.
     me þynkeþ] β; it semeth α.
502 trauaille wolde] L&rC;

trauailed wM.
&] ?α (*cf.* C); to βF.
503–9, 528–31 *Ll. copied after*
     532–68 β, *after* 502a α (532–68
     om α); *re-arr* K–D (C).
503 and . . . bileueþ] βC; to on
     persone to helpe α (to²] of F).
504 In . . . God] In þe holy grete
     god β; On o god þei greden α (On]
     & on F) (C).
     grace] αCK–D; grace þei β.
506 lyueþ] LαC; leue wgM(C).

And that is routhe for the rightful men that in the reawme wonyen,

pity; just; dwell

And a peril to the Pope and prelates that he maketh,   *?dire disgrace*
That bere bisshopes names of Bethleem and of Babiloigne.
510   'Whan the hye kyng of hevene sente his sone to erthe,
Many miracles he wroughte man for to turne,   *convert, cause to repent*
In ensaumple that men sholde se by sadde reson   *serious argument*
Men myghte noght be saved but thorugh mercy and grace,
And thorugh penaunce, and passion, and parfit byleve;
515   And bicam man of a mayde, and *metropolitanus*,   *(=archbishop)*
And baptised and bishined with the blode of his herte

?illuminated (C)

Alle that wilned and wolde with inwit bileve it. *'with mind and heart'*
Many a seynt siththen hath suffred to deye,
Al for to enforme the feith in fele contrees deyeden—   *teach; many*
520   In Inde, and in Alisaundre, in Ermonye, in Spayne,   *Armenia*
In doelful deth deyeden for hir feith[e] sake.   *miserable, painful*
In savacion of the feith Seint Thomas was ymartired: *To preserve*
Amonges unkynde Cristene for Cristes love he deyede,
And for the right of al this reume and alle reumes Cristene.

(cause of) justice in; kingdom

525   Holy Chirche is honoured heighliche thorugh his deying;
He is a forbisene to alle bisshopes and a bright myrour,

example; image, pattern

---

507   þe¹] ?αC; *om* βF.
508   a] W&r (*l. om* F); in a ?g (a)
    om GOC²).
    and] β; and to ?α.
509   of²] Hm&r; *om* WYLM.
510–27   *In* αCSk; *ll. om* β.
512   men] R; *om* F.
    by] *so* CK–D; þat by α (C).
514   beleve] FCSk; byle R.
515   man; *metropolitanus*] RC; *om*;
    m. after F.
516   And; bischined] RC; & was;
    ysygned F(C).

517   innewit] RC; wit F.
518   hath] R; haven F.
519   enforme; deyeden] R; ferme;
    dyȝen F.
520   and¹] RC; in F.
    in⁴] FC; and in R.
521   In; deyeden] R; & in; þey
    dyeden F.
    feithe] faith R; feyþis F.
522   Thomas] FCSk; *erased* R.
523   Amonges] RC; And am. F.
    loue] R; *om* F.
526   a forbysene] RC; beleve F.

And sovereynliche to swiche that of Surrye bereth the name,

supremely; Syria, pagan lands

And naught to huppe aboute in Engelond to halwe mennes auteres,

skip; sanctify; altars

And crepe in amonges curatours and confessen ageyn the lawe:

Nolite mittere falsem in messem alienam . . .

530 Many man for Cristes love was martired amonges Romaynes

the Romans

Er Cristendom were knowe ther or any cros honoured.

'It is ruthe to rede how rihtwise men lyvede—   *pitiful*

How thei defouled hir flessh, forsoke hir owene wille,   *mortified*

Fer fro kyth and fro kyn yvele yclothed yeden,   *went about*

535 Baddely ybedded, no book but conscience,

Ne no richesse but the roode to rejoisse hem inne:

Absit nobis gloriari nisi in cruce Domini nostri . . .

And tho was plentee and pees amonges poore and riche;

And now is routhe to rede how the rede noble

Is reverenced er the roode, receyved for the worthier

540 Than Cristes cros that overcam deeth and dedly synne.

the cross of C., who . . .

And now is werre and wo, and whoso why asketh—

For coveitise after cros; the croune stant in golde.

527–29a And supremely an example to bishops appointed to sees in Syria [sc.
to go there and preach Christianity at the risk of their lives] And not to run
all over England to consecrate altars And insinuate themselves into (the
affairs of) parish-priests, and hear confessions unlicensed [by the ordinary]:
'Do not put your sickle to another man's corn' (cf. Deut 23: 25).

536a God forbid that I should glory, save in the cross of our Lord (Gal 6: 14).

542 Because of desire for the cross [imprinted on the noble]; the prize [they
seek] is to be found in gold (C).

528 β *resumes.*
And . . . to¹] αC; That β (C).
aboute . . . to²] W&r (in) *om* OC²;
here in R)C; heere & þere for F.
mennes] βC; *om* αHm.

529 in] αCK–D; *om* β.
and] αWC; *om* β.
confessen] W&rC; c. men R;
confessyon GC²B.

529a *alienam &c*] WHmCCotLMC;
a. *&c* ?gF; *&c* R.

530 man] βC; a man αCrCot.
amonges romaynes] ?αCK–D; in
Romayne βF (Rom.] Rome CrCot;
greete roome F).

531 cristendom] αCK–D; any cr. β.
were] αCK–D; was β.

532–68 *In* β (*copied after* 502a *and
foll. by* 503–9, 528–31)C; *ll. om* α.

539 Rode] L&r; R. and WCrBC.
þe²] L&rC; *om* W.

Bothe riche and religious, that roode thei honoure
That in grotes is ygrave and in gold nobles.   *groats; engraved*
545 For coveitise of that cros [clerkes] of Holy Kirke
Shul torne as Templers dide – the tyme approcheth faste.   *fall*
    '[Mynne] ye noght, wise men, how tho men honoured   *Recall*
Moore tresor than trouthe? I dar noght telle the sothe;
Reson and rightful doom tho religiouse demede.   *judged*
550 Right so, ye clerkes, for youre coveitise, er [come aught] longe,
Shal thei demen *dos ecclesie*, and [depose youre pride]:
Deposuit potentes de sede . . .
    'If knyghthod and kynde wit, and the commune and conscience
Togideres love leelly, leveth it wel, ye bisshopes—
The lordshipe of londes [lese ye shul for evere],
555 And lyven as *Levitici*, as Oure Lord yow techeth: *the Levites*
Per primicias et decimas . . .
    'Whan Costantyn of curteisie Holy Kirke dowed
                                    Constantine; endowed
With londes and ledes, lordshipes and rentes,   *properties*
An aungel men herden an heigh at Rome crye: *aloud*
"*Dos ecclesie* this day hath ydronke venym,   *poison*
560 And tho that han Petres power arn apoisoned alle!"
A medicyne moot therto that may amende prelates,   *is needed*
That sholden preie for the pees; possession hem letteth. *hinders*
Taketh hire landes, ye lordes, and let hem lyve by dymes; *tithes*
If possession be poison, and inparfite hem make,
565 Good were to deschargen hem for Holy Chirches sake,   *unburden*

551–51*a* Shall they pass judgement on (those who hold) the temporal
     possessions of the Church . . . 'He hath put down the mighty from their seat'
     (Lk 1: 52).
555*a* By first-fruits and tithes (cf. Deut 12: 6).

545 clerkes] *so* CK–D; men β (C).
546 torne] W&r; ouerturne B (ouer]
     +Bm).
547 Minne] *so* CK–D; Wite β (C).
     wyse] L&r; ye wise wG.
549 þo] L&rC; þe w.
     demede] W&r; damneden B(*over
     erasure* Bm)C (C).
550 come auht] *so* CK–D; *om* β
     (C).
551 depose; youre pride] *trs* β (C).

552 þe] WC; *om* L&r.
     &³] B (+Bm)CK–D; by WCr
     +M; *om* L&r.
554 of] L&rC; of youre W.
     lese . . . euere] *so* CK–D; for e. shul
     ye l. β (shul ye) *trs* g) (C).
555 yow] L&rC; *om* W.
555*a* &c] L&rC; *om* YL.
556 kirke] WCrLMC; chirche gHm.
563 let] CrGOC²LC; leteþ
     WHmYCBM.

And purgen hem of poison, er moore peril falle.
If preesthode were parfit, the peple sholde amende,
That contrarien Cristes lawe, and Cristendom dispise.

                      act against; (their) Christianity

   'Every bisshop that bereth cros, by that he is holden   *obliged*
570 Thorugh his province to passe, and to his peple to shewe hym,
Tellen hem and techen hem on the Trinite to bileve,
And feden hem with goostly foode, and nedy folk to fynden.

                      spiritual; provide for

Ac Ysaie of yow speketh and Osias bothe,   *Isaiah; Hosea*
That no man sholde be bisshop but if he hadde bothe
575 Bodily foode and goostly foode to gyve there it nedede:
*In domo mea non est panis neque vestimentum, et ideo nolite
   constituere me regem.*
Osias seith for swiche that sike ben and feble,
Inferte omnes decimas in orreum meum, ut sit cibus in domo mea.
   'Ac we Cristene creatures, that on the cros bileven,
Arn ferme as in the feith – Goddes forbode ellis!—

               God forbid that it be otherwise

580 And han clerkes to kepen us therinne, and hem that shul come after
   us.
And Jewes lyven in lele lawe – Oure Lord wroot it hymselve
In stoon, for it stedefast was, and stonde sholde evere—   *permanent*
Dilige Deum et proximum, is parfit Jewen lawe—

                  (which) is; Jews', Jewish

575*a* . . . in my house there is no bread nor clothing: make me not ruler [of the
   people] (Is 3: 7).
577 Bring all the tithes into the storehouse that there may be meat in my house
   (Mal 3: 10).
583 Love God and your neighbour (cf. Mt 22: 37–40, Deut 6: 5, Lev 19: 18).

568   *After this* β *copies* 503–9,
    528–31, *and* α *resumes.*
569   he] βF; *om* R.
570   to³] WCrLMR; *om* HmgF.
571   techen] β; schewen α.
572*b–5a In* αSk; *om* β (572*a as one*
    l. with 575*b*).
572   fynden] R; feeden F.
573   Ac; of yow speketh] R; But; as
    how þou spekist F.
575   foode²] R; *om* F.
    to] α; and β.

nedede] ?α; nedeþ βF.
575*a* me] W&r; me in g.
    Regem] W&r; r. &c HmYB; regem
    y 3 Lα (y.] ysa. F).
577   decimas] L&r; *om* W.
    sit] CrOC²Sk; *om* W&r.
    mea] wLMF; mea &c HmR; &c g.
579   ferme] β; for me R; formed F.
580   vs²] WLMR; *om* HmCrg.
581   it] W&r; *om* g.
582   was] W&r; ys g.

And took it Moyses to teche men, til Messie coome;

                                gave; the Messiah should come

585 And on that lawe thei leve, and leten it the beste.   *believe; consider*

And yit knewe thei Crist, that Cristendom taughte,

And for a parfit prophete that muche peple savede

Of selkouthe sores; thei seighen it ofte—   *strange*

Bothe of miracles and merveilles, and how he men festede,   *fed*

590 With two fisshes and fyve loves fyve thousand peple—   *loaves*

And by that mangerie thei myghte wel se that Messie he semede;

                                      feeding

And whan he lifte up Lazar, that leid was in grave,

                              raised to life Lazarus

And under stoon deed and stank, with stif vois hym callede,

                                      loud voice

Lazare, veni foras,   *Lazarus, come forth* (Jn 11: 43)

Dide hym rise and rome right bifore the Jewes.   *(And) made; walk*

595 Ac thei seiden and sworen, with sorcerie he wroughte,

And studieden to struyen hym – and struyden hemselve, *destroy(ed)*

And thorugh his pacience hir power to pure noght he broughte:

                               absolutely nothing

Pacientes vincunt.

  'Daniel of hire undoynge devyned and seide,   *prophesied*

Cum sanctus sanctorum veniat cessabit unxio vestra.

600 And yit wenen tho wrecches that he were *pseudo-propheta*

                                   a false prophet

And that his loore be lesynges, and lakken it alle, *teaching; disparage*

And hopen that he be to come that shal hem releve— *redeem, rescue*

Moyses eft or Messie hir maistres yit devyneth.

                            again; learned men foretell

---

599 When the Saint of Saints shall come, your anointing [*sc.* the special relation of the Jews with God] shall come to an end (cf. Dan 9: 24, 26).

584 men] β; it hem α.

585 leuen] Hm&rCK–D; lyue WL. and²] αC; ʒit and β. it] βR; it for FC.

587 And] αC; *om* β.

589 he] βF; *om* R.

591 þei] αK–D; men β.

593 deed and stank] β; st. and dede R; he st. ded F.

hym] W&r (he h. F); & G; he y.

599 *So* β; *Cum veniat s. s. &c* α(*&c*] *om* F).

600 ʒet] L&r (*cf.* C); *om* WCr.

603 hir . . . ʒit] β; ʒit here m. dyu. α (m.] maystries R).

Ac pharisees and sarsens, scribes and Grekes
605 Arn folk of oon feith – the fader God thei honouren.
'And sithen that the Sarsens and also the Jewes
Konne the firste clause of oure bileve, *Credo in Deum patrem* *creed*
omnipotentem,
Prelates of Cristene provinces sholde preve, if thei myghte,

endeavour

Lere hem litlum and litlum *Et in Jesum Christum filium,*

To teach them little by little

610 Til thei kouthe speke and spelle *Et in Spiritum sanctum,*   *make out*
And rendren it and recorden it with *remissionem peccatorum,*
Carnis resurreccionem et vitam eternam. Amen.'

---

607 I believe in God the Father Almighty (first clause of Apostles' Creed).
609 And in Jesus Christ his (only) son, our Lord (second clause of Ap. Cr.).
610 And (I believe) in the Holy Ghost (seventh clause of Ap. Cr.).
611–11a And construe it and declare it, with 'the forgiveness of sins' (tenth
    clause of Ap. Cr.) The resurrection of the body and the life everlasting
    (eleventh and twelfth clauses).

604   pharisees; Sar3ens] W&r; *trs* g.   & l. F.
   Grekis] L&r; Iewes WHm.   610   *et*] β; and R; *Credo* F.
607   *omnipotentem*] W&r; *o. &c*   611   rendren] L (*cf.* C); reden W&r
   HmR; *&c* OC²; *om* Cr?g?C.   (C).
608   prouinces] βF; *sg* R.
609   Lere] L&rC; To lere WCrBM;

Passus XVI

'Now faire falle yow,' quod I tho, 'for youre faire shewyng!
For Haukyns love the Actif Man evere I shal yow lovye.
Ac yit am I in a weer what charite is to mene.'   *doubt, perplexity*
  'It is a ful trie tree,' quod he, 'trewely to telle.   *choice*
5 Mercy is the more therof; the myddul stok is ruthe;   *root; trunk*
The leves ben lele wordes, the lawe of Holy Chirche;   *faithful*
The blosmes beth buxom speche and benigne lokynge;   *kind*
Pacience hatte the pure tree, and pore symple of herte,
And so thorugh God and goode men groweth the fruyt Charite.'
10 'I wolde travaille,' quod I, 'this tree to se, twenty hundred myle,
    travel
And to have my fulle of that fruyt forsake al other saulee.   *food*
Lord!' quod I, 'if any wight wite whiderout it groweth?'
    out of which place
  'It groweth in a gardyn,' quod he, 'that God made hymselve;
Amyddes mannes body the more is of that stokke.   *root; trunk*
15 Herte highte the herber that it inne groweth,   *arbour, garden*
And *Liberum Arbitrium* hath the lond to ferme,   *tend*
Under Piers the Plowman to piken it and to weden it.'   *hoe; weed*

'Piers the Plowman!' quod I tho, and al for pure joye
That I herde nempne his name anoon I swowned after,   *mentioned*
20 And lay longe in a love-dreem; and at the laste me thoughte

---

8 The actual tree itself is called 'Patience and humble simplicity of heart' . . .

Collation WHmCrGYOC²CB
(56–91 *om* CB)LMRF.
RUBRIC *Passus xvjᵘˢ &c et primus
de dobet* W&r (*&c . . . dobet*] *om*
YOC²M; *xvjᵘˢ . . . et*] *om* Hm; *pr.*]
secundus BHm); *Passus xvᵘˢ de
visione vt supra* R; *om* G; *Incipit P.
xijᵘˢ* F.
4 trewely] β; treuthe ?α (good t. F).
8 þore] L&r (p. and B); pure wG
YOC².

9 and²] CrgαK–D; and þoruȝ
WLM; and pure Hm.
11 to] Cr²³gαK–D; for to wLM.
pal . . . saulee] L&r; alle oþere
saulees WG.
12 -out] β; -out þat ?α; *om* HmF.
16 to] L&r; þe W.
17 Vnder] β; And vnder α.
to²] W&r; *om* gF.
20 loue] W&r; lone Cr¹(C).
dreem] W&r; deerne C.

That Piers the Plowman al the place me shewed,
And bad me toten on the tree, on top and on roote.   *gaze*
With thre piles was it underpight – I parceyved it soone.

props; supported

'Piers,' quod I, 'I preie thee – whi stonde thise piles here?'
25 'For wyndes, wiltow wite,' quod he, 'to witen it fro fallyng – *keep*
Cum ceciderit iustus non collidetur quia Dominus supponit manum
suam—
And in blowyng tyme abite the flowres, but if thise piles helpe.

(they) nip off

The World is a wikked wynd to hem that wolden truthe:
Coveitise comth of that wynd and crepeth among the leves
And forfret neigh the fruyt thorugh manye faire sightes.

almost nips off

30 And with the firste pil I palle hym doun – that is *Potencia Dei Patris.*

strike; the power of God the Father

'The Flessh is a fel wynd, and in flouryng tyme, *fierce; i.e. in youth*
Thorugh likynge and lustes so loude he gynneth blowe *sexual desire*
That it norisseth nyce sightes and som tyme wordes, *fosters; foolish*
And wikkede werkes therof, wormes of synne,
35 And forbiteth the blosmes right to the bare leves.   *eats away*
Thanne sette I to the secounde pil, *Sapiencia Dei Patris—*

proceed; the wisdom of God the Father

That is the passion and the power of oure prince Jesu.
Thorugh preieres and thorugh penaunces and Goddes passion in
    mynde,
I save it til I se it ripen and somdel yfruyted.   *somewhat in fruit*
40 'And thanne fondeth the Fend my fruyt to destruye   *tries*

25a When the just man shall fall he shall not be bruised: for the Lord putteth
     his hand under him (Ps 36: 24).
26 . . . in the blossoming season (or, possibly, in time of blustery weather).

22   me] L&r; me to wYC.
25   witen] β; kepen α.
25a *manum suam*] L&r (*m.*]
     misericordiam B); ma (*cropped*)W.
27   *So* βC; *run together with* 28 α.
     to . . . truthe] βC (wolden] LC;
     willen wGM); *om* α.
28   Coueitise . . . wynd] βC; *om* α.
29   -frete] YCLMα; -freteþ W&r.

30   And] ?α (*om* F)C; Thanne β
     (That CB).
     palle] WCrYLMRC; pulle ?g (*om*
     Cot); call F.
     þat ys] βR; ys F; *om* GC.
     dei patris] L&r (*p.*] *om* F)C; de
     (*cropped*) W.
38   Thoru3[1]] β; with α.
     þoru3[2]] W&r; *om* gF.

With alle the wiles that he kan, and waggeth the roote,   *shakes*
And casteth up to the crop unkynde neighebores,   *throws; top*
Bakbiteris brewecheste, brawleris and chideris,   *'Start-fight slanderers'*
And leith a laddre therto – of lesynges are the ronges—   *rungs*
45 And feccheth awey my floures somtyme bifore bothe myne eighen.
Ac *Liberum Arbitrium* letteth hym som tyme,   *hinders*
That is lieutenaunt to loken it wel, bi leve of myselve: *guard*
Videatis qui peccat in Spiritum Sanctum numquam remittetur . . .
hoc est idem, qui peccat per liberum arbitrium non repugnat.

'Ac whan the Fend and the Flessh forth with the Worlde
Manacen bihynde me, my fruyt for to fecche,   *threaten*
50 Thanne *Liberum Arbitrium* laccheth the thridde planke   *seizes*
And palleth adoun the pouke pureliche thorugh grace   *devil; wholly*
And help of the Holy Goost – and thus have I the maistrie.' *victory*

'Now faire falle yow, Piers!' quod I, 'so faire ye discryven *describe*
The power of thise postes and hire propre myghte.
55 Ac I have thoughtes a threve of thise thre piles—
                                    number (lit. bundle); about
In what wode thei woxen, and where that thei growed,
For alle are thei aliche longe, noon lasse than oother,   *equally; smaller*
And to my mynde, as me thynketh, on o more thei growed; *one root*
And of o greetnesse and grene of greyn thei semen.'   *width; colour*
60 'That is sooth,' seide Piers, 'so it may bifalle.
I shal telle thee as tid what this tree highte.   *at once; is called*
The ground there it groweth, goodnesse it hatte;
And I have told thee what highte the tree: the Trinite it meneth'—
                                                         signifies
And egreliche he loked on me, and therfore I spared *sharply;refrained*
65 To asken hym any moore therof, and bad hym ful faire *courteously*

47a You may see (by this that) 'He who sins against the Holy Ghost, it shall
     not be forgiven him' [Mt 12: 32]; which is the same (as saying), 'he who sins
     through his free will does not resist [sin, as he should]' (source unidentified).

43 brewe-] ?α (& boosteris &   planke] αK–D; plante β.
    F)K–D; breke β (brokke M; b. þe   51 pureliche] β; priueliche α.
    W).   54 my3te] L&r; my3tes WHmF.
45 by-] αGCCotC; to- BmBo; a-   55 Ac] W&r (but F); And Crg.
    W&r.   56–91 *Ll.* om CB; GYOC² =?g.
46 hym] W&r; hem HmCr²³R.   57 are þei] W&r; om ?g.
47a *rem. &c*] β; *re &c* ?α (om F). 58 growed] W&r; growe ?g.
48 whan] β; what α.   59 of¹] β; al of F; om R.
50 thridde] Lα (*cf.* C); firste wgM. 60 seide] Lα; quod wgM.

To discryve the fruyt that so faire hangeth.   *describe*
  'Heer now bynethe,' quod he tho, 'if I nede hadde,
Matrimoyne I may nyme, a moiste fruyt withalle.   *take*
Thanne Continence is neer the crop as kaylewey bastard.

top; a Cailloux pear (C)

70 Thanne bereth the crop kynde fruyt and clennest of alle—
Maidenhode, aungeles peeris, and rathest wole be ripe, *peers; soonest*
And swete withouten swellyng – sour worth it nevere.'   *becomes*
  I preide Piers to pulle adoun an appul, and he wolde,   *if*
And suffre me to assaien what savour it hadde.   *allow; try*

75   And Piers caste to the crop, and thanne comsed it to crye;

?reached; began

He waggede widwehode, and it wepte after;   *shook*
And whan he meved matrimoyne, it made a foul noise,
That I hadde ruthe whan Piers rogged, it gradde so rufulliche.

shook; cried; piteously

For evere as thei dropped adoun the devel was redy,
80 And gadrede hem alle togideres, bothe grete and smale—
Adam and Abraham and Ysaye the prophete,   *Isaiah*
Sampson and Samuel, and Seint Johan the Baptist;
Bar hem forth boldely – nobody hym lette—   *He carried; hindered*
And made of holy men his hoord *in Limbo Inferni*,   *verge of hell (C)*
85 There is derknesse and drede and the devel maister.
  And Piers, for pure tene, that a pil he laughte,   *anger; one; seized*
And hitte after hym, happe how it myghte,   *struck out*
Filius by the Faderes wille and frenesse of *Spiritus Sancti*,
To go robbe that rageman and reve the fruyt fro hym.   *coward*
90   And thanne spak *Spiritus Sanctus* in Gabrielis mouthe   *spoke*

---

70 Finally, the uppermost part bears a natural fruit, the finest / most pure of all.

88 The Son, by the will of the Father and grace [*lit.* generosity] of the Holy Spirit.

69 Thanne] W&r; And M; þat ?g.
73 I preide] βF; In priede R.
   to] L&r; þo to W.
76 He] A ?αC; And βF (& anoon F).
77 he] α (*cf.* C)K–D; it β.
78 þat I had] L&r (I] *om* R); þan had y F; And I WHm; I Cr.
   rogged] β; rused R; rusched F.

81 Abraham] W&rC; eue ?g.
83 hym] W&rC; hem ?gR.
   lette] αCrC; letted β.
86 þat] L&r; of þat WCr; þo F.
   lau3te] L&r; rau3te W; caught Cr.
87 And] L&r; He w.
   happe] L&r; hitte WCr.
88 faderes] αCrC; fader β.
89 reue] βC; reuend R; bereue F.
90 Gabrielis] βFC; gabriel R.

To a maide that highte Marie, a meke thyng withalle,
That oon Jesus, a justice sone, moste jouke in hir chambre   *rest*
Til *plenitudo temporis* tyme comen were *'the time of the fulness of time'*
That Piers fruyt floured and felle to be rype.   *should happen*

95 And thanne sholde Jesus juste therfore, and bi juggement of armes,
                    joust; (to settle) by trial-at-arms
Wheither sholde fonge the fruyt – the fend or hymselve.   *Which*
   The maide myldeliche tho the messager graunted,
                                        humbly; consented to
And seide hendeliche to hym, 'Lo me his handmaiden   *courteously*
For to werchen his wille withouten any synne:
Ecce ancilla Domini, fiat michi . . .'

100   And in the wombe of that wenche was he fourty woukes,
                                        girl; weeks
Til he weex a faunt thorugh hir flessh, and of fightyng kouthe,
                                        grew; child; learnt
To have yfoughte with the fend er ful tyme come.
And Piers the Plowman parceyved plener tyme,   *the fullness of time*
And lered hym lechecraft, his lif for to save,   *taught; medicine*
105 That though he were wounded with his enemy, to warisshen
    hymselve;   *cure*
And dide hym assaie his surgerie on hem that sike were,
                                        try; medical skill
Til he was parfit praktisour, if any peril fille; *practitioner; should befall*
And soughte out the sike and synfulle bothe,
And salvede sike and synfulle, bothe blynde and crokede,   *lame*
110 And commune wommen convertede and to goode turnede:
Non est sanis opus medicus, set male habentibus . . .

99*a* Behold the handmaid of the Lord; be it done unto me [according to thy
    word] (Lk 1: 38).
110*a* They that are in health need not a physician, but they that are ill (Mt 9:
    12).

92   iustice] L&r; Iustices WHm
     OC²Cot?C.
93   tyme] αCK–D; fully β.
95   and²] & ?αC; *om* βF.
96   fonge] W&r (song Cr¹); foonde
     YCBLR (C).
99*a* &c] W&r; *secundum verbum
     tuum* HmGBF (t.] t. &c HmBo).
103 plener] β; þe p. ?α (þe] in þat

     F).
106 -gerye] L&r; -genrie
     WHmBmBo.
110 And] βFC; *om* R.
110*a* -cus] W&r; -co CrOC²CotM;
     -ci R; -cine G.
     male . . . &c] ?α (m. h. &c R; &c]
     om F); in &c ?β (in] *infirmis* OC²;
     om CrM).

Bothe meseles and mute, and in the menyson blody—

Ofte he heeled swiche, he ne held it for no maistrie, *great achievement*

Save tho he leched Lazar, that hadde yleye in grave   *when; cured*

Quatriduanus quelt – quyk dide hym walke.

115 Ac as he made that maistrie, *mestus cepit esse*,   *miracle*

And wepte water with hise eighen – ther seighen it manye.   *saw*

Some that the sighte seighen seiden that tyme

That he was leche of lif, and lord of heigh hevene.

Jewes jangled therayein that juggede lawes,   *objected violently to it*

120 And seide he wroghte thorugh wichecraft and with the develes

    myghte:

Demonium habes . . .

'Thanne are ye cherles,' quod Jesus, 'and youre children bothe,

And Sathan youre Saveour – yowself now ye witnessen:

For I have saved yowself, and youre sones after,

Youre bodies, youre beestes, and blynde men holpen,   *helped*

125 And fed yow with fisshes and with fyve loves,   *loaves*

And lefte baskettes ful of broke mete – bere awey whoso wolde—'

        fragments of food

And mysseide the Jewes manliche, and manaced hem to bete,

        rebuked; boldly; threatened

And knokked on hem with a corde, and caste adoun hir stalles

        of those

That in chirche chaffareden or chaungeden any moneie,   *traded*

130 And seide it in sighte of hem alle, so that alle herden,

'I shal overturne this temple and adoun throwe,

And in thre daies after edifie it newe,   *rebuild it*

And maken it as muche outher moore in alle manere poyntes

        great; respects

As evere it was, and as wid – wherfore I hote yow,   *wide; bid*

---

111 Lepers and the dumb, and those suffering from a bloody flux.
114 Four days dead – made him walk alive (Jn 11: 39).
115 (Jesus) wept [*lit.* became sad] (cf. Mt 26: 37, Jn 11: 35).
120a He hath a devil [and is mad] (Jn 7: 20, 8:48; cf. 10: 20) (C).

112 he[1]] L&r; *om* W.
115 þat] αC; þe β.
119 þat] ?α (þo þat F)K–D; and β.
120a habes] L&rC; habet W.
121 Jesus] ?α (ihc R; crist F)CS*k*;
  ich β.

122 yow-] YLMR(*cf.* C); your-
  Hm&r; ye W.
123 and] αCK–D; seiþ crist and β.
125 fisshes] L&r; two f. wFM(ij
  +M).
126 mete] W&rC; brede g.
131 throwe] L&r; þ. it W; it þ. F.

135 Of preieres and of parfitnesse this place that ye callen:
    Domus mea domus oracionis vocabitur.'
        Envye and yvel wil ar[ne] in the Jewes: *welled up (C)*
    Thei casten and contreveden to kulle hym whan thei myghte;
                                                         schemed; plotted
    Eche day after oother hir tyme thei awaiteden,
                                              opportunity; watched for
    Til it bifel on a Friday, a litel bifore Pasqe.   *occurred; Passover*
140 The Thursday bifore, there he made his cene,   *held; supper (C)*
    Sittynge at the soper he seide thise wordes:
    'I am sold thorugh so[m] of yow – he shal the tyme rewe *one (C); rue*
    That evere he his Saveour solde for silver or ellis.'
        Judas jangled therayein, ac Jesus hym tolde   *remonstrated, protested*
145 It was hymself soothly, and seide, '*Tu dicis.*'
                                      '*Thou hast said it*' (Mt 26: 25)
        Thanne wente forth that wikked man and with the Jewes mette,
    And tolde hem a tokne how to knowe with Jesus,   *sign to recognize*
    The which tokne to this day to muche is yused—
    That is, kissynge and fair countenaunce and unkynde wille.   *looks*
150 And so was with Judas tho, that Jesus bitrayed: *then*
    '*Ave, raby,*' quod that ribaud, and right to hym he yede,
                                      '*Hail, Rabbi*' (Mt 26: 49); *villain*
    And kiste hym, to be caught therby and kulled of the Jewes.
        Thanne Jesus to Judas and to the Jewes seide,
    'Falsnesse I fynde in thi faire speche,
155 And gile in thi glad chere, and galle is in thi laughyng.   *expression*
    Thow shalt be myrour to many, men to deceyve,

135*a* My house shall be called the house of prayer (Mt 21: 13).
156 You shall be an example to many of (what it is to be) a deceiver of men.

136   *arne*] *so* CK–D; aren R; was βF   143   he] βF; *om* R.
      (C).   148   þe] α; And β.
140   cene] αK–D; maundee β (C).   150   þat] wYLMα; he ?g.
141   he] β; and R; hymselue F.   152   of] β; þoru₃ α.
142   som] *so* K–D; summe α; oon β.

Ac the worse, and the wikkednesse shal worthe upon thiselve: *redound upon*

Necesse est ut veniant scandala; ve homini illi, per quem scandalum venit.

Though I bi treson be take, [and at] youre owene wille, *treachery*
Suffreth myne apostles in pays, and in pees gange.' *to go in peace (C)*
160 In a Thursday in thesternesse thus was he taken *darkness*
Thorugh Judas and Jewes – Jesus was his name
That on the Friday folwynge for mankynde sake
Justed in Jerusalem, a joye to us alle. *Jousted*
On cros upon Calvarie Crist took the bataille
165 Ayeins deeth and the devel, destruyed hir botheres myghtes—
the power of both of them
Deide, and deeth fordide, and day of nyght made. *destroyed*

And I awaked therwith, and wiped myne eighen,
And after Piers the Plowman pried and stared, *peered*
Estward and westward I waited after faste, *looked eagerly*
170 And yede forth as an ydiot, in contree to aspie *seek, inquire*
After Piers the Plowman – many a place I soughte.
And thanne mette I with a man, a myd-Lenten Sonday,
on; 4th Sunday in Lent
As hoor as an hawethorn, and Abraham he highte. *hoary(-headed)*
I frayned hym first fram whennes he come, *inquired of*
175 And of whennes he were, and whider that he thoughte.
intended (to go)
'I am Feith,' quod that freke, 'it falleth noght me to lye, *man; befits*
And of Abrahames hous an heraud of armes. *herald*

157a For it must needs be that scandals come; but nevertheless woe to that
   man by whom the scandal cometh (Mt 18: 7).
159 Let my apostles alone, and let them go in peace (Sk).

157 þe²] HmOC²Mα; þi W&r (*om*   162 -kynde] L&r; -kyndes
   Cr²³).   WHmCr³.
157a *scandalum venit*] W&r; &c g. 166 deth] L&r; deed W.
158 and at] and ?α (þorgh F); at β 168 þe] W&r; *om* gF.
   (C).   175 þouȝte] L&r; souȝte W.
159 pays] L&r; pees WCrGCF. 176 þat] W&rC; þis g.
   & in pees] L&r (p.] pays WCr);   nauȝt me] ?α (*trs* F)C; noȝt β.
   priuyly forþ to F (C).
160 In¹] α; On β.
161 his name] βR; þan taken F (C).

I seke after a segge that I seigh ones,   *man; once*
A ful bold bacheler – I knew hym by his blasen.'
                                  young knight; blazon, arms

180   'What berth that buyrn,' quod I tho, 'so blisse thee bitide?'
                                          bears; warrior

'Thre leodes in oon lyth, noon lenger than oother,   *persons; body*
Of oon muchel and myght in mesure and in lengthe.   *size; power*
That oon dooth, alle dooth, and ech dooth bi his one.
                                        That (which); self

The firste hath myght and majestee, makere of alle thyng:
185   *Pater* is his propre name, a persone by hymselve.   *Father*
The secounde of that sire is Sothfastnesse *Filius*,   *Truth the Son*
Wardeyn of that wit hath, was evere withouten gynnyng.
                                          what; beginning

The thridde highte the Holi Goost, a persone by hymselve,
                                          alone (distinct)

The light of al that lif hath a londe and a watre,   *on*
190   Confortour of creatures – of hym cometh alle blisse.   *Comforter*
'So thre bilongeth for a lord that lordshipe cleymeth:
Might, and a mene [his owene myghte to knowe],   *means; ?express (C)*
Of hymself and of his servaunt, and what suffreth hem bothe.
So God, that gynnyng hadde nevere, but tho hym good thoughte,
                                      when it seemed good to him

195   Sente forth his sone as for servaunt that tyme,
To ocupien hym here til issue were spronge—   *be active*
That is, children of charite, and Holi Chirche the moder.
Patriarkes and prophetes and apostles were the children,

191–3 Likewise, three things are proper for a lord who lays claim to
   dominion: Power, and a means / intermediary to realize his power, Belonging
   to himself and his servant, and (also) something which sustains / endures (the
   action) of both (?) (C).

178   I¹] L&r; And W.
180   buyrn] W&r; barn g.
181   in] W&r; on Cr²³g.
182   and¹] W&r; and oon Cr²³yF
   (oon] of oon F).
   myght] W&r; m. & majeste ?g (m.
   &] om OC²).
184   thyng] y?α; þynges wGLMF.
185   propre] W&r; om g.
186   of þat sire; is] W&r (l. om F;
   þat] þa W); trs g.

189   The ... haþ] β; þat alle þe liȝt
   of þe lif α (of] & F).
192   a] L&r; om WHmOC²C.
   his ... knowe] cj K–D; to k. his o.
   m. β (o.] om Cr)R; kn.] om R); to
   his myght owiþ F (C).
193   -selue; soffret hem] αCK–D;
   om; þei suffre β (C).
196   occupien] L&rC; ocupie w.
198   children] βC; barnes α.

And Crist and Cristendom and alle Cristene Holy Chirche
200 In menynge that man moste on o God bileve,   *Signifying; one*
And there hym likede and lovede, in thre [leodes] hym shewede.

persons

And that it may be so and sooth manhode it sheweth:
Wedlok and widwehode with virginite ynempned,
In tokenynge of the Trinite was taken out of o man—   *Symbolizing*
205 Adam, oure aller fader; Eve was of hymselve,   *of us all; from*
And the issue that thei hadde it was of hem bothe,
And either is otheres joye in thre sondry persones,   *distinct*
And in hevene and here oon singuler name.   *sole, single (C)*
And thus is mankynde or manhede of matrimoyne ysprynge,
210 And bitokneth the Trinite and trewe bileve.   *symbolizes; faith*
'Might is in matrimoyne, that multiplieth the erthe,
And bitokneth trewely, telle if I dorste,
He that first formed al, the Fader of hevene.
The Sone, if I it dorste seye, resembleth wel the widewe:
Deus meus, Deus meus, ut quid dereliquisti me?
215 That is, creatour weex creature to knowe what was bothe.   *became*
As widewe withouten wedlok was nevere yit yseyghe,   *seen*
Na moore myghte God be man but if he moder hadde.
So widewe withouten wedlok may noght wel stande,   *properly exist*
Ne matrimoyne withouten muliere is noght muche to preise:

offspring

Maledictus homo qui non reliquit semen in Israel . . .

214a O God, my God . . .: why hast thou forsaken me? (Ps 21: 2, Mt 27: 46).
218–19a i.e. The idea of widowhood without marriage and that of marriage
    without offspring are both absurdities . . .: 'Cursed is the man who has not
    left offspring in Israel' (*Hereford Breviary*, II, 266: Lesson for St Anne's Day)
    (C).

199   alle] α; *om* β.
200   on] β; in αCr.
201   leodes] persones *All MSS* (C).
204   taken . . . man] L&r (o.] *om*
      GMF; man] mankynde F); out of
      man taken WCr.
205   Adam; Eue] L&r; Adam was;
      and Eue WF.
206   þei] W&r; he g (*om* Cot).
209   þus] β (þis L); þat α.
      or] L&r; and WHm.
210   In W&r; l. *om* g.

211   Miȝte] L&r; Mighty WCr.
      in] αK–D; *om* β.
212   if] W&r; yt if g; ȝow if F.
213   He] L&r; Hym wF.
214   if] wBLMα; is if ?g.
      it] WLRF; *om* HmCrgM.
      -eþ] W&r; -ant g.
      wel] W&r; to gF.
214a quid d. me] βF; quid me d. R.
217   Na] βF; Ne na R.
219a &c] WHmLMR; *om*
      CrgMFC.

220 'Thus in thre persones is parfitliche pure manhede—
  That is, man and his make and mulliere hir children,
          children born of woman(kind)
  And is noght but gendre of a generacion, bifore Jesu Crist in hevene;
  So is the Fader forth with the Sone and Fre Wille of bothe—
  Spiritus procedens a Patre et Filio—
  Which is the Holy Goost of alle, and alle is but o God.   *one*

225 'Thus in a somer I hym seigh as I sat in my porche. (Gen 18: 1ff.)
  I roos up and reverenced hym, and right faire hym grette. *greeted*
  Thre men, to my sighte, I made wel at ese,   *entertained*
  Wessh hir feet and wiped hem, and afterward thei eten *Washed*
  Calves flessh and cakebreed, and knewe what I thoughte.
230 Ful trewe toknes betwene us is, to telle whan me liketh.
            trusty covenant

  'First he fonded me, if I lovede bettre *tested; (to see) if*
  Hym or Ysaak myn heir, the which he highte me kulle. *Isaac; bade*
  He wiste my wille bi hym; he wol me it allowe; (Gen 22)
  I am ful siker in my soule therof, and my sone bothe.

235 'I circumscised my sone sithen for his sake— *afterwards*
  Myself and my meynee and alle that male weere *household*
  Bledden blood for that Lordes love, and hope to blisse the tyme.
              bless

  Myn affiaunce and my feith is ferme in this bileve, *trust; belief*
  For hymself bihighte to me and to myn issue bothe *promised*
240 Lond and lordshipe and lif withouten ende.
  To me and to myn issue moore yet he me grauntede—
  Mercy for oure mysdedes as many tyme as we asken:
  Quam olim Abrahe promisisti et semini eius.

---

220 Thus human nature subsists in its totality in (at least) three persons.
222–3*a* And is nothing else than one species related through one common
 nature ... Such is the relationship accordingly between the three persons of
 the Trinity – The Spirit proceeding from the Father and the Son (*C*).
233 He knew how I felt towards him [*sc.* how much I loved him]; he will hold
 it to my credit [that I obeyed his command to sacrifice Isaac].
242*a* As you promised to [our fathers;] to Abraham and to his seed [for ever]
 (from the *Magnificat*, based on Lk 1: 55).

220 puir] α (þorgh F)(*cf.* C)*K–D*; 223*a* filio] L&r; *f. &c* WHmGY
 om β.   BoCot.
221 her] Lα; *om* W&r.   228 and[1]; hem] βF; in; hes R.
222 a] WL?α; *om* HmCrgF.   241 me[2]] L&r (?men B)C; *om* W.

'And siththe he sente me, to seye I sholde do sacrifise,   *sent (word)*
And doon hym worship with breed and with wyn bothe,
245 And called me the foot of his feith, his folk for to save.

                                         support, founder
And defende hem fro the fend, folk that on me leneden.   *leaned*
  'Thus have I ben his heraud here and in helle,
And conforted many a careful that after his comynge waiten;   *look*
And thus I seke hym,' he seide, 'for I herde seyn late   *talk lately*
250 Of a buyrn that baptised hym – Johan Baptist was his name—   *man*
That to patriarkes and to prophetes and to oother peple in derknesse
Seide, that he seigh here that sholde save us alle: *(the one) who was to*
Ecce Agnus Dei . . .'
  I hadde wonder of hise wordes, and of hise wide clothes;
For in his bosom he bar a thyng, and that he blissed evere.   *carried*
255 And I loked on his lappe: a lazar lay therinne   *leper*
Amonges patriarkes and prophetes pleyinge togideres.
  'What awaitestow?' quod he, 'and what woldestow have?'

                                        are you looking at
  'I wolde wite,' quod I tho, 'what is in youre lappe.'
  'Lo!' quod he – and leet me se. 'Lord, mercy!' I seide.
260 'This is a present of muche pris; what prynce shal it have?'   *value*
  'It is a precious present,' quod he, 'ac the pouke it hath attached,
                              devil; arrested, claimed
And me therwith,' quod that wye, 'may no wed us quyte,   *release*
Ne no buyrn be oure borgh, ne brynge us fram his daunger;   *power*
Out of the poukes pondfold no maynprise may us fecche *pound; bail*
265 Til he come that I carpe of: Crist is his name   *speak*
That shal delivere us some day out of the develes power,
And bettre wed for us legge than we ben alle worthi—   *offer*

252*a* Behold the Lamb of God (Jn 1: 29).

245 þe] WHmL?α; *om* CrgMF.   hem α.
246 leneden] W&r; *l*eueden CrBF   254 For] βC; And α.
    (-eden] -eþ F) (C).   &] αC; *om* β.
248 a] W&r (*l. om* F)C; *om* g.   255 on] L&r; in wFC.
    -en] L&r (*cf.* C); -eden WY.   262 -with] αHmGCK–D; -myde β.
250 buyrn] αK–D; barn β.   weye] αC; man β.
251 to²·³] W&r (to²] *om* F); *om* g.   263 buyrn] WHmYLM?α; barn
252 seiȝ] βC; seyde α.   Cr?gF.
    sholde; vs] β(sh.] shul C)C; shul;   264 *In* β(no] ne no g)C; *l. om* α.

That is, lif for lif – or ligge thus evere   *(he must) lie*
Lollynge in my lappe, til swich a lord us fecche.'
270   'Allas!' I seide, 'that synne so longe shal lette   *obstruct*
The myght of Goddes mercy, that myghte us alle amende!'
     I wepte for hise wordes. With that saugh I another
Rapeliche renne forth the righte wey he wente.   *Quickly; very same*
I affrayned hym first fram whennes he come,   *inquired of*
275 What he highte and whider he wolde – and wightly he tolde.

                                                       with alacrity

---

270–3 *So* βC; *3 spurious ll.*: Allas   trewly to telle α.
thou3te I þo þat is a longe   274 I] W&r; þan y F; and y GC.
abydynge/ And sued hym for he   275 What] αCK–D; And what β.
softe 3ede/ þat he toek vs as tit ac

Passus XVII

'I am *Spes*, a spie,' quod he, 'and spire after a knyght*e*   *inquire*
That took me a maundement upon the mount of Synay

gave; commandment

To rule alle reames therewith – I bere the writ here.'   *realms*
   'Is it asseled?' I seide. 'May men see thi lettres?'
5   'Nay,' he seide, 'I seke hym that hath the seel to kepe—
And that is cros and Cristendom, and Crist theron to honge.   *hang*
And whan it is asseled so, I woot wel the sothe—
That Luciferis lordshipe laste shal no lenger!'
   'Lat se thi lettres,' quod I, 'we myghte the lawe knowe.'
10 He plukkede forth a patente, a pece of an hard roche,   *rock*
Whereon was writen two wordes on this wise yglosed: *glossed*
Dilige Deum et proximum tuum . . .
This was the tixte trewely – I took ful good gome.   *text; note*
The glose was gloriously writen with a gilt penne: *splendidly*
In hiis duobus pendet tota lex et prophetia.
15   'Is here alle thi lordes lawes?' quod I. 'Ye, leve me,' he seide.

12, 14a Thou shalt love . . . God . . . and thy neighbour On these two
dependeth the whole law and the prophets (Mt 22: 37, 39, 40).

Collation WHmCrGYO(97–344
om)C²CBLMRF.
RUBRIC *Passus xvij^us &c et ij^us de
dobet* W&r (*&c . . . dobet*] om
YOC²M; *de visione* Cr; *ij^us*] *tercius*
B); *Passus iij^us de dobet* Hm;
Passus xvj^us de visione vt supra R;
om GF.
1   a¹ . . . he] αCK–D; quod he a β
(he a] þat M).
   and] βFC; om R.
3   þere-] αCK–D; om β.
   writ] βR; rolle F.
4   (*and* 7) as-] L&r; en- WCrG.
   þi] WHmL?αC; þe CrgMF.
5   I] L&rC; om W.
7   So βC; *run together with* 8 α.

I . . . soþe] βC; om α.
8   So βC; sathanas power schal last
no lenger R; s. haþ lost his power F.
After this a line: And þus my lettre
meneth ?α (men.] m. men mowe
knowe yt al F) (C).
9   þi lettres] βC; þat lettre α.
10 A plucked] α (A) & he F)CK–D;
   Thanne plukkede he β.
11 was] LαCK–D; were W&r.
13 gome] ?α (keepe F)C; yeme β.
14a pendet . . . lex] ?αC; *mandatis
tota lex pendet* βF.
   prophetia] WHmL?α; *prophete*
CrgMF.
15 Is] LαCK–D; Ben W&r.
   me] αCrGCK–D; me wel ?β.

'And whoso wercheth after this writ, I wol undertaken,
Shal nevere devel hym dere, ne deeth in soule greve.   *harm; afflict*
For though I seye it myself, I have saved with this charme
Of men and of wommen many score thousandes.'

20   'He seith sooth,' seide this heraud, 'I have yfounde it ofte.
Lo! here in my lappe that leeved on that charme—   *(those) who*
Josue and Judith and Judas Macabeus,
And sixti thousand biside forth that ben noght seyen here!'   *seen*
'Youre wordes arn wonderfulle,' quod I tho. 'Which of yow is
    trewest,

25   And lelest to leve on for lif and for soule?   *most trustworthy*
Abraham seith that he seigh hoolly the Trinite,   *saw wholly*
Thre persones in parcelles departable fro oother,
And alle thre but o God – thus Abraham me taughte—   *one*
And hath saved that bileved so and sory for hir synnes,
                                    (those) who (were) sorry

30   He kan noght siggen the somme, and some arn in his lappe.   *total*
What neded it thanne a newe lawe to brynge,   *What need was there*
Sith the firste suffiseth to savacion and to blisse?
And now cometh *Spes* and speketh, that hath aspied the lawe,
                                    examined
And telleth noght of the Trinite that took hym hise lettres—   *gave*

35   To bileeve and lovye in o Lord almyghty,   *believe in and love*
And siththe right as myself so lovye alle peple.
'The gome that gooth with o staf – he semeth in gretter heele
                                    walks; better health
Than he that [teeth] with two staves, to sighte of us alle.   *goes*
And right so, bi the roode, reson me sheweth

40   It is lighter to lewed men o lesson to knowe   *easier for; one; learn*

---

27 Three separate persons distinguishable from each other.

16   And] W&rC; *om* g.
19   þousandes] L&r; þousand W.
20   He seith] L&rC; Ye seien WHm.
     þis] W&r; þe gF.
     yfounde] W&r; founded YCB.
21   on] βFC; of R.
22   Iosue] βR; Boþe I. FC.
23   And] αC; Ye and β.
24   þo] W&r; *om* gF.
25   on] L&rC; so WHm.

26   hoolly] W&rC; holy GYCBmBo
     LR.
29   -ed] βC; -eth αGC².
31   bringe] αCK–D; bigynne β.
33   cometh] W&r (co-] bico- CB)C;
     bigynneth YOC².
     hath] L&rC; *om* WG.
37–47   *In* β (*cf.* C); *ll. om* α.
38   teeth] gooþ *All MSS* (C).
40   It] L&rC; That it W.

Than for to techen hem two, and to hard to lerne the leeste!

while (it is) too

It is ful hard for any man on Abraham bileve,
And wel awey worse yit for to love a sherewe. *much worse still*
It is lighter to leeve in thre lovely persones
45 Than for to lovye and lene as wel lorels as lele. *give (to); wastrels*
Go thi gate,' quod I to *Spes*; 'so me God helpe, *way*
Tho that lernen thi lawe wol litel while usen it!' *practise*

And as we wenten thus in the wey, wordynge togideres, *talking*
Thanne seighe we a Samaritan sittynge on a mule,
50 Ridynge ful rapely the righte wey we yeden, *hastily; very same*
Comynge from a contree that men called Jerico— *district, place*
To a justes in Jerusalem he chaced awey faste. *joust; hastened*
Bothe the heraud and Hope and he mette atones *arrived together*
Where a man was, wounded, and with theves taken. *robbed by*
55 He myghte neither steppe ne stande, ne stere foot ne handes, *stir*
Ne helpe hymself soothly, for *semyvif* he semed, *(barely) half-alive*
And as naked as a nedle, and noon help abouten.

Feith hadde first sighte of hym, ac he fleigh aside, *hurried*
And nolde noght neghen hym by nyne londes lengthe. *approach*
60 Hope cam hippynge after, that hadde so ybosted *hopping*
How he with Moyses maundement hadde many men yholpe; *helped*
Ac whan he hadde sighte of that segge, aside he gan hym drawe
Dredfully, bi this day, as doke dooth fram the faucon! *Fearfully; duck*
Ac so soone so the Samaritan hadde sighte of this leode, *as; man*
65 He lighte adown of lyard and ladde hym in his handes,

got down from his grey

And to the wye he wente hise woundes to biholde,
And parceyved by his pous he was in peril to dye, *pulse*
And but if he hadde recoverer the rather, that rise sholde he nevere:

'immediate treatment'

---

59 And would not come any nearer him than the distance of the breadth of
nine ridges in a ploughed field (after *Sk*).

45 lele] W&rC; *pl* g.
46 to] W&rC; *om* g.
47 wol] WLCC; wel HmCrYBM;
om GOC².
48 þus in; wey] W&r; in; w. thus
CrFC.
50 Rydynge] βC; & Rydende F;
Ryden R.

57 aboute] αCK–D; a. hym β.
58 of] βC; on α.
65 handes] αC; hande β.
66 to þe] βFC; with þat R.
67 by] βFC; in R.
68 if] L&r?C; *om* WCrGBF.
rather] L&rC; rapelier W.

And breide to hise boteles, and bothe he atamede.   *hastened; broached*
70 With wyn and with oille hise woundes he wasshed,
Enbawmed hym and bond his heed, and in his lappe hym leide,
Anointed; bound up

And ladde hym so forth on lyard to *Lex Christi*, a graunge
the Law of Christ; farm-house

Wel sixe mile or sevene biside the newe market;   *A good six miles*
Herberwed hym at an hostrie and the hostiler called,
Lodged; inn; inn-keeper

75 And seide, 'Have, kepe this man, til I come fro the justes,   *look after*
And lo here silver,' he seide, 'for salve to hise woundes.'   *ointment for*
And he took hym two pens to liflode as it weere,
pence; in payment for his keep

And seide, 'What he [moore speneth] I make thee good herafter,
For I may noght lette,' quod that leode – and lyard he bistrideth,
80 And raped hym to Jerusalemward the righte wey to ryde.
hastened; towards J.; direct

Feith folweth after faste, and fondede to mete hym,   *tried*
And *Spes* sp[r]akliche hym spedde, spede if he myghte   *nimbly*
To overtaken hym and talke to hym er thei to towne coome.

And whan I seigh this, I sojourned noght, but shoop me to renne,
delayed; set myself

85 And suwed the Samaritan that was so ful of pite,   *followed*
And graunted hym to ben his gome. 'Graunt mercy,' he seide,
offered; man; Thank you

'Ac thi frend and thi felawe,' quod he, 'thow fyndest me at nede.'
And I thanked hym tho and siththe I hym tolde
How that Feith fleigh awey and *Spes* his felawe bothe
90 For sighte of the sorweful [segge] that robbed was with theves.
'Have hem excused,' quod he, 'hir help may litel availle:
May no medicyne under molde the man to heele brynge—   *health*

---

69 *In* αCSk; *l. om* β.
And breide] R (*cf.* C); he breyded
F.
74 þe] αK–D; to þe β.
78 moore speneth] *trs All MSS* (sp.)
YOLR; spendeþ W&r) (C).
79 -ideþ] W&r; -ode g.
81 folweth] LR; folwede W&rC.
82 sprak-] spak- ?β; spark- α.

85 þe] αC; þat β.
86 gome] αGK–D; groom β (*alt.
from* gome Bm).
87 quod he] W&r (he seide YCB);
om CrOC²M.
88 I²] βR; þus I F.
90 þe] L&r; þat WCr²³.
segge] *cj* K–D; man *All MSS* (C).
92 vnder] αK–D; on β.

Neither Feith ne fyn Hope, so festred be hise woundes,   *festered*
Withouten the blood of a barn born of a mayde.   *child*
95 And be he bathed in that blood, baptised as it were,
And thanne plastred with penaunce and passion of that baby,
     treated with a healing plaster
He sholde stonde and steppe — ac stalworthe worth he nevere
     sturdy; will be
Til he have eten al the barn and his blood ydronke.
For wente nevere wye in this world thorugh that wildernesse
100 That he ne was robbed or rifled, rood he there or yede,
     plundered; walked
Save Feith and his felawe *Spes* and myselve,
And thiself now and swiche as suwen oure werkes.   *follow*
     'For Outlawe is in the wode and under bank lotieth,   *lurks*
And may ech man see and good mark take   *note*
105 Who is bihynde and who bifore and who ben on horse—
For he halt hym hardier on horse than he that is a foote.
     holds; (who is) on horseback
For he seigh me that am Samaritan suwen Feith and his felawe
On my capul that highte *Caro* — of mankynde I took it—
     horse; Flesh; humanity
He was unhardy, that harlot, and hidde hym *in Inferno.*
     fearful; rogue; Hell
110 Ac er this day thre daies, I dar undertaken
That he worth fettred, that feloun, faste with cheynes,   *will be; chains*
And nevere eft greve gome that gooth this ilke gate: *trouble; same way*
O Mors ero mors tua . . .
     'And thanne shal Feith be forster here and in this fryth walke,
     forester; wood

---

110 But before three days from today [have passed]; (cf. Mt 27: 63).
112a O death, I will be thy death; [O hell, I will be thy bite] (Osee 13: 14).

95   be he] β(*trs* CrgM); be α.
96   and²] β; and þe R; with þe F.
97–344   *def.* O (3 *leaves lost*); g=
      GYC²CB.
99   wye] βF; wiȝt RB.
100   or¹] β; ne R; & F.
102   as] βF (*cf.* C); þat RC².
103   outlawe is] ?α; an outlaw
      Cr²³F; Outlawes β.

104   may] αCrL; mowen ?wgM.
      take] β; taketh α.
106   a] LR; at C; on Hm&r (*om* W).
107   seigh] β(seeth Cr²³); seiþ αGC².
109   vnhardy þat] β; vn- R; but an F.
112a *In* α (*&c*] R; morsus tuus ero
      inferne F)Sk; *l. om* β.
113–24   *In* β; *om* α.

And kennen out comune men that knowen noght the contree,
guide (out of the wood)

115 Which is the wey that I wente, and wher forth to Jerusalem;
(Teaching them) which is . . .

And Hope the hostilers man shal be ther [an helyng the man lith],
a-healing; lies

And alle that feble and feynte be, that Feith may noght teche,
Hope shal lede hem forth with love, as his lettre telleth,
And hostele hem and heele thorugh Holy Chirche bileve
lodge; faith in H.C.

120 Til I have salve for alle sike – and thanne shal I returne,
And come ayein bi this contree and conforten alle sike
That craveth it or coveiteth it and crieth therafter.   *ask for; desire*
For the barn was born in Bethleem that with his blood shal save
Alle that lyven in Feith and folwen his felawes techynge.'

125 'A, swete sire!' I seide tho, 'wher I shal bileve—   *am I to believe*
As Feith and his felawe enformed me bothe—   *instructed*
In thre persones departable that perpetuele were evere,
distinguishable

And alle thre but o God? Thus Abraham me taughte;   *one*
And Hope afterward he bad me to lovye

130 O God with al my good, and alle gomes after,   *strength; men*
Lovye hem lik myselve – ac Oure Lord aboven alle.'
'After Abraham,' quod he, 'that heraud of armes,
Sette faste thi feith and ferme bileve;
And as Hope highte thee, I hote that thow lovye   *bade; bid*

135 Thyn evenecristene everemoore eveneforth with thiselve.
fellow-Christians; equally

And if conscience carpe therayein, or kynde wit eyther,
speak against it

Or eretikes with arguments, thyn hond thow hem shewe: *heretics*

---

114 out comune] wLM; out
commen Cr²³; comune ?g;
vnkummande Bo; vnkunnande Bm;
vnken Cot.
116 an helyng; þe man lith] *cj* K–D;
trs All MSS (C).
120 re-] L&r; *om* WHm.
122 or; and] L&r; *trs* W.
123–4 *So* wLM; *as* 3 *ll. div after*
mayde, feith g.

123 Bethleem] wLM; B. of a clene
mayde g.
124 his . . . techynge] wLM; þe t. of
hope þat is his Felaw g.
125 I shal] WL?α; *trs* Hm&r.
126 -ed] wLMC; -en g.
133 faste] L&r; fully WHm.
134 highte] β; bihiȝt α.
136 eyþer] W&r; other CrGCotR.
137 hem] WHmαC; hym CrgLM.

For God is after an hand – yheer now and knowe it.   *like; hear*
  'The Fader was first as a fust with o fynger folden,   *fist; one; bent*
140 Til hym lovede and liste to unlosen his fynger   *unbend*
And profrede it forth as with a pawme to what place it sholde.   *palm*
The pawme is purely the hand, and profreth forth the fyngres,

integrally

To ministren and to make that myght of hand knoweth;
And bitokneth trewely, telle whoso liketh,   *stands for*
145 The Holy Goost of hevene – he is as the pawme.
The fyngres that fre ben to folde and to serve   *bend*
Bitoknen soothly the Sone, that sent was til erthe,   *to*
That touched and tastede at techynge of the pawme   *felt*
Seinte Marie, a mayde, and mankynde laughte: *assumed human nature*
Qui conceptus est de spiritu sancto . . .
150   'The Fader is thanne as a fust with fynger to touche
(*Quia "Omnia traham ad me ipsum . . ."*)
Al that the pawme parceyveth profitable to feele.
Thus are thei alle but oon, as it an hand weere,
And thre sondry sightes in oon shewynge.
The pawme for he put forth fyngres and the fust bothe,   *because; puts*
155 Right so, redily, reson it sheweth,
How he that is Holy Goost Sire and Sone preveth.

?demonstrates, expresses

And as the hand halt harde and alle thyng faste   *holds; firmly*
Thorugh foure fyngres and a thombe forth with the pawme,
Right so the Fader and the Sone and Seint Spirit the thridde
160 Halt al the wide world withinne hem thre—

---

143 To execute and perform that of which the hand's power has knowledge.
149a Who was conceived of the Holy Ghost (fourth clause of Apostles' Creed).
150a For 'I will draw all things to myself' (Jn 12: 32).
153 And three distinct aspects in a single representation (C).

139   as] W&r (*cf.* C); *om* g.
    folden] α (*cf.* C); foldynge β.
140   louede] β; lykede HmC; leued
    R; lyþed F.
141   profered] αCK–D; profre β.
142   purely] βR; of F (C).
148   at] βC; and α.
150   þanne] L&r (*om* F)C; pawme
    W.

152   an hand] β; a fust α.
153   oon] βF; oen in R.
154   he] L&r; it WF; þe paume R.
    put] α; putteþ β.
160   *So* L&r (Halt) holden F; *om* W;
    thre] þre holden W; þre togydres
    F); Wythin hem three the wyde
    worlde holden CrM (*over erasure*
    a.h.) (C).
    -Inne] β; *om* α.

Bothe wolkne and the wynd, water and erthe,   *sky*
Hevene and helle and al that ther is inne.
Thus it is – nedeth no man to trowe noon oother—   *nothing else*
That [bilongeth thre thynges] in Oure Lord of hevene,
165 And aren serelepes by hemself, asondry were thei nevere,
                                            separately; apart
Namoore than may an hande meve withoute fyngres.   *move*
  'And as my fust is ful hand yfolden togideres,   *closed*
So is the Fader a ful God, formour and shappere—   *maker; creator*
Tu fabricator omnium . . .
And al the myght myd hym is in makynge of thynges.   *with*
170 'The fyngres formen a ful hand to portreye or peynten;   *draw*
Kervynge and compasynge is craft of the fyngres.   *Carving; designing*
Right so is the Sone the science of the Fader   *wisdom*
And ful God as is the Fader, no febler ne no bettre.
  'The pawme is pureliche the hand, hath power by hymselve
                                                   entirely
175 Otherwise than the writhen fust, or werkmanshipe of fyngres;
                                            clenched; activity
For the pawme hath power to pulte out the joyntes   *extend*
And to unfolde the fust, for hym it bilongeth,   *open; pertains to*
And receyve that the fyngres recheth and refuse bothe   *reach (to)*
Whan he feleth the fust and the fyngres wille.
180 'So is the Holy Goost God, neither gretter ne lasse

168a Thou art Creator of all things . . . (*Jesu salvator saeculi*, stanza 2) (C).

162 þere is Inne] Lα; therin is Cr&r
  (*trs* WHm).
163 is] W&r; *om* HmGCBα.
  to] LYC²α; *om* wGCB.
164 *bi*longeþ; þre þynges] *trs* All
  MSS (C).
165 -lepes] LMα; -lopes WCr¹;
  -ples HmCr²³g.
166 may an hand] αK–D; myn
  hand may β.
  fyngres] HmLα; my fyngres
  WCrgM.
167 yfolde] L&r; yholden WHm.
169 And] W&rC; *om* g.

171 and] β; or α.
  is] ?α (þat is F)CrK–D; as β.
176 þe pawme] L&rC; he WHm.
  pult] ?α?C; putte βF.
  þe] *so* αCK–D; alle þe β.
177 *So* αCSk; *run together with* 179
  β.
  þe] αCK–D; þe folden β.
  hym it bilongeth] α (h. it] it to h.
  F)C; *om* β.
178 *In* α (And¹·²] R; & to F)CSk; *l.
  om* β.
179 Whan . . . fust] α (*cf.* C)Sk; *om*
  β.
  and] αSk; at ?β (as GYCB).

Than is the Sire or the Sone, and in the same myghte, *of; power*
And alle are thei but o God, as is myn hand and my fyngres, *one*
Unfolden or folden, my fust and my pawme— *Open; shut*
Al is but an hand, howso I turne it. *one; however*

185 Ac who is hurte in the hand, evene in the myddes, *right; middle*
He may receyve right noght – reson it sheweth; *take (in his hand)*
For the fyngres that folde sholde and the fust make,
For peyne of the pawme, power hem failleth *pain; they lack power*
To clucche or to clawe, to clippe or to holde. *seize; grasp*

190 Were the myddel of myn hand ymaymed or ypersed,

  injured; pierced

I sholde receyve right noght of that I reche myghte;
Ac though my thombe and my fyngres bothe were toshullen *peeled*
And the myddel of myn hand withoute maleese, *pain*
In many kynnes maneres I myghte myself helpe *ways*

195 Bothe meve and amende, though alle my fyngres oke. *repair; ached*
 'By this skile,' he seide, 'I se an evidence *reasoning; indication*
That whoso synneth in the Seint Spirit, assoilled worth he nevere,

  against; absolved

Neither here ne elliswhere, as I herde telle—
Qui peccat in Spiritum Sanctum . . .
For he priketh God as in the pawme, that *peccat in Spiritu[m]
Sanctu[m].*

200 For God the Fader is as a fust; the Sone is as a fynger;

198a But he that shall sin [blaspheme, Vulg.] against the Holy Ghost [shall
  never have forgiveness . . .] (Mk 3: 29).

181 or] αCK–D; and β.
 in] βR; of FC.
182 are þei] W&r (*trs* GF); thre
 Cr²³C.
184 *So* CrLMαCSk; *run together
 with* 185 WHmg.
 howso . . . it] L&r (*over erasure, a.h.*
 M); *om* WHmg.
185 Ac . . . hande] LCr (Ac) And
 Cr) M(+ *a.h.*)α (Ac] But F)CSk;
 om WHmg.
186 *So* W&rC; *l. om* g; *run
 together with* 191 (*ll.* 187–91a *om*
 F).

190 ypersed] ?α (*l. om* F); yperissed
 β (-issed] -isched HmCr¹gM; -sshed
 LCr²³).
192 shullen] ?β; swolle αHmCr²³M.
196 he seyde] αCK–D; me þynkeþ
 β.
197 þe] WCrLMαC; *om* Hmg.
198a -um¹,²] CrC²CSk; -u, -o W&r
 (*l. om* F).
 &c] β; numquam *&c* R.
199 *spiritum sanctum*] *so* CSk;
 spiritu sancto W&r; *om* CrC (C).
200 a²] W&r; þe ?yC.

The Holy Goost of hevene is as it were the pawme.
So whoso synneth ayeyns the Seint Spirit, it semeth that he greveth
                                      injures

God that he grypeth with, and wolde his grace quenche.
  'For to a torche or to a tapur the Trinite is likned—   *compared*
205 As wex and a weke were twyned togideres,   *wick; twisted*
And thanne a fir flawmynge forth out of bothe.   *flaming*
And as wex and weke and warm fir togideres
Fostren forth a flawmbe and a fair leye   *produce; flame*
So dooth the Sire and the Sone and also *Spiritus Sanctus*
210 Fostren forth amonges folk love and bileve,   *Generate; faith*
That alle kynne Cristene clenseth of synnes.
And as thow seest som tyme sodeynliche a torche—
The blase therof yblowe out, yet brenneth the weke—   *flame; burns*
Withouten leye or light, that [lowe] the macche brenneth;
                                       flame; wick

215 So is the Holy Goost God, and grace withoute mercy
To alle unkynde creatures that coveite to destruye   *unnatural*
Lele love other lif that Oure Lord shapte.   *created*
  'And as glowynge gledes gladeth noght thise werkmen *coals; cheer*
That werchen and waken in wyntres nyghtes,   *work; watch/wake*
220 As dooth a kex or a candle that caught hath fir and blaseth,
                                       hemlock-stem

Namoore dooth Sire ne Sone ne Seint Spirit togideres
Graunte no grace ne forgifnesse of synnes
Til the Holy Goost gynne to glowe and to blase;   *blaze, burn (up)*
So that the Holy Goost gloweth but as a glede
225 Til that lele love ligge on hym and blowe.   *be (over)*
And thanne flawmeth he as fir on Fader and on *Filius* *flames; Son*
And melteth hire myght into mercy — as men may se in wyntre
Ysekeles in evesynges thorugh hete of the sonne   *Icicles; eaves*

---

203 . . . in the place where he grips.

202 aȝeynes] αC; in β.
204 For; to²] αC; And; *om* β.
207 warme] αCK–D; hoot β.
210 *In* L&rC; *l. om* WHm.
211 clenseþ] βFC; clensede R.
214 leye] W&rC; lowe C; lyght
  GC².
  lowe] *om All MSS* (C).

215 þe] L&rC; *om* W.
217 other] L&r; or WCr; to þe F.
218–44 *In* βC; *ll. om* α.
218 glowynge gledes] wLM; a
  glowynge glede ne g.
222 forg-] CrGCC; forȝ- W&r.
224 glede] L&rC; glade W.
227 into] W&rC; to g.

Melteth in a mynut while to myst and to watre.   *minute's time*
230   'So grace of the Holy Goost the greet myght of the Trinite
Melteth to mercy – to merciable and to noon othere. *for (the) merciful*
And as wex withouten moore on a warm glede   *immediately*
Wol brennen and blasen, be thei togideres,
And solacen hem that mowe [noght] se, that sitten in derknesse,

                                                     comfort
235   So wol the Fader foryyve folk of mylde hertes   *lowly, kind*
That rufully repenten and restitucion make,   *sorrowfully*
In as muche as thei mowen amenden and paien;   *make amends; pay*
And if it suffise noght for assetz, that in swich a wille deyeth,

                                                     satisfaction
Mercy for his mekenesse wol maken good the remenaunt.

                                                     remainder due
240   And as the weke and fir wol make a warm flaumbe
For to murthen men with that in merke sitten,   *cheer; darkness*
So wole Crist of his curteisie, and men crye hym mercy,   *(out) of; if*
Bothe foryyve and foryete, and yit bidde for us   *further; pray*
To the Fader of hevene foryifnesse to have.

245   'Ac hewe fir at a flynt foure hundred wynter—   *strike; from*
But thow have tache to take it with, tonder or broches,
Al thi labour is lost and al thi long travaille;   *effort*
For may no fir flaumbe make, faille it his kynde.
So is the Holy Goost God and grace withouten mercy
250   To alle unkynde creatures – Crist hymself witnesseth:
Amen dico vobis, nescio vos . . .
'Be unkynde to thyn evenecristene, and al that thow kanst bidde—

238–9 And if a penitent (who is truly sorry and tries) does not manage to
    make adequate (canonical) satisfaction, but dies wishing to do so, because of
    his humble intent, God's mercy will make good whatever remains to be paid.
246 Unless you have touchwood to light (from the spark), tinder or matches.
248 . . . if the substance [needed for fire – *sc.* kindling] be lacking.
250a Amen, I say to you, I know you not (Mt 25: 12).

229   Melteth] L&rC; Melte
  WHmCr[23].
231   non] L&rC; *om* WHm.
234   noȝt] *so* CK–D; *om All MSS*
  (C).
238   a] W&rC; *om* Cr[23]g.
240   make] L&rC; maken WHm.

warm] W&r; faire YC.
241   with] L&rC; myd WCr[1].
  in] L&rC; in þe WCr[12].
  merke] L&rC; derke W.
245   at a] βC; on a F; and R.
246   tache] αC; tow β.
248   his] L&rC; is WCBo.

Delen and do penaunce day and nyght evere,   *Give (alms)*
And purchace al the pardon of Pampilon and Rome,   *Pamplona*
And indulgences ynowe, and be *ingratus* to thi kynde,
                                     unkind; fellow-men

255 The Holy Goost hereth thee noght, ne helpe may thee by reson;
For unkyndenesse quencheth hym, that he kan noght shyne,
Ne brenne ne blase clere, for blowynge of unkyndenesse.   *bright*
Poul the Apostel preveth wher I lye:
Si linguis hominum loquar . . .

260 'Forthi beth war, ye wise men that with the world deleth, *take care*
That riche ben and reson knoweth – ruleth wel youre soule;
Beth noght unkynde, I conseille yow, to youre evenecristene;
For manye of yow riche men, by my soule, men telleth,
Ye brenne, but ye blase noght, and that is a blynd bekene!—
                                 lightless beacon (cf. Mt 5: 14–16)

Non omnis qui dicit Domine, Domine, intrabit . . .
265 'Dives deyde dampned for his unkyndenesse   (Lk 16: 19–31)
Of his mete and his moneie to men that it nedede.   *With*
Ech a riche, I rede, reward at hym take,   *advise; heed from*
And gyveth youre good to that God that grace of ariseth.   *arises from*
For that ben unkynde to hise, hope I noon oother   *(those) who; expect*
270 But thei dwelle ther Dives is dayes withouten ende.

'Thus is unkyndenesse the contrarie that quencheth, as it were,
The grace of the Holy Goost, Goddes owene kynde.   *nature*
For that kynde dooth, unkynde fordooth – as thise corsede theves,
Unkynde Cristene men, for coveitise and envye
275 Sleeth a man for hise moebles, with mouth or with handes.   *goods*

---

259 If I speak with the tongues of men, [and of angels, and have not charity] (I
Cor 13: 1).

264a Not every one that saith (to me), Lord, Lord, shall enter [into the
kingdom of heaven . . .] (Mt 7: 21).

273 For that which charitable people do/Nature (God) makes, uncharitable
people/unnaturalness destroys.

275 . . . by slander or by actual physical violence.

252 and¹] W&rC; or gF.
254 *ingratus*] β?C; ingrat α (C).
     kynde] βC; kynne αCr³.
256 quencheþ hym] βFC; quenche
     hem R.
258 wher] L&r (wheiþer w)C; þat y
     not F.

264 &] αC; *om* β.
264a *intrabit*] wCotLMα; *om* ?g.
266 his²] ?β (of his wGC²B)?C; *om*
     α (ne F)Y.
269 þat] LCr¹MαCK–D; þei þat
     W&r (þei) þo F).
270 þei] wLMRC; þei shall gF.

For that the Holy Goost hath to kepe, tho harlotes destruyeth—
                                                                protect; villains
The which is lif and love, the leye of mannes body.   *flame*
For every manere good man may be likned to a torche,   *compared*
Or ellis to a tapur, to reverence the Trinite;   *taper*
280 And whoso morthereth a good man, me thynketh, by myn inwit,
                                              murders; 'I truly believe'
He fordooth the levest light that Oure Lord lovyeth. *puts out; dearest*
    'Ac yet in manye mo maneres men offenden the Holy Goost;
Ac this is the worste wise that any wight myghte   *way*
Synnen ayein the Seint Spirit – assenten to destruye, *by assenting to*
285 For coveitise of any kynnes thyng, that Crist deere boughte.
How myghte he aske mercy, or any mercy hym helpe,
That wikkedliche and wilfulliche wolde mercy aniente?   *annihilate*
    'Innocence is next God, and nyght and day it crieth   *nearest to*
"Vengeaunce! Vengeaunce! Foryyve be it nevere   (*cf.* Gen 4: 10–11)
290 That shente us and shedde oure blood – forshapte us, as it semed:
                                                             unmade
Vindica sanguinem iustorum!"
Thus "Vengeaunce, vengeaunce!" verrey charite asketh;   *true*
And sith Holy Chirche and charite chargeth this so soore,
                                              insists on; strongly
Leve I nevere that Oure Lord wol love that charite lakketh,
                                              (the man) who
Ne have pite for any preiere [that he pleyneth there].'
                                              in spite of; utters (C)
295   'I pose I hadde synned so, and sholde now deye,
                                              put it that; were about to
And now am sory that I so the Seint Spirit agulte,   *offended*
Confesse me and crye his grace, God that al made,

290a Revenge the blood of the just! (*cf.* Apoc 6: 10).

276   þo] L&r?C; þe WHmGC².
278   man] L&rC; *om* W.
280   -so] Hmgα; þat CrM; *om* WL.
282   Ac] L&r (but C²F); for G; And
         WCrCC.
284   þe] WLMαC; *om* HmCrg.
285   kynnes] W&rC; *om* gF.
286   *In* L&rC; *l. om* WHmg.

290   vs¹] βC; *om* α.
         semed] α (-d] -þ F)C; were β.
294   that . . . there] þer þat he
         playneþ *All MSS* (C).
295   now] WCrYLMαC; not Hm?g
         (*canc* G).
296   now] β(*om* Cr)C; nouȝt α.
         am] L&r; am I WHmmMC.
         I] W&rC; *om* LR.

And myldeliche his mercy aske – myghte I noght be saved?'   *humbly*
'Yis,' seide the Samaritan, 'so thow myghtest repente *in such a way*
300   That rightwisnesse thorugh repentaunce to ruthe myghte turne.
                                                    justice; compassion

Ac it is but selden yseighe, ther soothnesse bereth witnesse,   *seen*
Any creature be coupable bifore a kynges justice,   *guilty*
Be raunsoned for his repentaunce ther alle reson hym dampneth.
                                                    redeemed; condemns

For ther that partie pursueth the peel is so huge
305   That the kyng may do no mercy til bothe men acorde   *agree*
And eyther have equite, as holy writ telleth: *each; justice*
Numquam dimittitur peccatum . . .
Thus it fareth by swich folk that falsly al hire lyves
Yvele lyven and leten noght til lif hem forsake.   *desist; leave*
Drede of desperacion thanne dryveth awey grace,
310   That mercy in hir mynde may noght thanne falle;
Good hope, that helpe sholde, to wanhope torneth—   *despair*
Noght of the nounpower of God, that he ne is myghtful   *impotence*
To amende al that amys is, and his mercy gretter   *wrong*
Thanne alle our wikkede werkes, as Holy Writ telleth—
Misericordia eius super omnia opera eius—
315   Ac er his rightwisnesse to ruthe torne, som restitucion bihoveth:
                                                    is needed

His sorwe is satisfaccion for [swich] that may noght paie.

---

304 For where the (injured) party prosecutes, the accusation is so grave (*Sk*).
306a The sin is never forgiven [until what is stolen is restored] (St Augustine;
    cf. V 272*a*).
309 A panic fear, then, arising from/amounting to pure despair.
312 Not from God's lack of power, from his being unable . . .
314a His tender mercies are over all his works (Ps 144: 9).
316 (To God), the sorrow of a sinner who cannot do canonical penance
    (because he is dying) is satisfaction enough.

299 so; mi3test] αC; so wel; myght
     β.
300 þoru3] βC; to α.
302 be] αCK–D; þat is β.
     by-] αCrMC; a- ?β.
303 repentaunce] βC; gilt F; *om* R.
304 pele] LαC; plee CrM; peple
     WHmg.

307 lyues] β; lyue α.
309–10 *In* αCSk; *ll. om* β.
309 Drede] RC; & drede F.
     þanne; dr. awey] FCK–D; *trs* R.
312 -power] βC; -per α.
314a eius] βC; domini α.
315 -wisnesse] W&rC; -fulnes g.
316 βC (sw.] CK–D; hym β); *l. om*
     α.

'Thre thynges ther ben that doon a man by strengthe   *'force a man'*
For to fleen his owene hous, as Holy Writ sheweth.
That oon is a wikkede wif that wol noght be chasted:
320 Hir feere fleeth hire for feere of hir tonge.   *spouse; fear*
And if his hous be unhiled, and reyne on his bedde,   *unroofed; rain*
He seketh and seketh til he slepe drye.
And whan smoke and smolder smyt in his sighte,   *fumes; strike*
It dooth hym worse than his wif or wete to slepe.
325 For smoke and smolder smerteth hise eighen   *sting*
Til he be bler eighed or blynde and [the borre] in the throte,

    hoarseness
Cogheth and curseth that Crist gyve hym sorwe   *Coughs; (saying . . .)*
That sholde brynge in bettre wode, or blowe it til it brende!   *burnt*
'Thise thre that I telle of thus ben understonde: *be understood*
330 The wif is oure wikked flessh, wol noght be chasted,   *disciplined*
For kynde clyveth on hym evere to contrarie the soule.   *nature; clings*
And though it falle, it fynt skiles, that "Frelete it made,"   *reasons*
And "That is lightly foryyven and foryeten bothe   *easily*
To man that mercy asketh and amende thenketh."
335 'The reyn that reyneth ther we reste sholde
Ben siknesses and othere sorwes that we suffren oughte,
As Poul the Apostle to the peple taughte:
Virtus in infirmitate perficitur.
And though that men make muche doel in hir angre,   *sorrow; pain*

---

324 It makes sleep even harder for him than does his wife's nagging or the rain.

337a For power is made perfect in infirmity (II Cor 12: 9).

318   hous] L&rC; *om* W.
319   -ed] LYCCotRC; -ised W&r.
320   hire] α?CK–D; fro hire β.
322   and sekeþ] wLMRC; al aboute Cr²³g; þanne F.
    slepe] W&rC; lygge g.
323   and²] W&rC; or g.
    sighte] βR; ey3en FC.
325   smerteth] αCK–D; smyteþ in β (in] *om* GCL).
326   þe borre] *so* CK–D; hoors β; cow3he α (a bold c. F) (C).
327   Cogheth] β (Than c. he C²)C; he k. α (þan kenely he F)G (he +G).
    hym] gMαC; hem wL.
329   þus ben] αC; *trs* β.
    vnderstonde] ?αC?C; to v. βF.
330   wol] ?αC; þat wol βF.
    -ted] CrYCLMRC; -tised W&r.
332   it³] wBLMαC; is Cr²³?g.
336   sikenesses] L&rC; *sg* WCrG YC²C.
    other] ?αC; *om* βF.
    ou3te] β?CK–D; ofte β.
337a   perficitur] αCrBmCK–D; *p. &c* ?β (p.) *om* C).

And ben inpacient in hir penaunce, pure reson knoweth   *tribulation*
340 That thei han cause to contrarie, by kynde of hir siknesse;
                                                  complain; virtue

And lightliche Oure Lord at hir lyves ende   *easily*
Hath mercy on swiche men, that so yvele may suffre.
    'Ac the smoke and the smolder that smyt in oure eighen,   *strikes*
That is coveitise and unkyndenesse, that quencheth Goddes mercy.
345 For unkyndenesse is the contrarie of alle kynnes reson;
For ther nys sik ne sory, ne noon so muche wrecche   *miserable*
That he ne may lovye, and hym like, and lene of his herte *give; from*
Good wille, good word – bothe wisshen and wilnen
Alle manere men mercy and foryifnesse,
350 And lovye hem lik hymself, and his lif amende.
    'I may no lenger lette!' quod he, and lyard he prikede,
                                                  delay; spurred

And wente away as wynd – and therwith I awakede.

---

342 ... that may suffer with such an ill grace *or* that may suffer evils in such a
    way.

339 ben] wα; *om* gLM.
340 cause] βC; resoun α.
343 *Here* O *resumes*; g=
    GYOC²CB.
344 That¹] W&rC; *om* g.
    is] βFC; *om* R.

þat quencheþ] W&r (þat] *om* R)C;
þey quenche F.
348 goed²; wilnen] αC; & good;
    willen β.
    bothe] L&rC; and W.
351 lyard he] W&rC; harde g.

Passus XVIII

Wolleward and weetshoed wente I forth after   *Shirtless; shoeless*
As a recchelees renk that of no wo reccheth,   *man; suffering; cares for*
And yede forth lik a lorel al my lif tyme,   *went; wastrel*
Til I weex wery of the world and wilned eft to slepe,   *desired; again*
5 And lened me to a Lenten – and longe tyme I slepte;   *idled till Lent*
Reste me there and rutte faste til *Ramis palmarum.*

         Rested; snored; Palm Sunday

Of gerlis and of *Gloria, laus* gretly me dremed

         children; Glory, praise (C)

And how *osanna* by orgene olde folk songen,   *hosanna; to the organ*
And of Cristes passion and penaunce, the peple that ofraughte.

         suffering; reached to

10   Oon semblable to the Samaritan, and somdeel to Piers the
Plowman,   *resembling; somewhat*
Barefoot on an asse bak bootles cam prikye,   *riding (C)*
Withouten spores other spere; sprakliche he loked,   *spurs; lively*
As is the kynde of a knyght that cometh to be dubbed,   *manner*
To geten hym gilte spores on galoches ycouped.   *slashed shoes (C)*
15   Thanne was Feith in a fenestre, and cryde 'A! *Fili David!*'

         window; Son of David (cf. Mt 21: 9)

---

1 With my skin towards the wool [i.e. with no shirt beneath my cloak] and
with wet feet [with feed shod with wet *rather than* with wet shoes].
6 . . . till Palm Sunday came (C).
7 C9th hymn by Theodulph or Orléans (*OBMLV*, no. 81) (C).

Collation WHmCrGYOC²CBLMR(*to*
412)F.
RUBRIC *Passus xviij^{us} &c et iij^{us} de*
dobet W&r (*&c . . . do.*] *om*
HmYOC²CM; *iij^{us}*] *quartus* B); P.
xvi^{us} de visione vt supra R; *Inc. P.*
xiiij^{us} F; *om* G.
2 As] W&rC; & as g.
reccheth] L&r (cf. C); recched G;
roughte WB.
4 to] βFC; *om* R.

6–8 *So ord* K–D; *after* 9 All MSS
(C).
8 Orgene] α (*pl* F)HmBC; Organye
β.
9 -rauȝte] W&r; -taughte Cr²³g.
10 þe²] WCrYLM?α?C; *om* Hm?gF.
-man] L&rC; *cropped* W.
11 cam] W&rC; gan g.
12 sprac-] αC; spak- ?β (sharp- B;
me- C²; apert- Hm).
14 on] F (?=α); or WHmLMR; *and*
CrgC (C).

As dooth an heraud of armes whan aventrous cometh to justes.
adventurous knights

Olde Jewes of Jerusalem for joye thei songen,.   *sang*
Benedictus qui venit in nomine Domini.
 Thanne I frayned at Feith what al that fare bymente,
asked; stir meant

And who sholde juste in Jerusalem. 'Jesus,' he seide,   *was to joust*
20 'And fecche that the fend claymeth, Piers fruyt the Plowman.'
the fruit of P.P.

 'Is Piers in this place?' quod I, and he preynte on me.   *winked*
 'This Jesus of his gentries wol juste in Piers armes,   *in his nobility*
In his helm and in his haubergeon, *humana natura.*
mail coat; human nature

That Crist be noght biknowe here for *consummatus Deus,*
25 In Piers paltok the Plowman this prikiere shal ryde;
P.P.'s jacket; horseman

For no dynt shal hym dere as *in deitate Patris.*'
 'Who shal juste with Jesus,' quod I, 'Jewes or scrybes?'
 'Nay,' quod Feith, 'but the fend and fals doom to deye.
Deeth seith he shal fordo and adoun brynge   *destroy*
30 Al that lyveth or loketh in londe or in watre.
Lif seith that he lieth, and leieth his lif to wedde   *lays; pledge*
That, for al that Deeth kan do, withinne thre daies to walke
And fecche fro the fend Piers fruyt the Plowman,
And legge it ther hym liketh, and Lucifer bynde,   *place*

17a Blessed is he that cometh in the name of the Lord (Mt 21: 9) (C).
24 ... openly acknowledged as fully and truly God.
26 For no blow [that his human body receives in this combat] will injure him
 in the divine nature that he shares with his Father/God the Father.
28 ... and a false condemnation to death.

17a *domini*] W&rC; *d. &c* Hmg.
19 sholde] βFC; *om* R.
22 gentries] ?βC; gentrie αHmCrB.
24 bi-] WLα; y- HmCrgMC.
 deus] W&rC; *est* g.
28 faith ... deye] α (but] non but
 F)CK–D; he þe foule fend and f. d.

and deeþ β.
30 or¹] β; and αW.
31 lieþ] ?β (liueþ] Cr²³)C; likth αL
 (C).
32 *So div from following* CK–D;
 after daies *All MSS* (to walke]
 W&r; *om* F).

35   And forbite and adoun brynge bale-deeth for evere:

bite through; baleful death (C)

    O Mors, mors tua ero, [*ero morsus*]!

    Thanne cam *Pilatus* with muche peple, *sedens pro tribunali,*
To se how doghtiliche Deeth sholde do, and deme hir botheres right*e*.

of both

The Jewes and the justice ayeins Jesu thei weere,   *judge*
And al the court on hym cryde '*Crucifige!*' sharpe.   *Crucify; loudly*
40   Tho putte hym forth a p[e]lour bifore Pilat and seide,   *accuser* (C)
'This Jesus of oure Jewes temple japed and despised,

made fun of; scorned

To fordoon it on o day, and in thre dayes after   *destroy; in one*
Edifie it eft newe – here he stant that seide it—   *Build; again*
And yit maken it as muche in alle manere poyntes,   *great; respects*
45   Bothe as long and as large a lofte and by grounde.'   *broad; on high*

'*Crucifige!*' quod a cachepol, 'I warante hym a wicche!'

officer; declare

'*Tolle, tolle!*' quod another, and took of kene thornes,   *some sharp*
And bigan of kene thorn a garland to make,
And sette it sore on his heed and seide in envye,   *painfully; malice*
50   '*Ave, raby!*' quod that ribaud – and threw reedes at hym,
Nailed hym with thre nailes naked upon the roode,   *(They) nailed*
And poison on a poole thei putte up to hise lippes,   *pole*
And beden hym drynken his deeth-yvel – hise dayes were ydone—

bade; bane

And [seiden], 'If that thow sotil be, help now thiselve;   *clever, cunning*
55   If thow be Crist and kynges sone, come down of the roode;   *from*
Thanne shul we leve that Lif thee loveth and wol noght lete thee deye!'

35*a* O death, I will be thy death (Osee 13: 14).
46–7 Crucify him! Away with him! (Jn 19: 15).
50 Hail, Rabbi (Mt 26: 49; [Judas' greeting to Jesus]).

35   forbite] ?α?C; forbete β (for) for
      to Cr²³gF (C).
35*a*   mors tua; ero¹] ?αC; trs βF.
    ero morsus] morsus tuus ero F; om
    β (&c Hmg)R.
36   muche] W&r (gret F)C; om g.
39   þe] W&rC; her LR.
40   pel.] so CK–D; pil. All MSS (C).

41   lewes] βC; om α.
    iaped] L&r (he I. F)C; haþ I. W.
42   on] W&rC; in αGBM.
45   a] αB (on FB)C; bi ?β.
50   þat rybaud] βC; þe ribaudes α
    (þe] þo F).
51   vpon] ?αC; on βF.
52   vp] βF; om R.
54   seiden] so CK–D (C).

'*Consummatum est*,' quod Crist, and comsede for to swoune,

'It is finished' (Jn 19: 30)

Pitousliche and pale as a prison that deieth;   *Pitiable; prisoner*
The lord of lif and of light tho leide hise eighen togideres.
60 The day for drede withdrough and derk bicam the sonne.
The wal waggede and cleef, and al the world quaved.

shook; split; quaked

Dede men for that dene come out of depe graves,   *noise*
And tolde why that tempeste so longe tyme durede.   *lasted*
  'For a bitter bataille,' the dede body seide;   *Because of*
65 'Lif and Deeth in this derknesse, hir oon fordooth hir oother.

Each of them is destroying the

Shal no wight wite witterly who shal have the maistrie   *for certain*
Er Sonday aboute sonne-risyng' — and sank with that til erthe.

Before; to the

   Some seide that he was Goddes sone, that so faire deyde:
Vere filius Dei erat iste.
And some seide he was a wicche — 'Good is that we assaye   *test*
70 Wher he be deed or noght deed, doun er he be taken.'   *Whether*
    Two theves also tholed deeth that tyme   *suffered*
Upon a croos bisides Crist — so was the comune lawe.
A cachepol cam forth and craked bothe hir legges,   *broke*
And hir armes after of either of tho theves.
75 Ac was no boy so boold Goddes body to touche;   *fellow*
For he was knyght and kynges sone, Kynde foryaf that throwe

As; granted; time

That noon harlot were so hardy to leyen hond upon hym.

scoundrel should be; bold

   Ac ther cam forth a knyght with a kene spere ygrounde, *sharpened*
Highte Longeus, as the lettre telleth, and longe hadde lore his sighte.

lost

80 Before Pilat and oother peple in the place he hoved.   *waited*

68a Indeed this was the Son of God (Mt 27: 54).

59   The lord] βC; Tyl þe l. F; Til lore
     R.
62   depe] βC; here α.
68a *iste*] WCrCotαC; *i. &c* L&r.
69   þat we] βC; we F; *om* R.

73   A] βC; Ac a α (Ac] But F).
74   her] L&rC; þe WCr.
75   boy] L&rC; body WGCot.
76   throwe] αK–D; tyme βC (C).

Maugree his manye teeth he was maad that tyme
To [justen with Jesus, this blynde Jew Longeus].
For alle thei were unhardy, that hoved on horse or stode,
                                                   lacked courage
To touchen hym or to tasten hym or taken hym doun of roode,
                                                   handle; from
85 But this blynde bacheler, that baar hym thorugh the herte.
                                                   knight; thrust
The blood sprong doun by the spere and unspered the knyghtes
   eighen.   *unbarred, opened*
Thanne fil the knyght upon knees and cryde Jesu mercy: *fell*
'Ayein my wille it was Lord, to wownde yow so soore!'
He sighed and seide, 'Soore it me athynketh!   *grieves*
90 For the dede that I have doon I do me in youre grace.   *put; mercy*
Have on me ruthe, rightful Jesu!' — and right with that he wepte.
Thanne gan Feith felly the false Jewes despise—   *cruelly; upbraid*
Callede hem caytyves acorsed for evere: *wretches; cursed*
'For this foule vileynye vengeaunce to yow alle!   *low, base action*
95 To do the blynde bete hym ybounde, it was a boyes counseille.
                                                 make; knave's
Cursede caytyves! Knyghthood was it nevere   *A knightly action*
To mysdo a deed body by daye or by nyghte.   *maltreat*
The gree yit hath he geten, for al his grete wounde. *prize; i.e. Christ*
'For youre champion chivaler, chief knyght of yow alle,
100 Yilt hym recreaunt rennyng, right at Jesus wille.   *Yields*
For be this derknesse ydo, Deeth worth yvenquisshed;
                                       at an end; defeated
And ye, lurdaynes, han ylost — for Lif shal have the maistrye. *villains*

---

81 'Despite his protests he was then forced . . .'
100 Admits that he has been defeated in the running (of the joust) (C).

82 iusten . . . Longeus] *so* CK–D; to   86 vnspered] βC; opned α.
   take þe spere in his hond and Iusten   þe kny3tes] W&rC; his Crg.
   wiþ Iesus *All MSS* (C).   87 ihesu] ?α(crist F)CK–D; hym β.
83 or] W&rC; & g.   93 for] βC; hem for α.
   stode] βC; stede α.   94 alle] L&r; falle WHmGC²C (C).
84 hym¹] βC; *om* αCr.   96 -tyues] αHmCrOBCK–D; -tif ?β.
   to²] W&rC; *om* gM.   101 deeth . . . Ivenkesched]
   hym³] L&rC; *om* wM.   αCK–D; his deeþ worþ avenged β.
85 þat] αC; þanne β(*om* WCrM).

And youre fraunchyse, that fre was, fallen is in thraldom,
                                      free condition; into

And ye, cherles, and youre children, cheve shulle ye nevere, *prosper*
105 Ne have lordshipe in londe, ne no lond tilye,   *ownership; cultivate*
But al barayne be and usurie usen,   *unproductive; practise*
Which is lif that Oure Lord in alle lawes acurseth.   *condemns*
Now youre goode dayes arn doon, as Daniel prophecied:
Whan Crist cam hir kyngdom the crowne sholde lese—   *lose*
Cum veniat sanctus sanctorum, cessabit unxio vestra.'

110   What for feere of this ferly and of the false Jewes,   *wonder*
I drow me in that derknesse to *descendit ad inferna*, *withdrew myself*
And there I saugh soothly, *secundum scripturas*,
Out of the west coste, a wenche, as me thoughte,   *region; girl*
Cam walkynge in the wey; to helleward she loked.   *toward Hell*
115 Mercy highte that mayde, a meke thyng with alle,
A ful benigne burde, and buxom of speche.   *kindly lady; courteous*
   Hir suster, as it semed, cam softely walkynge   *quietly*
Evene out of the est, and westward she lokede—   *Directly; east*
A ful comely creature [and a clene], Truthe she highte;
120 For the vertue that hire folwede, afered was she nevere.   *power*
   Whan thise maydenes mette, Mercy and Truthe,
Either asked oother of this grete wonder—   *Each; about*
Of the dyn and of the derknesse, and how the day rowed,   *dawned*
And which a light and a leme lay bifore helle.   *glow*
125   'Ich have ferly of this fare, in feith,' seide Truthe, *wonder at; event*
'And am wendynge to wite what this wonder meneth.'

109a 'When the Saint of Saints comes, your anoint[ed kingship] shall come to
    an end (cf. Dan 9: 24) (C).
111 ... into the depths of hell [*lit.* he descended into hell, eighth clause of
    Apostles' Creed].
112 ... according to the Scriptures (Gospel of Nicodemus; cf. Ps 84: 11).

104 ȝe²] L&r; *om* W.
105 Ne¹] L&rC; To WHm.
106 vsurie vsen] W&r; by v. ȝowr
    lyf lede Hm (*cf.* C).
109 hir] ?β (of hir WHmCr¹M (of
    +M)K–D; þe R; to his F.
    lese] αK–D; cesse β(iesse C; *om* L).
109a cessabit . . . vestra] βC; *om* α.
110 þe] βFC; þo R.

114 þe] βFC; þat R.
117 softly] L&rC; sooþly WYC²M;
    worthely Cr.
119 and a clene] *so* CK–D; *om All
    MSS* (C).
121 Whan] βC; And whan α.
123 of²] wOCotLMR; *om* ?gFC.
124 which] βC; swich α.

'Have no merveille,' quod Mercy, 'murthe it bitokneth.

             joy; portends

A maiden that highte Marie, and moder withouten felyng

             (sexual) contact

Of any kynde creature, conceyved thorugh speche *natural creature*
130 And grace of the Holy Goost; weex greet with childe;   *grew*
Withouten wem into this world she broghte hym;   *stain*
And that my tale be trewe, I take God to witnesse.

  'Sith this barn was ybore ben thritti wynter passed,
Which deide and deeth tholed this day aboute mydday— *suffered*
135 And that is cause of this clips that closeth now the sonne,

             eclipse; encloses

In menynge that man shal fro merknesse be drawe *sign; darkness*
The while this light and this leme shal Lucifer ablende. *glow; blind*
For patriarkes and prophetes han preched herof often—
That man shal man save thorugh a maydenes helpe,
140 And that was tynt thorugh tree, tree shal it wynne, *that (which); lost*
And that Deeth down broughte, deeth shal releve.' *raise up, restore*
  'That thow tellest,' quod Truthe, 'is but a tale of waltrot!

             absurdity

For Adam and Eve and Abraham with othere
Patriarkes and prophetes that in peyne liggen,
145 Leve thow nevere that yon light hem alofte brynge,

            shall bring them above

Ne have hem out of helle – hold thi tonge, Mercy!
It is but trufle that thow tellest – I, Truthe, woot the sothe. *nonsense*
For that is ones in helle, out cometh it nevere;
Job the prophete patriark repreveth thi sawes: *disproves; words*
Quia in inferno nulla est redempcio.'
150 Thanne Mercy ful myldely mouthed thise wordes: *uttered*
'Thorugh experience,' quod he[o], 'I hope thei shul be saved.

149*a* For in hell there is no salvation (C).
151 On the basis of practical experience I [found my] hope that . . .

129 kende] αC; kynnes β.
138 often] L&r; ofte WHmC.
141 doun] L&rC; adown W.
145 hem alofte] W&rC; alofte shall
  g (sh.] sh. hem O).
147 but] αC; but a β (but) *om* G).
  I] βC; *om* α.

148 þat] L&r; he þat WHmF.
  it] L&rC; he wC²F.
151 heo] *so* CK–D; he αCr¹; she β
  (C).
  þei shul] βC; þow shalt R; I shal
  FCr³.

For venym fordooth venym – and that I preve by reson.   *destroys*
For of alle venymes foulest is the scorpion;
May no medicyne [amende] the place ther he styngeth,   *heal*
155 Til he be deed and do therto – the yvel he destruyeth,   *placed upon it*
The firste venymouste, thorugh vertu of hymselve.   *poison; power*
So shal this deeth fordo – I dar my lif legge—   *destroy; wager*
All that Deeth dide first thorugh the develes entisyng;   *tempting*
And right as thorugh [gilours] gile [bigiled was man formest],

                                          (a) deceiver's; first

160 So shal grace that al bigan make a good ende
[And bigile the gilour – and that is good sleighte]:   *stratagem (C)*
Ars ut artem falleret.'

   'Now suffre we!' seide Truthe; 'I se, as me thynketh,   *let's be quiet*
Out of the nyppe of the north, noght ful fer hennes,

                                      cold region; from here

Rightwisnesse come rennynge; reste we the while,   *Justice*
165 For he[o] woot moore than we – he[o] was er we bothe.'
   'That is sooth,' seide Mercy, 'and I se here by sowthe   *(the) south*
Where cometh Pees pleyinge, in pacience yclothed.
Love hath coveited hire longe – leve I noon oother   *desired*
But he sente hire som lettre, what this light bymeneth   *means*
170 That overhoveth helle thus; he[o] us shal telle.'   *hovers over*
   Whan Pees in pacience yclothed approched ner hem tweyne,
Rightwisnesse hire reverenced for hir riche clothyng,

                                      saluted courteously

And preide Pees to telle hire to what place she wolde   *wished to go*
And in hire gaye garnements whom she grete thoughte?   *intended to*

161a That God by stratagem should foil The shape-shifting Destroyer's guile
(Fortunatus' *Pange lingua*, *OBMLV*, no. 54, line 8).

152 I preue] L&r (I) *om* Bo); *trs*
WCot.
154 amende] *so* CK–D; helpe *All*
MSS (C).
156 vertue] αCK–D; venym β.
157 fordo] βC; do α.
158 dyd] L&r (*cf.* C); fordide
WHm.
159 gilours ... formest] gile man
was bigiled *All MSS* (C).
160 all bigan] C²C (*trs*); he gan F;
bigan W&r (C).

ende] YGC²CK–D; sighte CB
+O; sleighte W&r.
161 *From C-text, so* K–D; *l. om All*
MSS (C).
165 heo[1,2]] *so* K–D; he W&r (she
F).
167 cometh pes] ?αC; *trs* βF.
170 heo] he α; she β.
171 ner] W&r (*om* F); neigh gCr23.
172 for] L&r; by WHm.
173 she] βC; he αG (*corr to* she).
174 she] βC; he α.

175　'My wil is to wende,' quod she, 'and welcome hem alle
　　　That many day myghte I noght se for merknesse of synne:　*darkness*
　　　Adam and Eve and othere mo in helle,　*more*
　　　Moyses and many mo Mercy shul have,
　　　And I shal daunce therto – do thow so, suster!
180　For Jesus justede wel, joye bigynneth dawe:　*Because; to dawn*
　　　Ad vesperum demorabitur fletus, et ad matutinum leticia.

　　　'Love, that is my lemman, swiche lettres he me sente　*beloved*
　　　That Mercy, my suster, and I mankynde sholde save,
　　　And that God hath forgyven and graunted me, Pees, and Mercy
　　　　　　　　　　　　　　　　　　　　　　　　'freely assigned to'
　　　To be mannes meynpernour for everemoore after.　*surety*
185　Lo, here the patente!' quod Pees, '*In pace in idipsum,*　*authority*
　　　And that this dede shal dure, *dormiam et requiescam.*'
　　　　　　　　　　　　　　　　　　　　document; be always valid

　　　'What, ravestow?' quod Rightwisnesse; 'or thow art right dronke!
　　　　　　　　　　　　　　　　　　　　Are you mad? dead drunk
　　　Levestow that yond light unlouke myghte helle　*unlock*
　　　And save mannes soule? Suster, wene it nevere!　*think, suppose*
190　At the bigynnyng God gaf the doom hymselve—　*gave; judgement*
　　　That Adam and Eve and alle that hem suwede　*followed, came after*
　　　Sholden deye downrighte, and dwelle in peyne after　*entirely, utterly*
　　　If that thei touchede a tree and of the fruyt eten.　*one; ate*
　　　Adam afterward, ayeins his defence,　*prohibition*
195　Freet of that fruyt, and forsook, as it were,　*Ate*
　　　The love of Oure Lord and his loore bothe　*teaching*
　　　And folwede that the fend taughte and his felawes wille　*i.e. Eve's*
　　　Ayeins reson – I, Rightwisnesse, recorde thus with Truthe　*declare*

180*a* In the evening weeping shall have place: and in the morning gladness (Ps
　　29: 6).
185–6 See, here is the letter of authorization, and [a text from the Psalms
　　signifying] that this document shall have lasting validity: 'In peace in the
　　selfsame I will sleep, and I will rest' (Ps 4: 9).

175　she] β; he ?α (*om* F).
179　*In* β (And] *om* g)C; *line om* α.
181　he] ?αC; *om* βF.
182　my suster] β (my] *om* O)C; *om*
　　α.
189　it] βC; þow it α.

190　At . . . god] L&r (At] Ac atte
　　Hm)C; For at þe fyrste god F; For
　　god þe bigynnere W.
192　peyne] αCr³C²BC; pyne ?β.
193　of þe] F (?=α)C; þe β (þe trees
　　Hm)R (C).
198　*In* β (I] L; *om* wgM)C; *l. om* α.

That hir peyne be perpetuel and no preiere hem helpe.
200 Forthi lat hem chewe as thei chosen, and chide we noght, sustres,
For it is botelees bale, the byte that thei eten.'   *incurable evil; mouthful*
'And I shal preie,' quod Pees, 'hir peyne moot have ende,
And wo into wele mowe wenden at the laste.   *happiness; turn*
For hadde thei wist of no wo, wele hadde thei noght knowen;
205 For no wight woot what wele is, that nevere wo suffrede,
Ne what is hoot hunger, that hadde nevere defaute.   *?hot/called; lack*
If no nyght ne weere, no man, as I leve,
Sholde wite witterly what day is to meene.   *properly; means*
Sholde nevere right riche man that lyveth in reste and ese   *a very rich*
210 Wite what wo is, ne were the deeth of kynde.   *natural death, mortality*
So God that bigan al of his goode wille
Bicam man of a mayde mankynde to save,
And suffrede to be sold, to se the sorwe of deying,
The which unknytteth alle care, and comsynge is of reste.   *start*
215 For til *modicum* mete with us, I may it wel avowe,   *'a little'*
Woot no wight, as I wene, what is ynogh to mene.
    'Forthi God, of his goodnesse, the firste gome Adam,   *man*
Sette hym in solace and in sovereyn murthe;   *content; supreme joy*
And siththe he suffred hym synne, sorwe to feele—   *allowed (to)*
220 To wite what wele was, kyndeliche to knowe it.   *directly; i.e. suffering*
And after, God auntrede hymself and took Adames kynde   *ventured*
To wite what he hath suffred in thre sondry places,
Bothe in hevene and in erthe — and now til helle he thenketh,
                                                            to; i.e. to go
To wite what alle wo is, that woot of alle joye.
225   'So it shal fare by this folk; hir folie and hir synne

215–16 For till they experience 'too little', none can know the meaning of 'enough'.

200 sustres] wLMC; sustre g.
202 I] W&rC; *om* YLR.
    preie] αC; preue β.
203 wo] L&r (we Cr)C; from wo
    WHm.
    wende] L&rC; wenden WF.
204 hadde þei¹] βC; þei α (hadd
    +F).
208 wite] L&r; neuere wite WHm.

213 suffrede] βFC; soffre RCr²³.
    to²] βC; and α.
215 mete] ?β; mette αHmGYOB.
216 is ynough] β (y.] ynought Y; *trs*
    WHm)C; is nouȝte ?α (it is F).
218 murþe] β; ioye α.
220 was] β; is α.
221 auntrede] W&r; graunted g.
224 þat . . . of] L&r (of] what G)C;
    and what is WHm.

Shal lere hem what langour is, and lisse withouten ende.   *pain; joy*
Woot no wight what werre is ther that pees regneth,   *war*
Ne what is witterly wele til "weylawey" hym teche.'   *misery ('alas!')*

Thanne was ther a wight with two brode eighen;   *wide*
230 Book highte that beaupeere, a bold man of speche.   *i.e. 'Bible'; elder*
'By Goddes body!' quod this Book, 'I wol bere witnesse
That tho this barn was ybore, ther blased a sterre   *when; star*
That alle the wise of this world in o wit acordeden—   *one judgement*
That swich a barn was ybore in Bethleem the citee
235 That mannes soule sholde save and synne destroye.
    'And alle the elements,' quod the Book, 'herof beren witnesse.
That he was God that al wroghte the wolkne first shewed: *heaven(s)*
Tho that weren in hevene token *stella comata*   *a comet*
And tendeden hire as a torche to reverencen his burthe;   *kindled*
240 The light folwede the Lord into the lowe erthe.
The water witnesseth that he was God, for he wente on it;
Peter the Apostel parceyved his gate,   *going*
And as he wente on the water wel hym knew, and seide,   *recognized*
"*Iube me venire ad te super aquas.*"
245 And lo! how the sonne gan louke hire light in hirselve   *lock up*
Whan she seigh hym suffre, that sonne and see made.   *sea*
The erthe for hevynesse that he wolde suffre   *grief*
Quaked as quyk thyng and al biquasshe the roche.   *a live; shattered*
    'Lo! helle myghte nat holde, but opnede tho God tholede,   *suffered*
250 And leet out Symondes sones to seen hym hange on roode.
                                                        Simeon's (C)
And now shal Lucifer leve it, though hym looth thynke;   *seem hateful*
For *Gigas* the geaunt with a gyn engyned

---

244 [Lord, if it be thou], bid me come to thee upon the waters (Mt 14: 28).
252 For Gigas the giant has contrived with an engine (of war) . . . (C).

226   lisse] βC; blisse ?α (*om*F)GY.   -eþ] gαC; -ed wLM.
233   wise of] β (w.] w. men Cr)C;   243   þe] βFC; þat R.
      men in α.   246   see] βC; mone α.
      acordeden] LORHmC; acorden   248   -quasche] αC; -quasshed β.
      W&r.   250   sones] L&r (*om* Y)C; sg
234   þe] WRC; *om* L&r.   WHmB.
238   -ata] L&rC; -eta WHmCr²³G.   251   leue] βC; leese F; *om* R.
239   hir] L&r; it WC.   252-3   *In* βC; *ll. om* α.
241   The] WCrOαC; þat L&r.   252   engyned] L&r; haþ e. W.

To breke and to bete adoun that ben ayeins Jesus.   *(those) who*
And I, Book, wole be brent, but Jesus rise to lyve   *burnt; unless*
255 In alle myghtes of man, and his moder gladie,   *powers; cheer*
And conforte al his kyn and out of care brynge,
And al the Jewene joye unjoynen and unlouken;   *Jews'; dissolve*
And but thei reverencen his roode and his resurexion,
And bileve on a newe lawe, be lost, lif and soule!'   *(they shall) be*
260 'Suffre we!' seide Truthe; 'I here and see bothe   *Let us be quiet*
A spirit speketh to helle and bit unspere the yates: *bids unbar; gates*
"*Attolite portas*."
A vois loude in that light to Lucifer crieth,
"Prynces of this place, unpynneth and unlouketh!   *undo; unlock*
For here cometh with crowne that kyng is of glorie." '   *(he) who*
265   Thanne sikede Sathan, and seide to Helle,   *sighed*
'Swich a light, ayeins oure leve, Lazar it fette;   *leave/belief; fetched*
Care and combraunce is comen to us alle!   *confusion*
If this kyng come in, mankynde wole he fecche,
And lede it ther Lazar is, and lightliche me bynde.   *easily*
270 Patriarkes and prophetes han parled herof longe—   *spoken*
That swich a lord and a light shal lede hem alle hennes.'   *from here*
'Listneth!' quod Lucifer, 'for I this lord knowe;
Both this lord and this light, is longe ago I knew hym.
May no deeth this lord dere, ne no develes queyntise,   *harm; cunning*
275 And where he wole, is his wey — ac ware hym of the perils!

                                                         let him beware

If he reve me of my right, he robbeth me by maistrie;

                                                          deprive; sheer force

For by right and by reson the renkes that ben here   *people*

261*a* Lift up your gates, [O ye princes] . . . (Ps 23: 9).

255 of] β; of a α.
258 -rencen] L&rC; -rsen WCr¹.
259 bileue] W&rC; leuen g.
After this an extra line g.
261 A] αC; How a β.
  bit] L&rC; biddeþ WF.
261*a* *So* βC; *as one line with* 262
  (*&c*) *om*) α.
265 helle] αCK–D; hem alle β.
266 it] L&rC; is B; out WCr.

267 com-] L&rC; encom- WB.
269 it] βC; hem α.
  laȝar is] αCK–D; hym likeþ β.
271 a²] L&r; *om* WHmC².
  schal] αC; sholde β.
274 þis lorde] αCK–D; hym β.
275 his] βFC; *om* R.
276 reueþ] L&rC; reueþ WYC²C.
  he robbeþ] βC; & robbe α.
  of] αCrC; *om* β.
277 þe] wCBαC; þo L&r.

Body and soule beth myne, bothe goode and ille.
For hymself seide, that sire is of hevene,   *lord*
280 That if Adam ete the appul, alle sholde deye,
And dwelle [in deol] with us develes – this thretynge he made.   *pain*
And [sithen] he that Soothnesse is seide thise wordes,   *since*
And I sithen iseised seven[ty] hundred wynter,
I leeve that lawe nyl noght lete hym the leeste.'
285   'That is sooth,' seide Satan, 'but I me soore drede;
For thow gete hem with gile, and his gardyn breke,   *got; broke (into)*
And in semblaunce of a serpent sete on the appultre,   *sat*
And eggedest hem to ete, Eve by hirselve,   *urged*
And toldest hire a tale – of treson were the wordes;   *treachery, deceit*
290 And so thou haddest hem out and hider at the laste.
It is noght graithly geten, ther gile is the roote!'   *duly obtained*
   'For God wol noght be bigiled,' quod Gobelyn, 'ne byjaped.

                                                               fooled

We have no trewe title to hem, for thorugh treson were thei
   dampned.'   *valid claim*
   'Certes, I drede me,' quod the Devel, 'lest Truthe wol hem fecche.
295 Thise thritty wynter, as I wene, he wente aboute and preched.
I have assailled hym with synne, and som tyme I asked   *once*
Wher he were God or Goddes sone – he gaf me short answere;
And thus hath he trolled forth thise two and thritty wynter.

                                                              wandered
And whan I seigh it was so, slepynge I wente   *in (her) sleep*
300 To warne Pilates wif what done man was Jesus;   *'make of' (Sk, q.v.)*
For Jewes hateden hym and han doon hym to dethe.

283–4 And (since) I was then put in possession [of them] . . . I am convinced
   that [his own] decree will not permit him [to overcome us by sheer strength].

279 *In* W&rC; *l. om* g.
280 þat] α (*cf.* C); *om* β.
281 in deol] *om All MSS* (C).
282 siþen] *cj* K–D; *om All MSS* (C).
     he] βF; *om* R.
283 And . . . I sessed] ?α (s. y was
     sesed F); And siþen I seised β(I] is
     ?g; he CrCB).
     seventy] seuene β (*many* YO); þise
     seue α (C).
287 on] L&r; vpon WCr.
290 so] βC; al so α.

294 *After this another line* Cr²³g.
295 he . . . aboute] αCK–D; haþ he
     gon β.
296 tyme] βC; *om* α.
     I²] *so* C; y- W&r(*om* CrGC²B); y
     have hym F (C).
297 Where] L&rC; Wheiþer W.
     gaf] L&rC; yaf WOC²BMF.
298 haþ he] βC; *trs* αCr.
299 slepyng] L&r (s *erased* M);
     lepynge WHmCr¹.

I wolde have lengthed his lif – for I leved, if he deide,   *prolonged*
That his soule wolde noght suffre no synne in his sighte;
For the body, while it on bones yede, aboute was evere   *walked alive*
305 To save men from synne if hemself wolde.   *(they) themselves*
And now I se wher a soule cometh [seillynge hiderward]   *gliding*
With glorie and with gret light – God it is, I woot wel!
I rede we fle,' quod he, 'faste alle hennes—
For us were bettre noght be than biden his sighte.   *await, endure*
310 For thi lesynges, Lucifer, lost is al oure praye.   *lies; prey*
First thorugh the we fellen fro hevene so heighe;
For we leved thi lesynges, we lopen out alle with thee;   *believed; fled*
And now for thi laste lesynge, ylorn have we Adam,   *lost*
And al oure lordshipe, I leve, a londe and a watre: *on*
Nunc princeps huius mundi eicietur foras.'
315   Eft the light bad unlouke, and Lucifer answerde,   *Again; unlock*
'*Quis est iste?*
What lord artow?' quod Lucifer. The light soone seide,   *are you*
'*Rex glorie,*
The lord of myght and of mayn and alle manere vertues—   *powers*
Dominus virtutum.
320 Dukes of this dymme place, anoon undo thise yates,   *at once; gates*
That Crist may come in, the Kynges sone of Hevene!'

314a Now shall the prince of this world be cast out (Jn 12: 31).
316, 318, 319a Who is this [King of Glory]? The Lord of hosts, he is the King
    of Glory (Ps 23: 10) (C).

302 I¹; leued] βC; And I; leue α.
303 nauȝt] α; *om* β.
306 seillynge; hiderward] *trs All
    MSS* (C).
308 we] L&rC; þat we CB.
309 his] βR; in his FC.
312–13 *So* α(*cf.* C)Sk; *run together*
    β.
312 þi] L&r; on þi WCrC.
    we² . . . þe] ?α (with þe] *om* F); *om*
    β.
313 And . . . lesynge] αC; *om* β.
    haue we] α; *trs* β.
314a *huius; mundi*] βFC; *trs* R.
    eicietur] W&rC; eicitur YBR.
316–19 *As* 2 *ll. div after* iste α.

316–18 *As* 2 *ll. div after* iste β;
    re-ord K–D (C).
    Quis . . . glorie] What l. artow
    quod Luc. *Quis est iste/ Rex glorie*
    þe light soone seide W&r(*Rex . . .
    seide*] þe Lyght seyde *Rex eterne* F;
    soone] *om* R).
319 *So* Hm&rK–D; *as one l. with*
    319a WOC²CBmBoL.
    þe] αCK–D; And β.
    mayne] L&rC; man WR; mani
    BmBo.
319a *So* β (*l. om* Y); *as one l. with*
    320 ?α (*l. om* F).
320 Dukes] β?C; Duk ?α(þow d. F).
321 þe] βFC; *om* R.

And with that breeth helle brak, with Belialles barres— *burst open*
For any wye or warde, wide open the yates. *despite; guardian*
Patriarkes and prophetes, *populus in tenebris,*
325 Songen Seint Johanes song, '*Ecce Agnus Dei!*'

Behold the Lamb of God (Jn 1: 36)

Lucifer loke ne myghte, so light hym ablente. *blinded*
And tho that Oure Lord lovede, into his light he laughte, *caught*
And seide to Sathan, 'Lo! here my soule to amendes *in satisfaction*
For alle synfulle soules, to save tho that ben worthi.
330 Myne thei ben and of me – I may the bet hem cleyme. *more validly*
Although reson recorde, and right of myselve, *declare; my own justice*
That if thei ete the appul, alle sholde deye,
I bihighte hem noght here helle for evere. *decreed, promised*
For the dede that thei dide, thi deceite it made; *caused it*
335 With gile thow hem gete, ageyn alle reson. *got; against*
For in my paleis, Paradis, in persone of an addre, *form; serpent*
Falsliche thow fettest there thyng that I lovede. *brought away from*
'Thus ylik a lusard with a lady visage, *serpent; woman's face*
Thefliche thow me robbedest. The Olde Lawe graunteth *Like a thief*
340 That gilours be bigiled – and that is good reson:
Dentem pro dente et oculum pro oculo.
Ergo soule shal soule quyte and synne to synne wende, *pay for (C)*
And al that man hath mysdo, I man, wole amende it. *done wrong*
Membre for membre [was amendes by the Olde Lawe], *satisfaction*
And lif for lif also – and by that lawe I clayme
345 Adam and al his issue at my wille herafter.
And that Deeth in hem fordide, my deeth shal releve,

destroyed; restore

---

324 The people [that walked] in darkness [have seen a great light] (Is 9: 2,
quoted Mt 4: 16); cf. V 494*a* (C).
325 Behold the Lamb of God (Jn 1: 36).
340*a* Eye for eye, tooth for tooth (Ex 21: 24, *trs*).

322 brak] βC; braste α.
323 open] ?β?C; opned αWHm.
331 Al]þough] L&rC; And þouȝ
WHm.
332 þei] L&rC; he WHm.
337 fettest] W&rC; fecchedest M;
fecchest R.
þere] L&rC; *om* WYO.

339 þe] L&r; and þe W.
342 man wole] W&r; may wel
OCr²³F (w.] it wel F).
it] αC; *om* β.
343 was amendes; by . . . lawe] *cj*
K–D; *trs All MSS* (by] in Cr) (C).
344 clayme] αK–D; clayme it β.

And bothe quyke and quyte that queynt was thorugh synne;
And that grace gile destruye, good feith it asketh.   *should; requires*
So leve it noght, Lucifer, ayein the lawe I fecche hem,   *believe; against*
350 But by right and by reson raunsone here my liges: *ransom; subjects*
Non veni solvere legem set adimplere.
     'Thow fettest myne in my place ayeins alle reson—
Falsliche and felonliche; good feith me it taughte,   *felonously*
To recovere hem thorugh raunsoun, and by no reson ellis,
                       no other method
So that with gile thow gete, thorugh grace it is ywonne.   *that (which)*
355 Thow, Lucifer, in liknesse of a luther addere   *treacherous, evil*
Gete bi gile thyng that God lovede;   *Got; those*
And I, in liknesse of a leode, that Lord am of hevene,   *human being*
Graciousliche thi gile have quyt – go gile ayein gile!   *let go against g.*
And as Adam and alle thorugh a tree deyden,   *one*
360 Adam and alle thorugh a tree shal turne to lyve;
And gile is bigiled, and in his gile fallen:
Et cecidit in foveam quam fecit.
Now bigynneth thi gile ageyn thee to turne
And my grace to growe ay gretter and widder.   *ever; wider*
The bitternesse that thow hast browe, now brouke it thiselve;
                       brewed; enjoy
365 That art doctour of deeth, drynk that thow madest!   *(You) who*
     'For I that am lord of lif, love is my drynke,
And for that drynke today, I deide upon erthe.   *because; for the sake of*
I faught so, me thursteth yet, for mannes soule sake;   *fought; I thirst*
May no drynke me moiste, ne my thurst slake,
370 Til the vendage falle in the vale of Josaphat,   *vintage take place*

---

347 And both give life to and make satisfaction for that which was quenched
     through sin [*sc.* eternal life for man and its loss through the fall].
350*a* I am not come to destroy the law but to fulfil (Mt 5: 17).
361*a* . . . he is fallen into the hole he made (Ps 7: 16).

347 quykke] L&r (quyt F); quykne
    wM.
348 -uye] ?β; -oyeth αCr; -oyed CB.
349 it] LαC; I wg; thow M.
350 by²] wCLM (*cf.* C); *om* ?gα.
350*a* ad-] βFC; *om* R.
351 alle] β; ryght & F; *om* R.

354 with] LαC; þoruȝ wgM.
    is] βC; was α.
356 Gete] αB; Getest β.
    þing] α; þo β.
357 I] W&r; *om* Crg.
360 turne] αCK–D; t. ayein β.
363 widder] βC; grettere α.
364 now] αCK–D; *om* β (*l. om* W).

That I drynke right ripe must, *resureccio mortuorum.*
And thanne shal I come as a kyng, crouned, with aungeles,
And have out of helle alle mennes soules.
   'Fendes and fendekynes bifore me shul stande   *minor devils*
375 And be at my biddyng wheresoevere me liketh.
Ac to be merciable to man thanne, my kynde it asketh,   *merciful*
For we beth bretheren of blood, but noght in baptisme alle. *by blood*
Ac alle that beth myne hole bretheren, in blood and in baptisme,

                                                                    entire

Shul noght be dampned to the deeth that is withouten ende:
Tibi soli peccavi . . .
380 'It is noght used on erthe to hangen a feloun   *customary*
Ofter than ones, though he were a tretour.   *once; traitor*
And if the kyng of that kyngdom come in that tyme   *came*
There the feloun thole sholde deeth or oother juwise,

                                                        suffer; judgement

Lawe wolde he yeve hym lif, and he loked on hym.   *should grant; if*
385 And I that am kyng of kynges shal come swich a tyme
Ther doom to the deeth dampneth alle wikked;   *(final) judgement*
And if lawe wole I loke on hem, it lith in my grace   *lies*
Wheither thei deye or deye noght for that thei diden ille.
Be it any thyng abought, the boldnesse of hir synnes,   *redeemed*
390 I may do mercy thorugh rightwisnesse, and alle my wordes trewe.

---

371 When I shall drink new wine [from grapes] thoroughly ripened – the
   resurrection of the dead (C).
375 . . . wherever it pleases me that they should be.
377 For men and I are brothers through the human nature we share, but not
   all are my brothers through baptism.
379a To thee only have I sinned . . . (Ps 50: 6).
383 Where the criminal is due to suffer death or a sentence of death (C).
389–90 If any circumstance mitigate the gravity of their sins, I have the power
   to show mercy as part of justice, and (still preserve) the truth of all I said.

374   fende-] L&rC; fynde- WC.
376   Ac] α (But F)CK–D; And β.
      to be] βC; not so F; *om* R.
      þanne] βC; *om* αY.
      it askeþ] β (it) *om* WO)R; it] þanne
      it R)C; may not aske F.
379a &c] βF; *om* R.
380   on] ?αC; in βF.

383   þe] L&r; *om* W.
      or] W&r; *om* CrMC.
      Iuwise] WHm?GC²C; wise
      YOCBLα; els CrM (C).
384   and] αC; if β.
386   Ther] W&r (& þ. F)C; where g.
389   abou3t] W&rC; *om* ?g (*l. om*
      CB).
390   may] LαC.

And though Holy Writ wole that I be wroke of hem that diden ille—
avenged upon

(*Nullum malum impunitum . . .*)
Thei shul be clensed clerliche and [clene] wasshen of hir synnes
clearly

In my prisone Purgatorie, til *parce* it hote.
And my mercy shal be shewed to manye of my bretheren;
395   For blood may suffre blood bothe hungry and acale,   *cold*
Ac blood may noght se blood blede, but hym rewe.'
    Audivi archana verba que non licet homini loqui.
    'Ac my rightwisnesse and right shal rulen al helle,   *'strict justice'*
And mercy al mankynde bifore me in hevene.   sc. *shall rule* (C)
For I were an unkynde kyng but I my kyn holpe—   *unless*
400   And nameliche at swich a nede ther nedes help bihoveth:
Non intres in iudicium cum servo tuo.
    'Thus by lawe,' quod Oure Lord, 'lede I wole fro hennes
Tho [leodes] that I lovede and leved in my comynge.   *people; believed*
And for thi lesynge, Lucifer, that thow leighe til Eve,   *lie; told to*
Thow shalt abyen it bittre!' – and bond hym with cheynes.   *pay for*
405   Astroth and al the route hidden hem in hernes;   *crew; corners*
They dorste noght loke on Oure Lord, the [l]este of hem alle,   *least*
But leten hym lede forth what hym liked and lete what hym liste.
leave

    Manye hundred of aungeles harpeden and songen,
'*Culpat caro, purgat caro, regnat Deus Dei caro.*'

391*a* No evil shall go unpunished [and no good unrewarded] (cf. IV 143 (C)).
393 . . . till (a command to) spare (them) bid it be otherwise (C).
395–6*a* For one may put up with one's kinsmen going both hungry and cold,
    But not with seeing one's kin bleed, without feeling pity. I heard secret words
    which it is not granted to man to utter (II Cor 12: 4) (C).
400–400*a* And especially in dire straits, when there is a great need for help:
    '. . . enter not into judgement with thy servant' (Ps 142: 2).
409 Flesh sins, flesh frees from sin, / As God now reigns, God flesh within
    (*Aeterne rex altissime*, stanza 4, Roman Breviary, Matins Ascension Hymn).

391 þat I] βC; I α (*om* F)G.
391*a* &c] β; *om* αB.
392 clene] *om All MSS* (C).
396 se] βC; se his α.
399 kyn] αC; kynde β.
  holpe] LGC²Bα?C; helpe W&r.

402 leodes . . . I] *so* ?CK–D; þat I α;
  þat me β (C).
403 til] βC; to αCr²³GC².
406 leste] *so* CK–D; boldeste *All
  MSS* (C).

410   Thanne pipede Pees of poesie a note: *song*
        '*Clarior est solito post maxima nebula Phebus;*
        Post inimicicias clarior est et amor.
        After sharpest shoures,' quod Pees, 'moost shene is the sonne;
        Is no weder warmer than after watry cloudes;
        Ne no love levere, ne lever frendes   *more precious; dearer*
        Than after werre and wo, whan love and pees ben maistres.
415   Was nevere werre in this world, ne wikkednesse so kene,   *fierce*
        That Love, and hym liste, to laughynge ne broughte,
        And Pees, thorugh pacience, alle perils stoppede.'
          'Trewes!' quod Truthe; 'thow tellest us sooth, by Jesus!   *Truce!*
        Clippe we in covenaunt, and ech of us kisse oother.'
                                        Let us embrace; concord
420   'And lete no peple,' quod Pees, 'parceyve that we chidde;   *notice*
        For inpossible is no thyng to Hym that is almyghty.'
          'Thow seist sooth,' seide Rightwisnesse, and reverentliche hire
          kiste,
        Pees, and Pees h[i]re, *per secula seculorum.*   *for ever and ever*
        Misericordia et Veritas obviaverunt sibi; Iusticia et Pax osculate sunt.
          Truthe trumpede tho and song *Te Deum laudamus;*
425   And thanne lutede Love in a loud note,   *(sang to the) lute*
        '*Ecce quam bonum et quam iocundum . . .*'

410*a* After much cloud the sun we brighter see/Love brighter, also, after
    enmity (Alanus de Insulis, *Liber parabolorum* (*PL* 210: 581–2)) (C).

423*a* Mercy and truth have met each other: justice and peace have kissed (Ps
    84: 11).

424 We praise you God (the *Te Deum* hymn) (C).

425*a* Behold how good and how pleasant it is [for brethren to dwell together
    in unity] (Ps 132: 1).

410*a* *solito*] βFC; *om* R.
    clarior² . . . *amor*] gαCSk; *&c*
    wLM.
411 scharpest] αC; sharpe β.
413 R *defective to* XX 26 (8 *leaves
    lost*); F *collated only selectively
    after this.*
416 That] Cr¹CBMFC; That ne
    W&r.
    ne] W&r?C; he F; it Hm.
417 stopped] L&r (-de *over erasure*
    Hm; -d *alt. to* þ M)C; stoppeþ WF
    (he s. F).

419 cusse] L&rC; clippe W.
420 lete] L&rC; leteþ W.
    chidde] WCrLFC; chide HmgM.
422 seyde] LMC; quod wgF.
423 hire] *so* K–D; here W&r (*l. om*
    F); there G.
423*a* *Iusticia* . . . *sunt*] β (*s. &c*
    Hm?g (*om* Bm)); su (*cropped*) W)C;
    om F.
425 þanne . . . loue] β (loue) *om*
    WHm)C; love lawhte of hym F.
425*a* *&c*] βC; *om* BF.

Til the day dawed thise damyseles carolden,   *dawned; danced (C)*
That men rongen to the resurexion – and right with that I wakede,
And callede Kytte my wif and Calote my doghter:
'Ariseth and go reverenceth Goddes resurexion,   *do honour to*
430 And crepeth to the cros on knees, and kisseth it for a juwel!   *creep*
For Goddes blissede body it bar for oure boote,   *bore; salvation*
And it afereth the fend – for swich is the myghte,   *frightens; power*
May no grisly goost glide there it shadweth!'   *where its shadow falls*

---

427 Until the bells of Easter Morning were rung . . .

426   carolden] F (?=α)?CK–D;
      dauncede β.
429   Ariseth] L&rC; And bad hem
      rise W.
      goo] F (?=α)C; om β.
      -ceth] L&r; -ce WCrGCC.

430   crepeth] L&r; crepe WCrGC.
      to þe cros; on knees] βC; trs F.
      kisseth] L&r; kisse WCrGFC.
431   goddes] βC; cristis BF.
433   shadweth] L&rC; schawyþ
      Hm; walkeþ W.

Passus XIX

Thus I awaked and wroot what I hadde ydremed,
And dighte me derely, and dide me to chirche,   *dressed tidily; went*
To here holly the masse and to be housled after.
In myddes of the masse, tho men yede to offryng,   *when; went*
5   I fel eftsoones aslepe – and sodeynly me mette   *again; I dreamed*
That Piers the Plowman was peynted al blody,   *painted*
And com in with a cros bifore the comune peple,
And right lik in alle lymes to Oure Lord Jesu.   *limbs, features*
        And thanne called I Conscience to kenne me the sothe: *teach*
10   'Is this Jesus the justere,' quod I, 'that Jewes dide to dethe?   *jouster*
Or it is Piers the Plowman! Who peynted hym so rede?'
        Quod Conscience, and kneled tho, 'Thise arn [hise] armes—
Hise colours and his cote armure; ac he that cometh so blody

                                                            coat-of-arms

Is Crist with his cros, conquerour of Cristene.'   *Christians' conqueror*
15   'Why calle ye hym Crist?' quod I, 'sithen Jewes called hym Jesus?
Patriarkes and prophetes prophecied bifore
That alle kynne creatures sholden knelen and bowen
Anoon as men nempned the name of God Jesu.   *At once; uttered*
Ergo is no name to the name of Jesus,   *Therefore; (compared) to*
20   Ne noon so nedeful to nempne by nyghte ne by daye.   *necessary*

---

3   To be present throughout mass and receive Holy Communion at the end (C).

Collation WHmCrGYO(238–361
    om)C²CBLMRF.
RUBRIC *Passus xix*ᵘˢ *et explicit
    dobet et incipit dobest* W&r (*et*¹
    ... *dobest*] *om* YOC²CM; *de
    visione* Cr; *et quintus de dobet* B);
    P. *v*ᵘˢ *et ultimus de dobet. Hic inc.
    p. j*ᵘˢ *de dobest* Hm; *Inc.* P. *xv*ᵘˢ
    F; *om* G.
3–4   *So* W&r (ho.] holyly; In] &
    F)C; *run together*, and ... after, In
    ... masse *om* g).
4   yede] W&rC; wente CrMF.

5   *So* β (*l. om* g)C; & y fel asl. and s.
    y drempte F.
8   lymes] L&rC; þynges W.
    ihesu] L&rC; Iesus WCr;
    hymselue F.
9   And] WHmLC; *om* CrgMF.
11   it is] β (*trs* Cr²³GC²; it Cr¹)C; ys
    he F.
12   hise] Piers β; cristis FC (C).
15   ʒe] L&rC; *om* W.
    called] Hm?g?α (named F)CK–D;
    calle WCrC²LM.
18   *After this a line like* 80a F.

For alle derke develes arn adrad to heren it,   *terrified*
And synfulle aren solaced and saved by that name.
And ye callen hym Crist; for what cause, telleth me?
Is Crist moore of myght and moore worthiere name *of greater power*
25 Than Jesu or Jesus, that al oure joye com of?'
      'Thow knowest wel,' quod Conscience, 'and thow konne reson,
That knyght, kyng, conquerour may be o persone.   *one single*
To be called a knyght is fair, for men shul knele to hym;
To be called a kyng is fairer, for he may knyghtes make;
30 Ac to be conquerour called, that cometh of special grace,
And of hardynesse of herte and of hendenesse—   *courage; courtesy*
To make lordes of laddes, of lond that he wynneth, *commoners; with*
And fre men foule thralles, that folwen noght hise lawes. *vile slaves*
      'The Jewes, that were gentil men, Jesu thei despised—
35 Bothe his loore and his lawe; now are thei lowe cherles. *base serfs*
As wide as the world is, wonyeth ther none   *dwells*
But under tribut and taillage as tikes and cherles; *taxation; villeins*
And tho that bicome Cristene bi counseil of the Baptiste
Aren frankeleyns, free men thorugh fullynge that thei toke, *baptism*
40 And gentil men with Jesu – for Jesus was yfulled   *baptized*
And upon Calvarie on cros ycrouned kyng of Jewes.
      'It bicometh to a kyng to kepe and to defende,   *befits; protect*
And conqueror of his conquest hise lawes and his large.
And so dide Jesus the Jewes – he justified and taughte hem
45 The lawe of lif that laste shal evere,   *'eternal life'*
And fended hem from foule yveles, feveres and fluxes,   *defended*
And from fendes that in hem was, and false bileve.
Tho was he Jesu of Jewes called, gentile prophete,   *Then; by; noble*
And kyng of hir kyngdom, and croune bar of thornes.   *bore*
50 'And tho conquered he on cros as conquerour noble;

---

43 And (it befits) a conqueror to maintain and guard his laws and his
   munificence by virtue of his act of conquest.

24 worthiere] F (?=α)C; worþi β.
30 Ac] ?β (And Crg)C; For F.
34 ihesu] L&rC; Iesus WHmC².
36 wonyeth . . . none] L&r (n.] n.
    therin CrM (th.] +M))C; noon of
    hem þer wonyeþ W.
38 þe baptiste] LC; þe baptisme
    W&r (om Hm; þe] om F).

40 Ihesus] L&r; Iesu WHmC²F.
43 his¹] F (?=α)CK–D; om β.
46 fended] L&rC; defended WCr.
    hem] OHmFC; yt GC²; om W&r.
47 was] LF (?=α)?CK–D; were
    W&r.
48 Iesu] F (?=α)C; Iesus β.

Mighte no deeth hym fordo, ne adoun brynge,   *destroy; defeat*
That he n'aroos and regnede and ravysshed helle. *But that; plundered*
And tho was he conquerour called of quyke and of dede,
For he yaf Adam and Eve and othere mo blisse   *gave*
55 That longe hadde yleyen bifore as Luciferis cherles. *lain (in hell); serfs*
And took [Lucifer the lothly], that lord was of helle, *terrible, fearsome*
And bond [hym] as [he is bounde], with bondes of yrene.   *bound*
Who was hardiere than he? His herte blood he shadde   *bolder; shed*
To maken alle folk free that folwen his lawe.
60 And sith he yeveth largely al his lele liges   *gives to; loyal subjects*
Places in Paradis at hir partynge hennes,
He may wel be called conquerour – and that is "Crist" to mene.
                                                what 'Christ' means (C)
    'Ac the cause that he cometh thus with cros of his passion
Is to wissen us therwith, that whan we ben tempted,   *instruct*
65 Therwith to fighte and fenden us fro fallynge into synne,   *defend*
And se bi his sorwe that whoso loveth joye,
To penaunce and to poverte he moste puten hymselven,
And muche wo in this world wilnen and suffren.   *desire, will*
    'Ac to carpe moore of Crist, and how he com to that name, *speak*
70 Faithly for to speke, his firste name was Jesus.   *Truly*
Tho he was born in Bethleem, as the Book telleth,   *When*
And cam to take mankynde, kynges and aungeles   *human nature*
Reverenced hym right faire with richesses of erthe.
Aungeles out of hevene come knelynge and songe,
Gloria in excelsis Deo! . . .
75   'Kynges come after, knelede, and offrede

74a Glory to God in the highest (Lk 2: 14).

56-9 *In* F (?=α)CK–D; *ll. om* β.
56 took . . . loþely] *so* CK–D; þanne
   took he lotthly l. F.
57 hym . . . bounde] *so* CK–D; his
   as his bondeman F.
58 he[1]] *so* CK–D; he þat F.
59 lawe] *so* CK–D; lawes F.
60 ʒeveþ] F (?=α)C; yaf β.
63 cros] β; his cros FC.
   his] WOLFC; þe Cr[1]M; *om*
   HmCr[23]?g.

64 þat] βC; *om* F.
   we] YBoCotFCK–D; þat we W&r.
65 fenden] L&rC; defenden
   WHmCotF.
   into] L&rC; to W.
66 -so] W&rC; *om* g.
68 wylnen] F (?=α)C; willen β (to
   w. W).
73 ryght] F (?=α)CK–D; *om* β.
74a &c] W&r; *om* CrOF.
75 offrede] W&r; o. sense Cot (s.]
   ?+ *a.h.*) (C).

Ensense, mirre and muche gold withouten mercy askynge
                                        myrrh; thanks, favour
Or any kynnes catel, but knoweliched hym sovereyn
Both of sond, sonne and see, and sithenes thei wente   *sand; afterwards*
Into hir kyngene kith by counseil of aungeles.   *respective kingdoms*
80 And there was that word fulfilled the which thow of speke— *spoke*
Omnia celestia, terrestria, flectantur in hoc nomine Iesu.
'For alle the aungeles of hevene at his burthe knelede,
And al the wit of the world was in tho thre kynges.   *wisdom; those*
Reson and Rightfulnesse and Ruthe thei offrede,
Wherfore and why wise men that tyme,   *For which reason*
85 Maistres and lettred men, *Magi* hem callede.
'That o kyng cam with Reson, covered under sense.
                                   hidden (in the form of); incense
The seconde kyng siththe soothliche offrede
Rightwisnesse under reed gold, Resones felawe.   *companion*
Gold is likned to Leautee that laste shal evere,   *fidelity, justice*
90 And Reson to riche[ls] – to right and to truthe.   *incense (C)*
'The thridde kyng tho kam, and knelede to Jesu,
And presented hym with Pitee, apperynge by mirre;
                                    under the appearance of
For mirre is mercy to mene, and mylde speche of tonge.
Ertheliche honeste thynges was offred thus at ones   *of earthly value*
95 Thorough thre kynne kynges knelynge to Jesu.   *kings of three races (Sk)*
'Ac for alle thise preciouse presents Oure Lord Prynce Jesus
Was neither kyng ne conquerour til he [comsede] wexe *began to grow*

80a That in the name of Jesus every [knee] should bow, of those that are in
    heaven, on earth, [and under the earth] (Phil 2: 10).

76   Ensens] F; *om* βC (C).
     mercy] W&r; mercede Cot (-ede
     over erasure); mede CrM (*over
     erasure*) (C).
77   -lechid] F (?=α)GCK–D;
     -lichynge β (-ynge) -e Cr¹M).
78   sonde] L&rC; sunne F; soule B;
     long WHmCr¹.
     sonne] βC; of sond F.
83   -ful-] LCB?C; -wis- W&r.
86   sense] β?C; ensense F.
88–9 *So* βC; *run together* F.

89   Golde] L&rC; For gold W.
90   And . . . richels] And resoun to
     riche golde β (*l. om* W)C; For it
     shal turne tresoun F (C).
91   & knelid] F (?=α)C; knelynge β.
94   Erthely] F (?=α)CK–D; Thre
     yliche β.
     was] LF (?=α)CK–D; were W&r
     (*om* CB).
96   prynce] L&rC; kyng W.
97   comsede] *so* CK–D; gan to All
     MSS (C).

In the manere of a man, and that by muchel sleighte—   *great skill*
As it bicometh a conquerour to konne manye sleightes,   *know*
100 And manye wiles and wit, that wole ben a ledere;   *stratagems*
And so dide Jesu in hise dayes, whoso hadde tyme to telle it.
    'Som tyme he suffrede, and som tyme he hidde hym,
And som tyme he faught faste, and fleigh outherwhile,   *readily; fled*
And som tyme he gaf good and grauntede heele bothe,   *money; health*
105 Lif and lyme – as hym liste, he wroghte.   *he pleased; did*
As kynde is of a conquerour, so comsede Jesu   *is the nature of*
Til he hadde alle hem that he for bledde.   *bled for*
    'In his juventee this Jesus at Jewene feeste   *youth; 'a Jewish feast'*
Turnede water into wyn, as Holy Writ telleth,   (Jn 2: 1–11)
110 And there bigan God of his grace to do wel.
For wyn is likned to lawe, and lif of holynesse;
And lawe lakkede tho, for men lovede noght hir enemys;
    was defective then
And Crist counseileth thus – and comaundeth bothe—   *as well*
Bothe to lered and to lewede, to lovyen oure enemys.
115 So at the feeste first, as I bifore tolde,
Bigan God of his grace and goodnesse to do wel;
And tho was he cleped and called noght oonly Crist but Jesu—
A fauntekyn ful of wit, *filius Marie.*   *child; son of Mary* (Mk 6: 3)
For bifore his moder Marie made he that wonder,   *performed; miracle*
120 That she first and formest sholde ferme bileve   *foremost; firmly*
That he thorugh Grace was gete, and of no gome ellis.   *conceived; one*
He wroghte that by no wit but thorugh word one,   *device; only*
After the kynde that he cam of; there comsede he Dowel.

---

100 And as (it befits) him who wishes to be a leader to know . . .
121 That he had been conceived by the (power of God's) Holy Spirit (*Grace*)
    and not by any human agency.
123 In accord with the nature of God his Father [who *created* by his word].

108 *So div from* 109 βC; *after*
    turnede F.
109 Turnede; water into wyn] ?α
    (T.] he t. F)C; *trs* β.
110 to] wC²LMC; *om* ?gF.
111 of] L&r; *om* WC (C).
113 þus] wLM?C; vs ?g (*l. om* C²);
    þus vs F (?=α) (C).
114 Bothe] L&r (*l. om* C²)C; *om*
    WHmF.

115 the] Cr&r; þat WHmC.
117 þo] L&rC; þanne WHm.
    cleped &] L&rC; *om* W.
    only] M(oo *over erasure*)
    CrFCK–D; holy W&r.
118 fantekyn] F (?=α)CK–D; faunt
    fyn β.
120 scholde; ferme] ?α (f.] f. þe F)C;
    trs β.
121 of] wLMFC; *om* Cr²³g.

'And whan he was woxen moore, in his moder absence,   *grown*
25 He made lame to lepe and yaf light to blynde,   *run; sight*
And fedde with two fisshes and with fyve loves   *loaves*
Sore afyngred folk, mo than fyve thousand.   *Very hungry*
Thus he confortede carefulle and caughte a gretter name,
        the distressed; got
The which was Dobet, where that he wente.
30 For deve thorugh hise doynges and dombe speke and herde,   *deaf*
And alle he heeled and halp that hym of grace askede,   *helped; mercy*
And tho was he called in contre of the comune peple,   *by*
For the dedes that he dide, *Fili David, Ihesus.*   Son of David (Mt 9: 27)
For David was doghtiest of dedes in his tyme,   *Because; bravest*
35 The burdes tho songe, *Saul interfecit mille et David decem milia.*
        damsels
Forthi the contree ther Jesu cam called hym *fili David*,   *Therefore*
And nempned hym of Nazareth – and no man so worthi
To be kaiser or kyng of the kyngdom of Juda,   *emperor*
Ne over Jewes justice, as Jesus was, hem thoughte.   *judge; it seemed*
40 'Wherof hadde Cayphas envye, and othere of the Jewes,
And for to doon hym to dethe day and nyght thei casten;   *schemed*
And killeden hym on cros-wise at Calvarie on Friday,   *by crucifixion*
And sithen buriede his body, and beden that men sholde   *ordered*
Kepen it fro nyghtcomeris with knyghtes yarmed,
45 For no frend sholde it fecche; for prophetes hem tolde   *So that*
That that blissede body of burieles sholde risen,   *from its tomb*
And goon into Galilee and gladen hise Apostles   *cheer*
And his moder Marie – thus men bifore demede.   *believed*
'The knyghtes that kepten it biknewe hemselven   *guarded; admitted*
50 That aungeles and archaungeles er the day spronge   *dawned*

---

135 Saul slew his thousands, and David his ten thousands (I Kg 18: 7).
144 Guard it with armed men against any who might come by night.

124 was woxen] L&rC; *trs* WHm.
130 &¹ . . . herde] F (?=α)CK–D;
  to here & dombe speke he made β.
133 *Fili dauid*; *Ihesus*] wLMC; *trs*
  gF.
135 The . . . þo] β (þo) þat g)C;
  þerfore men F.
140 Wherof] β; þerfore F.

hadde kayphas] F (?=α)C; *trs*
  β. of þe] β; konynge F.
142 &] F (?=α)BC; *om* β.
145 freend; it] F (?=α)CK–D; *pl*;
  hym β.
146 shulde *rise*] L&r (r.] r. vp F)C;
  trs WHm.
149 beknewen] F (?=α)C; b. it β.

Come knelynge to that corps and songen   *dead body*
Christus resurgens – and [it] aroos after,   '*Christ rising*' (Rom 6: 9)
Verray man bifore hem alle, and forth with hem he yede.   *True; went*
  'The Jewes preide hem of pees, and [preide tho] knyghtes
155 Telle the comune that ther cam a compaignie of hise Apostles *people*
And biwicched hem as thei woke, and awey stolen it.
  'Ac Marie Maudeleyne mette hym by the weye
Goynge toward Galilee in godhede and in manhede,
And lyves and lokynge – and she aloud cride   *alive; conscious*
160 In ech a compaignie ther she cam, "*Christus resurgens!*"
Thus cam it out that Crist overcoom, recoverede and lyvede:
Sic oportet Christum pati et intrare . . .
For that wommen witeth may noght wel be counseille!   *remain secret*
  'Peter parceyved al this and pursued after,
Bothe James and Johan, Jesu for to seke,
165 Thaddee and ten mo, with Thomas of Inde.   *Thaddeus; India* (C)
And as alle thise wise wyes weren togideres   *men*
In an hous al bishet and hir dore ybarred,   *locked up*
Crist cam in – and al closed, both dore and yates—   *gates*
To Peter and to hise apostles, and seide, "*Pax vobis;*" *Peace unto you*
170 And took Thomas by the hand and taughte hym to grope,   *touch*
And feele with hise fyngres his flesshliche herte;
Thomas touched it, and with his tonge seide,

---

154 The Jews begged them to say nothing about it, and beseeched the
    knights . . .
156 And cast a spell on them as they were keeping watch . . .
161a Ought not Christ to have suffered these things and so to enter into his
     glory? (Lk 24: 26).

151 *So div from* 152 F (?=α)   154 of] F (?=α)C; *om* β (be W).
     CotCK–D; *as one l.* β.   and . . . þo] *so* CK–D; and bisouȝte
     þat] F (?=α)C; þe β.   þe β (þe] þo Cot); al þo propre F.
     and] βC; & konyngly F.   158 in²] F (?=α)?C; *om* β.
152 *resurgens*] β?C; *r. a mortuis*   161a–2 *In* βC; *ll. om* F.
     FCot.   162 þat] LCrG?CK–D; þat þat
     and . . . after] *so* C?α (it) anoon he   W&r.
     F)K–D; *om* β (C).   wommen] W&r?C; womman Y.
153 man] L&rC; men W.   167 barred] W&r?C; sperred g.
     yede] βC; wente F.   168 and¹] W&rC; *om* g.
                                     169 his] L&r; þise WHm; þe B.

    "*Dominus meus et Deus meus.*
    Thow art my lord, I bileve, God Lord Jesu!
175 Thow deidest and deeth tholedest and deme shalt us alle,   *suffered*
    And now art lyvynge and lokynge, and laste shalt evere!"
      'Crist carpede thanne, and curteisliche seide,   *spoke*
    "Thomas, for thow trowest this and treweliche bilevest it,   *think*
    Blessed mote thow be, and be shalt for evere.
180 And blessed mote thei be, in body and in soule,
    That nevere shul se me in sighte as thow seest nowthe,   *at this time*
    And lelliche bileve al this – I love hem and blesse hem: *faithfully*
    Beati qui non viderunt et crediderunt."
      'And whan this dede was doon, Dobest he [thou]ghte,
    And yaf Piers power, and pardon he grauntede:
185 To alle maner men, mercy and foryifnesse;
    [To] hym, myghte men to assoille of alle manere synnes,
    In covenaunt that thei come and kneweliche to paye
    To Piers pardon the Plowman – *Redde quod debes.*
    Thus hath Piers power, be his pardon paied,
190 To bynde and unbynde bothe here and ellis,
    And assoille men of alle synnes save of dette one.
      'Anoon after an heigh up into hevene
    He wente, and wonyeth there, and wol come at the laste,   *dwells*

---

173 My Lord and my God (Jn 20: 28).
182*a* Blessed are they that have not seen and have believed (Jn 20: 29).
187–8 On condition that they come and acknowledge satisfactorily [i.e. meet
  the terms of] Piers the P.'s pardon – 'Pay what thou owest' (Mt 18: 28).
191 *i.e.* the binding obligation to make satisfaction [*not* the sin of debt].

173 *Dominus*] F
  (?=α)CrCotCK–D; *Deus* ?β.
  deus] F (?=α)CrBCK–D; *dominus*
  ?β.
180 be] F (?=α)GC²CK–D; alle be
  ?β.
181 seest] OCK–D; hast Cr¹; doost
  W&r (C).
182*a* *& crediderunt*] F(?=α)CK–D;
  & cr. &c Hmg; *&c* WCrLM.
183 thouhte] *so* CK–D; tauȝte β;
  took sone F (C).
186 To hym] Hym WCrOCLM?C;

hys GYC²; he HmB; *om* F (C).
myght] W&rC; m. may GC²;
power myȝte Y; & power F.
men] L&r (*erased* M)C; *om* WCr¹;
hem F.
synnes] L&rC; *sg* WHm.
187 -che] L&r; -ched WHmC (C).
189 be] L&rC; by WC²BoCot; for
  F.
190 and¹] W&r; and to C²L?C.
  ellis] LF (?=α)CK–D; elliswhere
  W&r.
192 heuene] wOLMF; þe h. ?g.

And rewarde hym right wel that *reddit quod debet*—

                                                'makes satisfaction'

195 Paieth parfitly, as pure truthe wolde.   *complete integrity*
And what persone paieth it nought, punysshen he thenketh,
And demen hem at domesday, bothe quyke and dede— *judge; living*
The goode to the Godhede and to greet joye,
And wikkede to wonye in wo withouten ende.'

200   Thus Conscience of Crist and of the cros carpede,   *spoke*
And counseiled me to knele therto; and thanne cam, me thoughte,
Oon *Spiritus Paraclitus* to Piers and to hise felawes.
In liknesse of a lightnynge he lighte on hem alle   *alighted*
And made hem konne and knowe alle kynne langages.   *kinds of*
205 I wondred what that was, and waggede Conscience,   *nudged*
And was afered of the light, for in fires liknesse
Spiritus Paraclitus overspradde hem alle.   *covered*
    Quod Conscience, and knelede, 'This is Cristes messager,
And cometh fro the grete God – Grace is his name.
210 Knele now,' quod Conscience, 'and if thow kanst synge,
Welcome hym and worshipe hym with *Veni Creator Spiritus!*'
Thanne song I that song, and so dide manye hundred,
And cride with Conscience, 'Help us, God of grace!'
    And thanne bigan Grace to go with Piers Plowman,
215 And counseillede hym and Conscience the comune to sompne:

                                               summon
'For I wole dele today and dyvyde grace   *share; apportion*
To alle kynne creatures that kan hise fyve wittes— *have use of their*
Tresour to lyve by to hir lyves ende,
And wepne to fighte with that wole nevere faille.
220 For Antecrist and hise al the world shul greve,   *Antichrist (C)*
And acombre thee, Conscience, but if Crist thee helpe. *overwhelm*
    'And false prophetes fele, flatereris and gloseris, *many; deceivers*

---

202 The Spirit, the Comforter (Pentecost Vespers Hymn).
211 Come Holy Ghost, Creator come (Pentecost Hymn at Terce).

205–7 *In* βC; *ll. om* F.
206 þe] wLM; þat g.
  lyk-] L&rC; light- W.
209 god] F (?=α)CK–D; god and β.
211b–13 *In* βC; *Veni . . . hundred*
  om F.
212 and] L&rC; *om* WHm.

216 dyuyde] L&rC; ȝyue diuine
  WHm.
217 kan] LF (?=α)CK–D; han
  W&r.
  hise] F (?=α)CK–D; hir β.
219 *So* W&rC; *as one l. with* 227,
  219b–227a om g.

Shullen come and be curatours over kynges and erles. *spiritual rulers*
And thanne shal Pride be Pope and prynce of Holy Chirche,
225 Coveitise and Unkyndenesse Cardinals hym to lede. *guide*
Forthi,' quod Grace, 'er I go, I wol gyve yow tresor,
And wepne to fighte with whan Antecrist yow assailleth.'
And gaf ech man a grace to gye with hymselven, *guide, direct*
That Ydelnesse encombre hym noght, ne Envye ne Pride:
Divisiones graciarum sunt.

230 Some [wyes] he yaf wit, with wordes to shewe— *men; declare*
Wit to wynne hir liflode with, as the world asketh, *earn their living*
As prechours and preestes, and prentices of lawe— *students*
They lelly to lyve by labour of tonge, *honestly*
And by wit to wissen othere as grace hem wolde teche. *instruct others*
235 And some he kennede craft and konnynge of sighte,
With [buggynge and sellynge] hir bilyve to wynne. *buying; living*
And some he lered to laboure on lond and on watre, *taught*
And lyve by that labour – a lele lif and a trewe. *honest*
And some he taughte to tilie, to dyche and to thecche, *plough; thatch*
240 To wynne with hir liflode bi loore of his techynge.
And some to devyne and divide, [of] noumbres to kenne; *make out*
And some to compace craftily, and colours to make; *design skilfully*
And some to se and to seye what sholde bifalle,
Bothe of wele and of wo, telle it [wel] er it felle— *before it occurred*
245 As astronomyens thorugh astronomye, and philosofres wise.
And some to ryde and to recovere that unrightfully was wonne:
He wissed hem wynne it ayein thorugh wightnesse of handes,
back; strength

229a [Now], there are diversities of graces, [but the same Spirit] (I Cor 12: 4).

224 þan . . . Pryȝde] F (?=α)CK–D;
  Pride shal β.
  &] F (?=α) Cr²³C; om β.
228 gye] L&r (gide WCr)C; go g.
229 ne¹] F (?=α)C; om β.
229a sunt] F (?=α)CrC; *s.&c* β.
230 wyes] *cj* K–D; om All MSS (C).
231 With; wiþ] β; & wit; om F.
236 bugg.; sell.] *trs* All MSS (C).
  bil.] W&rC; lyflode HmCrBMF.
237–8 So F (?=α)CK–D; *run
  together*, on¹ . . . watre, & . . .

labour *om* β.
239 thecche] wLM (*cf.* C); egge
  Cr²³g; þresche F.
241 of] *om* All MSS (C).
243 to²] wYLMFC; some to ?g.
244 wel] *om* All MSS (C).
246 to²] ?wLM?C; some to gHm;
  om Cr²³F.
  vnriȝt-] L&r (vn-) *om* Hm)C;
  wrong- W.
247 *In* β (wynne] to w. WOB)C; *l.*
  om F.

And fecchen it fro false men with Folvyles lawes.   =*by main force (C)*

And some he lered to lyve in longynge to ben hennes,   *sc. as ascetics*

250 In poverte and in pacience to preie for alle Cristene.

And alle he lered to be lele, and ech a craft love oother,   *true*

And forbad hem alle debat – that noon [be] among hem.   *quarrelling*

'Though some be clenner than some, ye se wel,' quod Grace,

more refined

'That he that useth the faireste craft, to the fouleste I kouthe have put

hym.   *practises*

255 Thynketh [that alle craftes,' quod Grace], 'cometh of my yifte;

Loke that noon lakke oother, but loveth alle as bretheren.

find fault with

And who that moost maistries kan, be myldest of berynge;

arts; humblest

And crouneth Conscience kyng, and maketh Craft youre stiward,

Skill; deputy

And after Craftes conseil clotheth yow and fede.

260 For I make Piers the Plowman my procuratour and my reve,   *agent*

And registrer to receyve *Redde quod debes.*   *registrar; 'what is owed'*

My prowor and my plowman Piers shal ben on erthe,   *purveyor*

And for to tilie truthe a teeme shal he have.'   *cultivate; team*

Grace gaf Piers a teeme – foure grete oxen.

265 That oon was Luk, a large beest and a lowe chered,   *humble-looking*

And Mark, and Mathew the thridde, myghty beestes bothe;

And joyned to hem oon Johan, moost gentil of alle,

The pris neet of Piers plow, passynge alle othere.

best animal; surpassing

And yit Grace of his goodnesse gaf Piers foure stottes—

horses, ?bullocks

270 Al that hise oxen eriede, thei to harewen after.   *ploughed; harrow*

Oon highte Austyn, and Ambrose another,

Gregori the grete clerk, and Jerom the goode.

Thise foure, the feith to teche, folweth Piers teme,

---

250 pacience] F (?=α)HmCK–D;   *om* **g** (C).
        penaunce β.   256   Loke þat] L&r (L.] Lokeþ
251 he] βC; *om* F.   WHm)C; & l. F.
252 be] *so* C; were *All MSS* (C).   264   foure] L&rC; of foure W.
254 *After this 4 more lines* F (C).   269   ȝit . . . peers] F (?=α)C (ȝ.]
255 þat . . . Grace] alle quod Grace   sethe C); Gr. gaf P. of his
        þat grace W&r (q.] now q. F); *l.*   goodnesse β.

And harewede in an handwhile al Holy Scripture   *short time*
275 With two [aithes] that thei hadde, an oold and a newe,   *harrows*
Id est, Vetus Testamentum et Novum.

   And Grace gaf Piers greynes — cardynales vertues,   *seeds*
And sew it in mannes soule, and sithen he tolde hir names.   *sowed*
Spiritus Prudencie the firste seed highte;   *The Spirit of Prudence*
That whoso ete that, ymagynen he sholde,
280 Er he dide any dede, devyse wel the ende;   *consider, ponder*
And lerned men a ladel bugge with a long stele   *buy; handle*
That caste for to kepe a crokke, and save the fatte above.   *watch*

   The seconde seed highte *Spiritus Temperancie*.   *Temperance*
He that ete of that seed hadde swich a kynde,   *nature, temperament*
285 Sholde nevere mete ne meschief make hym to swelle;
                         (over-)eating; illness
Ne sholde no scornere out of skile hym brynge;   *good-temper*
Ne wynnynge ne wele of worldliche richesse,   *profit; prosperity*
Waste word of ydelnesse ne wikked speche moeve;   *move, upset*
Sholde no curious clooth comen on his rugge,   *artfully cut; back*
290 Ne no mete in his mouth that Maister Johan spicede.   *i.e. a fancy cook*

   The thridde seed that Piers sew was *Spiritus Fortitudinis*; *Fortitude*
And whoso ete of that seed hardy was evere
To suffren al that God sente, siknesse and angres.   *sorrows*
Mighte no lesynges, ne lyere, ne los of worldly catel.   *lies; wealth*

275*a* That is, the Old Testament and the New (C).
279–80 ... think through in advance, with the help of his imagination, the
   purpose / result of his action.
282 Who intend to watch over a (stock)-pot and save the fat [by preventing it
   from boiling over].

275 aiþes] ?α (hay3tes F)C*K–D*;
   harewes β.
275*a* *Id est*] W&rC; *om* g.
276 peers greynes] F (?=α)C;
   greynes þe β.
   -ales] L&rC; -al w.
277 it] L&rC; hem WHmC².
   he] WCr¹LMFC; *om* HmCr²³g.
279 þat¹] F (?=α)C; and β.
   þat²] β; þat frut F.
280 did ... dede] L&rC; deide any
   deeþ W.

282 pat] ?β (To O; And WHmY)C;
   For he F.
   &] F (?=α)C; to β.
283–361 *def* O (*a leaf lost*); g=
   GYC²CB.
285 myschef] F (?=α)C*K–D*;
   muchel drynke β.
286 sholde] L&rC; *om* WHm.
   out] F (?=α)C; ne scolde out β.
287 *In* W&rC; *l. om* g.
292 -so; of] L&rC; *om* W.
294 ne¹] β; of F.

295 Maken hym, for any mournynge, that he nas murie in soule,
     And bold and abidynge bismares to suffre,   *patient; calumnies*
     And plete al with pacience and *Parce michi, Domine*,   *pleaded (C)*
     And covered hym under conseille of Caton the wise: *the advice*
     Esto forti animo cum sis dampnatus inique.

300   The ferthe seed that Piers sew was *Spiritus Iusticie*,   *fourth; Justice*
     And he that ete of that seed sholde be eve[n]e trewe *upright, righteous*
     With God, and naught agast but of gile one.   *afraid; deceit alone*
     For gile gooth so pryvely that good feith outher while

                                                    secretly; sometimes
     May nought ben espied [thorugh] *Spiritus Iusticie*.   *detected; by*
305   *Spiritus Iusticie* spareth noght to spille hem that ben gilty,

                                                         put to death
     And for to correcte the kyng if he falle in [any kynnes gilte].   *fault*
     For counteth he no kynges wrathe whan he in court sitteth

                                                    takes account of
     To demen as a domesman – adrad was he nevere   *judge (v. & n.)*
     Neither of duc ne of deeth, that he ne dide the lawe;   *'powerful noble'*
310 For present or for preiere or any prynces lettres,   *despite*
     He dide equyte to alle eveneforth his power.   *according to*
         Thise foure sedes Piers sew, and siththe he dide hem harewe
     With Olde Lawe and Newe Lawe, that love myghte wexe   *grow up*
     Among thise foure vertues, and vices destruye.

315 For comunliche in contrees cammokes and wedes   *rest-harrows*
     Foulen the fruyt in the feld ther thei growen togideres; *Choke; where*
     And so doon vices vertues – [f]orthi,' quod Piers,   *therefore*

---

295 Destroy his spiritual happiness through tearful anxiety.
297 And (one who) has taken no other legal action except to endure and (a
    prayer), 'Spare me, Lord' (Job 7: 16).
299 Be of brave heart when you are unjustly condemned (*Dist. of Cato* II, 14).
310 In spite of bribes, entreaties, or royal interventions.

297   plete] *so* ?C; he pletede F;
      pleieþ β (C).
301   euene] *so* CK–D; euere W&r;
      neuere Bo.
304   thorw] *so* CK–D; for W&r; fro
      Cr (C).
305–6   *So div* CK–D; *as* 3 *ll. div
      after* spille, correcte *All MSS* (C).

306   The . . . falle] β; þey men falle
      ageyn þe kyng F.
      any kynnes gilte] gilt or in trespas
      All MSS (C).
309   þe] LF (?=α)C; *om* W&r.
314   þese] F (?=α)C; þe β(þo WHm).
317   vertues forthy] *so* CK–D; v.
      worþi β; worthy fayre vertues F (C).

'Hareweth alle that konneth kynde wit by conseil of thise doctours,
And tilieth after hir techynge the cardynale vertues.'   *according to*

320 'Ayeins thi greynes,' quod Grace, 'bigynneth for to ripe,   *Before*
Ordeigne thee an hous, Piers, to herberwe inne thi cornes.'

                                               Prepare; store

 'By God! Grace,' quod Piers, 'ye moten gyve tymber,   *must*
And ordeigne that hous er ye hennes wende.'

And Grace gaf hym the cros, with the croune of thornes,
325 That Crist upon Calvarie for mankynde on pyned;   *suffered on*
And of his baptisme and blood that he bledde on roode
He made a manere morter, and mercy it highte.   *a kind of mortar*
And therwith Grace bigan to make a good foundement,   *foundation*
And watlede it and walled it with hise peynes and his passion,
330 And of al Holy Writ he made a roof after,
And called that hous Unite – Holy Chirche on Englissh.   *Unity*

  And whan this dede was doon, Grace devysede   *fashioned*
A cart highte Cristendom, to carie home Piers sheves,

                                   (=Baptism); sheaves

And gaf hym caples to his carte, Contricion and Confession;   *horses*
335 And made Preesthod hayward, the while hymself wente   *overseer*
As wide as the world is, with Piers to tilie truthe
And the lo[nd] of bileve, the lawe of Holy Chirche.

Now is Piers to the plow, and Pride it aspide,
And gadered hym a greet oost: greven he thynketh   *intends to harass*
340 Conscience and alle Cristene and Cardinale Vertues—
Blowe hem doun and breke hem and bite atwo the mores;

                                     in two; roots

And sente forth Surquidous, his sergeaunt of armes,   *Presumption*

---

318 kynde] β (kyndly g)C; *om* F.
320 greynes; Grace] β (G.] g. to
    Piers g)C; tyme; grace þat þy frut F.
321 Ordeigne] βC; Peers o. F.
    Piers] WHmCr³C; quod p. LCr¹²
    M; *om* gF.
    cornes] WHmBLMFC; *sg* Cr?g.
322 gyue] βC; gyve me FCot.
329 *So* β (hise peynes] his peyne
    W)C; & he peyntyde þe wallis wiþ
    þe woundis of his passion F.

333 home Piers] *so* CK–D; hoom F
    (?=α); Piers β (C).
337 *In* F (?=α)C (lond; the²] C;
    loore; & þe F)K–D; l. *om* β (C).
339 ost] F (?=α)CK–D; oest to ?β
    (to] for to W; hym to B; for Hm).
340 Conscience . . . cristene] β (l.
    om g)C; & C. & cristendom F.
342 Surquidous his sergeaunt] β;
    surquidoures were sergawntys F (*cf.*
    C) (C).

And his spye Spille-Love, oon Spek-yvel-bihynde.
   Thise two coome to Conscience and to Cristen peple,
345 And tolde hem tidynges – that tyne thei sholde   *were going to lose*
The sedes that [Sire] Piers sew, the Cardynale Vertues:
'And Piers bern worth ybroke, and thei that ben in Unitee   *will be*
Shulle come out, and Conscience; and youre [caples tweyne],   *pair of*
Confession and Contricion, and youre carte the Bileeve   *Creed*
350 Shal be coloured so queyntely and covered under oure sophistrie,
                          artfully

That Conscience shal noght knowe by Contricion
Ne by Confession who is Cristene or hethene;
Ne no manere marchaunt that with moneye deleth
Wher he wynne with right, with wrong or with usure.'   *gain; usury*
355   With swiche colours and queyntise cometh Pride y-armed,
                          banners/deceptions

With the lord that lyveth after the lust of his body—   *pleasure*
'To wasten on welfare and on wikked kepynge   *luxury; living*
Al the world in a while thorugh oure wit!' quod Pryde.
   Quod Conscience to alle Cristene tho, 'My counseil is to wende
360 Hastiliche into Unitee and holde we us there,
And praye we that a pees weere in Piers berne the Plowman.
                          P. the P.'s barn

For witterly, I woot wel, we beth noght of strengthe   *assuredly*
To goon agayn Pride, but Grace weere with us.'
   And thanne kam Kynde Wit Conscience to teche,
365 And cryde, and comaundede alle Cristene peple
For to delven and dyche depe al aboute Unitee   *dig and make a ditch*
That Holy Chirche stode in [holynesse], as it a pyl weere.
                          might stand; fort

---

343 spye; oon] βC; spyʒes; & F.

345 *So div from* 346 CK–D; *after*
    sedes All MSS (C).
    tyne þei sholde] βC; þey wolde
    stroye F.

346 sire] *so* CK–D; *om All MSS*
    (C).
    sew] *so* CK–D; plowman seew all
    F; þere hadde ysowen β.

348 caples tweyne] two caples *All*
    MSS (C).

350 owre] L&rC; your Cr¹Cot; *om*
    WF.

354 Where] L&rC; Wheiþer wCotF.

357 on²] L&r; in WC; *om* GC²F.
    wykked kepynge] β (k.] lyuyng);
    wikkednesse he meyntiþ F.

363 *Here* O *resumes*; g
    =GYOC²CB.

364 And] W&rC; *om* g.

366 and dyke] Hm&r?C; a dych
    WGLM.
    all] F (?=α)?C; *om* β.

367 in holynesse] *so* CK–D; in
    vnitee β; strong F (C).

Conscience comaundede tho alle Cristene to delve,
And make a muche moot that myghte ben a strengthe
                                    great moat; fortification
370 To helpe Holy Chirche and hem that it kepeth.
Thanne alle kynne Cristene, save comune wommen,   *prostitutes*
Repenteden and refusede synne, [right] save thei one,   *only them*
And [a sisour and a somonour] that were forsworen ofte; *perjured*
Witynge and wilfully with the false helden,   *deliberately*
375 And for silver were forswore – soothly thei wiste it!
Ther nas Cristene creature that kynde wit hadde—
Save sherewes one swiche as I spak of—   *evil-doers only*
That he ne halp a quantite holynesse to wexe: *helped; measure; grow*
Some thorugh bedes biddynge and some thorugh pilgrymage *praying*
380 And othere pryvé penaunces, and somme thorugh penyes delynge.
                                    private; almsgiving
And thanne wellede water for wikkede werkes,
Egreliche ernynge out of mennes eighen.   *Bitterly running*
Clennesse of the comune and clerkes clene lyvynge
Made Unitee Holy Chirche in holynesse stonde.
385 'I care noght,' quod Conscience, 'though Pride come nouthe; *now*
The lord of lust shal be letted al this Lente, I hope.   *prevented*
Cometh,' quod Conscience, 'ye Cristene, and dyneth,   *dine*
That han laboured lelly al this Lenten tyme.
Here is breed yblessed, and Goddes body therunder.
390 Grace, thorugh Goddes word, gaf Piers power,
Myght to maken it, and men to ete it after
In helpe of hir heele ones in a monthe,   *(spiritual) health*

---

389 Consecrated Hosts and Christ's body beneath (their appearance of bread).

372 right] *om All MSS* (C).
373 *So* CK–D; *as* 2 *ll.:* And false
     men flatereris vsurers and þeues/
     Lyeris and questemongeris þat were
     forsworen ofte *All MSS* (fl.] & fl.
     &; were] ben F) (C).
376 nas]ne was C;nas no β;was no
     F.
377 one] β (o. and Y; & GO);
     oonly & F.
     as; of] β; *om*; of toforehond F.
379 þoruȝ[1]] W&rC; by Cr.
     some[2]] β?C; *om* F.

þoruȝ[2]] W&r; by CrC.
pylgrymage] L&r; *pl* WC.
380 *So* βC (pen.] WC; *sg* L&r; *sg*
     paines CrM); Somme þorghȝ pens
     delyng & summe þorghȝ priue
     penaunces F.
381 welled] βC; walmede F.
383 of þe] L&rC; out of WHm.
384 stonde] F (?=α)YCK–D; to st.
     β.
390 gaue] L&rC; yaf WC[2]B.
391 Mighte] CCK–D; And m. CrF;
     Myȝtes ?β (And m. WHm) (C).

Or as ofte as thei hadde nede, tho that hadde ypaied
To Piers pardon the Plowman, *Redde quod debes.'*   *pay your debt*
395   'How?' quod al the comune. 'Thow conseillest us to yelde *give up*
Al that we owen any wight er we go to housel?'   *Holy Communion*
'That is my conseil,' quod Conscience, 'and Cardinale Vertues;
                                                    (that of the) C.V.

Or ech man foryyve oother, and that wole the *Paternoster*—
Et dimitte nobis debita nostra . . .

And so to ben assoilled, and siththen to ben houseled.'   *absolved*
400   'Ye? Baw!' quod a brewere, 'I wol noght be ruled,
By Jesu! for al youre janglynge, with *Spiritus Iusticie*,   *arguing*
Ne after Conscience, by Crist! while I kan selle   *know how to*
Bothe dregges and draf, and drawe it at oon hole—   *ale-leavings*
Thikke ale and thynne ale; for that is my kynde,   *nature, way*
405   And noght hakke after holynesse – hold thi tonge, Conscience!
                                                    grub about for
Of *Spiritus Iusticie* thow spekest muche on ydel.'   *to no purpose*
'Caytif!' quod Conscience, 'cursede wrecche!
Unblessed artow, brewere, but if thee God helpe.
[Save] thow lyve by loore of *Spiritus Iusticie*,   *Unless; teaching*
410   The chief seed that Piers sew, ysaved worstow nevere.   *will you be*
But Conscience be thi comune fode, and Cardinale Vertues,
Leve it wel, thei ben lost, bothe lif and soule.'
'Thanne is many a [leode] lost!' quod a lewed vicory.   *ignorant vicar*
'I am a curatour of Holy Kirke, and cam nevere in my tyme
415   Man to me that me kouthe telle of Cardinale Vertues,
Or that acountede Conscience a cokkes fethere or an hennes! *valued*
I knew nevere Cardynal that he ne cam fro the Pope;   *who did not*

---

394 'Pay what thou owest' (Mt 18: 28); cf XIX 187.
398a And forgive us our trespasses . . .
403 Both the sediment and the liquid covering it at the bottom of the cask
 (after the ale has been drawn off).

398 Or] F (?=α)CK–D; That β.
399 to ben²] gF (?=α)C; ben
      WHmL; *om* CrM.
403 it at] ?β (it] *om* O; it out W; at]
      om Hm); out an F.
404 for] β; *om* F.
408 þee god] β?C; *trs* F.
409 Save] But W&r; and but C²F.
411 be . . . fode] FC² (þyn] *om*

C²)?C; þe comune fede β (f.] seede
GO) (C).
412 it; þei ben] β (*l. om* Y)C([þei] we
C); *om*; þou art F.
413 a] W&r; *om* LC.
      leode] man *All MSS* (C).
414 kirke] W&r?C; chirche C²BF.
416 a] ?α (oon F)C; at a β.
      or an hennes] βC; *om* F.

And we clerkes, whan thei come, for hir comunes paieth,   *clergy; food*
For hir pelure and hir palfreyes mete and pilours that hem folweth.

                                                             feed; robbers
420 The comune *clamat cotidie*, ech a man to oother,   *'cries out daily'*
"The contree is the corseder that cardinals come inne,   *worse off*
And ther thei ligge and lenge moost lecherie there regneth!"

                                                             dwell; remain
Forthi,' quod this vicory, 'by verray God! I wolde
That no cardynal coome among the comune peple,   *came*
425 But in hir holynesse helden hem stille   *remained quiet/always*
At Avynoun among Jewes – *Cum sancto sanctus eris . . .*   *Avignon (C)*
Or in Rome, as hir rule wole, the relikes to kepe;
And thow Conscience in kynges court, and sholdest nevere come
      thennes;
And Grace, that thow gredest so of, gyour of alle clerkes;

                                                          go on about; guide
430 And Piers with his newe plough and ek with his olde
Emperour of al the world – that alle men were Cristene.
      'Inparfit is that Pope, that al peple sholde helpe,   *Faulty*
And s[ou]deth hem that sleeth swiche as he sholde save.   *pays*
A[c] wel worthe Piers the Plowman, that pursueth God in doynge,
                                                            well be it (for)
435 *Qui pluit super iustos et iniustos* at ones,
And sent the sonne to save a cursed mannes tilthe   *sends; bad; crops*
As brighte as to the beste man or to the beste womman.
Right so Piers the Plowman peyneth hym to tilye   *takes pains; plough*
As wel for a wastour and wenches of the stewes   *prostitutes*
440 As for hymself and hise servaunts, save he is first yserved.

---

426 With the holy, thou wilt be holy (Ps 17: 26).
431 . . . and that all men were (true, not just nominal) Christians [*sc.* as they
      would be if Piers *were* emperor].
435 Who . . . raineth upon the just and the unjust (Mt 5: 45).

419 and hir] β (hir) *om* Cr)?C; *om*   432 peple] LB?C; þe peple Hm&r;
     F.   þe world WCr.
420 to] L&r C; til WHmF.   433 soudeth] *so* CK–D; sendeþ *All*
422 þat] βC; þere F.   *MSS* (C).
426 Iewis] F (?=α)CK–D; þe I. β.   hem; suche as] L&rC; swiche; hem
429 gredest] L&rC; graddest W.   þat W.
430 Piers; ek . . . his] βC; p.   434 Ac] ?α (But F)CK–D; And β.
     plowman; þe F.   437 or] WCrF (?=α)C; and L&r.
                                                439–40 *In* βC; *ll. om* F.

[So blessed be Piers Plowman, that peyneth hym to tilye],
And travailleth and tilieth for a tretour also soore *criminal; as hard*
As for a trewe tidy man, alle tymes ylike. *honest upright*
And worshiped be He that wroghte al, bothe good and wikke,
445 And suffreth that synfulle be til som tyme that thei repente.
And God [the Pope amende], that pileth Holy Kirke, *robs*
And cleymeth bifore the kyng to be kepere over Cristene, *guardian*
And counteth noght though Cristene ben killed and robbed, *cares*
And fynt folk to fighte and Cristen blood to spille *provides, maintains*
450 Ayein the Olde Lawe and the Newe Lawe, as Luc bereth witnesse:
Non occides: michi vindictam . . .
It semeth, bi so hymself hadde his wille, *provided that*
He ne reccheth right noght of al the remenaunt.
    'And Crist of his curteisie the cardinals save,
And torne hir wit to wisdom and to wele of soule! *minds, cunning*
455 For the comune,' quod this curatour, 'counten ful litel
The counseil of Conscience or Cardinale Vertues
But if thei sowne, as by sighte, somwhat to wynnyng.
Of gile ne of gabbyng gyve thei nevere tale, *lying; take no account*
For *Spiritus Prudencie* among the peple is gile,
460 And alle tho faire vertues, as vices thei semeth.
For ech man subtileth a sleighte synne to hide, *devises a stratagem*
And coloureth it for a konnynge and a clene lyvynge.'
                                  disguises it as; wise act
    Thanne lough ther a lord, and 'By this light!' seide, *laughed*

450a Thou shalt not kill (Ex 20: 13, quoted Lk 18: 20); Revenge is mine (Deut 32: 35, quoted Heb 10: 30).
457 Unless they (C. and the C.V.) visibly result in some sort of financial gain.
462 And passes off sharp practice as prudence and honest dealing.

441 So CK–D; *l. om All MSS* (C).
445 til . . . repente] L&r [som] *om* F)C; *erasure* W.
446 the Pope; amende] *trs All MSS* (C).
450 þe²] F (?=α)C; *om* β. beriþ witnesse] F (?=α)CK–D; þerof witnesseþ β.
452 he] F (?=α)CK–D; That he β. ne] L&r; *om* WHmC. of . . . remenaunt] βC; how þe remnaunt fareþ F.
454 wele] L&r?C; welþe W; hele Cot. of] β; to F.
457 sowne] F (?=α)CK–D; sowe L; seiჳe W&r (C).
460 þo] wLMFC; the Crg (*l. om* B). semeþ] WCr²³OBLFC; semed Hm&r.
461 For ech] *so* C; Ech β; For euery F (C). to] F (?=α)CK–D; for to β.
462 for] W&rC; with Cr²³g.

'I holde it right and reson of my reve to take   *sensible; from*
465 Al that myn auditour or ellis my styward   *accountant; steward*
Counseilleth me bi hir acounte and my clerkes writynge.
                                                  Advise me (to); records
With *Spiritus Intellectus* thei toke the reves rolles,   *of Understanding*
And with *Spiritus Fortitudinis* fecche it – wole [he, nel he].'
                                                          i.e. by force

And thanne cam ther a kyng and by his croune seide,
470 'I am kyng with croune the comune to rule,
And Holy Kirke and clergie fro cursed men to defende.   *evil*
And if me lakketh to lyve by, the lawe wole I take it
Ther I may hastilokest it have – for I am heed of lawe: *most promptly*
For ye ben but membres and I above alle.
475 And sith I am youre aller heed, I am youre aller heele,
                                                  of you all; protection
And Holy Chirche chief help and chieftayn of the comune.
And what I take of yow two, I take it at the techynge
Of *Spiritus Iusticie* – for I jugge yow alle.
So I may boldely be housled, for I borwe nevere,
480 Ne crave of my comune but as my kynde asketh.'
    'In condicion,' quod Conscience, 'that thow konne defende,
And rule thi reaume in reson, right wel and in truthe,
That thow [have thyn askyng], as the lawe asketh: *request; requires*
Omnia sunt tua ad defendendum set non ad deprehendendum.'
    The viker hadde fer hoom, and faire took his leeve;   *far (to go)*
485 And I awakned therwith, and wroot as me mette.   *as I (had) dreamed*

---

469 *by* 'with reference to' (*Sk*) *or, more likely,* an oath.
479–80 So I may confidently (go forward and) receive Holy Communion, for I
    never borrow Or make demands from my subjects except as my position as
    king requires.
483a What's yours is yours to keep (in trust)/Not seize according to your lust (*C*).

467 þei] W&r (*l. om* Hm)C; to g.
    tooke*n*] F (?=α)C*K–D*; seke β.
468 wole . . . he²] *so* C*K–D*; I wole
    ?β (I] *om* CrY; w.] w. after W); to
    presoun F (*C*).
471 kirke] wYLMFC; chirche ?g.
    defende] L&rC; fende WHm.
474 For] L&r; And WC.
476 chirche] L&rC; chirches
    WHmCr³OM.

481 konne] β?C; kunne hem F.
482 right . . . in] βC; as right wyll
    & Cr; in ryght & in FHm (*C*).
483 That . . . askyng] *so* C; þat þou
    þyn lykyng have F; Take þow may
    in reson β (may] mayst W; might
    CrHm).
    þi] β?C; þe CrOF.
483a *sunt tua*] F (?=α)C; *trs* β.

Passus XX

And as I wente by the way, whan I was thus awaked,
Hevy chered I yede, and elenge in herte;   *Sad-faced; desolate*
For I ne wiste wher to ete ne at what place,
And it neghed neigh the noon, and with Nede I mette,

5 That afrounted me foule and faitour me called. *accosted; rudely; knave*
   'Coudestow noght excuse thee, as dide the kyng and othere—
That thow toke to lyve by, to clothes and to sustenaunce,   *What*
Was by techynge and by tellynge of *Spiritus Temperancie*,
And that thow nome na moore than nede thee taughte,   *took*

10 And nede ne hath no lawe, ne nevere shal falle in dette
For thre thynges that he taketh his lif for to save?—
That is, mete whan men hym werneth, and he no moneye weldeth,

                                       refuse; possesses

Ne wight noon wol ben his borugh, ne no wed hath to legge;
And he ca[cch]e in that caas and come therto by sleighte,   *take*

15 He synneth noght, soothliche, that so wynneth his foode. *obtains*
And though he come so to a clooth, and kan no bettre chevyssaunce,

                             bargain (i.e. can't pay)

Nede anoon righte nymeth hym under maynprise.

---

13 And nobody will stand surety for him, and he has nothing to pledge
(against a loan).
14 If in those circumstances he obtains anything by underhand means . . .
17 (The fact of) his need immediately 'stands bail for him'.

Collation WHmCrGYOC²CB
(356–87 *def* Bm)LMR(*from* 27)F.
RUBRIC *Passus xx^us de visione et
primus de dobest* W&r (*Passus . . .
et*] *om* G; *de¹ . . . do.*] *om* OM; *de
vis.*] *om* CrYCBL; *de v., de do.*] *om*
C²); *Passus ij^us et ultimus de do
best* Hm; *Incipit Passus xvj^us* F.
1 And] F (?=α)C; Thanne β.
3 For] F (?=α)C; *om* β.
6 Coudestow] L?α (& seyd c. F)C;
Kanstow W&r.

7 lyve by] F (?=α)C; þi bilyue β.
8 Was] *so* CK–D; & þat was F; As
?β (And WHmg) (C).
by²] wLMC; *om* gF.
9 þat] F (?=α)C; *om* β.
10 ne¹] W&rC; *om* CrYOC²MF.
11 þat] F (?=α)C; *om* β.
13 noon] ?β (ne BmBo; *om* GCot);
þat CrF.
no wed haþ] F (?=α)C; wed hath
noon to β.
14 cacche] *so* CK–D; cauȝte β;
caste F (C).

And if hym list for to lape, the lawe of kynde wolde   *if he wish; drink*
That he dronke at ech a dych, er he [deide for thurste].

20 So Nede, at gret nede, may nymen as for his owene,   *take*
Withouten conseil of Conscience or Cardynale Vertues—
So that he sewe and save *Spiritus Temperancie*. *Provided; follow; keep*
  'For is no vertue bi fer to *Spiritus Temperancie*— *far; (compared) to*
Neither *Spiritus Iusticie* ne *Spiritus Fortitudinis.*

25 For *Spiritus Fortitudinis* forfeteth ful ofte: *fails, goes wrong*
He shal do moore than mesure many tymes and ofte,

                                     'act immoderately'

And bete men over bittre, and som body to litel,   *too severely*
And greve men gretter than good feith it wolde.

And *Spiritus Iusticie* shal juggen, wole he, nel he,   *tends to judge*
30 After the kynges counseil and the comune like.   *According as*
And *Spiritus Prudencie* in many a point shal faille
Of that he weneth wolde falle if his wit ne weere.
Wenynge is no wysdom, ne wys ymaginacion: *Supposition, opinion*
Homo proponit et Deus disponit—
[God] governeth alle goode vertues;

35 And Nede is next hym, for anoon he meketh,   *makes (men) humble*
And as lowe as a lomb, for lakkyng that hym nedeth;   *what*
For nede maketh nedé fele nedes lowe-herted.   *necessarily humble*
Philosophres forsoke welthe for thei wolde be nedy,
And woneden wel elengely and wolde noght be riche. *very wretchedly*
40   'And God al his grete joye goostliche he lefte,   *really*
And cam and took mankynde and bicam nedy.   *human nature*

---

32 Concerning what he thinks would happen if his wisdom did not exist (C).
33*a* Man proposes, God disposes (proverbial; see XI 37–8).

18 for] W&rC; *om* g.
19 ech a] YC²MC; ech W&r; euery F.
   deide; for thurste] *so* C; *trs All MSS* (th.] þurst W) (C).
23 fer to] βC; fore F.
24 Neither] L&rC; Ne W.
26 tymes] F (?=α)G?C; tyme β.
27 *Here* R *resumes*; α=RF.
28 it] W&r?C; *om* Hmg.
33*a*–5 *So div* K–D?C; *as* 2 *ll. div after* vertues β, *after* alle α (C).

34 God] *so* CK–D; *and All MSS* (C).
35 And] ?α (*om* F)CrGC; Ac ?β.
36 þat] αC; of þat β.
37 *In* αCK–D; *l. om* β.
   fele; -herted] RC; fele for; of herte F.
38 Filosofres] αCK–D; Wise men β. welth] αGC²C; wele ?β.
39 wel elengly] αCK–D; in wildernesse β.

So he was nedy, as seith the Book, in manye sondry places,
That he seide in his sorwe on the selve roode,   *the cross itself*
"Bothe fox and fowel may fle to hole and crepe,
45 And the fissh hath fyn to flete with to reste,   *fin; swim*
Ther nede hath ynome me, that I moot nede abide
                             Whereas; seized; endure
And suffre sorwes ful soure, that shal to joye torne."
Forthi be noght abasshed to bide and to be nedy,   *endure*
Sith he that wroghte al the world was wilfulliche nedy,   *voluntarily*
50 Ne nevere noon so nedy ne poverer deide.'   *poorer*

Whan Nede hadde undernome me thus, anoon I fil aslepe,
                             reproached
And mette ful merveillously that in mannes forme
Antecrist cam thanne, and al the crop of truthe   *upper growth*
Torned it [tid] up-so-doun, and overtilte the roote,   *quickly; upturned*
55 And made fals sprynge and sprede and spede mennes nedes.   *prosper*
In ech a contree ther he cam he kutte awey truthe,   *region*
And gerte gile growe there as he a god weere.   *made*
    Freres folwede that fend, for he gaf hem copes,
And religiouse reverenced hym and rongen hir belles,
60 And al the covent cam to welcome a tyraunt,
And alle hise as wel as hym – save oonly fooles;
Whiche fooles were wel gladdere to deye
Than to lyve lenger sith Leute was so rebuked,   *Fidelity*
And a fals fend Antecrist over alle folk regnede.   *reigned*
65 And that were mylde men and holye, that no meschief dradden,
                             feared

---

42 needy in many ... *or* as says the book in many ...

42 So ... nedy] ?α (he was so n.
    F)CK–D; So n. he was β.
45 to²] β (& to G)C; or to α.
48 bide] wC²LM?C; bydde ?gR;
    bowe F (C).
51 had] L&rC; haþ W.
    me] β (+M)FC; *om* RO.
53 þe] βFC; *om* RCB.
54 it tid] *so* CK–D; it W&r; *om*
    CrGCF.
55 made] αCSk; *om* β.

59 Religiouse] W&rC; *pl* R;
    religiouns Hm.
60 cam] αCK–D; forþ cam β.
    a] ?α?CK–D; þat βF.
62 *So div from* 63 CK–D; *after* lyue
    All MSS.
    wel] βC; *om* αG.
    gladdere] αCK–D; leuere β.
63 leute] αHmCr¹BCSk; Lenten ?β.
64 a] L&rC; as a W.
65 And] L&rC; Saue W.
    were] βC; we α.

Defyed alle falsnesse and folk that it usede; *practised*
And what kyng that hem conforted, knowynge h[ir] gile, *supported*
They cursed, and hir conseil – were it clerk or lewed.
   Antecrist hadde thus soone hundredes at his baner,
70 And Pride it bar boldely aboute, *bore*
With a lord that lyveth after likyng of body,
That cam ayein Conscience, that kepere was and gyour *leader*
Over kynde Cristene and Cardynale Vertues. *true*
   'I conseille,' quod Conscience tho, 'cometh with me, ye fooles,
75 Into Unite Holy Chirche, and holde we us there.
And crye we to Kynde that he come and defende us
Fooles fro thise fendes lymes, for Piers love the Plowman.
And crye we on al the comune that thei come to Unitee,
And there abide and bikere ayeins Beliales children.' *fight*
80   Kynde Conscience tho herde, and cam out of the planetes,
And sente forth his forreyours – feveres and fluxes, *foragers*
Coughes and cardiacles, crampes and toothaches, *heart-attacks*
Rewmes and radegundes and roynouse scalles,
Biles and bocches and brennynge agues,
85 Frenesies and foule yveles – forageres of Kynde *vile diseases*
Hadde ypriked and prayed polles of peple; *preyed on; heads*
Largeliche a legion lees hir lif soone. *Fully; lost*
   There was 'Harrow!' and 'Help! Here cometh Kynde, *Alas!*
With Deeth that is dredful, to undo us alle!'
90 The lord that lyved after lust tho aloud cryde
After Confort, a knyght, to come and bere his baner.
'Alarme! Alarme!' quod that lord, 'ech lif kepe his owene!'
To arms; everybody
   Thanne mette thise men, er mynstrals myghte pipe,
And er heraudes of armes hadden discryved lordes, *named*

83–4 Colds and running sores and unwholesome scabs, Boils and swellings
and burning agues.

67 hir] *so* CK–D; hem W&r; hym F
(C).
   gyle] αCK–D; any while β.
70 it bar] W&r?C; bar yt bare F;
bar þe baner Y (C).
73 -ale] βFC; -ales R.
78 on] αCK–D; to β.

83 scalles] L&r; scabbes WC (C).
86 of] WHmLRC; of the CrgMF.
87 Largeliche] αCK–D; That l. β.
   lese] L?α (lose R)C; loste wGF;
loren yM.
91 Confort a] βC; *om* R; a komely
F.
93 þanne] αCK–D; And þ. β.

95 Elde the hoore; he was in the vauntwarde,   *grey-haired; vanguard*
    And bar the baner bifore Deeth – bi right he it cleymede.   *claimed*
    Kynde cam after hym, with many kene soores,   *sharp*
    As pokkes and pestilences – and muche peple shente;   *plague-sores*
    So Kynde thorugh corrupcions kilde ful manye.   *diseases; killed*
100 Deeth cam dryvynge after and al to duste passhed   *dashed*
    Kynges and knyghtes, kaysers and popes.   *emperors*
    Lered ne lewed, he lefte no man stonde
    That he hitte evene, that evere stired after.
    Manye a lovely lady and [hir] lemmans knyghtes   *lover-knights*
105 Swowned and swelted for sorwe of Dethes dyntes.   *died; blows*
      Conscience of his curteisie [th]o Kynde he bisoughte
    To cesse and suffre, and see wher thei wolde   *desist; whether*
    Leve Pride pryvely and be parfite Cristene.   *true, sincere*
      And Kynde cessede tho, to se the peple amende.
110 Fortune gan flatere thanne tho fewe that were alyve,   *those*
    And bihighte hem long lif, and Lecherie he sente   *promised*
    Amonges alle manere men, wedded and unwedded,
    And gaderede a greet hoost al agayn Conscience.   *host*
    This Lecherie leide on with laughynge chiere   *pressed on; expression*
115 And with pryvee speche and peyntede wordes,
    And armede hym in ydelnesse and in heigh berynge.   *lofty demeanour*
    He bar a bowe in his hand and manye brode arewes,

                               broad-tipped arrows
    Weren fethered with fair biheste and many a fals truthe.

                               promise; troth
    With untidy tales he tened ful ofte   *indecent; hurt*

102–3 No man whatever whom he struck with a direct blow was left standing
    or ever stirred again.

95 hoore] β (*l. om* g)C; horel α.
    he] L&rC; þat W.
    þe²] βFC; *om* R.
96 *In* W&rC; *l. om* g.
97 hym] αC; *om* β.
100 passched] W&r (*alt. to* daschte
    R)C; he daschede hem F.
102 ne] L&rC; and WCr¹².
    left] αC; leet β.
103 euere stired] WLMαC; stered
    neuere HmgCr (*trs* OCr).

104 and . . . knyȝtes] *so* CK–D; and
    lemmans of kn. βR (of] *om* R); for
    hire levis sake F (C).
105 dethes] L&rC; dentis F; hise W.
106 þo] *so* CK–D; to *All MSS* (C).
109 þo] βRC; sone F.
114 with] αCK–D; with a β.
    laugh-] L&rC; langl- WHm.
117 brode] WHmFC; blody L&r
    (C).
119 with] α (& w. F)C; W. hise β.

120 Conscience and his compaignye, of Holy Kirke the techeris.
   Thanne cam Coveitise and caste how he myghte   *schemed*
Overcome Conscience and Cardinale Vertues,
And armed hym in avarice and hungriliche lyvede.   *'in miserly fashion'*
His wepne was al wiles, to wynnen and to hiden;
125 With glosynges and gabbynges he giled the peple.   *deceptions; lies*
Symonye hym s[ue]de to assaille Conscience,   *followed*
And preched to the peple, and prelates thei maden
To holden with Antecrist, hir temporaltees to save;   *temporalities*
And cam to the kynges counseille as a kene baroun,   *bold*
130 And kneled to Conscience in Court afore hem alle,
And garte Good Feith flee and Fals to abide,   *made*
And boldeliche bar adoun with many a bright noble   *brought down*
Muche of the wit and wisdom of Westmynstre Halle.
He jugged til a justice and justed in his eere,   *rode up to; jousted*
135 And overtilte al his truthe with 'Tak this up amendement.'

                                     overturned

And in to the Arches in haste he yede anoon after,
And tornede Cyvyle into Symonye, and siththe he took the Official:
                                       bribed

And for a menever mantel he made lele matrymoyne *fur; true wedlock*
Departen er deeth cam, and a devors shapte.   *Dissolve; made*
140 'Allas!' quod Conscience, and cryde tho, 'wolde Crist of his grace
That Coveitise were Cristene, that is so kene to fighte, *bold in fighting*
And boold and bidynge the while his bagge lasteth!'

                                   steadfast; money-bag

---

135 'Take this (bribe) to amend your judgement [in my favour]'.
137 (He) made civil law subservient to simoniacal purposes, and then gave
    (some bribe) to the bishop's officer (after *Sk*).
143 And then (the Pride of) Life laughed, and had his clothes curiously cut (C).

120   kerke] αCr*K–D*; chirche β*C*.
122   -ale] β*FC*; -ales R.
123   *h*ungriliche] β*FC*; vngriseliche
     R.
125   and] ?α*gCK–D*; and wiþ
     w*LMF*.
126   seude] ?α*CK–D*; sente β
     (soughte Hm)F (*C*).
127   maden]Cr*MCK–D*; hem m.
     W&r.
132   bright] β*C*; rede α.
134   iugged] L&r; Iogged W*C*;

Iusted F; iustled Cr.
til] W&rC;to WHmCr³;ageyn F.
136   into] αHm?*C*; to β.
138   & . . . mantel] α*CK–D*; (&] *om*
     R*K–D*); for a Mantel of Meneuer β.
139   a] α*C*; *om* β.
140   þo] βR?*C*; *om* F.
     his] β*F*; *om* R.
141   to fiȝte] α*CK–D*; a fightere β.
142   þe] α*C*; *om* β.

And thanne lough Lyf, and leet daggen hise clothes, *be 'dagged' (C)*
And armed hym in haste in harlotes wordes, *lascivious speech*
145 And heeld Holynesse a jape and Hendenesse a wastour, *Courtesy*
And leet Leautee a cherl and Lyere a fre man; *considered; noble*
Conscience and counseil, he counted it folye.
Thus relyede Lif for a litel fortune, *rallied; (good) fortune*
And priked forth with Pride — preiseth he no vertue, *esteems*
150 Ne careth noght how Kynde slow, and shal come at the laste *slew*
And kille alle erthely creature save Conscience oone. *alone*
　Lyf lepte aside and laughte hym a lemman. *took; mistress*
'Heele and I,' quod he, 'and heighnesse of herte *Health; presumption*
Shal do thee noght drede neither Deeth ne Elde, *make; old age*
155 And to foryyte sorwe and yyve noght of synne.' *forget; care nothing for*
　This likede Lif and his lemman Fortune,
And geten in hir glorie a gadelyng at the laste,

(they) begot; presumption; base fellow

Oon that muche wo wroughte, Sleuthe was his name.
Sleuthe wax wonder yerne and soone was of age, *grew; quickly*
160 And wedded oon Wanhope, a wenche of the stuwes. *Despair; brothels*
Hir sire was a sysour that nevere swoor truthe— *juror*
Oon Tomme Two-tonge, atteynt at ech a queste. *found false; inquest*
This Sleuthe was war of werre, and a slynge made, *wary, cautious*
And threw drede of dispair a dozeyne myle aboute. *despairing fear*
165 　For care Conscience tho cryde upon Elde, *anxiety, trouble*
And bad hym fonde to fighte and afere Wanhope. *try; frighten (off)*
　　And Elde hente good hope, and hastiliche he shifte hym, *moved*
And wayved awey Wanhope and with Lif he fighteth. *drove*
And Lif fleigh for feere to Phisik after helpe,
170 And bisoughte hym of socour, and of his salve hadde, *help; remedy*
And gaf hym gold good woon that gladede hir hertes; *a-plenty*

144　in; in] L&rC; an; wiþ W.
147　and] L&rC; and his W (h.]+).
　　it] Cr²³gR (?=α)C; it a HmLM; at
　　Cr¹; at a W; but F.
149　priked] L&r; prikeþ W.
150　Ne] Wα (Ne he F)C; he
　　Cr?gLM; and HmB.
151　kille] βC; calle α.
　　creature] LY?α?C; *pl* w?gMF.
152　lepte aside] βC; sei*th occide* α.
155　sorwe] W&r; deþ MCr¹.

158　wo] βC; *om* α.
162　a queste] L&rC; enqueste W;
　　qwestis F.
163　This] βC; þus BoCotR; *om* F.
　　was] W&rC; wex g.
166　hym] βC; *om* α.
168　fighteþ] ?wOLMαC; fyghted
　　?g; faught Hm.
170　hadde] L&rC; he hadde WF.
171　And] L&rC; He W.
　　here hertes] ?α?C; his herte βF.

And thei gyven hym ageyn a glazene howve.   *in return; glass hood (C)*
Lyf leeved that lechecraft lette sholde Elde,   *believed; stop*
And dryven awey Deeth with dyas and drogges.   *remedies; drugs*
175   And Elde auntred hym on Lyf – and at the laste he hitte
                                                       set off against

A phisicien with a furred hood, that he fel in a palsie,
And there dyed that doctour er thre dayes after.
    'Now I se,' seide Lif, 'that surgerie ne phisik
May noght a myte availle to medle ayein Elde.'   *engage against*
180   And in hope of his heele good herte he hente   /   *took*
And rood so to Revel, a riche place and a murye—
The compaignye of confort men cleped it som tyme—
And Elde anoon after hym, and over myn heed yede,
And made me balled bifore and bare on the croune: *bald in front*
185   So harde he yede over myn heed it wole be sene evere.   *visible*
    'Sire yvele ytaught Elde,' quod I, 'unhende go with the!
                                              ill-bred; discourtesy
Sith whanne was the wey over menne heddes?   *men's*
Haddestow be hende,' quod I, 'thow woldest have asked leeve!'
                                                           leave
    'Ye – leve, lurdeyn?' quod he, and leyde on me with age,   *sluggard*
190   And hitte me under the ere – unnethe may Ich here.   *scarcely*
He buffetted me aboute the mouth and bette out my wangteeth,
                                                     beat; molars
And gyved me in goutes – I may noght goon at large. *shackled; freely*
And of the wo that I was inne my wif hadde ruthe,   *plight; sorrow*
And wisshed wel witterly that I were in hevene.   *most assuredly*
195   For the lyme that she loved me fore, and leef was to feele—
                                                   member; loved
On nyghtes, namely, whan we naked weere—   *particularly*

---

172 ... an imaginary protection (*Sk*), a nostrum, a placebo.
189 'Oh, yes – permission, rascal?'

174   Dyas] βC; dayes α.
176   a³] WHmGLαC; the Cr&r (*om*
         O; +M).
178   Surgerie] wOLMαC; surgiens
         ?g.
179   medle] L&rC; mede W.
180   he] βFC; *om* RBoCot.
181   so to] L&rC; forþ to a W.
182   confort] wLMαC; courte Cr²³g.

183   hym] αCK–D; me β.
190   may] L&rC; myȝte W.
191   and ... my] L&r (and] þat W;
         bett] buscht F; *om* W; out] *om*
         Hm; out my] me on þe g).
       wange teeth] αCK–D; tethe β (teeþ
         he bette W; t. owt beet Hm).
194   wel] ?α (often F)C; ful β.

I ne myghte in no manere maken it at hir wille,
So Elde and he[o] it hadden forbeten.   *she; enfeebled*
 And as I seet in this sorwe, I saugh how Kynde passede,   *sat*
200 And deeth drogh neigh me – for drede gan I quake,   *drew*
And cryde to Kynde, 'Out of care me brynge!   *affliction*
Lo! Elde the hoore hath me biseye: *visited*
Awreke me if youre wille be, for I wolde ben hennes!'   *Avenge*
 'If thow wolt be wroken, wend into Unitee,   *avenged*
205 And hold thee there evere, til I sende for thee;
And loke thow konne som craft er thow come thennes.'   *see; learn*
 'Counseilleth me, Kynde,' quod I, 'what craft be best to lerne?'
 'Lerne to love,' quod Kynde, 'and leef alle othere.'   *leave all else*
 'How shal I come to catel so, to clothe me and to feede?'
210 'And thow love lelly, lakke shal thee nevere   *If; faithfully*
Weede ne worldly mete, while thi lif lasteth.'   *Clothing; food*
 And there by conseil of Kynde I comsed to rome
Thorugh Contricion and Confession til I cam to Unitee.
And there was Conscience conestable Cristene to save,   *governor*
215 And bisegede, soothly, with sevene grete geaunts   *truly*
That with Antecrist helden harde ayein Conscience.
 Sleuthe with his slynge an hard saut he made.
Proude preestes coome with hym – passynge an hundred
In paltokes and pyked shoes and pisseris longe knyves
220 Coomen ayein Conscience – with Coveitise thei helden.
 'By the Marie!' quod a mansed preest, was of the march of Irlonde,
                ?defrocked; province
 'I counte na moore Conscience, by so I cacche silver,   *esteem; provided*

---

219 [Dressed up like blades] in jackets and peaked shoes, and wearing long
  tapering daggers.

198 heo] so CK–D; hee ?α (þe
  gowte & she F); she sooþly β.
  it hadde] ?αC; *trs* βF.
199 as] βC; was α.
202 me] βC; my lif α.
  bi-] βFC; *om* R.
207 -eileth] ?αC; -eille βF.
  be . . . to] ?α (y myȝhte F)C; is best
  to β.
208 leue] αCr¹CK–D; leef of β.
210 lakke] αCK–D; quod *he* l. β.
211 Wede; mete] αCK–D; *trs* β.

212 I] βC; he F; *om* R.
214 was Conscience] βC; was R; he
  was mad a F.
217 saut] LHmC²αC; assaut
  WCr?gM.
  he] WHmLαC; *om* CrgM.
218 passynge . . . hundre*th*]
  αCK–D; mo þan a þousand β.
221 þe¹] ?αCK–D; *om* βF.
  was] αCK–D; *om* β.
  yrlonde] L&rC; walys W.

Than I do to drynke a draughte of good ale!'
And so seiden sixty of the same contree,
225 And shotten ayein with shot, many a sheef of othes,   *oaths*
And brode hoked arwes – Goddes herte and hise nayles—
And hadden almoost Unitee and holynesse adown.
      Conscience cryede, 'Help, Clergie, or ellis I falle
Thorugh inparfite preestes and prelates of Holy Chirche!'
230 Freres herden hym crye, and comen hym to helpe—
Ac for thei kouthe noght wel hir craft, Conscience forsook hem.
Nede neghede tho neer, and Conscience he tolde
That thei come for coveitise to have cure of soules.   *i.e. church livings*
'And for thei are povere, paraventure, for patrymoyne hem failleth,
235 Thei wol flatere, to fare wel, folk that ben riche.   *prosper*
And sithen thei chosen chele and cheitiftee, poverte—*cold; destitution*
Lat hem chewe as thei chose, and charge hem with no cure! *burden*
For lomere he lyeth, that liflode moot begge,   *oftener; a living*
Than he that laboureth for liflode and leneth it beggeres.   *gives to*
240 And sithen freres forsoke the felicite of erthe,   *renounced*
Lat hem be as beggeris, or lyve by aungeles foode!'
      Conscience of this counseil tho comsede for to laughe,   *at; advice*
And curteisliche conforted hem and called in alle freres,   *cheered*
And seide, 'Sires, soothly welcome be ye alle
245 To Unitee and Holy Chirche – ac o thyng I yow preye: *one; beg*
Holdeth yow in unitee, and haveth noon envye
To lered ne to lewed, but lyveth after youre reule.
And I wol be youre borugh, ye shal have breed and clothes
                                                        will guarantee
And othere necessaries ynowe – yow shal no thyng lakke,   *enough*

---

234 . . . because they lack endowments (to provide a steady income).
237 Let them lie on their beds as they've made them, and don't burden them
    with the responsibilities of a parish.

225 wiþ] W&r (*l.* †F); hym with
     YOCBC.
     many a] WCrC²LMRC; many Hm;
     with many ?g.
231 Ac] W&r (but F)C; And Crg.
233 for] βC; for no α.
234 hem failleth] L&rC; þei faille
     WHm.
235 to] L&rC; and WHm.
     folke] L&r?C; of f. F; wiþ f. W.

236 cheitif*tee* pouertee] W&r (ch.]
     HmCr?gM)?C; pore cheytiftee ?B
     (pure chastite Cot); chastite &
     pouert F.
238-9 *In* βC; *ll. om* α.
240 And; þe] βC; *om* α.
242 þo] βC; *om* α.
249 yow] βC; þow R; for ȝee F.
     lakke] αCK–D; faille β.

250 With that ye leve logik; and lerneth for to lovye!   *Provided that*
    For love lafte thei lordshipe, bothe lond and scole—   *abandoned*
    Frere Fraunceys and Domynyk – for love to be holye.
       'And if ye coveite cure, Kynde wol yow telle *wish to be parish priests*
    That in mesure God made alle manere thynges,   *proportion*
255 And sette it at a certein and at a siker nombre,   *definite; fixed*
    And nempnede hem names newe, and noumbrede the sterres:
    Qui numerat multitudinem stellarum . . .
       'Kynges and knyghtes, that kepen and defenden,   *protect*
    Han officers under hem, and ech of hem a certein.

                                    definite (number of men)
    And if thei wage men to werre, thei write hem in noumbre;
260 Wol no tresorere taken hem wages, travaille thei never so soore,
    [But hii ben nempned in the noumbre of hem that ben ywaged].
    Alle othere in bataille ben yholde brybours—   *robbers*
    Pylours and pykeharneys, in ech a parisshe ycursed.
       'Monkes and moniales and alle men of religion—   *nuns*
265 Hir ordre and hir reule wole to han a certein noumbre;   *requires*
    Of lewed and of lered the lawe wole and asketh
    A certein for a certein – save oonliche of freres!   *except only from*
    Forthi,' quod Conscience, 'by Crist, kynde wit me telleth *plain reason*
    It is wikked to wage yow – ye wexen out of noumbre!   *too numerous*

256a [Praise ye the Lord . . .] who telleth the number of the stars: and calleth
    them all by their names (Ps 146:4).
259 And if they undertake to pay the wages of soldiers, they keep a written
    record of their (exact) number.
261 Unless they are included by name in the payroll of enlisted men.
263 Pillagers (of the fallen) and plunderers of (dead men's) armour.
267 A fixed number to each particular category.

253 telle] αCK–D; teche β.
255 it] L&rC; hem WCrF.
256 hem] αCK–D; om β.
     newe and] β; trs α (C).
     noumbrede] βFC; nombre R.
     sterres] W&rC; preestes ?g (p.
     sterreȝ C²).
256a Qui] βFC; Quis R.
     &c] so C; et omnibus eis &c β
     (&c] nomina &c YC²CBmBo;
     nomina vocat Cot)F; om ?α.

257 kepen] βFC; kepten R.
258 a] WHmOB+MFC; om
     CrGYC²LR.
260 So L&rC; after 263 in WHmB.
261 So CK–D; but he kunne rekene
     ariȝt her names in his rollis C²; om
     W&r (C).
263 parische] αCK–D; place β.
265 Hir . . . and] βC; heraude R;
     þer is in F.
269 out of] βC; of on R; ouer ony
     F.

270 Hevene hath evene noumbre, and helle is withoute noumbre;
    Forthi I wolde witterly that ye were in the registre   *list*
    And youre noumbre under notarie sygne, and neither mo ne lasse!'
                                                  officially recorded
        Envye herde this and heet freres go to scole   *ordered; university*
    And lerne logyk and lawe, and ek contemplacion,
275 And preche men of Plato, and preve it by Seneca   *from*
    That alle thynges under hevene oughte to ben in comune. *in common*
        He lyeth, as I leve, that to the lewed so precheth;
    For God made to men a lawe and Moyses it taughte— *taught it to M.*
    Non concupisces rem proximi tui.
280 And yvele is this yholde in parisshes of Engelonde;   *badly; observed*
    For persons and parissh preestes, that sholde the peple shryve,
    Ben curatours called to knowe and to hele,
    Alle that ben hir parisshens penaunces enjoigne,   *bid (to do)*
    And be ashamed in hir shrift; ac shame maketh hem wende
285 And fleen to the freres – as fals folk to Westmynstre,   *dishonest*
    That borweth, and bereth it thider, and thanne biddeth frendes
    Yerne of foryifnesse or lenger yeres leve.
        Ac while he is in Westmynstre he wol be bifore   *forward (to spend)*
    And maken hym murie with oother mennes goodes.
290 And so it fareth with muche folk that to freres shryveth,
    As sisours and executours: thei shul yyve the freres

---

270 i.e. the number of the blessed is fixed (predetermined), that of the damned
     is indeterminate (C).
272 And the number (allowed) you noted in a formal document, and your
     (actual) numbers in agreement with it.
279 Thou shalt not covet thy neighbour's goods [*domum* 'house', Vulg.] (Ex
     20: 17).
284 And (penitents) should experience in confession the sense of shame (which
     is part of true penance), but their (fear of) shame causes them to go (away).
287 Earnestly for remission, or a longer period of grace (to repay it).

271 þe] W&r; þat F; *om* OC; *erased*
     M.
272 -arie] LHmGαC; -aries W&r.
273 go] Hm&rCK–D; to go WCL.
277 He] αCK–D; And yet he β.
279 *tui*] WCrC²LMFC; *tui &c*
     Hm?gR.
283 penaunces] αC; *sg* β.
     enioynen] ?αCK–D; to e. βF.
284 be] *so* CK–D; beþ α; sholden

be β (be) *om* W).
286 it] WHmLαC; *om* CrgM.
287 yeres] W&r (yere R)C; þey F.
     leue] L?α (bleve þere F)C; loone
     wgM.
289 maken] βC; makeþ α.
     mennes] βF; men RC.
290 to] αCrCK–D; to þe β.
     freres] L&r?C; f. hem WOF.
291 schul] αCK–D; wol β.

A parcel to preye for hem, and [pleyen] hem murye

portion; enjoy themselves

With the residue and the remenaunt that othere [renkes] biswonke,

men; toiled for

And suffre the dede in dette to the day of doome.

295   Envye herfore hatede Conscience,   *for this reason*

And freres to philosophie he fond hem to scole,

The while Coveitise and Unkyndenesse Conscience assaillede.

In Unitee Holy Chirche Conscience held hym,

And made Pees porter to pynne the yates   *fasten; gates*

300   Of alle tale-telleris and titereris in ydel.   *To; tatlers*

Ypocrisie and h[ii] an hard saut thei made.   *they; assault*

Ypocrisie at the yate harde gan fighte,

And woundede wel wikkedly many a wise techere

That with Conscience acordede and Cardynale Vertues.

305   Conscience called a leche, that koude wel shryve,   *doctor*

To go salve tho that sike were and thorugh synne ywounded.

Shrift shoop sharp salve, and made men do penaunce   *prepared*

For hire mysdedes that thei wroght hadde,

And that Piers [pardon] were ypayed, *redde quod debes.*

pay what you owe

310   Some liked noght this leche, and lettres thei sente,

If any surgien were in the sege that softer koude plastre. *more gently*

Sire Leef-to-lyve-in-lecherie lay there and gronede; *Love-to-live-in-l.*

For fastynge of a Fryday he ferde as he wolde deye: *acted*

'Ther is a surgien in this sege that softe kan handle,

315   And moore of phisik bi fer, and fairer he plastreth—*(knows) far more*

---

294 And leave the dead man (still) in debt till doomsday (*Sk*).
296 And made provision for friars to study philosophy at universities (C).
300 Against [*OED s.v. of*, XVI, 58] all gossip-mongers and idle chatterers.

292 pleyen hem] make hemself β;
make hem ?βC; with þe remnaunt
make F (C).
293 Wiþ . . . rem.] βR; Of þe
residue of þe good F.
renkes] men *All MSSC* (C).
296 hem] L&r (*om* O)C; þanne W.
300 -rers] L&rC; -leris WCrCF.
301 hij] *cj K–D*; they C; he W&r (*l.
om* F) (C).
302 *In* L&rC; *l. om* W.

303 a] WCr[1]BαC; *om* L&r.
304 -ale] βFC; -ales R.
305 koude wel] W&rC; *trs* g.
306 Go] L&r (To go W); To
C[2]CBFC.
were] αC; ben β.
and] w+MαC; *om* gL.
309 pardon] *so* CK–D; þe
ploughman B; þe C; *om* W&r (C).
311 in þe sege] αCrCSk; þe segg β.
312 leef] βC; lif αHmCr.

Oon Frere Flaterere, is phisicien and surgien.'

   Quod Contricion to Conscience, 'Do hym come to Unitee;
For here is many a man hurt thorugh Ypocrisye.'

   'We han no nede,' quod Conscience, 'I woot no bettre leche

320 Than person or parissh preest, penitauncer or bisshop—   *confessor*
Save Piers the Plowman, that hath power over alle,
And indulgence may do, but if dette lette it.
I may wel suffre,' seide Conscience, 'syn ye desiren,   *permit; since*
That Frere Flaterere be fet and phisike yow sike.'   *fetched; treat*

325   The frere herof herde and hiede faste   *hurried*
To a lord for a lettre, leve to have to curen   *heal/act as a parish-priest*
As a curatour he were, and cam with his lettre
Boldely to the bisshop, and his brief hadde,   *authority obtained*
In contrees ther he coome, confessions to here— *districts; should come*

330 And cam there Conscience was, and knokked at the yate.

   Pees unpynned it, was porter of Unitee,   *unlocked; (who) was*
And in haste askede what his wille were.

   'In faith,' quod this frere, 'for profit and for helthe   *benefit*
Carpe I wolde with Contricion, and therfore cam I hider.'   *Speak*

335   'He is sik,' seide Pees, 'and so are manye othere;
Ypocrisie hath hurt hem – ful hard is if thei kevere.'   *recover*

   'I am a surgien,' seide the frere, 'and salves can make.
Conscience knoweth me wel and what I kan do bothe.'

   'I praye thee,' quod Pees tho, 'er thow passe ferther,

340 What hattestow? I praye thee, hele noght thi name.'

                                      are you called; conceal

   'Certes,' seide his felawe, 'Sire *Penetrans-domos*.'

                                      Surely; companion

   'Ye? Go thi gate!' quod Pees, 'by God, for al thi phisik,   *way*
But thow konne any craft, thow comest nought herinne!   *some skill*

---

322 . . . unless the sinner's unfulfilled penitential obligation prevent it.
323 (However), I suppose that since you wish it, I can allow . . .
341 'Sir Piercer-of-Homes' (alluding to II Tim 3: 6, and with possible sexual
    pun).

320 pen*i*t-] W&rC; pen- R.
321 alle] αGC*K–D*; hem alle β.
326 to³] WLMαC; *om* HmCrg.
327 As] W&rC; and as gF.
    his lettre] αC*K–D*; hise lettres β.

329 coome] Wα?C; c. inne L&r.
    to here] βFC; *om* R.
337 frere] αC*K–D*; segge β.
343 any] ?α (more F)C*K–D*; som β
    (s. ooþer W).

I knew swich oon ones, noght eighte wynter passed,   *once; ago*
345 Coom in thus ycoped at a court there I dwelde,   *manor-house*
And was my lordes leche – and my ladies bothe.   *physician*
And at the laste this lymytour, tho my lord was oute,

licensed mendicant

He salvede so oure wommen til some were with childe.'*salved/greeted*
  Hende-Speche heet Pees tho, 'Opene the yates.   *Good Manners; bade*
350 Lat in the frere and his felawe, and make hem fair cheere.   *welcome*
He may se and here here, so may bifalle,   *hear here; happen*
That Lif thorugh his loore shal leve coveitise,   *teaching; abandon*
And be adrad of deeth and withdrawe hym fram pryde,
And acorde with Conscience and kisse hir either oother.'

each of them; the o.

355   Thus thorugh Hende-Speche entred the frere,
And cam in to Conscience and curteisly hym grette.   *greeted*
'Thow art welcome,' quod Conscience, 'kanstow heele sike?
Here is Contricion,' quod Conscience, 'my cosyn, ywounded.
Conforte hym,' quod Conscience, 'and take kepe to hise soores.

inspect

360 The plastres of the person and poudres ben to soore,   *dressings; harsh*
And lat hem ligge overlonge and looth is to chaunge hem;

(he) lets; remain

Fro Lenten to Lenten he lat hise plastres bite.'
  'That is overlonge!' quod this lymytour, 'I leve, I shal amende it'—
And gooth, gropeth Contricion and gaf hym a plastre   *handles*
365 Of 'A pryvee paiement, and I shal praye for yow,   *secret*
And for al[le hem] that ye ben holden to, al my lif tyme,   *bound*
And make yow [and] my Lady in masse and in matyns
As freres of oure fraternytee for a litel silver.'
  Thus he gooth and gadereth, and gloseth there he shryveth—

'plays down (sin)'

---

344   passed] L&rC; hennes WG.
346   lordes; ladies] W&rC; *trs* g.
349   þo] α (þoo to F)C; to CrYO;
  om W&r.
350   þe] βFC; *om* R.
351   *her* so] α (h.)er F)C*K–D*; so it
  β.
356–87   *def* Bm; B=BoCot.
356   in] W&r; *om* CrC.
357   syke] αC*K–D*; þe sike β.

360   ben] ?αC; biten βF.
361   And] ?αC*K–D*; He βF.
364   goth] ?αC*K–D*; g. and βF.
366   And] CrgF (?=α)C*K–D*; *om*
  WHmLMR.
  alle hem] *al All MSS*; hem C (C).
367   yow . . . Lady] yow my lady
  βRC; of ȝow memory F (C).
368   freres] L&rC; frere WHmO;
  suster Y.

370 Til Contricion hadde clene foryeten to crye and to wepe,
    And wake for hise wikked werkes as he was wont to doone.

                                                    watch (in prayer)

    For confort of his confessour, contricion he lafte, *sorrow for sins; left*
    That is the soverayneste salve for alle kynne synnes.   *all kinds of (C)*
      Sleuth seigh that, and so dide Pryde,
375 And comen with a kene wille Conscience to assaille.

                                                  came; fierce intent

    Conscience cryed eft and bad Clergie helpe hym,
    And also Contricion [come] for to kepe the yate.
      'He lith [adreynt] and dremeth,' seide Pees, 'and so do manye
        othere;   *drowned (in torpor)*
    The frere with his phisyk this folk hath enchaunted,   *bewitched*
380 And plastred hem so esily [hii] drede no synne!'
      'By Crist!' quod Conscience tho, 'I wole bicome a pilgrym,
    And walken as wide as the world lasteth,   *extends*
    To seken Piers the Plowman, that Pryde myghte destruye,
    And that freres hadde a fyndyng, that for nede flateren
385 And countrepledeth me, Conscience. Now Kynde me avenge, *oppose*
    And sende me hap and heele, til I have Piers the Plowman!'

                                                       luck; health

    And siththe he gradde after Grace, til I gan awake.   *cried aloud*

---

384 (And who might bring about) that friars should have some proper
    endowment, instead of being led to resort to flattery through their need for
    money.

371 was] βFC; *om* R.
373 kynne] W&rC; kinnes CrG (C).
376 hym] W&rC; *om* g.
377 come] *so* CK–D; *om All MSS*
     (C).
378 adreynt and dremeþ] *cj* K–D;
     adreynt CotCx; and dremeþ W&r
     (C).
379 haþ] βC; hath so α.
380 hii] þei *All MSS* (C).

383 myȝte] α (he m. F)CK–D; may
     β.
386 þe] βR?C *om* F.
387 And siþþe] βC; So sore F;
     illegible R.
     til I gan] βRC; þat he began F.
COLOPHON *Explicit hic dialogus
     petri plowman* W&r (*dial.*) *visio*
     Hm); *Explicit* (*hic*) B; *Explicit* F;
     Passus ii^us de dobest R; *om* Cr.

COMMENTARY: A TEXTUAL AND LEXICAL

TITLE There is no authoritative title for any version of the poem; I follow Crowley, the poem's first publisher, in calling it *The Vision of Piers Plowman*.

Prologue

The **rubric** *prologus* appears only in an A-MS, Oxford, Bodleian Library MS Rawlinson Poet. 137 (R). **2** *sheep*: 'sheep' not 'shepherd', for which no lexical support exists. **10** *sweyed*: 'sounded' (so ZA) goes better with *murye* than the yL variant *sweyued* 'flowed along', which is unlikely to represent Bx here. **11** *me to meten*: the line scans *xa/ax* in AxBx and Z, a pattern I judge inauthentic (see Appendix). C Pr 9 has *merueylousliche me mette*, and that L's preferred construction was with the impersonal form (see *MED s.v. meten* v. (3), 2) is suggested by B VIII 68 and XIX 485, *qq.v.* The emendation here offered presupposes an unusual threefold repetition of error in the Z copy and the archetypes of the successive revisions. **13** Bx presumably read zero, (∅), like Z and revised C, *And* in WCMH being a scribal intrusion. **22** *þese* F could show contamination (⊗) from // AC, since β here agrees with Z; but it may be one of six instances in Pr where F represents α in the absence of R. **29** Whether showing asyndeton after preceding *holden* (28) or suppressed relative pronoun, ZAC show Bx to be scribal here. **34** *Wr*'s emendation of *synnelees* (also the preferred reading for **A**) to *giltles* is unnecessary on metrical grounds. If the suffix *-lees* has contexual rhetorical stress, the line is the first example in the poem of the metrical pattern *aaa/bb*, or, preferably, the line scans as Type IIa, see Appendix on Langland's verse). **41** The Bx form is a scribal misunderstanding of the ZAC spelling *bret-* (acceptably preserved in H, perhaps by ⊗ from **A**) occasioned by the context of food and eating. **48** As at **29** above, a scribally intruded pronoun affects the characteristic *usus scribendi* attested by ZAC. **50–2** Not in **A**; they were either omitted in the C revision or are spurious (the metre seems awkward and alliteration heavy) and could be Bx expansion of **49**. However the imagery is characteristic of L, and used again at XIV 309, *q.v.* **59** *Prechynge*: Bx apparently read *preched* (so **Z**), mistaking the participial form *prechend* for *precheden*. The source of the error is the unexpectedness of a participle in a sequence of preterites. WHm correct independently, not necessarily from C or A. *the wombe* appears original in the light of Z(A)C; *her wombys* H will be by ⊗ from A (as with *mete* at 63 below). **67** *up*: β may have inserted *wel* for ∅ Bx (so F, ?=α), as G inserted *up*, by ⊗ from A rather than correction from a superior lost B source (see Intro. p. lxxi). **76** *ʒe; ʒoure*: Bx could have read ∅; *hire*, and correction from agreed ZAC is secure, as is *helpe* ZAC, which will have come into H from an A source. **82** *peple*: Bx read ∅, omitting by eyeskip from *pore* to *par-*. β and ?α supply divergently. **94** F's extra line after this could =α (and hence Bx), but its absence from // C suggests (?memorial) ⊗ from A, of which F shows many signs in much smaller details (see Intro., p. lxiv). **99** *hys* H, accepted on grounds of sense (*Consistorie* is here metaphorical) and support from C (from which H shows no ⊗ elsewhere), could have been in α (no witness here). **108-9** The sense is rendered hard by the distance between *of the cardinals* and the verb *impugnen*, and by the rareness of the construction. Translation (a) seems preferable as L is more concerned with the electoral college's power to 'create' St Peter's successor (a power held to have been invested in him by Christ) than with its capacity to invest the Pope with Petrine authority generally, as K–D's parenthesizing of *impugnen I nelle* requires. *Bn*'s 'took (on themselves)' does not fit with *in hem*, which points to the cardinals' (sin of) presumption that they really do possess the power in question. **117** Bx is metrically defective in the b-half; reconstruction is after C. **125** Hereafter α denotes R unless indication is given to the contrary. **143** has 'cognative' alliteration on |g|, |k|, |k|, i.e. a voiced stop with its unvoiced counterpart: cf. XIX 213, 323; and see further Sch, *Clerkly Maker*, pp. 40–1. **147** scans as Type IIIa (so in C); W's scribe attempts to 'correct' the metre. **148** Emendation of Bx is directed by the ease of the error and the superior sense of C; the number describes the whole gathering, not just a portion of it. **152** K–D needlessly read *dedes*; but there is no tautology, since *drede* 'danger, source of fear' is well instanced in *MED s.v.*, 5a from Chaucer (*CT* VII. 2517). **159** *Seide* is perhaps absolute 'spoke' (*OED s.v.*, 3(e)); if not, *quod he* 160 is pleonastic but need not be scribal. The b-half *hemselven alle* is reconstructed as Bx from the 'split variants' attested by β and α. The line scans as Type Ie with 'counterpoint' (Sch, *Clerkly Maker*, p. 62). **171** *rometh*: Y may preserve β through direct descent from g, but more probably is a happy guess or a reminiscence of C; Bx could have so read, but α is absent. **182** *tho* is not strictly necessary for the metre but looks original in the light of C and will have been lost from Bx by haplography before *thoughte*. G has it from C, from a lost B source distinct from Bx, or by felicitous conjecture. **189-92** K–D (p. 176) show convincingly that the lines have been misordered, on grounds of inconsequence in the argument. **201** scans, like 147 above, as Type IIIa; C revises *wille* to *reik*. **206** *so*: *cj* as the stave-word for which Bx ⇒ the expected *to*. F's *slen* (so K–D) is metrical 'improvement': the mouse does not say that the cat should *kill* them (cf. 185) but that he will stick to rabbits if he is not vexed by a constraint. 213 *poundes*: the reading, certain in ZC and here accepted for all four versions, plays on the senses 'money' (noun) and 'pulverize, beat' (verb in the present tense). FH seem contaminated from an A source. 231 *I seigh*: G's correct subject–verb order is most probably a happy chance or else an echo from A.

Passus I

4 *the castel*: Bx's *a* misses the reference to *tour* (Pr 14). 11 *may . . . meene*: a reconstruction of Bx's unmetrical b-half on the basis of C. H is perhaps contaminated from an A source, several A-MSS having its reading. 41 *seeth*: Bx is satisfactory in sense and confirmed by C. G is contaminated from an A source of the r-family and sophisticated F's b-half echoes the corrupt Ax a-half. 42 scans on |*th*| as a two-stave Type IIIa line. 44 Both *holdeth* and *kepeth* are acceptable and supported by other traditions; since no major difference of sense is involved, β is retained. 45 Bx *madame* is rejected as scribal on the basis of ZAC agreement. F here may show influence from A. 48 Bx has an awkwardly heavy three-syllable penultimate dip in revising A's Type II to a Type I line. GH appear contaminated from A. 60 *bemeene*: Bx's exemplar **be mene* could have invited smoothing to *be to meene* (not obviously wrong in itself). Assuming GHF contaminated from A and C^2Cr^3 from C, decision rests on the certain reading of C. 64 *and* Bx may be a smoothing of its exemplar's *a* (=*he*), as in A; C points to the ∅-reading as the probable original. 70 The α reading looks to =Bx in the light of ZA, but β is closer to revised C. G here presumably contaminates from A rather than correcting from an α source and H ⟹ a near-synonym for its β original. 73 F has presumably corrected α from A or C; *hasked* R is a spelling variant of Bx *asked*. 96 G's (erroneous) *trespacers* appears a ⊗ from an A source (or possibly a C group-variant). 98–9 C has 98–9 in the Bx order; but the passage is extensively revised, and on balance the ZA order is preferable. 112 seems necessary to the sense and is echoed in C I 106a. The form adopted here is that of Z, with the correct *lyght* for Ax *siȝt* in the a-half (as *cj* by K–D, p. 104; and cf. *Ka²*, p. 462). 121 The needed stave-word *for* could have been omitted as otiose. 123 The Bx a-half was rendered unmetrical by transposition to prose order. The emendation gives a Type IIIa line. 127 Adopting harder *hym* makes pride the (personified) subject and gives an apter sense for *pulte*. L here = β, R = α and Cr has contaminated from C. 136 The harder reading *thus* seems secure and *his* an easy visual error. 141 In R's absence for over 100 lines, F is cited only where clearly not sophisticated but likely to represent α. 142 *quod she* appears from ZAC to have been scribally intruded in Bx. 152 *plante*: not clearly A's reading, but arguably (spelled *plonte*, as in C) is that of the B original, of which Bx has failed to grasp the metaphor,

partly through unconscious association of 'plenty' and 'peace'. 154 Cr seems to have C's reading (='begotten') by ⊗; to retain Bx *fille* (and consequently *(y)eten*) avoids anticipating the explicitly incarnational statement of 155 and strengthens the pregnant metaphor of *heavenly* love as drawing sustenance from *human* nature. 160 *inmiddes*: *cj* as the necessary stave-word in the b-half, gives a line of 'T' type (see Appendix). The rare prepositional use of the adverb (see *MED s.v.*, 2) would have invited substitution. (For the form cf. C IX 122.) 165 *comseth a myghte*: Bx would scan on 'cognative' staves (see note on Pr 143 above) with G's transposition; but *bigynneth* looks a scribal substitution for a harder synonym; *myghte* needs to be disyllabic as in // C. 176 *myghty*: G contaminates from A, Cr from C, but Bx looks scribal. 186 *feet*: F's variant *fewte*, perhaps contaminated from an A source like sub-archetypal **m** (=EAM), shows failure to understand the lexical pun on 'deed' and 'feet'. The unmetrical b-half may reflect Bx's objection to the logic; H contaminates from A, but destroys the metre by synonym substitution. 191 *hardere*: G contaminates from A, but ZAC agreement makes the reading secure. *hii*: from // A and (revised) C I 187b, the vocalic pronominal form gives a Type I line, which seems preferable to Bx's Type II line (with inferior stress-pattern here). 200 The emendation of both unmetrical halves of the Bx line is secure on the basis of (Z)AC agreement. 206 *sighte of*: GH contaminate from A, but the emendation seems secure from ZAC agreement.

Passus II

1 *courbed*: Bx substitution for *kneled* or a revision later rejected in C. 8 *wonderliche*: looks an original B reading, G having acquired it from A; Bx is not clearly determinable here. 22 *hym*: β's error may arise from recalling the grammatical gender of nouns like *leautee* in French and Latin. 28, 43 *heo*: not strictly necessary metrically, but the Western form gives a better stress-pattern. 36 *caccheth*: an unusual use of the same word instanced at XI 173 (cf. also XIII 298); Bx ⇒ an unmetrical synonym. 47 *þow ... tonge* Bx seems a deliberate substitution influenced by the sense of 48a and stylistic objection to repeating *alle* 45. 75 *upon*: GHF all show ⊗ from A *vpon*; ZAC agreement indicates absence of *þis* in B. 84 will scan with *and* as a mute stave in the b-half, but *wraþe* appears probably a Bx substitution of the commoner synonym regularly used in Passus V as the name of this sin. 89 *With*: Bx ⇒ *And* to avoid the (characteristic) repetition. 91 *wenynges*, 'hopes, expectations', whether it represents α or is an F smoothing, seems in comparison with C closer to the presumed original (a mental term) than the contextually (possible but) less apt *wedes*. 119 *engendred*: the *-th* of YCLR indicates a Bx spelling variant of the same past participle, not 3rd pers. pres. 120 *graunted*: the tense is best resolved

as preterite, the -*th* form being an erroneous reflex of ambiguous **Bx** **grauntet*, or an assimilated form like **Cx** *grante* (cf. *folweth* at 186 below). **123** H here shows obvious ⊗ from an A source of r-type. Its unmetrical and otiose extra line, 'Worþi is þe werkman his mede to haue', looks clearly scribal. **130** *feithlees*: the H (and, surprisingly, C) form *feytles* seems an echo of a possible A family reading, conjecturally meaning 'without deeds', though probably a spelling variant, with loss of *h*, for *feythles*. **143** The b-half's feeble sense suggests either a damaged exemplar or deliberate censorship (the *sele*s would have been the bishop's). Reconstruction from C with support from one A family and Z gives satisfactory sense. **153** *wittes*: GHF's singular is presumably by ⊗ from A. **166** *fetisly*: the G variant *feytlyche* may be a corrupt reflex of a difficult original *feyntly*, 'deceptively' (as in A family **m**) or a spelling variant of *feetly*, 'neatly', a word closely related to **Bx**. **180** *drawe*: **Bx** *lede* seems deliberate or unconscious scribal substitution, perhaps induced by *leden* 182. **181** *oure*: **Bx** *vs* looks like an attempt to avoid repetition (cf. 89 above). **198, 200–3** The succession of **Bx** errors (of over-emphasis in 198, of metre in 200, of word and line order in 201, 203, of misunderstood syntax in 202) may all be securely emended in the light of // **ZAC**. **210** *feeris*: F may represent α here or, more probably, be ⊗ from A or C. Once again, **Bx** ⇒ through objection to the near-repetition in the original's wordplay (cf. 181, 189 above). **222** The word-order of **Bx** is not objectionable in itself but looks scribal on comparison with agreed **ZAB**. **229** *withhelden*: preferable on grounds of sense. In both **Bx** and **Z** initial *with-* could have been lost by eyeskip to *with* at 230 (**Z** 210) below.

Passus III

10 The line is Type III (as in A), with staves on |*b*|. F's *mente* is a characteristic attempt to 'regularize' the alliteration. **15** *Conforteden*: if the verb was finite, **Bx** *To conforten* could result from smoothing of an exemplar reading with omitted preterite morpheme that was mistaken as infinitive. HB are smoothed reflexes of A or ⊗ from C. **41** *erende*: the back-spelled form in H is by ⊗ from A, which is indicated by C as the original of **Bx**'s pointless synonym substitute. **46** *brocour*: G's *baud*, of which H appears a smoothed reflex, is a ⊗ from A, and **Bx**'s revision a suggestive euphemism, anticipating the tone of XX 346ff. **48** *stonden*: H's reading, presumably by ⊗ from A, is accepted on AC agreement as the original replaced in **Bx** by a common near-synonym. **51–62** are witnessed only in β, but on AC evidence are clearly original. The α lines in their place are a clumsy expansion of A III 50–1, the only case in either sub-archetype of recourse to another version. **71** *gyve*: **Bx** substitution of an aurally induced non-alliterating synonym *dele* renders the b-half unmetrical. **75** Transposition of the subject and verb to the intended prose order restores the metre of the a-half, giving a Type IIIa line. 76–81 Syntax anacoluthic as it stands; possibly 80–6 should be parenthetical, as J. A. Burrow has suggested to me, with a very idiomatic resumption of the main sentence at 87, *mayr* taking up plural *maires* at 76. 87 *heo bisoughte*: the plausible Bx corruption could have arisen mechanically through misreading the exemplar's pronominal form **a* (so C) as intended for *hath*, and then smoothing. 98 *forbrenne*: the AC form is adopted to give a Type IIb line. Loss of the metrically necessary proclitic intensive could have been through visual distraction (from *fir* to *for-*). 103 *That*: agreement of W with AC is accidental; A is revised in B, as B is by C. 107 scans more smoothly if the stave-sound is |w|; but conjunctive use of the (normally interrogative) *whan* is unusual, and both Bx and Cx will scan on the voiced |δ| or |v| with b-half stresses on either adverb or pronoun and a possible wrenched-stress stave-sound on *nevére*. The Hm GF *whan* is either ⊗ from A or independent metrical 'correction'. 113 *ellis*: Bx *soone* looks like an over-emphatic substitution for neutral and firmly attested *ellis*. 114 *And* W&r a scribal connective, presumably deleted in H's ancestor by reference to A. 117 *What*: the original elliptical form has been spelled out by Bx. 118 *quod the kyng*: possibly a Bx intrusion (G again following A), but not obviously scribal, and could have been deleted in C. 124 The line, acceptable enough in itself, is to be reconstructed on the solid evidence of ZAC. G retains *In* by reference to A, F includes *she* as part of a wider rewriting. Bx replaced the indefinite verb with a more explicit one, H then substituting its own near-synonym. The error was perhaps induced by the suggestion of initial *tr-* in the a-half. 132; 141 Bx's b-half is in each case metrically acceptable but reveals scribal over-emphasis on comparison with ZAC. 151 *holde*: the Bx reading *have* may be, like *habbe* Z, a visual error for *halde*, although it could be a pointless substitution. 160 *mote*: used absolutely, appears original (in GF by ⊗); Bx missed the construction, and H has smoothed further. 222 *kenne clerkes*: Bx ⇒ a more common verb and then smooths to generalize (and change sense). 224 *at þe meel tymes* seems over-explicit and rhythmically uncharacteristic on comparison with AC. 226 *Marchaundise*: H may have corrected here from A or C; Bx's reading is an easy visual error. 255 *lowe lewede*: diagnosis of split variation across the sub-archetypes is slightly confused by HmC²H (β-MSS) agreeing with α, but γLM agreement seems secure if M and Cr²³ are regarded as individual synonym substitutions for *lowe*. 260 *fel²*: a characteristic punning adjectival homograph as the needed second stave-word is posited as having been lost through haplography. Cf. V 171 (C) below. 283 *sothest* seems preferable on grounds of style (balance with *sonest*). WG have made individual corrections, not necessarily in knowledge of // C. 292 *trewe men*: necessary to provide a key-stave. Bx *trupe* has come in from 293. 298 *lordeth*: cj as the needed key-stave, for which Bx ⇒ an unmetrical near-synonym, finding the usage difficult (not found transitively before C16th, but intransitively at X 86) and/or objecting to repetition of *lord*. 303 *come into*: the first example of a 'liaisonal stave', a common resource of L (see Sch, *Clerkly Maker*, p. 38). 316 *-carke*: adopted as the needed first stave-word. The rareness of the word would have prompted substitution of an unmetrical alternative. 319 *moot*: conjectured as the needed key-stave, a 'strong' word which Bx's substitution weakens. 322 *That*: necessary for the sense. Possibly Bx's exemplar read *Tha*, which was thoughtlessly mis-expanded. Bm presumably corrects from C. 339 scans with 'cognative' second stave and long onset (*omnia próbáte*). 342 *felle*: Bx's error is visually induced (so in several C-MSS here). G's variant may be a simple modernization of spelling, but Cr will have corrected from C. The sense may be *MED s.v.*, 2: 'subtle, wise', rather than 'fierce, harsh' as at V 168. 343 scans with anomalous a-half (because macaronic) and 'compensating' |t| stave in the b-half. 344–5 fail to scan in Bx, but simple transposition (in 345 from prose order) restores both as Type III lines (345 as IIIb). 346 *tidy*: cj as the needed key-stave, with *OED* sense 3a, 'good, useful' (cf. 322 above) for which Bx ⇒ the exact lexical equivalent. 351 scans as Type III with 'counterpointed' a-half (*abb/ax*) and F's *tale* is a characteristic attempt to 'correct' the metre.

Passus IV

4 *rather*: presumably replaced by W&r (= ?Bx) to avoid repetition in 5, perhaps by inducement from an exemplar reading **er* (for *arre*), a synonym of *rather*, which has been adopted by the others perhaps from A or C. 10 Line missing from Bx (for no apparent mechanical or other reason) and added by the ancestors of Y and OC[2] (from A or C) and Cr[23] from C. 15 *seide*[2]: was adopted by F from C, since A reads *sente* and Bx evidently *bad*. Emendation is tentative, but a second |s| stave seems likely in the light of ZAC. 38 An unmetrical scribal line follows in Bx; but *capones* is retained in the reconstructed 38 on the showing of revised // C. 47 *vp* H is by ⊗ from A and is adopted as the probable B original replaced in Bx by a common synonym. 75 F's form of the b-half *may* represent α but more probably is an intelligent scribal 'correction', and Bx preserves a line awkwardly scanning on vocalic staves (the // versions also scan on vowels, but not awkwardly). Whether B itself read like F must remain uncertain. 86 *suffre hym*: the conjecture supplies the needed first stave-word, for which non-alliterating *lete* would be an unconscious substitution. The C revision, closer to ZA, would provide a less drastic emendation. 91 *withseide*: cj in the light of C's |w| verb as a difficult original lost through influence of preceding *-wiþ*. The word itself is instanced at A IV 142. 105 *er I*: the HG readings presumably from companion with A but look original on the showing of ZAC. 145 *on Englissh*: H adapts a form of the A reading with homoeoarchic loss of *on*

(as in Z). Bx smoothed from the same defective reading in its exemplar. **158** *Kynde*: a necessary conjecture, finding some support in (much-revised) // C, that enables confusion with Wisdom's companion Witty (27 above) to be avoided. **190** *hennes*: on the showing of ZAC, the adverb looks original and Bx's phrase scribal over-emphasis. H presumably derives from A.

Passus V

9 scans as Type III with a-half 'counterpoint' (*abb/ax*). **23** The ?Bx b-half fails to scan through inversion to prose order. F's reading, whether reflecting α or an independent 'correction', gives a form close to the probable original. **32** The line is present in one A family (**m**, supported by the r MS J), from whence F might have derived its reading by ⊗. **44** Bx probably read *lyuen*, but no change is made in W's spelling as homography better enables a play on the senses of two distinct lexemes. **47** *stewed*: possibly the rare verb meaning 'restrain, check' (*OED s.v. stew* v., 1), with pun on *styward*, or the more common *stowed* 'established (in order)'. **70** *that*: F's reading is either an independent correction or by ⊗ from A or C. **111** *litheth*: 'eases' is *cj* as an original hard enough to have invited substitution of Bx *liketh* (or, by its form, to have been mistaken for *lighteth*, a variant in // A). **128** *biggyng*: 'residing', the *cj* key-stave word, is unusual enough to have invited substitution of a commoner synonym. **136** scans on 'cognative' staves: |k|g|g|. **165** *purveiede*: the *cj* third stave-word gives a term with one of two apt senses, either 'foresaw', with *for* as conjunction, or, more probably, 'provided', with *for* as preposition. It both matches the metrical structure of Bx's synonym and accounts for the substitution. Cr could be an intelligent scribal attempt to correct the metre, or an echo of a lost B source (no // in C). **171** *faste²*: 'severely; diligently' (*MED s.v.*, 4, 6) is *cj* as the necessary second stave-word lost by haplography (cf. *fel²* at III 260 above). **172** α is reconstructed from the split variants of R and F as the Bx reading identical with C. **174** Transposition from prose order enables the line to scan as Type IIa. **176** *and whan*: reconstructed from the split variants *and*, *whan*; *wel* is preferred to *wyn* on comparison with *late* in // C. **179** *coughe*: is the substantive lexeme in C and, given the metaphorical context, is likely to be not a revision but the B original, of which Bx's (arguably no less apt) *coupe* is an error due to ʒ/þ confusion. **188** Bx shows mis-division on account of the line's length; the second line is of Type IIa and not objectionable metrically, but it adds nothing to the sense and looks like scribal padding on comparison with C and A-r (the A-family **m** is contaminated from **Bx**). **190** alliterates on |s| / |ʃ|, *his chyn* and *chyveled* being pronounced |ʃ|. **193** The over-emphatic scribal extra line contains in *torn* an echo of the posited B original behind Bx *tawny*. **194** *leve I*: the needed key-stave is conjecturally restored as the

intervening phrase presumed lost through homoarchy with *lepe* imme-
diately before at the caesura. **208** scans 'cognatively' on |b|b|p|. **223** Bx's
b-half is metrically acceptable but appears scribal flattening of a phrase
perhaps judged inappropriately specific. **232** *be*: was lost severally in L, R
and M's exemplar by homoarchy; or else they preserve an elliptical Bx
form. **253** Bx has transposed the b-half to prose order; restoration gives a
Type I line scanning 'cognatively' on |p|p|b| (cf. 208). **259** Bx inverts the
clause order to give an unmetrical line; reconstruction repairs the metre
and brings the main verb into syntactic contiguity with its object. **266**
scans 'cognatively' in ?Bx on |p|p|b| with mute key-stave. **276a** The α line
that follows looks clearly spurious on grounds of metre and redundancy;
one of two spurious lines in α (cf. XVIII 8). **277** Rejected as spurious by
K–D but satisfactory in sense and metre. **282** Possibly a scribal addition
'introducing' a Latin line, but acceptable as a Type III line with
'counterpointed' a-half (*abb/ax*) if *goddes* is emended to *his*, giving a
closer translation of **282a** *eius* (*goddes mercy* could be Bx scribal
explicitness induced by *mercy of God* at following 284a. **284** *inmiddes*:
Bx omits the second half of the *cj* preposition, evidently finding the word
difficult (cf. I 160 (C)). Restoration is on the showing of revised // C. **300**
Bx is unmetrical; transposition of verb and adverb gives a Type IIIb line
with counterpoint (*abb/aa*). **304** The Bx phrase *ought . . . purs* looks like
a scribal padding-out of an exemplar reading that lacked *quod he* (added
independently by W and F). **328** Bx omits; reconstructed from C VI 384
(// A VI 178, uncertain in the b-half). **330** Bx can be reconstructed in the
light of C from the (disordered) split variants in R (=α) and β (*by, þe*
(for *hy* or *þei*)). **338** Bx omits this line for no evident mechanical or other
reason. Linking of *bargayne* and *beverage* suggests here for the former its
usual sense or else 'undertaking' (= 'bet') rather than 'contention' (*MED*
s.v., 5). **345** *wexed*: 'polished' rather than 'stopped up'; hunters' horns
were polished to improve their tone (see *OED s.v. wax* v.[1,2]). **351**
thrumbled: a rare word, possibly L's own nonce-blend of 'thrust' and
'stumble' or 'tremble', both attempted resolutions of B's presumed form,
here reconstructed from // C (also in A-MS V). **363** *warp*: by normal
criteria of AC agreement (with *was* as the second stave) Bx here should be
scribal, but the reading is harder in itself and could be a B revision itself
revised again in C for clarity's sake. **364** The Bx line is likely to have had
wit as the subject, w having ⇒ *wif* under influence from A or C; but the
latter's presence in C's revised *wif and his inwit* suggests that both *wif* and
wit also appeared in B, giving it one stave more than A. The Bx scribe
presumably judged the Type Ic line overloaded and so dropped one
subject, perhaps also converting a simple preterite verb (as in AC) to the
pleonastic form with *gan*. **375** *feestyng*: *cj* as necessary for the sense and
of a form easily open to substitution under inducement from the
contextually commoner term (378 below). **377** scans as T-type or
'cognatively' as Type Ib on |t| |t| |d| |d|. The sense is satisfactory and no

emendation is required: Glutton has his meals only in order to drink and gossip. 378 *it*: *cj* as the needed vocalic key-stave; an idiomatic usage of L's with plural verb. 394 scans as Type IIb with 'liaisonal' stave on *quod_þé (aaa/bb)*. Sloth expresses *wanhope* here, not terror of death as in revised C. 400 *sithenes*: *cj* as the needed key-stave. The difficult sense is that Sloth feels no continuing sorrow for sin *after* confession; Bx, in substituting the simpler *yet* 'furthermore', damages the metre. 405 *pure*: needed as the key-stave; on the showing of C, Bx ⇒ a more commonplace non-alliterating adverb. 412 *mengen I of*: the needed stave-phrase *cj* in the light of // C's *haue Y a memorie at*. Sloth recalls that he can arrive at the friary church as the service ends without risk of rebuke. 415 *telle*: the conjecture, based on C, provides the necessary stave-word for which Bx ⇒ the more explicit and emphatic unmetrical *shryve*, smoothing with subsequent inversion of verb and adverb. 420 *clausemele*: the simple adverb sounds more original than the form with *it*, an α scribal reflex; β has a more radical smoothing after mistaking adverb for noun + adverb. 440 *yarn*: the alliterating preterite of *yernen*, *cj* in the light of // C (and found also at XI 60), provides the needed first stave, lost through Bx substitution of the advancing verb form. 441 *be*[2]: *cj* as the needed key-stave, with the relatively uncommon sense 'through' (*MED s.v.*, 7). The same substitution of *for* occurs in // Cx, for the same reason. Reversing the Bx order of verb and noun in *beggere be* establishes the form likeliest to have generated the diagnosed error; *be*[2] having been lost in Bx's exemplar, the resultant ∅-reading would invite intrusion of another causal preposition. 456 Bx is here reconstructed from the split variants preserved in β and α. The verb *yelde* thus has a noun-clause object preceding and one following (457); the 'split' will have been occasioned by the length of the line and the (relative) complexity of the syntax. The C revision, however (VI 309–10), seems to echo only the β remnant of the postulated B reading. 466 scans awkwardly as extended Type III, on |δ| (*Tho, the*). *Dysmas*: the well-authenticated name of the 'good thief'; *bysmas* (also in some C-MSS) may be a scribal attempt to make the line conform to a commoner metrical type. 468 *Roberd*: the proper name, well attested in // ZAB, provides a better grammatical fit with the first-person verb. 487 *us*: Bx *and* is deleted as grammatically otiose. 488 *sute*: W's coincidental agreement with (revised) C is induced by *secte* (491). 492 *sight*: preferable for metre and sense (see Literary Commentary below *ad loc.*), is the probable Bx reading. Cx repeats the error through visual confusion of *l* with long *s*. 495 *And*: Bx *þoruȝ* is omitted on grounds of grammar and sense. β has smoothed the construction preserved in ?α and unambiguously attested in C. Possibly *it* was added by α, F reflecting the ∅ form of Bx (passive *blente* is not recorded.) 497 *ther-*: the proclitic is not strictly necessary on grounds of sense or metre, but on the showing of C was probably present in B and lost through distraction from preceding *þridde* and following *þow*. 512

The unmetrical b-half is reconstructed to accord with clearly attested ZAC. 514 *baches* 'valleys': replaced by commoner (but less appropriate) topographical terms in **Bx** and **Ax**, but supported by **ZC**, is the hardest reading and the one likeliest to be original. 526 *the sépúlcre*: with two lifts, forms the whole b-half after a 'strong' (three-syllable) dip. **Bx**'s exemplar will have expanded with *of oure lord* (as in **Z** and **C** family x), of which **Bx** itself retains the awkward reflex *oure lordes sepulcre*. The hardest form seems securely attested in **Ax**, though two m-MSS and one other include the final phrase in its **Z** and **C** family x form. Presumably this was a marginal gloss in the earliest version, incorporated in **Bx** first and then in **C** family x. 532 *quod they*: will have been omitted from **Bx** and **Z** on account of the length of the line. 533 *wissen*: omission of *auȝt* in g and F may be independent correction or ⊗ from **A** or **C**; **Bx** intrusion of the word repeats a habit of expansion earlier instanced at 304 above (*q.v.*). 537 *heved*: the unapocopated form of the noun in **ZC** (which descend from dialectally purer exemplars) is here adopted as providing **L**'s customary feminine line-ending. 540 *siththen*: will almost certainly have been present in **Bx** on the joint showing of **ZAC**; lost through homoarchy with following si*kerly*. 555 *the wey wel right*: reconstructed as the form preserved in **Z**, as split variants in the **Ax** tradition, and revised in **C**, in preference to the emphatic and more clearly scribal **Bx** form with *witterly*. 556 The unmetrical line that follows in **Bx** can be emended to scan by reading for *dwellyng* the less usual *wonyng*: but it appears a piece of scribal explicitation interrupting the movement from the pilgrims' offer to Piers's angry response. 565 *hii*: in the light of **C** the reading is best resolved as the plural pronoun in its plainest Western form (**Z** has the ambiguous unstressed *a*, the possible original for **AB**). 567 *Forto*: the unusual conjunction is restored as the form likely to have been replaced by the advancing *Til*. 591 *of o wombe*: present in **A** and, a line later, in revised **C**; presumably in **B** but dropped by **Bx** as otiose and as overweighting the line. 597 *woot*: the indicative is clearly attested as the required form, corrupted in **Bx** through misunderstanding the sense. 609 *Wrathe-thee*: 'Get angry' is to be judged a correct reflex of **B**'s revision of **ZA**'s less logical 'Don't get angry'. The **C**-tradition is divided between this latter form and the simpler 'Anger', with an ambiguous spelling *Wratthe*. Whichever form was intended, the sense is the same: 'beware of Anger'. 617 The unmetrical **Bx** line can be easily emended by transposing object and verb in the b-half; but on comparison with agreed **ZAC** it looks like a scribal rewriting, perhaps based on objection to the supposed moral laxity of the condition set out in the original a-half. 628 *any*: the curt and elliptical **AC** form looks original, **Bx**'s variant a scribal explicitation; omission of *quod Piers* by GF may be due to ⊗ from an **A** source. 638 *so*: WG need not here show ⊗ from **A** or **C**; *bi*, which does not affect the sense, was in **Bx** but is probably not original on the showing of **AC**.

Passus VI

8 *the*: WHmYOC² probably reflect the γ reading, which is a correction from C of inferior ?Bx *þere*. **17** Metrically emendable, the Bx line following appears a piece of scribal expansion, on comparison with ZAC. **33–4** *conseyved*: easily the most likely reading to have generated the A and C variants, and Bx has probably ⇒ the same unproblematic *comsed* found (in present-tense form) in some A-MSS. If the sense here is 'uttered' (*MED s.v.*, 8c) rather than 'grasped' (*Ka*) then *quod he* is to be omitted as in ZAC. **37, 38, 41** The variation between singular and plural pronouns, paralleled in C, is probably non-significant, and F's regularization to the sg may reflect influence from A. **59–61** On the showing of ZAC, Bx's alteration to first person and present tense appears a scribal error, perhaps induced through misreading initial *A* (= *He*) as *And* and subsequently smoothing. **74** *forther*. Bx's exemplar may have lacked the concluding *-er*, inviting substitution of a metrically superior final disyllable. Bx conflates C and B readings. **88** The Bx word-order is unobjectionable in itself but appears probably scribal on comparison with ZAC. **119** *here*, not strictly needed but improving the sense, is added in M from a C source and appears original from ZAC. **123** *pleynt*: *cj* on the guidance of *pleyneden* ZA as the needed first stave-word, for which *mone* is a Bx substitution, probably already in *B¹*, since C uses it in revising the whole line to scan on |*m*|. **128** *noȝt*: Bx may have resolved an exemplar reading lacking terminal *-er* as the simple negative, through confusion of *þ* and *ȝ*. BCr may have corrected from C. **137** scans vocalically as Type Ie with mute key-stave (*and*), and needs no emendation. **138** *garisoun*: *cj* as the key-stave, for which Bx ⇒ the unmetrical synonym *amendement*. Its sense fits deliverance from both sickness and imprisonment (see **136** and *MED s.v.*, (b)) and its form may owe something to suggestion from that of the original verb in the parallel half-line *gare hem to arise* in AZ, from which L was revising. **148** *receyve*: *cj* as supplying a needed stave-word for which Bx ⇒ the commoner near-synonym and F a sophisticating metrical correction (as at **150** below). **150** *putte*: *cj* as the needed stave-word for which Bx ⇒ a synonym more familiar as part of a common collocation. F's variant is unlikely to be anything other than sophistication. **154** *alse*: a form with metrically necessary final vowel is posited on the model of ZA rather than revised C. **162** Transposition of adj. and noun restores the metre lost through Bx inversion to prose order; F is a sophisticating metrical correction. **179** In the light of ZAC, Bx's final phrase reveals scribal over-explicitness and over-emphasis. **182** The unmetrical Bx line following seems a clear piece of enthusiastic scribal elaboration. **192** On the showing of A VII 180, C VII 189, K–D plausibly suspect a B line missing here in Bx but rightly eschew conjecture, since extensive revision renders its probable form irrecoverable. **197** A line corresponding to this occurs at C VIII 197 and again at 203, with a-half word-order as in ZA. No need to emend arises. 198 The Bx line, not itself defective in metre or sense, looks suspicious on the uniform showing of ZAC, is altogether more cautious in sentiment, and suggests scribal intervention. 200: *evere: cj* as lost from Bx through haplography (þere < euere) and F may have supplied a near-synonym by ⊗ from A or C. 215 *Abave*: a very rare word that invited Bx substitution of the contextually more obvious *abate* (not a synonym). 218 *Fortune*: the apparent contradiction between βZA and αC may be explained as due to α having anticipated *false* in 219 following, which becomes otiose if α is authentic. 219 *Other*: the expanded form of the conjunction is posited to provide an internal |v| (*Other*) eliding with *any* to form the first full stave. 221 *kynde wolde*: Bx's *god techeþ* is a scribal attempt to increase the authority attaching to the injunction, which (as Hunger's) more properly expresses natural law. 223 *norisse: cj* as the needed key-stave, an unusual extended use which might have invited substitution of the more obvious Bx *help*. 242 *after: cj*, in the light of AZ *siþen* and C *thenne*, as the needed first stave-word, for which unmetrical *wiþ* was (?unconsciously) ⇒ by Bx. 257 *that*: B's agreement with ZAC in the preferred reading could be accidental. 271 *lest . . . faille*: the clash between ZB and AC challenges the hypothesis of Z's priority to A and of 'linear' revision (see Intro. lxxvi). Either Z here shows a 'scribal' level (of ⊗ from the Bx tradition), or C has revised back to an A form, itself a revision of Z, rejected by B. Both explanations have their difficulties, and leave open the possibility that Z is a scribal product, with the B phrase a conflated Bx reminiscence of Pr 86 and the same phrase (of the form in AC), or that L had access to Z at the time of revising to B. 272 The Bx line is difficult to reconstruct. If *morareres* α is a corruption of *murþereris* β, it will have been strongly reminiscent of Z VII 263–4. But both variants (unlike Z) are metrically defective in the b-half and *mo [li]eres* is *cj* as giving a Bx line identical with A (a presumed revision of Z). The R variant could be a reflex of α **mo ::eres*, F a smoothing, and β another attempt to make sense of its exemplar with prompting from the sense of 273. 278 *Er*: Bx's *Til* is another case of agreement with Z that calls in question the hypothesis of 'linear' revision (see 271 above). But the substitution could have been unconscious in both versions, since the words were in free variation. 281 *ek: cj* as the key-stave lacking in Bx; the mechanism of loss is unclear, but the proposed word (also *cj // A*) avoids the more drastic recourse to the (? revised) reading *a cake of otes* at C VIII 305. 285 *plaunte coles: cj* as the necessary stave-phrase that has undergone transposition in Bx through misunderstanding of the sense (Z confirms the reading of A family *m*). The F variant represents further metrical smoothing of α's presumed reading preserved in R. 305 *brewesteres*: another case of contradiction between ZB and AC, on which see 271 above. The Z reading could once again be derived from a B source during the scribal phase of Z's transmission, or may indicate Z's status as an A-MS contaminated from a post-Bx MS. 312 *warie*: Bx's *waille* is a substitution of a milder and less critical term in a highly sensitive context. 317 *noon of hem*: metrically awkward and perhaps a Bx reflex of the exemplar's *her noon*. 321 *thorough*: another case of Bx (*wiþ*) agreeing with Z against AC. The two words were contextually in free variation, and the agreements need not indicate dependence of Z on B. 325 *merke*: *cj* as the needed key stave-word, for which Bx will have unconsciously ⇒ the commoner verb.

Passus VII

24 *And bad hem*: the BxZ reading scans satisfactorily, but looks suspect on the showing of AC. If Bx is scribal, Z could have derived it from an exemplar contaminated from a B source, a circumstance in accord with the view that interest in A and (*a fortiori*) in Z would only have arisen after B had been published and become well known (see Intro., p.lix. 33 *angel*: the ?Bx reading looks, on the showing of ZAC, like scribal over-emphasis, also weakening the metre; HmF correct perhaps by reference to A or C. 34 *drede*: *cj* in the light of ZA, C as the needed key stave-word, for which Bx ⇒ a non-alliterating synonym. 39 scans on $|l|$, with internal key-stave in the consonant group *pl* of *pleteden*, a rare metrical licence (cf. examples at VIII 106 and X 300); but a case for emendation is possible. 45 *preve*: *cj* as the needed key stave-word ('you will find by experience', rather than the more obvious 'believe') for which Bx ⇒ a similar-sounding equivalent. 49 *for*[1] *... sheweth*: the C-text, despite substituting the synonym *declareth*, retains the alliterative structure of ZA, suggesting the unoriginality of Bx's (Type IIa) line, with its added mention of 'learning'. 56 *the deth*: preferred on the showing of C, though Bx seems to have omitted the article (perhaps through associating the phrase with the Great Plague). Group *y* may show influence from C or independent correction. 59 *if I lye witeth Mathew*: the three Bx lines are clearly corrupt in sense and metre, with the third line mere padding. K–D's economical conjecture (='blame Mathew if I'm in error') is accepted here as the best available, although not based on the reading adopted for A in *P-T*. 69–70: re-divided to give better rhythm than Bx's with minimal interference. Line 70 now reads as Type IIIc. 81a Where MS variation obscures the exact form of the Biblical quotation, the fuller version of F is often closest to the Vulgate text, though not always adopted as here (cf. 87, 138a below). 104 *upon this pure*: the α reading scans satisfactorily and could be adopted as = Bx, but appears on the showing of agreed ZAC a scribal response to a word found difficult (or objectionable) in this context. The Z-text ends here, and henceforth criticism of Bx's readings is carried out with reference only to A and C. 109 *In*: G may be contaminated from A. *lettre*: obviously preferable on grounds of sense, and Bx an unintelligent substitution for greater emphasis. 125 *be fooles*:

α is preferred to β as supported by A family **m** (where **A** family **r** reads *be another*) and offering the harder, more pregnant reading. The phrase looks forward to the idea of 'God's fools' in XX 61, 74, perhaps not without some play on *foweles* 'birds' (in allusion to the following 129), which has been wrongly resolved in β . 155 scans as Type III (contrast // A); so 171 below (also in AC). 174–5 F's correct line-division here may be an independent judgement on metrical grounds, a reflex of α, or the result of comparison with A or C. 193 *fyve*: preferred as the (harder) B revision, retained in C. F and β could be scribal 'corrections' of a supposed error. **Colophon** The *explicit* was lacking in γ MF but its presence in the A- and C-traditions suggests that it may have been in Bx, as R's extended form of the title (=α) and L's marginal note (=β) in VIII indicate (see next note).

Passus VIII

Title In addition to the R evidence, L's marginal note *Ps viijus de visione, & hic explicit, & incipit inquisicio prima* points to a possible Bx colophon of the same type as those of AC. But the opening connective *Thus* negates the notion that a new poem begins here (cf. Intro, pp.xxx–xxxi). 6 *wight as I wente*: appears the probable Bx reading, but R's *in þis worlde* will then be either a ⊗ from C or (as is just possible) a coincidental substitution of a familiar phrase for α's reading (here retained by F). 18 F's reading is that of A, presumably by ⊗, the first of some 14 instances in this passus (see 25, 28, 38, 43, 49, 74, 76, 78, 80, 101, 103, 105, 106), and the Bx line is unexceptionable. However, a slight piece of evidence that Bx may have censored an original oath in the a-half is the presence of C's asseveration *Sothly* in the same position as A's *Marye*. 23 *seide*: Bx scans satisfactorily as Type IIb, and emendation by adding *certis* (present in // AC) would not be easy without major reconstruction of the line. Bx's explicitness here seems to reflect a syllogistic precision that replaces A's anacolouthon and is itself retained in the revised C line. 25 *at hoom*: not metrically necessary but adopted on the showing of AC. F presumably has it from A. 28 Bx scans acceptably as Type II, but the F form (without its addition of *tyʒ de*) is preferred on the strength of AC agreement. 35 *raughte*: appears to be preterite subjunctive of *rechen*, but the sequence of tenses in both protasis and apodosis is present. 38 *fareth*: both F and G are presumably contaminated from A but share the harder reading, supported by AC. 44 The A reading is adopted to restore the metre of the b-half, which Bx's transposition damages. 49 The sense does not strictly require the extra line following in F (a sophisticated version of A); it was either deleted by B or unconsciously omitted by Bx. 61 *men to worthe*: Bx's b-half seems blunter in tone than that of F, which seems based on either *lif to ende* A or *ende to deye* C (which is closer to A than to Bx); but it could be revision, and F a contaminated reading. 69 The a-half in Bx scans *xa* and the proposed emendation gives an (abrupt but) acceptable Type IIIb line, which leaves the last lift in the same position as in A. F attempts to smooth the metre, but here shows no trace of the difficult a-half in A that was being revised. **74** *who art thow*: the F reading is metrically better than Bx's and confirmed by agreed AC, from one of which it may derive. **78** The word-order of Bx, though not unmetrical, looks unoriginal on the showing of AC, and F's reading, whether by ⊗ or not, is more likely to represent B. **80** The extra F line here corresponds to A IX 71, its probable source. The b-half's sense is partly in 80*a*, and this may explain its deletion in B. **93** Bx omits the needed first full stave attested in A and C, with subsequent smoothing. **99** The Bx b-half fails to scan, through inversion to prose order; the |*d*| stave needs to be in key position as emended. **100–10** show disordered sequence in α, with omissions; F's divergences from R probably represent attempts to correct α errors, with occasional reference to the A-version. **100** *kepen*: correction of the β (and presumably Bx) error (characteristically replacing the key stave-word with a more explicit non-alliterating term) depends on A alone, but revised C shows the line to be original. **101** F's extra line after 101 (which R lacks) seems a rewriting of A IX 93, and the revised line at // C X 102 can be thought of as reflecting Bx 101 rather than the supposedly lost line. **102** R being defective, the F readings preferred to β's (not in themselves objectionable) cannot be affirmed as α's, but agreement with A must decide the issue in the absence of // C, assuming that F is not contaminated here. That this is possible seems clear from the extra line in F (identical with A IX 95), presumably deleted as otiose in B. **105** The b-half in F looks strongly like ⊗ from A, given that the Bx form is confirmed by C and is not in itself objectionable. **106** The BxC lines scan normatively with an 'internal' |*r*| stave in the b-half, a device noted at VII 39 above. **107** The Bx line will scan as Type III, but it seems likely that the phrase providing a second lift in the AC lines, both identical and standard, which repeats for emphasis, was omitted as supposedly redundant. **109–10** The Bx line, unmetrical in its b-half, has on the evidence of AC lost 109b, 110a, presumably through syntactic anticipation of 111a. Whether or not derived from A (not from C; but cf. 113 below) F must correspond to lost B material. **113** scans as Type III, as does Ax, though the latter can be tentatively emended to Type I, and C revises to scan on |*k*| (F either borrows from C or, most probably, conjecturally 'regularizes').

Passus IX

4 *wittily*: OC²'s exclusive ancestor has corrected independently or from C. **7** *to . . . envye*: Bx is not obviously wrong in sense or metre, but the reading is rejected because evidently easier than that of agreed AC with its verb-phrase preceding the complex subject. **15** *biddeth*: *cj* as used absolutely in sense 'directs' (*MED s.v. bidden* v., 4b); appropriate to a bishop, and providing characteristic wordplay on *bit*. 16 The Bx line is metrically acceptable as 'licensed', i.e. varying from L's customary types, because of its Latin first lift; but on the showing of C transposition to prose order may be diagnosed. 22 *alle*: Bx *forsope* seems an over-emphatic scribal attempt to avoid repeating *alle* (17, 18). 23 scans on |*v*| or else on |*s*| with liaisonal key-stave; if F is contaminated from A, it is from an A source of family r which has *sixe*. 24 Bx's b-half has a non-alliterating key-stave; F has presumably corrected from A. 27 scans with a 'liaisonal' stave on *of al* or mute *pat* as Type I. 32 *spak*: an easier reading than *warp* A, but Bx scans as Type III; for further discussion of *warp*, see V 363 (C) above. F hereafter sophisticates on the basis of A X 34. 33 *moost lik*: provides a Type IIb line; Bx ⇒ the more for the less common superlative. 38 *ne*: *cj* as necessary for the sense of the figure, preceding *and* having been mistaken to mean 'if', whereas it specifies the first of the conditions required for successful letter-writing. 39 *welde*: Bx scans minimally on vowel staves with two blank staves in the a-half; but the natural stresses fall on *write*, *wel*, and *welde* is therefore *cj* as the needed stave-word, apt in sense but hard enough to have invited substitution of the more straightforward *hadde*. 41–2 Bx is not obviously corrupt in sense or metre in 41, but the macaronic 42 uncharacteristically has no full staves. If *there he seide* is omitted, in the light of A, as scribal padding, the Latin quotation becomes free-standing and there is no metrical problem. Presupposing mislineation on account of the line's length, reconstruction gives a Type II line with vowel staves, the third possibly muted (an unusual pattern), unless *there he seide* is omitted, yielding better rhythm. The Latin quotation is reconstructed on the basis of A, from which F may have derived its (correct) quotation. *Dixit* is presumed original, but *& facta sunt* a mis-expansion citing the wrong scripture, Ps 148: 5 (perhaps through anticipatory recollection of XIV 60*a*, where it is correctly quoted). This concerns the non-human creation, whereas the right text, Gen 1: 26, is on God's creation of man in his image and likeness (so given in A and F). 55 *heo*: *cj* as the correct pronominal form; *he* is an erroneous reflex of presumed **a*. 77 scans as an extended Type IIIb line with counterpoint (*abb*/*aa*); possibly the key-stave in B was *hij* (for Bx *pei*). The emendation *preve* for *have* in the a-half, though attractive, is not strictly necessary (cf. VII 45 above). 87 Bx's missing key-stave cannot be restored by simple transposition in the b-half, as this gives a masculine ending. The proposed emendation gives a form easily liable to undergo prose-order inversion. 88 scans as Type IIIa with 'cognative' staves generated from liaison of *As Jewes* and *Shame* (key-stave). 91 Bx is unmetrical (*xa*/*ax*) but will scan as Type IIIa on transposition from prose order. 98*a* The quotation from Js 2: 10 reads *vno*, not *verbo*, and M, following γ, has presumably corrected accordingly. But the Lα (= ?Bx) reading may be original, L having misremembered or else consciously altered the text to specify 'custody of the lips.' *Space* balancing *speche* in the English which 98*a* illustrates allows either possibility, and F (perhaps influenced by the sense of 98) tries to have it both ways with *vno verbo*. **99** *Tynynge*: *cj* as a lexically harder word for which **Bx** ⇒ an unmetrical equivalent. **108** scans as Type IIIa. The emendation first proposed (*Sch*, pp. 95, 278, following K–D) produces an unacceptable masculine ending to the line. **111** *cherles*: the minority reading (?BF), perhaps derived from A X 137, seems more suitable in what appears a list of honourable social orders, and *cherles* may be a scribal substitution prompted by the collocation; but it is metrically acceptable and may be original. **113** *wye*: an uncontentious alteration of the ambiguous spelling instanced also in the C-text for this word. **121** scans as Type IIIc on |*k*| and vowels. **124**; **127** *Seem* is a (possibly original) confusion of Adam's son Seth with Noah's son Sem. In 127 the name should perhaps be read as first stave-word, thereby corresponding more closely to A X 159; but *some* makes acceptable sense, given *hir* at 129. **152a** *uva*: w's grammatically correct singular is adopted to fit the sg passive verb. **154 Bx** has lost the key-stave by transposing to prose order from the more unusual postulated form. **155 Bx** is reconstructed from the split variants *men* α, *þat* β. **163 Bx**'s substitution of the more expected term seems to have caused loss of the needed key-stave, a palatal glide. **166 Bx**'s sense is acceptable, but AC's superior order is presumed original for B. **188** *leel*: *cj* in the light of A and (especially) revised C's *lele* [*wedlok*] as the needed stave-word for which **Bx** has ⇒ a more obvious and emphatic non-alliterating term.

Passus X

28 The **Bx** form is tentatively reconstructed from the split variants (also tentatively) recoverable from β and α. A simpler form would omit *good*[1], placing the stress on *gyveth*, but the exceptionally long line postulated here is likelier to have caused the split diagnosed. As it now scans, *God* forms part of both the first and the second dip. (For a line of comparable syllabic length, cf. XIII 255.) **36** *or lete by*: on the showing of AC this phrase is presumed lost from **Bx** (which scans as Type Ia) by eyeskip (*lete* >*lesson*). **50** *game*: *cj* on the basis of // A XI 37 as the needed key-stave for which **Bx** ⇒ the non-alliterating synonym *murþe*. M's *glee* appears an independent attempt to correct. **53** *how . . . thridde*: the powerful but blasphemous image will have invited scribal censorship, which **Bx**'s bland phrase covers successfully (and in correct metre for once). **57** *gnawen . . . with*: 'defame God with their words' (*Sk*; and see Stanley, pp. 445–6); there is no need to emend to A's *gnawen . . . in*. **60** *nyme hym in nor*: M's reading is a happy guess that restores the sense of // A and (revised) C (*haue hym in*), that of 'taking in' the poor man (as a charitable act). The construction *nymen hym neer* in **Bx** could mean 'betake oneself to, go' (*MED s.v. nimen* v., 4a) but is probably a smoothing of *ne* to *neer* after loss of *in* through assimilation to preceding *nym*en. **68** *in Memento*: Bx's *ofte* ⇒ vaguely for the precise (but not obvious) Psalm reference securely attested in AC. **69** *othere kynnes men*: appears inferior compared to A's *kete men*, for which it could be a Bx substitution and C's *knyhtes* a sharper revision. But *kete* 'acute' was difficult enough for the B reading to be a (weak) authorial revision. **70** *hire*: not essential for the sense, but adopted as original on the showing of AC, from which FG may have it, and lost from Bx by alliterative attraction (mu*che*>mou*þ*). **72** *tyme*: the division of support for the sub-archetypes indicates either that α accidentally omitted *tyme* from Bx, and C's revision (to plural *pestilences*) coincidentally *required* its omission, or, less probably, that Bx omitted *tyme* and β added it through recollection of A. **73** *for . . . clerkes*: 'because of sheer ill-will towards the clergy', *clerkes* here having the sense of 'secular clerks' – i.e. in contrast to the friars themselves, who are also 'clerks' (regulars). The opposition between friars and 'clergy' in this sense is dramatized in XX 376 (with which cf. XX 228–30, which reveals the ambiguity of the term). **78–9** Possibly omitted from β through censorship. The rare verb *forgrynt* '?grinds to nothing' is unrecorded in *OED* or *MED*. **90** *loke*: cj on the guidance of C's *loke by þy lyue* (XI 74) as the needed key-stave for which Bx ⇒ a commoner term, perhaps under aural suggestion from *weldeth*. The line scans as Type III. **108** *biwiled*; *wye*: Bx seems to have ⇒ for the key-stave a commoner non-alliterating noun and for the first stave-word a commoner form of the verb, well attested in XVIII 292, 340, 361; the Anglo-Norman variant is attested in *Sir Gawain and the Green Knight* (*SGGK*) 2425. **131** *havylons*: the tricks of the hunted fox doubling back to throw off his pursuers (cf. *SGGK* 1708). *ablende*: found later in XVIII 137 and proposed as providing the needed vowel stave (here 'muted'; see Appendix), easily lost after preceding *to*. **139** *deeth*; *arere*: the readings of F and C^2 (here visibly corrected) suggest ⊗ from A; see also C^2 at 153 below. **171** *the Bible*: securely attested in AC, this could have undergone replacement in Bx through objection to the notion of any other author for the Bible than God. **172** *glosed*: supported by AC, this is a better reading than Bx's (it is the Psalms themselves that Scripture studies, with the *aid* of the gloss). B and Hm presumably derive from C or are independent corrections. **186** Bx scans as Type III, with internal rhyme. Though *therinne* is not strictly necessary, its presence, suggested by // A XI 141a, sharpens the sense, and its loss may be cj as due to terminal *inne* 185 (this would have been easier if *therinne* and not *nere* had been in final position in B, giving identical end-rhyme). **190** *kennyng*: Bx *kynne* reads weakly in the context, which seems to require not a relationship word but one which emphasizes the supremacy of love as a *teacher*. Parallel *scole* in A and *doctour* in (revised) C indicate a word such as *kennyng* 'training, discipline' (*MED s.v.*, b; see also 198 below), easily mistaken visually for *kynne* if the line-end had been cropped. **204** *nameliche* 'especially': **Bx** has a flatter word than // A XI 249 *souereynliche* 'supremely, above all', producing an unmetrical a-half. It could be a **Bx** scribal substitution, but **L** may have wished to avoid repeating the latter word, which occurs adjectivally at 212 in the sense 'supreme' and at 208 in the sense 'most efficacious'. **211** *two*: **Bx** refers only to geometry and geomancy, whereas *the science* 212 seems to include all three, and **A** indeed reads *three*. Either *two* is officious scribal 'correction' or **L** changed his view of astronomy (apparently = 'astrology' in **A**) as necessarily connected with sorcery. (Omission of **A**'s line on conjuring demons makes Study's tone about '(natural) science' lighter and less censorious; **K–D**'s argument for its restoration is doubtfully persuasive). **242** *animales*: cj here as the rare original needed to provide an |*m*| stave in key position where **Bx** ⇒ the common word *beestes* to give a line with the inauthentic pattern *aa/bb* (see *MED s.v. animal*, citing Trevisa's *Bartholomew c.* 1398: '*animal, a best*'). *bothe*: in identical end-rhyme with 241, but with different sense, 'as well, too'. **246** *Gospelleres*: cj as the needed key-stave (scanning 'cognatively' with |*k*| in the a-half) for which **Bx** has ⇒ a commoner non-alliterating synonym. An earlier conjecture, *same*, assuming scansion of the line on |*s*|, is rejected as reducing to a dip two important lexical words in the a-half. **248** *lewed*: evidently the **Bx** reading, but perhaps suspect as failing to stress that *all* must believe, as revised // C makes clear (XI 157 *alle*). The g reading *men* could reflect γ *ledes* 'men' but cannot = **Bx**, which is retained as possibly a first thought later modified. **249** *dispute*: the sense 'expound; maintain, defend' (*MED s.v.*, 1 (c), 3 (a)) rather than 'dispute against' (*Sk*; *MED s.v.*, 3 (b)), seems fitter for a *freke* of *fyn wit*. **251** *Siththe*: cj as the needed first stave-word in a line scanning on |*s*|. The sense is 'next', introducing the second of the three Do's being described in order. **266** The line that follows in **Bx** (scanning as Type IIIc) appears spurious in its over-emphatic attempt to list the ranks of the higher clergy without any logical connection to what precedes or follows. **271** *lost:* the sense is superior, in the light of 272, to that of *boste* '(idle) noise', which seems to indicate a common source for **L** and **R**. This would have to be **Bx**, unless each has erred independently through visual confusion of *l* with *b*. (One of some half-dozen readings where **L** and **R** appear to agree in error (see Intro, p. lxviii).) **273** The emendation is required to provide the key stave-word, which **Bx** has characteristically damaged by adopting a common form of the phrase. **279** *barnes*: cj as the needed key-stave word for which **Bx** ⇒ a more expected term, perhaps objecting to the literal meaning 'children' (but here used in its special 'Biblical' sense) or, if the original reading was *burnes*, to a word of restricted lexical distribution. **291–302**, which appear in α only but correspond to A XI 204–10, C V 146–55, are important evidence for the nature of α as an independent branch of the **Bx** tradition (see further K–D, pp. 63–9). **297** Re-division and emendation are based on rejecting as spurious a line which is metrically unobjectionable but appears scribally over-emphatic in context. *roileth*: an unusual word with much the same sense as that of the R and F variants, 'strays about'. 301 scans *aa/xx* in α; if this represents **Bx**, it shows familiar substitution of a non-alliterating synonym for a difficult original at key-stave position. K–D conjecture *carpe*, but *querele* is preferred here, though not instanced elsewhere in *PP*, as a harder possible original (see *MED s.v.* n. and v.). The archetype of the C-MSS (**Cx**) also reads *chide* in this (apparently unrevised) line (C V 154). This may be a reflex of **L**'s use of a scribal B-MS (B^1), and if *chide* was in B^1 and in α it is likely to have been in **Bx**. Either **L** overlooked the error in composing C (which seems unlikely, as there is detailed revision in the immediate vicinity, at C V 151, 155) or else **Cx** ⇒ *chide* for the original (***carpe* or ***querele*) as had **Bx**. Possibly the unfamiliar *querele* was first *glossed* marginally or supralinearly in the exemplars and the gloss then mistaken for a correction by **Bx** and/or **Cx** and incorporated in the text. There are no grounds in the rest of the poem for thinking that **L** 'could have tolerated an imperfect line on occasion' (*Sch*, p. 281). 303 The ?α-reading, more meaningful though more elliptical than β's, is here accepted as that of **Bx**; C cannot confirm, as it is completely revised. 304 *lereth*: **Bx** repetition of *loueþ* in the b-half is rightly suspected as scribal by K–D. Like their conjecture *loweþ hym to*, the present one reconstructs after // C, not after the a-half but after the b-half *lykyng to lerne*, which optimistically adduces the clerks' learning as a reason for their not fighting. 307 *upon*: cj as providing a needed second stave in the a-half of what is now a Type IIb line, following the pattern of A XI 213, which has an equivalent (but imperfect because unstressed) stave syllable *pópèriþ* in this position (C revises to Type I). 320 *biyeten*: 'acquire possession of' (*MED s.v.*, 1 (a)) is cj as the difficult original to which α and β offer variant resolutions. The direct object is now *That* 321, and while *hem* could be retained as 'for themselves', it is better omitted (since the barons presumably reclaim the lands for their *heirs*) as consequential smoothing after substitution of a verb seeming to require an immediate pronominal object. 323 *which . . . inne*: transposition to prose order here restores to key position the stave-word *catel*, which **Bx** has made non-structural through moving to the end. 324 scans (somewhat weakly) on *Grégòries* (cf. *pópèrith* cited at note 307 above); emendation to *gan despende* (so *Sch*) seems barely justified, as does K–D's *ungodly* for *yvele*. 337 The line is reconstructed as Type IIb, with the caesura coming after *it*. The α and β substitutions of an extra lift respectively before and after *nede* result from placing the caesura after *naught*. Neither diverges from a likely reading preserved by the other from **Bx**, which is here cj as ∅. 348 *an*: possible, and not necessarily an easier reading than *arn*, a variant in A family **r**, from which C^2 has presumably been contaminated. 366 *Non mecaberis*: 'thou shalt not commit adultery', not 'slee noght'. Despite the three variants in the β family, **Bx** clearly read *mecaberis*, as did **A**, and the translation error is presumably authorial (cf. Lk 18: 20 in Vulgate). **367** *also*: cj as the key-stave word from which **Bx** varied (?unconsciously) to the commoner collocation of *al* with *for*. **385** *in helle*: **Bx**'s *ydampned* appears a substitution of a near-synonymous expression slightly toning down the harshness of the original. **393** *men*: cj as the needed stave-word for which **Bx** ⇒ non-alliterating *þei* (**C**'s b-half is revised but has an |*m*| key-stave). **421** *who myghte do*: the agreed **AC** reading scans better than **Bx**'s (perhaps prompted by anti-feminism here), which requires wrenching the stress in *wommán* so as to avoid the inauthentic pattern *aa/bb*, and also gives better contrast (of *do*) with *dide* in 422. **424** *Muche* β: not necessarily = **Bx**: the point is *that* the (future) apostle 'killed' Christians, not how many he killed. The line's tight brevity invited scribal expansion (cf. **Cx**, which ran C XI 269–70 into one long line). **425** scans awkwardly as Type III with two lifts in *sóveréyn(e)s* and a five-syllable first dip. It appears to be Type I in both **A** and **C** (of different form) and possibly a word like *(al)so* was omitted from before it in **Bx**'s exemplar by haplography before *so-* and replaced in **Bx** by *as*. **435** *wote*: harder and thus more probably = **Bx** (< L = β, R = α) and γ may have regularized to produce concord of both tense and sequence. **440** On the showing of A XI 293, C XI 277–8, there may be a line missing after this, which K–D restore from **A** (so *Sch*). But the evidence, and direction as to reconstruction, are both uncertain. **446** *with*: cj as the needed key-stave for which **Bx** ⇒ *and* (unless R = α and **Bx**, in which case β and F independently filled the Ø reading). The line is now 'T'-type and is divided after *hem* for better rhythm and syntax. **464** scans as Type I on 'cognative' staves |*b*|*p*|*p*|. **465** scans vocalically as Type Ie with blank third stave. **467** is not suspect as tautological because the two verbs here mean respectively 'learnt' and 'knew', the *clerkes* recalling when they knew no more than the *lewed*. **472** scans as Type III, though possibly **Bx** has replaced original *ledes* with *men* (**C**'s revision has *laborers*).

Passus XI

From here, comparison of **Bx** is made only with the C-text, **A**'s parallel text having ended with B X. **5** *worth*: **Bx**'s reading may be a metathesis of **warþ* (the C spelling) induced by preceding *wraþe* in 4b. **6** *mette me thanne*: β's reading seems likelier to be that of **Bx** on the showing of revised C XI 167 (*wonderliche me mette*), although α's half-line would scan with a mute *me* as a 'cognative' 'T'-type (|*t*| |*d*|). **8** *and love*: the β error *allone* shows smoothing of an exemplar *loue* misread as *lone* (cf. the ambiguous reading at XVI 20 (C) below). **41** *graithly*: preferable as the **Bx** and original adverb for its harder and more subtle meaning. β 's *gretly* is either an error repeated in **Cx** or a C revision to a simpler reading. **49** *of the leste*: 'of the least', **Bx** *if* being diagnosed as a visual error for *of* after mistaking the grammar, and the phrase 'if you like' seen as unoriginal redundancy. 'Least', however, presupposes more than the two 'Do's' mentioned; the half-line would give better logic and rhythm if *of* and *ought* were omitted, and if *leste* meant 'the least thing, anything'. **60** *foryat*: for the appropriate sense of 'lose recollection of', see *MED s.v. forȝete* v., 4 (c), rejected as unapt by K–D, who emend to *foryede* 'left' or 'lost' (which is certainly harder). **Cx** agrees with **Bx**, though the x-group spelling for *forȝet* is suspicious. **67** *cristned were*: transposition of participle and verb is necessary to obtain a first stave-word in this (Type IIIa) line. It would scan 'cognatively' as Type Ia if **Bx**'s exemplar read *gome* for *man* (cf. 86 (C) below). The prose line that follows in **Bx** looks like an inept attempt to emphasize Conscience's axiom by extending it to cover a man's whole life. **70** scans as Type IIa with a liaisonal first stave on *Ac‿yet* (and a 'supplemental' fourth |k| stave); no emendation is needed. **82** *be so*: transposition of **Bx** *so be* (metrically unobjectionable in itself) is *cj* as giving a better rhetorical pattern (*so* is contextually 'promoted' above *be*) and better rhythm; the line now also becomes 'T'-type. **84** *lough*: **Bx** *loke* is acceptable for sense, but on comparison with **C** looks like scribal substitution, perhaps induced by *loked* 85b. **86** *amonges men*; *quod I*: transposition of **Bx**'s order gives a smoother first half, reducing the seven-syllable dip to one of three syllables. **103** *nevére*: scans with a wrenched stress in **Bx** and ?**Cx**; HmF, like C family **p**, intrude the same word to obtain an extra voiced fricative in first-stave position (cf. *thow* at 105 below). **106** *laude*: of the five variants (omitting F's sophisticating paraphrase), *preise* appears a non-alliterating synonym of a word judged difficult; *laude* or *looue* is such a word; *lab* a ⊗ from C; and *lakke* is nonsense induced by the verb in the b-half or, possibly, by visual error for *labbe*, *b* and *k* being frequently confused. If the last case were true, α's reading would be identical with C's and so probably original. But it must remain speculative, and ?β *laude* seems satisfactory as an English equivalent of *lauda* at 106*a* and, though lacking its chime with *love*, is as rare as *loove*. (The latter reading is also found in the C group *t*, where presumably it expresses scribal dissatisfaction with *labbe* 'broadcast, blab'.) **110** *The . . . Oure*: **Bx** is inaccessible in the absence of β, but R perhaps preserves α, since F is evidently a smoothing of a nonsense reading like R's. C's reading provides a satisfactory solution. **127** *chatel*: **Bx** (typically) ⇒ a commoner, non-alliterating term, in this case a mere phonological variant rather than a synonym, for the required stave-word in key-position (most C-MSS make the same error). **141** *Highte*: makes good sense in **Bx**, though producing an abrupt shift to direct speech at 143b. Cr here, as occasionally elsewhere, shows ⊗ from C. **148–9** Better rhythm is obtained for 149, which has a seven-syllable first dip in **Bx**, by dividing the lines after *grace*. **181** F's reading here (adopted *Sch* and, with some reconstruction, first by K–D) could seem good enough to reflect possible correction from a superior B source distinct from Bx (no // in C). But it probably arises from objection to a double reference to a single category, the poor, without any mention of one's neighbour in general. L seems to have had a 'Biblical' notion of one's neighbour as specifically the poor (see C IX 71: *Ac þat most neden aren oure neyhebores*). *principally: cj* as the needed first stave, as at XIV 195 below (in a line now of Type IIb), for which **Bx** ⇒ a commoner, non-alliterating synonym. **184** *juele*: the line could scan as Type IIIc in β F, with Cr and F being modernizings of *hele*; but R's variant, orthographically impossible for *hele*, would have been mistaken for the contextually impossible *evel*, whereas it is very plausibly resolved as *iuel*, giving a line of Type Ia. **196** The α line is reconstructed from the split variants of R and F by diagnosing R's loss of *myȝte* and F's of *Almiȝty*. The argument, that 'all-powerful God could have achieved this', pivots on the word play (*Al-, alle*; *miȝty, myȝte*). **202** The integrated grammar of this macaronic line requires omission of **Bx** *and*. **204** The line seems on the showing of identical C to have been misdivided; but the metre remains problematic in both texts, as there seem to be four and not three lifts in the first half of (what should be) a Type IIa line (*In, olde, as, lettre*). Presumably *the . . . telleth* is in some way to be treated as a notional dip (cf. the awkwardness of *silver* in the a-half of 289 below). Final *echone* appears a **Bx** attempt to fill out the b-half of the now excessively short second line. **216** *in commune*: 'publicly, openly' (*MED s.v.*, 11 (e)), with play on earlier *commune* (cf. *saven, salven* in 217, alluding to Lk 7: 50). **239** *lowe be*: inversion of Bx's prose order gives a line scanning as Type IIIa. **281** *wise*: gives better metre but less good sense than *parfit* β, which would be preferable if *siluer* **Bx** were seen as a substitution for, e.g., *pitaunce* or *paiement*; but emendation here is not justified. **287** The word-order of WHm, presumably felicitous correction in their immediate ancestor or else severally made, is metrically preferable, and scansion of **Bx** with three staves in the a-half is to be rejected on the showing of almost identical C. **289** *nyme*: *cj* as the necessary third stave-word, with a rather awkward following two-syllable dip (if *silver* comes before the caesura, as it must; cf. 204 (C) above). **Bx** will have ⇒ *take* as more commonly used in literal contexts (cf. *nymen hede* at 321 below; and contrast XI 430 below). **299–302** are rejected by K–D as 'untranslatable' (p. 114) and reconstructed, but they are acceptable in both sense and form (see text for translation). The explicitness of 301 (perhaps echoed by C XIII 184–5) and the Type IIIa structure of 302 could both be original. **301** *at*: *cj* as the original behind the four variants of which *and* is probably archetypal. **322** *wondres*: suitable in context (cf. Pr 4) but possibly influenced by 328b, 349b below, and *wordis* may be the harder reading, alluding to the notion of the 'book of creation' (*worchynge* is more probably a scribal response to *wordis* than to *wondres*). But the possibility remains of simple visual error in R and B. **324** scans vocalically as extended Type IIIa with counterpoint on |f| (abb/ax). K–D's plausible conjecture *forbisenes* would fit with Bx's tendency to substitute non-alliterating synonyms at the key-stave position, but is not strictly required. **325** *creature*: cj on comparison with C as the original to which Bx added *and* through misunderstanding *kynde* as 'natural creation', not as a name for the Creator of nature. **338–9** Both sense and metre seem acceptable, with **339** scanning on vowels and |m| as Type IIb. K–D argue that *amorynges* should read *al mornynge* (= 'melancholy [*post coitum*]'); C-MS D has *mournyng* and B-MS Hm *al mornyng*, but Cx clearly read *amorwenynge*, and no attempt was made at revising B **338–9** to eliminate ambiguity so as to obviate recurrence of the 'error'. The elaborate reconstruction proposed by K–D (so *Sch*), therefore, though attractive, does not impose itself. *yede*: clearly a verb of motion is required, and ?α's reading (to which // C's *ferddede and drowe* corresponds) is supported by L (an imperfect reflex of the verb). The γ reading shows ʒ / þ confusion, (ʒe > þe, as in gM) with smoothing in w, which supplies a verb (*ben*). **343** *mid*: cj as the needed key-stave for which Bx ⇒ the advancing form *with* (cf. XII 203). The F reading may be an echo of // C XIII 153a, or else a sophisticated attempt to regularize the metre. **353** scans vocalically as Type IIa or else as Type Ia, if *hii* is read as original for Bx *þei*. **371–2** As divided in Bx the lines scan as Type IIIa and anomalous *aa/bb*. If 371 is seen as the basis of C's revised line 182, the b-half *neither riche ne povere* may be tentatively accepted as having been lost in Bx through eyeskip (*Reson > Reson*). **385** *the quod*: reconstructed as the α original of the split variants *þe, quod*. **386** *if thyn*: reconstructed from *if þow* and *þyn* as giving the best sense in context. **388** The sense of both R and F, and the metre of R are defective. A likely α original is hard to reconstruct from the variants, so *Cristen* is cj on the evidence of revised parallel C. The point seems to be that if man were not dependent on God for both his creation and his redemption, there would be nothing to stop him being perfect. **406** *chydde*: perhaps a Bx substitution for an original *sherewede* (cf. XIII 331), or else pronounced |ʃ| and thence alliterating 'cognatively' with the |s| staves. F's variant is an evident scribal attempt to 'regularize'. **420** *no . . . he*: transposition to prose order of the cj form explains the anomalous metre (*xa/ax*). The line is Type IIIa. **429** *To blame*: omission of the first lift by Bx seems logically necessitated by the presence of the initial *or*, and the emendation from C seems inevitable. **430** *noye*: cj as the difficult key-stave for which *doute* was ⇒ by Bx as a non-alliterating near-synonym. Another possibility is *nede*, which Bx might have rejected as repetition. C's revised b-half indicates the probability of an |n| stave in B, and while vocalic scansion in a Type Ia or Type IIa line remains possible for Bx, this produces unnatural stress on three non-lexical words. **435** *shonyeth*: the reconstruction in the light of C presumes that Bx contained both *shonyeþ* and a word meaning 'company'. Both β and α seem to have shortened the **Bx** line and then smoothed it. Cr's *ech* (? after **C**) would give a smoother rhythm. **438–9** show extensive damage to the metre in **Bx**, **439** being completely unmetrical. In **438** *raughte* is *cj* as an unusual verb of motion (see *MED s.v. rechen* v.5 (a)), for which *folwed* was ⇒, an unlikely choice if **Bx**'s exemplar had read *reuerensed* as in **C**, with *after* having a temporal and not a spatial sense. In **439**, two stave-words in |*k*|, both well attested in **L**'s usage, are *cj* as the originals of the non-alliterating synonyms *preyde* and *telle*. The presence of the latter in **C** XIII **248** may suggest that B^1 also contained the error; but the line is otherwise completely revised.

Passus XII

4 *mynne*: *cj* as the needed stave-word for which **Bx** ⇒ the commoner non-alliterating synonym. **24** *places manye*: the transposition presumes **Bx** inversion to prose order causing loss of the needed key-stave. Though not absolutely required if *ben* is read as a 'cognative' third stave in a Type IIa line, the syntactic structure of the a-half suggests that *to ben* forms part of a strong dip and that the key stave-word should be *places*. **60** *gomes*: *cj* as the needed key-stave, lost perhaps through preoccupation with the notion of humility and distraction from terminal *groweth* **61**. Also possible is *goode*, which could have been deliberately censored as too restrictive. **95** *as mirours ben*: transposition presumes **Bx** inversion to prose order with loss of the first stave. **124** *medle we*: reconstruction of **Bx** is in light of **C**, retaining the pronoun but omitting the redundant particle. **125** *chafen*: securely restored as **Bx** on grounds of sense; α's error will have been confusion of *f* with long *s*. **127** *Com*: *cj* on the basis of **128a** *cometh* as the needed first stave for which **Bx** ⇒ a more obvious non-alliterating synonym. **129–30** The (single) **Bx** line has the unacceptable pattern *aa/bbb* and reconstruction proceeds by restoring a required b-half alliterating on |*b*| from // **C** XIV **80**. The rest of the line scans as standard with a 'cognative' key-stave in a word (*décéites*) of characteristic structure (cf. *sépúlcre* V **526**). **131** *Olde*: *cj* as the needed vocalic first stave, its loss by **Bx** is hard to explain, unless it was judged redundant. The term specifies the wise men of pagan antiquity who developed 'natural science' from empirical observation. **144** *hexte*: the presumed β form seems authentic and gives better rhythm in the strong five-syllable dip than the standard Southern form *hyeste*. **161** *sikerer*: the grammatically correct γ form is here preferred to ?**Bx** (and perhaps original) *syker* (with assimilation of the comparative morpheme), since elision makes possible the same syllabic value. **162** scans vocalically as Type Ie with muted key-stave and 'semi-counterpoint' on |*k*| (the second |*k*| coming in an unstressed syllable within the post-caesural dip). The // **C** line is identical. **183–4** Re-division after **C** restores the last lift to **183** while removing what is clearly an important word from its unemphatic position in the prelude dip of 184. Mis-division in **Bx** will have been occasioned by the extreme length of 183. **193** *graith ... evere*: the emendation explains the presence of *redy*, an easier **Bx** substitution, in a line that appears, from C, to have been intended to scan on |g| (scansion on vowels allows a passable Type IIIa line in **Bx**, but de-stresses the important *grace* in the a-half and gives poor syntax). ?**Bx** *and* may be a smoothing of the exemplar's ∅ relative clause; W's *þat*, an intelligent scribal guess, is retained as making the construction clearer. **203** *mid*: *cj* as the needed key-stave (here mute) presumably omitted by **Bx**, unless F's *with* is not a scribal intrusion but here preserves α. C revises with a new |m| stave but retaining *with* (cf. also 295 below and the revised C XIV 143 which changes *mid* to *wiþ* with new key-stave in *m*). **210** *by the thef*: reconstruction here in the light of C's *leue Y þat thef* retains the presumed original *be* by seeing it as the preposition, not the verb, as do both sub-archetypes and as **Bx** seems to, although the latter's exact form is irrecoverable. The Cx reading is simpler but has prompted in one group (p^1) effectively the same variant as that adopted here (with *of* for *be*). **245** *taille* is the probable α and β form (altered by M under influence from a γ source). As K–D rightly recognize, the senses 'tally' / 'account' / 'reversion' are uppermost (though a pun on *tail* is also to be recognized). The phrase refers to 'the end of the rich / the account they must make to God'; but their encumbering wealth is figured by the peacock's (splendid but) useless tail. **251–2** Re-division of **Bx** enables *I leve* to become the first lift of 252, where it brings better rhythm to the line. The disyllabic oblique form of *wille* is therefore necessitated here at the end of 251. In 252, the **Bx** line gives satisfactory sense and rhythm, w's interjection of *chiteryng* being an attempt to fill out a b-half judged incomplete because the caesura was mislocated (it comes after *be*, not *ere*). **265** scans as extended Type III with cognative counterpoint (|g| |k|) and a 'supplemental' theme-stave (|t|, assuming the pronunciation *Aristótle* here; cf. X 176). **270** *weyes*: either 'ways' or a spelling-variant of *wyes* 'men', or a play upon both. *wisshen*: *cj* on grounds of sense and in the light of C *wenen* 'hope'; **Bx** *vs* then becomes redundant. The original presumably intended a play on 'guidance' and 'desire' and in L's idiolect |ss| may well have had a sound like |sh|, to judge by spellings in, especially, the C-text tradition. **288** Both text and meaning are clear in both B and C (identical) (see the footnote translation). K–D's emendation to And *wheþer it worþ [of truþe]* or *noȝ t, [þe] worþ [of] bileue is gret* is metrically doubtful, textually unnecessary and doctrinally misleading. The notion that 'the intrinsic value of faith is great, whether it actually comes to be faith in the true religion or not' is significantly different from Imaginatif's case, that if one's 'faith' produces a just life it must be, if only implicitly, faith in 'the true religion'. **290** *eternam vitam*: transposition of adjective and noun by **Bx** conceals the riddling message hidden in the Latin name DEVS and found, as Professor J. A. Burrow informed me, in a MS gloss on Evrard the German's rhetorical treatise the *Laborintus* (Faral, *Les Arts poétiques*, p. 65). The line may be amplified thus: 'God is called *DEVS* because his very name spells out salvation to those who believe in Him: "*d*ans *e*ternam *v*itam *s*uis", that is, "giving eternal life to his own." '

Passus XIII

2 fey: 'doomed to die', is evidently the right word on the secure showing of C, from which B's exemplar will have corrected. The α and β variants seem attempts to make sense of a possible **Bx** *fe(r)*. **8 peple:** the needed first stave, secure in // C, for which **Bx** presumably ⇒ the commoner, non-alliterating synonym under inducement from *folk* 7b. **40–1 flessh; mete:** ordinary, merely nourishing meat, contrasted with elaborately cooked, 'gourmet' dishes. **49 Dia:** probably archetypal in B and // C (?deliberate mis-spelling of the adverb *diu* 'long' which plays on the sense 'drug or potion' (cf. XX 174)). **52, 53a–4:** re-arrangement of the order of 52 and 53, and re-division of 53a give the best sense and metre, requiring 53a to read as an 'appended' Latin line so as to make 53 scannable as a true macaronic (see *Clerkly Maker*, pp. 88–102). Line 53 would certainly read better if *he brou3te vs forþ* were omitted, as in K–D, the seven-syllable dip being awkward and adding nothing to the sense. **63 egges . . . yfryed:** transposition is required to supply the needed key-stave (here mute |*w*|), which Bx has lost by inversion to prose order. **79–80** The lines present a major crux in B and revised C, the reading of the B sub-archetypes, which both make good sense, appearing also in C. The rejected reading requires a full-stop after *yvele*; in the one adopted, *That* is an elliptical relative and *yvele* unambiguously adverbial. Either reading could have given rise to the other, *and* α being a mis-expansion of **a* 'he', or *he* being a misreading of the ampersand as **a*. There is no very great difference of sense involved in B. By contrast the x^1 group in C, in what could be an authentic revision of a B^1 reading identical with α's, offers *compacience* 'compassion', a very rare word, for *to Pacience*, the reading of the other C-MSS. There seems no sufficient reason, however, to follow K–D in rejecting the latter as unoriginal in B. **82 this . . . bifore:** cj as providing the needed key stave-word, which Bx has lost by transposing preposition and noun phrase to prose order. **85 preve:** tentatively suggested as the first stave-word in a Type I line. Bx scans adequately as Type IIIa, and the initial dip is not excessively long; but *telle* seems weak in context as a response to an angry challenge, and *preve* has the advantage of playing on the senses 'demonstrate by argument' and 'show to be true by example', echoing 80 above. **86 preynte:** cj as the necessary stave-word in the key position, its sense preserved in non-alliterating *wynked* β, while α offers a possible 'cognative' stave but an insufficiently precise verb, and not one which could have generated *wynked*. The word *preynte* appears securely attested at XVIII 21. **95** *forel* 'box': preferable on the showing of C as the original for which Bx ⇒ a term perhaps induced by the context of food references (a *frayel* 'basket' held fruit etc). But *leef* 96 (see next note) implies that the 'box' contained a book, presumably one with an account of friars' eating-habits that would accommodate those of the Doctor. **96** *leef*: the clear reading only of OC²Cot, quite possibly by correction from C of a g-group reading of ambiguous meaning. G's *leyeffe* reflects uncertainty as to what the exemplar intended. Whether or not g read substantively a word cognizable as 'leaf', this seems to be the required term on grounds of sense and the showing of // C, which seems unrevised from XV 96–107 (=B XIII 87–98). The Bx form could have been spelled *lyue* as in w, the *u* being understandably misread as *n* in LMα , and w would therefore reflect a γ spelling still evident in the uncorrected members of g. (The converse error is made at C III 490, where Cx has ⇒ *leef* for required *lyne*, presumably because its exemplar had a reading which was visually ambiguous in the same way as Bx here.) **100** *rubbede*: either a past participle (as punctuated here) or a preterite, requiring a comma after *rose*. C's *rodded* 'ruddied, reddened' looks like a revision, and Hm a ⊗ from C, F the same with smoothing. Visual confusion of *bb* with *dd* seems unlikely, but *rodded*, unusual compared to *rubbede*, might have invited a simplifying substitution in Bx. **121** *hym*: i.e. the 'Lord of Life', seems the probable Bx reading. which γF have levelled to the nonsensical *hem*. But Clergy's sons the Seven Arts are teachers of others, they are not teaching themselves. **136** *by*: *cj* as the necessary ('cognative') key-stave, omitted in Bx through *þo* > *so* attraction. **139** *taughte*: the key stave-word scanning 'cognatively' with the |d| staves of the a-half. **153** *aboute*: the adverb seems clearly what Bx read, *a bounte* and *a beaute* being attempts to generate a grammatical object for the transitive verb *bere*. This object is *Dowel*, and the referent for *therinne* may be Patience's scrip, the *speche* of 151, or the Latin phrase of 152b. The conjecture *bouste* of K–D (='the pyx for the Host'), accepted in *Sch*, is ruled out because Patience is not a priest, and only a priest would be authorized to 'bear' the Host. **158** *se if*: reconstructed from the substantive α variant *se* (also the original of L before alteration) and β *if*, in contention with its virtual synonym *wher*. The reading *deme* is presumably that of γ, from which L has corrected, and may be the original or a more emphatic substitution for *se*. The latter, on the showing of L, was the original reading of β and so of Bx. **167** Division after *thee* prevents the direct object from being isolated with its complement at the beginning of 168. F's word-order might be preferable if creation of too heavy a b-half could be avoided by omission of *ne*, an idiolectal possibility in L after *þat* in this construction. **171** scans as Type Ie on |δ| with counterpoint on |j|, i.e. *aab/ab*; the syntactically elliptical b-half means: 'inasmuch as they recognize you as the best governor'. **175** *parformen*: reconstructed on the showing of // C as the required stave-word, for which **Bx** has ⇒ non-alliterating and (in context) more familiar *conformen*. 203 *to*: the probable β reading, from which four MSS have varied through missing the sense of *take* 'give'. The α variant, whether *and* or *ne*, may (like β) be a response to an archetypal ∅ reading, possible after this construction. 255 Restoration of the line's metrical structure is on the model of // C XV 226 (identical except for lacking *hymself*). **Bx** scans *abb/aa* which is acceptable, and *xa/ax*, which is anomalous; but it seems likely that the unusual length of the original line gave rise to division followed by a padded-out extra b-half. 270 *thritty*: LR (= β, α) alone retain the reading which on metrical and factual grounds appears original. M obtains the right date by correction (of a possible γ reading *twies*) and achieves a passable metrical pattern; but this cannot be what **Bx** read. 284 *pope holy*: 'pretending to great holiness . . . sanctimonious, hypo-critical' (*OED s.v.*). 299 *loos*: the inevitable emendation of R *losse*, an aberrant spelling that gives an obviously nonsensical reading. 300 *go*: *cj* as the needed key stave-word lost through homoarchy (*gomes . . . go*). Possible alternatives are *carpe* or *gabbe* for the verb, either difficult enough to invite substitution of the commoner *telle*. 326 *to . . . it*: the *cj* transposition restores the key-stave lost through **Bx**'s inversion to prose order. 330–1 Re-division of **Bx** after // C VI 74–5 retains the adverb with its verb phrase, and eliminates an awkward dip at the beginning of 331. 341 *God ne*: the extra word adapted from // C VI 84 is not strictly necessary since the line could scan as Type IIIa, but its omission through attraction to following *Goddes* and subsequent corruption of *ne* to *no* would account for the unsatisfactory rhythm of **Bx** and the shape of (revised) C's a-half. 391 *conscience*: puns on the senses 'inward intent/feelings' (as at III 67), retained in *herte* β, and 'the moral reason in act', the dominant sense in L (as at XV 31–2, 39*a*). As well as the basic contrast between outward act and inner disposition, the wordplay ironically points up Haukyn's *negative* scruples about suffering material loss through generosity, which corrupt his 'kind' act into an occasion for further spiritual sin. 407 *worth*: a case of metathetic corruption by α followed by sophistication in F; cf. the earlier case at XI 5 (C) above. 411 *Is whan a man*: the nonsensical reading *his woman* appears to have been that of **Bx**, the result probably of visual confusion, perhaps prompted by inaccurate recollection of Glutton's wife in V 358–64. The ancestors of (OC²) and B have evidently corrected from C. 424 *in hope*: *cj* on the showing of C as the needed key-stave in a line of double-counterpointed extended Type IIIa (*abb/ab*). 444 *thy*: a key-stave now is required bearing stress, and // C's *thy* is *cj* as the original corrupted to a reading lying behind the two α variants. The sense of the a-half seems to require stress on *for* 'in place of', but *sittynge* fits awkwardly whichever side of the caesura it is located. 454 *for he wroghte so*: the stave-phrase *cj* on C evidence as omitted is not strictly necessary as Bx could scan as Type IIIa; but the rhythm is improved and the sense greatly sharpened if it is restored (450–7 are otherwise completely unrevised in //C VII 109–16), except for *loved* at 456 (= C 115 *lythed*).

Passus XIV

7 The grammar of 7b is defective, requiring some connective particle and verb. Reconstruction is directed by F's (presumably conjectural) attempt at correction, with inversion of verb and indirect object to ease the rhythm. The line now scans as Type IIIc (with 'cognative' b-staves). 8 *gome*: *cj* as the needed third stave in this Type IIa line, Bx having ⇒ the commoner non-alliterating noun for the regionally restricted *gome*. 9 *for . . . me*: transposition of verb and adverbial phrase provides the needed key-stave, lost by Bx's inversion to prose order. 22 Of the two lines that here follow in F, the first is adopted by K–D (so *Sch*); but though acceptably written it is not necessary for the sense and is rejected here. 23 *myte*: *cj* as more appropriate in sense and, if written *myȝt* in the exemplar, easily liable to be visually mistaken for Bx *myste*. (For association of mites and moths as threats to fabrics, cf. Chaucer, CT III. 560). 36 *yow either*: reconstructed for α from the RF variants as more precise in context than β. 48 scans as Type IIb with a 'half-stressed' suffix as the third a-stave (perhaps an acceptable licence because of the supplemental b-staves on |p|). 49 scans as a macaronic line with either a normal a-half on |p| and a non-alliterating b-half, or as an extended Type III line with counterpoint, the theme-stave being |v|: *abb/ax*. 61 *bothe*: *cj* on the evidence of //C's b-half as the needed second stave in the a-half; presumably lost by Bx through attraction of *mowen* to *men*. 77 apparently scans as extended Type III on |δ|: *axx/ax*. No particular emendation proposes itself as inevitable and as explaining the form of Bx. 123 *riche were*: transposition provides the needed key-stave which Bx has lost by inverting the phrase to prose order. The line scans somewhat woodenly with a heavy five-syllable dip before the third lift. Reading *renkes* for *men* (K–D) would certainly improve the rhythm. 131 Although macaronic, appears to scan as Type Ia. 131*a* is reconstructed to include the important word *ymaginem*. The Bx form *sompnum* 'sleep' for Vulgate *somnium* 'dream' (so F) is supported by Cx and may be original (cf. *Eice* for *Ejice* at VII 138*a*, X 264*a* above). 190 *He*: possibly a reflex of Bx *a, which F has 'logically' altered to *we* to fit with *us* 189. The referent is either Christ (at the Last Judgement; so *Sk*) or the sinner (*he* being used as generic indefinite for 'any man'). L presumably does not envisage the Passion as a 'once-for-all' release of each individual but is thinking of the penitent's continuing sorrow after confession, which enables God's forgiveness to act as a valid 'document' empowering him to require the Devil to drop his suit. 196 *wroghten*: *cj* as preferable on grounds of sense

since what 197–9a specify is *actions*. Bx *writen* may be a visual error partly induced by *writeth* 199b and the contextual references to documents. **198** *welle*: evidently original for both B and // C, a metaphor which puns on the near-homophone *wille*, of which *welle* was still an acceptable variant (Kentish) in the language familiar in the capital. **202** The Bx reading is identified as the (harder) majority variant, which Cx retains (from *B¹*), though adding a second *þat* before *ben*, which destroys the grammar. Original B may have had Ø relatives. **223** *ben*: adopted as the needed key stave-word for which both Bx and Cx ⇒*arn*, perhaps under unconscious inducement from the surrounding vowel forms at the beginning of lines. F, like two C-MSS (W and N) provides a felicitous conjecture. **248** scans either as standard on |b| with 'inverse' counterpoint in the a-half (see *Clerkly Maker*, pp. 63–4) or as Type IIIa on |l|. **253** *noon*: preferred as the harder and therefore more probably original reading, preserved in L from β . *were*: either ⇒ by L to avoid repetition of the verb or, as judged here, the β reading for which γ (and M from γ) ⇒ under inducement from 252. **260** *asken*; *cleymen*: transposition restores the needed key-stave lost in Bx by promotion of the concept judged more important (*cleymen*). As restored the line scans as extended Type IIIa with standard counterpoint (*abb/ax*). **267** *of hym*: gives a vowel stave in a Type IIIa line; *a man* as key-stave in C improves the line as a whole by enabling the a-half stresses to fall on the |m| words and may be a B original for which Bx unconsciously ⇒ the pronoun. **284–6** The reconstruction here is K–D's in 284b and in the transposition of 286, 286a to give a better sequence of thought; it also follows their guidance in the form of 285 while preferring |s| as the stave-sound and seeing the reference to the *body* as authorizing conjecture of a balancing reference to the *soul* in 285a. **300** *lowe*: cj as giving the best sense in context ('poverty is "medicinal" to the humble') and, if spelled *lawe* in Bx's exemplar, as explaining the form of probable Bx **lawd* (of which *lawde*, *land* are both unapt reflexes). The ?g conjecture *lewde* does not seem fitting in context, nor does the sense of F's *lawe* which may, nonetheless, come adventitiously close to the earliest discernible form. Total revision in C conceals the possible shape of *B¹* here. **304** *lighter*: Bx *hardier* is tolerable in context, and the line will scan vocalically as Type Ib. But the C word (giving a Type IIIa line) is more appropriate in corresponding closely to the sense of the Latin line following, and *hardier* may have come in by inducement from 305a, where it is collocated with *herte*. **304a**: re-ordered to give better sense in parenthetical position between the two English lines that translate its sense and before 306 with its logically conclusive *Forthi*. **311** *so*: cj in the light of revised C (*sothly*) as the needed first stave-word lost in Bx by distraction from following *deserue . . . somer*. **316–17a** Re-division after C gives better metre and rhythm by removing the important *Seint Austyn* from the prelude dip of 317.

Passus XV

17 *a party* 'in part', 'partly': the sense is that all souls were created by God, some are Christian, all are 'known' in heaven (in that Christ died for all), and some (the just) will enter there (with the thought, cf. XVIII 378–9). **25** *mens thoughte*: the α reading, like Cx, correctly incorporates *thoughte* as an *internal* gloss on the Latin, using the disyllabic by-form of the noun to give the last lift its required feminine ending. β's omission of *thoughte*, like that of three C-MSS (UDN²), is presumably due to judging it a *marginal* gloss (an easy error since it is the last word in a long line). **55a** *opprimatur* 'let him be overwhelmed': the probable original (confirmed by C) corrected to the Vulgate future indicative form in F and to the present indicative in β. **73** The **Bx** reading can be reconstructed from the joint witness of the sub-archetypes: 'it would be better, in the case of many theologians, to abandon that kind of teaching'. **84** scans as Type IIIa on |f| or possibly as Type Ia on |s| with liaisonal stave in *as‿it* and a (clumsy) caesura before or after *ye*. **109** *hem that thei*: R's awkward syntax is less awkward than βF's, which would require a comma after *hem*, making *that mysdoon* qualify *men* 108. **111** Transposition of *in Latyn* and *ypocrisie* restores the needed first stave-word, lost in **Bx** through placing the dominant noun first in normal prose order. The line scans as Type IIIa. **115** could scan normatively on 'cognative' staves (|b|b|p|), but at the cost of placing the caesura in the middle of the French phrase. On the showing of C, *ben* is to be *cj* as the first stave-word, **Bx**'s substitution *aren* being a form doubtless more familiar in the archetypal scribe's idiolect (cf. a similar case at XIV 223 (C) above). **123** *ech*: *cj* as affording a 'cognative' stave for the voiced palatal fricatives in the a-half. Omission in **Bx** could have been induced by the syntactical movement from dual subject to verb. Pronunciation of *girdel* with initial |dʒ| seems phonologically excluded. **126–7** The **Bx** line, whether read with *have* α or *saue* β, affords passable metre and sense. But a more complex argument seems to underlie **Bx**: not that 'a bad priest (a) never saves money to buy a breviary and (b) always says his offices unwillingly', but that '(a) he has never had a breviary for his offices and (b) he always says it unwillingly unless he is paid' (i.e. he is presumably willing enough to do it when he *is* paid). The proposed reconstruction avoids the contorted syntax and idioms of **Bx** and sufficiently explains generation of the latter through omission of the postulated 127a as a consequence of assimilating *have²* to *have¹*. The OC² variant looks like a piece of scribal conjecture. **138** scans vocalically as Type Ia if verb and noun are transposed in the b-half. Loss of the key-stave is the result of **Bx** inversion to prose order. **213** scans as Type Ie with counterpoint, the theme-stave |n| being mute in key position after elision (*ne‿in*) and the contrapuntal staves being in third and fourth positions. F's *loveþ* is a characteristic attempt to 'regularize' the metre to Type Ia. **224** *stille*: a key-stave in |s| is required for the metre, and unless this is intended to be *ch* in *charite* pronounced |ʃ| and scanned 'cognatively', *so* α must represent Bx. But this is semantically weak and cannot have generated *tyl* or w-group *for*. K–D's conjecture *stille* 'continually, always' as the original helps to explain the form of β , which could = Bx, α then becoming an alliterative substitution for *tyl*; or, alternatively and preferably, both *so* and *tyl* could be reflexes of Bx *stille*, *so* the result of failure to grasp the meaning. Something of the sense of *stille* remains in revised C's b-half *all here lyues*. **234** scans vocalically as Type III (*-oúten, hír*) with contrapuntal staves in the b-half. Emendation, though possible, is not strictly necessary: the line's terse structure appears original. **268** *verray*: F's *verred* challenges consideration for harder meaning and smoother metre; but *verray* makes good sense, and probably represents Bx, R preserving α and F having 'improved' independently. **289** scans as Type Ia with liaisonal stave on *of͜Austynes*. The B reading seems an echo of revised C XVII 15b, 16b. **312** *hath ben*: *cj* as providing the needed key-stave, for which Bx ⇒ the more obvious *was*. The emendation *yborwed was* (K–D) fails to give L's required feminine ending. **313** *foweles*: acceptable here despite the paradoxical notion of metaphorical 'birds' being fed by real birds (314). Cr's conjecture *foles* fits well enough with the thought developed at XX 61–2 and adumbrated at VII 125 (C) above (*q.v.*) with its converse punning on *foweles*; but Anima's fowl imagery here is related to that he develops at 471–9, and while it punningly alludes to *foles*, the substantive reading is acceptable as in Bx. **314** *by lyve*: transposition of verb and particle restores the needed key-stave lost by Bx through inversion to prose order. **320** *moore* 'further': *cj* in the light of revised // C *amorteyseyd eny more* as the needed first stave lost through partial haplography before *amortisede*. The line scans as Type IIa. **352** *myd*: *cj* as the needed key stave-word for which Bx ⇒ the standard Southern form *with*. **355** *unresonable* 'against reason': i.e. the weather is disordered like men's actions (for the weather/morality parallel, cf. Reason's sermon, V 13– 20). Cr²³'s commonplace substitution does not merit consideration as a possible original. **370** *clemat* 'weather-region': *cj* on the evidence of // C as the form underlying *clement* α and *element* β, both visual errors perhaps induced by a mistaken nasal suspension in Bx. **377** *to . . . under*: *cj* as the phrasal form partially inverted to prose order by Bx with consequential loss of the needed key stave-word *fourmen*. F's 'regularizing' of the metre obliterates the original sense. **393** *Lede*: *cj* as the (contextually difficult) word (see *MED s.v. lede*, 1 (c)) needed for the key-stave, for which Bx ⇒ a non-alliterating synonym (see ibid., 1(a)). The motive was perhaps objection to the *human* connotations of *lede*, nonetheless used of the persons of the Trinity at XVI 181 below, which caused no trouble to the Bx scribe. **394** *bileveth . . . God*: transposition (here) to *prose* order provides the needed key stave-word lost by Bx's inversion to the most frequent order in such phrases as in 395 (stress *oón God*). 395 scans 'cognatively' as Type Ia |*k*|*k*|*g*|. **421** *bothe* 'likewise': *cj* after K–D (who place it in first-stave position) as the needed third stave in a Type IIa line, omitted by Bx through partial haplography (*boþe* < *þe*). **450** *fourmed*: *cj* as the needed first stave-word in this Type Ia line. A simpler emendation, providing a Type IIa line, would be to read *was and* for *and*; but *fourmed* is unusual enough to have invited substitution of a commoner (but contextually less apt) near-synonym. **461** *mynnen*: evidently right on grounds of sense and metre, but perhaps severally corrected in various β-MSS, with β itself having read *nymmen* as in Bx (through minim confusion), for which α has ⇒ the commoner synonym. **470** *mowen*: *cj* as the stave-word necessary in first position, for which Bx ⇒ the commoner *don*. A simpler emendation would be *men rightfulle*, but *mowen* has the right sense, forming the elliptical 'so may just men [be said to] desire . . .' **471** *is*: possibly R's *his* is a spelling for *is*, with *understonde* a past participle, here to be taken as referring to God, with *is* understood. **479** *wissynge* 'guidance, teaching': *cj* as giving better sense than identical-rhyming *whistlynge*, which may be a simple visual error induced by homoteleuton. **503–9, 528–31** An emendation of major importance proposed by K–D on grounds of inconsequence in the argument, resulting from 'early corruption by dislocation in the archetypal text of B XV 50[3]–6[8]'. They emend 'by reconstruction as the criterion of sense and the suggestion of revised C direct' (pp. 178–9). Their detailed case is on balance convincing, and the result is to make the B-text as coherent as C, even though it is evident that C itself was revising from a B-MS (*B¹*) with the same dislocation as had occurred in Bx. (As K–D observe, a single C-MS, M, also has the corresponding C lines in an order like that to which they transpose Bx, 'whether . . . by sophistication or by good correction' (p. 179n.).) The omissions in β (510–27) and α (532–68) during the sequence 503–68, however, appear to be unconnected with the posited archetypal displacement (*K–D*, p. 178n.). **504** *grete holy*: inversion of the adjectival order is *cj* on the showing of // *grete hye* in C XVII 256 for the sake of the rhythm in the a-half. Bx's order is unknown, since α has what appears to be a smoothed reading after omitted 532–68. **506** *lyveth* 'live': elliptical, with understood verb 'believe' following *and* (so // C); γM read *leue* 'believe', but also a dialectal variant of 'live'. Lα (?=Bx) depend on wordplay, γM on unifying both objects (*feith*, *mene*) after the same verb. **512** *by*: the emendation adopted on the showing of C eliminates the possible meaning 'see that by steadfast reason(ing) men might not be saved, but only through grace' for the stronger and more likely one, 'see through [the] serious argument [of Christ's life and passion] that men could be saved only by grace'. The point is that Christ's miracles confirmed the authority of his teaching on the need to suffer for the salvation of oneself and others; the lesson drawn is that if the modern apostles would *suffer*, they might perform miracles, too (such as converting the Moslems). **516** *bishined*: presumably the weak preterite of a transitive verb derived from the intransitive base form *shinen*, which has a strong preterite. The form *bissheinede* in identical // C makes clear that the word means 'shined' and not 'signed' as in F's variant *ysygned*. The term should not be pressed for a precise sense in terms of sacramental theology, as it occurs in a metaphor involving Christ's blood: baptism brings a *general* 'illumination' (or 'brightness') to the believer, not the *specific* infusion of the spiritual graces connected with confirmation. **528** *And ... to*: the β reading *That* is a scribal smoothing after the omission of 510–27. The sense is elliptical: Thomas was an exemplar of some action (risking his life to save men's souls) that contrasts with these titular bishops' useless wanderings. **545** *clerkes*: *cj* as the needed key stave-word lost by Bx substitution of a more familiar expression. **547** *Mynne*: *cj* as the required first stave-word (as in C), supplanted in Bx through inducement from following *wise*. Alternatively, but less probably, *men* read *wyes*, and the line alliterated on |*w*|, *men* in // C XVII 210b being a revision. **549** *demede* 'condemned': revised in C to stronger *dampnede*, from which B is doubtless contaminated (C also revises *demen* 551 to *dampne*). **550** *come aught*: *cj* on evidence of // C as the needed key-stave omitted by Bx through inducement from the common shorter expression *er longe*. **551** *depose youre pride*: transposed (here) to prose order to provide the needed key stave-word. Possibly Bx's anomalous scansion (*aax/bb*) is due to the line being macaronic, but so is revised // C, which has the order here *cj* (*youre* becoming *yow for youre*). **552** *and*[3]: not strictly needed for sense (and present in B, doubtless through ⊗ from C) but improves the style and may have been omitted through assimilation to preceding and following *and*. **554** *lese ... evere*: reconstructed after revised // C to provide the needed key stave-word lost in Bx through (partial) movement towards prose order. **567** *the peple*: notwithstanding earlier doubts (*Sch*, p. 292) the referent must be 'the Christian people' in both versions, and not 'the Moslems' in either Bx or C (which revises XV 567 *twice*, once at XVII 233, and then again at 250, only the second mention of *peple* possibly referring to non-Christians (although its most natural sense is '*all* people, (nominal) Christians and Moslems alike'; cf. 249: *alle maner men*). This closeness to the sense of Bx is evidence that L was here using a B-MS which closely resembled the latter (i.e. '*B*[1]'). **604** *Grekes*: presumably (some of) the pagan Greeks, not the (Greek) Orthodox, who were of course Christians as well as just monotheists like the Jews and Moslems. The revised line in // C mentions the latter but not the Greeks, and the ancestor of WHm was presumably influenced by *Iewes* at 606b. **611** *rendren* 'expound': the harder and (in the light of slightly revised // C) original reading, preserved in L alone. If L here = β, then α will have varied to coincide with γM; alternatively, L may be contaminated from C, though it shows no sign of this elsewhere.

Passus XVI

20 *loue dreem*: despite the palaeographical ambiguity of *loue/lone*, the true reading is established on metrical grounds: the compound has a stress on the *first* element, and this is possible only with the reading *loue*. **33** scans as Type Ia, with wrenched stress on *norisséth*, awkward but firmly established here and in identical // C. 66 scans as Type IIIa on |s| with semi-counterpoint on |f|.**71** scans vocalically as a 'T'-type line, with first stave on wrenched suffix *-hode*, a blank third stave, and secondary thematic staves on |r|. **96** *fonge* 'get, obtain': the Bx reading is likelier to have been *foonde* 'try for', but the felicitous correction by wGOC²MF seems more appropriate in sense and closer to C's *fecche*. Both Christ and Satan will 'try for' the fruit but only one will 'win' it. **136** *arne*: clearly established on comparison with C; *aren* R is a mistaken spelling, βF represent an attempt at smoothing on the basis of a supposed verb *to be*. **140** *cene* 'supper': the β variant *maundee* 'commandment to love' (i.e. act of washing the disciples' feet on Maundy Thursday), is not less hard than *cene*, but could be the β-scribe's attempt to avoid repetition by substitution of a different word for one known to mean 'supper' (mentioned in **141**). **142** *som* '(some) one': mis-spelled in α, replaced in β by unambiguous *oon*. The straightforward emendation is secure even in the absence of support from C. **158** *and at*: reconstructed in the light of *and to* C as the Bx reading of which *and* α, *at* β are split variants. **159** *pays; pees*: identical except for spelling: 'leave them alone, and let them go unmolested'. **161** *his name*: the hero is being 'named' here, as later he is to be given his 'title' by Conscience ('Christ', in XIX 62). F's variant was induced by associations of *name* with *(y)nome* (past participle of *nymen*) and preceding *taken* 160. **192** *his ... knowe*: *cj* as necessary to provide the key-stave lost by Bx through transposition to prose order. The sense of *knowe* is passive ('to be known') or elliptical ('for men to know'). Impersonal uses of *suffre* are unrecorded, and β's 'correction' attempts to clarify the sense, which is 'to make known his own power, that of himself and that of his agent, and what both can experience/ undergo/ suffer'. **198–201** Punctuation of these lines is difficult, but *Wr*'s comma and *SkK–D*'s stop after *chirche* 199 do not make them easier. The evidence of // C XVIII 210 (formally the same as 210 but actually corresponding to 200) points to the three nouns of 199, taken with *In menynge that* 200, meaning 'are to be understood to signify . . .' In *SkK–D* these nouns must share one of two complements, *Holy Chirche* 199 or (taking *Holy Chirche* as part of the phrase 'Cristene Holy Chirche'), *children* 198. Thus Christ and his religion *are* God's offspring and Holy Church *is* his daughter (cf. II 29–30); but if Holy Church is also 'mother' of the 'children of charity' (197), L's notion must be that of Christ as the Church's bridegroom, not as her (divine) father. What emerges is a (rather strained) parallel between two arbitrary triads, for the OT figures can be regarded as 'children' of the *Christian* Church only by (retrospective) adoption. **201** *leodes*: *cj* as the necessary stave-word for which **Bx** ⇒ the non-alliterating synonym gloss *persones*. The verb *lovede* (without pronoun subject) is 'carried' by the force of a well-established impersonal idiom *hym likede* (cf. XVII 140 below). **231** scans as Type Ia with a liaisonal stave on *if I*. **246** *leneden*: the best resolution (on grounds of sense) of a word palaeographically and contextually ambiguous, since 'lean' goes better with the *foot* metaphor of 245.

Passus XVII

3 The key stave is found 'internally' in *writ*, a licence abandoned in the C revision of this line (cf. VII 39 (C) above). **8** The extra line in α is accepted by K–D as original, but on the evidence of C, which omits, and the absence of content in the line, it is rejected as a scribal addition. **38** *teeth*: *cj* as the rare first stave-word for which **Bx** has ⇒ a familiar non-alliterating synonym. The key-stave is either |s| or |t| (in mute *to*) and another possibility is *steppeth* (less difficult than *teeth*). Unemended, the line has a clumsy five-syllable prelude dip including a lexical verb (but cf. 75 below, which has the same pattern), and no full stave in the b-half. **52** *chaced*: the unvoiced palatal affricate alliterates 'cognatively' with the voiced and emendation to the revised C verb *jaced* is unnecessary. **71** scans as a 'T'-type line with vowel staves in the a-half. K–D's attractive conjecture *barm* for *lappe* would create a smooth and characteristic Type Ie line. **78** *moore speneth*: transposition *cj* to provide the needed first stave-word in this Type IIIa line (which could otherwise scan, unsatisfactorily, as Type IIIb on the vowels of grammatical words *he, I, -after*). **81** *folweth*: perhaps a mis-resolution of **Bx** *folwet*, a tense-ambiguous spelling, or else γM may have corrected to the preterite later adopted in the C revision. The mixture of tenses seems more likely to be original (cf. 79). **88** scans as Type Ia with liaisonal key-stave (*siththe I*). **90** *segge*: *cj* as the needed third stave in this Type IIa line for which **Bx** ⇒ the commoner non-alliterating synonym. **101** scans as an extended Type IIIb line with counterpoint (*abb/aa*). **116** Transposition in the b-half restores the key-stave lost by **Bx** through inversion to prose order. **140** *hym lovede*: an impersonal use of this verb (on the analogy of *likede*, to which // C revises), unlikely to have arisen from the latter as it occurs earlier at XVI 201 above (C) along with *likede* and is not open to question. **153** scans as Type Ia with two lifts in the final word: *shéwýnge* '[mental] representation, image'. **160** scans vocalically with key-stave *hem, thre* de-emphasized, and counterpoint in the a-half (*abb/aa*). **164** is reconstructed to provide the needed first stave in the a-half lost by **Bx** through inversion to prose order. The line scans as extended Type IIIa with counterpoint on |θ|. Unemended, it could scan as normal Type IIIc, but only with a clumsy caesura after *in*. **190** *ypersed* 'pierced': the required sense, though the β spelling was presumably an ambiguous one with |ʃ| for |s|. **199** The ablative -*u* and -*o* in Bx yield nonsense and presumably result from missing the nasal suspension and then smoothing (the same error occurs in the preceding 198*a* and is there corrected by two MSS). The revised C line (with correct cases) shows L's awareness that Latin *in* here means 'against', a sense of English *in* instanced at 197 above (*MED s.v.*, 9 (a)) and cf. the β variant at 202 for *ayeyns* (perhaps induced by recollection of the occurrence at 197). **208** The extra line here in C XIX 174 could have been originally in B (so K–D, *Sch*) but is not strictly necessary to the sense and could have been added in revision. **214** *lowe* 'low': *cj* as the needed key-stave word lost by Bx though assimilation to preceding *yblowe* 213*a* or (if the exemplar had the dialectal variant *lowe* for *leye*) to the preceding noun meaning 'fire' in 214*a*. **224** scans vocalically as an extended Type III line with counterpoint (*abb/ab*) (identical in // C), the key-stave being the stressed comparative adverb *as*. **234** *noght*: required for the sense, and surprisingly not inserted by any of the MSS. Omission could have been occasioned by the length of the line, or possibly Bx's exemplar read the unemphatic negative *ne* (placed before *mowe* and lost through visual confusion). **240** scans as type IIIc (*ab/ab*) and Y's variant *faire* agreeing with revised C (which has a 'T'-type line) is probably an accidental convergence prompted by objection to *warm* with *flame*. **254** *ingratus*: preferred as supported by C, though *ingrat* α, only instanced here, is strictly the 'harder' reading. The line scans vocalically as a 'T'-type with 'cognative' macaronic b-half (|g| |k|) after a mute stave on *in-*. **294** *that ... there*: transposition to restore the key stave-word *pleyneth* displaced to last position in Bx, here from prose order. Final *-e* is added to the spelling (in accord with W's usual orthography) for the required feminine ending. **297** scans 'cognatively' on |k| |g|; emendation of *God* to *Crist* (so K–D) is unnecessary, and explanation of the possible causes of the substitution (*Sch*) otiose. **326** *the borre*: *cj* on the showing of C as the key stave-word replaced because of its difficulty by an easier adjective *hoors* in β and *couȝ he* in α (sophisticated to alliterate by addition of an adjective in F). Neither sub-archetypal variant is hard enough to have generated the other, and though the line could scan as Type IIa (counting *be* as first stave) in both α and β, the likeliest archetypal (and original) reading is that preserved in // C.

Passus XVIII

6–8 re-ordered on the showing of C and the requirement of a verb (*dremed*) for the noun-phrase object in line 9. **14** *on*: suits the context as an intelligent correction of Bx. The gCr smoothing of Bx's poor sense anticipates C's revision, which is, however, historically less correct (it was obtaining the spurs, not the shoes, that formed part of the knighting ceremony). **31** *lieth*: fits better contextually with the challenge-cum-threat of Death, and is confirmed by C. The α reading ('is willing, satisfied [to accept the challenge]') gives equally good sense, and L's agreement may point to β's having read the same, so that M will then have presumably corrected from a γ source (as elsewhere). The source of the error was presumably an ambiguous medial spirant in Bx (*gh* for *ʒ* in *lʒ eþ*) mis-resolved in α (? and β) and corrected in γ independently or by reference to C. **32–3** Re-division after C gives better rhythm, sense and phrasing for both lines; Bx will have mis-divided because of the length of l.32. **35** *forbite*: preferred as the harder reading, confirmed by Latin *morsus* 35*a* and the general 'fit' with such imagery at, e.g., XVI 35, XX 56. **40** *pelour*: the harder and more legally precise term, liable to replacement by a familiar term of abuse. **49–50** *seide; envye; quod*: the verb *seide* is taken absolutely (= 'spoke') by K–D, who print a semi-colon after *envye*; alternatively, *quod* may be taken as pleonastic after preceding *seide* 'said' (identical in C). **54** *seiden*: syntactically necessary after *And*, perhaps omitted through influence of preceding *beden*. **76** *throwe*: the harder reading, unlikely to have been ⇒ for the much commoner *tyme* to which C (doubtless) revises, and which β seems to have anticipated. **82** The Bx line is unmetrical and could be emended by conjecturing for *spere* a word *javelot*, not attested before 1440 but perhaps known as a rare usage, and therefore vulnerable to scribal substitution. But a possible occasion for wholesale rewriting by Bx is objection to Longinus as a Jew (he was honoured as a Christian saint), and K–D's proposal to read C's line here is accepted as the best available solution. **94** *alle*: severe, and not to modern religious taste, but probably the reading of Bx and quite possibly original. The milder C reading, which confines the curse to the Jews present and their offspring, is anticipated by WHmGC², perhaps under influence from C. **119** *and a clene*: cj as furnishing the needed third stave in this Type IIa line; lost from Bx because of the line length and position after a subject already provided with an adjective. **151** *heo*: elsewhere in this passus, the Western and Southern form of the feminine pronoun is restored to avoid ambiguity (so 165 below). **154** *amende*: cj as the needed third stave-word in this Type IIa line; lost through Bx substitution of a commoner non-alliterating (near)-synonym. **159–61** Defective in Bx in both metre (159) and sense (160). Reconstruction of 159*a* proceeds on the presumption of loss of a needed stave-word through homoarchy, with subsequent inversion to prose order in 159*b*. This is cj as *gilours*, although an alternative *the gilour* placed after *gile* would be closer to // C. The b-half is emended on the basis of C, adapting to the a-half's passive construction. Line 161 is adopted from C on grounds of sense as having been lost through eyeskip (*good* 160, 161), and *ende* YGC², *all* C² (both probable contaminations from C) as giving better sense after restoration of the lost 161. This is one of the serious corruptions in Bx where correction without major recourse to C is impossible, but the archetypal sense is unacceptable. 193 scans vocalically as Type Ie, with enriched last lift and the other lifts on the important grammatical words *a* 'one particular' and *of*. 198 *I*: preserved in L alone as the β and presumably **Bx** reading, confirmed by one C-group, x^1 (most C-MSS omitting *I*) but lost in γM through variation to the stock phrase, and misconstruction of the mood of *recorde* as imperative. L's reading here should be contrasted with XIII 385, XVII 296 above, where it omits *I* (with R). 238 scans as a (macaronic) Type IIIa with a liaised first stave *that‿weren*. 281 *in deol*: *cj* on the basis of revised C XX 304 *Sholde deye with doel* as the needed second stave in this Type IIa line, presumably lost in **Bx** through attraction from *dwelle* and to *deueles*. 282 *sithen*: not absolutely necessary for the metre, since the line scans as Type IIIa, but greatly improves the sense if given as the first of Lucifer's two reasons for feeling confident; lost through anticipation of *sithen* in 283. 283 The sense, clear in α, is confirmed by revised C XX 309. 'And I, afterwards, given possession . . .' 294 scans 'cognatively' on $|d|d|t|$ as in (unrevised) C. 296 I^2: better construed as the pronoun not the past participial proclitic morpheme as in **Bx**, an error induced by the perfect-tense form of the first verb phrase. 306 *seillynge hiderward*: transposed to provide the needed key stave-word lost in **Bx** (here) by inversion to 'normal' verse order, with adverb before the participle at the line-end. The sense of *seillynge* 'sailing' is inferior to C's *sylinge* 'gliding', of which it may be a mis-spelling, though C could be a revision of the kind common in this section. 316–19*a* Divergent corruptions in the sub-archetypes result from the presence of 'appended' Latin phrases; but **Bx** also seems to have read unmetrically in 316–18, suffixing the question to 317a and prefixing the answer to 317b. K–D's reconstruction both places question and answer in their logical order (Lucifer's question *Quis . . . ?* answers Christ's *command*, Christ's answer Lucifer's *question*) and gives correct metre in the English lines, which are not macaronics at all. A further result is to make 315 and 317 read concordantly with their (lightly) revised counterparts C XX 359, 360. 343 *was . . . Lawe*: transposition of the two phrases restores the key stave-word lost by **Bx** inversion through fronting of the adverbial phrase. 351 scans vocalically (but none too satisfactorily) as Type IIIa (*in*, *álle*). Possible emendations are *maugree* for *ayeins* (K–D) or *alle maner* for *alle*; but want of a C// argues for caution. 375 scans as Type IIIa either vocalically or on $|m|$ with a- and b-half lifts in rhythmically parallel pairs: *mý bíddyng / mé líketh*. A lost stave-word *be* before *me* (*cj Sch*) gives an excessively heavy post-caesural dip. 379 scans as a Type Ia line with caesura after *deeth* and a 'cognative' liaisonal stave on *that‿is* ($|d| d|t|$) or, possibly, as 'T' type, if the liaisonal stave is also muted (*that‿is withóuten énde*). 383 *juwise*: the **Bx** reading may well have been *wise*, which looks easier than *iuwise*, the revised C reading, from which WHmGC^2 may be contaminated (cf. 94 (C) above). Either reading is acceptable, though if *iuwise* = 'sentence', not 'death sentence', both here and in // C, the requirement that law 'give him life' becomes logically applicable only to the *first* punishment (*deeth*). But *or* here may = *vel* rather than *aut*, as MSS CrM seem to take it. The scansion of the line is as Type IIa on |*f*θ| (clearly the scansion of // C), but optionally as Ia with (muted) liaisonal stave (*deeth ̣or oóther*). Possibly the root of the confusion was authorial uncertainty about the exact sense of *iuwise* at the time of writing B. In both texts it stands in apposition with *doom* [= *iudicium*] at 386 (C XX 427); in C there is a clearer contrast between the execution itself and the passing of the (death) sentence. 392 *clene*: *cj* as the necessary stave-word lost in Bx through assimilation to preceding clens*ed*, cler*liche*. The line may be Type Ia, with *clene* in key-stave position, or Type IIa with caesura before *wasshen* and the adverb modifying *clensed*. 402 scans in BxCx very awkwardly as Type IIIa on the vowel staves *I* and *in*. The first stave, found only in C group *t*, may be scribal conjecture but accords with the context and provides apt wordplay on *lede* 401 (=C XX 443). The metrical difficulty in 402 is removed if *me* β is read for *I* α, giving a Type IIIa line of pattern closely resembling 375 above. But C tells against this, and *I* generally gives better sense, Christ's *love* for the patriarchs balancing their *belief* in him. 406 *leste*: *cj* as the necessary key stave-word lost in Bx by substitution of a non-alliterating term occasioned through failure to grasp the logic (subtle, but clear enough, and missed by *Sch*): that the *minor* devils would have *less* to fear from Christ than the greater ones. C need not be seen as revision to make this different point, nor need any alliterating equivalent of *boldeste* be *cj*. 413 During the absence of R as chief witness to α, MS F is cited *only* where it seems likely to preserve the family readings; most of its sophisticated variants are omitted from the apparatus and are not discussed here.

Passus XIX

12 *hise*: *cj* as the difficult and (deliberately) ambiguous reading which has generated a 'logical' variant *Piers* (the figure *looks* like Piers; cf. XVIII 23–5) and a 'theological' one *Cristis* (either α's or contaminated from a C source), which is contradicted by *ac* 13b. L's (profound and subtle) point seems to be that the 'arms' belong to *both*, to divine and human natures united in one person. 38 *Baptiste*: obviously right on grounds of sense and confirmed by C, shows L's independent descent from β; α is uncertain, since F may have varied coincidentally with γM. 56–9 F's text here is assessed on comparison with C in the light of its recognized tendency to sophisticate α's reading. 60 scans either as Type Ib with two lifts in *lárgelíche* or (preferably) as a vocalic 'T'-type line with counterpoint. 75–6 Omission of *ensense* from both β and Cx may indicate its absence from both Bx and *B¹*. F and Cot will therefore have added by conjecture, and the word's proper position is undeterminable. If placed after *offrede*, it gives line 75 a Type IIb structure; if before *mirre*, 75

becomes standard and 76 forms its dip from the major lexical word *Ensense*, a not unparalleled pattern (cf. 89 below). The form adopted here accepts that F's word and order may both be conjectural (like that of MS R in the C-tradition, which inserts *Rechels* at this point); but the original must have contained a mention of incense. (For further difficulty with this 'gift', cf. 90 below.) 76 *mercy* 'thanks': the Cot variant *mercede* (reflecting knowledge of C III 290ff.) and *mede* CrM are scribal responses to the apparent inappropriateness of 'mercy' here; but the kings could hardly be supposed to be asking for a *reward* from the infant Christ. 90 *richels* 'incense': *cj* as a difficult stave-word corrupted to *riche* and then smoothed (illogically) to *riche gold* (but gold = justice, and incense = reason). The crux is one of the stronger indications that B^1 was the basis of the C revision and may not have been revised throughout in XXI–XXII. However, if written in the form *riche les* the word may have seemed nonsensical and invited substitution of a term (*gold*) which gave sense, if not logic. F's variant b-half appears an attempt to explain the anomaly by removing Reason altogether to make the line deal with the supposed power of *leautee* (though the natural referent of it seems to be *gold*), producing a different, and unsuitable, meaning. 97 *comsede*: *cj* on the showing of // C as the likely key stave-word for which Bx ⇒ the commoner *gan to*, not itself unmetrical since it can alliterate 'cognatively', but arguably less likely to be a case of a B original revised by C. 101 scans as a Ib line with 'cognative' b-half staves ($|d|\ |d|\ |t|\ |t|$); but *hadde tyme to* could be the result of Bx scribal objection to the tone of *durste* C, otherwise to be regarded as a revision. 111 *of*: could be original here and revised in C, which is slightly better; W presumably agrees by coincidence. 113 *thus*: preferable on metrical grounds, though an original BC *thus us* as in F could have generated the split variants *thus, us* as found in both the Bx and the Cx traditions. 148 *demede* 'believed, expected' (*MED s.v.*, 11 b-c); possibly original and not necessarily a Bx substitution for an original *deuyned* as in C. 152 *and . . . after*: credibly to be judged, on the showing of C, the α original sophisticated by F (perhaps through objection to calling Christ's risen body *it*). 181 will scan as Type IIa on $|s|$ in Bx, but O's contaminated reading from C gives what is possibly the B original for which Bx ⇒ the more expected *doost*. 183 *thoughte*: the obviously original reading, *taughte* having no special relevance here in this context. 186 *To*: the sense requires a preposition to indicate the contrast between the gifts given to *all* (185) and those given to Piers alone (*hym* 186). *To* will have been lost through assimilation to *To* in 185 above. Pardon is given to all men, but the power to absolve (the agency of the pardon) to the Apostle Peter. Presumably the absence of *To* in B^1 indicates that L overlooked it, or else accepted *Hym* as an elliptical form of *To hym*. 187 *kneweliche*: present subjunctive after *come* (same tense and mood) is as acceptable as C's double preterite, to which WHm have varied. 213 scans as Type Ib on 'cognative' staves $|k|\ |k|/\ |g|\ |g|$. 230

wyes: *cj* as the needed first stave-word, which Bx omits and for which Cx reads unmetrical *men*; the latter was presumably in B^1, and was overlooked, whether or not revision took place. 236 *buggynge*; *sellynge*: transposed to provide a first stave in this Type IIIa line. The conjecture here is also that of a single C-MS (N^2), but Cx clearly read as Bx, and the error is thus likely to have been in B^1. 239 scans 'cognatively' $|t|$ $|t|$ $|d|$, unless to^2 is the (mute) key-stave, as in C, which has *theche* for *dyche*. 241 *of*: *cj* to provide the (liaisonal) key-stave lost through failure to see the sense of the particle (= 'about'). Since Cx makes the same error, it was presumably also in B^1. 244 *wel* 'accurately' or 'long': *cj* as the necessary key stave-word lost in Bx through attraction to *wele, telle, felle*. C appears revised here in the b-half. 252 *be*: *cj* as the necessary key stave-word lost in Bx through substitution of *were* (to rationalize the tense-sequence after preterite *forbad*). The b- half phrase, like (? revised) // C, is 'semi-direct' speech. 254 The extra lines (printed K–D, p. 223) are clearly spurious on grounds of sense, metre and style. 255 is reconstructed in the light of // C *That alle craft and connyng cam of my ȝefte* to give a standard line scanning 'cognatively' $|k|$ $|g|$ $|k|$, retaining the crucial idea of the arts/ skills given by the Holy Spirit to the community, which was lost through inattention to copy and distraction by the dominant term *grace*. 279 *that²*: the harder reading, supported by C family x (family p reading *þat seed*). F's *frut* must be rejected as a sophistication (of ?possibly α *seed*), in the absence of support from R. 297 *plete*: the tense is reconstructed on the showing of // C *plede* and accounts for the present tense in β. The verb must mean 'goes to law', as this is how the man with fortitude 'pleads', by enduring injustice. β 'plays' destroys the metaphor. 301 *evene*: a stronger reading in context than Bx *euere*, an easy visual error. 304 *thorugh*: makes much better sense than *for* (a visual or auditory error in Bx) since Justice is the means of finding out guile, not the reason why it is *not* found out. The line scans 'cognatively' on $|b|$ and $|p|$, the $|p|$ staves being internal to the initial consonant group $|sp|$. 305–6 are mislineated in Bx, giving three lines theoretically scanning as Type IIIb, *xa/xa*, Type IIIa, the first and third not impossibly original, but the whole sequence appearing scribal in the light of // C. The line now scans as an extended Type Ie with enriched 'cognative' b-half. The exact form remains doubtful as Cx here is uncertain, the sub-archetypes reading *any þynge gulty* p / *any agulte* x. In reconstruction, *kynnes gilte* is postulated as the underlying form of which *gilt or in trespas* Bx is scribal explicitation of the faults through which kings become subject to legal justice. 317 *forthi* 'therefore': to be discerned on the showing of C as the exemplar form (perhaps written *uorthi*, with *u* representing the voiced labial spirant) mistaken in Bx through grammatical misconstruction and/or visual error. 319 scans 'cognatively' on $|t|$ $|t|$ $|d|$, the third stave being mute (*cardinále*). 324 scans 'cognatively' on $|g|$ and $|k|$ as Type Ic ('extended standard'). 333 *home Piers*: the *cj* Bx reading (preserved in C) of which F (?=α) and β are clearly split variants. **337** *lond*: the C reading fits the context better than *loore* F, presumably an error induced by preceding *truthe* and following *bileve*, and by failure to grasp the metaphorical figure. **342** *Surquidous*: as sg seems preferable, his companion in 343 becoming one villain with two names. F's plural could represent α or be contaminated from C (also plural), the villains of 343, who are the antecedent referents of *Thise two* 344, then becoming *two* people. But sg 'sergeaunt' makes better sense in the context. **345–6** Division after C provides the needed first stave for 346; *sire*, also necessary for the metre in this Type IIa line, may have been lost from Bx through visual distraction from *Piers* or else through objection to applying the knightly/priestly title to a ploughman; *sew*: on metrical and stylistic grounds preferable to β and probably the reading lying behind F's sophisticating elaboration. **348** *caples tweyne*: *cj* as providing the necessary key stave-word lost by inversion to prose order; *tweyne* gives the needed disyllabic form usual in post-nominal position, *two* being a substitution following inversion. The error, found also in Cx, will have been in B^1. **351–2** are awkward in rhythm, both scanning as Type IIIa, 351 with a caesura after *noght*, 352 with caesura before or possibly after *who*. Emendation is possible but hazardous. **367** The Bx reading is rejected on grounds of sense and on the evidence of C. The image is of a fortified tower standing in a moat (cf. 381–4 below). **372** *right*: *cj* as the needed key stave-word lost in Bx (and in B^1, since it is lacking in C) through *synne* >< *saue* attraction. **373** a^1 ... *somonour*: *cj* on the evidence of C as the original a-half in B corrupted in Bx by scribal expansion into two lines attacking six separate groups of hardened professional sinners. **379** scans either as extended Type IIIa on |s| with 'cognative' counterpoint in both halves or more probably as a standard ('cognative') line on |b| |b| |p|. **391** *Myght*: the sg supported by C?α is preferable to the pl, and *And* may be regarded as scribal easing of the transition (cf. 186 above). **398** *Or* 'first, beforehand': clearly the harder reading and rightly so adopted by K–D (see *MED s.v., er*, 3). **409** *Save*: *cj* as the needed Type IIIa first stave for which Bx like B^1 (since C also reads *Bote*) ⇒ a more familiar conjunction. The line could in principle scan, again as counterpointed Type IIIa, |b| alliterating 'cognatively', with an internal |p| stave in *Spiritus*; but on balance the emendation seems preferable, and *But* may have been picked up from 411 below. **411** *be ... fode*: accepted as the α (and so Bx) reading, confirmed by the reading of C family x as this C group is reconstructed from the split variants of x^1 and t. The β reading rationalizes (like p) by changing the noun *fode* to a verb after loss of *be*. **413** *leode*: *cj* as the needed key-stave lost in Bx, which ⇒ the familiar non-alliterating synonym, under the influence of the common collocation *many man*. **416** *or an hennes*: β's reading is shared by C, only the *t* group and

DWF omitting it, so it will have been in B^1 and may be original. Omission in ?α will have been on account of the length of the line and apparent metrical completeness of the first b-half phrase. **433** *soudeth*: the harder and more precise reading, perhaps visually confused in **Bx** through anticipation of *sent* 436 (and cf. 449 below). **441** Though not strictly necessary for the sense, the line serves to introduce 442 effectively, and loss would have been easy since the last phrase is identical with that of 438, and *tilye* re-appears as the second stave-word in 442. The a-half anticipates 444a balancing God's role with that of his deputy Piers. **444** scans as Type IIIc on |*b*|, unless the original read the less usual *wikke and goode* in the b-half, which underwent transposition in B^1 and **Bx**. **446** *the Pope amende*: transposition is required to provide the first stave in this Type IIIa line, lost through inversion to prose order in **Bx** (and also in C, from B^1). **457** *sowne*: a case of L witnessing imperfectly what was the probable form of β, γM having corrupted to *seȝ e* through inducement from following *sighte*. **461** *For ech*: reconstructed after C from the split variants in F and β. **468** *wole he nel he*: C makes the best sense, F's variant being a sophistication and β's a smoothing after presumable loss of *nel he* at the line-end. **482–3** The BxCx reading in 482, rejected by K–D*Sch*, is here retained as making acceptable sense.

The difficulty of the lines is grammatical, since the conditional subjunct-ive of the protasis would normally be followed by an indicative in the apodosis (e.g. *thow may*, as in β). But in fact it is followed in C by another ('jussive') subjunctive, a construction retained from α in F, which has characteristically replaced *askyng* α with a synonym (β, having altered the grammar, has gone on to smooth the sense.) There is no need, therefore, to see the latter as a purpose clause and so emend *wel* to *wol* (K–D*Sch*).

Passus XX

8 *Was*: adopted from C as preferable on grounds of sense, the β and α variants (and whatever **Bx** form they derive from) the result of reading *That* 7 as a conjunction introducing an indirect clause (after understood 'saying') and not as a relative pronoun (=*that which*). The error may have been partly due to the presence of this construction in line 9, though here too *that* could be a relative. **14** *cacche*: the present fits better with the tense-sequence of the main verbs (and subjunctive *come* following must be present). **19** *deide for thurste*: the C order gives a line firmly scanning on lexical stave-words, whereas **Bx** would scan vocalically only on (here unimportant) grammatical words. Inversion, here *from* prose order, will have occurred in **Bx** through influence from the common order (adverbial, verb) in such phrases (see XVII 294 above). **33ᵃ–35** The proposed relineation establishes the Latin line as free-standing and reconstructs the first lift of 34 on the evidence of C. Only one C-MS (U) has the reading *cj* as original, and if Cx's form is that preserved in C-groups **p** and *t*, then α in the B-tradition is identical with it and may preserve Bx, as against β. **48** *bide*: harder in context and supported by C-group x^1 (and cf. 46 above); the theme seems to be 'patient waiting' not 'mendicancy' as an answer to 'need'. **67** *hir*: at first sight the easier reading, but *hem gile* Bx (making *gile* a verb) sounds unidiomatic, and *hem* may be a visual error for *her*, a common and perhaps original spelling. **70** scans 'cognatively' on |*p*| and |*b*| as Type Ib. F's variant looks like an ingenious attempt to 'regularize' the metre (*bare* = 'displayed'), and is unlikely to represent α. **83** *scalles*: *scabbes* W is a coincidence, perhaps a visual error due to *l/b* confusion, and not ⊗ from C. **104** *hir lemmans knyghtes*: the two nouns in qualifying apposition ('their lover-knights') give the original sense against the repetitive β, which refers twice to ladies. **106** *tho*: gives better sense and rhythm than *to* Bx, a probable visual error which makes the verb unidiomatically intransitive. **117** *brode*: preferable on grounds of sense, and WHmF may all have corrected independently here after registering the inaptness of ?Bx *blode*. **126** *suede*: spelled *seude* as in R (=α) Bx would have easily been misread as the preterite of *sende* with voiced stop (see *MED s.v.* senden, v. (2)). **256** *newe*: evidently lost in C or omitted; would have been easier had Bx read as α, producing potential homoeoarchy through juxtaposing *newe noumbrede*. **261** is necessary to complete the sense of 260; C^2's line is a guess, perhaps prompted by recollection of C. The line scans vocalically as extended Type III with counterpoint in the a-half. **292; 293** *pleyen*; *renkes*: *cj* as the needed key stave-words for which Bx (and presumably B^1, since Cx has the same error) have ⇒ non-alliterating synonyms, the first forming part of a familiar collocation. **298** scans as Type IIa with an enriching vowel stave in the b-half and strong a-half stress on *In* 'within, inside'. The line would be smoother if not necessarily more effective with inversion of subject and verb. **301** *hii*: a plural is obviously required by the sense, and the form of *he* Bx suggests this was the Southern and South-Western form rather than *they* as in C. **308** scans awkwardly on |*f*|/|δ| in both Bx and Cx but would be much improved if *thei* read *hii* (cf. 301 (C) above). Other conjectures are -*fetes* for -*dedes* (K–D) and *wrong* for *mys*-. **309** *pardon*: on the showing of C this was likely to have been the needed second stave-word (also required to complete the sense) in this Type IIa line, lost by attraction of *Piers* >< *ypayed*. **366** *alle hem*: conjecturally reconstructed as the original of which Bx *al* and Cx *hem* are split variants. **367** *and*: *cj* as lost through inattention to the sense and assimilation to preceding *And*, the archetypal scribes having taken *yow* as addressed to *my Lady*. Friar Flatterer is offering membership of the fraternity to both master and mistress. **373** scans as extended Type III with contrapuntal |*s*| staves in both halves (*abb*/*ab*). But better rhythm is obtained if *alle kynne* is emended to *alleskynnes* with medial liaisonal stave, giving a Type Ia line. **377** *come*: *cj* on the showing of // C as the needed second stave; scansion as Type IIIa is possible without emendation, but is very awkward here. **378** *adreynt and dremeth*: convincingly *cj* by K–D (and mistakenly rejected by *Sch*) as the original of which *adreint* Cx, *and dremeth* Bx are split variants. Cot's *adreynt* may be identified as ⊗ from C. **380** *hii*: *cj* as the needed key stave-word in this vocalically scanning Type Ia line, lost through substitution of the pronominal form usual in the dialect of the archetypal MS. The // C line *And doth men drynke dwale, þat men drat no synne* is sufficiently different to represent major revision, the last example in the poem (and one of the clearest), though it is arguably also difficult enough to have been the β original that invited rewriting in the more explicit form witnessed in Bx.

Supplementary Notes

Passus XIV, 28 *Haukyn wil: cj* on grounds of sense, since it is he who is *Activa Vita* and comparison between his wife and other minstrels pointless. The error could have come in by aural/visual suggestion from following *waf-* and confused recollection of *wif* at 1. 3, with subsequent smoothing to *Haukyns*.

Passus XVIII, 283 *seventy hundred: cj* in the light of revised C as closer to the traditional number (four or five thousand) and, as having been in the less familiar form, easily liable to corruption. It is likelier that *sevene* was misread for *seventy* than that *hundred* was substituted for visually dissimilar *thousand*.

B   LITERARY AND HISTORICAL

Prologue

1–22 The opening lines echo several earlier alliterative poems such as *Wynnere and Wastoure* (ed. Turville-Petre in Ford, *Medieval Literature*). **2** *shep*: because dressed in a woollen garment (cf. X 1, XX 1), the characteristic garb of hermits. The outer *habite* may suggest humility, but he is to prove far from docile. **3** On false hermits, see Jusserand, pp. 140–3. **5** *Malverne Hilles*: the setting of the vision, but not of the visionary events themselves; an 'authenticating' detail or a cultural flourish like the references to Western localities in *Wynnere* or *Richard the Redeless* (see Kane, *Evidence*, pp. 38–41). **6** On Fairy Land as a source of marvellous dreams, cf. *Sir Orfeo*, in Sch and Jacobs, lines 133ff. **11** Medieval dream-vision poems, deriving from the C13th *Roman de la Rose*, generally have the dreamer in bed; L follows *Wynnere*, setting his visions mainly outdoors and motivating them by the Dreamer's fatigue after wandering (Passus XIX, set in church, is exceptional). **13–14** *eest*; *tour*: symbolic of the direction of sunrise (= light as a symbol of God), and of divine strength (see Ps 42: 3, Ps 60: 4). **17ff.** On L's picture of society generally, see the references under *PP* in Mann, Jusserand and Du Boulay. **38–9** alluding to Eph 5: 3–5 (*Bn*). L's hostility to false minstrels echoes *Wynnere* (24–8). **44** *Roberdes knaves*: 'Roberdesmen' was a contemporary name for thieves of no fixed abode; cf. Robert the Robber, V 462ff. **46** *palmeres*: strictly, pilgrims to the Holy Land, who returned with palm branches. On pilgrims, see Jusserand, pp. 338–403; Adair. **47** The shrine of St James at Compostella, north-west Spain; the relics of apostles and martyrs in Rome. **54** The shrine of Our Lady at Walsingham, Norfolk, the most famous English shrine after Thomas Becket's at Canterbury. See also V 226, Adair, pp. 114–20. **58** The Dominicans, Franciscans, Carmelites and Augustinians; cf. VIII 9 and esp. XIII 61ff. for the collocation of greed, gluttony and insincere preaching. See Jusserand, pp. 279–309. **64** *charite*: ?St Francis, the great exemplar of this virtue, and so (metonymically) his order. **68ff.** *pardoner*: empowered by the Pope to supply an indulgence remitting part of the temporal punishment for sin imposed by the local clergy in return for some payment towards the general work of the Church. He required the local bishops' licence to preach in their dioceses. L attacks the practice, which had come to be popularly seen as a means of buying absolution without contrition or sacramental penance. On pardoners, see II 220–3, V 639–42, and Jusserand, pp. 309–37. **75** *rageman*: a long parchment document with a ragged edge; see *Bn*. **80** *by the bisshop*: my translation (cf. *MED s.v. bi*, 8b(a)) allows the bishop responsibility for granting the pardoner the seal but *not* any authority to preach in his diocese (a duty of the parish priest); pardoners were laymen or in minor orders); but *Bn* 'with the bishop's permission' (with evidence that they could obtain the seal without his knowledge) is equally consonant with 78–80 and overcomes *Sk*'s objections to the (natural) sense of *bi* here. **84** *pestilence*: the Black Death, a catastrophic combination of bubonic, the more lethal pulmonary or pneumonic, and septicaemic plague, reached England in 1348, with further outbreaks in 1361–2, 1375–6 (see McKisack, pp. 331–3; Ziegler, esp. pp. 27–9). In 1349 it killed perhaps half the clergy and reduced the population by about a third, leaving many parishes unable to support their priests with tithes. **87** Specifically the 'curial' bishops, who received their office as a reward for serving the king (*Bn*); but all absentee bishops may be intended here. **96** *styward*: the lord's chief official on the manor, who could deputize for him in the manor courts (Bennett, *Manor*, pp. 157–61). **99** *Consistorie*: (a) the bishop's court, for cases involving ecclesiastics; (b) the Pope's solemn council of cardinals; (c) (figurative and ironic) Christ's court on Judgement Day (cf. Mt 25: 41). **100–6** The divine ratification of Peter's authority is described in XIX 190, the giving of the Cardinal Virtues (Prudence, Temperance, Fortitude and Justice) in XIX 276–310; see also VII 176*a*, citing the text, and XIII 255. **107–11** may allude to the French cardinals opposed to Urban VI who in Sept 1378 elected an antipope (Clement VII, a Frenchman), thus causing the Great Schism (see Bennett, 'Date', p. 56, and Intro., p. xxv,. **114** *Kynde Wit*: natural and practical intelligence, based on the senses (as opposed to speculative intellect), and responsible for the proper ordering of society (see Quirk, '*Kind Wit*', Morgan, 'Kind Wit', and White, *Nature and Salvation*, ch. 1). **122, 126** *leaute*: justice in society; law-abiding citizens; see Alf*G, s.v.*, and Kean, 'Love, Law, and *Lewte*' and 'Justice . . . in *PP*'. **132–8** These anonymous Leonine verses, which appear in an early C14th sermon MS (see *Bn*), sum up concisely L's view of proper social order. *Pietas*: 'mercy' (ME *pite*); but L contrasts law as a human institution subject to the will of earthly rulers, and law as a reflex of divine justice. The Christian ruler will show mercy but must also rule *religiously*, i.e. with an abiding sense of what is owed to God by his earthly deputy. Mercy is not an arbitrary *deflection* of (strict) justice; rather, justice is to be seen as 'law administered with Christian goodness'. The play on 'measure' and 'reap' is lost in translation. *Ius* here = 'the law', 'legal justice' rather than justice absolutely. Of the Biblical texts alluded to, Mt 7: 1–2 is important; for the later development of the contrast (and possible conflict) between *divine* justice and mercy, see XVIII 110–228. **139–42** The words of the goliard or vagabond clerk echo and complement those of the lunatic, and reflect the author's shrewd practical sense. They may be original, but for an earlier form see Wright's *Political Poems*, i. 278. **145** The ignorant common people's utterance of this absolutist maxim from Roman law (the *Lex Regia*) suggests their helplessness and contrasts with the educated goliard's attitude. *Precepta*: found in this form (preceded by *Et* or *Hec*) as part of a couplet in Richard of Wetheringsette's *Summa* for parish clergy of the early C13th (Wenzel, in Alford, *Companion*, p. 161n.). **146ff.** L here re-tells a traditional fable, also used topically by Bishop Thomas Brinton in a sermon of 18 May 1376 (ed. Devlin). The cat has been interpreted as John of Gaunt, the rats and mice respectively as the Lords and Commons, the rat of renown as the Speaker, Sir Peter de la Mare, the mouse as a spokesman for the author, the kitten as the young Richard (nine years old in 1376 when his father the Black Prince died), and the bell and collar as constitutional restraints warning the commons of the King's threatening intention. But L's sceptical and ironic treatment is original: the topical application should not be overdone (see Intro. p. xxxviii, and L's tale has a general validity. **196** Richard II was a boy of ten when he was crowned king in July 1377. **225** The song may allude to the 'wise woman' Dame Emme of Shoreditch referred to in XIII 339 rather than Canute's virtuous queen, who survived trial on a false charge of unchastity. **230** *Rochel*: La Rochelle, a fortified port on the Atlantic coast of France, a centre for the export of Bordeaux wines.

Passus I

1 *mountaigne*: in Biblical tradition Mt Sion, a symbol of the heavenly Jerusalem and later of the Christian Church (Mt 5: 14). **3** The traditional image of the Church as a beautiful woman, deriving from Apoc 19: 8, also owes something to literary personifications of simple or complex ideas as authoritative female instructors, from Philosophy in Boethius' *De consolatione Philosophiae*, to Alan of Lille's Nature in his *De planctu Naturae* and Raison in the *Roman de la Rose* and De Guilleville's *Pèlerinage de la vie humaine*, a work L knew. **12** *Truthe*: a deeply Biblical name for God (Ps 30: 6, Jn 14: 6); in this application it means both 'the real object of knowledge' (*veritas*) and 'the object and source of faith and trust, fidelity' (*fidelitas*). **15** *fyve wittes*: the senses, to be used soberly; their 'right uses' are the sons of 'Inwit' (IX 20–2). **20** *three thynges*: the three necessities of life, to be properly satisfied according to the natural law established by God. The example of Lot's incest with his daughters (27) illustrates disobedience to God through ignoring the law of nature. **35** *Mesure is medicine*: to live by nature and reason is to live moderately, and avoid the ills that come from excess. The Deadly Sins later described are aberrations, through excess or defect, from a norm of moderate sufficiency. As the 'cardinal' virtue Temperance, *measure*, derives from

Plato, but the medieval conception of virtue as a mean derives from
Aristotle, *Ethics* II. 6–9, and is influenced by the Biblical idea that God
created 'everything in measure' (Wisd 11: 21). **38–9** *likame; liere; world*:
Flesh, Devil and Worldly Pleasure, the three enemies of man's spiritual
nature. **41** *soule*: the life-principle (*anima*), under the governance of mind
(*inwit*), and located in the *heart* (see IX 55–9). **44** *moneie*: a man-made
value, not a 'good of nature', hence not self-evidently for common
possession. **64** *Fader of falshede*: 'a murderer in whom there is no truth
. . . the father of lies' (Jn 8: 44). **66–78** Cain the first murderer and Judas
the supreme traitor sum up diabolic activity for L – the obstruction of
God's love and truth (see Jn 8: 44). *elder*: popularly believed to be the tree
on which Judas hanged himself. **85** *treuthe*: as the supreme value, is to
live by faith in God and 'fidelity' towards one's fellow-man. 'Knowing
truth' is not merely intellectual understanding, as illustrated by the
example of the fallen angels. That Truth (= God) can only be 'known' by
being *lived*, with its implied warning of the danger of mere knowledge, is
the central doctrine developed through the figure of Piers Plowman. **98**
David: the Biblical warrior-king 'chivalricized' in the Middle Ages as one
of the 'Nine Worthies'. **99** *truthe*: the special virtue of knights, much
discussed in contemporary chivalric literature (Chaucer's *FranT* and *Sir
Gawain and the Green Knight* (*SGGK*)). **105** *tene*: the number of
completed creation. **115–16** The fiends are damned forever and their
number is not fixed (cf. XVIII 332, XX 270). **119** *Ponam pedem*: from
Augustine, *Enarrationes in Psalmos* (*PL* 36: 69), on the basis of Is 14:
13–14 (Robertson and Huppé, *Tradition*, p. 44 n. 52: Kellogg). **120**
Echoed by 153, *q.v.* (*Bn*). **124–5** On the traditional belief (Eph 6: 12) in
devils and spirits infesting earth and afflicting mankind, see Lewis,
Image, pp. 135–6. **138** *kynde knowynge*: a natural, instinctive understanding; or, a 'proper knowledge', on which see White, *Nature and
Salvation*, ch. 2, esp. p. 51. **142–5** 'Truth and love have become identical'
(*Bn*): by loving God we obtain direct 'natural' knowledge of him; but
man only knows God because God has revealed himself to man, in the
OT Law and Prophets (*Moyses* 151), finally through his Son (167). God's
love for man is the 'motive' of the Incarnation (Jn 3: 16). **148ff.** On the
imagery, see Smith, *Imagery* and Kean, 'Incarnation'. The remedy for the
bite of the diabolical 'serpent' must be made from the powdered skin of a
serpent (tyriacon = *triacle*). Following traditional exegesis of Num 21:
8–9, L sees the Incarnation as God's way of 'becoming the serpent',
which through his sacrificial death and sacramental life in the Eucharist
of the Church provides the healing remedy for man's wounded nature.
For further commentary on this passage, see *Bn ad loc*; on the *plant of
peace*, an early rendering of Ezech 34: 29, see Adams, 'Lectio', pp. 12–
13. **185–7a** True religious 'works' are not empty observances or even
passive 'holiness' but active, urgent *concern* for the welfare of individuals
in need. The attack focuses on the sin of avarice, antithesis of the God

whose generosity is revealed in the Incarnation, and the most hateful form of avarice is that of churchmen, who are particularly called to charity. Thus, the ideal or spiritual Holy Church is not to be identified simply with the institution and its functionaries. 188–9 *chastite . . . inne*: from St Bernard, Epistle 42, with some possible influence from Chrysostom (Sch, 'Complex Echo').

Passus II

5–7 *left*: traditionally the 'bad, inferior' side, regardless of 'direction' (see *MED s.v. lift* adj (2) and (3); and cf. *luft* at IV 62, also V 578); also the *north* (the 'Devil's quarter', cf. I 118*a*) (*Bn*) because Will is facing *east*. 8–19 allude to the Whore of Babylon (Apoc 17: 4–5) and probably also to Alice Perrers, Edward III's extravagant mistress (cf. 10) and her marriage to William of Windsor, the king's deputy in Ireland, in 1376 (18). 14 *Orientals*: either *specifying* the sapphires of 13, or 'pearls', perhaps confirmed by *margaritas* (Apoc 17: 4) (*Bn*). L here refers to the healing properties attributed to some jewels (see Evans and Serjeantson, *Lapidaries*). 16 The redness of gold was traditional (cf. *Sir Orfeo* 150) but its factual basis was the addition of copper as an alloy (*Bn*); pure gold is yellow. 20 *Mede the mayde* 'Reward the virgin': she *ought* to be 'pure' (i.e. neutral, honest) but Conscience's accusation at III 121–33 suggests otherwise. (On Mede generally, see Mitchell; on her literary antecedents, see Yunck; and on her nature, see Morgan, 'Status'.) 23 *Popes paleis*: since 1309 at Avignon, which became the court of final appeal for all ecclesiastical cases and, as the church's administrative, also a major financial centre. From 1379 it was the seat of the antipope, Rome becoming the papal seat again. 24 *soothnesse*: the principle of truthfulness, perhaps here personified as at 189 below. 25–6 The Fals who is a liar and Meed's father is the same as Wrong (I 63–4); the Fals proposing to marry Meed is Wrong's representative, son (see 41), 'incarnation' almost, anticipating Antichrist in XX 53. 30 *doughter*: as Meed is the Devil's (cf. Jn 8: 44); see also XVI 197. 33 *leef* 'portion' (*Bn*; *MED s.v.* n. (1), 2d): in context 'beloved' (ibid. n. 2) is more natural. 39 Ps 14 promises salvation to the man who speaks and lives truth and 'hath not put out his money to usury, nor taken bribes [*munera* "Meed"] against the innocent'. The *context* of the Biblical quotations L uses is always relevant to his pattern of thought; on their importance, see AlfQ. 56 repeats Pr 18; lovers of Meed are found in all sections of society. 59–60 specify officials especially prone to taking 'bribes against the innocent': *sisour*, member of the sworn assize of inquest, the precursor of the modern jury; *somonour*, the official who summoned defendants for trial in the church courts, which dealt with a variety of offences against morality and such matters as wills; *sherreve*, the chief administrative officer of the Crown in each shire; *bedel*, a minor manorial official with

duties of summoning tenants to court, collecting fines, etc; *baillif*: chief
representative of the lord of a manor; *brocours*: retail traders, or agents
in business transactions between two parties. 61 *Forgoers*: purveyors
concerned with 'pre-empting for the King' and 'impressing labour and
materials for [his] building operations' (*Bn*); *Arches*: the provincial court
of the Archbishop of Canterbury which sat at St Mary Arches in Bow
Street. 63 *Symonie*: the sin of buying and selling church offices or
spiritual benefits. Here he seems conceived as a corrupt canon lawyer
linked with his counterpart, Cyvylle (*Bn*; and see Gilbert, p. 57, and
Barratt). 66 *brocour*: often corrupt because he arranged marriages to the
financial advantage of the bride's father (here allegorically the Devil). 69
chartre: a 'deed of conveyance of landed property' (*OED s.v. charter*,
2(b)), the lands being (loosely) equated with five of the Seven Deadly Sins
in 80–9 (the metaphor changing at 93). Sources of the figure include
Grosseteste and the *Roman de Fauvel*. 74a The standard opening of a
charter. This and passages like XI 303–5 attest L's knowledge of legal
forms and procedures (cf. Kirk, and AlfG, p. 140). 87 Usury as 'lending at
exorbitant interest' was forbidden to Christians, and 'distress loans' to
people at need, commonly at 43% interest, were officially made by Jews
only. Loans (*mutua*) with 'compensation' for loss arising (*interesse*) were
permissible for Christians (Gilchrist, pp. 64–5, 68). 96 The Church's
rules allowed only one solid meal on fast-days; 'full time' was reckoned as
noon (the usual time for the main meal was evening; see Bennett, *Life*, p.
236). 100–1 On end-rhyme and other forms of rhyme, see Sch, *Clerkly
Maker*, pp. 75–9, esp. p. 78. 105 Alluding to the custom of annual tenure,
L sees the sinner as having to yield up his soul in payment for his sins, with
perhaps the suggestion that a life passes as quickly as a year. 109
Paulynes: a minor order of friars among those suppressed in 1370;
though friars were not usually pardoners (*Bn*), this one could have been,
and *doctrine* plainly implies an order or profession. 111 *Reve*: an official
with important duties in the manorial economy, elected by the peasants
from their own number (see Bennett, *Life*, pp. 166–78), and prone to
amass debts of his own (cf. X 471, XIX 463). 113 These words (?spoken
by Wrong) parody the normal dating formula ('. . . of Our Lord'; cf. XIII
269) and point to Wrong's affinity/identity (see (C) on 25–6) with Satan.
115 Theology, who takes over Holy Church's role (*Bn*), personifies her
doctrine systematized and applied to society (cf. X 182–99). 119
Amendes: Meed's 'true' (i.e. ideal) parent, in the sense that *heavenly*
reward is for those who repent and make amends for their sins. Meed is
'lawfully born' in that this, ideally, ought to be the case. In reality, as
Meed's words and actions show payment and reward are unjust. The
context of the quotation is Christ's statement of the right of apostolic
preachers to get food and shelter in return for their work. That it is at
Theology's behest that Meed goes to London – where she nearly suceeds
in becoming accepted by the King – seems a tart comment on the

likelihood of justice being realized in our world. **131** *Belsabubbe*: 'prince of the devils' in Mk 3: 22–6; perhaps another name for Satan. **139** *Conscience*: the disposition responsible for applying the rules of reason to particular moral acts (as at III 120); defined at XV 31–2 below. **144** *floryn*: gold coin worth six silver shillings, introduced by Edward III in 1344 (illustrated Poole, pl. 34). **156** *London*: actually Westminster, at this time a separate city, for the court in question is the King's, not the Archbishop's in Cheapside. **162** *caples*: the 'riding' metaphor is traditional, appearing in Nicole Bozon's *Char d'orgueil* and *The Simonie* (line 326). For other developments, see IV 16–23, XVII 108. **163** If L here puns on *foles*, then the 'worldly-wise' who follow Wrong are 'fools in the eyes of God', whereas the *fooles* of XX 61–3 (which recapitulates Passus II) are, though 'foolish in the eyes of the world, wise in God's eyes', and do *not* follow Antichrist (= Wrong). **171** *provisours*: clergy appointed directly to benefices by the Pope. The Statute of Provisors (1351) only slightly reduced petitions for benefices from English clerics to the papal court – petitions accompanied by payments (see McKisack, pp. 280–3). **173–4** *Denes*; *southdenes*: officers of the bishop especially prone to corruption (accepting bribes or using blackmail), who as churchmen abusing their office would count as simoniacs. *Erchedeknes*: ecclesiastical judges who made parochial visitations and imposed fines for offences against sexual morality and church discipline (*Bn*); *official*: the bishop's representative in the consistory court; *registrers*: clerks of the church courts in charge of records, citations and receipts (AlfG *s.v.*). **176** These matters, within the jurisdiction of the church courts, were the Archdeacon's special concern. He could be bribed to overlook adultery and to effect separations under the guise of canonical annulment (the sense of *divorce* here; see AlfG *s.v.*). Secret or *derne usurie*: the practice of *occulta* as opposed to *manifesta usura*, i.e. not publicly licensed lending, but lending, at exorbitant rates, under the pretence of a trading transaction – e.g. buying wheat from a vendor (actually, a debtor) paid more than the real value, the excess constituting a secret loan on which interest became due (see Gilchrist, under 'usury', esp. p. 108). **180** *commissarie*: the bishop's legate exercising jurisdiction in far-flung parts of the diocese. **181** *fornicatores*: the officials will provision themselves at the expense of fornicators and adulterers by fining them (*Sk*). Taking *mede* for overlooking such cases among the clergy is criticized in *The Simonie* 49–52. **189** *Sothnesse*: truth, *veritas*, especially the perspicaciousness of integrity (cf. 24 above) which can recognize Gyle. **196** *maynteneth*: aids and abets them through money, protection or influence; alluding to the abuse of 'maintenance' of retainers by great lords. **199** *constable*: 'an officer of the king's peace' (AlfG *s.v.*). **200** *tyraunts*: 'vicious rogues, villains' (cf. XX 60); not in the political sense. **205** *pillory*: the standard punishment for breaches of trade regulations. *Drede*: 'fear of earthly punishment' (by the king); not the salutary *drede* (of God) Wit describes at IX 95–6. 206 *doom*: *Bn* questions the reading as no judgement has been passed; but the tone of 193–8 makes plain that the king sees the wrongdoers' condemnation as assured once they come to trial. 211 The first attack on friars since Pr 58–65. For balanced comment on their condition at this time, see McKisack, pp. 309–10; and for the background of satire on the friars, see Szittya, ch. 7. 217 A line that seems echoed by Chaucer in *CYT* (*CT* VIII. 658). 229 *half a yeer and ellevene dayes*: the exact length of Edward III's French campaign of 1359–60, 'a period when rumour was rampant' (and spread by minstrels and messengers) (*Bn*).

Passus III

12 *Westmynstre*: the seat of the royal law-courts, full of judges and lawyers presumably ready to accept 'meed'. 22 *coppes*: suggesting the gold cup held by Babylon in Apoc 17: 4, which Walter Map glosses as *avaritia* in *De mundi cupiditate* 18 (Wright, *Mapes*, p. 167). 24 *moton*: a gold coin worth about five shillings, bearing the impression of a lamb. 31 Judicious bribery will help procure employment for them in the church courts. 36ff. The abuse of confession by a friar will be recapitulated in XX 364ff. The essence of the abuse on the *penitent's* part is formally confessing without true contrition (*shamelees*). 45 *noble*: a gold coin worth 6s 8d (= £⅓) (Poole, pl. 34e). 53 *lordes . . . lecherie*: to be recapitulated at XX 312ff., where such a lord seeks easy absolution from Friar Flatterer. 58 The seven capital sins (deadly = mortal, 'destroying sanctifying grace in the soul'); developed in full in Passus V. *Lecherie's* rather brief treatment in V 71–1 may be due to L's already having personified the sin here in Mede. Her special fondness for it underlines her affinity with the Whore of Babylon, with her 'cup of fornication' (see 22 above). 63 *suster . . . house*: i.e. enrolled as a member of his order by letters of fraternity 'entitling the [benefactor] to special privileges and benefits' (*MED s.v. fraternite*, 1 (c)). In XX 367, which recapitulates this scene, Friar Flatterer makes the same promise to the sick Contrition. 66 *pride*: the other deadly sin only briefly treated in V 62–70, again perhaps because partly anticipated here in the person of Meed. 77–86 *Bn* suspects this passage as 'not clearly related to its context'. Abrupt it is, but it describes the presence at Meed's trial of those who had followed her to London (II 56; III 80 echoes II 187). Meed had bribed the lawyers and clergy (III 20, 29); now she bribes the civic authorities. 76 *Maires*: the municipal government of which the mayor was head had the special duty 'to check dishonest dealing' (Poole, pp. 251–5, fig. 56; pl. 24 depicts the civic mace and the punishment of dishonest traders). 83 *regratrie*: not simply *selling* retail but (the illegal practice of) *buying* in rings from the producers so as to depress the price they obtained and then go on to make large profits at the expense of the poor. 93 *Salomon*: regarded as the

author of the *sapience bokes*, i.e. Proverbs, Ecclesiastes and Wisdom (and cf. V 39). L here loosely attributes to him an utterance of Job (the greatest 'wisdom-writer'; see *Jerusalem Bible*, pp. 723–5). See also Prov 15: 27 (*Qui autem odit munera vivet*) and cf. 336 (C) below. 100 *yeresyeve*: a toll or payment 'or rather a . . . bribe . . . to connive at extortion' (*Sk*) taken by a royal officer (sheriff, judge) upon entering office, and renewed annually on New Year's day. Cf. VIII 52 (metaphorical) and XIII 185. 124 A line echoing 170 and associating Conscience's judgement with that of Holy Church. 127 *fader*: the reigning king when these lines first appeared in the Z-and A-texts was Edward III, and even in B it is he who is in question, not the young Richard, though the latter was crowned in July 1377. His *fader* is thus presumably Edward II, murdered in 1327. Edward, however, was not destroyed through *avarice*, and the lines are ironically more applicable to *Richard's* father, Edward the Black Prince (d. 1376), 'whose troubles arose from the failure of Don Pedro [the Cruel of Castile] to supply him with the money he had promised' (*Sk* – i.e. for restoring him to his throne (see McKisack, p. 144). 128 *popes*: Benedict XI was said to have died by poison (1306), but the allusion is a more general one to the Donation of Constantine, 'poison' to the Church (*Sk*). See XV 558–9 (C). 138 *grote*: 'great' silver coin (worth 4d) introduced in 1351 (Poole, p. 293, pl. 35a). 140 *Trewthe*: here not God (as in I 12 etc.) but a 'collective personification' of God's loyal followers, the just men like Piers Plowman who do *not* take meed (see V 556–9, VI 38–40). 146–8 *secret seel . . . provisours*: the king's personal seal accompanied a letter granting abbey or cathedral chapters permission to proceed to an election or a bishop leave to appoint to a benefice. It could be circumvented by a provisor (see C on II 171) who had secured a prior claim through a papal bull (obtained by payment, hence by simony). See *Bn* and *Sk, ad loc.*, with apt citations from Wycliffite writers. 152–62 On corruption in the law at this period, see McKisack, pp. 205–7. 158 *lovedaies*: set apart for the amicable settlement of differences in the manor court, furnished occasions for bribery. Cf. also V 421. 165 *coupleth*: suggests 'married, united' not just 'linked'; cf. I 195–7. 176 *Sk* notes Meed's respectful *ye* used to the king, and the familiar (and in this context disrespectful) *thow* 178 used to Conscience, who replies in kind at 259, 338, returning (sarcastically) to the polite plural at 344ff. 189–208 *Normandie*: alluding to Edward III's Normandy campaign and identifying Conscience with the king's policy of abandoning his claim to France in return for Aquitaine and a money payment of three million crowns (Treaty of Brétigny, 8 May 1360). Meed argues (207–8) that the king should have maintained his claim, because of the great wealth to be got from France. 191–4 *cold*: refers to the severe hailstorm and cold of 'Black Monday' (14 April 1360), which contributed to Edward's decision to make peace. 196 *bras*: plunder of copper utensils on the way back to Calais (*Bn*). 201 *marchal*: commanding officer of the king's army. 211

aliens: mercenaries or foreign messengers or traders (*Bn*). 230–1 Conscience's denial and the formal distinction he makes recall the procedure of scholastic debate (cf. also VIII 20 (C)). 234ff. From the psalm first quoted by Holy Church at II 39 Conscience develops his doctrine of integrity to refute Meed's specious argument that all forms of *mede* are simple rewards for service. 241*a* is the verse of Ps 14 alluded to by Holy Church in II 37. See further AlfQ, p. 7. 243–5 probably allude to Lk 6: 35: the unjust seek immoderate gain, the just receive (from God) reward beyond what is strictly due (*Bn*). 258 Conscience does not seem to recognize legitimate *profit* in trade (*lucrum*), which was allowed by the theologians; but he may imply it under *permutacion* (see *commutatio*, *ST* II, 2, 77: 4); cf. also AlfG, *s.v.* 259ff. The Scriptural moral of the first Book of Kings (= I Sam), ch. 15, is that Saul was punished for disobeying God through listening to the voice of the people (15: 24), who kept the cattle, etc. for sacrifice. Conscience interprets 'Saul's' sin as avarice, thereby perhaps implying that Edward III might have incurred divine wrath if he had refused to make peace with France and persisted in his claim to the 'richeste reaume' (208). 263 *dede*: the Amalekites' attacks upon the Israelites in the wilderness (Ex 17: 8, 16). 276–7 refer to the destruction of Saul and his sons after their defeat by the Philistines (I Kg 31: 2,4). 280 *culorum*: the *ende* (281b) of the phrase *in saecula saeculorum* 'for ever and ever' with which many liturgical prayers ended. It is unclear exactly what implication Conscience finds in the *cas* and therefore what he might fear beyond general disfavour for his bluntness. 285–9 After killing Agag, Samuel anointed David (I Kg 16: 13), who was to succeed Saul as king. The prophecy is general and millennial; no direct contemporary application appears, since Richard was Edward's lineal heir. 297ff. are not in the // A-text (which ends at 300). *Sk* associates the lines with the jubilee of 1377, Edward III's fiftieth year as king, *Bn* links the prophecy of just times to come with Is 2: 2–5 (cf. 308*a*, 324*a*). It is a vision of an ideal state of affairs, possibly in the 'last days' before the Second Coming of Christ. In X 318ff. the reign of general justice foretold is to be preceded by the coming of *Caym* (328), perhaps the Antichrist who actually appears in XX 53. By contrast, the portents of III 325–9 seem benign, and the prevailing optimistic tone recalls that of the chancellor's speech at the opening of Parliament in Jan 1377, when Prince Richard entered as president, and the atmosphere at his coronation (see McKisack, pp. 395–6, 399). 308*a*: referring to the Last Judgement as understood in the OT. 320 *Kynges court*: the Court of King's Bench, the chief criminal court originally presided over by the sovereign; *commune court*: the Court of Common Pleas, the high court for civil actions. 322 *Trewe-tonge*: a personification of the Just Man of Ps 14: 3 who 'speaks truth in his heart', an appropriate judge in Truth's court. 324*a* completes the verse at 308*a*: Conscience favours peace with France because his vision of an end to *all* war is the 'Messianic' one of

Isaiah. 325–30 Riddling prophecies were common at the time (e.g. those of 'John of Bridlington' in Wright, *Political Poems* I; cf. also VI 320–9, XIII 152–7). The passage is discussed by *Sk* and *Bn*, who notes (after Bradley) that a sheaf contained 24 arrows, a multiple of the 12 and 6 mentioned here, and that sun, moon and arrows occur in Hab 3: 11. Developing Bradley's hint (with *Bn*'s gloss), the ship may be thought of as symbolizing the Church (*navis* 'ship', whence 'nave'), seen perhaps in the form of Christ's cross (the mast). The number twelve may suggest the apostles come to judge the tribes of Israel (Mt 19: 28). The six suns remains a vague dire portent. The *myddel of a moone* may be the Paschal full moon (as at XIII 155) 'with the events of the crucifixion' (*Sk*). The general underlying sense may be that when Christians are prepared to love one another and lay down their lives for their friends (Christ's discourse at the Last Supper (Jn 15: 12–13) *ante diem festum Paschae*, Jn 13: 1), that is, live out the Christian faith, the Jews will be converted and the pagans (?Moslems) at that sight ('Christians living virtuously in peace and charity' [*Bn*]) will believe in Christ (sing *Gloria* (Lk 2: 14)). The signs at 326 seem to suggest that this will occur only at the end of the world, i.e. that ideal justice will not be established in our time (cf. also Bloomfield, *Apocalypse*, pp. 211–12). *Makometh*: associated with the *coveitise* of clerics at XV 395, 413–14 (*Bn*). 336 Meed's quotation, which comes from a mere eight verses after that of Conscience at 330, shows that she knows how to employ Scripture for her own purposes. It is not, *pace Bn*, inaccuracy she is guilty of in attributing *Proverbs* to Solomon (see Prov. 1: 1, also 1: 2, which calls the work *sapientiam*, and also 96 (*C*) above) but dishonesty: she quotes only partially, because the text will justify *giving* gifts (unobjectionable in itself; cf. 346) but not *receiving* them (*sc.* as bribes). Conscience seems to attack only *hem that taketh mede* (*accipientium . . . munera*; cf. the just man of Ps 14: 5, *Qui . . . munera . . . non accepit*).

Passus IV

5 Conscience, the soul in its capacity to say 'no' or 'yes' to a course of action (XV 31–2, 39*a*) must get from Reason the power to make (moral) judgements (XV 27–8, 39*a*), 'the knowledge on which to act' (*Bn*, who gets them the wrong way round, however). See esp. Harwood, *Belief*, pp. 92–5, on Conscience, and Alford, 'Idea of Reason', for the philosophical, legal and theological background to this figure. 11 *acounte*: an exact term, because Conscience is *Goddes clerk and his notarie* (XV 32) and will have to render accounts to God on Judgement Day for the king and his subjects. 17 If *Caton* here = the (supposed) author of the *Distichs of Cato* (?C4th), then he must stand for practical commonsense morality, day-to-day prudence (see X 191–6), something close to the dubious 'prudence' which 'among the peple is gyle' at XIX 458, and certainly not

'elementary learning' (*Bn*). But L may here have in mind something more general and, through the association with True-Tongue, presumably creditable (contrast the characters Waryn and Witty). 27 *Waryn*; *Witty*: '*merely* worldly knowledge and intelligence', habitually associated with Meed (34) and Wrong (63ff). 29 The Exchequer court dealt with 'cases arising from the audit of the revenue'; *Chauncerye*, the Lord Chancellor's court, was coming to be a court of equity dealing especially with grievances arising from the other courts (McKisack, p. 199). These characters have evaded taxes and need Meed's help to get them out of trouble. 36a; 37a Psalm 13 as a whole describes the ways of evil-doers who have no fear of God. 38 suggests especially those who become *riche* (40) by profiteering, e.g. in the food trade (cf. Ps 13: 4 'they eat up my people like bread'). 41 Conscience, who *knew* ('recognized') this pair at 32, does not *know* ('acknowledge') them here (alluding to Mt 7: 23 (*Bn*), where *vos . . . qui operamini iniquitatem* echoes *omnes qui operantur iniquitatem* in Ps 13: 4a). 45 *sone*: retained from ZA, written when the Black Prince was alive. The *importance* of Reason's 'central' place is what matters in the allegory. 47 *Pees*: a pliable figure all too ready to compromise with strict justice, as later in XX 335, when he agrees to admit Flatterer into Unity. *parlement*: not clearly distinguishable from the great council of lords temporal and spiritual meeting as a court under the king to hear complaints and petitions from private individuals (cf. Pr 144; see McKisack, pp. 193–4). 48 *Wrong*: this diabolical figure (see II 25–6, 113 (*C*)) is here personified as a king's purveyor, forcibly requisitioning and engaging in rape and violence. His acts echo and 'pre-echo' those of the first robber Lucifer (described in XVIII 286–91, 335–40); but they appear also to be 'a catalogue of crimes *contra pacem regis* . . . not only against the victim but also against the king, who prosecutes[s] even if the wronged individual fail[s] to do so', rejecting Peace's petition for mercy and continuing the action against Wrong (104–5) (Alf*G s.v.* Wrong); see further Baldwin, *Theme*, ch. 3, Simpson, *Introduction*, pp. 56–9. 55 *maynteneth*: here implies that he arms as well as aiding and abetting his retainers. 56 *Forstalleth*: buys up goods before they come to market (perhaps with the aid of threats) so as to re-sell them at a profit or to avoid paying customs duties; statutorily condemned as an offence against the common good (Alf*G s.v.*). 58 *taille*: the tally-stick, marked with notches indicating the amount due, was so split that buyer and seller each retained one half as a record of the transaction. Peace complains that the debt was never honoured. 75 *handy-dandy*: in this game one player shakes an object between his hands, then shuts his fists, the other having to guess which hand it is in. Wrong will pay Wisdom 'with closed hands' (i.e. secretly), as he may go on to bribe the judges. 82 *overcomen*: the attempt is recapitulated at XX 122, when Coveitise tries to *overcome* Conscience (*Bn*). 116 *Pernelle*: 'Petronella', a proudly dressed rich lady, enjoined by Reason at V 26–7, appears ready at V 62ff.

to do this. But Reason's 'conditions' are ideal ones, and only if they are realized will he have 'ruth' on Wrong; and since he will *never* do that, the implication is that the conditions will remain unfulfilled. **117** The *act* of spoiling (implying agents, the parents) will be chastized: *they* ought to be beaten for *not* beating their children. **121–2** *St Benedict*: the founder of monasticism; *St Bernard of Clairvaux*: founder of the Cistercian order; *St Francis*: founder of the Friars Minor. Francis did not prescribe an enclosed life for his followers; L means roughly 'all orders should observe their rule' (*Bn*), but the view that *prechours* **122** = the Dominicans, the Order of Preachers, is too specific: as at V 42, all preaching clergy, including parish priests, are meant. **124–5** Elliptical: instead of keeping expensive mounts and hawks, like secular lords, bishops should house and feed the poor as is their duty. **126–7** *Seint James*: should be 'visited' not through (repeated) pilgrimages to his shrine at Compostela, in Galicia, north-west Spain, but through the works of charity specified in his own definition of 'Religion clean and undefiled ... to *visit* the fatherless and widows' (Js 1: 27): **127** seems, however, to acknowledge the validity of a single pilgrimage at the end of one's life or else a perpetual, purely spiritual pilgrimage (*Bn*). **128–33** refer to clerics taking money to the officials of the papal court in consideration of benefices and promotions, as well as the proceeds of papal levies in England (*Pe*). The Curia was still at Avignon (II 23) when the lines appeared in ZA, but the term *Rome* was a set one. The excepting of provisors at **133** sorts oddly with lines like II 171; but if not satirical it covers those who 'go to receive benefices or offices already given', with no necessary implication of simony (*Bn*). *Dovere*: pilgrims could here be examined to ascertain whether they were carrying gold or silver abroad. **139–40** Reason here represents the uncompromising principle of retributive justice in law (*lex est ratio*), anticipating the axiom of Truth's pardon at VII 110*a* (Alford, 'Idea', pp. 206, 208). **143–4** The Latin phrases come from Innocent III's definition of the just judge who leaves no evil man unpunished and no good one unrewarded (*De contemptu mundi* iii, 15). It is this (divine) standard of justice that Conscience invokes in distinguishing the two 'meeds' (III 232–45): if Reason ruled, this standard would prevail and have the results described in **147–8**. The response to *this clause* of clergy and lawyers in **149–53** contrasts with that of the people and the *grete* (= ?'the lords judging' (*Bn*)) at **157–9**. **168** *sherreves clerk*: liable to being bribed to refrain from serving writs (*Bn*). **172** Reason's actions here accord with his nature as later defined at XV 27–8 (*q.v.*). Alford, 'Idea', p. 206 stresses his nature as *ratio*, the principle of rational order in which the eternal law of truth exists, and the faculty to which that law is revealed. **175** *chetes*: property reverted to the Crown if there were no heirs; if lawyers dishonestly produce bogus heirs, the king is defrauded of the revenue from reversion. **179–end** Though Meed is apparently defeated, the king's commitment to Reason and Conscience indicates how things ought to be rather than how they are or will be. Conscience's recognition of realities at 182–4 is elaborated in Passus V, where the *commune* (= the folk of the field) will not find the quest for reformation easy; in V 556 they even offer Piers *huyre* 'meed' to show them the way to Truth.

Passus V

8 *bedes*: 'prayers', as at 401, not 'rosary-beads' (*Bn*), but the Creed's muttered clauses, acting like the *sweying* of water in Pr 10 to 'bring him asleep'. 11 Reason (here an ideal archbishop, divine *ratio* embodied in the Church's teaching authority) preaches a sermon to the whole realm urging general repentance. The structure of this passus, beginning with the sermon, is analysed by Burrow, 'Action' (in his *Essays*). 13 L agrees with Brinton, Bromyard and other contemporary writers in seeing the plague and similar natural disasters as a divine punishment for the sins of the people. 14 *wynd*: a memorable tempest on 15 Jan 1362, a Saturday, which occurred during the second plague and lasted five days. It is seen as an act of God serving as a portent (*tokenynge*) of the Last Judgement and a warning to repent. The storm as a symbol of divine wrath against human pride is found in such OT texts as Is 28: 1–3 (*Dominus turbo confringens*), Ezech 13: 13 (*spiritum tempestatum*), and esp. Ps 48: 8, on the wind and other elements 'which fulfil his word'. The image of the uprooted tree is recapitulated in Antichrist's attack on the 'crop of truth' in XX 53–4. 24 *Wastour*: a destructive parasite, possibly a traditional 'type-name'; not the rich profligate of *Wynnere and Wastoure*. Cf. VI 130, 152ff. 29 *wyvene pyne*: by beating his wife he may save her from exposure to jeers or being ducked in the pond. 31 *marc*: not a coin, but a money of account worth 160 pence, a skilled workman's wage for a fortnight (*Bn*). 34–8: echo a sermon verse preserved in the C14th *Fasciculus morum* (Wenzel, in Alford, *Companion*, p. 162). 39a The quotation continues 'but he that loveth him correcteth him betides' (cf. 38). 45–7 *religion*: the religious orders collectively, who lived according to a formal Rule. The threat of royal intervention in lax monasteries anticipates the famous prophecy at X 316–27 (in the C-text, a part of Reason's sermon here) which made Crowley in the C16th see L as a precursor of the Reformation. L, however, advocates not suppression but right observance. 49 *tryacle*: the Commons' love is a remedy for (possible) lack of support from lords and clergy; the image echoes I 148 above. The allusion to the possibility of popular treason is omitted in the C revision of this passage, when it had become actual in the Peasants' Revolt. 50 *have pite on*: a heartfelt cry; 'deal gently with' (*Bn*) is unjustified in the light of XIX 431, 445, qq.v. 55 is from the Parable of the Virgins, but L may have thought of the (more appropriate) Mt 7: 23 *Quia nunquam novi vos*, said to those *qui operamini iniquitatem* (cf. C on IV

41). 57–8 'The Holy Spirit' for Seynt Truthe (Bn) is perhaps over-specific, though L's awareness of the root sense of *seynt* is clear from I 84, and he may be echoing such passages as Jn 15: 26 and I Jn 4: 6. *Qui &c* is, however, formulaic and need not have Truth as grammatical antecedent. Reason is the living voice of Holy Church, who at I 12–14 has described Truth as (God) the Father; 'Truth' is here not an individual but a personified principle, a life lived in accordance with God's will. 61 *Wille*: 'a momentarily personified abstraction of the human will' (Bn); but since the poet-dreamer is called Longe Wille at XV 152, perhaps the repentance, and so the sins, are his own, though he is also meant to stand as a representative of sinful humanity (cf. 184–5 below). *wepe*: an important symbolic act in the poem, weeping is the authentic outward sign of genuine inward contrition. 62 The tradition of the Deadly Sins is traced by Bloomfield, *Sins*. Contemporary parallels appear in confessional treatises on sins and their remedies (e.g. Chaucer's *ParsT* (CT X. 385–958)) and sermons (e.g. no. 9 in Ross, which relates the sins to the seven petitions of the Our Father, as in the York Paternoster Play). *Pernelle*: the only sin who is personified as feminine, though both Envy and Wrath below *illustrate* their character with female examples (109, 151ff.), and has a personal name (on which see 26 (C) above). In medieval iconography, pride is usually depicted as a woman (see Katzenellenbogen, figs 9, 5, 66). 65–6 *heyre*: the hair-shirt worn in place of a lining (Bn) will tame (the desires of) her flesh, which is (as) fierce (as a hawk or other wild creature; cf. VI 31). 71–4 The Virgin Mary is invoked as patron of chastity (cf. *SGGK* 1769) and intermediary between God and the sinner (see 635 below). Apart from these passages, L's religious focus is on Christ, with no special concern to stress Mary's place in the life of the Church. The penance of a Saturday fast (a special devotion to the Virgin) aims to curb the bodily excesses that lead to lust as in the Lot exemplum at I 25–35. 76 *mea culpa*: from the *Confiteor*, the prayer of penitence at the opening of mass. 80 *freres frokke*: L sees the friars as motivated by envy of other clergy who receive benefits from the laity (cf. X 71–3, recapitulated at XX 273, 295). *Envy* here = 'resentment' and 'hostility' and is close to 'hate' (*invidia*). 122 *diapenidion*: sugar twisted into a thread, used to relieve phlegm in the throat. 137 *listres*: friars whho read a Scriptural text and 'gloss' it so as to make its hard moral demands more acceptable to the rich and powerful. 147–8 plays on the senses 'church properties and dues', 'endowments' (Bn); or the first *spiritualte* means 'church dues', the second 'spirituality' (ironic): preoccupation with the money to be got from the laity distracts friars and parish priests from their true spiritual concerns. 158–9 *Dame Pernele*: this lady's situation would be considered in the chapter court before being brought before one of the diocesan church courts. 164–6 Possibly authorial (and apparently echoed at XIX 162), or else tart comment from the speaker's experience of such ladies. Gregory IX (Pope 1227–41) forbade abbesses to hear their nuns' confessions. Wrath here denies that they could keep them secret. 167–79 With the favourable view of monastic discipline here, cf. X 305ff. 184–5 *Esto sobrius*: St Peter warns against the Devil as a roaring lion, an apt image of wrath. *me*; *my*: not scribal slips (*Bn*) but bold re-enforcements of the Dreamer as representative man, prone to all the sins. 199 The metaphor is that of 'learning' the vices as one might virtues or skills by reading from a book (*leef* = folium). 201 Weyhill, near Andover, Hants, had a large autumn fair, as did Winchester. 205 *Donet*: the Latin grammar of Donatus (C4th). Having learnt to 'read' in the book of fraud (199–200), he advances to the subtler lessons in deception. 206–14 Greed racked or stretched the cloth in a frame, lengthening but also weakening it; his wife spun her yarn loosely, making it easier to rack, then used a pound weight of 1¼ lbs, paying the spinners for only 1 lb. worth of wool. Greed's own steelyard weighed accurately, but the device was banned because thought open to fraudulent use, and only the balance (= scales) was permitted. Deut 25: 14–15 specifically forbids false weights and measures and prescribes true ones. 216–21 Thin ale sold at one penny a gallon, thick ale (the best) at fourpence. By bringing it in by cupfuls from her 'chamber' Rose could mix both secretly and sell the mixture at the higher price, the customers having already sampled only the best ale. 227 Bromholm Priory, near Walsingham (Pr 54 (C)), had a relic of the true cross, to which Greed will pray for release from his *dette* (of sin). 231 *restitucion*: with Greed's failure to understand the term, cf. Envy's with 'sorrow' at 126 above. Both failures symbolize spiritual obtuseness. 235 *Northfolk*: i.e. he knows *no* French (*Bn*), 'Norfolk' being so remote from the capital that knowledge of French was not to be expected there. This, the above reference and his oath at 224 imply he is from Norfolk, whose people had a reputation for parsimoniousness. 236–48 *usurie*: see II 87, 176 (C); highly developed in Lombardy where economic prosperity made surplus cash available (Gilchrist, p. 93); C IV 194 specifies the Lombards of Lucca as living 'by lone as Iewes'. Either usury or coin-clipping is called a horrible crime in a Commons petition of 1376 (*Rot. Parl* 2: 332). 240 Greed lends for love of money itself (the 'cross' on the coins; see Poole, pls 32, 34) and not for charity (the cross of Christ which, ironically, he will pray to, 228 above; cf. amplification of the image in XV 538–46). Greed's aim is for the borrower to lose his pledged security by failure to pay on the day assigned. 243–4 He lends *goods* and buys them back at less than true value to conceal the interest charged (*Bn*); cf. *derne usurie* II 76 (C). 246 *lese*: i.e. in interest. 247–8 *Lumbardes lettres*: bills of exchange used by Lombard bankers by which money due in Rome (to the papal exchequer) was paid in England and the corresponding sum disbursed in Rome on production of the credit-note. Greed presumably doctored the bills and paid in less at Rome than he got in England, keeping the difference for himself. 249 *mayntenaunce*: Greed bought the 'protection' of lords, or less probably, lent them money to enable them to maintain their position. 251–2 *mercer*: the knight might have to forfeit clothes laid in pledge or sell back those bought by feigned sale (*Bn*). *gloves*: a typical gift-offering made to the master of a craft on becoming apprenticed. 275 *Sauter glose*: the *Glossa ordinaria* interprets these verses to mean that God will not compromise his truth by letting sin pass unpunished, but demands satisfaction from the sinner in the form of mercy shown to others. 284*a*: found in this form as a C14th preaching commonplace, in Holcot, John of Grimestone and the *Fasciculus morum* (Wenzel, in Alford, *Companion*, p. 156). 305–6 *pepir ... fenelseed*: could be chewed, possibly, without breaking the fasting rule. 312–13 *Clarice*; *Pernele*: prostitutes (Cock's Lane was a haunt of theirs). *Pridie*: 'on the day before', a phrase occurring at a solemn moment in the consecration prayer, was the point in the mass at which a priest who had forgotten the bread and wine had to recommence (*Bn*); hence the name may mean 'incompetent priest'. 320–36 *Clement; Hikke*: the parties to the barter (the 'new fair'), they ask the chapmen to assess the value of cloak and hood. Helped by an umpire, Robin, they make the exchange, Clement paying the agreed difference in value with a drink for all three. Whoever has second thoughts is to pay a fine of a gallon of ale. 339–42 *evensong*; *Paternoster*: point up Glutton's failure in his religious duty (cf. 395 below). 360 *accidie*: from the Latin technical name for the sin of sloth, *accidia*, to which gluttony, and esp. over-drinking was held to lead. 369–71 These are the 'great oaths' that accompanied Gloton at 307. Swearing is traditionally rebuked by the preachers as one of the 'sins of the tavern' (cf. Chaucer, *PardT* (CT VI. 629–60)). 372 *soper*: the last meal of the day: *nones*: the meal midway between breakfast and supper. On medieval meals, see Bennett, *Life*, pp. 234–7. 391 'Bless me father, for I have sinned': the words with which the penitent began his confession. 396 *rymes*: this (earliest) vernacular reference presupposes the existence of ballads about Robin Hood (see Sargent and Kittredge, no. 117). The Earl of Chester (1172–1232): another popular hero; Sloth was presumably familiar with taverns, where such ballads were recited. 406 *feble ... fettred*: two of the seven corporal works of mercy; see Mt 25: 36. 412 *Freres*: implying that they would not mind Sloth's putting in a token appearance before the end of mass, whereas his parish priest would rebuke such laxity as grave sin. 415 *twyes*: i.e. not even once a year, as he was canonically obliged to do. 419 *Beati ...* : both Psalms describe the kind of conduct required for salvation. 422 *Canoun*: ?the *Corpus iuris canonici*, the official body of papal decretals determining points of canon law; *Decretals*: perhaps the *Decretum* of Gratian (1140) (AlfG *s.v. Canoun*, takes them the other way round) or a general name for a collection of papal decrees (AlfG *s.v.*). The passage may allude to the poor quality of priests ordained after the Black Death. 433 *lured*: the hawk's lure was usually 'a bundle of leather and feathers resembling a bird' (*MED s.v.*). Sometimes it had a piece of meat attached, and Sloth may mean by *ligge &c* 'unless there is something in it for me.' **443** *Vigilate*: may allude to such passages as Mk 13: 33–7, 14: 38, I Cor 16: 13, I Pet 5: 8, where it occurs after the text at 184 above; see Alf*Q s.v.* **451** Sloth vows devotion on Sunday, as Lechery had for Saturday (73), Glutton for Friday (383). **453–5** *matyns*: at dawn, followed by mass. He will not drink between midday and evensong at 3 p.m. **460** *Rode*: formerly on Rood Eye (Cross Island) in the Dee at Chester. **461** *seken truthe*: Sloth's acceptance of Reason's injunction at 57 closes the confessions and states the major new theme of 'pilgrimage' as inward conversion or change of heart. **462–77** A transition from confession to absolution. Robert is not 'an eighth sin' or 'a generic name for a slothful waster' (*Bn*), but sums up all sinners as those who are 'in debt' to God: all have 'stolen' like the thief Lucifer (477) and must beg mercy from the crucified Saviour. **473**'s echo of 61 links Robert with the Human Will of which all the sins are expressions: Robert 'is' Wille, humanity 'in debt' and totally dependent on divine mercy. **466** *Dysmas*: the penitent thief's name, as given in the apocryphal Gospel of Nicodemus (*GNico*). **468** Having *no* means of satisfaction, he depends on God's mercy, like the creditors in Lk 7: 42 (*Bn*). **475** *Penitencia*: specifically sacramental penance, which must accompany man through his earthly life. The staff image also points to the notion of 'pilgrimage' as 'satisfaction for sin' (510), the part of penance equated with 'Dobest' by Patience at XIV 2, a first recapitulation of this scene (with 472–7 cf. XIII 450–60). **478ff.** The liturgical echoes, 'in particular the services of Holy Week' (*Bn*), have the effect of 'locating' the Sins' repentance in the season of Lent and 'orientating' it towards Easter, the climax of the Church's year, when the cycle of redemption begun at Christmas is completed (also the time of compulsory confession before the Easter communion). The passage recapitulating this scene in XIX is specifically set towards the end of Lent (XIX 370–98). **487a** Genesis describes the creation of the first man, John the 'new creation' of man through a life of charity (cf. Holy Church at I 85–91, 148ff.). **488** *oure sute*: plays on the senses 'in our cause, action-at-law' (*Bn*) 'in pursuit of us' and 'in our fleshly form'. Both chivalric and legal meanings are apposite to Christ's encounter with Lucifer in XVIII, esp. 349–350a, 368, 401, and the metaphor of Christ's incarnation as a 'disguise' begins at XVIII 23–5 and is explicit at XVIII 358. **488–501a** are recapitulated in XVIII 36–63, 324–6 and XIX 157–60. **489** Christ's death occurred at 3 p.m. according to the Synoptic Gospels, and the phrase for this, *nona hora* 'ninth hour', later took on the meaning *noon* 'midday'. But *ful tyme* may also suggest, anticipating XVI 93, the death of Christ as balancing his conception, 'at the proper, appointed time/in the fullness of time'. **490–1** The somewhat elliptical thought seems to be that it was not the divine nature of Christ that suffered crucifixion (because it could not) but the human nature (*oure secte*) united with it in the person of Christ. *it ladde*: i.e. Christ led it away (from damnation), but also it led (or carried) the divine nature, as his 'capul that highte *Caro* [human nature]' (XVII 108). **491a** St Paul's quotation from Ps 67: 19, sung as an antiphon on Ascension Day. It alludes to the belief (enshrined in the 5th clause of the Apostles' Creed, and based on I Pet 3: 19 and early tradition) that Christ descended into the underworld and released the souls of the just from Limbo. The theme proposed here in a prayer is enacted as vision–narrative in XVIII 407. **492** *sonne . . . sight*: the primary reference is to the 'darkening of the sun' from the sixth to the ninth hour during the crucifixion of Christ (Lk 23: 45); but L's image is that of the sun, the eye of heaven, becoming temporarily blind. For full discussion, see Sch, 'Crucifixion', pp. 185–8. The image 'foreshadows' the saving power of the eucharist, and may show influence from the legend of the pelican reviving its young with blood from its breast (*Pe*). But more probably, it relies on the notion of the cross as made from the Tree of Life (in Genesis 2: 3) and placed above Adam's grave, into which the blood of Christ trickled. For a visual representation, see Schiller 2: pl. 479. **493–4** *mydday*: the time of this meal, 'when most light is', becomes that at which the patriarchs in the 'darkness' of hell receive the saving effects of Christ's sacrificial blood, freshly shed. **494a** *Populus . . .*: this Isaian quotation from the lesson of the Monday in the fourth week of Advent, here linked with the narrative of the Harrowing of Hell deriving from (*GNico*), is repeated in the account of that event in XVIII 324. **495–6** *lepe . . . blewe*: Christ is envisaged as lightning (Daniel's vision, Dan 7: 10) and storm-wind; his *birth* as 'light of light' (Nicene Creed, and cf. Jn 1: 5) is made known to the dead after his *death*. Ideas of divine love 'leaping' from heaven and of its arrival on earth as the descent of light are associated at XII 140, 153, *qq.v.* **498** *synful Marie*: i.e. Mary Magdalen, 'out of whom he had cast seven devils' (Mk 16: 9). The reference is to Jn 20: 14, recounted in XIX 157–62. **499a** *Non veni . . .* L's point is that the resurrected Christ by *first* appearing to the Mary who was the type of sinners (see X 421) and not to (the Blessed) Mary, the type of holiness, provided special comfort for sinners. **501** *armes*: the first use of the great structural metaphor of chivalric action to describe the incarnation and its climax, the crucifixion and resurrection; cf. XVIII 22–6. **504** Christ is man's *brother* through the human nature he had (cf. XI 199–203, XVIII 377). The term *fader* seems unsuited to God the Son; but if *with* in 487, 488 above is taken literally, it seems that Christ *qua* divine is being thought of as of one nature with his Father and so (somewhat confusingly) identical in person with him. In L's thought it is 'God' simply who becomes man (compare XVIII 221 with XVIII 217), and so an extreme theological precision is not to be expected in the context of an extended poetic metaphor. **507** *Deus . . .*: Ps 70, esp. 1, 5, 14 is a hymn of hope in God. Though the horn image could be from the Easter *Exultet* (*Bn*) the phrase *horn of salvation* is the more likely source (in Ps 17: 3, the *next* verse of which appears in the mass after the priest's communion, just after the words *sperabo in eum*; see Burrow, 'Action', p. 84). 508 *Beati* . . . : a verse which is the 'breath of (spiritual) life' to the man whose hope is restored through the forgiveness of sin. 514 *beestes*: perhaps suggested by *iumenta 509a* above; they are like lost sheep (cf. Mt 9: 36, Ps 77: 52–3). 515–31 This pilgrim is a type figure who has been to nearly all the shrines and brought back stamped pewter ampullae from Canterbury (Jusserand, p. 338); souvenirs of the relics at St Francis's shrine in Assisi; shells commemorating a miracle of St James (see Anderson, pl. 60); patterns of cross and (St Peter's) keys from the Holy Land and Rome respectively; a copy of the cloth image of Christ's face supposedly taken by Veronica when she wiped it on the way to Calvary, also kept at Rome (see Anderson, pl. 38, for the scene). 527 *Babiloyne*: near Cairo, where 'a faire churche of oure lady' (*Mandeville's Travels* (ed. P. Hamelins, EETS OS 153 (1919), p. 21)) commemorated the Flight into Egypt. 528 *Armonye*: Mt Ararat, where Noah's ark had rested and supposedly did still; *Alisaundre*: where St Catherine was martyred. 542 *fourty wynter*: 'many a long year' (*Bn*); at VI 83 Piers is 'old and hoor'. 547–8 The ascription to Truth of the ordinary 'secular' crafts here is recapitulated in XIX 239–57 in Grace's actual distribution of graces and skills. 552 *hire . . . even*: as commanded in Lev 19: 13, with some allusion to the parable of the vineyard (Mt 20: 8). Figuratively, the sense is that, since virtue is its own reward, payment is immediate. 558 *Seint Thomas shryne*: pilgrims' offerings had made it a veritable treasure-house (despoiled at the Reformation). 563–5 allude to Christ's summary of the Old Law (Mt 22: 37–9) run together with 7: 12, recalling Deut 6: 5, Lev 19: 18. 567ff. 'Honour thy father and thy mother', the fourth commandment (Ex 20: 12); 570, the second; 573–4, the ninth and tenth; 577, the seventh and fifth (the sins they forbid, theft and murder, are to be passed on the left: cf. II 5–8 (C)); 579, the third; 580–4, the eighth, alluding to the perils of bribery leading to perjury (*Bn*). 585–608 Observing the commandments of the Old Law prepares the soul for Christianity; God's mercy is shown to those who show it (Ex 20: 6) (*Bn*), a teaching restated in the fifth petition of the Lord's prayer. The castle is the tower of Truth glimpsed at Pr 14. The image is possibly derived from Robert Grosseteste's *Chasteau d'Amour*; the motif is discussed in Cornelius, 589: alludes to the opening of the Athanasian Creed: faith (in Christ and his Church) is necessary for salvation. 601–4 repentance or conversion (*Amende-yow*) obtains the grace through which alone holiness/heaven can be achieved. 606–8: alludes to Col 3: 14 (*charitatem . . . vinculum perfectionis*), Mt 18: 3 (*nisi . . . efficiamini sicut parvuli*, quoted after XV 149). 606 echoes I 163–4 and refers to the indwelling of God's spirit in the Christian. 607: in the context the image of a chain seems to suggest '(loving) servitude' rather than a 'chain of office'. 609–17 stress the new peril of *spiritual* pride as opposed to worldly pride (the Pride of Life), that may threaten a Christian who 'does well', and the continuing need for humble dependence on God's grace. 615: time spent in purgatory making reparation for sin. 618–24 *seven sustren*: the seven virtues which are remedies against (in order) the Deadly Sins of Gluttony (and Sloth), Pride, Envy, Lechery, Wrath, Avarice. 632 The wafer-seller anticipates (the more receptive) Haukyn in XIII 227; they were of ill-repute (*Bn*). 635 *Mercy*: a moat in the castle allegory of 586 (cf. the moat of 'religious tears' in XIX 380–3, which recapitulates this image but also stands as its correlative: mercy is experienced through contrition), is now seen as a heavenly intermediary, the Blessed Virgin Mary, obliquely referred to by her characterizing quality, as God has been referred to as 'Truth'. 639–41 Linking pardoner with prostitute (*suster*, a euphemism here for 'concubine'), underlines the low view L had of the former's profession.

Passus VI

4 *half acre*: the average area of one strip in the open-field system of ploughing (*Pe*). 7 *scleyre*: the veil covering head and chin worn by ladies of rank (Poole, pl. 108). 10–12 *silk and sandel*: the embroidery done by English ladies was thought the best in Europe; see Boase in Poole, 508–9 and pl. 107a (early C14th). 16 *comaundeth Truthe*: alludes to Mt 25: 63, 'Naked, and you covered me' (one of the corporal works of mercy). 21 On conceptions of the knight in contemporary literature, see Mann, pp. 106–15; and on the 'idea' of chivalry, Keen, *Chivalry*, pp. 1–7. 30 *bores; bukkes*: beasts of the warren like foxes and hares could be hunted only by manorial lords, but the peasants could hunt deer ('beast of the forest') over 'warren-land' (Bennett, *Life*, p. 94). 34 *trouthe*: a solemn word from a knight, whose duty is *to serven truthe evere* (see I 94–104 on the duties of knights). The two words are of identical etymological origin and closely associated in the poem. 38 *tene*: a knight could *tene* his tenants by tallage (arbitrary rates of rent), heriot (a customary claim on the best chattel of a dead tenant) and amerciaments (discretionary fines) (*Bn*). For the wordplay on *tene*, see Sch, *Clerkly Maker*, pp. 130–1. 43 *one yeres ende*: earthly privilege, such as rank, is like a lease with a fixed date, the end of one's life. 47a *Amice . . .* : the text applies only obliquely to the relation between knight and bondman, but more exactly if read in the light of Js 2: 6 (on not oppressing the poor). The knight's avowal *by Seint Jame* (55) is appropriate in context. 48–9 *charnel*: the vault under the church for bones brought to light when a graveyard was dug over for new burials. The notion here derives from St Ambrose, and was widely used by preachers in the period (see Fletcher, pp. 350–4). 57 *apparaille*: Piers's pilgrim garb is no special dress but his ordinary working clothes; his pilgrimage is to be not a journey but a way of life (cf. IV 126 (C) above). 62 *busshel*: 8 gallons dry measure, the amount of seed required to sow a half-acre. 63–4 imply a literal pilgrimage for a literal pardon; but 102–4

make clear that Piers understands by 'pilgrimage' a life of labour performed in charity, so this first reference, too, may be figurative. 75–6a *Deleantur . . . scribantur*: closely echoed by Apoc 3: 5, and found as early as Ex 32: 32–3 (cf. also Dan 7: 10). 76 *tithe*: not accepted by the Church from income earned immorally (cf. V 264–8 above). L seems certain about the fate of such characters, whose 'sin's not accidental, but a trade'. 77 *good aventure* 'by good luck': ironic since they escape paying tithes only at peril to their souls (*Pe*). The sense of 77 may be 'they have not yet felt God's wrath; may they repent (before they do).' 86 *In . . . Amen*: the standard formula in making a will; this was usual before a pilgrimage (*Bn*) but here the action is equally apt if Piers is preparing for death. 87–90 Piers bequeathes his soul to God who made it, alluding perhaps to the last petition of the Paternoster, and the Creed article on Christ as judge of living and dead. 90 *rental*: a register of rent due from tenant to landlord; the 'record' believed in is the Creed, with its final clauses promising forgiveness, resurrection and eternal life. 91–5 Piers paid his parish priest (*he* 92) tithe from his corn and profit arising from his trades (*catel* V 547–8). As Truth's servant, he paid promptly, like his master (93 echoes V 551) and so now trusts in Truth's final repayment. He hopes to be remembered in the *Memento* prayer for the faithful departed, in the canon of the mass. While his *faith* is not in question, Piers clearly relies also on his works to support his claim to salvation, in accordance with Js 2: 24. 99 *borwed*: alludes to Deut 24: 12–13 (*Bn*); cf. V 551–2 (C) above, and contrast Sloth at V 423–6. 100 *residue*: the third of the legacy remaining after the widow had received one-third and divided the other among the children. *Rode*: the wooden Rood of Christ crowned in Lucca. 103 *plowpote*: a stick with pointed or forked end (see fol. 6 in Hassall (*Ka*, p. 447)). This second allegorical pilgrim's staff (cf. V 475) concretely symbolizes Piers's spiritual intention to labour for his fellow-Christians. The scene is recapitulated in XIX 262–3, which echo these lines. 107 *balkes*: earth thrown up by the plough's action, which became weed-filled and needed digging over. 113 *oversen*: Piers's role is that of overseer, 'reeve' (*Bn*), 'head-harvest-man' (*Sk*). 116 *How trolly lolly*: recalls the song of the bad workmen in Pr 226. 117 *pure tene*: the righteous anger, called *ira per zelum* by Gregory the Great (*Moralia*, ch. 45, in *PL* 75: 726), which was found in Christ (*ST* II, 2, 158: 2; III, 15: 9). The phrase recurs at VII 115, XVI 86, both referring to Piers. 122 *legges aliry*: 'the calf against the back of the thigh, so that it appears to be cut off' (*Bn*; cf. 124, which indicates their pretence of having lost a limb). 131 *hyne . . . warne*: Piers's rôle here in society is recapitulated at XIX 260, where he is made *reve* of the Christian *societas*, the Church. 133–8 mirrors social conditions after the Black Death had caused a scarcity of labour leading to huge rises in workmen's wages and inducing some not to work at all (see Ziegler, ch. 15; McKisack, pp. 331–42), despite the high incidence of crop failure and consequent scarcity of food in the years

1350–75, on which see Frank, 'Agricultural Crisis'. **145** *ancres*: lived enclosed in anchorholds, sometimes attached to churches; *heremites*: lived in solitary places such as forests. Both depended on the charitable support of laypeople for their simple bodily needs. **147** *that han cloistres*: i.e. religious with responsibility for the upkeep of conventual buildings. **148** *Robert Renaboute*: probably a 'wandering hermit' (*Bn*) as in Pr 3; cf. 187 below. **151** *unresonable Religion*: a 'religious' way of life intrinsically lacking in rational proportion (Alford, 'Idea', p. 214); recapitulated by Conscience at XX 264–7. **152** *Wastoure*: 'destroyer', 'despoiler' rather than 'spendthrift' as in *Wynnere and Wastoure*. **154** *Bretoner*: had a reputation for boastfulness (cf. alliterative *Morte Arthure* 1348). **164** *Curteisly*: in accordance with contemporary ideals of knighthood (cf. 33 above, Chaucer, *GP* (*CT* I. 70–1)). **182** *benes and bren*: used to feed horses (193); cf. 282, 302 below. **212–17** *wisdom*: Hunger's practical solution is to feed the (able-bodied but idle) beggars with food so unattractive they will become convinced it is better to work. **221–21a** St Paul sees concern for one's neighbour as commanded by Christ (hence the Bx reading; see Apparatus, and Textual Commentary *ad loc.*); but the ZAC reading makes such concern part of *natural* law. In 207 Piers sees all men as his brothers because Christ *died* for all, here (it is implied) because God *created* all. The 'law of Christ' (Gal 6: 2), seen in his epitome of the commandments (Mt 22: 37–40), is the 'eternal law' in which 'natural law is contained' (*ST* I, 2, 71: 6). Gal 6: 2 refers in context to putting up with one another's faults; here it is applied to sharing one's neighbour's material burdens. **225a** *Michi vindictam*: the OT text is present here partly through the influence of Gal 6: 1, which urges *not* condemning others' faults, through remembering one's own. **227a** *Facite ... iniquitatis*: the money is not 'ill-gotten' in Piers's case, but all earthly *tresor* is tainted or at best intrinsically valueless, so should be used for the good of others, the question of their 'true' desert being left to God. **231** *Genesis the geaunt*: the longest book of the Bible (excluding Psalms), which describes the 'engendering' or creation of mankind (*Bn*). **237** *mannes face*: according to tradition, the 'four living creatures' of Ezech 1: 10, Apoc 4: 7 were interpreted as symbolizing the evangelists: Matthew a man, Mark a lion, Luke an ox, John an eagle (cf. also XIX 264–8 and see Mâle, pp. 35–7). **238** *servus nequam*: from Lk, but the occurrence of *piger* in Mt 25: 26 as well as // Prov 20: 4 may have confused L's recollection of the source (*Bn*). **248** *Contemplatif ... actif*: 'ditching' and 'delving' are forms of the active life, 'travailing in prayers' of the contemplative (cf. VII 118–30). Both 'lives' involve *work* of different kinds. **249–51a** *Beati ...* : Hunger misinterprets the psalm, which says that the man who fears the Lord shall eat, i.e. that *righteousness* will be blessed with prosperity, not that *labour* as such is blessed. **269–70** Phisik's expensive clothes are either payment in kind or evidence of the large fees he charges. Hunger's attribution of most illness to excess (=

gluttony) helps to equate *hele* with the opposite virtue to gluttony, temperance, thus echoing the teaching of Holy Church at l 35–7, a doctrine recapitulated at XIX 283–390. The greed and dishonesty of Phisik meet a grim end at XX 169 (and see esp. 176–7). **277 hennes . . . wende**: on the 'hungry gap', the period of scarcity before the arrival of harvest, when the last year's supply had dwindled, see Frank, 'Crisis', pp. 89–90. **287 droghte**: that of March (cf. Chaucer, *GP (CT* I. 2)), the time for manuring the fields (*Bn*). **288 Lammesse** (Loaf-mass) *tyme*: harvest (on 1 Aug a loaf of new wheat was offered at mass). **298 neghed neer**: litotes for 'came', unless a reference to the release by merchants of wheat hoarded from the previous year (*Bn*). **302 noght werche**: hints at recognition of excess as inevitable after a long period of restricted supply. **313a** The *Distichs of Cato*: maxims in four books dating from the C4th, formed part of the grammar school course and were studied after Donatus (see V 205). **316 lawes**: the Statute of Labourers (1351), designed 'to ensure a supply of cheap labour by pegging wages [which increased by over 90% between 1340 and 1360] at pre-plague rates' (McKisack, p. 335), was much resented. Enforcement was at first successful, though 320 implies that hunger was the only effective long-term answer to peasant discontent. **320–end** The prophecy is serious, but not offered as formal prediction of disaster in five years' time. The passages *Bn* adduces to show Langland's belief in 'astronomy' only prove that contemporary astronomy was considered unreliable (XV 358–9; cf. X 209–11) though it was once a true, God-given art (XIX 243–5). **321 chaste**: seems the operative word which makes the prophecy consonant with Reason's earlier interpretation of calamities that have *already* taken place (V 13–20). **324 Saturne**: considered the malign planet linked with natural disasters like flood and drought. *Bn* ventures interpretations of 325–6 which do not really fit the enigmatic and arbitrary details: 'eclipse' seems too quotidian for the *sonne amys*, and a possible alchemical sense of *multiplied* very hard to apply to a *mayde* of unknown identity. The obscure details may be intended merely to suggest mysterious future happenings which will discipline mankind. **327** says that in the *future* God's instrument of chastisement will be not, as it was before, *deeth*, but *derthe* (the two are associated in Apoc 6: 8). The prophecy of famine can be read as a warning against the sin currently in question, avarice (and perhaps also sloth), just as the plague was interpreted at V 13–15 as a punishment specifically for pride (cf. also the warning to wasters at 130–5 above). But this is prophecy more in a Biblical sense (warning and reminder of God's presence) than in the popular sense of an exact 'prediction'.

Passus VII

1 Treuthe herde: the virtuous life of Piers becomes known to God, who sends him his reward, forgiveness of sin. 3 *a pena et a culpa*: 'from punishment and from guilt'. In theory, guilt was forgiven in sacramental confession and only canonical temporal punishment (e.g. fasting) could be remitted through a pardon. If incomplete, it might have to be completed in purgatory. But in practice it was widely believed that a papal pardon obtained, say, through pilgrimage, absolved from both punishment and guilt. It was therefore prudent to go on pilgrimage towards the end of one's life. But Truth's 'pardon' is granted not for a specific penitential act but for a *life* lived in 'truth' and 'love'. 18–22 *margyne*: i.e. 'trade was dangerous for the soul' (*Bn*); but III 257–8 show that L condemns the merchants only for impiety and false swearing (20–2), which he doubtless thought a special danger of their trade. Line 19 should be read ironically (in the light of 173ff.): 'only an ideal pope would not, the actual pope (probably) would'. 23ff. *secret seel*: the privately sealed letter allows the merchants a symbolic 'let-out' in the use of their profits for socially beneficial works, without sanctioning their underhand practices. More specifically, merchants, to make satisfaction for *dishonest* trading, should use (legitimately earned) profits for charitable ends. On these charitable works, see Thomson, and Rosenthal. 42–3 urges another class of men who have misused their skill to use the same skill now to make amends (compare 50 with 34): lawyers should give their services free to the helpless and be paid by the Crown (or perhaps by God). Aquinas (*ST* II, 2, 71: 2) sees this as an act of mercy. The source of 43*a* is probably a commentary on Ecclus 38: 2, referring to doctors, but here transferred to the legal profession (Alf*Q*, pp. 53–4). 44–59*a*: a digression on law and lawyers following from the above. The account of the pardon resumes at 60, after which begins a digression on false beggars, 71–97. 44 *Johan*: may be less effective in context as 'common fellow' (*MED s.v. Jon*, (b)) than as a female name; however, the offence of prostitution was tried in the Church's courts, not before justice and jurors, and some more complicated proceeding involving a woman may be in question. 52 *wit*: to class 'knowledge', 'intelligence' as an elemental gift of God is to argue analogically that it belongs to men in common and cannot be bought or sold (cf. XIII 151). 67 Such beggars are guilty of *false* 'suggestion' (a legal notion); cf. 65, AlfG *s.v.* 73–3*a Stories*: the *historiae* of the *Historia scholastica* by Peter Comestor (d. 1179), a re-telling of sacred history (ed. *PL* 148: 1049–7722; and see Daly). Together with Cato, it provides a prudent, 'this-worldly' view of charity as alms. The quotation is a variant of a common proverb found in penitential and canonical sources (see Alf*Q s.v.*). 75*a*: not from Gregory: traced to Jerome's Commentary on Eccl 11: 6 (*PL* 23: 1103) (*Bn*), but attributed by Richard Maidstone to Isidore of Seville (Alf*Q s.v.*) and used in the anti-mendicant controversy (Scase, pp. 72–3), it evidently has no direct bearing on the friars here. 78 *reste*: in heaven, by charitable acts which shorten his time in purgatory. 81 *usure*: has a paradoxically favourable sense here, like *mede* at III 224–5 (contrast III 240); generosity to beggars is an investing of the wealth given by God, who will take the interest but restore it to him in heaven (cf. Prov 19: 17 (*Bn*)). 84*a*: from Jerome's Epistle 125 (*PL* 23: 1085), logically the *Book* of 83, but the latter looks forward to the Biblical source of 86*a* (Psalms). 85–6 *solas*: from the accounts of God's direct provision for the saints' necessities (see XV 269ff.). Ps 36, one of total trust in God, prohibits begging only by implication: 'the Lord . . . will not forsake his saints' (verse 28); cf. XI 277. 101–4 *myschief . . . purgatorie*: it is not the suffering of the handicapped but the patience and humility they bear it with that wins God's favour. On *suffraunce* as the 'sovereign' virtue, see also XI 378. 110–14 The lines from the Athanasian Creed echo Mt 25: 46; this concludes a long passage (verses 31ff.) on the Last Judgement which mentions various forms of 'doing well', specifically the corporal works of mercy. Truth's words do no more than ratify Holy Church's teaching at I 128–33; but the priest's failure to recognize this divine promise of salvation/threat of damnation as a true pardon is a measure of the spiritual decay into which L judges the actual institutional Church of his day to have fallen. 112–13 *Do wel . . . Do yvel*: too general to need specific sources, but see Ps 33: 15, Is 1: 16–17, which both preface the command to do (or learn to do) good (or well) with one to turn from (doing) evil. 115 Earlier interpretations of the tearing of the pardon are surveyed by Frank, *Scheme*, pp. 28–9, who in 'Pardon Scene' convincingly interprets the tearing as a symbolic act of accepting the content of Truth's pardon while rejecting (inefficacious) paper pardons. For other views, cf. Woolf, 'Tearing'; Schroeder; Adams, 'Pardon', and for a subtle and suggestive reading of the whole controversial scene Simpson, *Introduction*, pp. 71–88. 116–17 Ps 22 is one of faith in God's support and *mercy* (= ultimate forgiveness, 'pardon'). See XIII 291 (C) below. 120 *plough*: 'striving', 'concern' recalls the image of penance as the pilgrim's staff at V 475. But Piers does not *abandon* ploughing for 'travaillynge in preieres', active for contemplative life (VI 247–8); *cessen* 118 taken with *so harde* and *so bisy* 119 must mean 'desist (for a time)' rather than 'renounce (permanently)'. Piers's later function may be primarily spiritual, but the hyperbolic language of 120–30 need not mean he is now choosing to be a hermit, only that he is giving priority to prayer over work. Piers does not take prayer and penance as the *bona* (*opera*) of the pardon (*Bn*): prayer was normally contrasted with works, and what 'works' are is suggested by the context of the Matthean discourse from which the 'pardon' text comes, esp. the use of one's gifts (Parable of the Talents, 14–30) and the corporal works of mercy (35–40). Piers is resolving to replace agricultural work as his main activity in life with prayer and penance, free from anxious preoccupation with more than he needs (cf. 126–7). His attitude is not one of indifference to these needs, which would be irresponsible, but of detachment from worldly cares: the *foweles* of 129 are like the lark of XII 261–4 and the poor man of XIV 317, *absque sollicitudine felix* 'blessed withouten bisynesse'. **136–7** *divinour . . . Dixit*: the priest taxes Piers with presumptuousness in being so confident, though a mere ploughman, about the meaning of Scripture, like a skilled exegete. *Lewed* has ironic bite, since Piers understands the pardon's spiritual meaning better than the *lered* priest who can construe its Latin (106). The ploughman's 'knowledge' of the Latin Bible has a symbolic not a realistic significance (see further Sch, *Clerkly Maker*, pp. 85–8). **140–1** *thorugh hir wordes*: for naturalistic waking of the Dreamer by noise *within* the dream, cf. *Parliament of Fowls* 693–5. *south*: 'so it is almost noon' (*Bn*), some six hours having elapsed from the 'inner time' of dawn (Pr 13) at the start of the first vision to the 'outer time' of his waking, recalled at the start of the last vision (XX 4). **144–201** Both 'epilogue' to the first and prologue to the poem's second main section. Its two themes are the validity of dreams (149–67) and the validity of pardons (174–95). It concludes by suggesting that dreams can be true and by declaring that the only true pardon is Truth's. **146** *pencif in herte*: suggests love-melancholy, which turns to *pure joye* the next time the Dreamer meets Piers (XVI 18–20), in a *love-dreem*. **148** *two propre wordes*: presumably *Dixit insipiens* 136. **150–3** L again sets one weighty authority against another, as at 74–5. 'Caton' regularly stands for mundane prudence as opposed to (sometimes imprudent) Christian charity and faith. **154** *Nabugodonosor*: the dream is his (Dan 2: 36ff.), but it is his ?son Baltasar (Belshazzar) who 'lees the lordshipe' (Dan 5: 30–1). **162–4** Not what the Bible says (*Sk*); but L may be reading into Gen 37: 11 ('but his father considered [the dream] with himself') the implication that Jacob believed it might come true. **170** *demed*: although the subject could be *the preest* 169, with *Dowel* being the object, it probably has an implied subject *I*, given the sense of 172–3 ('Dowel surpasses papal pardons'). **171** *Biennals*; *triennals*: masses said for the repose of a person's soul for a period of two/three years after his death. *lettres*: to license the preaching of indulgences (*Bn*). **174–9** appear 'orthodox enough' (*Bn*), but are not without irony. L affirms the Pope's power to grant salvation to men *without* penance on their part, and supports this with an appeal to Christ's words entrusting the 'power of the keys' to St Peter. But his protestation of belief at 177 seems ironic in an almost 'Chaucerian' way (cf. *GP* (*CT* I. 661)) since he then affirms that pardon causes souls to be saved (only when linked) *with* penance and prayer (180–1 sounds tongue-in-cheek). His true aim, then, would seem to be to *deny* the view of the papal plenitude of power first affirmed; if that makes L 'unorthodox', such he is. **192–3** *provincial*: head of all the houses of a religious order in a particular area or province, who could admit a lay person to all the privileges of the order in his province (see also III 63 (C)). *fraternite*: an offer also made to the unstable Contrition by Friar Flatterer (XX 368) and accepted by him, recapitulating in the final scene of (what the C-text calls) the *Vita* the final scene of the *Visio*. **194 Dowel**: here personifies the good deeds of the man facing judgement; but at 200 is more suggestive of Christ the king speaking for the just (Mt 25: 31ff., *q.v.*). A third sense, 'a way of life in which to do good deeds', is introduced in VIII 13.

Passus VIII

1–5 That VIII is a new *prologue* to the poem's second major part is confirmed by the echoes in 2, 1 of Pr 1, 3 (season, clothing). But now the Dreamer wanders not to 'hear wonders', but to 'seek Dowel'. *russet*: rough, homespun woollen garb worn by shepherds (*Sk*), the *shroudes* of Pr 2. **9 Maistres of the Menours**: the Franciscan order produced such leading C14th theologians as Scotus and Ockham; see Courtenay, pp. 66–9, 185–90, 193–218. **20–6 as a clerc**: Will answers in scholastic style with a (foreshortened) syllogistic argument: a two-part major premiss, an assertoric proposition (from Scripture = statement of fact) and an apodictic proposition (*whoso . . . yvele*, necessarily true); an apodictic minor premiss (*Dowel . . . togideres*); a conclusion. The latter is only partly true; indeed Dowel cannot always be with the friars, but *if* 'Dowel' is incompatible with sinning, and *if* even the just sins, Dowel cannot be 'at home' with any man – i.e. is no man (cf. 5). **21 Sepcies . . . iustus**: cf. also Eccl 7: 21, 8.12. Line 24 line recalls Boethius, *De consolatione Philosophiae* IV, pr. ii: 'But for to mowen don yvel and felonye ne mai nat ben referrid to good' (Chaucer's *Boece* IV, pr. ii, lines 247–9). **29 forbisne**: ultimately from Augustine's Sermo 75, ch. 3 (*PL* 5: 475) (*Sk*). This allegory of the Church as a ship is developed from Mt 14: 24–33 (Christ's stilling of the storm) in the light of I Pet 3: 20–1. The application of the 'boat' to the friars themselves is attacked in a Wycliffite sermon on Mt 24 (*Pe*); but L develops his image in a way that seems independent and original here. **30ff. Lat brynge**: the friar's exemplum (an illustrative story) here functions in the manner of a scholastic *distinctio*: he accepts the truth of Will's major premiss, but distinguishes the *just* man's sins as venial, not mortal, and so not contrary to Dowel. Though orthodox, he appears not to give due weight to the need to avoid venial sin, the links between venial and mortal, and the danger (in fighting *wanhope*, an aspect of *accidia*) of falling into spiritual complacency (cf. *sleuthe* 52). L appears to find laxism characteristic of the friars. The inevitability of falling into sin seems, nonetheless, to be a cardinal feature of L's thought, as at XIV 322–3 and (by implication) in XII 277–8, a passage correlative to VIII 20–1. **53–4** The notion of free-will in animals may come from the C12th Gandulph of Bologna (Sch, 'Philosophy', pp 145–9). The thought is close to *De consolatione Philosophiae* IV, pr. ii; at XI 334ff. the unerring instinct displayed by animals and their apparent 'reason' are contrasted with the unreason of fallen man. **57 Will**

cannot grasp the argument or feel it on the pulses. It is less that the friar's reasoning is hard than that it fails to meet Will's *likyng* or taste, a point he makes at 111 below, and is rebuked by Anima for making again at XV 49ff. See also I 138 (C) above. 70 *muche*: cf. *Longe Wille* XV 152. To see an aspect of oneself personified as a double appears common in dream experience (see Freud, pp. 505–6), and is a well-known pathological phenomenon of waking experience (autoscopy), but is not elsewhere found in dream-vision literature. 74 *Thought*: the mind as knowing power, as in XV 25, translating *Mens*, and in Chaucer's *House of Fame* II. 523, translating Dante's *mente* 'mental power, mind' in *Inf.* II. 7–9; (see Sch, 'Philosophy' 151 and n. 99). 75 *seven yeer*: probably an indefinite period of time, as at IV 86, V 204, or (possibly) here the period from the beginning of the age of reason (age 7) to that of commencement of university studies (around 14), and so covering the years of his schooling. 78–107 Dowel is the virtuous secular life; Dobet the life of the devout clergy; Dobest that of the conscientious episcopacy. For discussion, see Kean, 'Justice', pp. 79–84. 90 *religion*: perhaps here covers priesthood generally (*OED s.v.*, 1b) though the passage is cited by OED under 1(a) 'religious order' (see also *MED s.v.*) *rendred*: 'read aloud and expounded', not 'translated'. 93–4 misread *suffertis* as imperative and accordingly miss Paul's irony (cf. also I Cor 4: 10). 114–23 concisely dramatize the experience of a period of 'thought' terminating in 'knowledge' or 'understanding' (*OED s.v. wit*, 11). *thre daies*: either another indefinite period (see 75 (C)) or, as with the Biblical sense of 'the third day', 'the critical, decisive day' (cf. I Cor 15: 4), the encounter with Wit thus coming as the resolution of a mental crisis. The next two major time references mark the lapse of much longer periods (XI 47, XIII 3). 116 *Wit*: the knowledge derived from experience, the understanding that comes from reflection on what we sense and are (informally) told by others. Wit seems to correspond to Latin *sensus* in Anima's list of the soul's names, *the welle of alle craftes* XV 30, *q.v.*

Passus IX

2 *Kynde*: Nature's creator, *natura naturans*, not created Nature, *natura naturata*. See White, ch. 3, 'Kynde as God'. 3–4 *eyr*: probably the traditional fourth element, fire, L's 'air' being Latin *aether* 'the upper air', which he took as fiery, ?because fire rises upward (*Sk*), not the 'breath of life' of Gen 2: 7 (Goodridge), which L calls *spirit* at XV 36, 39*a* (see also Wittig, p. 217 n. 29). 6–7 The allegory of God as a lover 'wooing' the human soul was traditional (*Ancrene Wisse* in Bennett and Smithers, pp. 239–40; see Gaffney; Woolf, 'Lover-Knight'). The figure is developed as a chivalric one in XVIII 10ff, *q.v.* 7ff. *Anima*: the Latin name for the soul in its most comprehensive meaning and also in its specific sense as the life-principle of human nature (XV 24, 39) (see Sch, ' "Anima" and

"Inwit" '); here feminine less because of the noun's grammatical gender than because she is the *object* of the desire of both God and Satan (whereas in XV Anima is the *subject* governing the whole discourse of that passus). In the detailed allegory, she seems envisaged as a (royal) ward entrusted to the care of a great lord. 8 *Princeps huius mundi*: a title recalled by the Devil in the Harrowing of Hell scene (XVIII 314*a*). This peculiarly Johannine name for Satan denotes his operation through the lure of worldly delights, as emblematized in a haughty French nobleman; in XI he follows Fortune as the Pride of Life and in XX as Pride, Antichrist's bannerer. 17–22 *Constable*: 'governor or warden of a royal castle' (*MED s.v.*, 3(b)). *Inwit*: at 18 'Conscience' (*MED s.v.*, 4) though at 53 'Mind' or 'the collection of inner faculties' (*MED s.v.*, 1(a), 3(a)); see also Quirk, who equates it with the rational power generally. Since the word's common neutral, non-specific sense could expose it to a bad use, as in XIII 289 (= *MED s.v.*, 3*a*, in opposition to *outwit*), that sense is ruled out here, where Inwit is *wis* and his sons not just the senses, the (*out*)*wits*, but the right uses (of sight, speech, hearing, touch and motion). Harwood and Smith identify it with *synderesis*, while Harwood, *Belief*, p.60, emphasizes more 'the knowledge that enables people to support themselves'. But over-precision would be out of place. The term does not occur as an English equivalent of any of Anima's nine Latin names at XV 23 ff. (any more than 'soul' does) and is perhaps best regarded in a general sense as 'the rational power' (Quirk), intended for good by God but capable of going astray (its affinity with Conscience, a common contemporary synonym, is thus obvious). 35–43 *Faciamus*: important not because the person is plural (*Sk*) but because it means 'Let us *make*' (implying for L an action), in contrast with *Dixit* 32*a*, the (merely) verbal command that created the beasts. So the question of the Persons of the Trinity is not the issue. The nature of the action (*myght* 37 expressing itself in *werkmanshipe* 45) appears from the verbs *Formavit, inspiravit, aedificavit* in Gen 2: 7, 22. In 43 *with* thus signifies 'along with, in addition to', not 'by means of', and the purpose of the 'writing' analogy is that in addition to the 'slime of the earth' (= *parchemyn* in the metaphor) and his knowledge (*wit*), God required in 'forming, breathing, building' the active exertion of his power, regarded as it were instrumentally (*penne*), because man, unlike the animals, has an immortal rational soul made in God's image. 49 *Caro*: man's living body or physical nature; so at XVII 108. 53 If *Inwit* here means 'man's rational (judging) power', rather than 'conscience' in the narrower sense, it is perhaps easier to see how it can be both abused by gluttons and lacked by idiots, children and women without protectors (Sch, ' "Anima" and "Inwit" '). Yet 59, which does suggest 'conscience', is hard to reconcile with the allegory of 10–24, where Inwit's role was to *save* 'protect' (23) Anima not 'lead' (58), a function earlier given to Dobest (16). 65–6 *fordo; shoop*: to destroy reason, God's 'likeness' in man, is to uncreate the Creator's work. The juxtaposed ideas of destroying, creating and redeeming anticipate the lines against murder (XVII 274–81) as does the notion of the Creator/Redeemer withdrawing his grace from his rebellious creature. 73–4 *foure doctours*: Ambrose, Augustine, Jerome and Gregory. *Luc*: Acts 6: 1 speaks of widows (Goodridge), but an apter Scripture would be Js 1: 27, which links widows and fatherless, echoing Deut 16: 11–14. 85 *Judas felawes*: because thought collectively responsible for the death of Christ, on the basis of Mt 27: 25. L here criticizes Christians who fail to live up to their beliefs as Jews do to theirs. His knowledge of social solidarity among the Jews (on the Continent presumably) is by hearsay, since they had been expelled from England in 1290. 90–1 *Bisshopes . . . Judas*: bishops who patronize bawdy minstrels but will not feed ragged beggars are thought of as 'betraying' Christ; that Judas was the apostles' purse-keeper (Jn 13: 29), sharpens the point of the comparison. 95–8 Wit's first definition of Dowel, Dobet and Dobest, like his third and fourth (200–3, 204–7) specifies *inward* dispositions: Dowel = fear of God/keeping the Law; Dobet = fear of God out of love of God/loving friend and enemy/suffering (? = patience); Dobest = (?)contemplative withdrawal/active works of charity/humility bringing power over evil. 98a *verbo*: the alteration of Js 2: 10 *uno*, if deliberate, stresses not that one serious sin can destroy a man's state of grace but that a single idle word, however seemingly slight, can have grave effects. 108 A definition of Dowel only, as faithful marriage, an *outward* state, though reflecting an inner disposition (cf. Thought's account at VIII 81–4). This objective definition introduces the second theme of Passus IX, right and wrong sexual relations between men and women, the sustainers of the social fabric. 114, 117 *And thus*: seems to imply that L sees the existing marriage arrangements as divinely instituted, as right and good in contrast to the irregularities and disorders to be described. 118 *witnesse*: not 'present at' (whence the allusion to the Marriage at Cana, Jn 2:2 (*Sk*)), but 'bearing testimony to' the 'paradisal' quality of marriage, the allusion being to Gen 2: 18–25. Cf. the very similar thought in *Purity* 697–704, and Sch, 'Natural and Unnatural Love', pp. 119–21. 121 *Caym*: 'born during the period of penitence and fasting to which our first parents were condemned for their breach of obedience' (*Wr*), a story told in the apocryphal *Vita Adae et Evae*, of which a ME tanslation appears in Blake, pp. 109–10. The *yvel tyme* was that of Cain's conception, before the period of penance was complete. 123 *yvel ende*: alluding literally to the destruction of Cain's progeny in the Flood (Gen 6–7), and symbolically to the unrighteous in all generations, who will be overwhelmed by God's wrath, as in I Jn 3: 12, Jude 11 (*Pe*). The verbs may be preterite, but if L's *sherewes* are metaphorically Cain's kin, they could be present. 124–6 Some early Latin Christian writers (e.g. Augustine, *De civitate Dei* xv, 23) interpreted 'the sons of God' and 'the daughters of men' in Gen 6:

2, 4 as respectively Seth's offspring and Cain's. This tradition appears in Comestor's *Historia* (dealing with Gen 31) from which L probably got the idea of God's prohibition to Seth (*Sk*). Cf. Wilson, *Gawain-Poet*, pp. 88–92. **145** *Gospel*: actually Ezekiel (but distantly echoed by St John): the text affirms each individual person's responsibility for his own actions, while **152a** recognizes the influence of both heredity and upbringing in the moral development of that same individual. The *ellere* **149** may be specified as the tree on which tradition had it that Judas hanged himself (cf. I 66–8, where he is linked with Cain). **154–5** To marry for the wrong reasons is to act 'against God's will' by re-enacting the sin of the Sethites (*thei* 154), who 'imped their apples' on the Cainite 'elders'. The analogy lends force to *unkyndely* **157** and the pun on *good(e)* in **160**, which highlights the perversion of values involved in confusing virtue with wealth (on this see Sch, *Clerkly Maker*, p. 136). **161** *avaunce*: the idea of Christ as fount of nobility anticipates the account of him as the conqueror who ennobles his followers in XIX 32ff. (cf. Chaucer, *WBT* (*CT* III. 1117–18). **167** *the pestilence*: Wit's comment on the effect of the Black Death upon marriages may be compared with Reason's on the upbringing of children (V 35–6). **169** *no children*: would imply, unless *no* is pure exaggeration, that fewer children were born. Marriages and births rose after the Black Death in 1348, but by the time of the B-text the previous trend of decline had returned (Postan, p. 43, and see 167 (C)). **107–2** *Dunmowe*: in Essex, where a flitch of bacon was awarded to a couple married for a year who could swear they had never quarrelled. **179** *seculer*: not the secular clergy (*Sk*); *MED* s.v., 1(d) gives ample contemporary support for the meaning 'lay' (as opposed to clerical); L does not hold the uncanonical view that priests might marry. **181** *lymeyerd*: a twig smeared with thick glue to trap birds, with perhaps a pun on *yerde* (*OED* s.v. *yard*, 11, 'penis'; cf. the witty play on *wepene* and *wreke* in 182–3). The sentiment echoes I Cor 7: 2. **183a** The proverb is found in this form with a ME verse translation in a MS at St George's Chapel, Windsor (AlfQ, citing S. Horrall in *MS* 45 (1983) 375) and seems to have been proverbial (Walther, no. 4447); the second line appears in a couplet of John of Bridlington (*Sk*). **186** *untyme*: fasting-times or any period when either partner might not be in a state of grace. **187–8** specify the conditions for virtuous intercourse: chastity, charity and canonical wedlock. **189** *derne dede*: for a parallel to the thought, cf. *Purity* 697–700, Sch, 'Kynde Craft', 116–18. **192** *Bonum est . . .* : a somewhat negative reason for marrying, which does not seem to accord with 117–18; but L may also have been remembering Gen 2: 18, *Non est bonum esse hominem solum*, and the Pauline statement is accorded the same authority as Gen 1: 28, 2: 23–4, establishing human marriage in Eden. **196** *wasten*: the behaviour of *wastours* (cf. Pr 22) is traced back to their origins in illicit (not necessarily illegitimate) sexual intercourse. **200–end** *Dowel . . . Dobet . . . Dobest*: on these definitions, see the analysis at 95–8 (C).

Passus X

1 *Studie*: a personification of the disciplines preparatory to philosophy and theology, i.e. grammar-school education and the university study of the Liberal Arts: as an activity, married to 'knowledge'; as the knowledge itself, 'married' to Wit as the faculty of understanding. With her acerbic tone, compare Anima's criticism of the state of contemporary education at XV 370–4. **6** *frenetike ... of wittes*: the actual condition of the Dreamer at the opening of Visions 4 and 5 (XIII 1, XV 3, 10). **12** *paradis*: the Earthly Paradise was believed to be full of precious stones which 'grew'; see Gen 2: 12 for the basis of the idea, and cf. *Pearl* 73ff. **18** *card*: comb out impurities in wool and straighten the fibres for spinning with a metal instrument having the hooks of teasels attached to it. Intellectual ability will not succeed unless 'dressed' with ambitious greed. **30–50** An attack on the decline of minstrelsy (on which see Poole, pp. 605–10; Strutt, pp. 152–66; Southworth, pp. 119ff.; Sch, *Clerkly Maker*, pp. 5–11. **33** *Tobye*: the Book of Tobias (or Tobit) in the Vulgate Bible tells the story of a figure of exemplary life, a suitable model for edifying the nobility in domestic piety (see further 87–95 below). **36–7** *he*: perhaps an indirect allusion to L himself, who recounts just this story in XVIII 36ff. **44** *Munde*: a type of the coarse, unspiritual man, familiar from Chaucer's Miller (and cf. Mann, pp. 160–1). **54** *Bernard*: of Clairvaux (1090–1143), the great monastic reformer and the emblem of theological orthodoxy. The story is presumably one of the type re-told by Chaucer in *PardT*, blasphemously applied to the Persons of the Trinity. **66** This is graphically illustrated by the gluttonous Doctor at XIII 100ff. **68a** *eam* [the Ark]: glossed *caritatem* in // C IX 51a. The sense is that true charity is found amongst the humble and simple country people. *Effrata*: Bethlehem in the famous messianic prophecy of Mi 5: 2, and as the place of Christ's birth in a stable, an apt symbol of humility. **71** *questions* 'theological problems': friars who raised them in the early C14th were the Franciscan Peter Aureole and the Dominican Durandus of Saint-Pourçain (see Leff, pp. 272–9). **73** *Seint Poules*: the cross just north of the east end of old St Paul's Cathedral was used for open-air preaching; possibly alluded to at XIII 65–6. **75–84a** reflect the social and moral disintegration occasioned by the plague. Study links the cleric's *intellectual* pride with ordinary worldly pride (cf. Reason at V 13–20). Her twin themes are laymen's arrogance in theological matters (fostered by friars' preaching and influence) and the decay of the social fabric. **79** *girles*: the outbreak of plague in 1361–2 was 'known as the *mortalité des enfants*' (McKisack, p. 331) because it took a special toll of children (doubtless earlier alluded to at V 36). Children will suffer for their parents' *giltes*; cf. IX 143–4, and see Ex 20: 5). **95** A celebrated specimen of a friar of this type occurs in Chaucer's *SumT* (*CT* III. 1709–60). **96–102** A vivid glimpse of domestic life in the manor house (on which see Colvin, in

Poole, pp. 41–50; Girouard, pp. 29–80, esp. p. 30). L attacks eating in private less as an undesirable social innovation than as a practice destructive of charity (see 99). **117** *Ymaginatif*: Study's striking reference to a character who only appears at XI 408 shows L's careful planning and use of each interlocutor for a definite purpose in the task of bringing Will to know Dowel. (Ymaginatif does not in fact explain why men suffer death, but he does defend *clergye* (divine learning which teaches about God), attacked by the lay *maistres* at 115 and implicitly by Will at XI 367–73 when he rebukes Reason, as noted at 421–8.) **118–18a** 'to be wise unto sobriety': Augustine in *De baptismo contra Donatistas* attacks the 'human temptation' to wish 'to know a thing as it is in itself (*aliquid sapere quam res se habet)' (Sk)* in what seems a critique of the *kynde knowyng* Will insists on in VIII 57–8 and 110–11. **129–30** *as he wolde*: Study's stress not just on the absolute supremacy of God's will but on the need to accept it in faith may reflect Bradwardine's stand earlier in the century against Ockham's followers (see Leff, pp. 286–9). Her attack on the quest for distinctions between Dowel and Dobet implies that those who really do well do not need to ask, and that the way to *do* well is 'love' (189–90, 205–6 below). **149–50** *kenne . . . Clergie*: because Will's request is now made in *mekenesse* 'humility' Study undertakes to guide him. He has too precipitately sought *wit*, which is inseparably 'wedded' to, can only be possessed by, *study*. After a course of study, he will be able to approach *clergie* 'learning', 'wedded' to God's written word (*Scripture*). **152** *the sevene arts*: the *trivium* (grammar, rhetoric, logic: mastery of language and reasoning) and the *quadrivium* (arithmetic, geometry, astronomy, music: substantial sciences). Scripture formed part of the advanced university course for a theology degree. The seven arts are, as it were, her younger sisters. By the late C14th, the course in logic led on to further study in Aristotle's works on natural, moral and metaphysical philosophy (see Courtenay, pp. 30–66). Since theology was for those destined for holy orders, the 'clergy', the metaphor of marriage for the relationship of Clergie and Scripture (= the Bible and the Fathers) is apt. **156** *gold*: Will's improved disposition is shown in his valuing wisdom more than gold (Prov 8: 10). The 'earthly' gift of gold in XIX 88–9 stands for righteousness; but here 'gold' still pertains to Mede's world as an 'earthly (worldly) treasure' in opposition to truth, the proper object of learning (on the gold/wisdom antithesis, cf. Chaucer, *GP* (*CT* I. 297–8)). **159–69** The 'signpost allegory' here recalls Piers's directions to the pilgrims. *left half* **164**: wealth and sex as temptations to fall from the pursuit of learning (like theft and murder at V 578, or worldly pride personified in Mede at II 5) are aptly situated on this, the traditional side of weakness and evil. **171** *wroot*: i.e. wrote down; Study claims the literary skills needed to write down Scripture, not authorship of the Bible *per se*. **174** *musons*: the time and rhythm of *mensurable* music (as opposed to *immensurable*, e.g. plainchant), denoted by various signs.

But 'music' as part of the university arts course at this time was based on Boethius' *Institutio musica*, largely theoretical, though touching on the practice of the art in Bk IV (see Chadwick, pp. 84–8). **175** *poete*: 'author', 'writer', used here of Plato as of Aristotle at XII 260. **179–85** *alle kynne craftes . . . dymme . . . derker*: though Study looks weak-sighted(ly) as a result of her efforts, she is the source of the crafts (or practical skills) as well as the arts (or 'sciences'). But these pursuits affect only the physical eyes; Theology tests the inner vision, its mysteries perplexing the intellect. **186** *Theologie*: Study's disquiet about the academic subject (properly the preserve of Clergie and not quite identical with the authoritative figure of II 115, the approved teaching tradition of the Church) may reflect contemporary unease caused by the speculations of advanced thinkers like Holcot, Buckingham and Adam of Woodham and the opposition to the new 'Pelagians' by Bradwardine earlier in the century (see Leff, pp. 291–3.) **191** *oother science*: everyday practical wisdom, prudential morality, not the morality based on love taught by Theology. **210** *Geomesie*: 'divination by means of earth, dots and figures written in the ground' (*MED s.v.*); see Chaucer, *KnT* (*CT* I. 2045), and note. Its connection with geometry and astronomy seems unjustified, let alone the addition of magic; but contemporary literature frequently associates astrology, divination and various secret arts with study of the stars and plants (cf. Chaucer, *MilT* (*CT* I. 3191–7), *FranT* (*CT* V. 1117–62)). **213–14** *fibicches*: '?some kind of alchemical manipulations or tricks' (*MED s.v.*, following Quirk's derivation from *Pebichios*, an early alchemist) is supported by 214. Cf. Chaucer's *CYT* (*CT* VIII. 1391– 1425). **219** *kyndely*: belongs metrically in the a-half (= 'kindly') but also looks semantically to the b-half to form the phrase *kyndely to knowe*. **232–59** Clergie's definition of Dowel (*It* 230) is: 'to believe in God'; of Dobet, 'to live out one's belief (by acts of charity)'; of Dobest, 'to rebuke sinners' (implying the right to do so, i.e. the previous two, and perhaps though not necessarily, also, the authority of holy orders). **240a** *Deus . . .*: from the Athanasian Creed, clause 15, said at Prime on Sundays. **243** *Austyn . . . bokes*: the fifteen books of his *De Trinitate* (completed AD 417) IV, XV, 20 attacks the pride of intellectuals who mock 'the mass of Christians who live by faith alone'. Clergie argues that all must believe in the doctrine of the Trinity but none need understand it (for none can). **260–327a**: a long digressive diatribe against unworthy religious. With Clergie's strict attitude to moral criticism from clerics compare that of Lewte the layman at X 103. **266** *bosard*: 'an inferior kind of hawk, useless for falconry' (*OED s.v. buzzard* sb.l). L's figure compares the ignorant priest to a bird lacking the falcon's keen sight and training. **267** *person* (Lat *persona*): 'a holder of a parochial benefice in full possession of its rights and dues, a rector' (*OED s.v. parson*), here distinguished from the vicar (see XIX 413), acting in place of the rector, and the curate, as at XX 327: elsewhere *curatour* = 'priest-in-charge (whether curate or vicar)', a temporary paid assistant to the rector or vicar (see McKisack, pp. 302–3). **278–80 two badde preestes**: Ophni and Phinees, sons of Heli the priest, stole the sacrificial meats for themselves, rousing God's anger. When Israel was fighting the Philistines, they brought the Ark of the Covenant into the battle and were killed, and the Ark was taken. When Heli heard the news he fell backwards and broke his neck. Clergie's point is that unless priests desist from rapacity, the mere fact of their being priests will not save them from God's wrath in the end. **286 burel clerkes**: 'homespun scholars', laymen who can perhaps read (*Sk*), a meaning that fits well with the sense of 287–9. **287a Canes**: like the Ophni and Phinees example above, a warning against greed, this Isaian attack on the Jewish priesthood serves as a warning to the Christian clergy, here against sloth. Clergie's argument for the exemplary force of priestly holiness anticipates Anima's at XV 92ff. **290–1** The sentiment is in keeping with Gregory's teaching on *stabilitas mentis* (Straw, pp. 66–89), and he is an apt authority for 'the rule of religion', as the pope who sent the monk Augustine to England in 597 (*Pe*, p. 324; and see below). The exact source in Gregory (if any) is untraced, but the semi-proverbial 'As a fish without water lacks life, so does a monk without a monastery', attributed to Pope Eugenius by Gratian (*Sk*), appears in the *Legenda aurea* (*LA*), ch. 21, sect. iv, which L uses at XV 269ff. (cf. also Chaucer *GP* (*CT* I. 179–81)). **293 Morales**: Gregory's major theological work, his massive commentary on the Book of Job, the *Moralia in Job*. **300 cloistre . . . scole**: a sentiment found in L's contemporary Bishop Thomas Brinton: 'si sit vita *angelica* in terra, aut est in studio, vel in claustro' (Orsten) and in Petrus Ravennus, 'Si paradisus in hoc mundo est, in claustro vel in scholis' (Kaske, '*Paradisus*', pp. 481–3), which is closer to L. **303–5 scole . . . Religion**: an unfavourable contrast between the lax monasteries and the rigorous universities (cf. the more approving view of monks in V 169–79). On monasteries at the time, see McKisack, pp. 305–9. **309–10 knele . . . curteisie**: the monk expects the same respect as a knight, to whom it was customary for a serving-man to kneel (cf. XIX 28). **312 reyne . . . auters**: an image paralleled in Wycliffite writings attacking *friars* (rather than monks) whose churches receive support from the people at the expense of their own parish churches (*Sk*). **313–15 persons**: the rector, whether individual or corporation (e.g. a monastery), owned the greater (predial or agrarian) tithe. Clergie speaks of (absentee) monastic rectors who do not repair their churches (310) and of incumbents, possibly canons regular rather than monks, who simply exploit their property like lay lords. **316 kyng**: this famous 'prophecy' of the Reformation is really an 'apocalypic' threat that the pride and negligence of religious will be chastized by king and nobles, who will resume the lands given to the orders in former times. **319 Ad . . . ire**: a phrase found in Isidore of Seville's discussion of the penitential doctrine of the revival of merit (*AlfQ s.v.*). The figure is to be interpreted as a threat of royal and baronial dispossession of the orders, their formal 'penance' being a return to their 'original state' of material simplicity, which will also constitute (an opportunity for) return to the spiritual purity of their founders. 321a *Hii* . . . : alludes to the fall of the rich monks who now ride about in state (307–8). 322–4 *freres . . . Costantyns cofres*: if friars have a share in ecclesiastical, especially monastic, wealth they will have no need to beg, with the evils that brings (cf. XX 384). Clergie's case is developed by Anima at XV 556ff. On the 'Donation of Constantine' (the endowing of the Roman Church with property), see note on that passage. 'Gregory's god-children' are the monks, since he was a monk before (reluctantly) becoming Pope. 325 *Abyngdoun*: now in Oxfordshire, one of the oldest and richest abbeys in England, was completely levelled at the Dissolution. 327a *Quomodo* . . . : Isaiah foretells the fall of the king of Babylon through pride, and Clergie associates the monks with him as receivers of large revenues from their many lands (*exactor, tributum*). *Caym*: a type of Antichrist, suggests a great upheaval before the new age. This prophecy is not seen being fulfilled in XX, where Antichrist comes (23), since the plight of the Church as a whole is there the main theme. 330 *dominus*: Will's naïve question, provoked by Clergie's (apparent but not real) equation of the future reforming king with Dowel, occasions the transition to Will's argument with Scripture in the remainder of the passus. 340–2 *poverte with pacience*: Scripture introduces a major theme, later to be developed by Patience (XIV 218); the present lines are echoed directly by XIV 108–9. 340 *Apostles*: the blessedness of the poor is Dominical rather than specifically apostolic doctrine (Lk 6: 20), but is echoed in an important source for L, the epistle of James (Js 2: 5). Cf. XIV 276. 343 *Contra*: a scholastic offer of a refutation with supporting proof, cf. VIII 20. 344–5 *Peter . . . Poul*: alluding perhaps to I Pet 3: 21, Gal 3: 27–9, texts which assert the efficacy not the sufficiency of baptism for salvation. 346 *in extremis*: at the point of death, when a pagan, Moslem or Jew desiring baptism may have no Christian at hand to administer it. The disputation has continued in scholastic style: Scripture has not refuted Will's Scriptual proof-text but distinguished the narrower sense in which it can be absolutely true (i.e. when baptism can be all that is both necessary and sufficient for salvation). What Christians need is *to lovye* (354). 366 *Non mecaberis*: literally, 'thou shalt not commit adultery', confused here with 'thou shalt not kill' (*Non occides*) perhaps through unconscious confusion with *necare* 'kill'. 371–6a Scripture has said only that charity, shown in good deeds, is necessary for salvation, but Will is oppressed that theologians have found in Scripture the frightening doctrine of predestination; so he goes on to attack 'learning' (knowledge of Scripture) as useless and dangerous. 382 *Aristotle* (384–322 BC): admired in this period as 'The Philosopher' (Aquinas), 'master of those who know' (Dante); he would be in hell as a pagan (cf. also the tradition of his suicide at XII 43 (C)), *Salomon* on account of his idolatry in his later years (III Kg 11: 1–11). But since the true reason for their being damned was their failure in virtue rather than their lack of baptism, their exceptional intellect does not tell for or against the possibility of their salvation (contrast Trajan at XI 140, whose just life *does* give grounds more relative than this). Will's error in reasoning may be deliberately intended by L (cf. 419, 454*a* below). **405** *Holi Chirche ... Goddes hous*: an image anticipating the *hous Unite* in XIX 330. Here the image of the Church as the ark of salvation breasting the waves of the world and time goes back to I Pet 3: 20, which compares Noah's family, 'the eight souls ... saved by water', to Christians saved by baptism, the sacrament of initiation into the Church. The laity might be saved through the clergy's preaching while the clergy are damned through not living up to their own words. The verse from Ps 35: 7 here, already quoted at V 509*a*, associates the *beestes* of the ark with the Folk of the Field (see *beestes* V 514 (C)). The focus of the poem has now shifted from reform of the laity to reform of the clergy as the more urgent priority (see 474 below). **410** *deluvye ... fir*: the fiery flood of the last days (II Pet 3: 5–12), typologically foreshadowed by Noah's flood (cf. Mt 24: 37ff, seeing the flood as a type of the Last Judgement (*Pe*)). **416** *sonner ysaved*: alludes to Christ's promise in Lk 23: 43. In G*Nico*, ch. 26 (Hennecke, pp. 475–6) the patriarchs to their surprise meet the thief in paradise (ME version, ed. Hulme, lines 1573ff.). **421** *Maudeleyne*: seen as the type of all grave sinners, since the 'seven devils' cast out of her (Mk 16: 9) came to be interpreted symbolically as the Seven Deadly Sins. Like David's and Paul's, Mary Magdalen's great sinfulness cannot be legitimately set in opposition to the great learning of clerks, since it is the former's *repentance* that led to their being saved. Again, the logical flaw in the reasoning may be of set purpose. **438** *quant OPORTET ...*: the macaronic French proverb is associated with the theme of (final) judgement (Alf*Q* *s.v.*). **440** *Nemo bonus*: acquires a more pessimistic tone when taken out of context, where Christ is refusing the description 'good' of *himself*, reserving it to God alone. **455a** *Ecce ipsi ...*: 'The unlearned start up and *take heaven by force* [alluding to traditional interpretation of Mt 11: 12], and we with our learning and without heart [*sine corde*], lo, where we wallow in flesh and blood' (*PL* 32: 757, tr. Keble). If L was not using some other Augustinian source, then he has omitted *sine corde* (which leaves learning *per se* blameless) and replaced 'flesh and blood' with 'hell'. He thus appears to attack learning as dangerous in itself, a distortion perhaps meant to be recognized by readers who could appreciate the extremism of Will's position. **462** *Paternoster*: the basic prayer the layman needed to know; like Haukyn, he could say it at mass on Sunday with his fellows (XIII 237). **467** *Credo*: another fundamental prayer for the Christian believer (cf. XV 609–12), but less essential than the Lord's prayer. **474–5** *tresor*

. . . *soule to save*: echoing Will's demand of Holy Church at I 83–4. The 'treasure' the clerks keep is, of course, still 'Truth'.

Passus XI

3 *Multi . . . nesciunt*: the opening of the pseudo-Bernardine *Cogitationes piissimae de cognitione humanae conditionis (PL* 184: 485); see Wittig, pp. 212ff, Simpson, 'Scientia', pp. 49–51, on this tradition of self-understanding as the knowledge of God's image in the soul and of the need to avoid vain knowledge of merely external things. 7 *Fortune*: described as 'thilke merveyelous monstre . . . sche useth ful flaterynge famylarite with hem that sche enforceth to bygyle, so longe, til that sche confounde with unsuffrable sorwe hem that sche hath left in despeer unpurveied' (Chaucer's *Boece* II, pr. i, lines 17–21). 8 *lond of longynge*: the linkage with *love* after the caesura makes clear that the 'longing' is worldly or carnal 'desiring'; but the collocation with preceding *lond* suggests the metaphor of Will's spiritual plight as a being carried off into the distant land (*terra longinqua*) of alienation from the divine image and likeness, the *regio dissimilitudinis* 'land of unlikeness' of Augustine's *Confessions*, vii, 10 (see Wittig, pp. 232–4). The phrase may also contain a sardonic pun on the author's name (cf. XV 152, which has the same inverted order), suggesting the pride underlying the Dreamer-persona's self-ignorance. 9 *Middelerthe*: the earth thought of as placed between heaven and hell. A *mountaigne* at 323, here it is almost equivalent to the Field of Folk, and *merveillous metels* 6 echoes Pr 11, *wondres* 10 recalls Pr 4. The world's pleasures are gathered into a panoramic spectacle before him, as in a magic mirror (cf. Chaucer's *MerT* (*CT* IV. 1582ff.)). Js 1: 23–4 links failure to know oneself (see 3 above) and the image of a mirror in describing mere hearers, not doers, of the word, who are like men who look in a mirror and then forget what they look like (their true features or nature). Will becomes such a man, hearing the word but not doing it (for discussion see Wittig, pp. 236–7). The idea of *nature* as an instructive mirror of human life is found in the poem *Omnis mundi creatura* (*OBMLV*, no. 242) of Alan of Lille (from whom L quotes at XVIII 410*a*) and was given wide currency as the title of Vincent of Beauvais's encyclopaedia, the *Speculum naturale*. The image may also owe something to I Cor 13: 12, where man's knowledge of God is compared to looking into a mirror (*speculum*; partially quoted at XV 162*a, q.v.*) (Carruthers, pp. 94–5). The Pauline passage goes on to name immediately the 'holy' triad of faith, hope, and charity. 13–15 *Concupiscencia . . .* : described as 'all that is in the world' (I Jn 2: 16, with which cf. X 161–3 above). The three were often associated respectively with the triads Gluttony (or Lechery)/the Flesh, Avarice/the World, and Pride/the Devil (*Pe*; and cf. Howard, pp. 43–53). *Parfit*: heavily ironic, 'luxury' rather than the 'perfect living' of Christian tradition, with its

renunciation of worldly goods (cf. XI 271–6). King Life is the main
character in the late C14th morality play *The Pride of Life*. Life reappears
in XX 143, closely connected with Pride and 'his lemman Fortune' and
also with Antichrist, as in I Jn 2: 18. The whole sequence recapitulates
this one, Elde making Will's *croune* bald at XX 184, and Fortune
resuming her false promises at XX 111. **27** *Elde*: the character Elde in
The Parlement of the Thre Ages is close to this one and in line 290 warns
Youth and Middle Eld, 'Make ȝoure mirrous bi me'. **34** *Rechelesnesse*:
an attitude of total abandonment to what may come, not necessarily bad
in itself if attuned to Truth. **39** alludes perhaps to Mt 6: 25–34 and the
train of thought connected with Piers's words at VII 125–30 (quoting this
verse) and Anima's at XV 313–14, echoing it. **42** *Faunteltee*: the childish
irresponsibility into which such an attitude can degenerate (Donaldson,
C-Text, pp. 171ff.). **47** *fourty . . . fifte*: implies Will was young before his
'wit' began to 'torne' and wasted forty years after his youth (this goes well
with *elde* 60 and makes him about 65 at this stage in the inner dream, a
condition he 'actually' reaches in XX 182ff.). *Sk* takes 45 as his *total* age,
partly from XII 3 (not quite parallel), but this fits less well with the
context, Will becoming guilty of these sins even as a child, and with 60,
which does not mention a *further* 20 years spent with Fortune. **58** *pol by
pol*: each friar individually will pray for him; cf. VII 192–3, III 63 and XX
365–8, which recapitulate these lines. **76–7** *confesse; burye*: both were
more profitable, with hope of gifts from the dead man's relatives, or a
legacy from the living. *catecumelynges*: properly, young people receiving
instruction, either converts or in preparation for confirmation; but most
baptizands would have been infants. **87** *Peter*: perhaps I Pet 1: 22, on
sincere brotherly love, but with its corollary, sincere rebuke, only
implied. On the interchange with Lewte, see Sch, *Clerkly Maker*, pp. 11–
14. **91** *Lewtee*: 'Fairness, Justice', a term with several contextually
varying senses, but here the general one of 'equitable fairness, justice,
good faith' as at *SGGK* 2366, 2381. The senses 'law-abiding people' (*Ka*)
and, even more, 'strict adherence to the letter of the law' (Donaldson), are
quite inapplicable here (cited Alf*G s.v.* III, who properly notes the word's
'rich ambiguity'). **100** *synne*: i.e. sins told to them in the secrecy of the
confessional. **101–6** Lewte licenses Will to criticize notorious abuses but
not to expose individuals' faults, and since Scripture confirms him, this
may express L's own view of the legitimate scope of satiric and polemical
poetry. **117–18** *Holy Chirche*: referring back to I 75–8. She had not
taught him that baptism guaranteed salvation; a life of truth and love is
needed to make his 'claim' to heaven more than conditional. **120–2**
souke for synne: the image is of Christ offering his blood, mother-like,
and pelican-like, as a healing potion for sinners to drink (cf. XVIII 364–
73 and V 494 (C)); but the image is primarily baptismal, not
eucharistic, alluding to patristic interpretation of Jn 19: 34 (see 202 (C)
below). A possible source for this image of Christ as 'nurse' suckling the

sinner is the *Fasciculus morum* v, 7 (Wenzel, in Alford, *Companion*, p. 162). **127–36** *cherl*: boldly compares the Christian who lapses to the bondman who quits his manor; he has no 'right' to do so, and will have to pay for it in the end, just as the lapsed Christian will have to face his Creator's judgement. The bondman or villein could not own property and was legally bound to the land. On villeins, see McKisack, pp. 326–8, and on the implications of this figure, Simpson, *Introduction*, pp. 122–4. **140** *baw for bokes*: the quiet dialogue is broken by a dismissive cry against the *bokes* 139 of which Scripture is custodian. Not all of Trajan's speech, which is here understood to run as far as 318, would be strictly apt to the Roman emperor; but he is a figure from heaven with supernatural authority and knowledge, and *oon* at 319 below, recalling *oon* at 140, may be evidence of the limits of the speech (*K–D* give line 170 to Trajan, breaking the syntax incomprehensibly to ascribe what follows to an unknown speaker). Emperor AD 98–117, he was famed for his justice and integrity. The story of his release from hell through the prayers and tears of Pope Gregory goes back to early lives of the latter, though L gives his own source at 160 (on the background see Wittig, pp. 249–54, Whatley, 'Legend', esp. pp. 50–6). The point of L's use of the story has been much discussed, Gradon, 'Trajanus', Whatley, 'Notes', and Burrow, 'Thinking', pp. 8–14, tending to see in L's treatment an unorthodox, 'Pelagian' view: Trajan as saved by good works alone; while Simpson, *Introduction*, pp. 125–8, sees it as 'semi-Pelagian', Trajan's *lewte* or *truthe* meriting salvation not 'condignly' or absolutely but 'congruently', i.e. 'by doing what is in him'. **147** *soothnesse*: cognitive truth (*veritas*), perceived by Gregory as homologically present in Trajan's *leautee* or *truthe*, a disposition of the *will*. The stress on willing, like that on weeping, is crucial (146, 148, and cf. 262 below). Trajan is saved *by* 'sheer *fidelitas*' (*pure truthe*) but *through* the instrumentality of the Pope's tears and desire (cf. Wittig, pp. 254–5). **160** *legende*: the *LA* of Jacobus a Voragine (1230–98), Archbishop of Genoa, tells the story in the life of St Gregory (46, 10). **163** *truthe*: 'semi-personified', is at once God's power breaking into hell (cf. XVIII 322–3, which recapitulates this event, XVIII 294b, where Truthe *is* a person, Christ) and something hard to distinguish from the man's *truthe*, which enabled him to 'break *out* of hell' (140 above). **166ff.** *Love and leautee . . . book*: do not contradict Scripture's *bokes*, since she taught Will the same lesson at X 351–7 (cf. also Wittig, pp. 254–5). Trajan's argument that learning without love is valueless does not condemn learning *per se* but, esp. at 170–1, is close to the true teaching of Augustine, not Will's distorted understanding of it at that stage. Gradually the teaching on the primacy of love, adumbrated by Holy Church at I 148–51 (which 168–9 here restate) comes to the forefront. **175a** *Quia non diligit*: directly from I Jn 3: 14, but perhaps recalling verse 10, which pregnantly equates *justice* with love by the logic of negation, and the just works of Abel with love of one's brother. Trajan

can affirm that John's words are *sothe* (175) because his own *works* are
(147 above). 181 *povere peple ... enemyes*: Trajan's care for the first
appears in his redress to the widow, which moved Gregory; but he did not
love his *enemies* in life, so his knowledge of Christ's injunction to love
one's enemies has been acquired after his release from hell. 185 alludes to
Mt 25: 35: Christ is served in 'one of these my least brethren'. This is
developed at 198–203 below, with which cf. VI 207–9: Trajan's teaching
is at one with that of Piers, is exemplified at 230–5 below, and looks
forward to Christ's own words at XVIII 376–9. 202 *quasi modo geniti*:
from the introit for the mass of the Sunday within the Octave of Easter.
The Lesson of the day, containing the passage from I Jn 5: 6 on the 'water'
and 'blood' (from Christ's side), symbolizing baptism and eucharist, may
have suggested 200. *gentil*: free and noble, because brothers of Christ,
sharing in his *gentries* 'nobility' (XVIII 22). 203 *synne*: makes the sinner a
slave, and it is not the slave but the son who will inherit eternal life; see Jn
8: 34–6 (the sense is elliptical: since we are now Christ's *brethren* though
baptism, we are now 'sons of God'). 204 The phrase 'sons of men' (*filii
hominum*) is confined to the OT (*Sk*). 218 *bileve*: corresponding to *fides*
at 217, and a synonym for *truthe* (they are significantly combined at XIII
288b, *q.v.*). The 'faith' of the sinful woman in Lk 7: 37–50 is seen not in
her knowledge but in her love (shown in her *tears*, 44); hers, too, is an
'implicit faith' (or *trewe wille*) like Trajan's, on whose case her story
sheds light. 229 *Melius ...* : not traced in Gregory, but the following,
attributed to Augustine by Peter Lombard (*Collectanea*, in *PL* 191:
1601) is close: 'Melius est enim scire infirmitatem nostram, quam naturas
rerum. Laudabilior enim est animus cui nota est infirmitas sua, quam qui
ea non respecta, siderum viam *scrutatur*, et terrarum fundamenta, et
coelorum fastigia ...' (Robertson and Huppé, p. 141n.). The lines are the
source of a passage in ch. 5 of the pseudo-Bernardine treatise quoted in XI
3. 240 *pilgrymes*: wanderers, *peregrini*, until we find our true home,
heaven (cf. Heb 13 :14). 248 *Maudeleyne*: here confused with Mary of
Bethany, called in Jn 11: 2 'she that anointed the Lord with ointment', the
woman of Lk 7: 38, referred to at 217 above, who was commonly
identified with Mary of Magdala (cf. XIII 195, where she is another type
of *trewe wille*). 253 *poverte*: in the extended sense 'poverty of spirit,
humility' (cf. 239 above) which is fitly used of one 'who, sitting at the
Lord's feet, heard his word' (Lk 10: 39). Exegetes often took Martha as
representing the active, Mary the contemplative form of life, as at XV
294–5. 255 *poverte ... pacience*: the theme to be developed in XIII.
Trajan's teaching foreshadows that of Patience in XIV; with 267a cf. XIV
304a. 284a *Iudica me*: from the entrance psalm at mass, verse 1 ending *ab
homine iniquo et doloso erue me*. Such men, whom the celebrant should
not take gifts from (see 281), are mentioned again in the *Lavabo* psalm of
the offertory as 'impiis ... in quorum manibus iniquitates sunt; dextera
eorum repleta est *muneribus*' (Ps 25: 10). Since this same psalm also

begins with the words *Iudica me*, it is easy to see how L should have thought of Ps 42 (of which *Spera in Deo* is verse 5) as relevant to the question of priests' worldly resources, some commentators, like Peter Lombard, seeing in 42: 6 (quoted at 285) a warning *contra pressuras saeculi* 'worldly preoccupations' (Robertson and Huppé, p. 143). **288 title ... avaunced**: priests should have a guarantee of material support from a lay patron or the bishop so as to be able to concentrate on their spiritual responsibilities and not be distracted by need for money (Revard). **293 or ... strengthe**: if the subject of *foond* is *kyng* the sense is (a) 'or he maintained him for his prowess in battle'; if *knyght*, it is (b) 'or provided for his needs as a man-at-arms'. The third condition (in 295b) 'reputation for valour' indicates that L is not stipulating here that the knight *must* be financially independent, if the king thinks him worth supporting. This establishes a parallel condition with that in 291b and creates an analogy between king and bishop (see 311–12 (C)). **296 the same ... preestes**: reflects the decline in the quality of new priests ordained after the loss of perhaps as many as 60% through the Great Plague. **310 sapienter**: those who skip portions of the mass or offices do *not* 'sing wisely'. **312 Goddes knyghtes**: perhaps playing on the sense 'servant' for *knyght* (*MED s.v.*, 3 (a)), but developed as a metaphor from the analogy above at 291–5 (and recalling Holy Church's figure of the archangels as 'God's knights' at I 105). **315–16 *Ignorancia* ... :** a maxim of canon law, recalling the opening of Archbishop Peckham's *Constitutions* (AlfG, pp. 71–2). **ydiotes**: here adjectival, takes a plural like a French adjective. **319 oon**: echoing *oon* at 140, probably to indicate the conclusion of that figure (Trajan's) long speech. **320ff. the wondres of this world**: the vision of the plenitude of creation as here treated may owe something to two major C12th traditions, that of the philosophical School of Chartres, and of poets like Alan of Lille, and that of the contemplative Victorine School; on L's possible debt to Richard of Saint-Victor's *Benjamin major*, see White, '*Benjamin*'. **334 Reson**: the divine law or *ratio* as embodied in the natural order, with some possible influence from the Roman law tradition of natural law as 'that which nature teaches all living things' (Alford, 'Idea', p. 211). As the spokesman of God's providential purposes, he is obviously coherent with the Reason of IV and V, who is concerned with the moral behaviour of rational man. **357 at the bile**: perhaps alluding to the billing of pigeons before mating. **368–407 meved me ... mood**: for discussion, see Sch, 'Philosophy', p. 148, on Will's confusion of natural instinct with human rationality, and 'Inner Dreams', pp. 33–5, on the underlying theodicy. For the source, see Ecclus 11:4. An important passage contrasting fallen man's sexual lot with that of the animal creation is Alan of Lille in *De planctu Naturae* (*PL* 210: 448, *q.v.*) **378 Suffraunce**: the mysterious 'patience' of God that tolerates human sin for its own (obscure but ultimately 'reasonable') purpose. The notion foreshadows the treatment of patience in XII and closely recalls VIII 51–6. 384 *Bele vertue*: the unidentified French proverb offers a 'prudential', Cato-like wisdom ('oother science') to supplement that of Scripture (contrast VII 71, X 191). 386 *lakke . . . preise*: a 'Christian' version of the thought in Ecclus 11: 7; *my* here has the universalizing sense 'the life of any man', as well as referring to Reason's apparent 'behaviour'. 394–5 *fair or foul*: from Ecclus 11: 2. 410 *se . . . suffre*: this new definition of Dowel takes up elements of Wit's at IX 95–8a (C). Will has not yet learnt patience, but he has learnt to appreciate its value.

Passus XII

1 *Ymaginatif*: the *vertu imaginatif*, 'the ability to form images of things not experienced, e.g. of past or future events' (*MED s.v. imaginatif*, 4 (c)): perhaps corresponding to the *vis imaginativa* in one of the late medieval theories of imagination. See for thorough discussion of earlier interpretations, Harwood, 'Imaginative', who sees it as personifying 'the mind's power for making similitudes' (p. 249); Minnis, 'Theories', who shows its rôle in providing images and examples as means to understand the truth; Wittig, esp. p. 271, who sees it as 'actively or vividly representing to oneself'; White '*Benjamin*', who connects it with the Victorine view of imaginative contemplation leading to wonder and love of God; Kaulbach, who relates it to the Augustinised Avicennism that sees *vis imaginativa* as equivalent to thought in man and as having prophetic powers. It is not one of the names Anima applies to himself, and L perhaps saw it as intermediary between the bodily senses and the rational soul, providing images from which the intellect draws ideas by abstraction. 3 *fyve and fourty*: the peak of 'middle life', the time of critical decision; cf. XI 47 (C) above and see Burrow, '*Cammin*'. 9a *vigilia*: the time of Christ's Second Coming, which is unknown. He equates the three watches of the night with the Three Ages of Man: 'if death does not come at the first or second, it will come at the third: be prepared' Robertson and Huppé, p. 149 citing *Glossa ordinaria* (*PL* 114: 298). For further discussion, see Burrow, *Ages*, pp. 69–70. 11 *poustees*: recalling the prophetic meaning of these signs as examples of 'realized eschatology', the apocalyptic 'end-time' being experienced now, as at XX 97–8, where Kynde brings the plague. 12a *Quem diligo*: conflates Heb 12: 6, Apoc 3: 15, the one stressing the educative, the other the admonitory function of adversity. Apoc 3: 20 links the phrase with 9a: public and private afflictions are God's signs to sinners to repent in time. 13a *Virga . . . consolata*: the shepherd's 'rod and staff' (for guiding the sheep) are here instruments for beating; but God's corrections become consolations (*Sk*). 19 *peire*: friars often went about in pairs, e.g. those at VIII 8, XX 341. 29–31 *Dowel*: the definition of this comprehensive term covering faith (*Dowel*), hope (*Dobet*) and charity (*Dobest*) develops into a defence of

learning (*clergie*). 36 *Rochemador*: for illustrations of Our Lady's shrine at Rocamadour, in Lot, southern France, see Jusserand, pp. 338, 365. 40 *what* . . . : the answer to the question may be 'self-esteem' (which makes girls wish to marry). 43–4 *Aristotle*: said by Eumelus to have killed himself by drinking hemlock ('The Myth of Aristotle's Suicide', ch. 14 in Chroust). *Ypocras*: in *The Seven Sages* (ed. K. Brunner, EETS 191 (1932), lines 1040ff.) dies of dysentery sent as a divine punishment for murder. *Virgile*: said to have died in a sudden tempest, also to have had himself cut to pieces as part of a magical attempt at self-rejuvenation, which failed (Comparetti, p. 367). *Alisaundre*: in common medieval tradition was poisoned. These four represent respectively Philosophy, Medicine, Literature and Earthly Empire. 46 *Felice*: heroine of the popular romance *Guy of Warwick*, who contemplates suicide when Guy leaves her on pilgrimage, and dies of grief soon after his death. 47 *Rosamounde*: Walter, Lord Clifford's daughter and Henry II's mistress, allegedly poisoned by Queen Eleanor (1177), was buried at Godstow nunnery. 50a *Sunt homines* . . . : the Latin continues *Non hos sed verbum pectore fige tuo* 'Fix not the men in your heart, only their words' (AlfQ, from Wright, *Anglo-Latin Poets* 2: 130). 54a *Date* . . . : first quoted at I 201 (*q.v.*) apropos clerical greed; the context makes clear that 'unto whomsoever much is given [*sc.* the rich and the wise; cf. 6: 38], of him much shall be required' (Lk 12: 48); see 57–8. 59–60 *grace . . . gras*: the image of grace as a herb growing from humility (patient poverty) anticipates that of the tree of charity at XVI 5–9, and looks back to that of the plant of peace at I 152. All are recapitulated in the image of the crop of the virtues at XIX 276ff. 63–9a refer closely to Jn 3: 8–16; *greet love* 68: God's for the world (Jn 3: 16). 72–5 *God wroot*: Ex 31: 18, Lev 20: 10; but the command to *stone* is specified in Deut 22: 23–4 as the punishment for an espoused girl who is willingly unchaste. 77–8 *clergie*: Augustine (Homily 33 on St John, vii, 6 (Library of the Fathers (Oxford, 1848), p. 477; Latin in *PL* 35: 1649) states that Christ 'is the Lawgiver . . . What else doth he signify . . . when with his finger he writeth on the ground? For with the finger of God was the law written' (*Sk*). *caractes*: interpretation of them as announcing the Pharisees' sins comes from Jerome, *Dial. adv. Pelag.* (*PL* 23: 553). 84 *mansede*: 'excommunicated' (cf. X 278, XX 221, both of priests). The warning, which recalls that at X 463–5 and anticipates Anima's at XV 67–9, may be especially intended for the priest of immoral life who in performing the rite of mass necessarily 'eateth and drinketh judgement to himself' (I Cor 11: 29); see 90–1. 89a *Nolite*: from Lk 6: 37 but perhaps suggested for use here by the meaning of Jn 8: 1–11 and the wording of I Cor 11: 31, 22 *qq.v.* 90 *bretheren*: the plural, out of place here, may be unconsciously retained from I Cor 11: 2, 33. 95 *mirours*: a comparison perhaps suggested by Js 1: 23–4 (see also XI 9 (C)); both sense-perception and learning can be means to self-knowledge. 105 *a blynd man*: perhaps alludes to the action of the blind King John of

Bohemia, killed at the Battle of Crécy, 26 Aug 1346; see Froissart, tr. Lord Berners, ch. 130 (*Sk*). **113** *Levites*: ministers of the sanctuary in early Israel; the Ark was in their charge. L sees the Church's priests as their counterparts; see Num 1: 50–1, 3: 31; II Kg 15: 24. **116** *Saul*: see I Kg 13: 9; an implied warning to the secular power against interference with the prerogatives of the clergy. **125–5a** *Nolite . . .* : Ps 104: 15, referring to the Israelites, is here applied to priesthood, anointing forming part of ordination; a standard text cited to support clerical privileges (Alf*Q s.v.*). **136; 139a** *kynde knowynges*: do not avail for salvation because concerned only with the empirically knowable, i.e. the natural world. *Sapiencia*: here not so much knowledge of the natural world ('science') as worldly wisdom or philosophy in general, as against revelation. The wisdom of those who know only this world is counted as *folye* because it gives no knowledge of God. Paul advises the Corinthians to become fools (i.e. humble) that they may be wise in the eyes of God (verse 18). **141** *lepe out . . . erthe*: a direct echo of I 153–5, itself echoed at XVIII 240 (on the star at Christ's birth). On the patristic theme of the 'leaps' of Christ, based on exegesis of Cant 2: 8, see Smith, *Imagery*, 30. **142** *clennesse*: the Virgin Mary, type of all purity; see *Purity* 1070–88. *clerkes*: logically this anticipates the Magi (**144a** and see 153 below), but as a trans-linguistic pun on *Pastores* (**142a**) bears the sense 'clergy' (pastors of the Church; see *MED s.v. pastour*, 2(a), and XV 43 below). **147a** *et . . . diversorium*: possibly L's addition: the Gospel statement 'there was no room in the inn' implies that Joseph and Mary were seeking a room at an inn, and therefore cannot have been beggars; Ymaginatif denies the claim that mendicancy can in any way be traced back to Christ himself. **148** *pastours; poetes*: an association due to recollection that David, the Biblical 'poet' *par excellence*, was a shepherd (I Kg 16: 11) or to knowledge of Virgil's Fourth Eclogue, with its 'prophecy' of a saviour, often taken in the Middle Ages as referring to Christ (*Sk*). **153** *Clerkes*: i.e. the Magi, called at XIX 75 *Kynges*, according to the common medieval tradition. **156** *contrariedest*: i.e. at X 441–75a. **162ff.** *swymmen*: possibly imitated from Boethius (Chaucer *Boece* IV, pr. ii, line 105) (*Sk*); but the comparison is not close, since L speaks not of a natural power, the use of feet, but of a learnt skill (a kind of *clergie*). **176–7a** *Beati*: earlier quoted at V 508, and later in part at XIV 93: the point is that sorrowful acknowledgement of one's sin to God, even without formal confession, brings forgiveness, as is made plain in Ps 31: 5; and this is something that a clerk (who can read his Psalter) knows. The deeper implication is that the clerk ceases to be dependent on his (possibly incompetent) parish priest. **188** *Dominus*: quoted in the ceremony of tonsuring new clerks (Alf*Q s.v.*). Ps 15 begins aptly 'Preserve me, O Lord', ability to read which enabled a man to claim 'benefit of clergy' and so escape hanging for certain offences on a first conviction (the 'neck-verse', as it came to be called, was more usually Ps 50: 1, the *Miserere*).

189 *Tybourne*: near Marble Arch, in the Edgware Road, where a permanent gallows stood, was the chief place of execution. 191 *thef*: refers back to Will's argument at X 413–20, not to disparage the Good Thief's faith but to counter Will's extremism (on which see X 454*a* (C)) and failure to see the need for continual striving after holiness rather than relying on last-minute repentance. 206*a De peccato* . . . : Ecclus 5: 6–9 goes on to warn against further sin after forgiveness and to remind of the suddenness of death. 215*a Quare* . . .*quia*: the two phrases occur in Peter Comestor's discussion, *Historia scholastica*, ch. 24 of the folly of a question such as, why did God allow man to be tempted (*PL* 198: 1075) (*Sk*), a passage already alluded to by Studie at X 126–9 above, after her anticipatory reference to Ymaginatif's forthcoming 'answer' to Will (X 117). The phrases may echo the emphasis in earlier C14th theology on God's absolute power. 242 *flessh*: peacocks were still eaten at this time; but their popularity was waning. 256 *Avynet*: generically a collection of fables (*Wr*). Avienus was a C4th writer of Latin fables. Fable 39 in Robert's *Fabliaux* (on the peacock who lost his voice) contrasts the fate of the earthly rich, who will be poor in heaven, with that of those who live poor but just on earth, who will enjoy riches in heaven. The detail of the peacock's ugly feet, attributed to Aristotle by Bartholomaeus Anglicus (*Sk*), is untraced. 261–7 *larke*: Aristotle (*Historia animalium* IX, 25) notes that it is edible, but does not make the moral comparison. *logik* 266 seems chosen for the metre and perhaps because of Aristotle's fame as a dialectician. 277 *Contra*: a reply in scholastic mode (see VIII 20–6 (C)). 279 *salvabitur*: stressed rather than *vix*, perhaps implying that *if* Aristotle, Socrates and Solomon are found just at Judgement Day, their salvation, however narrowly, will be assured. 280 *trewe knyght*: echoing XI 141 and reminding of the special appropriateness of the virtue of *truthe* to knights (cf. I 99–100). 282–3*a* On the three kinds of baptism, see Dunning, 'Salvation'; baptism of blood is that of the martyr, who might not have received formal baptism; baptism of fire a baptism by direct infusion of grace into the soul of a man of *trewe wille*, generating the faith, and thence the hope and love (the three 'theological' virtues) necessary for salvation. *Ac* 282, 284: has the force of *Sed* in scholastic debate, ('but) now', not of *sed contra* 'but by way of opposition'; contrast Burrow, 'Thinking': following Whatley, who takes *Ac* as introducing a way of being saved distinct from all three baptisms, he translates *Ac* 'but however that might be', and reads *For* for *Ac* at 282 (but see Textual Commentary). *that* 283 has as antecedent either the third mode of baptism alone (= 'and that is solid belief') or the whole statement from *Ac ther* 282 to *fullyng* 283 (= 'and that [third baptism] is sure faith'). *ignis* . . . *illuminans*: referring to Acts 2: 3 (the descent of the Holy Spirit to *confirm* the apostles' faith) but also recalling Mt 3: 11 (baptism by spirit and fire), which has a bearing on the case of Trajan and his 'faith'. 284–7 *Ac truthe*: Ymaginatif argues that Trajan's *trewe truthe* (shown in

his just life) is homologically related to baptism (necessarily to the third mode, since baptism by water or blood is excluded in his case): that is, God, who is Truth (as both *veritas* and *fidelitas* (see I 12 (C)) will credit/ commend Trajan's 'will to justice' (*fidelitas*) as if an implicit belief in the 'truth' (*fides*) that places him among the *fidelibus* of 290. The rich ambiguity of *allowed* 287, which suggests 'the blending of reward (cf. 289b) and praise' (AlfG *s.v.*) is lost in translation. **289** *hope*: as the second theological virtue deriving from and dependent on the 'faith' inherent in just living (*truthe*), and at least implying the possibility of charity (as in Trajan's act for the widow; see XI 181 (C)). **290** *Deus dicitur quasi . . .* : on this see the Textual Commentary p. [390] above. This promise of eternal life to the faithful is *open* and forms part of his providential dispensation (*potentia ordinata*); but limitless divine power (*potentia absoluta*) lies hidden in God's nature, to which the secret meaning of his name (one of the *archana verba* of XVIII 396a) is, however, a clue. **291** *Si ambulavero . . .* : the quotation, describing total trust in God, is completed in its first appearance, at VII 117 (C). The effect is to associate the *trewe* knight/emperor (Trajan) with the *trewe* ploughman, who in turn becomes in XIX an emblem of the ideal pope (cf. the contrast at XIX 431-3 and the use of *Emperour* in relation to Piers at XIX 430). If Piers's tearing of the pardon ratifies *bona agere* as leading to *vitam aeternam*, Trajan (Ymaginatif implies), who has done the one, would seem to deserve the other. This suggests that if pagans of just life *would* have believed in Christianity, had they known it, they had an *implied* faith (= 'baptism of fire') which may justify them in the sight of God. Verses 3 and 6 of Psalm 22, on justice and mercy respectively, are crucial.

Passus XIII

1-20 summarize XI and XII from the inner dream to the end of Vision 3. Will's *wo and wrathe* XI 4 have become *fey* witlessness, a long-lasting mental anguish overshadowed by forebodings of death and damnation. Will's description of the vision of Kind's generosity to his creatures is explored by White, '*Benjamin*', esp. pp. 244-6. **24** *clergie*: Will's eagerness is the fruit of Ymaginatif's instruction, which has reversed the hostility displayed in his long diatribe in X 371-475a. But after meeting the Doctor he will have many of his earlier misgivings shockingly confirmed and withdraw from intellectual learning into the company of a spiritual virtue, Patience, to find the *kynde knowyng* of Dowel he has sought in vain elsewhere. On the stages of Will's progress, see Simpson, 'Reason to Affective Knowledge', pp. 14-19. **25** *maister*: a doctor of divinity, representing the highest academic degree in the most senior faculty of the university; cf. Pr 62, VIII 9. **39** *Ambrose* (339-97): bishop of Milan, friend of Augustine, author of a treatise on the sacraments; one of the Four Doctors of the Western Church (see XIX 271), whose authoritative commentaries on the Four Evangelists 'fed' the Church. 39a *Edentes* . . . : Christ's instruction to his disciples is dramatically realized: the just man's food is to be 'every word that proceedeth from the mouth of God' (Mt 4: 4), i.e. the Scriptures and the Fathers (Owen p. 103; cf. XIV 47a, where Patience quotes it). 44 *Post mortem*: 'after death, in purgatory' (AlfG); but possibly in hell, if there is an allusion to 'sinful receipt and abuse of bequests ("*Post mortem*")' (Scase, p. 105). 45–5a *synge . . . wepe . . . Vos*: warns that friars who profit from dishonestly won wealth will themselves be punished after death unless they do penance and say mass for the souls of their dead benefactors. The notion of 'eating sins' may come from Huon de Méri's *Tournoiment de l'Antichrist* (*Sk*, after Warton; see Owen, pp. 104–7). The Latin quotation remains unidentified, but the source of the thought is probably Osee 4: 8 and, more fittingly still, a passage in Gratian (*Corpus* I, 391): *Sacerdotes . . . peccata populi comedunt* 'the priests eat the sins of the people' (i.e. thrive on their wrong-doing) (AlfQ, p. 82). 48 *Agite*: so in Job 21: 2, Ezech 18: 30, which promises relief from punishment for wickedness (AlfQ). 49 *Dia perseverans*: 'the potion of long-persevering', playing on *dia* 'medicine' (as in XX 174) and *diu* 'long'; possibly based on Mt 10: 22 and the notion of suffering as a bitter/sweet drink (cf. XX 47, XIV 315). For discussion, see Sch, *Clerkly Maker*, p. 92, *PP Transl*, pp. xli-xlii. 52–3 *Beati; Miserere*: two of the Penitential Psalms, especially prescribed for recitation in Lent (AlfQ). The whole scene may be meant to be taking place in Lent, and so contrasting Patience's physical and spiritual self-denial with the indulgence of the friar (see next note). 54 *derne shrifte . . . confitebor*: confession was compulsory at least once a year, and especially before the Easter Communion. 56 *hac*: forgiveness for sin. 61a *Ve vobis*: the preceding verse (Is 5: 21) well accounts for the one quoted: 'Woe to you that are wise in your own eyes, and prudent in your own conceits' (appropriate for the Doctor). 73a *Unusquisque* . . . : the source of the allusion to the Corinthians verse at 70 remains unidentified, but it probably belongs to anti-mendicant writing of the period. 83 *Mahoun*: a corruption of 'Mahomet,' popularly believed (though not by L) to be worshipped by the Moslems as a god (whence *maumet* 'idol'); here = 'the Devil himself'. 84 *jurdan*: a possible allusion to the Dominican friar William Jordan (see Marcett) does not seem in tune with L's methods and views as a satirist (see XI 101–6); but the contextual relevance of the larger conflict between Jordan and his monastic opponent Uhtred of Boldon has been urged (Middleton, 'Averoys', pp. 31–2n). 91 *Pocalips*: the parodistic *Apocalypse of Golias* attributed to Walter Map, which has a description of greedy abbots (ed. Wright, *Mapes* 2: 341–80). *Avereys*: either a corruption of Aurea or Avoya, who was fed bread from heaven (*Sk*), or an imaginary 'saint' with a name suited to the Doctor, whose own 'passion' (cf. *penaunce* 88) can be imagined as over-eating. Middleton, 'Averoys', suggests that the name is a form of 'Aueroys' (*Aueroy* in // C-text), = 'Averrhocs', the C12th Moslem Aristotelian philosopher whose preference for natural science over spiritual and moral had been supposedly adopted by the Dominicans. **94** *trinite*: 'triad', presumably Dowel, Dobet and Dobest (98); the certainty of this (?Dominican) friar on the question echoes that of the Franciscan earlier at VIII 18–20. **95–6** *leef*: suggests that the *forel* contained a *book* (rather than 'provisions' (*Pe*)) defending the friars' way of life. The metaphor of a 'leaf of lying' repeats Coveitise's words at V 199. **109–10** *fare so*: i.e. if the friar leaves the sick in his infirmary to eat 'penitents' food' while he eats *mortrews*, there will be violent protest. It is not clear whom exactly *yonge children* refers to, possibly novices in the friary. **111** *permute*: a sardonic expression, given the word's specialized sense in canon law and penitential writings: exchange of benefices between two clerics, whereby one receives material compensation as part of the exchange (see AlfG *s.v.*). **116–17a** After defining Dowel at 105 as 'Do no evil' (an improvement on the friar at VIII 45), he equates it implicitly with obedience to the clergy; Dobet with the clergy *qua* teachers; and Dobest with doing as one preaches, a confused mixture. **120–30** *sevene sones*: the Seven Arts, that laid the basis for learning philosophy and theology; see X 152 (C) and cf. V 618, where the seven sisters who serve Truth are moral virtues, not intellectual *sciences*. The comment on Piers, who did not attack learning *per se*, is probably a loose recollection of the quarrel with the priest, and need not presuppose knowledge of the former ulterior to that supplied in the text, e.g. recognition of an implicit symbolic value in the Plowman. *castel*: recalling Wit's allegory (IX 2), where 'Life' (*Anima*) is a lady. Certainly this attitude is more sympathetic than that of the priest at VII 134–6. **127** Ps 14 is generally a psalm about 'dowel', negatively and positively expressed (verses 3, 5). **128** *infinites*: 'limitless, boundless things'; see Middleton, 'Two Infinites'. **135a** *Pacientes vincunt*: found in the apocryphal *Testament of Job* (ed. R. A. Kraft (Montana, 1974), p. 53) (identified Baldwin, 'Patience', p. 72). An idea of Stoic origin with a Christian sense in context and some echo of texts like Rom 2: 6–7, which link patience with 'doing well': '[Deus] reddet unicuique secundum opera eius: iis quidem qui secundum patientiam boni operis, gloriam'. The collocation of Piers (133) and Pacience (134) is significant; but (137–9) Patience does not 'set science at a sop', since learning and teaching are steps to Dobest. **140** *Love*: fleetingly personified here and later at XVIII 181 (as male, a *figura* for Christ). **149–72** Patience's riddle is discussed by Kaske, ' "*Ex vi*" ', revised version in Blanch; Schweitzer; Smith, 'Riddle'; and Goodridge, Appendix C. The grammatical 'power of transitivity' is that 'by which a verb "rules" its direct object in the accusative case' (Kaske, ' "*Ex vi*" ', p. 236). On the background to the terminology of the system for analysing syntax called *regimen*, see Bland,

'Langland's Use'; at least one of the sources quoted (130–1), Villedieu's *Doctrinale*, was known to L (see XI 267a). This may be a pun on *transitus* 'passage' in Ex 12: 11 (Schweitzer, p. 315) involving an allusion to the Pasch, which celebrated the Hebrews' deliverance from Egypt, and hence to Christ's passion, death and resurrection. *laumpe lyne* 152 plays on grammatical and liturgical significances, alluding to the phrase from Priscian's grammar *Tene hanc lampadem* 'illustrating grammatical "rulership" by the *ex v.t.*' (Kaske, ' "*Ex vi*" ', pp. 240–1) and *half* of the priest's words to the baptizand in the rite of solemn baptism during the Easter vigil: 'Accipe lampadem ardentem et irreprehensibilem: custodi baptismum tuum: serva mandata' (*Sarum Manual*, quoted Schweitzer), the candle symbolizing good works (cf. Mt 5: 15–16). Reading *a bouste* 'box', Kaske interprets its symbolic meaning as '*patientia . . .* or the heart . . . fortified by *patientia*' (p. 250), thereby avoiding the unacceptable sense 'pyx' for *bouste* proposed by *K–D* and rejected here (see Textual Commentary). But the *bouste* is non-existent, and no emendation required: *therinne* at 153 (and 158) refers back to *Kynde love* 151 (Charity, as *Sk* recognized), as does *herwith* (157); and *Undo* (158) has the figurative sense 'interpret' (*OED s.v.*, 7). Schweitzer explains *signe* 154 as referring to the sacramental *sign* of confirmation, administered on Holy Saturday, the vigil of Easter, from the date of which the dates of the Church's movable feasts were reckoned; *wit* 155 as referring to the significance or meaning of the mass of the Wednesday of Easter Week, i.e. the fulfilment of Christ's promises in the Second Coming and Judgement, and also the necessity of his suffering (Acts 3: 18, read in the epistle of the day); the full or Paschal moon (= Easter) as standing implicitly for the power of baptism and confirmation, both sacraments deriving their efficacy directly from Christ's redemptive sacrifice (cf. Kaske ' "*Ex vi*" ', p. 245). **164a** *Caritas . . .* : 'Kynde love', the answer to the riddle: *it* 164 is the *it* of 158; to 'undo' *Dowel* is to find *Caritas*. The other relevant text is I Cor 13: 4–7, esp. *Charitas patiens est, benigna est*, which illuminates the link between Patience and (his own definition of Dobest) *Dilige* 'Love' (139). **173** *dido*: the well-known story of Dido, queen of Carthage, in Bk IV of Virgil's *Aeneid*, re-told by Chaucer in *The House of Fame* I. **175–6** *Pope . . . Cristene kynges*: alludes to the Great Schism of 1378 and the continuing war between France and England. France supported the Avignonese contender to the papacy, Clement VII, and England the Roman Pope Urban VI, so the two issues were closely entangled (McKisack, pp. 145–7). **179** *lye*: a trait of pilgrims already noted (in Pr 46–51). The Doctor does not distinguish between the pilgrim–hermit (whose dependence on God recalls that of Piers at VII 120) and 'professional' pilgrims like the one at V 515. **193** *goode wil*: echoing the conclusion of Ymaginatif's words on Trajan at XII 286 (and see XI 146–8 (C)). **194** *trewe wille*: echoes I 85–93: 'truth' and a well-disposed human will have been shown to be closely connected. **195** *Maudeleyne*:

the woman of Lk 7: 47, often identified with the Magdalen, who has 'Many sins ... forgiven her because she hath loved much'. The implication is that those who give 'all their living' (Lk 21: 4) for love of God, like the 'poor widow,' will be saved. Like Mary Magdalen she represents the passive dependence on and total commitment to God that Conscience intuitively recognizes in Patience. 210 *Sarsens and Surre*: either both expressions = Moslems or one (cf. *MED s.v. Saracen* n., 1 (b)) means 'pagan'. 220 *hungry contrees*: recalls the topographical allegory of II 86–9, and that used by Piers in V 566ff. 225 *Activa Vita*: represents an inferior form of the 'active life', which might be called 'practical life', based on, and judged by, purely temporal conceptions of goodness' (Maguire, in Blanch, pp. 195, 200). 225–7 *mynstral*; *wafrer*: near-synonyms (as in '*wafferariis & menestrallis*' in Webb; and cf. Southworth, pp. 80–1; and see *MED s.v. minstrel*, 2: 'servant, function-ary'). Haukyn is a real *wafrer*; the kind of minstrel he denies himself to be could be either an honest maker of *glee* (Pr 334) or a *japere* (Pr 35), but his list of activities at 229–34 confounds the two categories (see, on minstrels, Bullock-Davies; Southworth, ch 4). 247 *pardon*: the lead seal (*bulla*, whence 'bull', 250 below) of the papal pardon was stamped with the heads of SS Peter and Paul. 250 *bocches*: boils or tumours in groin or armpit, the commonest symptom of the plague. Their reappearance at XX 84 indicates that the Black Death has returned (cf. XX 100–5). 255–5a *pot*; *hoc*: the gift of healing left by Christ to Peter and the other apostles (250a above), perhaps alluding obliquely to the story of the woman who anoints Christ's feet with a pot of costly ointment, an action found wasteful by Judas in // Jn 12: 4–6. The implied identification of a venal papacy with the false apostle Judas undermines the assertion of 257b in a manner reminiscent of VII 174–9, on the *spiritual* efficacy (or otherwise) of papal pardons. 260 *payn defaute*: recalling XII 11, VI 322–3. 267 *Stratford*: Stratford-atte-Bowe in East London, whose bakers supplied bread for the people of London. 271 *maire*: John de Chichester was Mayor of London during the great dearth of 1370. 274 *Cristendom*: alluding to the white robe of baptism worn by the infant or neophyte. 275 *moled*: recalling the 'spotted garment (*maculatam tunicam*) which is carnal' of Jude 23 (Frank, *Scheme*, p. 71n.), with perhaps an allusion to Mt 22: 1–14 (and cf. the version of this in *Purity*, esp. lines 29–50, 135–52). 313a *Si hominibus* ... : Haukyn's gospel is *secundum hominem* 'according to men, worldly' (Gal 1: 11); he serves worldly interest (mammon): cf. also 398–9a below. 340 *Soutere* ... *Dame Emme*: unknown but no doubt famous characters (the latter perhaps the same as at Pr 225); Haukyn's failure to pray is a cause of physical as much as a symptom of spiritual sickness. The image of Christ's grace as *lechecraft* 338 is a commonplace, much exploited by L, e.g. in XVII 92–9; see also XVI 104, 118. 349 *forboden nyghtes*: fast days and vigils, but perhaps also including periods of pregnancy and menstruation. **371–3** *pynched so narwe*: encroached on strips of land or stole corn growing on such strips directly adjacent to his. **392–3** *Brugges*: a great market-town and centre of the Flemish cloth-trade; *Prucelond*: 'the chief distributor of English cloth in Poland and west Russia' (McKisack, p. 359). **399a** *thesaurus*: the contrast of spiritual and worldly values in the Sermon on the Mount is relevant to understanding Haukyn (see Alford, 'Coat'). The 'treasure' theme recalls the discussion between Holy Church and Will in I, esp. 44–5. **410** *braunches*: sin commonly seen as a tree with branches and twigs (*Ayenbite of Inwit*, ed. R. Morris, EETS OS 23 (1866), p. 17; Chaucer, *ParsT* (CT X. 388); and see Katzenellen-bogen,·figs 65, 66). **423** *fool-sages*: 'wise fools' licensed to make sharp satirical comments. **424a** *ridetis*: the condemnation of 'foolish' laughter is a standard Biblical notion (see Eccl 7: 5–7). **433–6** Ps 100 mentions walking 'in the unspotted way' and excluding the proud and perverse from one's house. **437** *kynges minstrales*: a privileged class: 'The permanent salary of the royal minstrels of Edward II was 7½d a day' (Strutt, p. 164), '20 shillings a year' in the time of Edward III (Southworth, p. 103). **445–6** *suffred . . . save*: the infinitive of purpose depends both on *suffred* and *to lere*: both Christ's suffering and the poet's account of it will help to save the wise man's soul from hell.

Passus XIV

1–15 *oon hater*: 'Haukyn's one garment symbolizes the carnal nature of man, which requires shrift in the same way that a garment needs to be washed' (*Sk*); see Alford, 'Coat' on the allegorical interpretation of *uxor* in the quotation as 'concupiscence'; and cf. XVII 330–1. **16–21a** *Contricion*: the sacrament of penance has three parts: contrition of heart; oral confession to a priest; satisfaction through prayers and good works; see AlfQ, p. 87 and Gray. Cf. Chaucer's *ParsT* (CT X. 106–9). **43–4** *the criket*: probably the salamander (see *MED s.v.*). *corlew*: persuasively identified as the European quail (*coturnix*), in exegetical tradition often a symbol of spiritual pilgrimage and the need to rely on faith in God (Spearman), perhaps with some echo of the quails sent by God in Ex 16: 13. Gower, *Confessio Amantis* VI. 943, says the same of the plover. **59a** *Si quis . . .*: the first part of a couplet from the *Cartula*, one of the grammatical texts making up the collection *Auctores octo*. It is based on I Jn 2: 15 and continues *sed quasi fetorem spernens illius amorem* 'despising the love of it like a foul stench' (AlfQ, p. 88). **62a** *Aperis*: Ps 144: 15–16 was a commonly used grace at meals. **63–4** *fourty wynter*: the wandering of the Israelites in the wilderness (Num 14: 33, 32: 13); *flynt . . . folk*: the rock struck by Moses from which water flowed and people and cattle drank (Num 20: 11, Ps 77: 20); in Pauline exegesis, a symbol of Christ as the spiritual sustenance of the faithful (I Cor 10: 4). **65** *Elyes tyme*: the drought inflicted as punishment for sin (III Kg 17: 1, referred to in Js 5: 17). **68–9** *Sevene*: the Seven Sleepers of Ephesus were Christians who were said to have slept in a cave from the Decian persecution to the time of Theodosius (AD 448), nearly 200 years, when they miraculously woke, in proof of God's power over life and death (*LA*, ch. 100). **75–6a** *meschief*: see as well as Gen 18, 19, Ezech 16: 49, Comestor's source. Gluttony and lechery were commonly linked (I 27–37; cf. Chaucer, *ParsT* (*CT* X. 839)). **81** *sheltrom*: the shield-wall defence formation. The image recalls Eph 6: 11–17, but the implication of *collective* defence is due to the faith being the faith of the Church, not of an indidividual alone (cf. the moat of communal tears at XIX 380–3). **84** *contricion*: one unable to make oral confession (e.g. because sick or wounded) may be saved from damnation if truly contrite; cf. XII 175–7. **88** *surgiens*: echoed at XX 311–14, when the 'surgien' Friar Flatterer invites monetary payment as a substitute for painful contrition. The whole passage (88–96), with its imagery of wounds, is recapitulated in XX 303ff. **91** *Per . . . peccata*: penitential maxim, source not identified. **97** *Where wonyeth . . .* : recalls V 532, the Folk's question about Truth, and VIII 13, Will's question about Dowel. Haukyn both recapitulates the former and stands as a surrogate for the latter. **103** *Ye – quis*: Ecclus 31: 9, *Quis est hic? et laudabimus eum*. The text goes on to praise the rich man who *could* have transgressed but did not. **104–8** *richesse . . . poore*: for a solemn contrast between the condition of rich and poor cf. Js 5: 1–11. **122** *Dives*: the 'rich man' (*dives*) of Lk 16: 19; cf. XVII 265–70. **131** *another stede*: Ps 72 deals less with the dangers of riches than with the prosperity of sinners and its effect on the faith of poor believers. **160** *midsomer*: 24 June. From then till Lammas (1 Aug) was a time of shortage; see VI 277ff. (C). **169** *ingrati*: a term having legal as well as theological associations (AlfQ, pp. 73–4; cf. XVII 254), with a 'clerkly' pun on the senses 'refusing to reciprocate one's lord's kindness'/'rejecting God's grace' (cf. *grace* 170, XVII 255–6). **180a** *Convertimini*: Is 45 describes God as creating both peace and evil (*malum*, in context 'affliction'), but it also includes a solemn promise of justice and salvation (23). **181** *in genere*: a term from grammar or scholastic logic, 'in the kind or genus of'. **191–3** *Pateat*: the opening formula in letters patent; *Per . . . Dominum*: specifying by whose warrant the *acquitaunce* is issued (AlfQ, p. 89). The power of Christ's passion, sacramentally applied to the sinner in confession, is described in terms of the sovereign's words in a letter patent; to be written at all, such words need a 'parchment', man's own humility (191, 194); cf. XVII 4–5, *Ancrene Wisse*, ed. Bennett and Smithers, 239/470, 471. **200** *fenestres*: recalling III 64–70 (the friar and Mede). **201** *in commune*: a doctrine not of communism but of charity, concern for others restraining the quest for personal wealth (see the attack on communism in XX 275–6). **209–10** *fer . . . bettre; rather yherd*: the 'gift of nature', *wit*, is distinguished here from the 'gift of fortune', *richesse* (cf. Chaucer, *ParsT* (*CT* X. 452–3)), in contrast to

Ymaginatif who linked them as *combraunces* (XII 45). 213*a*; 215*a* *Opera*: heaven is seen as reward not for earthly poverty as such but rather for the patient bearing of poverty, though the first beatitude has a form closer to Lk (which omits 'in spirit') than to Mt. (See also *Patience* 34–45, 528–31, which link patience and poverty, and XIV 276 (C) below.) 219ff. *sevene synnes*: Poverty is seen as a general remedy against the Deadly Sins (envy is left out). As 'humylitee, or mekenesse' (Chaucer, *ParsT* (*CT* X. 475)) it is the specific against pride, the 'root' of all seven; but the objective advantages of material poverty as against riches are also stressed. 256–7 *grettest help*: contrasts with Haukyn's admission at XIII 341–42 above; cf. Chaucer, *WBT* (*CT* III. 1201–2). 259 *secte* 'livery': because Christ was one of them, the poor belong objectively and irrespective of their virtues to the section of society he belonged to (see Js 2: 1–6, and cf. Lk 7: 25). 262–73 perhaps allude to St Francis, a 'rich young man' who *did* 'marry' Poverty (see 272), referred to admiringly by Anima at XV 231–2, where *secte* is used again. Cf. Mt 19: 21 (*Sk*). 275 *What is poverte*: the account here is moral and spiritual, drawing on Stoic and patristic writings on the benefits of poverty as well as on Scriptural sources. For the contemporary social background, see Shepherd; Aers, 'Perception of Poverty'; and Pearsall, 'Poor People'. 276–6*a* *Paupertas* ... : from the *Gnomae* of Secundus, quoted in Vincent of Beauvais, *Speculum historiale* x, 71, and others (Chaucer paraphrases in *WBT* (*CT* III. 1195–1200)). *donum Dei*: from the opening of Augustine's *De patientia* (Sch 'Two Notes'). 280 *point*: cf. *Patience* 1, 531; Sch, 'Langlandian Phrase', 155. 286 *cura animarum*: the canonical sense 'cure of souls' (Alf*Q*, p. 90) is here not relevant; contrition provides 'care' for souls in a purely spiritual and inward way, irrespective of whether the penitent actually goes to confession (though he should: cf. 87–92 above; Sch, *Clerkly Maker*, p. 111). 293 *unseled*: measures used by brewers and taverners had to be sealed with the alderman's seal to attest their true capacity (*Sk*). 300*a* *Sanitatis mater*: because it protects from excess, for L evidently a chief cause of illnesses; cf. VI 267–8. 301 *Aultoun*: the road or 'pass', on the Surrey–Hampshire border (then forest), was a haunt of outlaws who lay in wait for the merchant-trains travelling to Winchester; cf. the image at XVII 103–6. 304*a* *Cantabit*: translated by Chaucer in *WBT* (*CT* III. 1193–4). 306 *Seneca*: praises poverty in Epistles 2 and 8, the latter close to the phrase from Vincent (*Sk*). 309 *tempreth*: contrast the previous use of this musical figure at Pr 51–2. 312*a* *Negocium sine dampno*: business without worrying about 'loss' or risking 'damnation'; i.e. since profit is not his aim, he does not risk his soul to gain the world. 316–19 *Austyn . . . mene*: for explanation, see Sch, 'Two Notes', 86. 324 *wepte water*: recalls V, linking Haukyn with Will (V 61) and Robert the Robber (V 463), and is echoed at XV 192 (Charity), XVIII 91 (Longinus) and XIX 380–1: weeping here symbolizes 'conversion' (cf. XVI 116, Christ's tears of compassion, described in the same phrase as at 324). 329

clothes: referring to his *cote of cristendom*, recognizing failure to live up to the demands of the Christian calling emblematized in the white baptismal robe; the only garb he can claim is a material one. 332 *awakede*: Haukyn's loud weeping wakes Will as had the quarrelling at VII 140. On the links between Haukyn and the Folk, see Maguire.

Passus XV

3; 10 *fool*: Will's seeming a 'fool' before the world shows how he has changed; contrast the *daffe* of I 140, and cf. VII 125, XX 61–4. 5 *looth to reverencen*: recalling Js 2, a Scripture central to L's thought, here esp. 1–3 (quoted at 88 below). 18 *porter*: Peter was traditionally thought of as gate-keeper of heaven (cf. Mt 16: 19 and Pr 100–6); *fauchon*: a symbol of Paul's martyrdom (by beheading) and perhaps alluding to the 'sword of the spirit' (Eph 6: 17). 23–39a For an analysis of Anima's names, see Sch, 'Philosophy', pp. 151–2: 37 On Augustine here, ibid, pp. 142–3; on Isidore (*c.* 560–636), bishop of Seville and author of the encyclopaedic *Etymologiae*, see Leff, pp. 51–2. 50 *Prides knyghtes*: a follower of Lucifer, whose 'legions' fell through pride (I 127); when Pride's host appears at XIX 354, Will is not among them. 51a *Ponam . . .*: Isaiah's address to the king of Babylon was traditionally applied to Satan ('Lucifer', Is 14: 12; cf. also Lk 10: 18). 55a *opprimatur*: 'let him be overwhelmed', stronger than the Vulgate *opprimetur*: 'he will be over whelmed'; a threat rather than a prediction. 59 *double scathe*: cf. the correlative notion of 'double reward' at XIV 148; much is expected from those to whom much is given (cf. Lk 12: 48). The 'honey' is learning. 60 *Bernard*: representing faith, humility and love, rather than reason and intellect, as the *kynde* way to know God; see Leff, pp. 134–5. 64–9 repeats his teaching, which stems from Augustine and Paul. 67 *licames coveitise*: the 'wisdom of the flesh' (*sapientia carnis*) which 'is an enemy to God' (Rom 8: 7). 70 On these *freres*, see X 71 (C), and cf. XX 273–6. 82 *glose*: the *Glossa ordinaria* gives Cassiodorus' gloss on Ps 4: 3, which identifies idols with lies and false earthly goods that cannot fulfil what they promise (*PL* 113: 849). His *Expositio in XX primos Psalmos* (*PL* 114: 759) quotes without attribution the passage from Augustine given by *Sk* contrasting truth (which makes blessed) with vanity and falsehood (= love of worldly goods). 83 *brennyng*: a rhetorical phrase perhaps reflecting knowledge of the practice in France; heretics were not burnt in England before the statute of 1401, *De heretico comburendo* (*Sk*). Cf. Book's vehement expression at XVIII 254. 88 *Ne sitis*: see 3 (C) above; the words of Jesus L has in mind may be in Lk 14: 12. 111–13 The images of dunghill, wall and wolf-like behaviour appear 'clustered in a passage on hypocrisy in the C13th *Summa virtutum de remediis anime*' (Wenzel, pp. 94–6). The 'wall' image recalls Mt 23: 27, Acts 23: 3, and another passage linking snakes and hypocrisy is Mt 3: 7.

That snakes nest in dunghills is a fact of natural history (cf. the observations on birds' nesting-habits in XI 344–9). **115** *bele paroles ... clothes*: the double image of pure words and white clothes concealing a false interior has no identified source (Js 2: 2, cited *AlfQ*, p. 93, refers to a rich man, not a hypocrite, and certainly not a priest). **116–17** *wolveliche*: Mt 7: 15, and the immediately following image of the evil tree in verses 16–20, pseudo-Chrysostom's source; and cf. *wolveskynnes* VI 161: these priests are a spiritual equivalent of the *wastours* in Piers's field. **124** *ballok-knyf*: a fashionable ornamental dagger or a knife with a knobbed (= testicle-shaped) haft, covered with gilt studs. **125** *plow*: a figurative use of 'plough' recalling that of Piers at VII 120. **149** *childissh*: i.e. having the nature proper to a child of God; cf. 216 below, also V 607, XI 208; the essential feature is the guileless trust of *infantes ... sine dolo* (I Pet 2: 2); contrast with 'childishness' (*fauntelte* 150). **152** *Longe Wille*: a compact phrase giving us his stature, his persevering character and his name (as a syllabic anagram: see Intro., p. xxi). **155** *paied*: i.e. rewarded by God; their charity 'seeks its own', has an element of prudent self-interest. **162** *mirour*: a reflecting surface, whether the Creation or the Law (cf. Js 1: 25), in which man gets an imperfect but valid image of God's essence (*facies*). **168** *Tarse*: 'a rich and costly stuff of Oriental origin' (*OED*), from Tharsia (?Turkestan). **178** *frend*: a personification of the will of God and the grace that makes following it possible. **179–80** have a nexus of associations with texts on spiritual feeding: Jn 4: 34 (God's will), Mt 4: 4 (God's word), Ps 41: 4 (contrition), and cf. XIV 49 (prayer). **181** *portreye ... peynte*: in saying the rosary, the 'Our Father's are seen as the 'design' (the pattern of Christian faith) given 'colour' by the detailed meditation on the human life of Christ, the 'Hail Mary's. **183** *hir pardon*: it is not the poor and the prisoners who confer the 'pardon' (taking *hir* as a subjective genitive) since they cannot, and Charity, who *non querit que sua sunt* 'does not ask after his' (157–8 above), is acting out of love of Christ, seen in 'the least of these', and not like those who give 'ther thei leve lelly to ben paied'. Charity is occupied with *their* 'pardon', through his prayers and concern. **187** *lavendrye*: cf. the *lavacrum poenitentiae* image used by Alan of Lille (*PL* 210: 171); and cf. VII 120–1. **188–9** perhaps refer to doing penance specifically for the extravagant sins of youth. **200α** *Et vidit*: on the influence here of Augustine's *De Trinitate* XV see Simpson, '*Et vidit Deus*'. L heightens the effect by replacing the *he/Jesus* of Lk 11: 17, Mt 9: 4 by *God* and naming *Christ* only at 212. **210** *wordes ... werkes ... wil*: on the structural importance of this theme, see Burrow, 'Words'. **212** *Petrus, id est, Christus*: expressing the notion of Christ's authority fully embodied in Peter, here figuratively at one with Piers (as later in XIX 183–91). I Cor 10: 4 as a possible source text is tenuous; notwithstanding the *petra/petrus* pun in Mt 16: 18, the Pauline reference is to the OT (see 63–4 (C)). **214** *ancres*: perhaps metonymic for 'the anchorholds of anchorites', since they were in principle enclosed. 223 *Edmond*: the martyr, King of the East Angles (d. 869); *Edward*: the Confessor (d. 1066), who built Westminster Abbey. 227–9 Charity is nowadays more likely to be found in a rich abbot or bishop than an austerely dressed friar; with garments of fine material appropriate to a prelate (not the liturgical vestments, which all priests wear at mass), a skull-cap over his tonsured head and the hair curling round it. This is to take *ycrymyled* here as a form of *crimplen* (so cited in *MED s.v.*, (a)); but if derived from OF *cresmeler* (*Sk*, Glossary *s.v.*, and n., IV, p. 894), it means 'anointed with holy oil' (used at the consecration of a bishop or abbot), with perhaps some allusion to the injunction *unge caput tuum* 'anoint thy head' (Mt 16: 17, quoted at 219*a*), a warning against hypocritical austerity linked by *For* 220 to the argument on the indifferent value of outward appearance as a sign of inner charity. 231 *fern ago*: St Francis had died a century and a half before, in 1226. On his order's development, see Keen, *Europe*, pp. 156–61. 234*a* comes from the praise of the just rich man quoted XIV 102, drawn on at XIV 145–54. 242 *yknyt*: see Mt 19: 6, evaded by what were in effect divorces though obtained under guise of annulment. 254*a in idipsum*: the apparent antecedent in the psalm text is 'the light of [God's] countenance'; but in this context *Goddes passion* (255) is the source of the peace enjoyed by Charity. 266 *suffrede in ensample* . . . : echoes Reason at XI 378–81, developing the sense of *suffre* there ('tolerate') into the new, Christian sense 'endure suffering'. 267 *Pacientes vincunt*: Anima also gives a specifically Christian sense ('those who suffer, conquer') to a phrase of Stoic origin first introduced in XII 135*a* and used six times in XIII–XV as a leitmotif. The main Scriptural allusions are to Lk 17: 25, 24: 26; Mt 16: 21; Rom 8: 17, and esp. II Tim 2: 12; cf. also Mt 26: 54, referring to Is 53. 269–97 *Legenda Sanctorum*: the *LA*, chs 21, 125, 15, 56, 96. 272 *Antony* (d. 356): an early Desert Father and reputed founder of monachism. *Egidie* (Giles): lived as hermit and monk in Provence, d. 700. 285 According to the life of Paul, Antony was his guest when a raven brought bread. 286 *primus heremita*: the opening description of Paul (d. 342) in *LA*, ch. 15. 289 Anima repeats the Austin friars' claim to have been founded by Paul the Hermit. 290 Paul the Apostle's trade was tent-making (Acts 18: 3); like Chaucer in *PardPro* (*CT* VI. 445), L confuses him with the Hermit, who did make baskets (Jerome, *PL* 23: 28) but there was uncertainty about St Paul's trade. 294 Mary Magdalen, according to legend, came to Marseilles and after converting the pagans lived 30 years in solitude on angels' music. *dewes*: cf. the Rawlinson lyric *Maiden in the mor lay*, in Sisam, p. 167. 313 *foweles*: perhaps alluding to Mt 6: 26, comparing trusting Christians to the birds of the air, with a pun on *foles*, a term used of the believers who take refuge in Unity and place their trust in God (XX 61–2). 317*a Brutorum* . . . : the comment is close to one *Sk* quotes from St Bruno's *Expositio in Job* VI, 5. The passage deals with moderation in feeding, not sex, but it nonetheless recalls the sentiment of XI 334–43, esp. 341. 325 *prophecie*: 'utterance made by the prophet-king David.' 348 *lussheburwes*: the importation of these coins, forged abroad, was forbidden as treason by Edward III. 370 *clemat*: 'one of the regions [of the earth] dominated by certain zodiacal signs' (*MED s.v. climat*, 1 (b)); sense (c) 'often considered with respect to its weather' seems apt in context, where weather-forecasting is being discussed. 371 *the ground of al*: origo et fundamentum liberalium litterarum, Isidore, *Etymologies* 1, 1. 372 *newe clerkes*: cf. the complaint against bad poets in *Wynnere and Wastoure* 20–30, seen there as a sign of social decay. For a full discussion of the subject see Sch, *Clerkly Maker*, pp. 21–7. 373 *versifie faire*; *formaliche enditen*: see chs 2 and 3 in Sch, *Clerkly Maker*. 375 *any langage*: means that few know French; cf. Trevisa's comment in 1387, in Sisam, p. 149; and see Sch, *Clerkly Maker*, pp. 102–7. 381 *quodlibet*: 'any question in philosophy or theology proposed as an exercise in argument or disputation' (*OED*). The discussion was presided over by a *maistre*; see AlfQ, p. 96. 388 *sola fides sufficit*: the phrase from the *Pange, lingua* sung at Lauds on Corpus Christi is apt since the hymn is by the greatest of *divinite maistres*, Thomas Aquinas. Anima's point is that the priest's defective performance of the liturgy will not harm the lay-people as long as they have true faith. The feast occurs on the Thursday after Trinity Sunday, was instituted *c.* 1263, and became the occasion of the great miracle-play cycle called 'the play of Corpus Christi'. 396–410 *Makometh*: Hildebert of Lavardin's C12th life of Mahomet makes him ambitious *pontificari* 'to become patriarch' (= L's *ben a pope* 397) (Wr). 400 *dowve*: so in Vincent of Beauvais's *Speculum historiale* XXIII, 40. 406 alludes to the descent of the Holy Spirit as a dove at Christ's baptism (Mt 3: 16). 414 *Coveitise*: recalling earlier attacks on clerical greed, beginning with that of Holy Church (I 196–7). 424–6 *siknesse . . . pees*: Anima brings together healing and reconciliation as fruits of devout prayer, countering the scepticism of Haukyn at XIII 255–9 and the Doctor at XII 175–7. 437 *Ellevene*: Matthias, elected to replace Judas (Acts 1: 25–6), in fact made them twelve (Sk). 443–4 *Gregory*: sent Augustine to preach to the heathen English in 597, and in the same year the latter converted Ethelbert, king of Kent. 445 *rede*: in Bede's *Historia ecclesiastica gentis Anglorum* 1, 26 and 31. 450–2 *fullynge . . . fullyng*: baptism of the heathen is compared to the preparation of woollen cloth by an elaborate process of 'fulling', so as to raise the nap with teazles arranged on a frame and then thicken the cloth by moistening, beating and pressing. 457 *hethene . . . heveneward*: involve a play on words, since *th* and *v* are near-identical sounds in L's dialect. 458 *Hethen*: the etymology is correct, and the allusion is to the fact that remote country districts were the last to be Christianized. Here the figure compares baptism of pagans to the cultivation of wild land. 461 *Mathew*: the Parable of the Wedding-Feast has no mention of fowls, and L's invention of 'the whistling' figure is a means of promoting his lesson that the uneducated laity learn by the *example* of their leaders, the clergy. **465** *The calf*: regarded as clean in Lev 11: 3, Deut 14: 4 (*Sk*). **489a** *eam in Effrata*: the meaning is that the possibility of finding 'charity' (*eam*: see C on X 68a) in heathen lands (i.e. receptivity to the message of the Gospel) is a motive for missionary effort. **492** Clerics were sometimes appointed by the Pope to (non-existent) titular sees *in partibus infidelium* (such as the places named), territory held by the Moslems; they rarely if ever visited these places. **496a; 499** *Bonus pastor ...* ; *Ite vos ...* : both passages bear on the responsibility of 'pastors' to serve their people, if need be at the cost of their lives; see Jn 10: 11–18, and Mt 20: 18–23, coming after the verse quoted, where Christ foretells his death and warns the apostles of the cost of their discipleship. Mt 20: 4 was commonly interpreted as a summons to priestly mission. **508** *peril*: because such 'bishops' do not fulfil Christ's command to preach (quoted above). **522** *Seint Thomas*: Becket (?1118–70), Archbishop of Canterbury from 1162, was murdered in his own cathedral by knights of Henry II. **529a** *Nolite ...* : adapted from Deut 23: 25; here it warns against the kind of practice described at XIII 374, in the light of Mt 9: 37–8, to become a means of criticizing non-diocesan bishops who interfere with the rights and duties of parish clergy. **535** *no book but conscience*: the notion of conscience as a 'book' in which one's good and bad actions are written, to be opened on Judgement Day, originates in Jerome's Commentary on Dan 7: 10, though L may have found it in Alan of Lille's writings (see Sch, 'L's "Book" '). **542** *croune*: they seek a 'corruptible' crown (I Cor 9: 25) not the 'crown of justice' (II Tim 4: 8), for which martyrdom may be necessary. The obverse of the noble and groat showed a crowned king's head (Poole, pls 34, 35); there may be a further pun here on the *croune* 'tonsure' of clerics, a symbol of forsaking 'possession' (XI 274), not seeking it. **546–9** *Templers*: the order of Knights Templars was suppressed by Clement V in 1312 under pressure from the French king, who wanted their vast wealth in France (Keen, *Europe*, pp. 217–18). *dar* 548 may allude to the French charges against them 'of cloaking under oaths of secrecy a system of organized vice and communal sacrilege' (ibid., p. 217). *religiouse* 549: the Templars united 'monastic austerity with the martial spirit of chivalry' (ibid., p. 122); and on the Templars generally, see Partner. **555–5a** *Levitici; primicias et decimas*: the thought is traced to Num 18 by AlfQ, p. 95. L runs together the teaching of Num 18: 19 and 21, which prescribe that the first fruits be offered to the priests and the tithes to the Levites, since he uses 'Levite' figurally to refer to the Christian priesthood as a whole. **559** *Dos ecclesie*: the grammar is confusing since the subject of *hath ydronke* should be *ecclesia*, not *dos*: 'the Church, through being endowed, has drunk ...', i.e. through receiving worldly wealth and power the Church, which had flourished spiritually in apostolic poverty, suffered corruption from the head downwards. The 'Donation' was an C8th forgery purporting to be a letter from the Emperor Constantine to Pope Silvester I in 315 granting him lands and privileges (see Southern, pp. 91–3, Smalley, pp. 154–7, on contemporary citations). 562 *possession*: worldly pre-occupations prevent the clergy from prayer and charity. This leads logically to the demand that they be 'dispossessed'. 563 *Taketh hire landes*: the 'prophecy' of X 316ff. has become an explicit invitation to dispossess the clergy, not just the religious orders, for the sake of the Church as a whole. The position superficially resembles the Wycliffites', who also cited the 'Donation'; but it has a long (orthodox) tradition behind it (see Gradon, 'Ideology'). 573 *Ysaie . . . Osias*: Isaiah refers to a secular ruler; Osee is confused with Malachias perhaps because the prophecies are similar, Os 5: 1 threatening priests in terms close to Mal 2 and 3. The criterion of the material sufficiency of bishops is at one with Trajan's strictures on priests and knights without income at XI 285–95. 597a *Pacientes vincunt*: this final quotation of the phrase now specifies the content of patience as suffering unto death, since it is Christ's 'Passion' that overcomes the power of his enemies, including death (XVI 166). 599 *Cum sanctus*: based on Dan 9: 24 but directly derived from the pseudo-Augustinian sermon *Contra Judaeos* (PL 42: 1124), quoted in a lesson of the Fourth Sunday in Advent (*Pe*). 600 *wrecches*: Anima is pitying rather than attacking the Jews: he urges their conversion and that of the Moslems because, if the missionaries of old converted the heathen English, it should be all the easier to convert people who are already monotheists. *pseudo-propheta*: a phrase from Mt 24: 11, made familiar by anti-mendicant writings (Szittya, p. 56). 606–7 *Sarsens . . . Jewes . . . firste clause*: the thought is very close to Alan of Lille's statement in the *Contra haereticos* IV, 1 (PL 310: 421).

Passus XVI

2–3 *Haukyns love . . . mene*: Will takes over the rôle of Haukyn, who had asked Patience the 'meaning' of poverty (XIV 275). The answer comes at 63, from the person whose 'help' Anima had declared necessary (XV 196) if Charity was to be 'seen' in person. 4 *tree*: see Smith, *Imagery* and, for a penetrating and suggestive discussion, Aers, *Allegory*, pp. 79–109, who also surveys and criticizes earlier work. 6 *lele wordes*: the words of Christ and his Church; cf. the *Vitis mystica* of Bonaventure, *Folia vitis . . . Jesu verba* (PL 184: 651). 8 *Pacience*: the suffering humility which is the basis of divine charity, recalling '*Dilige* – Dobest . . .' at XIII 139–48. Cf. the tree of virtues in Katzenellenbogen, fig. 66, with *Humilitas* the root and *Caritas* the fruit. 9 *the fruyt Charite*: the source of this image is Augustine's *arborem charitatem* in his commentary on I Jn (PL 35: 1993, 2020, 2033), noted by Goldsmith, p. 59, and Dronke, p. 214. 15 *Herte*: cf. Holy Church, who locates Truth there at I 142ff. (and cf. 6 above), and also Piers at V 606–7. **16** *Liberum Arbitrium*: 'Free Judgement', 'Free Choice'; cf. Sch, 'Philosophy', esp. pp. 134–43, and ' "Free Wit" '. **19** *swowned*: suggests (like *ravysshed* XI 7 at the opening of the first 'inner dream') 'a spiritual vision or imaginatif' (*The Chastising of God's Children*, ed. J. Bazire and E. Colledge (Oxford, 1957), pp. 169–70) like the *gostly drem* in *Pearl* 790 (see Wilson, '*Drem*'). Sch, 'Inner Dreams', pp. 28–33; but the preferred reading at 20 is *love-dreem* (see Textual Commentary, p. 399). **27–52** *a wikked wynd*: a new image for the traditional 'Three Temptations' (see XI 12–16) encountered in the first 'inner dream', and a sign of the parallelism between the two. L may owe something to Alan of Lille's image of 'the four kinds of pride which blow through the whole world like winds' (*PL* 120: 133), or Bonaventure's of the 'winds of pride and vainglory' which blow down the 'house of [man's good] intention' in the *Vitis mystica* (*PL* 184: 665). There is also symmetry here in the opposition of each enemy of Charity to a person of the Trinity: the created world and the world's Creator; the flesh and God-made-flesh; the evil spirit and the Holy Spirit. **30** *Potencia*: 'might' (see 192) as the *propre myghte* (cf. 54) of God the Father as Creator. **35** *blosmes*; *leves*: if closely related to 6–7, the sense is that fleshly lust destroys kindness in the soul, leaving (perhaps only nominal) adherence to the Church's teaching, not necessarily 'the bare text of God's scriptures' (Salter, *PP*, p. 75; see also Aers, *Allegory*, pp. 91–2). **36** *Sapiencia* . . . : occurs in the heading of Augustine's *De Trinitate* VI, i, discussing I Cor 1: 24; see also ibid. VII, iii, and the morality play *Wisdom* (ed. Eccles, pp. 5–16). **46** *Liberum Arbitrium*: the human faculty which responds to grace, the special attribute 'appropriated' to God the Holy Spirit; see 47a below. **47a** *hoc est* . . . : evidently a comment on the preceding text, where *peccat* may come from a pre-Vulgate version (ÁlfQ, p. 102). The 'sin against the Holy Ghost' was usually understood as wilful refusal of grace, especially the grace of repentance, but L may be thinking ahead to XVII 251–2, 283–6 (*unkyndenesse*). **63** *Trinite*: that the tree 'means' the Trinity and grows in goodness is not incompatible with Anima's description of it as 'Patience' growing in man's heart; Piers's account is of charity's source and origin (in the divine nature), Anima's of its manifestation (in man). **68–72** *Matrimoyne*: the three possible human states in rising order of excellence are marriage, widowhood (see 76 and cf. I Cor 7: 8–9), virginity. See Bloomfield, 'Grades'; they are named in *Vitis mystica*, ch. 18 (*PL* 184: 672). *kaylewey bastard* 69: perhaps = grafted, cultivated, not growing naturally (*MED s.v. bastard*, 2 (c)). *Cailloux* in Burgundy produced a highly esteemed pear. *swellyng* 72: i.e. with desire or pregnancy; *peeris* seems a pun; see Biggs on the patristic sources. **81–2** *Adam . . . Johan*: these names stand for all the just from Adam to Christ's precursor, the Baptist. **84** *Limbo*: the Limbo of the Fathers was believed to be continuous with hell (*ST* III, 52, *Suppl.* 69: 4, 5; and see 254 (C) below).

Satan's *maistrie* there was nominal rather than real (cf. Lk 1: 79), the Fathers suffering from 'darkness' (lack of the Beatific Vision) but not 'dread' (since they lived in hope of it). **86** *pure tene*: recalling his action of tearing the pardon at VII 115. **88** The syntax leaves it doubtful whether *Filius* is in apposition to *pil* or to *Piers*, but though the ambiguity may be intended, the former fits better with the allegory, making the Divine Son the 'means' through which human nature (Piers) can be enabled to act against the dominion of evil. **92** *jouke* 'rest': a bold metaphor from the action of hawks, rich in suggestion; *justice son*: son of God the Father, judge of all, and 'son of justice' (*sol iustitiae*), as in Mal 4: 2 (cf. Lk 1: 78). **93** *plenitudo temporis*: quoted from Gal 4: 4–5, *q.v.* **95** *juste*: takes up *justice* 92; the metaphor is from the outset legal as well as chivalric (see 92). **101, 104** *fightyng*; *lechecraft*: metaphors of Jesus under a tutor, as a young knight and apprentice physician, perhaps suggested by the thought of Gal 4: 1–7, quoted at 93 above; cf. Lk 1: 80. **112, 115** *maistrie*: alludes to Christ's description of his act as 'for the glory of God' (Jn 11: 4, 40); echoed by Lucifer as he remembers this act (XVIII 276, 266). *mestus . . .*: transferred from Christ's words before the agony in the garden (*Pe*), and therefore connecting his own coming death with the fact of human mortality instanced in that of Lazarus. **120a** *Demonium habes*: the third appearance of this phrase in St John's Gospel (Jn 10: 20) occurs before the *maistrie* and is provoked by Christ's claim to have power over death, referring to his own resurrection, of which Lazarus' raising is a type. **131–5a** draws on both Jn 2: 14–22 and Mt 21: 13, the link being the rebuilding of the Temple as a symbol of Christ's resurrection (Jn 2: 21–2), which is prompted by the preceding story of Lazarus (see 120a (C)). **149** *kissynge*: the common salutation among friends in England at this time; see Chaucer, *PardT* (*CT* VI. 968). **157a** *Necesse est . . .*: not directly addressed to Judas, though appropriate to his case, and perhaps suggested by the reference to hanging in Mt 18: 6. **164–6** *bataille . . . fordide*: anticipating the chivalric metaphor of XVIII (see 64, and Death's boast at 29). **170** Will becomes more of a fool (*MED s.v. ydiot*, (b)) in the world's eyes as he himself sees more; cf. I Cor 1: 25, 3: 19, contrasting divine and worldly 'foolishness'. **172** *myd-Lenten Sonday*: 'Laetare Sunday', after the opening introit of the mass of the day, *Laetare, Jerusalem* 'Rejoice, Jerusalem' (cf. 163 above). The subject of the epistle (Gal 4: 22–32) is Abraham and his two sons, which St Paul interprets allegorically to refer to the Old and the New Law respectively. **181** *Thre leodes*: the blazon recalls the wording of 57; the Trinitarian theme of the inner vision has spread into the containing outer dream. **186** *Sothfastnesse*: truth as knowable (*veritas*), because revealed by Truth (God); cf. Jn 14: 6. **199** *Crist . . . Chirche*: invoking the doctrine of the Mystical Body of Christ, according to which, as its head, he is one with his Church united in 'one baptism, one faith and one lord'. **208** *oon singuler name*: i.e. humanity (on earth), divinity (in heaven). The family analogy occurs in

De Trinitate XII, v, 5, but Augustine rejects it as a misleading opinion (*Sk*). **210** *bitokneth*: Faith extends the analogy so that each Person of the Trinity symbolizes or corresponds to a category of humanity as seen on the tree in the inner dream. **214** *widewe*: because deprived of or separated from his other half (the divine nature united with the humanity) at the moment of Christ's death, just after he utters his cry (Mt 27: 46). **215** *creatour ... creature*: a line of cardinal importance in *PP*, marking L's paradoxical understanding of the theology of the Incarnation, his sense of God needing experiential knowledge of human suffering and death to 'complete' his already complete perfection through imperfection (cf. XVIII 221–4). The wording is close to that of the poem *Ave, mater, stella maris*, st. 3: *factor fit factura/et creator creatura*, by Walter of Châtillon, ed. Strecker (no. 10). **219a** *Maledictus ... Israel*: closely paralleled in a lesson for St Anne's day from the *Hereford Breviary* (II: 266), the speaker being the high priest addressing Joachim, father of the Virgin Mary, in the Temple (see AlfQ, citing Tavormina). **222** Taking *bifore ... hevene* as asseverative, the line stresses identity of substance between the divine persons ('gendre', 'generacion') while positing some conceptual (not metaphysical) 'priority' as between them. The sense 'human nature remained human before being joined to God's in Christ's person at the Incarnation' seems contextually excluded. The comparison (inevitably) fails in suasive force since the relation of a human child to its parents is contingent, while that of Holy Ghost to Father and Son is, in orthodox theology, a necessary one. The logic of analogy has led L to think of human nature in metaphysical rather than empirical terms. **223–3a** *Fre Wille*: L adapts from Augustine the analogy between the Holy Ghost and the human will, the faculty that loves (*De Trinitate* X, xii, 19 and XV, xxi, 41); cf. *frenesse* 'generous graciousness' 88 above. This may explain also why Piers links the Third Person with *Liberum Arbitrium* 50–2. *Spiritus procedens ...* : the standard Western understanding of the dogma of the Trinity, seeing the Spirit as proceeding from both Father and Son (Athanasian Creed; see AlfQ, p. 105). **224** expresses the thought in English. **225** *I hym seigh ...* : see Gen 18, the notion of Abraham's knowledge of the Trinitarian nature of God deriving from his encounter with the three angels (Vespers Antiphon for Quinquagesima, in the *Sarum Breviary*). **235** *I circumscised my sone*: either Ishmael or Isaac (Gen 17: 23, 21: 4), but both *before* the command to sacrifice Isaac. **244** *breed ... wyn*: L confuses Abraham's sacrifice (Gen 15: 9) with Melchisedech's (Gen 14: 18) (*Sk*), referred to in the canon of the mass in the prayer *Supra quae*. **245** *feith*: Abraham is the OT personification of faith and, as the recipient of God's promise of salvation, an apt *heraud*, as is John the Baptist, whose own 'heralding' of Christ fulfilled God's promise to Abraham (cf. Rom 4, esp. 11, 16–20, and Mt 3: 9–11). **249** *I herde*: i.e. in limbo where John the Baptist, the 'heraud' of Christ, will have joined Abraham at his death. **254** *bosom*: a vividly concrete metaphorical *shewyng* of limbo, drawing on Lk 16: 22. Aquinas (*ST Suppl.* 69, 4) specifies limbo (= 'Abraham's bosom') as the place of rest of the just before Christ's advent, free from the pains of punishment but deprived of the beatific vision of God, and so 'hell', not *per se* but *per accidens*. **255** *lazar*: leper, i.e. Lazarus the poor man in the parable of Lk 16: 19–31. **264** *maynprise*: the release of a prisoner to one who stands surety for his appearance in court when required (AlfG *s.v.*); an indication of the legal character of the forthcoming dispute over 'possession', of humanity in XVIII 1. Christ can make such a guarantee because the 'court' will be his own (at Judgement Day). **270–2** *Allas . . . I wepte*: Will's words recall Haukyn's at XIV 322–8; now he weeps 'religious tears' (see Vernet, pp. 120–5, and XIV 324 (C) above).

Passus XVII

1 On *Spes* 'Hope' and *spire*: a probable pun on French *espier* 'spy'/*espeir* 'hope' (see Saint-Jacques ' "Spes" '). *knyghte*: the beginning of the chivalric metaphor that will dominate XVIII. **2** *Synay*: the sacred place where God gave Moses the Ten Commandments (Ex 19: 20). That *Spes* should be identified with Moses, who looks to the future, seems implicit in Deut 34: 4. The Law itself is the law of love (I 150–1), to be fulfilled in Christ, the new Moses (Mt 5: 17–19). **5** *seel*: the ratification of God's promise that will come with Christ's saving death; seals often took the form of a cross. **10** *patente*: open to public view (not *privee* or closed), on the model of royal documents addressed to the realm (cf. 3). Letters patent were sealed with the Great Seal: cf. XIV 192. *hard roche*: the stone tables of the Law (Ex 24: 12, 31: 18). **11–15** *two wordes*: echoing the *two lynes* of the pardon (VII 109), which is another expression of the same law, and was sent to Piers from the same Truth who gave Moses the tablets (see I 15–1). **13** *tixte*: runs together Deut 6: 5 and Lev 19: 18 (where Vulgate has *amicum* 'friend', for *proximum* 'neighbour') to accord with Lk 10: 27, which allows for *sherewe* 43 below. **14** *glose*: 'splendid' as Christ's own authoritative interpretation of the law. Truth wrote the Commandments with his finger; Love writes his in letters of gold. **18, 21** *charme*: an ironic contrast to Haukyn's irreligious resort to magic at XIII 342. Cf. the ironic use of 'witchcraft' imagery at 95–8 below. *saved* 18: i.e. conditionally; they are waiting in limbo for Christ's death to seal their release. **40, 44** It is not that Will is unable to reconcile the doctrine that faith justifies with the command to do good works and practise charity (Goodridge, p. 42). Will's problem is simply finding *lighter* 'easier' Faith's message than the 'Law' of *Spes*: love of one's enemies, the distinctive moral doctrine of Christianity, is (not surprisingly) the hardest to follow. **49ff.** *Samaritan*: the parable in Lk 10: 30–6 answers the lawyer's question 'Who is my neighbour?' after Christ has answered his question 'What must I do to possess eternal life?' The

meaning is 'Show Charity, Dobest', the superlative act of the Samaritan
(= Christ) corresponding to the positive and comparative degrees of
doing well embodied in Faith and *Spes*. Most of the elements of L's
version not found in the Gospel go back to patristic exegesis, via the
medieval homilists, and especially the liturgy of the Thirteenth Sunday
after the Octave of Pentecost and the interpretations of liturgical
commentators (Saint-Jacques, 'Liturgical Associations'). The unique
'chivalric' view of the Samaritan-Christ may derive from the Gospel
account of Christ's entry into Jerusalem riding an ass and the imagery of
the Easter sequence *Victimae Paschali*, esp. the lines *Mors et vita duello/
conflixere mirando* 'There together Death and Life/Met in strange and
wondrous strife' (cf. *112a below*). **56** *semyvif*: a coinage for the metre,
translating Vulgate *semivivo* (Lk 10: 30). **72** *Lex Christi*: Gal 6: 2 makes
'bearing one another's burdens' (= Charity) the fulfilment of Christ's
law; cf. XI 210*a*. It is under this law (= Christian life in the Church; cf.
119 below) that sick humanity will recover. *graunge*: a *figura* of the
Church, the *hous* to be built out of Scripture and Christ's passion itself
(XIX 324–31, which recapitulates this image by supplementing Christ's
teaching (*lex*) with his sacraments ('wattle', 'mortar')). **95** *bathed*: the
main Scriptural sources are I Jn 1: 7, I Pet 1: 2, Apoc 7: 14. **98** *eten*: the
flesh and blood of the incarnate Christ must be eaten in the eucharist (Jn
6: 54, I Cor 11: 27), just as God the Son 'ate' the earth of human nature to
become man (I 154–5) and will thirst to 'drink' man's love (XVIII 366–
71). The imagery of the crucified and consumed baby, with its shocking
associations of witchcraft, is prompted by the notion of Christ's work as
having begun with his birth. **103** *Outlawe*: an apt image for Satan, exiled
from heaven, living beyond God's law and preying on his people. **108**
Caro: a traditional interpretation going back to Bede (Robertson and
Huppé, p. 205) and familiar through liturgical commentaries (Saint-
Jacques); *Caro* is the 'castle' of man's body at IX 43. The parable
essentially 'shows the ineffectualness of Faith and Hope without Charity
(I Cor 13: 13, cf. Rom 13: 10) and the Old Law of the Priest (= Abraham)
and Levite (= Moses, of the tribe of Levi) without the New Law of Christ'
(*Pe*). **112a** occurs in an antiphon at Lauds on Holy Saturday; from Osee
13: 14, and cf. I Cor 15: 54. **139–203** *as a fust*: the extended analogy may
be original, but the source of the fist image is presumably *mundum
pugillo continens* 'holding the world in his fist', applied to the Creator,
supernus artifex, in the anonymous C6th hymn *Quem terra, pontus,
aethera* used at matins in the Office of the BVM (*OBMLV* 59, quoted C
XIX 114*a*). **150a** *Omnia traham* . . . : spoken by Jesus himself; but cf. the
Father's voice at Jn 12: 28. **168a** *Tu fabricator* . . . : from a compline
hymn for the Sunday after Easter (*Hereford Breviary*, ed. W.H. Frere and
L.E. Brown, 3 vols (1904–15), 1: 342). **198a** *Qui peccat*: i.e. wilfully
rejects divine grace (cf. XVI 47*a* (C)). **203** *his grace quenche*: effects a
transition from the 'hand' to the 'torch' image; cf. I Thess 5: 19: *spiritum*

nolite extinguere. 204ff. *torche*: a twist of hemp soaked in wax; *tapur*: a wax candle. The development of the image here may be original, but the 'unity' of the three elements in the candle is noted by Bartholomaeus (ed. Seymour) XIX, 63: 10, and *LA* (37: 164–5) remarks on the wax as signifying Christ's flesh, the wick his soul and the flame his divinity (*Pe*). For discussion, see Intro., pp. lii–liv. 250a *nescio vos*: the bridegroom's words come from a parable especially apt in context, since it is *oil* (= *kyndenesse* 'charity') that the foolish virgins lack to fill their lamps; see I 188–9 (C). 253 *Pampilon*: indulgences granted by the Bishop of Pamplona (in Navarre) for issue by the Abbot of Rounceval were distributed from St Mary's Rounceval, at Charing Cross, the house of Chaucer's Pardoner (*CT* I. 670) (*Pe*). 254 *ingratus*: perhaps from Paul's description in II Tim 3: 2ff. of the *ingrati* who *resistunt veritati* 'resist the truth' (verse 8); cf. 264a below, from a warning against the same 'false prophets' Paul is attacking; and cf. *ingrati* used of the rich who refuse charity (XIV 169). 257 *blowynge*: takes up the earlier metaphor of the three winds (XVI 25ff.). The wind of *unkyndenesse* 'uncharitableness' which blows out God's flame of love is the absolute negation of *Goddes owene kynde* (272: 'God is love', I Jn 4: 8). L sees charity, like gratitude, as due to others in return for God's showing mercy towards us. 265 *Dives*: the rich man of Lk 16: 19–31, already alluded to at XVI 255, *q.v.* 272 *grace . . . kynde*: the customary antithesis between 'grace' and 'nature' is overcome in God, whose nature is 'gracious' because he is both creator and saviour. 274 *Unkynde Cristene men*: the juxtaposition is almost oxymoronic, since the *unkynde* sin against the very nature or essence of Christ's religion, which is to be *kynde* 'charitable'. 275 *Sleeth a man*: lack of charity is shown supremely in murder of a man's body or reputation, an undoing of God's creation (a human being; virtue) which stands at the opposite pole to God's own incarnation and sacrificial death (see 290, 285), the acts of charity which establish the new creation. 306–6a *holy writ*: here not the Bible but one of the Fathers, Augustine (see V 272a). God's justice is like the *equyte* growing up in the King's prerogative courts, which sought true fairness where legal claims failed to assure it. 311ff. *Good hope . . . wanhope*: describes the dilemma of the man whose life of (freely committed) sins leaves him at the end despairing of God's mercy and so failing to show in his last moments the contrition needed to turn God's (wrathful) justice into mercy. 317 *Thre thynges*: a proverb in Pope Innocent III's *De contemptu mundi* I, 18 which draws on Prov 19: 13, 27: 15 (comparing wife and leaky roof), 10: 26 (smoke) (*Sk*). Also very close are the Latin verses in Walter Map (ed. Wright, p. 83, lines 173–4); cf. Chaucer *WB Pro* (*CT* III. 278–80). 329–end The Samaritan distinguishes the three conditions in which men succumb to sin – through weakness of their bodily nature (on wife as *flessh*, cf. XIV 3a (C)), being weakened by outward afflictions, and deliberate evil in the will. The skilful use of *kynde* in 331, 340 shows how sins arising from the first two sources may find forgiveness while those due to *unkyndenesse*, being the 'contrarie' of 'reson', extinguish the fire of God's grace, just as wet wood, though kindled, cannot foster the flame and goes out. **332** *Frelete*: cf. Lady Meed's plea to the friar at III 55.

Passus XVIII

4 *wery*: Will's weariness (of the *world*) and desire to 'sleep' here signalize spiritual advance: he has left *bely-joy* (VII 119) for *mynde of God Almyghty* (XV 295), like the hermits of XV 269ff. In this vision, the content of the canonical and apocryphal Gospels is mediated through phrases and images drawn from the liturgy of Lent and Eastertide. **6–8** [*Dominica*] *in ramis palmarum*: Palm Sunday, when clergy and people processed round the church carrying blessed palm-branches and on re-entering sang the hymn, clergy and adults chanting the verses (*Hosanna* occurs in verse 1) and children (choir and others) the response *Gloria, laus*: 'Glory, praise and honour be to thee, Christ, Redeemer King'. *gretly me dremed*: could possibly refer to the depth or meaning of the dream; but *longe tyme* 5 and *faste* 6 clearly indicate the length of time spent dreaming: his whole life has become concentrated in single-minded pursuit (*wilned* 4) of his vision. **8** *orgene*: perhaps the portative organ, since they were processing; the β variant *organye* yields the sense 'organum', i.e. in parts, a fifth above or below the plainsong line (so *Pe*), also possible here if the choir is conventual; but the C-text too has *orgene*. **9** *ofraughte*: 'reached to' (or, possibly, 'got possession of'): the antecedent of *that* is either *passion and penaunce* or *Crist*, but the sense is the same. **10** *Oon*: Christ entering Jerusalem (Mt 21: 1–9, Palm Sunday Gospel) is the embodiment of Charity figured in the Samaritan of his own parable and the poet's fictional creation, Piers. **11** *bootles*: 'without boots' but not 'without a remedy for man's sin'; without spurs to 'prick' his mount, he is yet *the* knight seeking the supreme adventure, Death (personified 37; see also XVII 50 (C) above). **17a** *Benedictus* . . . which ends the *Sanctus* in every mass, also ends the second Palm Sunday antiphon *Pueri Hebraeorum*. **22** *armes*: perhaps in heraldic sense, with a pun; but Christ is not wearing the *blasen* Faith described at XVI 181: rather, like such knights as Lancelot in the romances, he disguises his divinity in the form of the humble ploughman, *habitu inventus ut homo*, 'in habit found as a man' (Phil 2: 7). L's debt to two allegorical crucifixion poems by the C12th Anglo-Norman poet Nicole Bozon is explored by Waldron, pp. 66–74, who summarizes earlier discussions. **23** *helm* . . . *natura*: the imagery is close to that in the C14th *Meditations on the Life and Passion of Christ*: 'þis haberion is þy body fre' (ed. D'Evelyn, l. 1603), a work based on the C13th Latin *Philomena* of John of Howden (XIX, 52), ed. Blume. **24** *consummatus Deus*: 'Supreme God' (*Pe*), eternal and impassible, but ironically anticipating 57, the 'supreme' moment of Christ's human adventure being, inescapably, death. **25** *paltok*: cf. Walter of Châtillon: *Dei prudentia . . . cum in substantia cerni non potuit,/nostre camisia se carnis induit* (ed. Strecker, 1. 7). **26** *in deitate Patris*: 'in his divine nature from [not 'as' (*Pe*), which confounds the Persons of the Trinity] the Father'. **29–31** *Deeth . . . Lif*: based on the theme *Mors et vita duello conflixere mirando: dux vitae mortuus regnat vivus* from the Easter sequence *Victimae paschali laudes*, and a text such as Heb 2: 14–15 (*Pe*). **35a** *Mors . . . morsus*: already quoted in part at XVII 102*a*; here Christ will 'bite down' the tree of death which is the antithesis of his own 'plant of peace' and Tree of Charity, a return for the fatal 'bite' of Adam and Eve (201 below) that brought death into the world. **36** *sedens*: 'sitting in the place of judgement' (Mt 27: 19), one of a cluster of Latin phrases from the Holy Week Gospels which keep the intense emotional experience of the liturgy firmly in the reader's consciousness. **46** *wicche*: one of many details from the *GNico* (ME version, ed. Hulme, lines 215–16). **52** *poison*: based on the mistaken notion that the drink offered Christ on the cross (Mk 15: 36 and //) was meant to hasten his death (so in *Meditations*, ed. D'Evelyn, line 1868 and Howden; see further Sch, 'Crucifixion', pp. 176–85). **59** *The lord . .* : cf. Howden's *Philomena* (ed. Blume), stanzas 194–5. **60** *derk . . . sonne*: recapitulates and 'realizes' V 492; for full discussion, see Sch, 'Crucifixion', pp. 185–8. **64** *bataille*: on this conflict as a 'civil duel of law', see Baldwin, 'Duel', pp. 66–72. **79** *Longeus*: so named in *GNico*, line 625, after Jn 19: 34 (*lancea* 'spear', Greek *longchē*). He was revered as a Christian martyr; see Peebles; Kolve, pp. 218–21. He is made a Jewish knight (82) to represent Christ's defeat of his opponents the Jews, whose 'blindness' in refusing to accept Jesus as Messiah is often represented by the figure of Synagoga blindfolded (Mâle, p. 189). **81** *manye teeth*: a nonce-variant on the phrase *chekes* (cf. VI 40), perhaps alluding to the tearing-out of his teeth and tongue for refusing to worship idols (*LA*, ch. 47, which tells his story briefly). **94** *vileynye*: a low, ignoble act, against the laws of chivalry and the *gentries* of Jesus, whose divinity they fail to perceive in his humble human form. **100** *recreaunt*: acknowledging himself defeated in battle (a dramatic instantiation of the power of divine charity), but etymologically 'unfaithful, giving up one's faith'; here punning paradoxically on the fact that Longeus' *faith* in Christ saved him (*LA*; and cf. XII 192, on the Good Thief Dismas). **104** *cherles*: the Jews will be without civil rights; forbidden to own land, they will have to live off usury, itself forbidden, thereby ensuring their condemnation. The irony of the passage depends on the speaker being Abraham, both father of the Jewish race and embodiment of the new faith they reject, ostensibly in defence of the old (he echoes Jesus' words at XVI 121). **109a** *sanctus . . . vestra*: see XV 599; since the Jews reject Jesus as Messiah, God will withdraw his protection from his chosen people, to let them lose their independence and become subject to hatred and persecution. On the condition of Jews in the Middle Ages, see Southern, p. 17; Cohn, pp. 76–81. **111** *derknesse*: see Mt 27: 45, and possibly alluding to the service of *Tenebrae*, said in the darkened church on the Wednesday, Thursday and Friday of Holy Week (*Sk*); but the dream-darkness is that of hell, as in XVI 251 (and cf. XVII 234), an outer condition corresponding to the sinner's spiritual state (destruction of light: XVII 281). **113–228** The motif of the Four Daughters of God and their debate derives from Ps 84: 11 (quoted at the climax of the passus, 423*a* below). The 'argument' between them, suspended at 260 and resolved at 410, represents not a supposed conflict within the Deity but the tensions and contradictions in man's understanding of the ways of God, the result of seeing only *hic in enigmate* 'through a glass darkly'. The 'directions' may owe something to Is 43: 6; a precise symbolic meaning for them is in this context unlikely (contrast Mede at II 5 (C)). The debates, as *Sk* notes, are adapted from Robert Grosseteste's *Château d'Amour* (ed. Murray; ME translation, ed. Sajavaara); cf. also *N-Town Play*, ed. Spector, I 111–23, *The Castle of Perseverance*, ed. Eccles, pp. 95–111 and bibl. note p. 200; Owst pp. 90–2. **113** *wenche*: although it could be neutral (= 'girl' as at XVI 100) its connotations were 'low'; on the tone of the passage see Coghill. **115** *Mercy*: foreshadowed in the allegory of Truth's castle in V, where the maiden Mercy is the Virgin Mary (635), embodiment of the divine quality which is 'above' all God's other works (cf. V 282–4*a*, which looks forward to Christ's triumph in XVIII and manifests his absolute power). **119** *Truthe*: like Righteousness, a personification of God's *potentia ordinata*, his law revealed under the constraints of language, time and history; to human eyes, at odds with his mysterious inner nature. (Truth's half-line at 147 echoes Theology's at II 122, who is, like her, an interpreter of the Biblical 'text'.) **122** *wonder*: the Harrowing of Hell is dramatized in miracle plays (York 37, Towneley 25, Chester 17). The main sources are *GNico*, lines 1160–1548, *LA*, ch. 54, 242–5. **140** alludes to Fortunatus' hymn *Pange, lingua* 1.6 (*OBMLV*, no. 54) sung on Passion Sunday and during the Adoration of the Cross at mass on Good Friday (quoted at 161*a* below). In medieval legend the wood of the cross was said to be that of a tree grown from seeds of the tree of knowledge in Gen 2: 17 (*Legends*, ed. Morris; and *Cross*, ed. Napier). **142** *waltrot*: L's reversal of *troteuale* (*Handlyng Synne* 9244). Both words are of doubtful origin but seem to mean 'an idle tale'; cf. *trufle* 147 (?pun), and *dido* XIII 173 (C). **149a** *Quia* . . . (Office of the Dead, Nocturn 3, resp. 7, from *Sarum Breviary* 2: 278). It continues *miserere mei Deus et salva me*. Based on Job 7: 9, the saying was widely instanced in penitential and vernacular literary works (see Alf*Q*, p. 110). **152–6** *venym*: see Bartholomaeus Anglicus (ed. Seymour), 1249–50. **161a** *Ars* . . : the 'stratagem' is God's assuming human form, as Lucifer did a serpent's (287), with the important difference that the Incarnation, though a mystery, is reality, not deception: *grace* is God's *sleighte*, not *gile*; see

355–8. **164–5** *Rightwisnesse . . . er we bothe*: it is apparent how God's justice is prior to his mercy, but not how it is prior to his truth, unless perhaps the latter is equated with his self-revelation to man (see 119 above). Righteousness will then be thought of as an aspect of God's unrevealed essence. But more probably it belongs with Truth as part of the especially ordained Law, and Mercy is later only in a temporal, not in a metaphysical sense (as belonging especially to the time of Grace). **180a** *Ad vesperum . . .* : in verse 4 the psalmist praises God for saving his 'soul from hell', the immediate cause of this rejoicing; this makes the psalm especially appropriate to the vigil of Easter Sunday, the time when the action to be narrated takes place. **181** *Love*: the cognomen for God which now replaces his earlier title 'Truth', as a fuller revelation of his nature and disposition towards man; the events sketched by Holy Church in I 148–74 have now been unfolded, and the reader (through the Dreamer) has acquired the *kynde knowyng* Will asked for at I 138. **185** *patente*: the New Covenant sealed in Christ's blood, which fulfils (not replaces) that of *Spes* (XVII 10), and is what Patience relied on at XIV 190–93. It brings mankind rest and peace because Love is the 'plant of peace' (I 152); cf. XV 254a (C). *In pace . . .* : the verse is the opening antiphon of Holy Saturday, matins. **213** *the sorwe of deying*: alludes to the doctrine of Christ's *kenosis* ('self-emptying') in Phil 2: 6–11, a passage of particular relevance here as it ends with Christ's exaltation recognized by the power of hell. **215** *modicum*: a passing semi-personification like those at IV 142–3. As there, *mete with* could mean 'equate' (*MED s.v. meten* v. (1), 4); but in both cases the allegory favours an encounter (*meten v.*, 4), the construction being as at XVI 172. Wordplay on the 'equate' sense is, however, quite likely. Peace is here teaching negatively what Holy Church had stated positively, that *Mesure is medicine*, but that (failing this), man must learn the evil of 'too much' (*sin*) by the contrary evil of 'too little' (*suffering*). **220** *kyndeliche . . . it:* 'to know it by direct experience/as in itself it really is' (cf. I 138); the familiar phrase brings home that the price of such knowledge is suffering: to 'know' man, God must become man, so to know God man must become like God. **229** *two brode eighen*: symbolizing the literal and spiritual sense of Scripture (Kaske, ' "Book" ', p. 127) or else perhaps the Old and New Testaments that make up the Bible ('Book'). **236** *elements*: the theme of the 'witnessing elements' goes back to Gregory's commentary on Mt 2: 1–2 (Kaske, ibid., 119). **238** *stella comata*: a (newly created) comet ('long-haired star') was the common interpretation of the star seen by the Magi in Mt 2 (see *ME Sermons*, ed. Ross, p. 227, cited AlfQ, p. 111). L's connecting the star with the angels (238–9) may be influenced by the account of the brightness (*claritas Dei*) at their appearance to the shepherds in Lk 2: 5. **250** *Symondes sones*: in *GNico*, Caryn and Lentin, sons of the Simeon of Lk 2: 25 who uttered the *Nunc dimittis*, are raised from the dead at Christ's resurrection and tell the story of the Harrowing in written form. 252 *Gigas* 'giant': Christ, whose breaking-down of the gates of hell (recalling Samson's carrying-off of the gates of Gaza, Jg 16: 3) is about to be witnessed (*Sk*). This is borne out by iconographic evidence (Anderson, fig. 11). Kaske ('*Gigas*') finds a reference to Ps 18: 6, uniformly interpreted as referring to Christ, who is a 'giant' because of his indomitability and more-than-human nature, and this is supported by the comment of Hugh of Saint-Cher: 'Whence he is called a *Giant*; of double nature, true God and true man'; the *gyn* he has 'devised' is his dual nature as 'god–man' (Alf*Q*, p. 111). 254–9 On these lines, see Donaldson's convincing arguments in 'Grammar'; *but* 'unless'; *to lyve* 'to life' or 'to live'; Book wagers his existence on the certainty of Jesus' resurrection and victory, and the Jews' discomfiture unless they believe in him. His vehement assertion, similar to Anima's at XV 83 (though obviously more apt to a book than to the soul), confirms the sense of *but* as 'unless' (Donaldson, 'Grammar') not 'but' (Kaske, 'Book'). 261 Ps 23, a royal processional psalm, was sung at matins on Holy Saturday; the phrase, applying 'gate' to the gates of hell (Mt 16: 18), is used in *GNico* and *LA* 54. On its use in semi-dramatic church ceremonies, which might have influenced L, see Young, ch. 5, index. 265 *Helle*: personified in the sources (*Inferus*); perhaps another name of Lucifer, who replies to Satan. 266, 269 *Lazar*: i.e. Lazarus of Bethany (XVI 113); Satan may think the patriarchs are going back to earth, or else to heaven. 276–7 *right . . . reson*: 'a well-grounded right in law'. Satan will need to be convinced, not just conquered, and his stance is that of Truth and Justice earlier, against Mercy and Peace. The former call to mind the principles of common law, based on inflexible precedent, and the latter those of chancery law, where concepts of equity and fairness prevail (Birnes). By the theory of the 'Devil's right' over man, the Devil was granted possession (283) over the human race after Adam's sin. He might lose this by attempting to seize a sinless soul (the 'abuse of power theory', formulated by Augustine in *De Trinitate* XIII (*PL* 42: 1025–31)); or, he might have it annulled by an offer of such a soul in ransom for the souls of men (the 'ransom' theory). L's Christ appeals to the latter at 353, and his Satan tries to avoid the former by preventing Christ's death (302–5). 281 *thretynge*: Gen 2: 17, 3: 19 specify death, not damnation; cf. 333 below. 282 *Soothnesse*: the 'revealed' Truth, *Veritas*. 283 *seventy hundred*: perhaps chosen for the metre, and see Textual Commentary; the commoner figure was four or five (thousand); cf. the familiar *Adam lay y-boundyn* 2. *iseised*: a legal term (see Alf*G*) indebted at this point to the English Version of Grosseteste's *Château* (ed. Sajavaara, p. 294). 297 *short answere*: at the temptation in the desert (Mt 4: 4,7). 299–300 L here follows the legend, developed from Mt 27: 19, that the Devil in a dream urged Pilate's wife to save Jesus in order to stop him dying to redeem mankind (see no. 30 in *York Plays*, ed. Beadle, lines 158–76, Kolve, pp. 228–30). 314a *Nunc . . .* : spoken by Christ in the source, here becomes an admission of defeat by the Devil. The battle here between Christ and Lucifer may be seen as a 'duel of chivalry' (Baldwin, 'Duel', pp. 72–6). 316, 318, 319a: these quotations from Ps 23 appear in *GNico* and *LA*, as does 325b. 338 *lusard*: here = serpent (cf. *addre* 336, 355), though the standard medieval representation was of a standing lizard-like creature with a woman's face. 341 Christ gives his soul in payment for Adam, but answers Lucifer's original *gile* by giving him tit for tat: hell cannot *hold* his soul (he thus fulfils the *lex* of 50). *synne to synne wende*: only the unjust will henceforth go to hell, the abode of sin. 361a comes from a psalm in praise of the justice of God's judgements. 365 *drynk*: a concrete actualization of the threat at 35a above. 366 *love is my drynke*: for full discussion, see Sch, 'Crucifixion', pp. 181–4. 370–1 *Josaphat*: 'Jehovah has judged' (Joel 3: 2, 12); traditionally understood as the place assigned for the Last Judgement. The vintage metaphor comes from verse 13, but L, drawing on other harvest and vintage images from the Gospels (e.g. Mt 13: 39), has transformed Joel's grapes of wrath into grapes of righteousness: God will save as well as judge. 371 *resureccio mortuorum*: the 11th clause of the Nicene Creed (cf. the clauses quoted at 111–12 above), occurs in I Cor 15: 12–13 and elsewhere (AlfQ). 378 *hole*: already his 'half-brothers' through the humanity Christ shares with them, they become his 'whole' brothers through adoption as sons of his heavenly Father (Rom 8: 15–17), alluding perhaps also to the chivalric custom of 'brotherhood-in-arms' (Baldwin, 'Duel', p. 758, n. 38). 379a *Tibi soli peccavi*: from the *Miserere*, the great penitential psalm of mercy: 'since sin is only an offence against himself ... [Christ] may forgive it if he chooses' (Goodridge). 380–4 allude to the custom at law of pardoning a criminal who had somehow managed to survive hanging. Edward III's pardon of one Walter Wynkeburn, hanged at Leicester in 1363, could be the actual incident alluded to (*Sk*). The point of the illustration is that the King of Kings can hardly be *less* just than a human king; man has already suffered *juwise* once (death) and there is no call for a second 'hanging' (damnation): a spell in prison (purgatory) will suffice to satisfy justice. 393 *til parce it hote*: from the first lesson of the Office of the Dead for matins, from Job 7: 16 (AlfQ; Alford, ' "Til *Parce*" '). 396a *Audivi*: L implicitly identifies himself with St Paul through the verb, referring here to the privileged apostle's experience of mystical *visiones et revelationes Domini* (II Cor 12: 1) when he was *raptus* 'ravished' or 'caught up', into heaven (verses 2, 4). This is perhaps L's boldest claim for the value and validity of his own 'visions and revelations'. 398 *al mankynde*: does not necessarily imply that all men *will* be saved, any more than 373 (which refers to judgement rather than election); but Christ retains the right, as judge and king, to show mercy to all men, thus giving them a chance to gain heaven. 400a *Non intres*: the whole of Ps 142, with its cry for deliverance from hell, is relevant here. 405 *Astroth*: Ishtar, the Babylonian Venus (Jer 7: 18); in medieval usage, a devil. 410a The quotation from

Alanus, appearing in this exact form in *Auctores octo* (Alf*Q*, p. 113), may
have been connected in L's mind with Tob 3: 22, a passage of special
relevance in this context (*Sk*). **419** *covenaunt*: a word redolent of the
theological implications of Christ's death, which establishes a 'new
covenant' (Heb 12: 24) between man and God that reconciles the
apparently irreconcilable (cf. 431b) and will be everlasting (423; cf. Heb
13: 20). **423a** *Misericordia* . . . : the psalm verse on which the whole
allegory of the Daughters of God is constructed. **424** *Te Deum*: the great
hymn of praise, formerly attributed to St Ambrose; not sung at the offices
during the penitential season. Its triumphant appearance signalizes the
end of Lent and the dawning of Easter, the greatest feast of the Church.
425a *Ecce* . . . : foreshadowing the image of the Church as Unity in XIX,
an interpretation of this is found in Brinton, *Sermons* (ed. Devlin, 2: 58,
114) (Alf*Q*, p. 113). **426** *carolden*: 'danced in a ring, in a round dance
(carole)'; a word with strongly secular associations which was altered to
daunseden in one tradition of both the B- and the C-texts. This is 'sacred
mirth', the Incarnation having healed and hallowed man's natural life.
428 *Kytte*; *Calote*: for discussion of these names' possible pejorative
associations, see Mustanoja, pp. 72–4; Alford, 'Coat', p. 136. That the
names may be fictitious need not suggest (*pace Pe*) that wife and daughter
are too. **430** *crepeth* . . . : alludes to the penitential practice of creeping
on one's knees to venerate the cross (part of the liturgy of Good Friday
and possibly also performed on Easter Sunday). Will's cry to perform this
act on Easter morning expresses his understanding that the continuing
cost of Christ's victory over death is participation by his followers in the
suffering that made that victory possible. *Pace* Harbert (p. 68), *juwel*
need not suggest that the cross venerated on Easter Sunday is not a
'crucifix' (cf. at XIX 63 *cros of his passion*, though he has now
conquered). The 'jewel' is a symbol of Christ himself, so called at XI 158.
For L's sense of liturgy as *anamnesis* 'making present again', cf. Vaughan.

Passus XIX

3 *housled*: all were required to receive communion yearly, preferably at
Easter, after confession. Will's resolve implies that he has confessed and is
in a state of grace. **4** *offryng*: i.e. at the offertory, when the people brought
their offerings to the priest. **6** *Piers* . . . *al blody*: recalling XVIII 24–5,
where Christ-as-Piers rode to the joust; the allusion is to the patristic
figure of 'Christ of the Winepress' developed in Bonaventure's *Vitis
mystica* (*PL* 184: 739; see Sch, 'Crucifixion', pp. 183–4). The image is
based on Is 63: 1–7, which begins with *Quis est iste?* (the question asked
by Lucifer at XVIII 316 about the *glorious* Christ). The image stresses the
notion (similar to that in *Pearl* 1135–40) that Christ in a manner
continues to suffer in the members of the Church of which he is head. **7**
with a cros: recalling V 12, though now it is not Reason preaching God's

wrath and the need for repentance but Conscience proclaiming God's love and mercy and the reward awaiting those who do repent. **14** *cros; conquerour*: alluding to the cross as a symbol of victory over God's enemies, as in Constantine's vision before the battle of the Milvian Bridge of a cross with the inscription *in hoc signo vinces*. **17** *knelen*: see Phil 2: 10, quoted at 80*a* below; on the nexus of kneeling images, of which this forms the centre, see Weldon, esp. pp. 56–8. **19; 25** *the name of . . . Jesus*: object of a devotion popularized by Richard Rolle, for whom naming it brings 'joy' (ed. Allen, p. 108); cf. XVI 161–3; Sch, 'Inner Dreams', pp. 31–2. **23–5** *Crist*: cf. Aquinas: 'in this name *Christ* are understood both the divinity which anoints and the humanity which is anointed' (*ST* III 16: 5), i.e. Christ = 'God-made-man'. **32–3** *lordes . . . thralles*: as conqueror, Christ can ennoble and enslave (*lordes* and *thralles* are antithetical); a notion of 'theological nobility', conferred by divine grace, is developed by the C14th legist Bartolus in his treatise on heraldry (Keen, *Chivalry*, p. 149). **37** *taillage*: on the civil disabilities of the Jews, see Cohn, pp. 79–80; Gilchrist, p. 111. **39** *frankeleyn*: 'a landowner and member of the gentry ranking immediately below the nobility; a freeman, a gentleman' (*MED s.v.*); cf. *generosus*, Intro, p. xx and *gentil men* 40, 'noble men'. Through baptism, men become 'free' (liberated from sin), through sanctifying grace 'noble' (= holy). **44** *justified*: 'brought them the means of justification', i.e. the *lawe of lif*. **62** *Crist*: L need not have thought *Christ* meant *conquerour* (*Sk*), merely have associated the ideas of 'the Anointed One' with the anointed *king* (David, II Kg 3: 39, or the king of England, anointed in the coronation service), moving on to the notion of *conqueror* as the 'superlative degree' of *knight* (see 27–30 above). **64** *to wissen us therwith*: reiterating the teaching of his *partyng felawe* Patience at XIV 190–5. **75** *Kynges*: LA calls the Magi kings, naming them Caspar, Balthasar and Melchior (ch. 14). **86** *covered under*: LA proposes gold = royalty/love; incense = divinity/prayer; myrrh = humanity/mortification of the flesh. L's symbolic meanings are his own but the virtues fit a king-conqueror. The apparent 'contradiction' (*Sk*) in 90 is removed by reading *richels* (see Textual Commentary *ad loc*). **92** *Pitee*: a near-synonym of *Ruthe* (83), *mercy* (93), but with the range of Latin *pietas* in the angel's speech (Pr 135). **103–4** *faught; gaf*: metaphors designed to keep the 'conqueror' analogy, alluding to Christ's arguing, driving out the sellers from the Temple, turning water to wine, (cf. 108). **111–12** *wyn is likned . . .* : Conscience interprets this miracle (water = the Old Law; wine = love, the New Law; cf. Jn 13: 34) as signifying the extension of love to one's enemies, which L recognizes as the distinctive ethical precept of Christianity. **116–200** *do wel*: Conscience makes Dowel Christ's act of *power* (changing water to wine 116), Dobet his acts of *compassion* (feeding, healing, 128), Dobest his acts of *pardon* to all mankind to come (through giving Peter his own power, 183). **133, 136** *Fili David*: the cry of the two blind men (Mt 9: 27) is run together with that of the crowds (*the contree*) at 21: 9, sung several times on Palm Sunday at the procession (see 138), Christ's entry into Jerusalem being compared to David's return after defeating Goliath. **152** *Christus resurgens*: 'Christ, rising again from the dead, dies now no more' (Rom 6: 9); sung as an antiphon during Easter (AlfQ p. 114). **161a** *Sic oportet . . .* : the quotation conflates Lk 2:26 *oportet* with 46 *oportebat*, the latter concluding *et resurgere a mortuis,* echoing *resurgens* 160 (AlfQ, after *Pe*). **165** An early tradition, going back to the C3rd Gnostic Acts of Thomas, made Thomas the apostle of India; see *LA*, ch. 5 on his life. **169–70** *Pax vobis . . . grope*: ironically recalled at XX 364; Friar Flatterer's act destroys contrition, where Thomas's creates faith. The greeting was that adopted by friars, on the basis of Lk 10:5. **181** *in sighte*: recalling XV 162, where Will has sought what is now revealed. **184** *Piers*: here identified with the apostle Peter, though at 188 with the Plowman, and at 11 with Christ; those who imitate Christ become one with him as he is with the Father (cf. Jn 14, esp. 20–3). **190** *and ellis*: 'in heaven (as well as earth)' rather than 'in the future (as well as here and now)' (referring to Mt 16: 19), recapitulating Pr 100–6. **202–5** *Spiritus Paraclitus*: from stanza 1 of *Beata nobis gaudia* (AlfQ, p. 15). *lightnynge . . . langages*: based on stanza 2, *ignis vibrante lumine/Linguae figuram detulit/Verbis ut essent proflui.* **209, 211** *Grace*: the Holy Ghost is the grace-bringer in stanzas 1 and 7 of *Veni, creator,* quoted at 211. **214** *Piers Plowman*: not here 'still Christ' (*Sk*), since Christ has ascended, the scene appears to be Pentecost and Piers can only = St Peter. **220** The idea of an Antichrist goes back to I Jn 2: 18, 22, 4: 3 (cf. also II Thess 2: 3–9). On medieval developments, see Cohn, pp. 33–6; Emmerson pp. 193–203. **229a** *Divisiones. . .* : the inclusion here of 'natural' talents, where Paul names spiritual graces, attests L's ideal of the oneness of religious and secular in 'Unity', seeing the world of the first two visions in a theologically profounder perspective. **248** *Folvyles lawes*: a sardonic allusion to the violent practices of the Folville family, a criminal gang active in Leicestershire in the early years of Edward III (McKisack, p. 204). Knights are to *recover* stolen goods from men like the Folvilles by the same methods the criminals use, for, as shown by the experience of the courteous Knight with Wastour in VI 164–8, who 'leet light of the lawe', only 'law' that law-breakers understand will work. To read *with* as 'against' (*OED s.v. with* prep. 2) renders the line commonplace; while the 'grace' in question corresponds to the obligation specified at I 94–6, the moderate *reson* has to yield to *wightnesse of handes* if circumstances require it. **260–3** recapitulate Passus VI–VII; the ploughing now has an allegorical (spiritual) sense because Piers is now head of a community directed to a spiritual end, without specific concern for the material basis of life: he is to *tilie truthe*. **261** *registrer*: specifically 'the clerk of an ecclesiastical court' (AlfG); what he 'receives' is an account of whether those 'on erthe' have made satisfaction for their sins. **264** *foure grete* *oxen*: especially apt since the ox was the traditional 'symbol' of the Evangelist Luke (*Sk*); see VI 238 (C). The usual number in a full team was eight, but four are depicted in the Luttrell Psalter illustration of ploughing (fol. 170r, Blanch, p. 21), a probably symbolic icon. **274–5a** *two aithes*: the Bible is to be used to interpret itself, precisely what the Fathers' commentaries set out to do, and especially implying the typological method used by L himself. **276** *greynes*: traced to Gregory's Homily 3 on Ezechiel, *PL* 76: 807–9 (Kaulbach, p. 136). *cardynales vertues*: the 'natural' (as opposed to the infused, supernatural) virtues on which the others depend (*cardo* 'hinge'). The Christian view of them was influenced by Is 11: 2–3, the list of the gifts of the spirit, prophetically applied to Christ. Of these, Aquinas regarded counsel, fortitude and piety as 'corresponding' to the cardinal virtues prudence, fortitude and justice. *Prudence*: 'foresight, sagacity' (from *providentia*); *Temperance*: not plain 'moderation' but restraint of the passions, as the necessary foundation of asceticism; *Fortitude*: the virtue that resists pain and fear; *Justice*: rectitude of judgement, a virtue close to *truth*, and so to God (cf. 300–1); Conscience describes it as the *chief seed* 410, and it runs through the poem as a major theme, an argument fully presented by Stokes; see AlfG, pp. 76–7. **312–14** Harrowing breaks the earth and covers the seeds against birds: the natural virtues need the help of revealed truth (the Bible interpreted by the Fathers) to foster *the plante of pees, moost precious of vertues*, which alone is powerful enough to destroy the choking weeds of vice. L here allows the tightly compressed metaphor of I 152 to flower out into an expansive recapitulating allegorical action. **331** *Unite*: an oblique English name (cf. 'Truth' for God) for the real essence of the actual Church, aiming to awake attention to the doctrine of the Church as Christ's body (the crucial source here is Eph 4: 1ff.). 'Unity' would have had poignant significance in 1378, the year in which Christendom was rent by the Great Schism. **336** *Piers*: now signifies '[Christ's] faithful pastors and teachers' (*Sk*), whom the Holy Spirit will accompany everywhere they preach and who will meet opposition from 'Antichrist', all the evil forces opposed to the religion of Jesus, from the period of the Neronian persecutions to the present day and so on till the end of time. **337** *bileve ... lawe*: the dogmatic and the moral teaching of the Church ('truth' and 'love'; cf. I 76, XVI 6). **338–end** recapitulate in reverse the actions of Vision 1 and (to some extent) Vision 2 (esp. Passus V–VI, III–IV). The Deadly Sins now return in force to assail Piers's barn, and eventually (in XX) they prevail. **342** *Surquidous*: presumption is personified as 'an officer (usually armed) in the service of the king', in ill-repute at the time for 'great extortions and oppressions' (AlfG *s.v.*). **349** *Confession ... Bileeve*: links the corruption of the sacrament of confession (by friars, it will be made clear) with the growth of false belief, moral evil (vice) leading to intellectual evil (heresy). **361** *pees*: 'unity of the spirit in the bond of *peace*' (Eph 4: 3); without *internal* peace, the

Church cannot well stand against enemies from outside; another probable allusion to the Schism, but also echoing Scriptural texts on the dangers of division (cf. I Jn 2:19). **367** *pyl*: the castle of the Church (see Wilkes on the image, referring to *Ancrene Wisse* (ed. Mabel Day, EETS OS 225 (1952), pp. 109–10) as the source). The whole Christian community is now under siege from a diabolical army, recapitulating IX 1–24, where the individual soul ('the castel . . . *Caro*') had been described as under siege from 'the Prince of this World'. L's vision is not simply of a correspondence between microcosm and macrocosm, individual and community; the health of the whole *depends* on that of each member. **371–5** recapitulate moments in Visions 1 and 2, esp. II 59, V 641. As the action draws near the present, the world depicted increasingly recalls the Field of Folk; **380–3** echoes the repentance of the Folk of the Field in V. **386** *lust*: 'sensual pleasure'; Alan of Lille writes of the 'army of the flesh' which fights against the soul (*PL* 120: 141). **395–6** allude to Christ's words in Mt 5: 23–4; cf. also I Cor 11: 28. Since *housel* is the sacrament of unity between the communicant and Christ, it requires complete accord between each Christian and every other (cf. the connection of 'a pece of the Paternoster' with spiritual 'feeding' at XIV 49). **400–4** recall the deceptions practised by Coveitise's wife in V 215ff. **413** *lewed vicory*: a character whose shrewd questioning of the actual state of the Church echoes the narrator's comment at Pr 107–11 contrasting the cardinals with the Cardinal Virtues. **420** *clamat cotidie*: 'a formula used to initiate legal proceedings against a public enemy' (Alf*Q*, 116; Alf*G*, pp. 28–9). **426ff.** *Avynoun . . .* : the vicar attacks venal cardinals who associate with Jewish money-lenders and merchants instead of looking after the churches in Rome possessing important relics from which they took their formal titles. Avignon, the papal residence until 1377, was the centre of papal taxation and litigation. The papacy raised loans from bankers, who may have included Jews (see Gilchrist, under 'Avignon'); in addition, Jewish merchants were major suppliers to the papal court and in June 1379 a Jew transported to Avignon the cardinals who supported the antipope Clement (Bennett, 'Date'). **432–52** *Inparfit is that Pope . . .* : this contrast between Piers, the ideal of what a pope should be, and the graceless actuality, may allude (432, 435–8) to both the Great Schism of 1378 and the war between Urban VI and the antipope Clement VII in April 1379 (Bennett, 'Date', p. 63). The vicar's expression 'the Pope' ironically leaves open who *is* the 'true' Pope; but England stood by the Roman Pope Urban against Clement, who had French support, and who returned to Avignon in September 1378. **455** *the comune . . . ful litel*: reiterates Anima's assertion that evil example from the clergy, here from its highest levels, acts to corrupt the whole Church (*Inparfit* 432 echoes XV 95). **467** *Spiritus Intellectus*: on the 'spirit of understanding' (ironic here) see 276 (C). The attitudes of the lord and king here are perversions of the knight's in VI 55 and the king's in IV 194–5. **473–4** *heed of lawe*

. . . *above alle*: effectively a statement of absolutism such as that uttered by the *comune* at Pr 145 but warned against by the angel (Pr 131–8) as inadequate without *pietas*. It runs the risk of confusing public authority with personal power, as the *vicory* claims has happened to the papacy (447–52 above). 483a *Omnia sunt . . .* : exact source untraced, but a close analogue is in a summary of the penitential treatise on the vices by Peraldus (AlfQ, p. 116, citing Wenzel).

Passus XX

10–11 *nede ne hath no lawe*: translating the maxim of natural law (see below) *Necessitas non habet legem*, quoted at C XIII 43a (see AlfG, p. 103). Dire need or extremity is meant: the man who uses force or theft to preserve his life does not incur the *dette* of sin. 18 *lawe of kynde*: here less *lex naturalis* ('natural law'), in the sense of principles of (moral) conduct forming part of man's nature as created in God's image, than 'the natural instinct of self-preservation', also ordained by God and prior to (and, in some circumstances, superior to) any man-made *lex*. 21–2 *Cardynale Vertues*: see XIX 283–90 (*C*); Nede sees temperance as intrinsically incapable of perversion: one cannot, by definition, be *too* temperate. The thought is very close to Alan of Lille: 'O what a glorious virtue is temperance, which makes virtue hold the middle, lest it should fall into diminution or develop to excess' (*Summa de arte praedicatoria*, PL 210: 162). This does not involve 'depreciation of the other virtues' (*Pe*) though it does recall Holy Church's teaching on *mesure*. 33a *Homo . . . disponit*: close to Prov 16: 9, which is more providential than fatalistic, and suggesting the attitude of dependence on God proposed by Need (cf. also verse 20: *qui sperat in Domino beatus est*). 35 *is next hym*: i.e. a state that brings man closest to God, the referent of *hym* (not Temperance (*Pe*)). Need's nearness to God derives from its capacity to induce humility; cf. also 40. 38 *Philosophres*: notably Diogenes the Cynic, famous for his scorn of riches; but Need in stressing the voluntariness of poverty (cf. also 49) recalls the traditional ascetic, not solely Franciscan, ideal as well as the resignation taught by Patience earlier (with *forsoke*, cf. XIV 265). 44 *Bothe fox and fowel*: not spoken at the crucifixion but to a scribe asking to be Christ's disciple (Mt 8: 20). That may, however, be fittingly seen as Christ's moment of *moost nede*; cf. als Ps 39: 18, 40: 2, 68: 30. Need's use of these words, and his whole position, appear suspect to most commentators. Adams connects him with Antichrist in the dream immediately following, and the *egestas* of Job 41: 13 and Gregory's comment on it, seeing him as expressing the friars' views on poverty and mendicancy ('Nature of "Need" '); Burrow (*Fictions*, pp. 95–100) sees Need as 'necessitous deprivation', the condition mentioned by Piers at VII 66, having a right to a share in the produce of God's earth, as recognized by Holy Church (I 18–21). For a positive view of Need, setting him and his argument in the traditional context of discussion of 'the poverty of the cross', see Sch, 'Crucifixion', pp. 188–92. When Need reappears at 232 (within the dream) he is *against* the friars' wish to have *cure* and wants them to live in the poverty they profess: he opposes their *coveitise*, as Conscience does their *envye* (233, 246). **53** *Antecrist*: corresponds to Mede in Vision I, his victory answering her defeat; but if Mede was worldly and carnal, he is diabolic. The allegory develops Mt 13: 24–30, 39, with some possible influence from a well-known French C13th poem, Huon de Méri's *Tournoiement d'Antéchrist* (Owen, pp. 145–7). He gives an apocalyptic feel to the attack, since he was seen as harbinger of the Second Coming of Christ. But this is 'realized eschatology': judgement is in every moment, not on a particular date in history. **70** *Pride*: with a lord like those favoured by Meed in III 53. **74** *fooles*: the spiritual, who regard worldly wisdom as folly in God's sight (I Cor 3: 18–19), in contrast to the sensual, who find spiritual things folly (I Cor 2: 14). The Pauline conception of the 'fool' is crucial to L's view of the religious man. **76** *crye ... Kynde*: recalling IX 24, where the individual soul is threatened by the Prince of this World, a type of the *fend* Antichrist (54). The Church's situation is now desperate because the Devil has human allies, including churchmen. In Passus IX Anima was entrusted to Inwit's protection until called by Kynde (at death: see 205 below); Conscience's only weapon against human pride is an appeal to old age, disease and the *deeth of kynde* (recalling XVIII 210). The sequence recapitulates Piers's resort to Hunger in VI 172–3. Kynde, who here sends disease rather than hunger to chastize sinning man, is L's final oblique cognomen for God, as 'Piers' (77) is for Christ and his faithful representative on earth. **80** *planetes*: alluding to the belief that the origin and cause of disease were influenced by the conjunction of planets and their 'aspects' at a patient's birth. **93–4** *mynstrals ... heraudes*: as in a tournament; this time the Death defeated by Christ in a joust returns to triumph over those whose 'Life' is sensual, not spiritual like that of his former adversary at XVIII 65 (see Tristram, pp. 158–83). **95** *Elde*: an appropriate figure as Death's bannerer (cf. Chaucer's Old Man in *PardT* (*CT* X. 713ff.)). **109–10** *to se*: either '(in order) to see' (cf. 106–8), or 'at seeing', and so ironical (*Sk*). In either case, 110 refers to the confidence, expressed in dissipation, of the survivors of the plague. The assault of the Deadly Sins recapitulates and reverses the confessions of the latter in V, as do 126–39 the defeat of Mede in Passus IV. **126–30** The lines briefly recapitulate II 52–233, but with the position of Fals (131) here successfully reversed. **130** *kneled to*: an ironic gesture of mockery (contrast Conscience's sincere kneeling at III 116, XIX 12). **143** *daggen*: cutting the edges of garments into elaborate patterns in the fashionable style was attacked by moralists as both vain and wasteful (cf. Chaucer, *ParsT* (*CT* X. 416–20)). **153** *heighnesse of herte*: reversing Pernel's rejection of this vice at V 67. **156** *Fortune:* the fickle character of XI joins

Life here, showing how the temporary respite afforded the worldly survivors is not used for repentance. **167** *good hope*: like the *welhope* of XIII 454 is based on the good deeds done in life and on forgiveness of sin, with which L associates it (cf. V 507). **172** *glazene howve*: the proverbial glass helmet, like the physicians' nostrums, provides no real protection. **176** *furred hood*: recalling VI 268. **183** *myn heed*: dramatically brings Will back into the action. Old age being universal, Will can here stand as a representative of common humanity, as he did in 60–1. **193** *my wif*: sardonically identified with fleshly desire, as in its allegorical meaning at XVII 330–1. **198** *and heo*: a characteristic clerkly slur on woman's appetite: cf. Map, *Golias de conjuge* . . . 149–56 (ed. Wright, *Latin Poems*, p. 88). **203** *ben hennes*: Will has learnt by *kynde knowyng* 'the knowledge derived from experience' to desire what the ascetics of XIX 249 (*q.v.*) knew from the outset, detachment from the transience of worldly things. **207** *what craft* . . . : Will's blunt question about the 'best' gets an equally direct and authoritative answer from Kynde/Truth (*the beste* I 207/God); but it has taken his whole life to learn the meaning of the 'craft' *kyndeliche*. **212–13** *by conseil of Kynde*: warned by the voice of God operating through natural experience, Will reconciles himself to the Church by penance and communion. **214** *conestable*: as governor of Unity, recapitulates the function of the knight Inwit, his *alter ego*, at IX 7–18; the focus is now on leadership of the Church as a whole. **215** *geaunts*: the Deadly Sins, against whose leader Dowel had marshalled his sons to protect Anima (IX 23). The term is an ironic 'reverse-echo' of XVIII 252, where it is used of Christ. **232** *Nede*: insists that the friars 'eat' (*chewe*) their chosen food of poverty, or else 'angel's food' (God alone: like Mary Magdalen, XV 295). See 44 (C) above. **250** *logik . . . lovye*: the friars have turned from their founders' intentions towards a subject which weakens both faith and social order (cf. XI 223–4, XV 70–2, and 275–6 below). 'Logic' probably means 'philosophy', as at XII 266; 250b echoes Kynde's injunction at 208, underlining the link between Kynde and Conscience (80, 151). **254** *mesure*: a rule that limits, in accord with a rational judgement of what is 'proper' – whether stars, soldiers or friars. **270** alludes to the notion that there is a fixed and 'even' number of the blessed (cf. Apoc 7: 4), with a pun on *Hevene/evene* (homophones in L's language), while in hell there is *nullus ordo* 'no order' (Job 10: 22), including limitlessness of number, a sign of chaos: a Biblical and Neo-Platonic idea of *nombres proporcionables* familiar from Wisd 11: 21 and Boethius (*Boece*, III, metrum ix; Chadwick, pp. 75, 234). Since friars are mendicants they need have no natural limit imposed by the number of religious houses available. **275** *Plato*; *Seneca*: neither philosopher taught pure communism, though Plato (*Republic* III, 416e) required his Guardians to possess no more property than was strictly necessary, and Seneca (*Epistles* IX, 3) stated that avarice destroyed the Golden Age (when ownership was in common). The peasant leader John Ball was said to have taught the doctrine of primeval common possession (Lord Berners' translation of *The Chronicles of Froissart*, ed. G. C. Macaulay (1913), p. 251) and was not unsympathetic to the mendicants (McKisack, p. 421); but Owst (p. 288) found no such doctrine in the extant sermons of friars. **279** *Non concupisces* . . . : in this form, a maxim of canon law based on Ex 20: 17, Deut 5: 21 (AlfQ) and used in Richard FitzRalph's polemic against the friars' claims to jurisdiction (Scase, pp. 24–31). **296** *scole*: on some of these friar-philosophers, see Leff, pp. 279–94; Coleman, pp. 151–8. **311** *in the sege*: 'present at the siege' (i.e. somewhere outside the barn). Sire Leef is *within* Unitee; Friar Flatterer enters from outside. Despite the apparent oddity of seeking a physician amongst the enemy, this is what the allegory requires, and Sch, *PP Transl* (p. 252) is mistaken in attempting rationally to accommodate the friars, as already, in a sense, in Unity, as members of the Church (244–7). Paradoxically, they are within the Church (as a community of the baptized) but some of them, like Flatterer, are outside the Church (understood as 'fools' vowed to holiness) and prefer *scole* to *Unite*. Conscience is, however, unwilling to condemn them unconditionally; despite knowing Flatterer's name (324) he takes the risk that any kind of sacramental penance might be better than none ('I may wel suffre' 323 echoes the tolerance attributed to God at XI 379–81: it is a form of *hendenesse* (145; cf. 349)); however, though not deceived by Mede, he succumbs to a hypocritical friar (perhaps L's strongest statement of the danger in the friars' fluent address). For a general discussion of Conscience in *PP* and esp. in XX, see Jenkins; and on the difficulty of his admission of Flatterer, Harwood, *Belief*, p. 136; Simpson, *Introduction*, pp. 241–2. Interpretation of Conscience's failure depends on seeing him as both fallible and indestructible (151). **331** *Pees* . . . *porter*: perhaps based on Eph 4: 3. **341** *Penetrans-domos*: a text often cited in antifraternal writings (Szittya, esp. ch. 7; Scase, pp. 32–9); according to the friars' opponent, William of Saint-Amour, they break into the *domus conscientiae* (Szittya, p. 305). **355–6** *Hende-Speche*: both the gracious politeness incumbent on Christians and, from another standpoint, the 'glib and oily art' of the mendicants themselves. The word *curteisly* 356 succinctly indicates that the friars win men's confidence through their persuasive talk. **365–8** *praye for yow*: recapitulate the words of the flattering friar to Mede at III 35–50. **378** *adreynt and dremeth*: Contrition, instead of being vigilant, as *Vigilate* had warned Sloth, has become confused about the real condition of his soul, sleep here being an image of ignorance and spiritual decay. **384** *fyndyng* . . . *for nede flateren*: they require some formal endowment to live on, since in reality they cannot live on *cheitiftee, poverte* (236) but resort to corrupt means of livelihood. Conscience is in fact rejecting Need's solution not as wrong, but as unrealistic. **385–end** Conscience should not be taken over-literally as intending to 'leave' the (corrupted) Church. That would be entirely against his nature as the true conscientious Christian, tuned to the good, though not infallible, receptive to grace, but humanly limited. His resolution resembles that of Piers to set out as a pilgrim at VI 58. His last cry is an expression of total dependence on God the Trinity (*Kynde*, 'the Creator' (Father), *Piers*, 'God Incarnate' (the Son), Grace (the Holy Spirit), the final and sole supports of the individual conscience and the Christian community alike.

BIBLIOGRAPHY

The Bibliography includes all books and articles referred to by short title or author in the Introduction and Commentary and a selection of the main works consulted but not specifically mentioned. The place of publication of books is London unless otherwise specified. Useful aids to study are: K. Proppe, *PP: An Annotated Bibliography for 1900–1968*, *Comitatus* 3 (Los Angeles, Calif., 1972), pp. 33–90; A. J. Colaianne, *PP: An Annotated Bibliography of Editions and Criticism 1550–1977* (New York and London, 1978); D. Pearsall, *An Annotated Critical Bibliography of L* (New York and London, 1990); A. Middleton, 'XVIII. *PP*', in A. E. Hartung, ed.: *A Manual of the Writings in Middle English 1050–1500*, vol. 7 (New Haven, Conn., 1986), 2211–34, 2417–43; and the 'Annual Bibliography' in *The Yearbook of Langland Studies* (East Lansing, Mich., 1987–); and for a general introduction to L, J. A. Alford, ed: *A Companion to PP* (Los Angeles and London, 1988) (reviewed Schmidt, *JEGP* 89 (1990) 214–15). C. D. Benson and L. S. Blanchfield, *The Manuscripts of 'Piers Plowman'* (Cambridge, 1997). T. Matsushita, ed.: *A Glossarial Concordance to William Langland's The Vision of Piers Plowman: The B-Text*, Vol. I (2 parts), (Tokyo, 1998). C. Brewer, *Editing 'Piers Plowman'* (Cambridge, 1996). Articles where revised and reprinted are referred to in their latest published form. Items of particular help to the student are asterisked.

Abbot, C.C., ed.: *The Letters of Gerard Manley Hopkins to Robert Bridges* (Oxford, 1935).

Adair, J.: *The Pilgrim's Way* (1978).

Adams, R.: 'The Nature of Need in *PP*', *Traditio* 34 (1978) 273–301.

—— 'Piers's Pardon and L's Semi-Pelagianism', *Traditio* 39 (1983) 367–418.

—— 'The Reliability of the Rubrics in the B-Text of *PP*', *MÆ* 54 (1985) 20–31.

—— 'Editing and the Limitations of the *Durior Lectio*', *YLS* 5 (1991) 7–15.

*Aers, D.: *PP and Christian Allegory* (1975).

—— *Chaucer, L and the Creative Imagination* (1980).

—— '*PP* and Problems in the Perception of Poverty: a Culture in Transition', *Leeds Studies in English* 14 (1983) 5–25.

Alford, J.: '*PP* B XVIII 390: "Til Parce It Hote" ', *MP* 69 (1972) 323–5.

—— 'Haukyn's Coat: Some Observations on *PP* B XIV 22–27', *MÆ* 43 (1974) 133–8.

—— 'Some Unidentified Quotations in *PP*', *MP* 72 (1975) 390–9.

—— 'The Role of the Quotations in *PP*', *Spec.* 52 (1977) 80–99.

—— 'The Idea of Reason in *PP*', in Kennedy *et al.*, eds, *Medieval Studies.*

—— *PP: A Glossary of Legal Diction* (Cambridge, 1988).

——* *PP: A Guide to the Quotations* (New York, 1992).

Allen, H. E.: *English Writings of Richard Rolle* (Oxford, 1931).

Anderson, M.D.: *History and Imagery in British Churches* (1971).

Arias, L., ed.: *Tratado sobre La Santisima Trinidad* (Madrid, 1968). [Augustine's *De Trinitate*].

Baldwin, A.: *The Theme of Government in PP* (Cambridge, 1981).

—— 'The Double Duel in *PP* B XVIII and C XXI', *MÆ* 50 (1981) 64–78.

—— 'The Triumph of Patience in Julian of Norwich and L', in Phillips, ed., *Essays . . . Hussey*, pp. 71–83.

Barr, H., ed.: *The PP Tradition* (1993).

Barratt, A.: 'The Characters "Civil" and "Theology" in *PP*', *Traditio* 38 (1982) 352–64.

Beadle, R., ed.: *The York Plays* (1982).

Bennett, H. S.: *Life on the English Manor* (Cambridge; 1937; repr. 1974).

*Bennett, J. A. W., ed.: *PP: B-text, Prologue and Passus I–VII* (Oxford, 1972).

—— 'The Date of the B-Text of *PP*', *MÆ* 12 (1943) 55–64.

—— 'The Passion in *PP* XX', ch. 4 of his *Poetry of the Passion* (Oxford, 1982), pp. 85–112.

—— *Middle English Literature*, ed. Douglas Gray (Oxford, 1986).

Bennett, J. A. W., and Smithers, G. V., eds: *Early Middle English Verse and Prose* (Oxford, 1966).

Biggs, F. M.: ' "Aungeles Peeris": *PP* B 16.67–72 and C 18.85–100', *Anglia* 102 (1984) 426–36.

Birnes, W. J.: 'Christ as Advocate: the Legal Metaphor of *PP*', *Annuale Mediaevale* 16 (1975) 71–93.

Blackman, Elsie: 'Notes on the B-Text of *PP*', *JEGP* 17 (1918) 489–545.

Blake, N., ed.: *Middle English Religious Prose* (1972).

*Blanch, R. J., ed.: *Style and Symbolism in PP: a Modern Critical Anthology* (Knoxville, Tenn., 1969).

Bland, C. R.: 'L's Use of the Term *Ex vi transicionis*', *YLS* 2 (1988) 125–35.

Bloomfield, M. W.: *The Seven Deadly Sins* (Ann Arbor, Mich., 1952).

—— '*PP* and the Three Grades of Chastity', *Anglia* 76 (1958) 227–53.

—— *PP as a Fourteenth Century Apocalypse* (New Brunswick, NJ, 1961).

Blume, C., ed.: *John Hoveden: Nachtigallenlied* (Leipzig, 1930).

Bradley, H.: 'Some Cruces in *PP*', *MLR* 5 (1910) 340–2.

Brown, C., ed.: *English Lyrics of the XIIIth Century* (Oxford, 1932).

Bullock-Davies, C.: *Menestrellorum Multitudo: Minstrels at a Royal Feast* (Cardiff, 1978).

Burrow, J.A.: 'Words, Works and Will: Theme and Structure in *PP*', in Hussey, ed., *Approaches*, pp. 111–24.

——*Ricardian Poetry* (1971).

——'L *nel mezzo del cammin*', in Heyworth, ed.: *Medieval Studies*, pp. 21–41.

——*Essays in Medieval Literature* (Oxford, 1984).

—— *The Ages of Man* (Oxford, 1986).

—— *Langland's Fictions* (Oxford, 1993).

—— *Thinking in Poetry: Three Medieval Examples* (1993)

Carruthers, M.: *The Search for St Truth* (Evanston, Ill., 1973).

Chadwick, H.: *Boethius* (Oxford, 1981).

Chambers, R.W., ed.: *PP: The Huntington Library MS (Hm 143)* (San Marino, Calif., 1936).

Chambers, R.W., and Grattan, J. G.: 'The Text of *PP*: Critical Methods', *MLR* 11 (1916) 257–75.

——'The Text of *PP*', *MLR* 26 (1931) 1–55.

Chroust, A-H.: *Aristotle*, 2 vols (1973).

Coghill, N.: 'God's Wenches and the Light that Spoke (some notes on L's kind of poetry)' in D. Gray, ed., *The Collected Papers of Nevill Coghill, Shakespearean and Medievalist* (Brighton, 1988), pp. 199–217.

Cohn, N.: *The Pursuit of the Millennium* (repr. 1972).

Coleman, Janet: *PP and the Moderni* (Rome, 1981).

*Colunga, A. and Turrado, L., eds: *Biblia Vulgata* (Madrid, 1965).

Comparetti, D.: *Vergil in the Middle Ages*, tr. E. F. M. Beneche (repr. 1966).

Cornelius, R. D.: *The Figurative Castle* (Bryn Mawr, Pa, 1930).

Courtenay, W. J.: *Schools and Scholars in 14th Century England* (Princeton, NJ, 1987).

Daly, S. R.: 'Peter Comestor: Master of Histories', *Spec.* 32 (1957) 62–73.

Davis, N., ed.: *Non-Cycle Plays and Fragments*, EETS, E.S. I (1970).

Davlin, Sr M. C.: '*Kynde Knowynge* as a Major Theme in *PP* B', *RES* n.s. 22 (1971), 1–19.

——*A Game of Heuene: Word Play and the Meaning of PP B* (Cambridge, 1989).

D'Evelyn, C., ed.: *Meditations on the Life and Passion of Christ*, EETS OS 158 (1921).

Devlin, M. A., ed.: *The Sermons of Thomas Brinton*, 2 vols (1954).

*Donaldson, E. T.: *PP: The C-Text and its Poet* (New Haven and London, 1949).

——'The Grammar of Book's Speech in *PP*', in *Schlauch Studies*, (Warsaw, 1966); repr. in Blanch, ed., *Style and Symbolism*, pp. 264–70.

Doyle, A. I.: 'Remarks on Surviving MSS of *PP*', in Kratzmann and Simpson, eds, *Medieval English . . . Russell*, pp. 35–48.

Dronke, P.: 'Arbor Caritatis', in P. L. Heyworth, ed., *Medieval Studies*, pp. 207–43.

Du Boulay, F. R. H.: *The England of PP* (Cambridge, 1991).

Duggan, H. N.: 'The Authenticity of the Z-Text of *PP*: Further Notes on Metrical Evidence', *MÆ* 56 (1987) 25–45.

Dunning, T. P.: 'L and the Salvation of the Heathen', *MÆ* 12 (1943) 45–54.

——* 'The Structure of the B-Text of *PP*', *RES* n.s. 7 (1956) 225–37; repr. in Blanch, ed., *Style and Symbolism*, pp. 87–100.

——*PP: An Interpretation of the A Text*, 2nd edn. rev. and ed. T. R. Dolan (Oxford, 1980).

Eccles, M., ed.: *The Macro Plays*, EETS OS 262 (1969).

Emmerson, R. K.: *Antichrist in the Middle Ages* (Seattle, Wash., 1981).

Evans, J.; and Serjeantson, M., eds: *English Medieval Lapidaries*, EETS OS 190 (1933).

Fletcher, A.J.: 'The Social Trinity of *PP*', *RES* 44 (1993) 343–61.

*Ford, B., ed.: *Medieval Literature: Chaucer and the Alliterative Tradition* (Harmondsworth, 1982).

Frank, R. W.: 'The Pardon Scene in *PP*', *Spec.* 26 (1951) 317–31.

—— 'The Art of Reading Medieval Personification-Allegory', *ELH* 20 (1953) 237–50.

——*PP and the Scheme of Salvation* (New Haven, Conn., 1957).

—— 'The "Hungry Gap", Crop Failure, and Famine: the C14th Agricultural Crisis and *PP*', *YLS* 4 (1990) 87–104.

Freud, S.: *The Interpretation of Dreams*, tr. J. Strachey (1954).

Furnivall, F. J., ed.: *Robert of Brunne's 'Handlyng Synne'*, EETS OS 119, 123 (1901–3).

Gaffney, W.: 'The Allegory of the Christ-Knight in *PP*', *PMLA* 46 (1931) 155–68.

Gilbert, B. B.: ' "Civil" and the Notaries in *PP*', *MÆ* 50 (1981) 49–63.

Gilchrist, J.: *The Church and Economic Activity in the Middle Ages* (1969).

Girouard, M.: *Life in the English Country House* (New Haven, Conn., 1978).

Godden, M.: *The Making of PP* (1990).

Goldsmith, Margaret E.: *The Figure of PP* (Cambridge, 1981).

*Goodridge, J. F., tr.: *Piers the Ploughman* (2nd edn Harmondsworth, 1966).

Gradon, P.: 'L and the Ideology of Dissent', *PBA* 66 (1982 for 1980).

—— '*Trajanus Redivivus*: Another Look at Trajan in *PP*', in D. Gray and E. G. Stanley, eds, *Middle English Studies presented to Norman Davis* (Oxford, 1983), pp. 71–103.

Gray, N.: 'L's Quotations from the Penitential Tradition', *MP* 84 (1986) 53–60.

Green, R. F.: 'The Lost Exemplar of the Z-Text of *PP* and its 20-Line Pages', *MÆ* 56 (1987) 307–10.

Greene, R., ed.: *A Selection of English Carols* (Oxford, 1962).

Greg, W. W.: *The Calculus of Variants* (Oxford, 1927).

Hanna, R.: 'Studies in the MSS of *PP*', *YLS* 7 (1993) 1–25.

Harbert, B.: 'Langland's Easter', in Phillips, ed., *Essays . . . Hussey,* pp. 57–70.

Haren, M.: *Medieval Thought: The Western Intellectual Tradition from Antiquity to the Thirteenth Century* (1985).

Harwood, B. J.: 'Clergye and the Action of the Third Vision in *PP*', *MP* 70 (1973), 279–90.

—— 'Liberum Arbitrium in the C-Text', *PQ* 52 (1973) 680–95.

—— 'Imaginative in *PP*', *MÆ* 44 (1975) 249–63.

—— *PP and the Problem of Belief* (Toronto, 1992).

Harwood, B. and Smith, R. F.: 'Inwit and the Castle of *Caro* in *PP*', *NM* 71 (1970) 48–54.

Hassall, W. O.: *The Holkham Bible Picture Book* (1954).

Hennecke, E.: *New Testament Apocrypha* I (1963).

Heyworth, P. L., ed.: *Medieval Studies for J. A. W. Bennett Aetatis Suae LXX* (Oxford, 1981).

*Holy Bible: Douay–Rheims Version (1956).

Hort, G.: *PP and Contemporary Religious Thought* (1938).

Howard, D. R.: *The Three Temptations* (Princeton, NJ 1966).

Hudson, A.: *The Premature Reformation: Wycliffite Texts and Lollard History* (Oxford, 1988).

Hulme, W. H., ed.: *The Middle English Harrowing of Hell and Gospel of Nicodemus,* EETS ES 100 (1907).

Huppé, B. F.: 'The Date of the B-Text of *PP*', *SP* 38 (1941) 36–44.

—— '*Petrus, id est, Christus*: Word Play in *PP*', *ELH* 17 (1950) 163–70.

Hussey, S. S.: 'L., Hilton and the Three Lives', *RES* n.s. 7 (1956) 132–59.

——'L's Reading of Alliterative Poetry', *MLR* 60 (1965) 163–70.

——*(ed.): *PP: Critical Approaches* (1969).

Jenkins, P.: 'Conscience: The Frustration of Allegory', in Hussey, ed., *Approaches,* pp. 124–42.

Jones, H. S. V.: 'Imaginatif in *PP*', *JEGP* 13 (1914) 583–8.

*Jusserand, J. J.: English Wayfaring Life in the Middle Ages (1899).

Kane, G.: *PP: The Evidence for Authorship* (1965).

——*The Autobiographical Fallacy in Chaucer and L Studies* (1965).

—— ed.: *PP: the A-Version,* 2nd edn (London and Los Angeles, 1988).

—— 'The "Z Version" of *PP*', *Spec.* 60 (1985) 910–30.

—— 'The Text', in Alford, ed., *Companion.*

Kane, G. and Donaldson, E. T., eds: *PP: The B-Version,* 2nd edn (London and Los Angeles, 1988).

Kaske R. E.: '*Gigas* the Giant in *PP*', *JEGP* 56 (1957) 177–85.

—— 'L and the *Paradisus Claustralis*', *MLN* 72 (1957) 481–3.

—— 'The Speech of "Book" in *PP*', *Anglia* 77 (1959) 117–44

—— ' "*Ex vi transicionis*" and its Passage in *PP*', *JEGP* 62 (1963) 32–60; repr. with revisions in Blanch, ed., *Style and Symbolism*, pp. 228–63.

—— 'Holy Church's Speech and the Structure of *PP*', in B. Rowland, ed.: *Chaucer and Middle English: Studies in Honour of R. H. Robbins* (1974).

Katzenellenbogen, A.: *Allegories of the Virtues and Vices in Medieval Art* (1939; repr. Toronto, 1989).

Kaulbach, E.: *Imaginative Prophecy in the B-text of PP* (Cambridge, 1993).

Kean, P. M.: 'Love, Law and *Lewte* in *PP*', *RES* n.s. 15 (1964) 241–61; repr. in Blanch, ed., *Style and Symbolism*, pp. 132–55.

—— 'L on the Incarnation', *RES* n.s. 16 (1965) 349–63.

—— 'Justice, Kingship and the Good Life in the Second Part of *PP*', in Hussey, ed., *Approaches*, pp. 76–100.

Keen, M.: *Pelican History of Medieval Europe* (repr. Harmondsworth, 1975).

—— *Chivalry* (New Haven and London, 1984).

Kellogg, A. L.: 'L and Two Scriptural Texts', *Traditio* 14 (1958) 385–98.

Kennedy, E. D. *et al.*, eds: *Medieval English Studies presented to George Kane* (Woodbridge, 1988).

Kirk, R.: 'References to the Law in *PP*', *PMLA* 48 (1933) 322–8.

Knott, T. A.: 'An Essay toward the Critical Text of the A-Version of *PP*', *MP* 12 (1915) 129–61.

Knott, T. A. and Fowler, D. C., eds: *PP: A Critical Edition of the A-Version* (Baltimore, Md. 1952).

Kolve, V. A.: *The Play Called Corpus Christi* (Stanford, Calif., 1966).

Kratzmann, G. and Simpson, J., eds: *Medieval English Religious and Ethical Literature: Essays in Honour of G. H. Russell* (Cambridge, 1986).

Lawlor, J.: 'The Imaginative Unity of *PP*', *RES* 8 (1957) 113–26; repr. in Blanch, ed., *Style and Symbolism*, pp. 101–16.

—— *PP: An Essay in Criticism* (1962).

Lawton, D., ed.: *Middle English Alliterative Poetry and its Literary Background* (Cambridge, 1982).

Leff, G.: *Medieval Thought: St Augustine to Ockham* (Harmondsworth, 1958).

Levy, B. S., and Szarmach, P. E., eds: *The Alliterative Tradition in the Fourteenth Century* (Kent, Ohio, 1981).

*Lewis, C. S.: *The Discarded Image* (Cambridge, 1964).

*McKisack, M.: *The Fourteenth Century, 1307–1399 (Oxford, 1959).

Maguire, S.: 'The Significance of Haukyn, *Activa Vita*, in *PP*', *RES* 25

(1949) 97–109; repr. in Blanch, ed., *Style and Symbolism*, pp. 194–208.

Mâle, E.: *The Gothic Image*, tr. D. Nussey (1961).

Mann, J.: *Chaucer and Medieval Estates Satire* (Cambridge, 1973).

Marcett, M. E.: *Uthred de Boldon, Friar William Jordan and PP* (New York, 1938).

Middleton, A.: 'Two Infinites: Grammatical Metaphor in *PP*', *ELH* 39 (1972) 169–88.

——'The Audience and Public of *PP*', in Lawton, ed., *ME Alliterative Poetry*, 101–23.

——'The Passion of Seint Averoys [B.13.91]: "Deuynyng" and Divinity in the Banquet Scene', *YLS* 1 (1987) 31–40.

——'Making a Good End: John But as a Reader of *PP*', in Kennedy *et al.*, eds, *Medieval Studies*, pp. 243–66.

Minnis, A. J.: 'L's Ymaginatif and late-medieval theories of imagination', in *Comparative Criticism: A Year Book* 3 (Cambridge, 1981) 71–103.

Mitchell, A. G.: *Lady Meed and the Art of PP*, Chambers Memorial Lecture 1956; repr. in Blanch, ed., *Style and Symbolism*, pp. 174–93.

Morgan, G.: 'The Meaning of Kind Wit, Conscience and Reason in the First Vision of *PP*', *MP* 84 (1987) 351–8.

——'The Status and Meaning of Meed in the First Vision of *PP*', *Neophilologus* 72 (1988) 449–63.

Morris, R., ed.: *Legends of the Holy Rood*, EETS OS 103 (1871).

Murray, J., ed.: Robert Grosseteste's *Le Chasteau d'Amour* (Paris, 1918).

Mustanoja, T.F.: 'The Suggestive Use of Christian Names in ME Poetry', in J. Mandel and B. A. Rosenberg, eds, *Medieval Literature and Folklore Studies: Essays in Honor of Francis Lee Utley* (New Brunswick, NJ, 1970) pp. 51–76.

Napier, A. S., ed.: *The Legend of the Cross* EETS OS 103 (1894).

Offord, M. Y.: *The Parlement of the Thre Ages*, EETS OS 246 (1959).

Orsten, E.M.: 'Patientia in the B-Text of *PP*', *MS* 31 (1969) 317–33.

——' "Heaven on Earth" – L's Vision of Life Within the Cloister', *American Benedictine Review* (1970) 526–34.

Owen, D. L.: *PP: A Comparison with Some Earlier and Contemporary French Allegories* (1912).

Owst, G. R.: *Literature and Pulpit in Medieval England*, 2nd edn (Oxford, 1961).

Partner, P.: *The Murdered Magicians: The Templars and their Myth* (Oxford, 1982).

*Pearsall, D., ed.: *PP: The C-Text* (1978).

—— 'The Origins of the Alliterative Revival', in Levy and Szarmach, eds, *Alliterative Tradition*, pp. 1–24.

—— 'The Alliterative Revival: Origins and Social Backgrounds', in Lawton, ed., *ME Alliterative Poetry*, pp. 34–53.

—— 'Poverty and Poor People in *PP*', in Kennedy *et al.*, eds, *Medieval Studies*, pp. 167–85.

Peebles, R. J.: *The Legend of Longinus in Ecclesiastical Art and in English Literature*, Bryn Mawr Monographs 9 (Bryn Mawr, Pa, 1911).

Phillips, H., ed.: *Langland, the Mystics and the Medieval English Religious Tradition: Essays in Honour of S. S. Hussey* (Cambridge, 1990).

Poole, A. L. ed.: *Medieval England*, 2 vols, (Oxford, 1958).

Postan, M. M.: *The Medieval Economy and Society* (1972; repr. Harmondsworth, 1975).

Proctor, F., and Wordsworth, C., eds: *Breviarium ad usum insignis ecclesiae Sarum* (Cambridge, 1857–86).

Quirk, R.: 'L's Use of *Kind Wit* and *Inwit*', *JEGP* 52 (1953) 182–9.

Raby, F. J. E., *The Oxford Book of Medieval Latin Verse* (Oxford, 1974).

Revard, C.: '*Title* and *Auaunced* in *PP* B. 11.290', *YLS* 1 (1987) 116–21.

Rickert, E.: 'John But, Messenger and Maker', *MP* 11 (1913–14) 107–16.

Rigg, A.C., and Brewer, C., eds: *PP: The Z Version* (Toronto, 1983).

Robert, A. C. M., ed.: *Fabliaux inédits* (Paris, 1834).

Robertson, D. W., Jr, and Huppé, B. F.: *PP and Scriptural Tradition* (Princeton, NJ, 1951).

Rosenthal, J. T.: *The Purchase of Paradise: Gift-Giving and the Aristocracy, 1307–1485* (1972).

Ross, W. O., ed.: *Middle English Sermons*, EETS OS 209 (1940).

Rotuli Parliamentorum, ed. J. Strachey *et al.*, 6 vols (1767–77).

Russell, G. H., and Nathan, V.: 'A *PP* MS in the Huntington Library', *HLQ* 26 (1963) 119–30.

Saint-Jacques, R.: 'The Liturgical Associations of L's Samaritan', *Traditio* 25 (1969) 217–30.

——'L's "Spes" the Spy and the Book of Numbers', *NQ* n.s. 24 (1978) 483–5.

Sajavaara, K., ed.: *The ME Translations of Robert Grosseteste's' Château d'Amour'* (Helsinki, 1967).

*Salter, E.: *PP: An Introduction* (Oxford, 1962).

Salter, E., and Pearsall, D., eds: *PP [Selections from the C-Text]*, York Medieval Texts (1967).

Salter, E., *English and International: Studies in the Literature, Art and Patronage of Medieval England*, ed. D. Pearsall and N. Zeeman (Cambridge, 1988).

Samuels, M. L.: 'L's Dialect', *MÆ* 54 (1985) 232–47.

Sargent, H. J. and Kittredge, G. L., eds.: *English and Scottish Popular Ballads* (Boston, 1932).

Scase, W.: *PP and the New Anticlericalism* (Cambridge, 1989).

Schiller, G: *Iconography of Christian Art*, 2 vols (1971–2).

Schmidt, A. V. C.: 'A Note on the Phrase "Free Wit" in the C-Text of *PP*, XI 51', *NQ* n.s. 15 (1968) 168–9.

—— 'A Note on L's Conception of "Anima" and "Inwit",' *NQ* n.s. 15 (1968) 363–4.

—— 'Two Notes on *PP*', *NQ* n.s. 16 (1969) 168–9.

—— 'L and Scholastic Philosophy,' *MÆ* 38 (1969) 134–56.

—— 'L and the Mystical Tradition', in M. Glasscoe, ed., *The Medieval Mystical Tradition in England* (Exeter, 1980), 17–38.

—— 'L's Structural Imagery', *EC* 30 (1980) 311–25.

—— 'L's "Book of Conscience" and Alanus de Insulis', *NQ* n.s. 29 (1982) 482–4.

—— 'L, Chrysostom and Bernard: A Complex Echo', *NQ* 228 (1983) 108–10.

—— * 'The Treatment of the Crucifixion in *PP* and in Rolle's *Meditations on the Passion*', *Analecta Cartusiana* 35 (1983) 174–96.

—— '*Lele Wordes* and *Bele Paroles*: Some Aspects of L's Word-Play', *RES* 34 (1983) 161–83.

—— 'The Authenticity of the Z Text of *PP*: A Metrical Examination', *MÆ* 53 (1984) 295–300.

—— 'The Inner Dreams in *PP*', *MÆ* 55 (1986) 24–40.

—— ' "Latent Content" and "The Testimony in the Text": Symbolic Meaning in *Sir Gawain and the Green Knight*', *RES* 38 (1987) 145–68.

—— '*Kynde Craft* and the *Play of Paramorez*: Natural and Unnatural Love in *Purity*', in P. Boitani and A Torti, eds, *Genres, Themes, and Images in English Literature* (Tübingen, 1988).

—— *The Clerkly Maker: L's Poetic Art* (Cambridge, 1987).

——*PP: A New Translation of the B-Text* (Oxford, 1992).

——*PP: A Parallel-Text Edition of the A, B, C and Z Versions*, vol. I: *Text* (1995).

Schmidt, A. V. C., and Jacobs, N., eds: *Medieval English Romances*, 2 vols (1980).

Schroeder, M. C.: '*PP*: The Tearing of the Pardon', *PQ* 49 (1970) 8–18.

Schweitzer, E. C.: ' "Half a Laumpe Lyne in Latyne" and Patience's Riddle in *PP*', *JEGP* 73 (1974) 313–27.

Seymour, M. C., ed.: *On the Properties of Things: John Trevisa's Translation of Bartholomaeus Anglicus De Proprietatibus Rerum*, 2 vols (Oxford, 1975).

Shepherd, G. T.: 'Poverty in *PP*', in T. H. Aston *et al.*, eds, *Social Relations and Ideas: Essays in Honour of R. H. Hilton* (Cambridge, 1983).

Simpson, J.: 'From Reason to Affective Knowledge: Modes of Thought and Poetic Form in *PP*', *MÆ* 55 (1986) 1–23.

—— 'The Transformation of Meaning: a Figure of Thought in *PP*', *RES* 37 (1986) 161–83.
—— **PP: An Introduction to the B-Text* (1990).
—— ' "Et vidit deus cogitaciones eorum": A Parallel Instance and Possible Source for L's Use of a Biblical Formula at *PP* B XV 200*a*', *NQ* 33 (1986) 9–13.

Sisam, K., ed.: *Fourteenth Century Verse and Prose* (repr. Oxford, 1962).

Skeat, W. W., ed.: *The Vision of William Concerning PP*, Vol. I: *Text A*, EETS OS 28 (1867); II: *Text B*, EETS OS 38 (1869); III; *Text C*, EETS OS 54 (1873); IV, i: *Notes*, EETS OS 67 (1877), IV, ii: *General Preface, Notes and Indexes*, EETS OS 81 (1885).

—— **The Vision of William Concerning PP in Three Parallel Texts*, 2 vols (1886; repr. Oxford, 1954).

Smalley, B.: *English Friars and Antiquity in the Early Fourteenth Century* (Oxford, 1960).

Smith, B. H.; 'Patience's Riddle: *PP* B XIII', *MLN* 76 (1961) 675–82.
—— *Traditional Imagery of Charity in PP* (The Hague, 1966).

Southern, R. W.: *Western Society and the Church in the Middle Ages* (Harmondsworth, 1970).

Southworth, J.: *The Medieval Minstrel* (Woodbridge, 1989).

**Spearing, A. C.: *Medieval Dream-Poetry* (Cambridge, 1976).

Spearman, A.: 'L's "Corlew": Another Look at *PP* B XIV 43', *MÆ* 62 (1993) 242–58.

Spector, S., ed.: *The N-Town Play*, 2 vols, EETS SS 11–12 (1991).

Stanley, E. G.: 'The B Version of *PP*: A New Edition', *NQ* 22 (1976) 435–7.

Straw, C.: *Gregory the Great* (Berkeley, Calif., 1988).

**Stokes, M.: *Justice and Mercy in PP: A Reading of the B Text Visio* (1984).

Strecker, K. ed.: *Die Gedichte Walters von Châtillon*, Vol. I (Berlin, 1925).

Strutt, J.: *The Sports and Pastimes of the People of England*, ed. J. Cox (1903 edn; repr. 1969).

Sumption, J.: *Pilgrimage: An Image of Medieval Religion* (1975).

Szittya, P. R.: *The Antifraternal Tradition in Medieval Literature* (Princeton, NJ, 1986).

Tavormina, M. T.: ' "Maledictus qui non reliquit semen": The Curse on Infertility in *PP* B XVI and C XVIII', *MÆ* 58 (1989) 117–25.

Thomson, J. A. F.: 'Piety and Charity in Late Medieval London', *Journal of Ecclesiastical History* 16 (1965), 178–95.

Tristram, P.: *Figures of Life and Death in Medieval English Literature* (1976).

**Turville-Petre, T.: *The Alliterative Revival* (Cambridge, 1977).

Vaughan, M. F.: 'The Liturgical Perspectives of *PP* B XVI-XIX', *Studies in Medieval and Renaissance History* 3 (1980) 87–155.

Vernet, F.: *Medieval Spirituality*, Eng. edn (1930).

Waldron, R. A.: 'L's Originality: The Christ-Knight and the Harrowing of Hell', in Kratzmann and Simpson, eds, *Medieval English*, pp. 66–81.

Walther, H., ed.: *Proverbia sententiaeque Latinitatis medii Ævi*, 6 vols (Göttingen, 1963–9).

Webb, J., ed.: *A Roll of the Household Expenses of Richard de Swinfield, Bishop of Hereford [during] 1298–90*, Camden Society (1854).

Weldon, J. F. G.: 'Gesture of Perception: the Pattern of Kneeling in *PP*', *YLS* 3 (1989) 49–66.

Wenzel, S.: 'Medieval Sermons and the Study of Literature', in P. Boitani and A. Torti, eds, *Medieval and Pseudo-Medieval Literature* (Cambridge, 1984).

Whatley, G.: 'The Uses of Hagiography: The Legend of Pope Gregory and the Emperor Trajan in the Middle Ages', *Viator* 15 (1984) 25–63.

—— '*PP* B. 12. 277–94: Notes on Language, Text, and Theology', *MP* 82 (1984) 112.

White, H.: 'L's Ymaginatif, Kynde and the *Benjamin Major*', *MÆ* 55 (1986) 241–8.

——*Nature and Salvation in PP* (Cambridge, 1988).

Wilkes, G. L.: 'The Castle of Unite in *PP*', *MS* 27 (1965) 334–6.

Wilson, E.: *The Gawain-Poet* (Leiden, 1976).

—— 'The "Gostly Drem" in *Pearl*', *NM* 69 (1968) 90–101.

Wittig, J. S.: '*PP* B Passus IX–XII: Elements in the Design of the Inward Journey', *Traditio* 28 (1972) 211–80.

Woolf, R.: 'The Theme of Christ the Lover-Knight in Medieval English Literature', *RES* 13 (1962) 1–16.

—— 'The Tearing of the Pardon', in Hussey, ed., *Approaches*, pp. 50–75; both repr. in H. O'Donoghue, ed., *Art and Doctrine: Essays on Medieval Literature* (1986).

Wordsworth, J.: 'Revision as Making: *The Prelude* and its Peers', in P. Fletcher and J. Murphy, eds, *Wordsworth in Context (Bucknell Review* (Lewisburg, 1992) 36:1), 85–11.

Wright, T., ed.: *The Latin Poems commonly attributed to Walter Mapes*, Camden Society (1841).

—— *Political Poems and Songs relating to English History*, 2 vols, Rolls Series 14 (1859).

—— *The Anglo-Latin Satirical Poets and Epigrammatists of the C12th*, Rolls Series 59 (1872).

Young, K.: *The Drama of the Medieval Church* (Oxford, 1933).

Yunck, J. A.: *The Lineage of Lady Meed: The Development of Medieval Venality Satire* (Notre Dame, Ind., 1963).

Ziegler, P.: *The Black Death* (repr. Harmondsworth, 1971).

Zupitza, J., ed.: *The Romance of Guy of Warwick*, EETS ES 42 (1883).

APPENDIX:
LANGLAND'S ALLITERATIVE VERSE

This Appendix is intended only as a concise guide to the scansion of the poem. A full account is given in my study *The Clerkly Maker: Langland's Poetic Art* (1987), pp. 21–80. The metrical criteria evoked in editing the text are set forth there and in my article, 'The Authenticity of the Z Text of *PP*' (1984).

Langland's alliterative line consists of not fewer than four and not more than five stressed syllables (*lifts*) separated by one or more unstressed syllables (*dips*). A dip may often precede the first lift, and may sometimes be omitted between lifts, usually at the caesura:

> Somme *p*útten hem to the *p*lóugh, // *p*léiden ful sélde. (Pr 20)

Every line has a feminine ending (i.e. terminates in an unstressed syllable).

Lifts that carry alliteration are *full staves* (*pútten, plóugh, pléiden*). Lifts *without* alliteration are *blank staves* (*sélde*). A *mute stave* is a syllable within a dip that carries alliteration but no stress, its purpose being to satisfy half the metrical requirement (alliteration) while the other half (stress) is satisfied by the lift that follows, which is accordingly a blank stave:

> And *w*ónnen that thise *w*ástours *w*ith glótonye destrúyeth. (Pr 22)

Here the mute stave *with* is shown without a stress mark. Mute staves are found especially in the position after the half-line break. The very rare *liaisonal stave* arises when the consonant of a preceding word is treated as if it belonged with the vowel of a following word, thereby generating a required full stave:

> Fírst he fónded me, if‿Í lovede béttre (XVI 231).

Except for a few lines with prose quotations in them or where the text remains doubtful, Langland's lines conform to *ten regular metrical patterns*, to each of which I give a descriptive name. These fall into three clear classes or types:

Type I (Standard)

a *Normative*
  I *sh*óop me into *sh*róudes as I a *sh*éep wére (Pr 2) *aa/ax*

b *Enriched*
  In a *só*mer *sé*son, whan *só*fte was the *só*nne (Pr 1) *aa/aa*

c *Extended*
  With *dé*pe *dí*ches and *dé*rke and *dré*dfulle of sí*ghte (Pr 16) *aaa/ax*

d *Enriched extended*
  And *lé*ne the *lé*de thi *ló*nd so *lé*aute thee *ló*vye (Pr 126) *aaa/aa*

e *Blank extended*
  A *dé*ep *dá*le bynéthe, a *dó*ngeon therínne (Pr 15) *aax/ax*

Type II (Clustered)

a *Single clustered*
  And *bé*re hire *brá*s at thi *bá*k to Cá*leis to sé*lle (III 196) *aaa/xx*

b *Double clustered*
  And *só*mme *sé*rven as *sé*rvaunts *ló*rdes and *lá*dies (Pr 95) *aaa/bb*

Type III (Reduced)

a *Minimal*
  The *nó*taries and yé *nó*yen the pé*ple (II 127) *ax/ax*

b *Enriched reduced*
  How thow *lé*rnest the pé*ple, *lé*red and *lé*wed (IV 12) *ax/aa*

c *Crossed*
  And whoso *bú*mmed the*ró*f, he *bó*ughte it the*rá*fter (V 219) *ab/ab*

In addition, a very rare type of line, apparently unique to Langland, may be described as *transitional* between Type I with 'muted' post-caesural stave (e.g. Pr 22 above) and Type IIb, which has a second stave-letter in the b half-line (e.g. Pr 95 above):

Ne nevere *wé*ne to *wý*nne *w*ith *crá*ft that I *knó*we (V 469) *aa/[a]bb*

The presence of the muted stave-word *with* establishes that V 469 is not of the *aa/bb* variety, found in other writers but not used by Langland. The existence of this 'T-type' line in the *Piers Plowman* text in MS Bodley 851 (ed. Rigg-Brewer) at III 158, VII 38 and 245 (lines not found in the A-, B- and C-texts) is evidence that this version of the poem, known as the 'Z'- text, is authentic (see Sch, 'Authenticity of the Z Text').

Some lines, usually of Type Ie, display *counterpoint*, i.e. the inter- weaving of alliterative sounds according to a set pattern. The 'standard' form of this employs a 'theme-stave' which appears in key-position and a 'contrapuntal stave' which appears in positions 3 and 5, as in IX 24, where the thematic stave-sound is $|k|$ and the contrapuntal stave-sound $|s|$:

Til *Kýnde* cóme or sénde to képen hire hymsélve.

There is occasionally some doubt as to which precise type a particular line belongs to, and Langland sometimes wrenches stress as well as muting staves. The most difficult examples are discussed in the Textual and Lexical Notes; for fuller discussion see ch. 2 of Sch, *Clerkly Maker*.

INDEX OF PROPER NAMES

Noe (Noah), IX 131, X 398 et passim
Normandie, III 189
Northfolk, V 235
Nynyve, XV 493

Offyn (Ophni), X 281
Oseye (Alsace), Pr 225
Osias (Hosea), XV 573, 576

Pacience, V 622, XI 255, XII 29 et
  passim, XIV 29 et passim, XVI 8
Pampilon (Pamplona), XVII 253
Paul the Hermit, XV 286, 290
Paul, St, Pr 38, VIII 91, X 202, 423,
  XI 92, XII 29, XIII 65, 69, XV 18,
  156, 265, XVII 259, 337
Paul's St (Cross), X 73
Pees, IV 47 et passim, V 622,
  XVIII 167 et passim, XX 299
Pernel, IV 116, V 26, X 62
Peter Comestor (Clerk of the Stories),
  VII 71
Peter, St, Pr 100, 109, VII 173, X
  443, XIII 255, XV 18, 265, 292,
  XVIII 242, XIX 163, 169
Phisik, VI 268, XX 169
Piers Plowman, V 556 et passim, VI 3
  et passim, VII 1 et passim, XIII 124
  et passim, XV 196 et passim,
  XVI 17 et passim, XVIII 10 et
  passim, XIX 6 et
  passim, XX 77
  et passim
Pilat, XVIII 80, 300
Plato, X 175, XI 37, XX 275
Pope, Pr 108, II 23, III 147, 215,
  V 50, VII 19, 174, 187, XIII 244,
  246, 257, XV 490, 492, 508,
  XIX 224, 432, 446
Poverte, XIV 243 et passim
Pride, XIV 280, XX 70 et passim
Pride of Parfit Lyvynge, XI 15 et
  passim
Prucelond (Prussia), XIII 393

Randolf, Erl of Chestre, V 396
Rechelenesnesse, XI 34 et passim
Religion, V 45, VII 32, X 305
Repentaunce, V 60 et passim
Reson, I 54, III 285, IV 5 et passim,

V 11 et passim, VI 314, X 114,
  XI 131, 334 et passim, XII 219,
  XIX 83
Rightfulnesse, XIX 83
Rightwisnesse, XVIII 187 et passim
Roberd the Robbere, V 462
Robyn Hood, V 396
Rochel, Pr 230
Rochemador, XII 36
Romaynes, XV 530
Rome, Pr 47, IV 128, V 56, 247, 461,
  522, XI 153, 162, XII 36, XIV
  197, XV 558, XVII 253, XIX 427
Rosamounde, XII 47
Ruthe, XIX 83
Rutland, II 111
Ryn (Rhine), Pr 230

Salomon, III 93, V 39, VII 138,
  IX 95, X 336 et passim, XI 268,
  XII 268
Samaritan, XVII 49 et passim,
  XVIII 10
Sampson, XII 41, XVI 82
Samuel, III 261 et passim, XVI 82
Sarsynes (Saracens), III 328, X 346,
  XI 120, 156, 164, XII 276,
  XIII 210, XV 389, 397, 604
Sathan, II 106, VI 324, IX 62,
  XI 164, XVI 122, XVIII 265 et
  passim
Satisfaccion, XIV 21
Saul, III 260 et passim, XII 116,
  XIX 135
Scripture, X 152 et passim, XI 1 et
  passim, XIII 26
Seem (Seth), IX 124
Seneca, XIV 306, XX 275
Shordych, XIII 340
Sleuthe, II 99, V 386 et passim,
  XIV 235, 254, XX 163 et passim
Sodome, XIV 75
Soothnesse, II 189, XVIII 282
Sortes (Socrates), XII 268
Southwerk, XIII 340
Spayne, XV 520
Spes, XVII 1 et passim
Spiritus Fortitudinis, XIX 291 et
  passim, XX 24 et passim

GLOSSARY

(*Compiled with the assistance of Judith V. Schmidt*)

The aim of this glossary is to list *each separate sense* of those words which are likely to cause difficulty, with at the minimum a reference to its first appearance. It is meant to be used in conjunction with the marginal glosses and footnote translations.

The following abbreviations are used:
a adjective, *av* adverb, *c* conjunction, *comp* comparative, *excl* exclamation, *i* intransitive, *imper* imperative, *n* noun, *p* participle, *pl* plural, *p.p.* past participle, *p.t.* past tense, *prep* preposition, *pres* present, *prn* pronoun, *refl* reflexive, *sg* singular, *subj* subjunctive, *t* transitive, *v* verb. An *asterisk* before a word or line-reference indicates that the reading is a conjectural emendation.

a, one, single XVI 86; on X 413, XVI 172

abave, confound VI 215

abide, stay VIII 64; endure XX 46

abidynge, long-suffering XIX 296

abien, pay for III 251; **abye,** IX 89

abiggen, pay II 128

abite, nip off XVI 27

*ablende (*v*), blind X 131; **ablyndeth,** blinds X 264

abosted, boastingly defied VI 154

aboughte, IX 143, *p.t. of* abi(gg)en; **abought** (*p.p.*), XVIII 389

ac (*c*), but Pr 5 et passim.

acale, chilled XVIII 395

accidie, attack of sloth V 360

acombre, oppress II 51; *p.p.* overcome I 32

acorden, agree V 329

acorse, condemn Pr 99; **acurseth,** XVIII 107

acounte, settle IV 11; *p.t.* valued XIX 416

acountes, reckoning VI 89

acouped, accused XIII 459

acquitaunce, document of acquittal XIV 190

aday, at morn VI 307; **adayes,** on a day XV 283

addre, serpent XVIII 336

adreynten (*v.i.*), drowned X 407; **adreynt** (*p.p.*), XX 378

af(f)aite(n), subdue, discipline V 66, VI 31

afereth, frightens XVIII 432

affiaunce (*n*), trust XVI 238

afrounted, accosted XX 5

after, according to XII 187; like XI 261

afurst, a-thirst X 59

afyngred, very hungry VI 266

agasteth, frightens XIV 281; **agast** (*p.p.*), XIX 302

agein, in return for X 197

agrounde, on the earth I 90

agulte, offend/sin against XIV 8; *p.t.* XVII 296

aiels, forefathers XV 322

aithes (*n*), harrows XIX 275

alarme, to arms! XX 92

alay (*n*), alloy XV 348; *v.p.p.* XV 353

alday, continually XV 358

aleggen, adduce (texts) XI 89

aliry, across VI 122

alkenamye, alchemy X 214
aller, of all XIX 475
alleskynnes, of all kinds (of) XX 373
al(l)owaunce, approval, favour
    XI 220
allowed (p.p.), assessed X 432
almaries, cupboards XIV 247
alough, low down XII 219
also, as III 331; als, likewise III 72;
    *thus X 367
amaistrye, dominate II 148
amende, improve V 265
amendement, conversion X 363
amendes, compensation V 325
amercy (v), fine VI 39
amonge (av), mixed in XIV 238
amortisede, conveyed in mortmain
    XV 320
amorwenynges, in the mornings XI
    338
ampulles, phials V 520
ancres, anchorites Pr 28
and, if IV 88 et passim; whilst X 407
angres, afflictions XII 11; v, V 116
aniente, annihilate XVII 287
anoonright, immediately XI 337
anoyed, harmed, troubled V 93
apaied, pleased, satisfied VI 195;
    apayed VI 108
apeire (v), harm, damage III 128,
    V 46, 564
apendeth, pertains I 100
apereth, reaches XIV 243
apertly, plainly, manifestly I 100
apeward, ape-keeper V 631
apostata, apostate I 104
appele, accuse XI 421
appose, (put) question(s) to III 5; p.t.
    disputed with VII 139
arate, reprove, correct XI
    102
arerage, debt, arrears X 470
arere, backwards V 348
aresonedest, argued with XII 217
armes, (coat of) arms, form V 501
arn, are XVII 30
arne (p.t. of ernen), welled up, ran
    XVI 136
arraye, prepare IV 16

artow (=art thow), art thou
    V 256
arwes, arrows III 326
askes (n), ashes III 98
asketh, requires Pr 19
aspare, spare XV 140
aspie, seek XVI 170
assay, trial X 255; assayen, try III 5
asseled, sealed XVII 4
assetz, adequate satisfaction XVII 238
assoilen, absolve Pr 70; solve, explain
    III 237
asterte, escape XI 400
astronomiens, astronomers XV 358
at, from III 25, XI 346; *as to XI 301
atamede, broached XVII 69
atones, at the same time XVII 53
athynketh, grieves XVIII 89
attachen, arrest II 200; p.t. claimed
    XVI 261
atteynt (p.p.), found false, attainted
    XX 162
attre, venom XII 255
auditour, accountant XIX 465
aught, something V 433
auncer, steelyard V 214
auntrede, ventured XVIII 221; set off
    XX 175
auter, altar V 108
avaunced, promoted, advanced I 191
aventrous, adventurous (sc. knights)
    XVIII 16
aventure, an, in case, lest perchance
    III 66
avoutrye, adultery XII 74
avowe, declare III 257; avowes (n),
    vows V 398
awayte, see, observe X 332
awreke, avenge VI 173; awroke
    (p.p.), VI 201
axe, ask IV 103
ayeins (prep), against III 92; towards
    IV 44; in return for V 431; av.c
    before XIX 320

baberlipped, thick-lipped V 188
bablede, mumbled V 8
bacheler, young knight XVI 179
baches, valleys V 514
baddely, badly XV 535

baddenesse, wickedness XII 48

bagge, money-bag XX 142

baillies, bailiffs III 2

bakbite, slander II 81

bakkes, cloaks X 360

baksteres, bakers Pr 219

bale, evil IV 89; misery XI 332; bale-deeth, baleful death XVIII 35

baleised, beaten with a baleys (q.v.) V 173

baleys, rod, birch X 178; baleises XII 12

balkes, ridges (on ploughed land) VI 107

balled, bald XX 184

ballok-knyf, knife with knobbed haft XV 124

banne, curse I 62; denounce X 7

banyer, standard-bearer XV 435

bar, bore II 3 (p.t. of beren)

barayne, unproductive XVIII 106

bare, openly displayed XX 70

bark, husk XI 258

barn, child II 3 et passim

baselard, dagger III 305; sword XV 121

batauntliche (av), with noisy eagerness XIV 214

bat-nedle, packing-needle V 208

batred, slapped III 199

baude, ?harlot, bawd III 129

baw, bah! XI 140

bayard, bay horse IV 53

beaupeere, elder XVIII 230

bedbourde, intercourse IX 187

bede (v), pray, intercede VIII 103

bede (n), prayer XI 149

bedelles, beadles, tipstaffs, II 60, III 2

beden, bade III 27 (p.t. of beden and bidden)

bedeman, beadsman, one who prays III 41

bedes, prayers V 9

bedreden, bedridden VII 100

beem, beam, plank X 264

beere, bore V 138 (p.t. pl of beren)

beflobered (v.p.t.), muddied XIII 401

beighes, necklaces Pr 161

bekene (n), beacon XVII 264

beknew, acknowledged X 415

belsires, ancestor's IX 143

belwe (v), bellow XI 341

ben, are VI 130

benes, beans VI 182

benigneliche, with good will XII 112

benyson, blessing XIII 236

beren, bear Pr 161; bere (p.t.), III 196; berth XVI 180

bernes, barns VI 183

beryng, manner X 256

bete, beat V 33; bette (p.t.), X 178

bete, relieve VI 236 (see boote)

beth, are III 27 (=ben); be X 445, XIII 421

bette, beat X 178 (p.t. of beten)

bible, book XV 89

bicche, bitch V 347

bicome, went V 642

bidde, pray V 227; -ynge, prayer(s), III 219

bidderes, beggars Pr 41

*biddeth, directs IX 15

bide, endure XX 48

bidraveled, beslavered V 191

bidropped, spattered XIII 321

bienfait, good turn V 430; pl good deeds V 612

biennals, biennial masses VII 171

bigge (a), strong VI 213

bigge (v), buy XIV 231; see buggen

*biggyng, residing V 128

bigile, deceive X 120; perplex XV 371

bigirdles, purses VIII 87

bigruccheth, complains VI 67

biheste, promise III 127

bihighte, promised III 29; see next entry

bihote (v), promise VI 230

bihynde, behind, overdue V 427

bikenne, commit, commend II 50

bikere, fight XX 79

biknowe, acknowledge V 196

bile, bill XI 357

biles (n), boils XX 84

bil(e)eve, creed V 7, XIX 349

bileve(n) (v), give up VI 179

bilieth, tell lies against X 22; p.t. II 22

bille, petition IV 47

bilongeth, is due IX 78

bilove, make beloved VI 227

bilowen, told lies about II 22

bilye, tell lies against V 408

biquasshed (*v.t.* or *i*) shattered XVIII 248

birewe, regret XII 249

bisette, bestow V 260; *p.t.* XII 47

biseye, visited XX 202 (*p.p.* of bisen)

bisherewed, cursed IV 168

bishetten, shut (something) up II 214; *p.p.* XIX 167

bishined, ? illuminated XV 516 (*see note*)

bisitte(n), oppress II 141; afflict X 359

bislabered, soiled V 386

bismere, calumny V 88; *pl* XIX 296

bisnewed, snowed over XV 112

bispered, locked up XV 143

biswatte (*p.t.*), covered with sweat XIII 403

biswynke, labour for; biswonke (*p.t.*), XX 293; biswynken, work at XV 487

bit, commands IX 15 (= biddeth)

bit, begs VII 66 (= biddeth)

bitelbrowed, with beetling brows V 188

bitit, it befalls XI 401; bitidde (*p.t.*), XII 116

bitter (*n*), bitterness V 118

bittre (*av*), grievously X 280

bityme, early V 638

biwicched, cast a spell on XIX 156

*biwiled, deceived X 108

biyete (*n*), offspring II 41

*biyeten, take over X 320

biyonde, abroad IV 128

blame (*v*), slander V 129

blancmanger, chicken stew XIII 92

blasen, coat-of-arms XVI 179

blenche, turn aside V 580

blente, blinded V 495 (*p.t.* of blenden)

blered, dimmed, bleared Pr 74

blisse (*v*), bless XVI 237

blisse (*n*), happiness, joy VIII 64

blisful, blessed II 3

blody, consanguineous VI 207

bloo, pale III 98

blosmede, blossomed V 139

blowyng tyme, blossoming time XVI 26

blustreden, wandered aimlessly V 514

bocches, plague-sores XIII 250

bocher, butcher V 323; *pl* Pr 219

body half, front part XIII 317

boldede, emboldened III 199

boldely, confidently XIX 479

boldnesse, strength, force V 612

bole, bull XI 341

bolk, belch V 391

bolle, bowl V 107

bolneth, swells V 118

bonched, struck Pr 74

bondeman, labourer, serf V 191

boon, bone VII 92

boone, request XI 149

boost, arrogance XIV 223

boot (*v*), bit (*p.t.* of biten) V 83

boot (*n*), boat VIII 30

boote, remedy IV 89 et passim

bootned, healed VI 191

borde, table VI 264

bordlees, without a table XII 200

borgh, surety IV 89; borwe XIV 191

*borre, hoarseness XVII 326

borwe, stand bail for IV 109; borrow I 77

bosard, oaf X 266

botelees, irremediable XVIII 201

bother, of them both II 67; botheres, XVI 165

botons, studs XV 124

botrased, buttressed V 589

boughte, redeemed II 3 (*p.t.* of biggen)

bouken, cleanse with lye, buck XV 190

bour, private room III 14

bourdeour, jester XIII 448

bourdynge, jesting XV 40

bowe (*v*), sink VIII 48; submit XIII 149

bowes, boughs V 575

boweth (*v. imper. pl*), proceed, turn V 566

boy, rogue, knave Pr 80

brak, broke I 113 (*p.t.* of breken)

brast, burst VI 178 (*p.t.* of **bresten**)

brawen, brawn XIII 63

brech, breeches V 174

bred corn, seed-corn VI 62

bredful, brimful Pr 41

breide, hastened XVII 69

breken, break VI 30; **breketh,** X 84

breme, powerful XII 223

bren (*n*), bran VI 182

bren (*v*), burn III 267 (*imper.* of **brennen**)

brent, burnished V 267

brevet, letter of indulgence Pr 74

brew, brewed V 215 (*p.t.* of **browen**)

brewecheste (*a*), trouble-brewing XVI 43

briddes, young (birds) XI 356

brocage, arrangement XIV 268

broche (*v*), sew V 208

broches (*n*), matches XVII 246

brocours, brokers II 60; *sg* go-between III 46; agent V 129

brode (*av*), extensively X 315

broke, torn V 107 (*p.p.* of **breken**)

broke (*n*), brook VI 135

brol, brat III 205

brotel, fragile VIII 43

brouke, partake of XI 122; enjoy XVIII 364

browe (*p.p.*), brewed XVIII 364

brugge, (draw-)bridge V 592

brunneste, darkest VI 305

brybours, robbers XX 262

bugge, buy Pr 168 (=**biggen**); **-ere,** purchaser X 306; **-ynge,** buying XIX 236

bukkes, male deer, bucks VI 30

bulles, mandates III 148

bummed, tasted V 219

burde, lady III 14

burdoun, staff V 517

burel, coarse, half-educated X 286

burgages, tenements III 86

burgeis, burgess XII 147; *pl* Pr 217, XV 342

burgh, town II 98

burieles, tomb XIX 146

burjoneth (*v*), shoot XV 75

burnes, men III 267; **buyrn** XVI 180

busked, went, betook themselves III 14

buskes (*n*), bushes XI 344

but (if), unless Pr 66, I 181

but (*av*), only V 74

buxom, obedient, willing I 110

buxomnesse, obedience I 113

by, concerning V 178; in accordance with Pr 80; with I 28; *by so,** provided XIII 136

byjaped, fooled XVIII 292

bymeneth, signifies Pr 209

bymolen (*v*), stain XIV 4

bynam, took away from VI 240; **bynomen** (*p.p.*), III 314

by wille, wilfully IV 70

cabane, shelter III 191

caccheth, take II 36; obtain XIII 299

cachepol, officer XVIII 46

cairen, wander Pr 29; proceed IV 24

calculed, calculated XV 370

cammokes, rest-harrows XIX 315

canonistres, canon lawyers VII 150

canoun, canon law V 422

caples, horses II 162; **capul** (*sg*) XVII 108

caractes, letters, characters XII 78

carded, combed X 18

cardiacle, heart-attack XIII 335

care, trouble, distress IX 153

cared, wanted, were concerned II 162

carefulle, full of anxiety I 203; *av* V 76

carolden, danced XVIII 426

caroyne, carcass, corpse Pr 189

carped, told II 192; **carpen,** cry out X 51

carpynge, talking Pr 204; speech XI 237

cartsadle, have harnessed II 180

cast (*n*), purpose III 19

casten (*v*), arranged (*p.t.* of **casten**); make VI 16; contrived XV 333

catecumelynges, catechumens XI 77 (*see note*)

catel, wealth Pr 205; food XV 428

caukede, trod, mated with XI 358

cawdel, mess V 355

caytif, wretch V 196; *a* wretched XI 294

cene, supper XVI 140

certein (*a*), definite XX 258
certes, assuredly II 152
cesseth, cease! IV 1
*chafen (*v*), heat XII 125
chaffare (*n*), trade Pr 31; goods V 243
chalangeable, open to dispute XI 303
chalangen, claim Pr 93; charged V 172
chalangynge, accusing V 87; criticizing XI 423; claiming XV 344
chambre, private room III 10
chanons, canons X 318
chapeleyns, priests VI 12
chapitle, chapter (-court) III 320
chapman, merchant Pr 64
chargeth (*v*), accounts XIV 312; insists on XVII 292; burden XX 237
charnel, charnel-house VI 48
chaste (*v*), discipline, chastize VI 51
chastilet, small castle II 85
*chatel, property XI 127
chaumbrere, chamberlain XIV 100
Chauncelrie, Chancery Pr 93
che(e)ste, angry quarrelling II 85 et passim
cheitiftee, destitution XX 236
Cheker, the Exchequer Pr 94
chekes, cheeks VI 40
chele, cold I 22
chepe (*v*), buy XV 31; -yng, market IV 56
chere, face, look IV 165
chered, looking, of appearance XIX 265
cherissynge, spoiling IV 117
cherl, villein, serf XI 127
chervelles, chervil VI 293
chese (*v*), choose XV 38
chesibles, chasubles VI 12
chetes, escheats, reversions IV 175
cheveden, succeeded Pr 31 (*p.t.* of cheven)
chevysaunces, loans at interest V 245; bargain XX 16
chewen, eat up, consume I 193
cheyne, chain V 607
chibolles, spring onions VI 293
chiden, complain I 193; quarrel

III 178; chidde (*p.t.*), XVIII 420
chidynge, scolding V 87
chief, foremost Pr 64
childissh, childlike XV 149
chirie-tyme, cherry-time, summer V 159
chivaler, knight XVIII 99
choppes, blows IX 169
chymenee, fireplace X 100
chyveled, trembled V 190
clausemele, clause by clause V 420
claweth, grasp X 281; scrape XIV 17; seize XVII 189
cleef (*v.i.*), split XVIII 61 (*p.t.* of cleven)
*clemat, weather-region XV 370
clene, pure V 511
cler, bright V 585
clergie, learning, the learned III 165
clergially, learnedly Pr 124
clermatyn, a fine white bread VI 303
cleymeth (*v*), claim I 93; *p.t.* XX 96
cliket, latch-key V 604
clippe, grasp XVII 189; embrace XVIII 419
clipse, eclipse XVIII 135
clokke, limp III 34
clomsest, are benumbed XIV 51
closeth, encloses XVIII 135
clouted, patched VI 59; cloutes, rags II 221
clyngest, are parched XIV 51
clyve, adhere XI 224
coffes, mittens VI 60
cofres, treasure-chests XI 198
cokeney, egg VI 284
cokeres, leggings VI 60
coket, a fine white bread VI 303
cokewold, cuckold IV 164
collateral (*a*), accompanying XIV 298
colled, embraced XI 17
colomy, grimy (with soot) XIII 356
coloppes, bacon and eggs VI 284
coloureth, disguises XIX 462
colvere, dove XV 403
combraunce, trouble XI 45
comeres, callers II 231
comly, fit XV 451
commissarie, bishop's officer XV 239

commune, common people Pr 115; communers, XV 331

communes, food Pr 117

commune womman, prostitute V 641

compaignable, companionable XV 219

compased, established X 180

compasynge, designing XVII 171

comsed, began III 104; comseth, arises I 139

comsynge, beginning XVIII 214

comune, in, in public XI 216

conceyve, take in, grasp VIII 57

conclude, confute X 446

conestable, constable XX 214

conformen, dispose XIII 209

confort (n), benefit IV 151

confortatif (a), agreeable XV 219

conforted, entertained XIII 57; supported XX 67

congeien, dismiss III 174; congeye, IV 4

congie (n), farewell XIII 203

conjured, required on oath XV 14

conseyved, uttered VI 33

contenaunce, appearance Pr 24; looks V 181

contrarieth, acts contrary to V 54

contrees, districts XX 329

contreve, devise, invent Pr 118

conynges, rabbits Pr 189

coped, clothed, robed II 231

coppes, cups III 22

corlew, curlew, ? quail XIV 44

correctours, (those) who correct X 283

corrupcions, diseases XX 99

cors, (living) body I 139, XV 23

corsaint, saint's shrine V 532

corseder, the worse off XIX 421

corseth (v), curses VI 315

costes, regions II 86, VIII 12

cote, coat V 109; c. armure, coat-of-arms XIX 13

cotes, cottages VIII 16

counseil, secret, confidence V 166

countee, county II 86

counteth, cares III 142

countreplede, argue against XII 98; oppose XX 385

coupable, guilty XII 88

coupe, sin, guilt V 298, 474

coupes, bowls III 22

courbed (v), bent I 79

cours, impulse III 56; skill XV 368

court, manor-house V 585, XX 345

courtepy, short coat V 79; pl VI 188

coveited, desired XI 125

coveitise, greed II 86; anxious concern XIV 11

covenaunt, condition V 333; agreement XIV 151

covent, convent V 153

covere (v), roof III 60

cowkynde, cattle XI 340

crabbede (a), ill-tempered X 106

cracched, carded XV 453 (see note)

cracchen, scratch Pr 154; snatch XI 144

craft, power I 139; skill II 4

crafty (men), crafts-, tradesmen III 225

craked (v), broke XVIII 73

craven (v), ask, require III 222; p.t. VI 92, *XI 439

creaunt (a), believing XIII 192

Cristendom, Christian faith, baptism V 588

croce, crosier VIII 95

croft, small field V 572

crokke, pot XIX 282

crop, upper growth, top XVI 42, XX 53

cropen (v), crept (p.t. of crepen) Pr 186; crope, III 191

crouch, cross-ornament V 522

crowne, hair XI 36; tonsure XI 297

crownynge, the tonsure Pr 88

cruddes, curds VI 281

cultour, coulter VI 104

cuppemele, by cupfuls V 221

curatours, parish priests I 195; spiritual rulers XIX 223

cure, benefice XI 300

curen (v), act as parish priest XX 326

curious, artfully cut XIX 289

cursed, condemned, excommunicated III 142; wicked XIX 436

curteisie, generosity I 20; graciousness XII 77

daffe, fool I 140, XI 425

daggen (v), tailor curiously XX 143

dampne, damn V 470; condemn XVII 303

damyseles, attendant ladies X 12

daunten, subdue III 288; make much of X 37

dawe (v), dawn XVIII 427

debate (n), quarrel, strife V 97, XV 427

decourreth, departs XIV 194

dedes, bonds V 241

dedly, mortal I 144, IX 207

deef, deaf X 132

deele, give, distribute I 199

deere, dearly VI 290

deeth, plague X 81

deeth-yvel, bane XVIII 53

defaute, deficiency II 140; lack VI 206

defence, prohibition XVIII 194

defendeth, forbids III 64

defie, digest Pr 230; v.i. V 383

defouled, mortified XV 533

delicatly, luxuriously V 375

delitable, pleasurable I 34

deluvye, deluge X 410

delven, dig VI 141; delveres, Pr 224

demen, judge Pr 96; claim III 188; believed XIX 148

dene, din XVIII 62

*deol, pain XVIII 281; see doel

departable, distinguishable XVII 127

departed, divided VII 157

depper (av), more deeply X 184, XV 199

deprave, revile, abuse III 179, V 143

dere (v), harm VII 34; (n), XIV 171

derely, tidily, properly XIX 2

dereworthy, precious I 87

derk, dark Pr 16; derkliche, obscurely X 372

derne (a), secret II 176; av XI 351; intimate IX 189

deschargen, unburden XV 565

despended, spent V 263

despiseth, pours scorn on XV 54

deve, deaf XIX 130

devinour, expositor VII 136, X 452

devoir, duty XI 284, XIII 213

devoutrye, adultery II 176

devyne, interpret Pr 210; ponder X 184; p.t. foretold V 597

devyse, indicate V 547; consider XIX 280; p.t. designed XIX 332

deyned, deigned VI 307

deynous, arrogant VIII 83

deyntee, pleasure XI 48

deys, daïs, upper table VII 17, X 56

diapenidion, cough-medicine V 122 (see note)

dide, made I 99 et passim; betook XIX 2

dido, an old tale XIII 173

dighte, prepare VI 290; p.t. dressed XIX 2

digneliche, honourably VII 172

disalowed, disapproved, refused credit XIV 130

disalowyng, disfavour, refusal of reward XIV 139

discryve, describe V 78, XVI 66; p.t., named XX 94

disours, minstrel's XIII 173

disputen, argue formally VIII 20; expound, maintain X 249

divined, expounded VII 153; divinour, VII 136

divorses, annulments II 176

do (it), appeal to I 86, III 188

doel, lament V 380; pain VI 120

doelful, painful XV 521

doke, duck V 74, XVII 63

doles, alms III 71

dolven, buried VI 180 (p.p. of delven)

done, what, what make of XVIII 300

Donet, grammar V 205 (see note)

donge, dung III 310

doom, judgement II 206

doon, do Pr 224; make V 94; put IX 11; (causative) have (something) done III 60–2

dorste, dared Pr 178

doted, foolish, silly I 140

doublers, platters XIII 82

doughtier, braver V 101

doute, fear Pr 152

downrighte, utterly XVIII 192

dowve, dove XV 400

doynges, actions XIX 130

dradden, feared (p.t. pl of dreden)

XX 65

draf, hog's-wash X 11; ale-leavings XIX 403

drat, fears IX 93 (=dredeth)

drawe forth, advanced X 37

dred, fear, treat with respect I 34; (n) *VII 34

dredful, terrible XX 89

dredfully, fearfully XVII 63

dremels, dream XIII 14

drenche, drown VIII 50

drevelen, slobber X 41

drighte, Lord XIII 269

drogges, drugs XX 174

droghte, dry weather VI 287

dronkelewe, drunken VIII 83

drough, betook V 205; drew V 350

drow, withdrew XVIII 111 (p.t. of drowen)

drury, treasure I 87

drye (n), dryness XIV 51

drynkes, potions VI 273

dryvele, slobber X 11; prate X 56

duc, duke, magnate IX 11, XIX 309

dureth, lasts VI 56; remain valid XVIII 186

dyas, remedies XX 174

dyche (v), make a ditch XIX 366

dykeres, ditch-diggers Pr 224

dym, dark III 193; weak-sighted X 181

dymes, tithes XV 563

dyngen, beat, strike III 312, X 329, XV 19; thresh VI 141

dynt, blow XVIII 26

dysshere, dish-seller V 316

dyvyde, apportion XIX 216

echone, each one I 17

edifie, build XVI 132

edwyted, reproached V 364

eft, again III 348; next time IV 107

eftsoone(s), again V 474

egre, fierce XIII 81

egreliche, sharply XVI 64; bitterly XIX 382

eighe! (excl) oh! XI 44

ek, also II 93, 237; XIII 165

elde, old age V 190, XII 8, XX 154

elenge, wretched Pr 194, X 96, XX 2

elengeliche, wretchedly XII 44, XX 39

eller(e), elder-tree I 68, IX 149

ellis, at other times Pr 91; otherwise, VIII 113, XIV 196

enbawmed, anointed XVII 71

enblaunched, whitened XV 115

enchauntede, charmed XV 404; XX 379

encreesse, increase XI 397

endited, accused, indicted XI 315; (pres) compose poetry or letters XV 373

enformeth, teaches III 241, XV 519; XVII 126

engendreth, breeds XII 238; p.p. XIII 18

engendrour, procreator, beginner VI 231

engendrynge, begetting XI 335

engleymeth, cloys XV 57

engreyned, fast-dyed II 15, XIV 20

engyned, contrived XVIII 252

enjoyned, joined II 66, IX 4; enjoin (upon) XIII 412, XX 283

ensamples, examples IV 136; parables VII 128

entente, aim, intention VIII 128

entisynge, provoking XIII 322; tempting XVIII 158

entremetten, interfere XIII 291; p.t. XI 416

entremetynge, interfering XI 414

envenymes (n), poisons II 14

envenymeth (v), poisons XII 255

envye, enmity, hostility V 610

equité, justice XVII 306

er, before Pr 155 et passim

erchebisshopes, archbishops XV 244; -dekenes, archdeacons II 174

erd, land, habitation VI 200

erende, message III 41

eretikes, heretics XVII 137

erie (v), plough VI 4; erye, XIV 29

eritage, inheritance X 341

ernynge, running XIX 382

ers, buttocks V 173; rear X 308

erst, first V 461

ertheliche, earthly, material XIX 94

eschaunges, monetary exchanges V 245

eschuwe, avoid VI 53

ese, comfort I 19, X 299

esily, at ease, comfortably II 38

ete, eat V 119; eten (p.t.), V 603

Evangelie, Gospel XI 189

evencristen, fellow-Christian II 95

evene, right, exactly XVII 185, XIX 301

eveneforthe, equally XIII 144; according to XIX 310

evesynges, eaves XVII 228

evidence, example XV 436; indication XVII 196

ewages, sea-coloured sapphires II 14

exciteth, urges XI 189

expounen, expound XIV 278

eyleth, afflicts, troubles VI 128

eyr, air Pr 128

faderlese, fatherless IX 68

faille, lack IX 81; p.t., missed XI 26

faire (av), properly I 4; courteously I 58

Fairye, land of enchantment Pr 6

faiteden, practised deceit Pr 42 (p.t. of faiten)

faiterie, deceit XI 92; faityng, X 38

faithly, truly XIX 70

faitours, deceivers, knaves II 183

falle (in), come upon IV 156

falleth, pertains I 166

falshede, dishonesty, deceit Pr 71

famed, slandered III 186 (= defamed)

fange, take V 558

fantasies, extravagant amusements Pr 36

fare (n), activity XVIII 18

faren, proceeded V 5 (p.p. of faren)

faren, behave XI 71

fareth, it happens VIII 38, XII 201

faste (av), firmly III 140; constantly XIV 274; * V 171

fauchon, sword XV 18

faucons, falcons VI 31; sg XVII 63

faunt, child XVI 101; pl. VI 282

fauntekyns, little children XIII 214; sg XIX 118

faunteltee, childishness XI 42, XV 150

fauten, lack IX 67

Favel, Flattery, Deceit II 6

fayn, pleased, content II 158; desirous II 78; av, gladly VIII 127

feble, weak V 175; w. with sickness V 406

feele, perceive XV 29; feel XIX 171

feere, spouse XVII 320; pl, companions II 6

feeris, affairs, doings V

feet, action, deeds I 186

feffement, deed of endowment II 73

feffeth, endows II 79

feires, chances of selling IV 56

feith, honesty III 157; feithful, honest VI 250

feitures, features XIII 297

fel (n), skin I 15

fel (a), fierce III 260, XVI 31; felle, V 168

felawe, companion VII 12

felaweshipe, company I 114, III 119

fele, many III 342, IX 73

feledest, felt V 490

felefold, many times V 490

felly, fiercely XVIII 92

felonliche, feloniously XVIII 352

femelles, females XI 339

fend, fiend, devil I 40

fendekynes, fiendlings, minor devils XVIII 374

fenden, defend XIX 65; p.t. XIX 46

fenestre, window XVIII 15; pl, XIV 200

fer, far VIII 79

ferded, assembled XI 339

ferde, fared III 344, IX 144; dealt XI 418

fere (n), companion IV 27 (= feere)

ferly, wonder, marvel Pr 6, X 387, XIII 109, XVIII 110

ferme, to, to tend XVI 16

fermed, strengthened X 74

fermerye, infirmary XIII 109

fernyere (av), formerly V 434; n, past years XI 5

ferthe, fourth VII 72

ferye, festival XIII 415

fesaunts, pheasants XV 462

fest, fastened II 124 (*p.p.* of festen, fasten)

festen (*v.t.*), feed XV 484, 341; *p.t.*, XV 589

festes, feasts, dinner-parties X 94; festynge, dinners XI 193

festred, festered XVII 93

festu, mote X 277

fet, fetched XI 324 (*p.p.* of fetten)

fetisli(che), gracefully, elegantly II 11

fette, fetched II 65 (*p.t.* of fetten)

fey, doomed to die XIII 2

feynen, pretend to be X 38

feyntise, faintness V 5

fibicches, tricks X 213

fikel, treacherous, deceiving II 25

fil, fell XIV 79 (*p.t.* of fallen)

fir, fire III 98

firses (pieces of) furze V 345

fithele, fiddle IX 103; *v.*, XIII 232

fithelere, fiddler X 94

flappes, blows, strokes XIII 67

flapten, threshed VI 184

flatte, dashed V 444

flawme (*v*), smell XII 254

flawmynge, flaming XVII 206

fleigh, flew, rushed XVII 58 (*p.t.* of fleen)

flete, swim XX 45; fleteth, floats XII 167

flex, flax VI 13

flicche, side of bacon, flitch IX 171

flittynge, changeable XI 63

flobre, sully XIV 15

florissheth (*v.t.*), prospers XIV 295

flowen, flew II 234 (*p.t. pl* of fleen)

flux, discharge V 177

fobberes, tricksters II 183

fold, times XI 256

fole, foal XI 343; *pl* II 163

foliliche, foolishly XV 77

follede, baptized XV 447 (*p.t.* of fullen)

folwen, pursue, follow I 40

folwere, follower V 542

fond, provided for XV 285 (*p.t.* of fynden)

fond (*v*), try, test VI 219

fondlynges, bastards IX 194

fondynge, temptation XI 399

fonge, receive XIV 139, XVI 96

fo(o)ld, earth VII 53, XII 254

fool sage, wise fool XIII 444; *pl* XIII 423

foon, foes V 95

for, to prevent I 24; in spite of V 382

forbar, spared III 274 (*p.t.* of forbere)

forbere, spare XI 209

forbeten, *p.p.*, enfeebled XX 198

forbisne, parable VIII 29; example XV 526

forbiteth, eats away XVI 35, XVIII 35

forbode, that forbid (*lit.* forbidden) III 152

forbrenne, burn up III 98

forceres, boxes X 213

fordide, destroyed XVI 166 (*p.t.* of fordoon)

fordo(on), destroy V 20; *p.p.* XIII 260

*forel, box XIII 95

foresleves, fore-part of sleeves V 80

foreward, agreement IV 14

forfaren, come to grief XV 135

forfeteth, fails XX 25

forfreteth, nips off XVI 29

forglutten, greedily consume X 83

forgoeres, purveyors II 61; guide II 188

forgrynt, destroys (= forgrindeth) X 79

formaliche, according to rule XV 373

formest, first of all X 217; foremost XIX 120

formour, creator IX 27

forpynede, wretched, damned VI 155

forreyours, harbingers XX 81

forsake, abandon V 425, XIV 265; turn down XV 84

forshapte, unmade, uncreated XVII 290

forsleuthed, spoilt through neglect V 439

forstalleth, buys up in advance IV 56

forster, forester XVII 113

forsworen, perjured XIX 373

forth (*n*), way, course forward III 157

forth (*av*), on X 437; also, further XIII 210

forthi, therefore Pr 111, *XIX 317
forthynketh, it me, I regret IX 130
forto, till V 567
forwalked, tired with walking
  XIII 205
forwanye, weaken V 35
forwhy, for which reason XIII 281
forwit, foresight V 164
foryaf, granted XVIII 76
foryat, forgot XI 60
foryelde, reward VI 275; repay
  XIII 189
foryete, forgotten I 398; foryyte,
  XX 155
foryifnesse, remission XX 287
fostren, produce XVII 208
foughten, fought Pr 42
foule (av), foully III 186; badly
  X 473; viciously XI 214; rudely
  XX 5
founde, try XI 192 (= fonde)
founde, thought up X 71
  (p.p. of fynden)
foundement, foundation XIV 200,
  XIX 328
fourmen, teach XV 377
fraternitee, religious brotherhood
  XI 56
frayned, asked I 58, V 525, VIII 3
fraytour, refectory X 322
fre(e), noble II 77; generous, X 74;
  freeborn XIX 33
freet, ate XVIII 195 (p.t. of freten)
freke, man IV 13, X 249, XI 26,
  XIII 2, XVI 176
frele, weak III 122; changeable
  VIII 43
freletee, frailty III 55, XVII 332
fremmed, stranger XV 141
frendes, relatives IX 115
frendloker, in a friendlier manner
  X 227
frenesse, generosity, grace XVI 88
frenetike, crazed X 6
freres, friars Pr 58
frete, eat II 96; p.p. XIII 330
fretted, adorned II 11
frith, wood XVII 113, XII 220
fro, from III 110, VI 88, VIII 96
frokke, gown V 80

frounces, creases XIII 318
frythed, hedged V 581
ful (av), very Pr 20, VI 44, XI 20
fullynge, baptism XII 282
fullyng stokkes, cleansing-frames
  XV 452
furlang, ten-acre field V 418
furwes, furrows VI 104
fust, fist V 84, XVII 139, 150
fuyr, fire XIII 163
fyle, concubine V 158
fyn, fin XX 45
fyn (a), subtle X 249; good XVII 93
fynde, find (in books) IX 68; read
  X 300
fynden, provide IX 68, XV 572
fyndyng, provision, endowment
  XX 384
fynt, finds IV 131; provides VII 129
  (= fyndeth)

gabbe, lie III 180; gabbynge, XIX
  458
gadelynges, rascally fellows IV 51; sg
  XX 157
gaf, gave XIV 9 (p.t. of gyve)
gailers, gaolers III 138
galoches, shoes XVIII 14
galpen, yawn XIII 89
game(n), play Pr 153, V 407; delight,
  entertainment IX 102, *X 50
gan, did I 173 (as auxiliary forming
  simple past tense)
gange, go II 168, XIV 161, XVI 159
*garisoun, cure VI 138
garnement, garment XIII 400
garte, made I 122, V 61, VI 300,
  XV 443
gat, begot I 33 (p.t. of geten)
gate, way I 205, III 156
gateward, gate-keeper, porter V 595
gaynesse, extravagance X 83
geaunt, giant VI 231
gedelyng, scoundrel IX 104
gendre, species XVI 222
generacion, (act of) generation
  XVI 222
gentile, noble, good I 185
gentilliche, courteously III 13;
  elegantly XIII 233

gentries, nobility XIV 181, XVIII 22

Geomesie, geomancy X 210

gerles, children I 33, XVIII 7; **girles**, X 79, 177

gerner, granary VII 130

gerte, made XX 57 (= **garte**)

gerthes, girths IV 21

gesene, scarce XIII 271

gest, guest XV 285

gestes, stories narrative(s) X 23, XIII 231

geten, begot XX 157 (*p.t.* of **geten**); *p.p.*, IX 193

Gile, guile, deceit II 145; **Gyle**, II 188

gileth, cheats VII 68

gilour, deceiver II 121

gilt, guilt, sin IV 101; **giltlees**, Pr 34

girdeth (*imper. pl*), strike II 202

girte, vomited V 373

glade (*v*), cheer VI 119; **gladie**, XVIII 255

glazene (*a*), of glass XX 172; *v*, glaze III 61

gleede, glowing coal II 12, V 284; *pl*, XVII 218

glee, singing Pr 34

gleman, minstrel IX 102, X 156, V 347

glorie, presumption X 115, XX 157

glose (*n*), gloss, commentary V 275

glosed, expounded Pr 60; **glossed** X 172

glosynges, deceptions XX 125

glubberes (*n* as *a*), gulpers IX 61

gnawen, revile X 57

go me to, let one go to X 192

goky, fool XI 306

goliardeis, buffoon Pr 139

gome, heed XVII 12

gomes, men II 74, *XII 60; *sg*, V 368, *XIV 8

gommes, (kinds of) gum II 227

good(e), wealth, goods III 169, V 296

goode, **to**, to good conduct III 223, V 634

goodliche, generously I 182; well XI 279

goost, spirit I 36, IX 46, X 390

goostliche, really XX 40

gorge, throat X 57

*gospelleres**, evangelists X 246

gossib, friend V 303

gothelen (*v*), rumble V 341, XIII 89

grace, favour III 108; mercy IV 141; success V 96; luck V 150

gracious, pleasing VI 226

gradde, cried aloud XX 387 (*p.t.* of **greden**)

graffen (*v*), graft V 136

graithe, direct I 205; *ready XII 193

graithly, quickly XI 41; duly XVIII 291

gramariens, scholars XIII 71

gras, herb XII 59

graunge, farm-house XVII 72

grave, stamped IV 130; *v*, engrave III 49

gravynge, engraving III 64

grece, fat XIII 63

greden, cry out II 74; call for III 71

gree, prize XVIII 98

greete, weep V 380

greetnesse, width XVI 59

grene, unmatured VI 280

greten, greet V 336

greven, injure Pr 153; offend Pr 203; take offence Pr 139; feel aggrieved VI 314

greyn, grain VI 119; seeds XIX 276

greyne, colour XVI 59

griped, clutched III 182

gromes, fellows VI 216

grope, feel, handle XIII 347, XIX 170

grotes, groats III 138, XV 544

growed, grew XVI 56

grucche, complain Pr 153, VI 216

grym, terrible V 354 **-ly**, fiercely X 261

grys, pork Pr 227; pigs VI 280

grys, fur of grey squirrel XV 221

gyde, guide VI 1

gyed, guided II 188

gyn, device XVIII 252

gynful, treacherous X 210

gynnyng, beginning II 30, IX 28

gyour, guide XIX 429

gyterne, gittern XIII 234

gyved, fettered XX 192

gyves (*n*) XIV 52

habbeth, have IV 147, XV 137

haddestow, had you XI 411, XX 188

hailse, greet V 100; *p.t.*, did obeisance to VII 161

hakeneyman, horse-hirer V 311

hakke, grub about XIX 405

half, hand, side II 5, III 181

haliday, holy day V 579

halidome, the holy relics V 370

halie (*v*), draw VIII 96

halp, helped XIX 131 (*p.t.* of helpen)

hals, neck Pr 170, VI 61

halsede, adjured I 73

halt, holds XVII 106 (= holdeth)

halwe, sanctify XV 528

handwhile, short time XIX 274

handy-dandy, by secret bribery IV 75 (*see note*)

hanged on, taken III 181

hanselle, gift, treat V 319

hap, luck XIII 106; *pl*, V 96

happe, happen III 286, VI 46, XVI 87

happily, perhaps V 615

hardie (*v*), embolden XV 436

hardier, more boldly XIV 262; hardiliche, boldly VI 29; hardy, bold IV 60

harewen (*v*), harrow XIX 270

harlotrie, obscene talk, story IV 115, V 407

harlottes, ribald fellows IV 118, VI 52; villains XVII 275

harmede, did harm, injury III 141

harmes, trouble, injury IV 31

harneis, armour XV 221

harrow!, alas! XX 88

hastilokest, most promptly XIX 473

hastow, have you (= hast thow) III 106

hater, cloak XIV 1; haterynge, clothing XV 78

hatie(n), hate VI 50, X 95

hatte, is called V 573

haubergeon, mail-coat XVIII 23

haukes, hawks IV 125; hawk's V 432

haunten, indulge in Pr 77, III 53

havylons, tricks X 131

hawes, hawthorn berries X 10

hayward, overseer XIX 335

hede, heed VI 15, XI 111, XV 91

heed, head I 164; *pl* heddes, XX 187

he(e)le, recovery XIII 342; health XIV 172, XVII 37; protection XIX 475

heeled, healed VI 192

heep, crowd Pr 53; number V 328

heeris, hair's X 333

heet, ordered XX 273 (*p.t.* of hoten)

heighe (*a*), great, ultimate V 274

heighe (*av*), loudly IV 162; aloud II 74; properly, duly V 579

heighnesse, exaltedness XX 153

heigh prime, the end of prime VI 112 (*see note*)

helden, thought Pr 180 (*p.t.* of holden)

hele (*n*), crust VII 195

hel(i)en, cover XII 230; conceal V 166, XX 340

hem, them Pr 45; themselves Pr 20

hemselven, themselves III 216

hende, courteous V 257; *av* -liche, graciously III 29; hendenesse, courtesy XIX 31

hennes (*av*), (from) hence III 109; -goyng, departure hence (= death) XIV 165

hente, seized V 5 (*p.t.* of henten)

heo, she II 28, III 29

heragein, against this IX 145, XIV 189

heraud, herald XIV 25, XVI 177

herber, arbour XVI 15

herberwe (*n*), shelter X 405; *v*, store, XIX 321; *p.p.*, lodged XVII 74

here, hear Pr 4

here-beyng, existence here XIV 141

hernes, corners, nooks II 234

heron, on this X 283

hestes, commandments II 83; *sg* command III 113

hethynesse, (a) pagan country XV 442

heved, head XIV 233, *V 537

heveneriche, the kingdom of heaven Pr 27, XIV 261

hevy, gloomy XI 27, XX 2

hevynesse, grief XVIII 247

hewe, workman V 552; *pl* hewen, IV 55

hewe (*v*), strike XVII 245

hexte, highest XII 144

heyre, hair-shirt V 65
hiede, hurried XX 325; **hyed,** V 378
highte, commanded Pr 102 (*p.t.* of **hoten**)
hii, they Pr 66, XX 301, *V 565
hiled, covered V 590; **hileden,** XI 351
hippynge, hopping XVII 60
hir(e), their Pr 28 et passim; of them XI 315; **her,** I 10
hire (*prn*), her II 1; *refl,* herself V 62
hire (*n*), reward, payment III 72
hitte, threw down V 322
hoen on, shout at X 61
hoked, crooked Pr 53
hokes, hooks V 594
holde, hold on to V 45; observe VII 20
holden (*p.p.*), practised V 223; considered III 212; obliged V 274
hole, entire VI 59, XVIII 378; **holly,** wholly III 113
holpen, helped (*p.t.* of **helpen**) VI 116; *p.p.,* VII 70
holwe, hollow(ly) V 187
homliche, at home X 95
honeste, honourable XIX 94
hoolly, entirely XVII 26
hoor, white-haired, hoary VI 83, XVI 173; **hore,** VII 98
hoper, seed-basket VI 61
hoppe, dance III 200
hors, horses XI 343
hostiler, inn-keeper XVII 74; ostler V 332
hostrie, hostelry, inn XVII 74
hote, command II 200
hoten, called II 21 (*p.p.* of **hote, hatte**)
houped, shouted VI 172
houres, the 'hours' of the breviary I 183
housbondrie, thrift I 57
housel, holy communion XIX 396
housled, be, receive communion XIX 3
housynge, house-building XV 78
hoved, waited about Pr 211, XVIII 80
howve, coif III 295; *pl,* Pr 211; hood XX 172
hucche, clothes-trunk IV 116
hukkerye, retail trade V 223

hulles, hills IX 139
hungrily, hungrily V 187; in miserly fashion XX 123
huyre (*n*), pay V 556
hyed, hurried V 375; **hyedest,** III 194
hyere, higher II 28
hyne, servant Pr 39; thing of low worth IV 118

Ich, I XIII 248
if, in case V 241
Ik, I V 224
ilke, same I 83
impe, graft IX 149; *n.pl* grafts V 136
impugnen, find fault with Pr 109
infinites, infinite things XIII 128
ingong, entrance V 629
***inmiddes,** in the midst of V 284; between I 160
inobedient, resistant XIII 282
inparfit, imperfect, faulty XV 50
inparfitly, imperfectly, incompletely X 465
intil, into XIII 211
Inwit, conscience, moral sense IX 18; intelligence, understanding IX 67
irens, irons, fetters VIII 102
iseised, put in possession of XVIII 283

jangle, argue Pr 130; quarrel II 95, VIII 120; utter IV 155
jang(e)leres, idle chatterers Pr 35, X 31
jangling, protestation IV 180; crying out IX 82
jape (*v*), jest, mock II 95; *n,* XX 145; japed, deceived I 67
japeres, jesters, buffoons Pr 35
jugged, rode up XX 134
jouke, rest XVI 92
journee, day's stint XIV 136
joutes, stews V 156
juele, jewel XI 184
jugged, concluded I 185; interpreted VII 162
jurdan, chamber-pot XIII 84
juste, bottle-shaped XIII 84
juste (*v*), joust XVI 95, XVIII 19
juttes, nobodies X 461

juventee, youth XIX 108
juwise, judgement, sentence XVIII 383

kaiser, emperor XIX 138; kaysers, IX 111
kan, know, have acquaintance with, know how to (passim)
kaughte, snatched Pr 107
kaurymaury, coarse garment V 78
kaylewey bastard, Cailloux pear XVI 69
kemben, comb X 18
kene, sharp IX 182; bold XX 129
kenne, teach I 81; guide, direct XVII 114
kennyng, instruction X 196; *discipline X 190
kepe, care III 280; protect VI 27; govern VIII 100; notice XI 336
kepe (n), notice, heed XI 336, XIII 272
kepere, guardian XII 126, XIX 447
kepynge, living, behaviour XIX 357
kerneles, crenellations V 588
kerse, cress X 17
kerve (v), cut VI 104
kerveres, carvers X 180; kervynge, XVII 171
kevereth, protects XII 178; recover XX 336
kex, dried hemlock-stem XVII 220
kidde, showed V 434 (p.t. of kithen)
kirk, church III 60, V 1, VI 91;
kirkyerd, churchyard XIII 9;
kirkeward, towards church V 298
kirtel, under-jacket V 79, XI 283
kith, kindred XIII 379; country XIX 79
kitten (v) cut (p.t. pl of kutten) VI 188
knappes, buttons VI 269
knave, servant IV 17; fellow Pr 44
knele, kneel X 309; knelynge, Pr 73
knewliched, acknowledged XII 192; knoweliched, V 474; knowlichynge, XIV 187
knowes, knees V 353
knytten, fasten Pr 169
konne, learn XV 45; know XV 53; know how to VI 68

konnynge (a), clever, learned III 34; n, knowledge XI 165; wise act XIX 462
kouthe, knew Pr 182; knew how to V 24
kultour, coulter III 308
kuttepurs, cutpurse V 630
kyen, cows, kine VI 140
kyn, kind; g.sg, kynnes, XIV 185 et passim
kynde (n), kind Pr 186; nature V 588; stock IX 126; people X 424; natural strength XI 260
kynde (a), natural I 138; right, own VIII 71
kyndely, kyndeliche, properly, in the right way I 81; naturally V 538; essentially XIV 87
kyngene, of kings XIX 79
kyngryche, kingdom Pr 125
kynrede, kindred IX 174

lacche, capture II 204; catch V 349; obtain VI 227; seize XVI 50
lachesse, negligence, sloth VIII 37
ladde, led Pr 112; carried V 247 (p.t. of leden); lad (p.p.), led, guided IX 16
laddes, ordinary people XIX 32
lafte (v.i.), remained III 197; v.t., left XX 251
laike (v), play Pr 172
lakke (v), criticize, disparage II 48; blame VI 224
lakkes (n), defects X 262
laklees, faultless XI 389
lambren, lambs XV 206
lang, long II 182
langour, pain XIV 117, XVIII 226
lape, lap up V 357; drink XX 18
lappe, portion II 35
large (a), wide, full X 164; liberal XIII 299; n, bounty XIX 43
largely, generously XIX 60; fully XX 87
largenesse, generosity V 623
largere (av), more amply XI 160
largesse, bounty XIII 449
lasse (a), lesser II 46; smaller XII 261; av, less X 265

lat, leads IX 58 (= ledeth)

lat (*imper.*), let V 337; late (*subj.*),
    let Pr 155

latter, later I 199

laude (*v*), praise XI 106

laughte, seized Pr 150 (*p.t.* of
    lacchen); took III 25; assumed
    XVII 149

laumpe, lamp XIII 152

launde, clearing, plain VIII 65; X 163

laved, washed XIV 5

lavendrye, laundry XV 187

layes, songs, lays VIII 66

layk (*n*), contest, sport XIV 244

lazar, leper XVI 255

leautee, justice Pr 122; loyalty II 21;
    right III 294; equity XI 84

leche, physician I 204, II 224

lechen (*v*), cure XIII 254; XVI 113

lechecraft, medicine VI 253, XVI 104

lede, person *XV 393; *XVI 201,
    *XIX 413; *see* leode

lede (*v*), draw II 182; lead, rule
    IV 148; manage X 20

ledene (*n*), vooice, cry XII 243, 252,
    261

ledere, leader I 161; guide XII 96

leed, lead V 591, XIII 83, 247

leef, leaf III 341, XV 102; part
    VII 176

leef (*a*), pleasing IX 58; fond XX 195;
    av, dearly III 18; *n*, beloved II 33

leel, faithful XI 161; leelly (*av*), I 78

le(e)re, face I 3

lees, lost (*p.t.* of lesen) VII 159

leet, caused (*p.t.* of leten) XX 143

leet, considered XX 146

leeve, dear IV 39

legende, book X 375

legge (*v*), lay V 240; wager II 34;
    l. on, lay on XV 191

legistres, legal experts VII 14

leide, pressed XX 114

leith, lays V 349

leighe, said falsely to XVIII 403

lele, honest X 432 (*pl* of leel)

lelly, faithfully VII 124

leme, gleam, light XVIII 124

lemman, lover V 411; XIV 300

lene, give, grant Pr 126, I 181; lend
    V 240

lenede, leaned Pr 9, XVI 246; idled
    XVIII 5

lenge (*v*), remain I 209, XIX 422; *p.t.*,
    dwelt VIII 7

lenger, longer III 340

lengthed, lengthened XVIII 302

lent (*v*), grants IX 106, X 62
    (= lendeth)

Lenten, season of Lent Pr 91,
    XIII 350, XVIII 5

leode, man I 141, *XIX 413; *pl*,
    persons XVI 181, *201, *XVIII
    402

lepe, run V 569; digress XI 317

lere, learn I 146; teach III 69, *X 304

lered, educated, learned IV 12, X 234

lerned, learnt I 199; taught V 295

lese, lose II 35, III 159

lese, glean VI 66

*leste, least XVIII 406

lesynge, loss V 111

lesynge, lie IV 19; *pl* II 125

let, considers X 187 (= leteth)

leten, consider XV 585; *p.t.*,
    IV 160; give up V 458; leave IV
    191

leten, caused II 159

lethi, empty, vain X 186

lette, impede, prevent III 32; *p.t.*,
    III 198; letted, XIX 386; delay
    IX 131

lettere, hinderer I 69

lettre, written assurance X 91; *pl*,
    letters of warrant IV 132

lettred, educated I 136, VII 132

lettrure, learning Pr 110; Scripture
    X 27; literacy, education XII 104;
    text X 377

lettyng, delay VI 7, X 221

leve (*n*), permission Pr 85, III 15

leve (*a*), dear V 556

leve (*v*), believe I 38; leveden (*p.t. pl*),
    I 118

leve (*v*), leave I 103; abandon VII 150

leved, leafy XV 97

level, (use of the) level X 181

leven, live V 44 (= lyven)

levere (*a*), dearer V 38; preferable X 11

levere (*av*), more dearly I 143, XV 195

leves, leaf's III 340

levest (*av*), most dearly V 563, X 355

leveste (*a*), dearest I 151

levynge, leavings V 357

lewed, uneducated, ignorant Pr 72; useless, worthless I 189

lewednesse, ignorance III 32

Lewte, Equity XI 84

leyd, laid (in pledge) III 202; leyen, lain III 38

leye (*v*), strike, lay on XIII 147

leye (*n*), flame XVII 208

leyes, fallow lands VII 5

libbe (*v*), live III 227

lich, like IX 63

liche, body X 2

liere, liar I 38; lyeres, IX 119

lif, living creature III 294, XI 213

liflode, living Pr 30; livelihood I 37; source of sustenance V 87; means of life V 458

lifte, sky XV 357

lige, liege, bound IV 184

liggen, reside Pr 91; liggeth, lies III 176; liggynge, lying II 52

light, lightly, at low value IV 161

lighte, descended XI 246; alighted XIX 203

lighter, easier XIV 249, XVII 40

lightliche, easily Pr 150

lightloker, more nimbly V 569

likame, body Pr 30, I 37

likerous, luxurious Pr 30; dainty VI 266; lascivious X 163

liketh, pleases I 43, II 232

likne, compare (disparagingly) X 42, 276

likynge (*n*), pleasure XI 21; *a*, pleasing XI 272

lippe, portion V 246, XV 501

liser, selvage, edge of cloth V 206

lisse, delight IX 29; joy XVIII 226

list, it pleases Pr 172, III 158, XX 18

liste, strip of cloth V 517

lith, lies (= lyeth), I 126

lithen, listen to XIII 424

lither, evil X 166; *pl*, X 437

litlum and litlum, by little and little XV 609

lixt, liest V 161

lobies, lubbers, ungainly fellows Pr 55

loke, behold I 112; protect I 209; govern VII 166; watch over XV 9; *behave X 90

lokynge, considering XI 317; conscious XIX 159

lolled, hung V 189, XII 190; lolleth, rests XII 212; lollynge, lying XVI 269

lomb, lamb V 553, VIII 85

lomere, more often XX 238

lond, land (passim); londleperis, vagabond XV 213

longe, tall Pr 55, XIV 244

longen, belong II 46

loof, loaf XIII 48

loore, teaching V 38, IX 71

lo(o)resman, teacher XII 182; *pl*, IX 88, XV 390

loos, reputation XI 295, XIII 449; *praise XIII 299

looth, reluctant, unwilling III 161, XI 222, XV 472; hateful IX 58

lopen, leapt I 117; ran Pr 223; lope, if he ran (*p.t. subj.* of lepen)

*lordeth, acts as lord over X 86, *III 298

lordlich, haughty XIII 302

lordshipe, domain II 46, III 20; *pl*, properties XV 557

lorel, wastrel VII 137, XV 5, XVIII 3; *pl*, XVII 45

loren, lost XII 120; lore XVIII 79 (*p.p.* of lesen)

losedest, praised XI 419

losels, wretches, wastrels Pr 77, VI 122

losely, loosely XII 212

losengerie, deceitfulness VI 143; flattery X 49

loseth (*v*), praises XV 253

lotebies, concubines III 151

lother, the more unwilling XV 391

lotheth, is hateful Pr 155

lothliche, loathsome I 117

lotieth, lurks XVIII 104

lough, laughed XIX 463, XX 143

loure, scowl, frown V 131, XII 277; *p.t.*, II 224; **lourynge,** V 82, 337

lous, louse V 194

loutede, bowed III 116, X 142

lovedaies, days of settlement out of court III 158, V 421, X 20, 306

lovelich, amiable, pleasing V 553, VIII 85; *av*, XIII 26

lovelokest, handsomest I 112, XIII 295

loves, loaves VI 282

lowe, humble V 553, *XIV 300; gentle V 591; *av*, XII 264

lowenesse, humility III 291

lowen, lied V 94

luft, worthless wretch IV 62

lurdaynes, villains XVIII 102; *sg*, sluggard XX 189

lusard, serpent XVIII 338

lussheburwes, light coins XV 348 (*see note*)

lust, pleasure XIX 356

lutede, sang to the lute XVIII 425

luther, bad, vicious V 117, X 434, XV 348; *see* lither

lyard, grey horse XVII 65

lybbynge, living Pr 223, VII 60, XII 264

lyme, limb V 98; *pl*, features XIX 8

lymeyerd, lime-rod, snare IX 181

lymitours, licensed mendicants V 137, XX 347

lynage, descendents IX 48, ancestry XI 295

lynde, lime-tree I 156, VIII 65

lyne, measuring-line X 181

lyth, limb (= body) XVI 181

lythe(n), listen to VIII 66, XIII 424

lyveris, people living XII 131

lyves (*av*), alive XIX 159

macche, wick XVII 214

maceres, mace-bearers III 76

magesté, majesty IX 52, XV 480, XVI 184

maires, mayors III 76; XIII 271, XIV 289

maistrie, advantage, upper hand V 102; miracle XVI 115; *pl*, acts of power IV 26; arts XIX 257

make (*n*), spouse III 119; mate XI 327

make (*v*), compose poetry XII 22

makynge, verse-making XII 16

maleese, pain XIII 77; **male ese,** XVII 193

males (*n*), bags V 230

mamelen, go on (about) V 21; *p.t.*, XI 416

manacen, threaten XVI 49; *p.t.*, VI 170

manere, kind of XIX 327

manere (*n*), estate, manor X 307; **manoirs,** V 242; **manoir,** manor-house V 586

manered, disposed, mannered XV 415

manged, eaten VI 257

mangerie, feast XI 112; feeding XV 591

manhod, humanity, human worth XII 295

mankynde, human nature XVII 149, XIX 72

manlich, charitable V 256; **manliche** (*av*), generously X 89; forthrightly X 284, XVI 127

mansed, wicked II 40; vicious, ? excommunicated X 278, XX 221

mansion, dwelling-place XIV 217

march(e), province XV 445, XX 221

marchal, marshalling officer III 201

marchaunden, do business XIII 394; **marchaundise,** goods, wealth V 285; **marchaunts,** merchants VII 18

mareys, marsh(es) XI 352

marke, observe XII 131

marked, allotted XII 185

massepens, mass-pence III 224

maugree (*n*), disfavour VI 239; ill-luck IX 155; *prep*, in spite of VI 40

maundement, commandment XVII 2

mawe, stomach V 123, VI 174

mayn, strength XVIII 319

mayne, household, retainers V 97

maynpernour, surety IV 112

maynprise (*n*), bail IV 88; *v* II 197

mayntene, support, maintain III 185

maze, dismay Pr 192; vain wanderings I 6

me, one, people X 192; **men,** XI 13, 204

mede, reward, hire, payment II 20 et passim; **medeth** (*v*), reward III 216

medled, mixed, had intercourse with XI 343; **medlest,** concern XII 16

me(e)ne (*n*), intermediary I 160, IX 34, XV 506

me(e)ne (*a*), lesser I 108; humble X 64

mees, mice Pr 147

mees, (dish of) food XIII 53, XV 316

meete (*v*), measure Pr 215

megre, thin V 127

meke (*a*), humble I 173

meke (*v*), humble V 69

mele, meal, ground grain XIII 261

meled, spoke III 36

melk, milk V 439

melleth, speaks III 105

mene (*v*), mean III 97; refer to V 276

mened, complained III 170, VI 2

menever, furred XX 138

menged, adulterated XIII 362

mengen, commemorate VI 95

menske (*v*), honour III 184

menynge, in, (as if) seeking XV 474

menyson, flux XVI 111

mercer, silk-dealer V 251

merciable, merciful V 504, XVII 231

merciede, thanked III 20

mercy, thank you I 43, X 145; *n*, thanks XIX 76

mercyment, fine I 162

mercymonye, reward XIV 126

meritorie, meritorious XI 79

merk(e) (*a*), dark I 1; obscure XI 159; merknesse, darkness XVIII 136

merk, imprint XV 349

merke (*v*), observe VI 325

meschief, ill-luck III 177; danger X 451; disease XV 98

mesel(e)s, lepers III 133, VII 101

mesondieux, hospitals VII 26

mestier, occupation VII 7

mesurable, moderate III 256

mesure, moderation I 35; measure I 177

mesurelees, immoderate III 246

met (*n*), measure XIII 359

mete (*n*), food I 24

mete (*v*), measure, mete out I 177

metelees, without food VII 142

metels, dream VII 143

meten (*v*), dream Pr 11; **metynge,** dream XI 319, XIII 4

meteyyveres, food-providers XV 147

mettes, dinner-companions XIII 35

meve, move VIII 33; urge VIII 120; stir up XII 124; **mevestow,** do you arouse X 263

meynee, troop I 108, III 24, X 93; household XVI 236

mildely, humbly III 20

mirre, myrrh XIX 92

misese, illness XIII 160; **myseisé,** sick VII 26

mitigacion, compassion V 470

mnam, pound VI 240

mo, more Pr 147, IV 10

modiliche, angrily IV 173

mody, the, the proud one IX 20?

m(o)ebles, movable goods III . , IX 84

moeve(n), adduce XV 70; upset XIX 288

moiste (*v*), moisten XVIII 369

molde, earth Pr 67, I 44

molde, pattern XI 349

moled, spotted XIII 275; **moles,** spots XIII 315

mone, prayer XV 26, 505

moneilees, moneyless VII 142

moniales, nuns X 318, XX 264

mood, feelings, anger X 263

moore (*a*), greater V 282

mooste, greatest Pr 67

moot (*v*), must XX 238 (= mote)

moot, moat V 586, XIX 369

moot-halle, council-chamber, court IV 135

more, root XV 98, XIX 341

mornede, sulked XIII 60, III 170

morthereth, murders XVII 280

mortrews, stews XIII 41

morwenynge, morning Pr 6

moste, must V 387; must go V 412; might IV 112 (*p.t.* of moten)

mote, must I 138; **moten,** might V 512

mote, litigate I 176; **motyng**, action at law, legal services VII 58

moton, a gold coin III 24

motyves, motions, ideas X 115

moustre, show XIII 362

mow(en), can Pr 170 et passim; *XV 470

muche, tall VIII 70

muchel (*a*), much Pr 202; great V 470

muchel (*n*), size XVI 182

muk, dung VI 142

muliere (*a*), legitimate II 119; *n*, legitimate offspring XVI 219

murie, pleasant II 154; merry (*euphemism*) XIII 352

murthe, entertainment Pr 33, III 11; joy XVIII 127

murthe(n) (*v*), gratify XI 398; cheer XVII 241

musons, measures X 174

must (*n*), new wine XVIII 371

myd, with Pr 147, I 116, IV 77; *XI 343, *XII 203, *XV 352

myddel, waist III 10

myghtful, powerful I 173

mynistren, have the use of XII 52

mynne, reflect XII 4; remember XV 461

mynours, miners Pr 222

mynstralcie, music(al entertainment) III 11

mynut while, a minute's time XVII 229

myrthes, delights XI 20

mysbede, injure VI 45

mysdo, maltreat XVIII 97; *p.t.*, mysdide IV 99

mysfeet, misdeed XI 374

myshappe (*v*), come to grief III 329

mysproud, arrogant XIII 436

mysruleth, abuses IX 60

mysse, be without Pr 192, XII 99

mysseide, rebuked XVI 127; *p.p.*, spoken against V 68

mysshapen, deformed VII 94

mysstandeth, is wrong XI 380

myswonne, wrongfully obtained XIII 42

mytes, mites, farthings XIII 197; *sg*, mite *XIV 23

na, no I 183, II 109

nale, atte, at the ale(-house) VI 115

namely, especially II 146; in particular V 258

nappe, fall asleep V 387

n'aroos, did not arise XIX 52

nat, not Pr 38; **naught**, I 101

neddres, adder's V 86

nede (*n*), need, necessity XX 4

nede (*av*), necessarily III 226; **nedes**, V 253

nedé, the needy XX 37

nedfulle, necessary I 21

nedlere, needle-seller V 311

neet, animal XIX 268

neghen, approach XVII 59; *p.t.*, XX 4

neigh (*a*), near XI 212; *av*, nearly III 145

neighe, closely related XII 93

nelle, do not wish Pr 109; **nel he**, if he does not wish XIX 468; **neltow**, if you do not wish VI 156 (= ne + wilt thou)

nempne (*v*), name I 21; **nempnynge**, IX 79

ner, nearly VI 178

nere, should not be V 331; were not X 186

nerhande, almost XIII 1

nevelynge, running V 134

next(e), nearest XIII 373, XVII 288

noble, gold coin worth £⅓ III 45

noght, not Pr 29 et passim

nolde, would not V 558, XI 64

nome, took XX 9 (*p.t.* of nyme)

nones, midday V 372

nonne, nun V 150, VII 29

noon, none VIII 113

norisseth, fosters XVI 33; *norisse, sustain VI 223

no(u)mbre, number XX 255, 259; *v. p.t.*, 256

nounpere, umpire V 331

nounpower, powerlessness XVII 311

nouthe, now III 290, VI 205

noy (*n*), trouble X 60; *danger XI 430

noyen, harm, vex II 127; *p.t.*, II 20

nyce, foolish XVI 33

nyghtcomeris, comers by night
XIX 144

nyght-olde, a night old, stale VI 307

nyme, take X 60, *XI 289, 430

nyppe, cold region, dark XVIII 163

nyste, did not know XIII 25 (= ne
wiste)

o(o), one II 30; one and the same
XVI 58; first XIX 86

ocupien, be active XVI 196

of, through Pr 118; from III 88; for
VI 127; by XVI 152

ofgon, obtain IX 107

ofraughte, reached to XVIII 9

ofsente, sent for III 102

ofter, oftener XI 50, XVIII 381

*ofwandred, worn out with
wandering Pr 7

oke (v), ached XVII 195

olofte (av), above Pr 157; up V 353

on cros wise, by crucifixion XIX 142

one, alone XI 297; self XVI 183

ones, once Pr 146; at one time III 145

oonliche, only IX 141

oost, host III 266, XIX 339

or, before X 417 (= ar, er); av,
beforehand XIX 398

ordeigne, prepare XIX 321; p.t.,
established Pr 119, VIII 99

ordre, order I 104; rank VI 166

orgene, organ, ? organum XVIII 8

orientals, oriental sapphires II 14

othergates, otherwise IX 193

othes, oaths II 93, V 307

oughte, owned III 68 (p.t. of owen)

oute (av), in existence XII 144, 266

outher, or III 306, V 53

outher (a as n), others IV 136

outherwhile, at (other, some) times
Pr 164, V 404, VIII 26

outwit (n), (physical) sense(s)
XIII 289

over al, especially XIII 291

*overcarke, over-burden III 316

overgilte, gilt over XV 124

overhoveth, hovers over III 208,
XVIII 170

overhuppen, skip over XIII 69,
XV 385

overlepe, spring on Pr 200; p.t., 150

overmaistreth, overcomes IV 176

over-plentee, superfluity XIV 73

overreche, encroach XIII 374

overse(n), oversee VI 116; look at,
study X 327; overseyen, forgotten
V 372

overskipped, omitted XI 305

overspradde, covered XIX 207

overtilte, upturned XX 54, 135

paas, pass XIV 300

paast, pastry XIII 251, XIV 29

paie (v), satisfy VI 308

paiere, paymaster V 551

palle, strike XVI 30

palmere, (Jerusalem) pilgrim V 535

paltok, jacket XVIII 25

panel, panel of jurors III 317

paniers, baskets XV 290

panne, brain-pan, skull IV 78

paraventure, perchance V 639

parcell, portion X 63; pl, XI 305

parcelmele, by retail III 81; by
portions XV 246

parceyved, comprehended Pr 100;
perceived V 152

parchemyn, parchment IX 38; deed
XIV 194

parentrelynarie, with interlineations
XI 305

parfit, perfect XI 271; parfitnesse,
perfect virtue X 202

parformen, establish XIII 175;
parfourneth, acts XIII 79; fulfils
XV 325

parisshens, parishioners V 420

parled, spoken XVIII 270

parroked, enclosed XV 286

parten (v), share Pr 81, V 42

partie, part I 7; party XVII 304; a
party, partly XV 17

Pask wyke, Easter week XI 232

passed, past, ago XX 344; passeth,
exceeds VII 173

passhed, dashed XX 100

passion, suffering XIII 91; XV 270

pastours, herdsmen X 460, XII 148

patente, deed XIV 192; document of
authority XVIII 185

Paternoster-while, time taken to say an 'Our Father' V 342
patrymoyne, patrimony XX 234
pawme, palm (of hand) XVII 141
paye, to, satisfactorily V 549
payn, bread VII 122 et passim
paynym, pagan, heathen V 516, XI 162
pays: *see* pees
pece, piece XIV 49; *pl*, cups III 89
peel, accusation XVII 304
peeren, appear Pr 173; are equal to XV 417
pees, peace I 152; pays, XVI 159
peire, pair IX 167, XII 19, XIII 197
peis, weight V 237; peised, weighed V 213
pelet, stone ball V 77
*pelour, accuser XVIII 40
pelure, fur II 9, III 296
penaunce, suffering X 34, XI 279
penauncelees, without punishment X 463
penaunt (*n*), penitent IV 133, XIII 93
pencif, pensive, thoughtful VII 145
penitauncer, confessor XX 320
pennes, feathers XII 246
pens, pence II 223; penyes, XIX 380
penyworthes, bargains V 327
pepir, pepper XV 203
peraunter, perhaps XI 11
percen, pierce, penetrate X 460
percile, parsley VI 285
permutacion, exchange III 258
permute (*v*), exchange XIII 111
perree, jewellery X 12
persaunt, piercing I 157
persone, form, character XVIII 336; *pl*, parsons III 150
pertliche, manifestly V 15; forthrightly V 23
pese, pea VI 169; *pl*, pesen 195; pescoddes, pea-pods VI 291
petit, little VII 57, XIV 243
peyne, pain I 169; peynen, take pains VII 42
phisike (*v*), treat medically XX 324
picche, cut VI 103
p(i)ere, equal III 205, IX 14; *pl*, VII 16

pik, pike-staff V 475; pikstaf, VI 103
piken (*v*), hoe XVI 17; *p.t.*, VI 111
pil, pile, prop XVI 30
pileth, robs XIX 446; pilour, robber III 195; *pl*, XIX 419, XX 263
pioné, peony (-seed) V 305
pisseris, pissers' XX 219 (*see note*)
pistle, epistle XII 29
pitaunce, portion, allowance V 266, XIII 55
pite, pity I 171
pitousliche (*a*), pitiable XVIII 58; *av*, forgivingly IV 98
plastred, treated with a plaster XVII 96
platte, threw (herself) flat V 62
*plaunte coles, greens VI 285
playte (*v*), folded V 208
plede, plead (at law) VII 42; pledours, barristers VII 42; pledynge, III 296
pleide(n), amused themselves Pr 20; played Pr 151
plener (*a*), full XVI 103; *av*, fully XI 108
plentevouse, bountiful X 82
plesynge, pleasure III 252
pletede(n), pleaded at law Pr 213, VII 39
pleye, be active with III 309; *enjoy (oneself) XX 292
pleyn, full, complete VII 102
pleyne, plead XIV 226; utter(s) XVII 294; *p.t.*, complained Pr 83
pleynt, complaint XI 248; *VI 123
plot, patch XIII 276
plowpote, plough-pusher VI 103
po, peacock's XII 256
Pocalips, Apocalypse (*see note*)
point, reason V 15; quality XIV 280; *pl*, respects XVIII 44; in p., ready XIII 111
poke, bag XIII 217; pokeful, VII 192
poketh, thrusts V 611; *p.t.*, urged V 634
pokkes, plague-sores XX 98
pol, head XI 58; *pl*, XIII 247, XX 86
polshe, polish V 475
pondfold, pound, pinfold XVI 264
poole, pole XVIII 52

pope holy, hypocritically holy XIII 284

poret, cabbage VI 297; *pl*, leeks VI 285

portatif, portable I 157

porte, demeanour XIII 278

porthors, breviary XV 120

portreye, draw III 62, XV 181, XVII 170

pose, put it, suppose XVII 295

possed, pushed, dashed Pr 151

possession, property XIV 271

possessioners, beneficed clergy V 143

posternes, side-doors V 619

postles, wandering preachers VI 149

potage, soup VI 150; **potagere,** stew-maker V 155

potel, pottle, ½-gallon measure V 342

potente, staff VIII 97

pouke, devil XIII 162, XIV 189

poundes, belabours Pr 213 (*see note*)

poundemele, (by) pounds at a time II 223

pous, pulse XVII 67

poustee, power V 36; *pl*, violent onsets XII 11

praktisour, practitioner XVI 107

prayed, preyed upon XX 86

preide, requested II 71

preiere, request VII 107

preien, pray XI 58; *p.t.*, asked for XI 245

preise (*v*), value V 324; praise V 611

prentices, students XIX 232

prentishode, apprenticeship V 252

prest, prompt VI 196, XIII 251, XIV 221

presumpcion, supposition X 55; presumption XI 421

preve, practise V 42; experience *VII 45; *demonstrate XIII 85

preynte, winked *XIII 86, XVIII 21

pried, peered XVI 168

priked, spurred II 190, XVII 351

prik(i)ere, rider IX 8, XVIII 25

prikye, riding XVIII 11

prime, heigh, 9 a.m. VI 112

pris (*n*), value II 13; *a*, chief XIX 268

prison, prisoner XVIII 58; *pl*, XV 183

procuratour, agent XIX 260

propre, fine VII 148; distinct X 239; excellent XIII 51; **propreliche,** really XIV 284

provendreth, provides prebends for III 150

provisours, provisors II 171 (*see note*)

prowor, purveyor XIX 262

pryvee, private X 99; intimate III 146

pryveliche, secretly III 82; quietly XIII 55

publice (*v*), make public XI 105

pulte, thrust I 127, VIII 97

punfolde, pen, pinfold V 624; *see* **pondfold** XVI 264

purchaced, obtained VII 38

pure (*a*), sheer X 464; *very VII 104; *av*, very XI 194; **purely,** integrally XVII 142; entirely XIII 260

purfil, furred trimming V 26; **purfiled,** II 9

purpos, line of argument VIII 122

purveie, provide XIV 29; *p.t.*, V 165

put, pit X 369, XIV 174; *pl*, dungeons V 406

pye, magpie XI 346; **pies,** magpie's XII 226

pyk, pike-staff V 535

pyked, peaked XX 219

pykeharneys, plunderers of armour XX 263

pykoise, pick-axe III 309

pyl, fort XIX 367

pylours, pillagers XX 263

pynched, encroached XIII 371

pyne, pain, punishment II 104

pyned, tortured V 209; **pynynge,** punishment III 78

pynne (*v*), fasten bolt XX 299

pyries, pear-trees V 16

quaved, quaked XVIII 61

queed, evil one XIV 190

quelt, dead (*p.p.* of **quelle**) XVI 114

*querele,** quarrel X 301

queste, inquest, jury XX 162

queynt, destroyed XVIII 347

queyntely, ingeniously XIX 350

queyntise, cunning XVIII 274, XIX 355

quod, said Pr 160 et passim

quyk (*a*), living XVI 114

quyk, as, as quickly as possible XIV 190

quyke (*v*), give life to XVIII 347; animate XV 23

quyte, requite XI 192; pay XIII 10; release XVI 262; *p.p.*, paid in full VI 98, XVIII 358

radde, advised IV 110, V 45 (*p.t.* of **reden**)

radde, read III 338 (*p.t.* of **reden**, read)

radegundes, running sores XX 83

rageman, bull with seals Pr 75; coward XVI 89

rakiere, scavenger V 315

rape (*n*), haste V 326; *v*, hasten IV 7; *p.t.*, XVII 80; *av*, **rapeliche,** quickly XVI 273

rappen (doun), strike down, suppress I 95

rathe (*av*), early III 73, IX 13; *comp.*, rather, earlier, sooner IV 5, VIII 75; *superl*, soonest XVI 71

raton, rat Pr 158; *pl*, 146; **ratonere,** rat-catcher V 315

raughte, obtained Pr 75; stretched IV 185; grasped VIII 35; *moved XI 438 (*p.t.* of **rechen**)

raunsoun, ransom XVIII 353; *v. p.t.*, saved XVII 303

ravysshede, carried off IV 49, XI 7; seduced X 457

raxed, stretched V 392

rayes, striped cloths V 207

reaume, realm, kingdom Pr 177; *pl*, I 96

reautee, royalty X 334, XIV 210

recche (*v*), care IV 33

recchelees, reckless XVIII 2; *av*, -ly, XI 130

rechen, reach XI 361; suffice XIV 231

reconforted, comforted again V 280

record (*n*), witness XV 87; *v*, declare XV 611; *p.t.*, IV 172

recoverede, came to life XIX 161

recoverer, means of treatment XVII 68

recrayed, recreant III 259

recreaunt, defeated XVIII 100

redels, riddle(s) XIII 168; *pl*, 185

rede(n), advise I 175; declare XI 102; interpret XIII 185; *p.t.*, **redde,** instructed V 478

redyngkyng, lackey, retainer V 316

reed (*n*), advice XIII 375

reed, red II 15; **rede,** XV 538, XIX 11

refuse, reject XVII 178; *p.t.*, XIX 372

registre, list XX 271; **registrer,** registrar XIX 261

regne, reign III 285; *p.t.*, became king XX 52

regrater, retailer V 222; **regratrie,** retail-trade III 83

reherce, declare V 160; *p.t.*, Pr 184

rekene, give an account of I 22; number II 62; make settlement V 270

rekketh, cares XV 177 (= **reccheth**)

relees (*n*), release; *v. p.p.*, -ed, III 58

releve, support VII 32; restore XV 602

religion, (the) religious order(s) V 45, VI 151

religious, member of religious order IV 125; *pl*, X 291; **religiouses,** X 316

relyede, rallied XX 148

remenaunt, rest XI 114, XVII 239

remes, realms VII 10

renable, eloquent Pr 158

rende, tear Pr 199

rendred, memorized V 207; expounded VIII 90; **rendren,** expound XV 611

reneye, abjure XI 125; **reneyed,** forsworn 160

renk, man Pr 197, V 393; *pl*, *XX 293

rennen, run II 183; **renneres,** runners IV 128; **rennyng,** (while) running (his course) XVIII 100

rental, record of rent due VI 90

renten, provide with incomes VII 32

rentes, income X 15, XIV 231

repented, had regrets V 335

repentedestow, did you repent? V 228

repreve, refute X 343; *p.t.*,
    condemned XII 137
rerages, arrears V 242
resembled, likened XII 264
reson, argument XIV 308
resonable, proper, rational XIII 286
rest, rests Pr 171; *p.t.*, reste, rested
    XVIII 6
retenaunce, retinue II 54
retorik, rhetoric, poetry XI 102
reve, reeve, bailiff II 111, XIX 260
reve (*v*), take away XIV 131, XVI 89
revel, revelry XX 181; *pl*, festivities
    XIII 442
reveris, thieves XIV 182
reward (*n*), heed XVII 267; *v*,
    recompense III 318; watch over
    XI 369; take for XIV 168
rewe, take pity V 468; rue XVI 142;
    it will grieve XVIII 396
rewful, compassionate XIV 148; *av*,
    -liche, XIV 152; pitiably XII 47
rewmes, colds, rheums XX 83
reyn (*n*), rain III 208; *v*, X 312
ribanes, ornamental bands II 16
ribaudes, sinners V 505; evil ones
    XIV 204; *sg*, villain XVI 151
ribaudie, obscenities Pr 44
ribibour, fiddler V 315
riche (*n*), kingdom XIV 179
riche (*a*), rich; richesse, richness II 17;
    riches III 90; *pl*, III 23; *v*, richen,
    grow rich III 83
*richels, incense XIX 90
riflede, rifled, ransacked V 230
right(e) (*a*), direct, very XVI 273; *av*,
    directly XII 295; straight XVI 151;
    exactly X 297; fully XVIII 371;
    *absolutely XIX 372
rightful(le), just Pr 127, III 342; -ly,
    justly VII 10; -nesse justice XIX 83
rightwisnesse, justice XVII 300,
    XVIII 164
ripe, (*a*), ready V 390; matured
    XVIII 371; *v*, ripen XIX 320
risshe, rush IV 170, XI 429
robeth, clothe XV 339
roche, rock XVII 10
rody, red XIII 100
rogged, shook XVI 78

roileth, strays about X 297
rolle (*v*), record V 271
romere, wanderer X 305; *pl*, IV 20
rometh, go forth Pr 171; *p.t.*,
    wandered VIII 1
rongen, rang XVIII 428, XX 59
ronges, rungs XVI 44
ronne, run VIII 90
roon, rained XIV 66 (*p.t.* of reynen)
roos, arose V 230
ropen, reaped XIII 374
ropere, rope-maker V 316
rored, roared V 392
roten (*v*), rot X 114; *p.p.*, XV 101
rotes, roots VI 103
rotey-time, rutting-time XI 337
roughte (ye), you would care XI 73
rouneth, whispers IV 14; *p.t.*, V 326
route, throng Pr 146, II 62
routhe, care X 312; pity XV 507
rowed, dawned XVIII 123
roynouse, unwholesome XX 83
rude, untrained XV 460
rufulliche, sorrowfully XVI 78,
    XVII 236
rugge, back XIV 213; ruggebone,
    V 343
rusty, foul, obscene VI 73
ruthe, pity I 175 et passim
rutte, snored V 392, XII 151, XVIII 6
ruwet, trumpet V 343
ryde, copulated XI 337
rymes, rhymes, ballads V 396
ryt, rides, goes about Pr 171
    (= rydeth)

saaf, safe VIII 34; saved X 345
sacrificed, offered sacrifice XII 116
sad(de) (*a*), upright VIII 28; grave
    VIII 119; sadder, firmer X 459;
    sadnesse, seriousness VII 151; *v*,
    confirm X 244
sage (*a*), wise III 93, X 378
saille, dance XIII 234
salve (*n*), ointment XVII 76; *v*, heal X
    270, XI 217, *see* save (*n*)
samplarie, exemplar XII 102
sandel, sendal, a thin rich silk VI 11
Sapience, the Book of Wisdom III 333

Sarsynes, Moslems III 328; heathens XI 120

saufte, safety VII 36

saughtne, be reconciled IV 2

saulee, food XVI 11

saunz, without XIII 286

saut, assault XX 301

saute, leap, tumble XIII 234

sauter, Psalter, Book of Psalms II 38

save (n), salve, remedy XI 121

save (v), protect Pr 115; preserve XV 428

savore (v), make tasty VI 262; savoreth, meet (one's) taste VIII 109

sawes, sayings VII 138, IX 94

scalles, scabs XX 83

scape, escape III 57

scarlet, fine fabric, usually red II 15

scathe, harm, injury III 57, IV 79

science, knowledge XV 62; wisdom XVII 172

scismatikes, schismatics XI 120

sclaundre, ill-repute III 57

scleyre, veil VI 7

scole, university X 230, XX 273; school, VII 31

scolers, schoolboys VII 31

scorne (v), jeer, speak scornfully X 331, p.t., XI 1

scryppe, bag VI 61

scryveynes, scribes, writers X 331

seche, search III 348; seek VII 164

secret, private VII 23

secte, class, division V 491; garb XIV 259

seculer, layman IX 179

see, sea IV 129, XI 326, XVIII 246

seel, seal Pr 79, III 146, XIII 249

seem, horse-load (8 bushels) III 40

seet, sat XX 199

sege, abode, ? siege XX 311, 314

segge, man III 63, V 608; pl, Pr 160

seigh, saw V 535, XI 363, XV 158

seint, holy I 84; saint Pr 27 et passim

seise, take possession XIII 375; iseised, put in possession XVIII 283

seketh, penetrates XIV 6

selde, seldom Pr 20 et passim

seles, seals Pr 69; seleth, seal III 148

self, himself XI 249; selve (a), very XX 43

selkouthes, wonders XI 363; a, selkouthe, strange XV 588

selleris, merchants III 88

semblable (a), resembling X 365, XVIII 10

semblaunt, appearance VIII 119

semen, seem XV 206; semynge, resembling XV 392

semyvif, half-alive XVII 56

sene, visible XX 185

sense, incense XIX 75

serelepes, separately XVII 165

sergeant, serjeant-at-law III 295, XV 5

serk, shift, shirt V 65

sermon, discourse III 93, X 454

sestow, do you see? I 5

seten (p.t. pl), sat V 339, VI 115, XIII 36

sette, plant V 541; settynge, planting Pr 21; proceed XVI 36; p.t., esteemed VI 169; established XIII 154

sew(e), sowed XIII 374 (p.t. of sowen)

seweth, follows Pr 45; sewe, XI 22

seye (thow), did you see? VIII 75

seyned, crossed V 449

shaar, ploughshare III 308

shadde (v. p.t.), shed XIX 58; shedde, XVII 290

shadweth, throws a shadow XVIII 433

shaft(e), form XI 395; figure XIII 297

shame, modesty XIV 330; shamedest, brought disgrace on III 190

shape, prepare III 17; cause VII 65; dispose XI 424; p.t., shapte, created XVII 218; engineered XX 139

shappere, creator XVII 168

sharp (a), causing smart XX 307; av, loudly XVIII 39

shedynge, dropping (through) VI 9

she(e)f, quiverful III 326, XX 225; pl, sheaves XIX 333

sheltrom, defence XIV 81

shenden, damage II 126; corrupt III

155; mortify XI 424; *p.p.*, **shent**, ruined III 135

shenfulliche, ignominiously III 277

shene, bright, glorious XVIII 411

shepsteres, dressmaker's XIII 331

shere, scissors XIII 331

sherewe, villain, evil person Pr 192 et passim; *v. p.t.*, cursed XIII 331

sherewednesse, wickedness III 44

sherreves, sheriffs II 59

sherte, shirt XIV 330

shete, sheet V 107; *pl*, XIV 234

shette, shut Pr 105; *p.t.*, V 602

sheweth, professes X 254; *p.t.* cited III 351

shewer, mirror, revealer XII 152

shewynge, representation XVII 153

shides, planks IX 132, 399

shifte, shifted XX 167

shilden (*v*), shield X 406

shonye, avoid V 167; **shonyeth**, shuns XI 435

shoon, shoes XIV 330

shoop, got Pr 2; created, IX 66; *pl*, Pr 122; got ready XI 437; XX 307 (*p.t.* of **shapen**)

shoures, storms XVIII 411

shrape, scrape V 123, XI 431

shrift(e), confession V 75, XIV 89

shrof, confessed III 44, X 415 (*p.t.* of **shryven**)

shroudes, garments Pr 2

shryve, confess Pr 64, 89, V 302, XX 281

shynes, shins XI 431

shyngled, clinker-built IX 142

sib, related V 625, X 152

sidder, lower V 190

siggen, say, declare XIII 307 (= **seggen**)

signe, stamp IV 129; *pl*, badges V 521

sike, sick XX 303; **siknessse**, VI 257

siked(e), sighed XIV 326, XVIII 265

sikel, sickle III 308, XIII 375

siker (*a*), sure I 132; *comp*, more secure, confident XII 161; *av*, **sikerer**, more surely V 502

seillynge, sailing, gliding XVIII 306

sire, father Pr 193; V 157

sisour, juryman II 165; *pl*, II 59

sith, since Pr 64, X 224; XIII 255

sithe, scythe III 308

sithes, times V 425, XIV 188

sithen, thereupon Pr 128; then I 146; **siththe**, V 488; *next X 251; *V 540; **sithenes**, afterwards VI 63

skile, argument XI 1; reason XII 215, *pl*, X 300; reasonable state of mind XIX 286

skipte, rose up hurriedly XI 107

sle(e), slay, kill V 577, X 365

sleighte, trick, stratagem XVIII 161; *pl*, XIII 365

slepe, slept XIV 68; *n*, **slepyng**, sleep Pr 10

sleyest, deftest XIII 298

sliken, make sleek II 99

slowe(e), slew X 53, XX 150 (*p.t.* of **slee**)

smaughte, smelled V 357

smerte (*v*), hurt III 168; *av*, sharply XI 434

smolder (*n*), fumes XVII 323

smyt, strikes XI 434; **smyte**, smitten III 324

smythye, hammer III 307; **smytheth**, forges III 324

so (*av*), as V 8; *c*, provided that IV 193

sobreliche, gravely XIII 204; **sobretee**, sobriety XIV 315

socour, help, succour XX 170

soden, cooked XV 293 (*p.p.* of **sethen**)

sodenes, sub-deans XV 132

softe (*a*), mild Pr 1; *av*, carefully XIV 211

soghte, sought III 130 (*p.t.* of **sechen**)

sojourned, delayed XVII 84

sokene, soke, district II 111

solas, comfort, encouragement XII 150; *v*, comfort V 499; amuse XII 22

soleyn, solitary person XII 204

solve, sing by note (*sol-fa*) V 417

*som, (some) one XVI 142

somdel, somewhat III 92, V 431

somme, sum, total XVII 30

somone, sompne, summon II 159,
III 316

somonours, summoners II 59,
XV 132

sond, sand, shore XI 326, XIX 78

sonde, bidding IX 127

songen, sang V 508, VI 115

songewarie, dream-interpretation
VII 149

sonken, sank XI 224

sonne, sun Pr 1, V 492, XI 326,
XV 48

soone (so), as soon (as) X 228; at
once III 47; **sonner,** sooner X 416;
sonnest, soonest III 283

soore (av), strongly XI 224; painfully
XVIII 49

sooth, truth Pr 52; **-fast,** true X 236;
-liche, truly III 5; **-nesse, -fastnesse,**
truth(fulness) II 24, XVI 186

sop, morsel XV 180; thing of small
value XIII 125

sope, soap XIV 6

soper, supper V 372, XVI 141

sorcerie, witchcraft X 212, XV 12

so (that), provided (that) XIII 136,
IV 102

sothe, truth I 86; *a,* **sothest,** truest
X 440; *av,* most truly III 283

sotil (a), skilful XIII 298; clever,
cunning XV 399, XVIII 54; subtle
XV 48; fine-drawn XV 12

sotile (v), argue subtly X 185; *p.t.,*
subtly planned X 216

sottes, fools, sots X 8

soude, payment III 353; **soudeth,** pays
XIX 433

souke, suck XI 121

soule, soul's XVIII 368

soupen, sup II 97, VI 217, XIV 160

soure (av), bitterly, harshly II 141,
X 359

souteresse, female shoemaker V 308;
souters, shoemakers V 407

sovereyn (a), supreme Pr 159;
efficacious X 208; *n. pl,* superiors
VI 80; princes X 425; *av,* **-ly, -**
liche, supremely XV 527

sowne, tend to XIX 457

space, opportunity III 171

spak, spoke V 212, XVI 90

sparen, save XII 51; *p.t.,* XV 143

specheless, without voice XV 36

spede, prosper III 171; succeed
XVII 82

speke, speak X 40; said XII 191;
spoke XIX 130

spekes (n), hollows, caves XV 275

spelle, make out XV 610

spelonkes, caves XV 275

spences, expenses XIV 208

sperhauk, sparrow-hawk VI 196

spie (n), scout XVII 1; *v,* look over
II 227

spille, destroy III 272; waste IX 98;
die XV 135; put to death XIX 305

spire (n), sprout IX 101; *v,* inquire
XVII 1

spores, spurs XVIII 12

sprakliche (a or av) lively,
energetic(ally) XVIII 12; *XVII
82

spredeth, spread XV 92

spryng, rod, switch V 40

spuen, vomit X 40

stable (v), cause to rest I 123

stale, stole XIII 367 (*p.t.* of **stelen)**

stalworthe, sturdy XVII 97

stant, stands XVIII 43; appears
XV 542

starynge, glaring X 4

stede, place Pr 96; *pl,* V 47

stede, horse XIII 294

stekie, stick fast I 123

stele, handle XIX 281

stere, stir XVII 55

sterres, stars VII 161, XI 362

sterve, die XI 430, X 297

stewed, established, ordered V 47

stif, strong XV 593; *av,* firmly VIII 33

stille, constantly XV 224

stiward, deputy XIX 258; *pl,*
stewards Pr 96

stok, trunk XVI 5; *pl,* stumps V 576;
stocks IV 108

stonden, cost III 48

Stories, History VII 73

stottes, plough-horses XIX 269

stounde, short time VIII 65

stoupe, stoop V 386, XI 36

streyte, strictly Pr 26

streyves, strays Pr 94 (see note)

strik, go V 577; strook (p.t.), Pr 183

struyen, destroy XV 596; struyden (p.t.), ibid.

studie, ponder VII 144, XII 222

stuwes, brothels VI 70, XIV 252, XIX 439

stynte, stop X 222

styvest, strongest, stiffest XIII 294

subtileth, devises XIX 461

suede, followed VIII 75, XX 126

suffraunce, long-suffering VI 144; patience XI 378

suffre, allow, tolerate I 146, II 175; p.t., V 483; *IV 86

suggestion, reason, motive VII 65

suppriour, sub-prior V 169

suren, give one's word V 540

Surquidous, presumptuous XIX 342

sustene, support IX 109

suster, sister in religion III 63; pl, sustren, V 618

sute, guise, attire V 488; retinue XIV 257

suwen, follow X 204; seek XI 422

swelte, die V 152; p.t., swelted, XX 105

swerye, swear XIV 35

swete, sweat VI 25, 128

swete, sweet Pr 86; swetter, sweeter XIV 313; av, VI 217

swevene, dream Pr 11, VII 162

sweyed, sounded Pr 10

swich, such IV 69 et passim

swithe, very V 463; quickly III 162; exceedingly V 449

swonken, toiled Pr 21 (p.t. of swynken)

swowe, faint V 152; swowned, fainted V 442

swynk (n), toil VI 233; v, Pr 55

sykir, certain III 49

symonie, simony Pr 86, II 63

sympletee, simplicity X 167

syn, since XX 323

synguler, alone, single IX 35; unique XIII 283; sole XVI 208

sysour, juror XX 161

sythenes, since X 259

sythes, times Pr 231

tabard, short coat V 193

taboure (v), play the tabour XIII 231

tacches, faults IX 148

tache, touchwood XVII 246

tail, number, train II 186; end III 351; sex(ual organs) III 131, XV 105; roots V 19

tailende, tail-end V 389; reckoning VIII 82

taillage, taxation XIX 37

taille, tally-stick IV 58; tally V 248, XII 245

take, give I 56, IV 58

tale, account, estimation I 9, XIX 458

tales, speeches Pr 48; gossip V 404

talewis, garrulous, tale-bearing III 131

tapur, taper XVII 279

Tarse, silken material XV 168

taseles, teazles XV 453

tastes, experiences, contact with XII 130

taverners, inn-keepers Pr 228

taxeth, impose I 162

taxour, assessor VI 39

teche, direct I 84

te(e)me, plough-team VI 134, VII 2, XIX 263

*teeth, goes XVII 38

tellen, keep account of Pr 92; speak III 104

teme, theme III 95, V 60, VI 22 (pun on teeme); proposition X 118

temporaltees, temporalities XX 128

tempred, tuned Pr 51; tunes XIV 309

tendeden, kindled XVIII 239

tene (n), anger VI 116; pain VI 133; v, grieve III 322; vex V 425, VI 38; p.t., became angry II 115; teneful, painful III 349

teris, tears XIII 45

termes, expressions XII 236

thanne, then VI 33, VIII 68; XVI 69, 70

that, that which Pr 38, III 84

thecche (v), thatch XIX 239

thee, prosper V 224

thef, thief XII 191; thefliche, like a thief XVIII 339

theigh, though Pr 192, I 144

thenke, think XI 158

thennes, thence I 73, II 230

ther, where Pr 194, IV 35; whereas III 197

therafter, accordingly VI 114, X 397; afterwards XI 25

therfore, for it IV 54, V 232

therfro, from there XI 353

thermyd(e), therewith VI 69, 158

therto, for that purpose XV 127

therunder, under (the form of) it XIX 389

thesternesse, darkness XVI 160

thider, thither, there II 162

thikke, thickly III 157

thilke, those same X 28

thirled, pierced I 174

thise, these Pr 62, II 171

tho (av), when Pr 176; then V 466

tho (prn), those I 21; they V 326

tholie, suffer, endure IV 84; p.t., XVIII 71

thonked, thanked VIII 108; **thonkyng,** II 149

thorugh, through, by II 41 et passim

thoughte, intended (to go) XVI 175

thresshfold, threshold V 351

thretynge, threat XVIII 281

threve, number XVI 55

threw, fell V 351

thridde, third Pr 121 et passim

throwe, time XVIII 76

***thrumbled,** bumped against V 351

thrungen, thronged V 510

thurst (n), thirst XVIII 369; v, **thursteth,** XVIII 368

thynke, think, intend I 21, X 211

tid, as, at once XVI 61

tidy, upright III 322, IX 105; *useful III 346

tikel, loose, wanton III 131

tikes, villeins, serfs XIX 37

til, to V 601, XI 35, XVIII 223

tilde, dwelt XII 209

tilie, cultivate Pr 120; **tilieris,** ploughmen, XV 363

tilthe, crops XIX 436

titereris, tattlers XX 300

tixte, text XVII 13

to (prep), after VI 29; for VII 136; on V 171; as, in the office of V 151, I 82

to (av), too VI 262, XIII 72

tobollen, swollen up V 83

tobroke, broken down VII 28; destroyed VIII 87

tocleve, cleave asunder XII 140

todrowe, mutilated X 35

tofore, in the presence of V 450

toforn, before XII 131

toft, hillock Pr 14, I 12

togideres, together I 197, II 84

toke (thei on), if they took III 85

tokene, sign, password V 597, X 158

tokenynge, in, as a sign, portent V 19, XVI 204

told, counted V 248

tolled out, stretched out to V 210

tollers, toll-collectors Pr 221

tolugged, pulled about II 217

tome, leisure II 186

tonder, tinder XVII 246

tonne, tun, barrel XV 337

took, gave III 45, XI 169, XVII 2

top, top of the head III 140

torende, be torn apart X 114

torne, subvert III 42; be converted III 327; be overturned XV 546; convert XIII 211; p.t., converted XV 437

toshullen, peeled, flayed XVII 192

to synneward, as if tempting to sin XIII 346

toten, gaze XVI 22

to trutheward, towards truth XIV 309

touchen, deal with XV 74

travaille, work VII 43; effort XI 194, XIV 153; v work VI 139; travel XVI 10

travaillours, labourers XIII 240

traversed, transgressed XII 284

treden, copulated with XI 355

treson, treachery XVIII 289, 293

tresorere, paymaster XX 260

tresour, treasure I 45

trespased, sinned, did wrong XII 284

tretour, traitor XVIII 381; criminal XIX 442

trewe, upright III 304; honest VII 54

trewe (*n*), truce VI 329; **trewes,** XVIII 418

treweliche, justly, honestly VII 61

triacle, healing remedy I 148, V 49

trie, choice XV 168, XVI 4; *av,* -**liche,** Pr 14

triennals, triennial masses VII 171, 180

trieste, choicest I 137

trolled, wandered XVIII 298

trompe, play the trumpet XIII 231; *p.t.,* XVIII 424

troneth, enthrones I 133

trowe, believe I 145; **trowestow,** do you think XII 164

trowes, trees XV 96

trufle, trifle XII 139; nonsense XVIII 147

trusse, pack up II 219

truthe, honesty VI 96; righteousness (= a just man) XII 284; troth XX 118

tulieden, tilled XIV 67; **tulying,** tilling XIV 63

tunycle, jacket XV 168

tutour, overseer I 56

twey(n)e, two, twain V 32, 199, *XIX 348

twyned, twisted XVII 205

tyd, as, quickly, at once XIII 319

tymbre, build XI 360; **tymbred,** would have built III 85

tyme, opportunity V 85; **in tyme,** at the right time X 184

tyne, lose I 113, IX 172; **tynt,** lost XVIII 140; **tynynge,** IX 99

umwhile, at times V 339

unblessed, vicious, accursed XIX 408

unbuxom(e), disobedient, rebellious II 83, XIII 276

unchargeth, unburdens XV 344

uncoupled, unleashed Pr 162, 207

uncristene, non-Christian, pagan X 348, XI 143

underfeng, received I 76 (*p.t.* of **underfonge**); -**fonged** XI 118; *p.p.,* -**fongen,** V 626, VII 172

undernome, criticized XIII 283; rebuked XX 51; *p.t.* of **undernymen,** V 114, XI 214

underpight, supported, propped XVI 23

undertake, affirm X 154, XIII 132; *p.t.,* **undertoke,** rebuked XI 91

unesiliche, uncomfortably XIV 233

ungracious, lacking grace IX 195; unpleasing X 390; *av,* -**liche,** disgracefully XV 133

ungrave, unstamped IV 130

unhardy, lacking courage Pr 180, XIII 123

unheled, uncovered XIV 233, XVII 321

unhende (*n*), discourtesy XX 186

unjoynen, dissolve XVIII 256

unkonnynge, unskilled, ignorant XII 183, XIII 13

unkouthe, strange, alien VIII 156

unkynde, ungenerous I 192, XIII 379; unnatural V 269

unlose, unloose, open Pr 214

unlovelich, disagreeable XII 243

unmesurable, unfathomable XV 71

unmoebles, immovable possessions III 269

unnethe, scarcely IV 60, XX 190

unpynned, unlocked XI 113; -**eth,** undo XVIII 263

unresonable, irrational XV 355

unrosted, uncooked V 603

unsavory, tasteless XV 432

unsavourly, ill-tastingly XIII 43

unseled, unsealed, unauthorized XIV 292

unskilful, unreasonable XIII 277

unspered, unbarred XVIII 86

untempred, untuned IX 103

unthende, small V 175

untidy, improper, indecent XX 119

untrewe, dishonest XV 107

untyled, untiled XIV 253

untyme, the wrong time IX 186

unwittily, foolishly III 106

up gesse, by guesswork, thoughtlessly V 415

upholderes, old-clothes men V 318

up-so-doun, upside-down XX 54

us selve, ourselves VII 128
usage, practice, custom VII 85
used, customary XVIII 380; usen,
    practise III 313, XVIII 106; *p.t.*,
    usedestow, V 236
usure, usury XIX 354; usurie, V 236

vauntwarde, vanguard XX 95
veille, watcher V 443
vendage, wine-harvest XVIII 370
venymousté, poison(ousness)
    XVIII 156
vernicle, image of Christ's face V 523
verray, true XV 268, XVII 291
verset, short text XII 188
vertues, power(s) I 152, XIV 38
vertuous, potent, powerful Pr 103
vesture, clothing I 23
vicory, vicar XIX 413
vigilies, vigils V 410
vileynye, base action XVIII 94
vitaillers, victuallers II 61
vitailles, foodstuffs V 437, XIII 217
voideth, removes XIV 94
vokettes, advocates II 61

wade, go XII 185
wafrer, wafer-seller XIII 227;
    wafrestere, V 632
wage, guarantee (by payment) IV 97;
    p.p., IV 100
waggeth, shakes XVI 41; *p.t.*,
    XVIII 61
waggyng, rocking VIII 31
waiten, look (to do); *p.t.*, VII 140;
    waitynges, lookings II 90
waken, wake, watch XVII 219
walkne, sky XV 361; wolkne,
    XVIII 237
walnote, walnut XI 258
Walshe, Welshman V 317
waltrot, absurdity XVIII 142 (*see
    note*)
walweth, toss VIII 41
wan, obtained V 457; warned
    XV 291; went IV 67
wangteeth, molars XX 191
wanhope, despair II 100, V 279, 445,
    XII 178

wanteth (hem), they lack XIV 173;
    wantynge, lack, XIV 177
wantounnesse, unchastity III 125;
    recklessness XII 6
wanye, wane VII 55; *p.t.*, XV 3
war, aware II 8; wary XIII 71,
    XX 163
warde, guardian XVIII 323
wardemotes, ward-meetings Pr 94
wardeyn, guardian I 55, XVI 187
ware (*v*), guard V 445, IX 180
wareyne, warren Pr 163
warie, curse V 313
warisshen, cure XVI 105
warner, warren-keeper V 309
warp, threw out (= uttered) V 86
warroke, fasten with girth IV 21
wastel, cake of fine flour V 286
wasten, destroy; wastours, destroyers
    Pr 22; wastyng, expenditure V 25
watlede, wattled XIX 329
wawes, waves VIII 40
wayte, look after V 198
wayven, open V 602; *p.t.*, drove
    XX 168
web, piece of woven cloth V 110;
    webbe, weaver V 211; webbesters,
    weavers Pr 220
wed(de), pledge IV 146, V 240
weder, weather XVIII 412; *pl*, storms
    VIII 41, XV 482
wedes, clothes XI 234; *sg*, XX 211;
    weeds VI 111
wedlok, wedlock XVI 203; *pl*,
    marriages IX 154
weend (*imper*), go III 266
weer, perplexity XI 116; doubt XVI 3
weet (*a*), wet XIV 42; *n*, V 530
weetshoed, wet-shod, with wet feet
    XIV 161, XVIII 1
weex, became III 331; fell V 279;
    arose XIV 76; increased XV 3 (*p.t.*
    of wexen)
wehee, horse's neigh IV 23, VII 90
weke, wick XVII 205, 207
wel, good III 70; very III 162; much
    V 113; nearly XV 187
welawo, misery XIV 236
Welche, Welsh (flannel) V 195

welden, possess, control X 24, XI 72, *IX 39

wele, happiness XVIII 203

welfare, luxurious living XIX 357

welhope, good hope XIII 454

welle, spring, source XIV 307, XV 30; v. p.t., XIX 381

wel libbynge, upright X 430

wem, stain XVIII 131

wenche, woman Pr 54; servant-girl V 358; maiden XVI 100, XVIII 113

wenden, go Pr 162; turn XVIII 203

wene, think, suppose III 302; p.t., wende, V 234, wendest, III 192; expect V 469

wenynge (n), (mere) supposition XX 33; pl, hopes II 91

wepe, weep V 61; p.t., wepte, XI 4; wepten, VII 37

wepene, weapon III 306, IX 182, XIX 219

werchen, do, practise IV 146; imper, work II 134

wer(i)e(n), wear III 295, XIV 329

werk, deed IV 146; -manshipe, (sexual) performance II 92; action IX 45, X 289

wernard, deceiver III 180; pl, II 129

werneth, refuse XX 12

werre, war XI 331, XIV 283, XX 163

werse, the, less III 175

wery, weary Pr 7, XIII 205, XV 186

wesshen, washed II 221, XIII 28 (p.t., of wasshen)

wete (n), wet weather XVII 324

weve, weave V 548; wevyng, XV 451

wex, wax XVII 205; wexed, wax-polished V 345

wexen, grow III 302; become XIV 323; increase VIII 39; spring up XV 459

wey, way, road Pr 48 et passim

weye, wey (portion of 3 cwt) V 92

weye (v), weigh V 200; p.p., weyen, I 178

weylawey, alas! XVIII 228

weyled, bewailed XIV 324

weyves, lost property Pr 94

what, what sort of II 18; partly XIII 317

what so, what(so)ever IV 155, X 130

wheither, which XVI 96; do . . . ? XV 197

whennes, whence V 525

wher, whether Pr 171 (contraction of wheither)

wherof, to what end XI 91; means XIV 41

whi, why IX 87; whyes, reasons X 124, XII 218

whider, whither XV 13; -out, from whence XVI 12; -ward, which way V 300

whilom, formerly XV 359

whitlymed, lime-washed XV 113

who, whose, whoever IV 131, Pr 144

wicche, witch XIII 338; sorcerer XVIII 46

widder, wider XVIII 363

wideweres, widowers IX 176

widewher, far and wide VIII 62

wight (n), thing X 274; person III 227; a, powerful IX 21; av, -liche, -ly, vigorously VI 20, briskly X 221; n, -nesse, strength XIX 247; *(no) wight, not at all X 274

wightes, weights XIV 293

wike, week VI 255, X 96; wyke, XI 232

wikkede, bad, difficult VI 1, VII 27; -ly, dishonestly V 200; -lokest, most evilly X 426

wilfulliche, voluntarily XX 49

wille (n), desire XIII 81

wilne (v), desire V 185; wilnyng, desiring XIII 280

wisloker, more carefully XIII 343

wispe, wisp, handful V 345

wisse, instruct V 146; direct V 555; guide VII 128; p.t., I 74; *wissynge, instruction XV 479

wiste, knew Pr 12; wisten, recognized XI 236

wit, understanding XI 322; wisdom V 587; judgement V 364; pl, senses XIX 217; wits X 6

wite, know III 74; learn VI 210

witen, preserve VII 35; protect XVI 25

with, by means of III 2; -alle, moreover Pr 123; -oute, on the outside XI 258

withdraweth, removes IX 97

withhalt, withholds (from) V 552; p.t., withhelden, kept II 229

*withseide, spoke against IV 91

with that, on condition that V 73, X 148

withwynde, woodbine V 518

witlees, out of my mind XIII 1

witte, laid the blame on I 31

witterly, certainly, to be sure I 74, III 176

wittily, ingeniously IX 4; witty, wise II 138; witynge, knowingly XIX 374

wo (n), trouble V 358; misery XIV 177; a, wretched, sorrowful III 153, V 3

wodewe, widow IX 164, 176

woke (v), moisten XV 338

wol(e), will V 246; desire VIII 49; p.t., wolde, wished I 169; woldestow, if you would III 49; wol he, nel he, willing or not XIX 468

wolle, wool VI 13; -ward, shirtless XVIII 1; wollen webbesters, wool-weavers I 220

wolt, wish XI 41 (= wilt)

wolveliche, wolveskynnes, wolf-like XV 116, VI 161

wombe, belly Pr 59; womb XV 455, XVI 100; -cloutes, tripes XIII 63

wonder, (a cause for) w. III 183; pl, marvels, strange events Pr 4, XV 482; av, wondrously XIV 6, XV 1; -wise, in wonderful manner I 124

wone, custom XV 235; woned, accustomed XV 182

wones, dwellings III 235; won(i)eth, dwell(s) II 75, 233

woon, plenty XX 171

woot, knows II 78, XVIII 205

wordeden, spoke, exchanged words IV 46, X 427; wordynge, speaking XVII 48 (pres. p. of worden)

worm, serpent X 107; worm XIV 42

worship, honour I 8; v. p.t., paid reverence to X 224

worstow, will you be V 613, XIX 410

wortes, vegetables V 160, VI 307

worthe, become I 26; be Pr 187; shall be II 40; became (= fell) *XIII 407; w. upon, redound upon XVI 157; w. up, mount VII 90

worthier, more honourable XIX 24; worthili, nobly II 19

wouke, week V 92; pl, XVI 100

wowede, solicited IV 74; woweris, suitors XI 71

wowes, walls III 61

woxen, grown XIX 124

wrastle, wrestle XIV 225

wrathe (v.t.), anger, enrage II 117, X 288; v.i., become angry III 183; p.t., IX 129

wrecche (a), miserable; n.pl., wretches X 80

wreke, avenge V 84; relieve, vent IX 183

wrighte, craftsman XI 348; pl, X 403

writhen, clenched XVII 175

wroghte, worked VI 113; made IX 154; caused X 34; acted X 426; *performed XIV 196; p.p., created VI 312, VII 97

wroken, avenged II 195, XVIII 391 (p.p. of wreken)

wrong, wrung (sc. hands) III 237; twisted VI 175

wroth, angry III 331

wrotherhele, misfortune XIV 120

wryngyede, twisted V 84

wryngynge, twisting V 84

wye, person V 533; man IX 113, XVII 99

wyghtliche, speedily II 209

wyn, wine Pr 229, V 176, XIII 61

wynkyng, sleep V 3; drowse XI 5

wynne, earn IX 109; wynnynge, profit XIX 287

wyved, married IX 184

wyvene, of women, women's V 29

wyvyng, marrying IX 193

yaf, gave I 15, 107 (p.t. of yyve)

ytouked, tucked XV 454
yvel (*a*), bad V 120; hard VI 48
yvele (*av*), badly V 166; wickedly
    X 324; poorly XII 98
yveles, diseases XX 85
ywasshen, washed IX 135

ywis, certainly XI 409
ywonne, won XVIII 354
yworthe, be (left alone) VI 84
ywroght, created IX 117
ywrye, twisted XIV 233
yyve, give V 106; give away X 311

GLOSSARY OF LATIN AND FRENCH WORDS

Amor, Love XV 34
Anima, the Soul IX 8, XV 23
Animus, Will XV 24
Archa Dei, the Ark of God X 282, XII 113
Aves, Hail Mary's XV 181
Beau fitz, fair son VII 163
Benedicite, Bless me V 391
caristia, dearth XIV 72
Caritatis, (of) Charity II 35
Caro, the flesh, body IX 49, XVII 108
chaud, plus chaud, hot, very hot VI 310
Contra, 'I deny that' VIII 20, X 343
culorum, conclusion III 280, X 408
douce vie, luxurious living XIV 122
episcopus, bishop XV 43
ergo, therefore VIII 25, XVIII 341
extremis, in, in extreme circumstances X 346
fornicatores, fornicators II 181
gazophilacium, treasury XIII 198
genere, in, in the nature XIV 181
infamis, of ill repute V 166
Inferno, in, in hell XVII 109
ingratus, unkind XVII 256; **ingrati,** ungrateful XIV 169
Ite, missa est, Go, mass is finished V 413
Latro, thief V 477
Lex Christi, the law of Christ XVII 72
licitum, allowed XI 96
Limbo Inferni, in, in the border-region of hell XVI 84
Magi, Magi, Wise Men XIX 85
mea culpa, through my fault V 76
Mens, Mind, Thought XV 25
metropolitanus, metropolitan XV 42

modicum, a little XVIII 215
multi, many XI 112
parce, the command 'Spare' XVIII 393
paroles, bele, fine words XV 113
Pater Abbas, father Abbot V 169
pauci, few XI 114
Paternoster, Our father V 342
pecuniosus, moneyed XI 58
Penetrans-domos, Piercer of Homes XX 341
Penitencia, Penitence V 475
Placebo, psalm III 311
pontifex, pontiff XV 42
Potencia Dei Patris, the Power of God the Father XVI 30
presul, prelate XV 42
pur charite, for the love of God VIII 11
quatriduanus, for four days XVI 114
Qui cum Patre et Filio, who with the Father and the Son V 58
quodlibet, general intellectual problem XV 381
Ramis Palmarum, Palm Sunday XVIII 6
Recordare, the offertory 'Remember' IV 120
Redemptor, redeemer XI 206
Regum, the Book of Kings III 259
Sapiencia Dei Patris, the Wisdom of God the Father XVI 36
sapienter, correctly XI 312
Sensus, sense-perception, XI 29
transgressores, lawbreakers I 96
turpiloquium, foul speech Pr 39, XIII 457
Vigilate, Keep Watch V 443